Universal Keys *for* Writers

THE MAIN ROUTES

▶ **Key to the Book** *(inside front cover and facing page)*
Menu-style directory to the book's ten parts.

▶ **Tabbed dividers** *(table of contents at the beginning of each part)*

■ Red tabs cover the writing process, writing in all your courses, and writing and technology issues.

■ Gold tabs cover nuts-and-bolts issues such as grammar and punctuation.

■ Blue tabs cover research and documentation.

▶ **Main Table of Contents** *(p. xix)*

▶ **Index** *(p. I–1)*
A comprehensive alphabetical list of topics and terms.

THE ALTERNATE ROUTES

▶ **Common Editing and Proofreading Marks** *(inside back cover)*

▶ **Correction Guide** *(page facing inside back cover)*

▶ **Specialized Indexes** for MLA *(p. 699)*, APA *(p. 766)*, CSE *(p. 805)*, *Chicago (p. 816)* documentation styles.

▶ **Glossary of Usage** *(p. 835)*
Clarifies the use of commonly confused words such as *affect* and *effect*, *principal* and *principle*, and *well* and *good*.

▶ **Glossary of Grammatical Terms** *(p. 848)*
Defines terms, provides examples, and gives page references of where more information can be found.

▶ **List of Boxes, Notes, and Source Shots** *(page following Index)*
A directory to

 Key Points boxes

 **Tech Notes**

 Language and Culture boxes

ESL Notes

Visit the Web Site for *Universal Keys for Writers*

HOUGHTON MIFFLIN
college division

Online Study Center

Universal Keys for Writers 2/e, Raimes | Jerskey

Navigate By Topic ▾ | Discipline Home | Bookstore | Contact Us

Research and Documentation

- Prepare For Class
- Improve Your Grade
- ACE the Test
- General Resources
- SMARTHINKING Tutoring Center
- Site Map

Product Information Center > Student Home > Research and Documentation > Improve Your Grade

Improve Your Grade

Work with these documents and activities to master chapter learning objectives. Some content requires software plugins. Visit our Plugin Help Center for help with downloading plugins.

:: **Quick Guide to Documentation Styles**
This quick sheet can help you format your Works Cited or References list.

:: **Research Schedule**
Manage your time and use this template to plan your work in advance.

:: **Recording Sources Template: Print Book**
Record the data you need to correctly cite every source you consult.

:: **Recording Sources Template: Print Article**
Record the data you need to correctly cite every source you consult.

:: **Recording Sources Template: Database Article**
Record the data you need to correctly cite every source you consult.

:: **Recording Sources Template: Web Sources**
Record the data you need to correctly cite every source you consult.

College Site Map | Partners | Press Releases | Company Home | Contact Us
© 2005 Copyright Houghton Mifflin Company. All Rights Reserved.
Privacy Policy | Children's Privacy Policy | Terms and Conditions of Use | Site Map

RESOURCES FOR STUDENTS AVAILABLE AT WEB SITE

▶ **Online handbook**   *Digital Keys Online,* by Ann Raimes, includes exercises, search function, and diagnostic self-tests. (Use free password provided with new copies of *Universal Keys.*)

▶ **ESL Center**

▶ **Downloadable Templates and Editing Exercises**

▶ **eLibrary of Exercises**   700 self-quizzes help you sharpen your grammar and writing skills.

▶ *Internet Research Guide*   Six tutorials help you use the Internet for research.

▶ **Usage flashcards, helpful links,** *American Heritage Dictionary's* **100 Words to Know, and more**

RESOURCES FOR INSTRUCTORS AVAILABLE AT WEB SITE

▶ **Instructor's Resource Manual**

▶ **Links to online composition journals**

▶ **ESL Center for instructors**

▶ **PowerPoint slides, diagnostic tests, online handbook access, and more.**

Second Edition

Universal Keys
for Writers

Ann Raimes
Hunter College, City University of New York

Maria Jerskey
Baruch College, City University of New York

Houghton Mifflin Company
Boston   New York

Publisher: Patricia Coryell
Editor-in-Chief: Carrie Brandon
Senior Marketing Manager: Tom Ziolkowski
Marketing Assistant: Bettina Chiu
Senior Development Editor: Meg Botteon
Senior Development Editor: Martha Bustin
Associate Editor: Jane Acheson
Editorial Assistant: Sarah Truax
Senior Project Editor: Rosemary Winfield
Editorial Assistant: Andrew Laskey
Art and Design Coordinator: Jill Haber
Cover Design Manager: Tony Saizon
Photo Editor: Jennifer Meyer Dare
Composition Buyer: Chuck Dutton

CREDITS (*credits continue on p. 858, which constitutes an extension of the copyright page*)

Printed in the U.S.A.   Library of Congress Catalog Card number 2006929610
1 2 3 4 5 6 7 8 9 - DOC - 10 09 08 07 06
Instructor's exam copy ISBN 0-618-77773-3 or 978-0-618-77773-0
For orders, use student text ISBN 0-618-75397-4 or 978-0-618-75397-0.

Preface

As we began talking about the second edition of *Universal Keys for Writers*, our conversations returned again and again to the strengths that today's students bring to college and the challenges they face. In their daily lives—on campus, at home, and at work—students think about and create texts, and they do so using a variety of media. This means that more than ever, students need to think critically about the variety of purposes and audiences they face in their writing, and to shape their texts accordingly.

Their diverse experiences, cultures, and languages—even their many Englishes—add rich and multiple perspectives to classroom discussions and online conversations. At the same time, today's students grapple to fulfill a range of academic, professional, and linguistic expectations as they communicate. And because of the ease with which they can search for and find information on the Internet, students need to practice the critical evaluation and scrupulous documentation of sources they use in all of their writing situations.

These strengths and challenges and our own students' willingness to share with each other and with us have informed and shaped our understanding of what today's students need in a writing handbook. They need a useful and accessible tool that they will turn to and use with ease. They need to connect their own strengths with the challenges they face as writers. And they need to produce texts (in college and beyond) that fulfill their intended purpose and their readers' expectations.

Our goals in writing the second edition of *Universal Keys for Writers* have been to offer

- a respectful recognition of the strengths that today's student writers bring to college;
- practical, efficient, and problem-solving support for producing texts in college and beyond;
- multiple opportunities to practice the writing process and critical thinking in multiple writing situations;
- the clearest possible grammatical explanations of Standard English; and
- up-to-date and straightforward guidelines for finding, evaluating, and documenting sources.

Distinctive Features

Accessible design The accessible design includes dictionary-style thumb tabs, a four-color design, a full index, part titles, and a full book table of contents on the inside front cover.

Three-part color-coded structure *Universal Keys for Writers* has comprehensive coverage, organized simply. The three main divisions of the text—Writing (red), Language (gold), and Research (blue)—allow students and their teachers to find what they need when they need it.

Ten parts, clearly titled The three main divisions of the text are subdivided into ten parts. Each part has a separate table of contents, making navigation of the text intuitive and simple.

Exercises Our exercises are calibrated for a continuum of student competencies and learning styles—from those who study examples, dive in, and apply what they've learned to those who welcome direct instruction and collaborative learning environments.

Key Points boxes Eighty-seven concise summary and checklist boxes highlight important information for quick reference and class discussion. These boxes encourage students to review and develop their critical thinking, reading, writing, editing, and viewing skills.

Distinctive Content

WRITING: Parts 1, 2, and 3

Parts 1, 2, and 3 form a comprehensive guide to the writing process.

Emphasis on thesis Central to successful writing in college and beyond is a clear understanding of how to build and support a good thesis. The development of a useful, even compelling, thesis statement involves creativity, judgment, critical thinking, and synthesis—skills that are part of lifelong learning. We recognize, in *Universal Keys*, that the thesis is not easily taught or quickly mastered. Our approach to the thesis is woven throughout the writing process, argument, and research chapters of this book.

Authentic student writing Drafts, papers, blogs, visuals, and other sample materials were generously submitted by college and university instructors and by students around the country. The sample student papers and extracts, both in the print text and at the Online Study Center, are supported with annotations, critical thinking exercises, and discussion. The authors worked with most of these student authors to revise and present their texts for *Universal Keys*. These are authentic students, writing with their own voices and from their own research and experience.

Enhanced coverage of argument Argument requires discovery of what one believes. Our approach to argument and persuasion naturally develops from what has been explored in Part 1 about critical reading, writing, and seeing. For example, the discussion of *claims* (7d) builds on previous discussions of thesis. This section also builds on earlier work on critical thinking and reading, with specific and clear examples of logical fallacies as well as guidelines for students to check the logic of their own arguments. A provocative student argument essay (7l) demonstrates how to use a variety of evidence—visual and online as well as print—to support a controversial claim. In addition, the sample MLA research papers (51g) are annotated to both highlight the students' development of their argument as well as MLA-specific features.

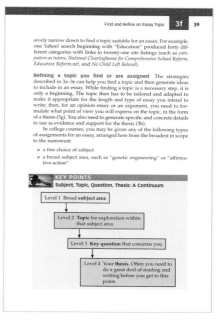

sively narrow down to find a topic suitable for an essay. For example, one Yahoo! search beginning with "Education" produced forty different categories with links to twenty-one site listings (such as *computers as tutors, National Clearinghouse for Comprehensive School Reform, Education Reform.net,* and *No Child Left Behind*).

Refining a topic you find or are assigned The strategies described in 3a–3e can help you find a topic and then generate ideas to include in an essay. While finding a topic is a necessary step, it is only a beginning. The topic then has to be tailored and adapted to make it appropriate for the length and type of essay you intend to write; then, for an opinion essay or an argument, you need to formulate what point of view you will express on the topic, in the form of a thesis (3g). You also need to generate specific and concrete details to use as evidence and support for the thesis (3h).

In college courses, you may be given any of the following types of assignments for an essay, arranged here from the broadest in scope to the narrowest:

- a free choice of subject
- a broad subject area, such as "genetic engineering" or "affirmative action"

KEY POINTS

Subject, Topic, Question, Thesis: A Continuum

Level 1 Broad **subject area**

Level 2 **Topic** for exploration within that subject area

Level 3 **Key question** that concerns you

Level 4 Your **thesis.** Often you need to do a great deal of reading and writing before you get to this point.

---

132 **7i** Sample Arguments: An Essay and a Persuasive Letter

False dichotomy or false dilemma Either/or arguments reduce complex problems to two simplistic alternatives without exploring them in depth or considering other alternatives.

► **After September 11, New York could do one of two things: increase airport security or screen immigrants.**

This proposal presents a false dichotomy. These are not the only two options for dealing with potential terrorism. Posing a false dilemma like this will annoy readers.

TECH NOTE

Logical Fallacies on the Web

Go to *Stephen's Guide to the Logical Fallacies* for lists of many more types of logical fallacies, all with explanations and examples. A link to this site and additional practices for identifying logical fallacies are at the Online Study Center.

Online Study Center Writing Process More logical fallacies

EXERCISE 7.7

Examine arguments.

For each of the following statements, determine whether the argument is logical or contains a logical fallacy. If it contains a logical fallacy, identify the logical fallacy and explain why it is a fallacy.

1. The new vice president of sales is untrustworthy because many years ago he was arrested for civil disobedience while in college.
2. Married couples without children often experience societal pressure to have or adopt children.
3. Mary can either matriculate as a full-time student in the fall or wait until the following fall to attend classes.
4. Keeping a diary is cathartic because writing on a daily basis releases bottled-up emotions.
5. All men like sports.

7l **Sample arguments: A student's essay and a persuasive letter in a community newspaper**

Here is a draft of Mara Lee Kornberg's argument paper on a vegan diet, annotated to point out the strategies in her argument. Note how she presents her thesis, supports it, considers and refutes opposing views, and varies appeals to readers. See 51g for MLA format for a final draft.

LANGUAGE: Parts 4, 5, 6, and 7

Throughout the writing process, students will turn to Parts 4, 5, 6, and 7 for support with style, grammar, punctuation, ESL, and other language issues.

The Five C's of Style Part 4 advises students in a straightforward way to Cut, Check for Action, Connect, Commit, and Choose Your Words. Widespread class testing has proven that this easy-to-remember approach works well with students and helps them to improve.

Thorough coverage of Standard English features for language learners and students who speak other Englishes *Universal Keys* features clear coverage of grammar and writing for English language learners as well as students who speak non-standard Englishes. Editing Guides for multilingual transfer errors and for vernacular Englishes examine the logical patterning of certain types of errors in written English if a student's original language is not standard American English. In addition, ESL Notes are integrated throughout the handbook, and Language and Culture boxes consider the interrelationship of language and culture, of interest to monolingual students approaching new languages as well as to multilingual students. Topics include language and dialect variations and different style preferences across cultures.

---

584 | **40d** | Editing Guide to Multilingual Transfer Errors

Language Features	Languages	Sample Transfer Errors in English	Edited Version
No distinction between subject and object forms of some pronouns	Chinese, Gujarati, Korean, Thai	I gave the forms to she.	I gave the forms to her. Or I gave her the forms.
Nouns and adjectives have same form.	Chinese, Japanese	She is beauty woman. / They felt very safety on the train.	She is a beautiful woman. / They felt very safe on the train.
No distinction between he and she, his and her	Bengali, Farsi, Gujarati, Spanish (his and her only), Thai	My sister dropped his purse.	My sister dropped her purse.
No plural form after a number	Creole, Farsi	He has two dog.	He has two dogs.
No plural (or optional) forms of nouns	Chinese, Japanese, Korean, Thai	Several good book . . .	Several good books . . .
No relative pronouns	Korean	The book is on the table is mine.	The book that is on the table is mine.
Different perception of countable/ uncountable	Japanese, Russian, Spanish	I bought three furnitures. / He has red hairs.	I bought three pieces of furniture. Or I bought three chairs. / He has red hair.
Adjectives show number.	Russian, Spanish	I have helpfuls friends.	I have helpful friends.
Negative before verb	Spanish	Jack no like meat.	Jack does not like meat.
Double negatives used routinely	Spanish	They don't know nothing.	They don't know anything. Or They know nothing.

EXERCISE 40.1
Identify transfer errors.
From samples of your writing marked by instructors, gather samples of transfer errors that you know you need to be aware of. Use a language notebook or blog to keep a list of transfer errors that you make, with an edited version (see p. 579).

Practical section on avoiding biased and exclusionary language More relevant than ever, this guide (20f) discusses sensible ways to avoid divisive and exclusionary language. It looks at language issues concerning gender, race, place, age, politics, religion, health and abilities, sexual orientation, and the word *normal*.

Neatly clustered grammar coverage Part 5 gives students one convenient place to turn when they have grammar questions or need to review the Top Ten Sentence Problems—a diagnostic checklist (p. 348). Our problem-solving approach to grammar encourages students to revise and edit for clarity, style, and accuracy.

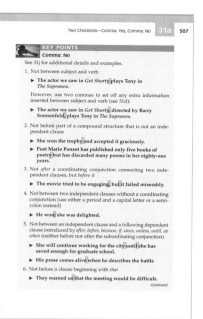

Two Checklists—Comma: Yes, Comma: No 31a 507

KEY POINTS
Comma: No
See 31j for additional details and examples.
1. Not between subject and verb
   ▶ The actor we saw in *Get Shorty* plays Tony in *The Sopranos*.
   However, use two commas to set off any extra information inserted between subject and verb (see 31d):
   ▶ The actor we saw in *Get Shorty*, directed by Barry Sonnenfeld, plays Tony in *The Sopranos*.
2. Not before part of a compound structure that is not an independent clause
   ▶ She won the trophy and accepted it graciously.
   ▶ Poet Marie Ponsot has published only five books of poetry but has discarded many poems in her eighty-one years.
3. Not *after* a coordinating conjunction connecting two independent clauses, but *before* it
   ▶ The movie tried to be engaging, but it failed miserably.
4. Not between two independent clauses without a coordinating conjunction (use either a period and a capital letter or a semicolon instead)
   ▶ He won; she was delighted.
5. Not between an independent clause and a following dependent clause introduced by *after, before, because, if, since, unless, until,* or *when* (neither before nor after the subordinating conjunction)
   ▶ She will continue working for the city until she has saved enough for graduate school.
   ▶ His prose comes alive when he describes the battle
6. Not before a clause beginning with *that*
   ▶ They warned us that the meeting would be difficult.
   (Continued)

RESEARCH: Parts 8, 9, and 10

The third main section of *Universal Keys* guides students through the research process with expert tips, up-to-date technology coverage, and a wealth of interesting examples. It offers the following advantages:

Clear, candid discussion of plagiarism You will find extensive coverage of plagiarism, including a distinctive chapter that explains the many ways in which plagiarism happens; succinct guidance on using sources responsibly; an engaging and enlightening list of the "Seven Sins of Plagiarism"; and exercises on summary, paraphrase, and defining the boundaries of a citation.

Source Shots Seven Source Shots—annotated screen captures and facsimiles of sources—*show* students where to find the information they need to correctly cite periodicals, books, Web sites, databases, and other kinds of sources they will consult as they do research.

Emphasis on evaluating sources A significant challenge for student writers is determining which sources have academic merit and which do not.

The latest documentation guidelines Covering the latest MLA, APA, *Chicago Manual of Style,* and CSE guidelines for print and electronic sources, *Universal Keys* helps students to understand that citation styles vary according to discipline, purpose, and audience. For reference, sample papers (complete and excerpted) show the document styles in action. Special indexes at the beginning of the MLA, APA, and other sections make it easy for students to locate sample entries such as a government publication, play, sound recording, or legal case.

Resources for Instructors

Online Teaching Center: Technology Tools for Instructors Access the **Online Teaching Center** at **http://college.hmco.com/ keys.html**. The following resources are available at this site:

- **Instructor's Resource Manual** The Instructor's Resource Manual is housed on the Online

---

47d Keyword searches

Use keywords to search for any material stored electronically. Keyword searching is especially effective for finding material in journal and newspaper articles in databases such as *EBSCO, InfoTrac, LexisNexis,* and specialized subject-area databases because a computer can search not only titles but also abstracts (when available) or full articles. See 47c for more on searching databases.

Keywords are vital for your Web searches, too. Spend time thinking of the keywords that best describe what you are looking for. If a search yields thousands of hits, try requiring or prohibiting terms and making terms into phrases. If a search yields few hits, try different keywords or combinations, or try another search engine or database. In addition, try out variant spellings for names of people and places: *Chaikovsky, Tchaikovsky, Tschaikovsky.* Some search engines, such as Google, automatically suggest alternate spellings.

Use the results to help refine your search. If your search produces only one useful source, look at the terms used in that one source and its subject headings and search again, perhaps using those terms with a different search engine or on a different database. Above all, be flexible. Each database or search engine indexes only a portion of what is available in the published literature or on the Web. Once you find a promising reference to a source that is not available online in full text, check whether your library owns the book or journal. If your search yields a source available only on microfilm or microfiche, you might need a librarian's help to learn how to use the reading machines and how to make copies.

KEY POINTS

Doing a Keyword Search

1. *Know the system used by the database or search engine.* Use the Search Tips or Help link to find out how to conduct a search. Systems vary. Some search for any or all of the words you type in, some need you to indicate whether the words make up a phrase (item 4), and some allow you to exclude words or search for alternatives (items 5, 6, and 8).

2. *Use Advanced Search features in a search engine or database.* Google (<http://www.google.com/help/refinesearch.html>) provides a simple grid to indicate whether you want to find results with all the words, with the exact phrase, with at least one of the words, or without the words, as shown in the

(Continued)

KEY POINTS

What to Cite

1. Cite all facts, statistics, and pieces of information unless they are common knowledge and are accessible in many sources.

2. Cite exact words from your source, enclosed in quotation marks.

3. Cite somebody else's ideas and opinions, even if you restate them in your own words in a summary or paraphrase.

4. Cite each sentence in a long paraphrase (if it is not clear that all the sentences paraphrase the same original source).

Note how James Stalker, in his article "Official English or English Only," does not quote directly but still cites the source of the specialized facts:

By 1745 there were approximately 45,000 German speakers in the colonies, and by 1790 there were some 200,000, nine per cent of the population (Anderson 80).

Citation is not necessary for facts regarded as common knowledge, such as the dates of the Civil War; facts available in many sources, such as authors' birth and death dates and chronological events; or allusions to folktales that have been handed down through the ages. When you are in doubt about whether a fact is common knowledge, cite your source.

TECH NOTE

The Instability of Internet Information

Information on the Internet is constantly changing. The source material you find today might disappear by tomorrow. The bounty, collaborative nature, and flux of online information mean that you have to be especially careful as you conduct Internet research and record information. When in doubt, even if you are using information from a blog to which you have contributed, always keep a copy of the source on your computer or in print and cite your source in your essay.

49e Keeping track of sources

The first step toward avoiding plagiarism is keeping track of what your sources are and which ideas come from your sources and which from you. You will find that the most frustrating moments for you as a researcher occur when you find some notes about an interesting

Teaching Center in five parts. It provides (1) an overview of the handbook and ideas on how to use it, (2) a section on teaching composition to ESL and multilingual students, (3) advice on using the Internet both within the composition classroom and throughout the course, and (4) diagnostic test handouts on five main areas of grammar.

- **PowerPoint slides** The PowerPoint slides are based on selected content from the Instructor's Resource Manual and allow instructors to adapt presentations for individual classroom needs.

Print Supplements for Instructors

- *Teaching Writing with Computers: An Introduction* Edited with an introduction by Pamela Takayoshi and Brian Huot, this is an up-to-date resource on integrating technology into writing instruction.

- *Finding Our Way: A Writing Teacher's Sourcebook* Edited by Deborah Coxwell Teague and the late Wendy Bishop, this is a unique and powerful collection of essays for new or relatively new composition instructors.

- *The Essentials of Tutoring: Helping College Students Develop Their Writing Skills* A supportive and comprehensive guide for writing tutors by Paul Gary Philips and Joyce B. Philips.

Additional Exercises to Accompany *Universal Keys for Writers* Additional exercises to accompany *Universal Keys for Writers,* Fifth Edition, may be found on the student Web site, *Digital Keys 5.0;* in *WriteSpace,* an easy-to-use Web-based writing program with hundreds of interactive exercises on over fifth grammar, writing, punctuation, and usage topics.

Resources for Students

Free Resources for Student Writers: *Universal Keys for Writers* **Web site**

college.hmco.com/keys.html

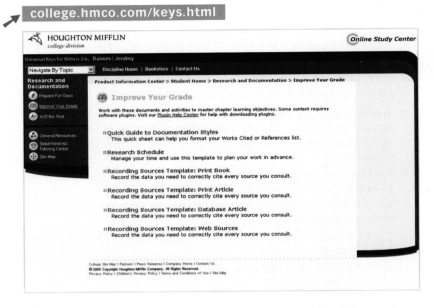

- <small>*Online Study Center*</small> Access the **Online Study Center** for this text by visiting **http://college.hmco.com/keys.html**. Resources at this site include the following:

  - Research templates for keeping track of different kinds of sources

  - Flashcards for quick review of usage issues

  - Additional ESL materials and information

  - Interactive exercises

  - Sources in 27 Subject Areas, with fully updated lists and links to frequently used reference works in print, print and electronic indexes, and Web sites. This extensive time-saving research source list, updated for this edition of *Universal Keys* by research librarian Trudi Jacobson at the University at Albany, SUNY, remains a tool that students can use throughout their college career as they work on papers across the curriculum.

- **Internet Research Guide** The second edition of this online guide by Jason Snart of the College of DuPage presents extended learning modules with practice exercises (tutorials) for using the Internet as a research tool. Topics include evaluating Web site information, building an argument with Web research, and plagiarism anddocumentation. It is available online at **http:// college.hmco.com/English/students/composition.html**.

■ **e-Exercises** This rich e-library of enjoyable self-quizzes lets students hone their grammar skills, go at their own pace, and work wherever is convenient for them—home, computer lab, or classroom. Exercises cover thirty areas within the broad categories of punctuation, mechanics, parts of speech, spelling, and sentence problems. It is available online at **http://college.hmco.clom/English/students/ composition.html**.

■ **Plagiarism Prevention Zone** The Plagiarism Prevention Zone provides a crash course of compelling tutorials on how to recognize and avoid plagiarism. It is available at **http://college .hmco.com/English/students/composition.html**.

Premium Technology Tools for Student Writers The multimedia edition of *Universal Keys for Writers*—the print textbook packaged with the new **Technology Guide for Writers** ensemble of technology products—provides four convenient and powerful aids for self-paced and personalized writing instruction on the computer:

■ *Digital Keys 5.0* This newly revised resource has a host of interactive tools and tips to help students work on all aspects of their writing, including grammar, punctuation, mechanics, and style. Use your online passkey for a twelve-month subscription to the *Digital Keys* site.

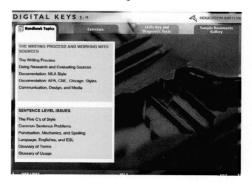

The core of this writing aid is an easily navigated handbook of writing instruction, practice exercises, examples, diagnostic tests, KeyTabs® for bookmarking, and hotlinks. When students look up a topic, they have two choices: they can read a brief explanation, or they can click a button for more detailed explanation and annotated examples. From either the brief screen or the detailed explanation screens, students can instantly access exercises and model documents.

- *WriteSpace* **online writing environment registration code** *WriteSpace for Composition* is an online course-management system with teaching and learning materials designed to enhance and extend your course. It offers (1) *Re:Mark,* an innovative online grading tool; (2) *Peer Re:Mark,* a new-generation peer-review environment that offers you and your students easy to use, flexible, and effective tools for collaborative writing; (3) *My DropBox Safe Assignment* plagiarism prevention that checks papers against four databases; (4) *Digital Keys 5.0,* a concise, complete handbook full of examples and exercises, four diagnostic tests, and model student papers; (5) *HM Assess,* an assessment program that provides diagnostic tests that, when graded, automatically offer each student in your course a personalized study plan; (6) twenty-four multimedia interactive news reports from the Associated Press, presented with a context building introductions and follow-up questions designed to develop visual literacy and critical thinking; (7) writing modules, or tutorials, covering the writing process, rhetorical modes, argument and persuasion, and research; and (8) a wide array of suggested writing assignments as well as exercises.

Print Supplements for Students

- **THEA and CLAST Preparation Manuals** These manuals include practice tests to help students pass the Texas Higher Education Assessment Test and Florida's College Level Academic Skills Test.

- *The American Heritage College Dictionary,* **Fourth Edition** This best-selling reference is an indispensable tool and desk reference.

- *The American Heritage English as a Second Language Dictionary* This reference is specially designed with additional sample sentences to suit the needs of intermediate to advanced ESL students.

Acknowledgments

For all their help with this book, we are grateful to teachers and students at our own colleges and across the country. When we do workshops and attend conferences, faculty members have been unfailingly generous with their contributions of advice and materials.

Heartfelt thanks go to Maria's colleagues at Baruch College— Cheryl Smith, Suresh Canagarajah, Jessica Lang, and Gerald Dalgish—for their eagerness to discuss the diverse learning needs of diverse populations of students. For his expert advice on technological matters and prompt replies to many e-mails, we are deeply grateful to Manfred Kuechler, Ann's colleague in the sociology department at Hunter College, whose knowledge of the workings of the Internet is truly astounding. Thanks go, too, to Hunter College librarians Tony Doyle and Jean Jacques Strayer for keeping us up to date on databases and search engines; to Trudi Jacobson at the University at Albany, SUNY, for so ably updating the listing of resources in twenty-seven subject areas; and to Scot Ober, Ball State University, who generously contributed to the section on writing for work. We also offer thanks to all the students whose writing appears in this book.

The writing process was much in evidence as the first edition and drafts of the new edition were reviewed by composition instructors. They gave the evolving manuscript the benefit of their experience, wisdom, and critical eyes. Their many excellent and tactful suggestions at each stage of development have been invaluable:

Cole Bennett, Abilene Christian Universtiy
Laura Carroll, Abilene Christian University
Erika Deiter, Moraine Valley Community College
David Dzaka, Messiah College
Jennifer Edbauer, Penn State University
Lindsay Lewan, Arapahoe Community College
Nancy McTaggart, Northern Virginia Community College
Jeff Rice, Wayne State Universtiy
Julia Ruengert, Pensacola Junior College
Eleanor Swanson, Regis University
Pavel Zemliansky, James Madison University

Our colleagues at Houghton Mifflin have been a pleasure to work with, and Maria is particularly grateful for their welcoming assistance throughout the production of this book. They are warm, supportive, responsive, and incredibly knowledgeable about textbook publishing. Special thanks go to Pat Coryell, Vice President, and Suzanne Phelps Weir, Executive Editor, and Carrie Brandon, Editor in Chief, for their leadership, energy, and enthusiasm for the project; to the team of Senior Development Editors, Meg Botteon and Martha Bustin, for their keen editorial eyes, contributions to the manuscript, and unfailing grace under pressure; to Jane Acheson, Assistant Editor, for her astute ability to keep us all on target; to Rosemary Winfield, Senior Project Editor, for coping with challenging deadlines during the production process; and to Cindy Graff Cohen, Annamarie Rice, and Tom Ziolkowski, for keeping us attuned to market needs. We also gratefully acknowledge the help and professionalism of others on the large *Universal Keys* team: Janet Edmonds, John McHugh, Sarah Truax, Katherine Leahey, Andrew Laskey, Jill Haber, Jerilyn Bockorick, Jennifer Meyer Dare, Lisa Jelly Smith, Mary Dalton Hoffman, Sarah Zobel, Sherri Dietrich, Priscilla Manchester, and Stephanie Gintowt's miracle workers at New England Typographic Service.

On a personal level, we want to thank our friends (Jane Ashdown and Brian Jermusyk were of particular help to Maria), colleagues, and family, who lived through our stress levels and distraction and made sure we got out and had fun. Two people were especially important to us: Gene Jerskey-Long and James Raimes had to put up with piles and piles of paper, frequent trips to the copy shop, and deadline dashes to make the last courier pick-up. They knew when to let us be obsessive and when to say, "Enough! Let's eat!" Without them, you would not now be holding this book in your hands.

About the Authors

Ann Raimes was born and educated in England and has been living in New York since 1967. She recently retired from full-time teaching at Hunter College, City University of New York, where she was a professor of English for thirty-two years. In addition to teaching undergraduate composition courses, ESL writing courses, and graduate courses in rhetoric and composition, she was in charge of the Developmental English Program (1,500 students) for ten years and held a variety of administrative posts in the English Department, including directing the first-year composition course. She also chaired a CUNY-wide ESL Task Force, 1993–94 and was chair of International TESOL's Publication Committee, 1989–91.

Author of eight textbooks for composition and ESL courses and translator of Hugo Ball's diaries, Ann Raimes has also published many research and theoretical articles and has been invited to give keynote addresses in Singapore, Hong Kong, Rome, Athens, and cities across Canada and the United States. Her research interests are the writing process, second-language writing, grammar instruction, writing across the curriculum, and Web-based instruction.

When not involved in and obsessing about teaching, researching, and writing, she spends time with her husband, family and friends, playing tennis, reading, going to movies, gardening, and cooking.

Maria Jerskey grew up in New Jersey and Wisconsin and lived in Paris, where she learned to speak French as a second language, write songs, and play electric guitar. She was the lead singer of rock 'n' roll bands in France, Japan, Sweden, and New York. She has taught writing to college students in New York City for ten years. Since 2003, she has directed the writing center at Baruch College, City University of New York, cited as the most diverse institution of higher education in the United States. With a PhD from New York University in English Education, she develops writing support curricula for students from multiple linguistic and literacy backgrounds and supervises the training and development of writing tutors from undergraduate to the doctoral level. Her collaboration with faculty, librarians, and various academic units and initiatives have enhanced collegewide student support in ESL, information technology, writing across the curriculum, communication and presentation, and academic integrity.

This is her second writing handbook in collaboration with Ann Raimes. Her research interests are writing pedagogy, English language learners, writing handbooks, textual analysis, and teacher education.

She loves writing, reading, listening to music, traveling, and, most of all, being Gene's mom.

Our collaboration has a rich history. Long before we were colleagues and friends, we were teacher and student. In 1994, Maria, then a graduate student in TESOL at Hunter College, signed up for a rhetoric and composition course taught by Ann. Through lectures, discussions, and workshops, Ann conveyed not only the importance of teaching writing but also the endlessly fascinating issues that teachers of writing grapple with as they encourage their students to think critically about what they want to say, how they want to say it, and to whom they want to say it. Maria was hooked. But it was through the writing assignments—reading logs and essay drafts—that our connection really developed. Ann's comments—incisive and alive—drove home the transformative power of what can happen between a reader and a writer and between a teacher and a student. These interactions were truly collaborative and mutual. We brought out the best in each other and we still do!

Main Table of Contents

PART 2
Writing through College 109

LANGUAGE
Style, Accuracy, Punctuation, Fluency

PART 4
The 5 C'S of Style 265

RESEARCH

PART 8
Writing a Research Paper 625

Writing

Communicating and Presenting Ideas

Writing is one of our oldest technologies. It was developed over 5,000 years ago—not as a form of torture for first-year college students but as a way to keep permanent records of who owned what land. In his book *What a Great Idea! Inventions That Changed the World,* Stephen M. Tomacek points out that modern writing evolved from an even older technology: pictures. Ancient artists would paint pictures to describe events. "The key to writing," Tomacek points out, "involved taking complex pictures and turning them into a set of standard symbols that had very specific meanings." The evolution of pictures into symbols, characters, and the alphabet truly transformed the world (at a slow pace, of course).

Fast forward to our age of digital technology. As a college student, you are accustomed to participating in environments where information is readily available to you—and demanded of you. You rely on visuals to illustrate and concretize that information—and you are expected to provide them as well. You have expectations of how different kinds of information will be displayed and how you will be held to similar expectations when you produce your own written and visual texts. Unfortunately, getting your ideas across is not as simple as using "standard symbols with specific meanings." Writing may be one of the oldest (and most versatile!) technologies, but it demands considerable skill.

Like many other skills, however, writing can be developed and strengthened by focusing on key goals. As you work through the first three parts of this book, focus on the following three goals:

- Understand that writing works as a *process.* (Part I)
- Be willing to practice the writing process in the variety of writing situations you find yourself in—both in college and at work. (Part II)
- Practice producing texts that fulfill the requirements of your writing assignment or presentation project. (Part III)

PART 1
Writing an Essay

3

Learning to write essays is important in a number of ways. To begin with, essays will be required in many of the courses you take during your college career. Understanding how to use the writing process to fulfill the many writing assignments you will encounter will be a significant achievement and save you much time and angst in the long run. Equally, if not more important, writing essays will develop and strengthen the critical thinking tools you use when you read and write. No matter what kind of writing or communication situations you find yourself in—academic or professional, local or global, online or face to face—you will need to use critical thinking tools to assess your audience, your purpose, and the best way to communicate your ideas.

Writing an essay is a sustained and focused effort that mirrors what you do in many of your everyday conversations and online communications. When you explain to a colleague at work why you prefer one Web site over another or discuss with friends the possible outcomes in a local election, you make decisions based on the information you have. You take a position. During your discussion, your friends may challenge you with information you didn't have before and persuade you to reconsider your position; they may agree with you, adding critical points to support your position; or they simply may not fully understand your point, in which case you will need to devise a better way to explain your position.

During the process of writing, you think critically every step of the way. You question your own position, you anticipate any position that others (your audience) might take, and you consider how best to get your point across. This shapes your writing and strengthens your ability to communicate your ideas effectively. The practice of writing essays gives you the opportunity to hone and refine the critical communication skills you use every day as you study, work, play, travel, and plan for your future.

Writing itself is often characterized as steps in a linear process of planning, drafting, and revising. In fact, no writer marches neatly through the writing process in a set sequence of steps. Rather, writing involves several overlapping and recurring activities.

As you work your way through Part I, Writing an Essay, keep these points in mind:

- The writing process is not step by step or formulaic.
- Writing is typically a messy and chaotic adventure.
- Few writers (and even fewer good writers!) achieve perfection on a first draft.
- The very act of writing helps you generate ideas.

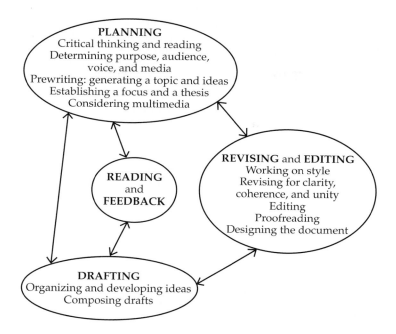

PLANNING
Critical thinking and reading
Determining purpose, audience,
voice, and media
Prewriting: generating a topic and ideas
Establishing a focus and a thesis
Considering multimedia

READING
and
FEEDBACK

REVISING and EDITING
Working on style
Revising for clarity,
coherence, and unity
Editing
Proofreading
Designing the document

DRAFTING
Organizing and developing ideas
Composing drafts

- The process of discovering what you know and what you need to know can be exciting.

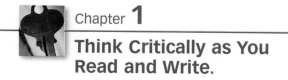

Chapter **1**

Think Critically as You Read and Write.

A few years ago, an advertising campaign for an automobile winningly demonstrated the pleasures of driving and announced, "In life, there are drivers and there are passengers. . . . Be a driver."

When you think critically as you read and write, you put yourself in the driver's seat. No longer satisfied to be sitting in the passenger's seat, you decide what ground you will cover, when to stop and get more information, and when to move on and see where the road will take you. When you think critically as a reader, you are no

Online Study Center   This icon will direct you to quick reference tools, Web resources, and research guides on the Web site at http://college.hmco.com/keys.html.

longer the passive recipient of someone else's information, knowledge, or meaning. Rather, you enter into an interactive conversation with the author you are reading. When you think critically as a writer, you are no longer just fulfilling a writing assignment. Instead, you make the piece of writing your own. When you think critically as you read and write, you also become more aware of language. You recognize varieties in the use of English and become more sensitized to when Standard English is practiced.

Thinking critically, like writing and reading, is a skill that becomes developed and strengthened with practice. Like driving, thinking critically is a skill that can be considered utilitarian. But when you are comfortable and confident in your skill, it becomes a pleasure. So go ahead; get into the driver's seat!

1a Read texts critically.

We often think of reading as linear: we start at the beginning and stop at the end. When you read for pleasure, this is often true. You give yourself over to the reading. When you read *critically*, however, your purpose is more complex. You may find yourself going back to a previous point or passage in order to fully understand the reading or to satisfy questions that come up for you. You may want to glance ahead to see where the writer is taking you. And you may want to re-read to better connect the reading to a writing assignment. Like writing, the act of reading can be a process, and you will read each piece in a different way, depending on its purpose, your plans, and the response you may be asked to provide.

Consider how you will read a passage that you will need to analyze and write about, which is often the case in college. You may be looking for pieces of information, a general overview, the claim the author is making, the author's use of language, or specific details. Try the following tactics.

KEY POINTS
Tactics for Effective Reading

1. With an informational work (not a work of literature), skim when you want to know "Is this worth a detailed reading?" Look at the table of contents, any blurb or summary, the preface, chapter introductions and conclusions, and the index in order to get a sense of whether the work meets your needs and how long it will take you to read and digest it.

2. Establish what background knowledge you need: What knowledge and information does the writer expect you to have? You may need to do some preliminary reading.

3. Give yourself large blocks of time for a long or complex work, allowing yourself to become immersed. Reading quickly in short sessions will lead to a sketchy or superficial understanding of a work.

4. Predict as you read. See how accurately you can predict what a writer will say next and how he or she will say it.

5. When doing focused research, read with the goal of finding a specific piece of information. For more on reading research sources, see 48a.

6. As you read, make inferences about what the writer intends and what assumptions the writer makes. Making an inference means "deriving conclusions that are not explicit in what is said" (*American Heritage Dictionary*).

7. Read more than once, especially with a challenging text, so that you are sure you have grasped all the text's complexities and so you can review its main points.

8. Read aloud a poem, drama, short creative work, or any section of a work that you find difficult to follow; this will help you hear the writer's voice more vividly.

9. Use a dictionary to find the meanings of words you do not know.

10. Write as you read—comments, notes, questions, highlights. See the Key Points box "Use Writing to Respond to Reading" on page 10.

11. Leave time after reading to respond informally to the text. (See 3a, 3b, 3c.)

Audience and purpose   When you read critically, ask yourself: Who is the audience of this text and what is the purpose of the reading?

Try to become aware of the different "voices" writers use when they address different audiences: a general audience (newspapers and magazines), an academic audience (scholarly articles and college textbooks), or different groups of people (a Web site about gaming will probably be written for a very different audience than will a Web site for a national monument). See also 2b.

Similarly, sensitize yourself to the purpose of the reading. Is it to inform? to persuade? to tell a story? An awareness of a writer's audience and purpose not only helps you read critically; it can help you become more aware of how others will read your writing (2b, 2c).

Respond to reading with critical thinking.   Reading critically is interactive. As you read, question, consider, agree, disagree, and mentally compare what you are reading with other points or texts you know. Bring your own knowledge and experience to your reading. That knowledge and experience may cause you to read and interpret the same passage differently from the way other readers do, offering you a unique point of view.

Similarly, when you read your own work, envision a reader who is critically reading your text. Keep the same questioning attitude to evaluate how well you have considered a critical reader's questions. (For more on audience, see 2b.)

KEY POINTS
Reader's Block

It is not uncommon for student readers to have the equivalent of writer's block: reader's block. If you or members of the group you are working with are not sure how to respond to a reading you have been assigned, try adapting the same techniques that writers use to generate ideas and break through writer's block (see 4f). Even if you don't think they apply to the reading, you will be surprised how these techniques can connect you to the reading and lead you and your group to more concrete ideas:

- Keep a reading journal or blog (3a).
- Freewrite (3b).
- Brainstorm, list, or map (3c).
- Break any rigid "reading rules" that might be holding you back (4f).
- Instead of getting snagged on each word you don't understand, try to move through the reading and get the "gist" of what the writer is saying, and then go back for a closer reading (4f).
- Talk to or e-mail a friend about what you've read. You'd be surprised at how much you do think about a reading when you can express your thoughts in a low-stakes context (4f).

Respond to reading by writing   When you read, annotate: Read with a pencil in hand (or, if you are reading on a screen, use your keyboard) so you can capture and record your ideas, questions, and associations. These annotations can be helpful starting points if you need to write a response to a particular reading.

While reading the following passage about the Ultimatum Game, a first-year college student annotated as she read. Notice how doing this increased her interaction with the article and provided her with ideas for her class discussion. Note, too, that she observes how the writers drew her in as a reader.

Direct approach caught my attention!

Imagine that somebody offers you $100. All you have to do is agree with some other anonymous person on how to share the sum. The rules are strict. The two of you are in separate rooms and cannot exchange information. A coin toss decides which of you will propose how to share the money. Suppose that you are the proposer. You can make a single offer of how to split the sum, and the other person—the responder—can say yes or no. The responder also knows the rules and the total amount of money at stake. If her answer is yes, the deal goes ahead. If her answer is no, neither of you gets anything. In both cases, the game is over and will not be repeated. What will you do?

Critical point

Good way to end the paragraph. Makes me want to continue reading.

Why do authors use feminine pronoun here?

How do the authors know this? Based on research?

Instinctively, many people feel they should offer 50 percent, because such a division is "fair" and therefore likely to be accepted. More daring people, however, think they might get away with offering somewhat less than half the sum.

Or should they say more greedy?

Before making a decision, you should ask yourself what you would do if you were the responder. The only thing you can do as the responder is say yes or no to a given amount of money. If the offer were 10 percent, would you take $10 and let someone walk away with $90, or would you rather have nothing at all? What if the offer were only 1 percent? Isn't $1 better than no dollars? And remember, haggling is strictly forbidden. Just one offer by the proposer; the responder can take it or leave it.

So what will you offer?

Ah! But since the organizers would know what I offered, it's not entirely anonymous.

I would take anything! I wonder what most people do— and why...

—Karl Sigmund, Ernst Fehr, and Martin A. Nowak, "The Economics of Fair Play"

Get into the habit of using writing to respond to reading. Consider using any of these key points:

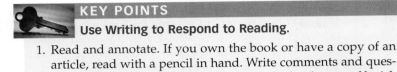

KEY POINTS
Use Writing to Respond to Reading.

1. Read and annotate. If you own the book or have a copy of an article, read with a pencil in hand. Write comments and questions in the margins. If you don't own the book, use self-stick notes.

2. Use a highlighter but do so sparingly—highlight only the important passages.

3. Read, pause, and make notes. Read a paragraph or a page at a time, pause, and write a brief summary and your own comments.

4. Write a summary or paraphrase of a significant work or passage on index cards or in computer files (49i).

5. Write questions about the writer's claims and assumptions (7i).

6. Write challenges to the writer's views: "But what about . . . ?"

7. Record in a journal or research notebook your reactions to what you have read.

8. Use a double-entry notebook to summarize the writer's ideas and how they relate to your own ideas and experiences (3a).

ESL NOTE
Responding to Reading in Other Languages

Attitudes toward written texts are influenced by culture, such as the culture of place, language, religion, race, class, and education. Be aware that the suggestions offered in this section refer to practices common in colleges and universities in North America, which may differ from practices common in countries using other languages as the language of instruction. You may have to be flexible in responding to texts if you have been thoroughly schooled in reading and responding to texts in another culture. To get a sense of linguistic and cultural differences, think of what a native speaker of English would need to know in order to write well in your language.

EXERCISE 1.1
Examine your own ways of reading.

List five of your recent reading experiences. What kinds of texts were they? Write down how and where you read each one and why you chose that method. Bring your list to class and share the results with your classmates.

EXERCISE 1.2

Read critically.

Read the following passage from Gloria Anzaldúa's "How to Tame a Wild Tongue" in *Borderlands: La Frontera: The New Mestiza.* Use the questions that follow to make annotations to guide a critical reading of the passage. Write your responses to each question.

Chicano Spanish sprang out of the Chicano's need to identify ourselves as a distinct people. We needed a language with which we could communicate with ourselves, a secret language. For some of us, language is a homeland closer than the Southwest—for many Chicanos today live in the Midwest and the East. And because we are a complex, heterogeneous people, we speak many languages. Some of the languages we speak are:

1. Standard English
2. Working class and slang English
3. Standard Spanish
4. Standard Mexican Spanish
5. North Mexican Spanish dialect
6. Chicano Spanish (Texas, New Mexico, Arizona and California have regional variations)
7. Tex-Mex
8. *Pachuco* (called *caló*)

My "home" tongues are the languages I speak with my sister and brothers, with my friends. They are the last five listed, with 6 and 7 being closest to my heart. From school, the media and job situations, I've picked up standard and working class English. From Mamagrande Locha and from reading Spanish and Mexican literature, I've picked up Standard Spanish and Standard Mexican Spanish. From *los recién llegados,* Mexican immigrants, and *braceros,* I learned the North Mexican dialect. With Mexicans I'll try to speak either Standard Mexican Spanish or the North Mexican dialect. From my parents and Chicanos living in the Valley, I picked up Chicano Texas Spanish, and I speak it with my mom, younger brother (who married a Mexican and who rarely mixes Spanish with English), aunts and older relatives.

With Chicanas from Nuevo México or Arizona I will speak Chicano Spanish a little, but often they don't understand what I'm saying. With most California Chicanas I speak entirely in English (unless I forget). When I first moved to San Francisco, I'd rattle off something in Spanish, unintentionally embarrassing them. Often it is only with another Chicana *tejana* that I can talk freely.

—Gloria Anzaldúa, "How to Tame a Wild Tongue"

QUESTIONS

1. What is a "secret language"?
2. Why does Anzaldúa use the first person plural pronoun *we*?
3. Why does Anzaldúa intersperse both Spanish and English words throughout this piece?
4. How many languages does Anzaldúa speak?
5. This excerpt is specific to "Chicano Spanish." Could it be applied to other languages?
6. Are there different languages you speak to different people at different times?
7. At the end Anzaldúa states, "Often it is only with another Chicana *tejana* that I can talk freely." To whom can you "talk freely"? Why?

EXERCISE 1.3

Respond to reading by annotating and brainstorming.

Annotate the following excerpt from Stephen L. Carter's "The Insufficiency of Honesty." Write your annotations on the page, on self-stick notes, or electronically. Compare your annotations with those written by your classmates. Then, as a group, conduct a brainstorming session on the topic of integrity.

A couple of years ago I began a university commencement address by telling the audience that I was going to talk about integrity. The crowd broke into applause. Applause! Just because they had heard the word "integrity"; that's how starved for it they were. . . .

When I refer to integrity, I have something very specific in mind. Integrity, as I will use the term, requires three steps: (1) *discerning* what is right and what is wrong; (2) *acting* on what you have discerned, even at personal cost; and (3) *saying openly* that you are acting on your understanding of right and wrong. The first criterion captures the idea that integrity requires a degree of moral reflectiveness. The second brings in the ideal of a person of integrity as steadfast, a quality that includes keeping one's commitments. The third reminds us that a person of integrity is unashamed of doing the right thing.

1b Read visuals critically.

Words are often used to generate images in our minds. When we say, "Picture this," we want our listeners to see what we see in our mind's eye. We want them to understand what we understand. Often, *I see* is synonymous with *I understand.* To make sure, we often ask, "Do you see what I am saying?"

More and more, your instructors may require you to call on your critical skills to consider visuals as texts to read and as evidence and support when you write. Visuals do not necessarily stand in place of print. They focus and direct readers' attention. They need to be powerful enough to withstand a critical reading.

All images—charts, graphs, maps, cartoons, photographs, graffiti, illustrations, and paintings—contain information and ideas that need to be interpreted. When considering a print text critically, readers typically examine it from beginning to end, in a linear way. Confronted with an image, however, we lose the traditional structure of linear progression. Think, for example, of films that reverse chronology, use fade-outs and flashbacks, and cut rapidly from one image to another. We "read" such visual texts differently from the way we read a print article or a piece of fiction. Continue to think about purpose and audience as you do when reading print texts critically, but now include a close look at the following features:

- the effect of spatial organization, in which elements of the image appear in relation to each other
- the visual focus, the part of the image that speaks to you most directly and expresses the main idea of the image

- the juxtaposition of visual and print text: what does one do to and for the other?
- the connections you (along with the originator of the image) make with other visual images in your experience and memory
- your response to color, to alignment, and (with multimedia images) to the sequence and progression of the images

The following photograph, used in an article exploring the causes of obesity in children in Starr County, Texas, makes a strong visual argument. Three children look trustingly into the camera— at us—as they sit in front of their hamburger lunches in a school cafeteria. The child on the left is obese; the other two appear small, even frail. A cut-out painting of a hamburger hangs emblematically on the gray cinderblock wall behind them. To its left, a poster displays a cartoon wizard waving a wand (the word *magic* can be discerned) over a loaf of sliced white bread. Are we to believe that bland foods can magically be transformed into something nutritious and wholesome? The image suggests that nutritional planning at the institutional level—no matter how well-meaning—has serious consequences for individual children. In Starr County, children are just as likely to be obese as they are to be underweight.

Heavy Questions

EXERCISE 1.4

Read a visual critically.

Consider the advertisement for the American Indian College Fund. As it appears in a magazine, the print along its bottom and side borders reads: "Carly Kipp, Blackfeet. Biology major, tutor, mom, pursuing a doctorate in veterinary medicine, specializing in large-animal surgery. Many of our graduates stay on the reservation. Economists project every dollar of their incomes will turn over two and a half times." Considering the aspects of critical reading of images discussed on pages 13–14, analyze how the advertisers have used the image of Carly Kipp effectively to persuade viewers to donate to the fund.

1c Write critically.

When you read critically, you subject your readings to close scrutiny: You ask questions beforehand and in the process of reading, new questions come up. You form ideas about writers, what they are saying, and how they are saying it. You connect their points and their ideas to other texts you know and to your own experiences.

When you write critically, you anticipate critical readers and the close scrutiny they will bring to your writing. You grapple with these questions:

- Who is my audience?
- What is my purpose?
- How can I communicate this most effectively?

During the process of writing critically, the answers to these questions will change and evolve. You may discover, for example, a purpose beyond fulfilling a composition assignment. As you imagine readers responding critically to your ideas, your concept of your audience may evolve from an instructor "correcting" your writing to a community of readers who never considered your particular point of view and are longing to talk further with you about your topic. Writing critically also means that you consider how best to convey what you want to say to your audience. From building paragraphs to building Web sites, writing critically increases the versatility you will need to succeed in the numerous communication opportunities you come across in college and beyond.

LANGUAGE AND CULTURE
Text Messaging

txtin iz messin,
mi headn'me englis,
try2rite essays,
they all come out txtis.
gran not plsed w/ letters shes getn,
swears i wrote better
b4 comin2uni.
&she's african

Hetty Hughes, a college student in Leeds, England, wrote this poem for a competition proposed by a British newspaper. She won first prize. Note how she adapts English to the limited number of characters allowed in a text message. Note, too, how she is able to convey her African grandmother's criticism of the effect text messaging has had on Hetty's English and how she connects it to Hetty's university education.

1d Standard English and its alternatives

In academic and professional environments, the norm for written and spoken English is called Standard English. *Standard English* is defined by the *American Heritage Dictionary (AHD)* as the "variety of English that is generally acknowledged as the model for the speech and writing of educated speakers." A Usage Note in the *AHD*, however, continues, "A form that is considered standard in one region may be nonstandard in another," and points out that *standard* and *nonstandard* are relative terms, depending largely on context. The Note concludes, "Thus while the term can serve a useful descriptive purpose providing the context makes its meaning clear, it shouldn't be construed as conferring any absolute positive evaluation."

In short, the concept of Standard English is complex. It is inextricably entwined with the region, race, class, education, and gender of both the speaker (or writer) and the listener (or reader). Standard English is continually and necessarily being supplemented (and challenged) by other ways of speaking and writing, such as those coming from digital technology, popular culture, and World Englishes. (To learn more about World Englishes, see 40a.)

Some instructors may encourage you to explore alternative discourses and nonstandard language in narrative and personal writing; some may insist on Standard English and traditional rhetoric from the outset; and others may give you options depending on the nature of the assigned task. As you read and write, continue to consider the context in which you are writing. Continue to ask yourself: Who is my audience? What is my purpose? How can I best convey what I want to say? For the most part, in academic and professional communities, you will be expected to communicate using Standard English, the focus of this book.

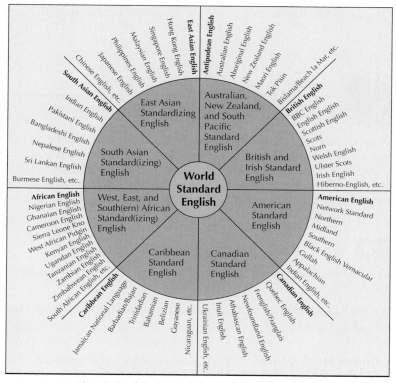

The Circle of World English (used with permission)

LANGUAGE AND CULTURE
The Englishes of North America

The Englishes of North America are living artifacts of rich cultural heritages. Dialects as diverse as African American Vernacular (also known as Black English Vernacular), Gullah, Chicano English, and Newfoundland English have developed over generations while contemporary cultural movements and technological advances have spawned new uses of language such as hip-hop and cyberspeech.

Even if English is your only language, you might well consider yourself multilingual when you think about all the Englishes you move back and forth among and how and when you use academic English. As author Amy Tan writes in her essay "Mother Tongue," "I am fascinated by language in daily life. I spend a great deal of my time thinking about the power of language—the way it can evoke an emotion, a visual image, a complex idea, or a simple truth. Language is the tool of my trade. And I use them all—all the Englishes I grew up with."

Chapter 2

Define the Assignment.

"I'm not sure what I'm supposed to be doing." "I wish I had a clearer sense of what my instructor wants." Have you often found yourself thinking or saying things like this? If so, you are not alone. In fact, a big part of writing an essay in college is understanding and fulfilling the terms of the assignment: its situation, audience, purpose, appropriate tone, and deadlines.

2a   What are the requirements?

Use the following questions to help you establish the requirements for your assignment.

- ▪ Have you been given detailed instructions about length, format, and organization?

Online Study Center   This icon will direct you to quick reference tools, Web resources, and research guides on the Web site at http://college.hmco.com/keys.html.

- What level of formality does your instructor expect? For example, how acceptable will informal language and abbreviations be?
- Will you be expected to write in Standard English, or will alternatives be accepted? (See 1d.)
- What sources of information are appropriate for your writing assignment? For example, should you plan to use required reading, interviews with experts, statistics, or critical essays?
- Will you be required to document sources according to a specific documentation style? (See Part VIII for more on documentation styles.)
- Will you present your writing as a hard copy (on paper) or online? (See Chapter 12.)
- How long will the final draft need to be?
- Who will read what you write? (See 2b.)
- How will the writing be evaluated?
- How long do you have to complete the assignment? (See 2f.)

Ask your instructor. If you cannot answer these questions, or need support applying what you do know, be sure to ask your instructor. In addition, do the following:

- Ask what background information should be included and what can safely be omitted. For example, for an essay about literature, find out if your instructor envisions an audience who has read the work of literature and will not expect a summary of the plot or an audience who has not read the work and would benefit from a summary. For an essay that includes statistics or measures, find out if you need to include tables or charts. For an essay about art, find a balance between description and analysis of a work of art.
- Ask if your instructor is willing to look at an early outline or draft of your paper to make sure you understand the requirements. Or ask your instructor if you can see model papers for the course—ideally a paper that would earn an A and a paper that would be considered unsatisfactory.

2b Who is your audience?

A good writer connects with his or her audience and keeps readers in mind at all times, as if in face-to-face communication. Achieving this connection, however, often proves challenging because not all readers have the same characteristics. Readers come from different regions, communities, ethnic groups, organizations, and academic disciplines, all with their own linguistic and rhetorical conventions (see 7f). Ask yourself the following questions about your audience.

- Who will read your piece of writing? What will those readers expect in terms of length, format, date of delivery, technical terms, and formality of language?
- What kinds of texts do your readers usually read and write, and what are their expectations of those texts?
- Will your audience expect formal or informal language? The expectations of teenagers online and college professors, for example, differ greatly.
- Will your audience expect you to use technical terms? If so, which terms are in common use?
- What characteristics do you and your audience have in common: nationality, language, culture, race, class, gender? Consider what limitations writing for this audience places on your use of dialect, vocabulary, and political and cultural expectations. Cultivate common ground, and try not to alienate readers.
- Is your instructor your main audience? If so, find out about the expectations of his or her academic discipline. Be sure to ask what background information you should include and what you can safely omit, and ask to see a sample paper.

For more on writing about literature or writing in academic disciplines, see 8 and 9.

TECH NOTE

Taking Accessibility Issues and Disabilities into Account

For documents you prepare for online audiences or for oral and multimedia presentations, issues of accessibility are important.

- Consider whether readers have a dialup or a broadband connection before you post large image files online.
- For any vision-impaired viewers, increase type size, provide a zoom function, and limit the number of visuals or describe them in words.
- Pay attention to color in visuals: Contrasting shades work better than different colors for some viewers.

Online Study Center **Design/Media** Accessibility

EXERCISE 2.1

Write for different audiences.

Write three passages on the general topic of "lying"—one for your eyes alone (a diary entry or a freewrite), one for an e-mail message to a close friend (for more on writing e-mail messages, see 11b), and one for a college instructor. Keep each version short—no more than two paragraphs each. How do the versions differ and why?

EXERCISE 2.2

Revise for a writing class assignment.

A student wrote the following passage on "lying" as a journal entry in response to the previous exercise. Circle key ideas that you think could be further developed or improved. Your purpose is to help the student locate good ideas that could be developed into a formal essay about lying.

Big lies, little lies, white lies, fibs, not truth, deception.

Lying annoys me. I hate when I'm lied to. I think it hurts the most when I am lied to by someone I care about and trust. Especially, if I don't know what I did. I can remember so many different times when friends were mad at me but didn't tell me why. They just stop taking phone calls, say they are busy and when I ask what's wrong, they don't say anything: "Nothin's wrong." But something is very wrong. I hate when I know someone is lying to me but I can't prove it. Why can't everyone just be direct? Lying is the opposite of communication; it's disconnection, building walls, distancing, and it hurts.

I don't agree with the theory that there is nothing wrong with a little white lie. There is no such thing as a little lie. Invariably, they lead to big lies. If you lie, even about a part of a story, then the entire story comes into question. The best policy is to speak your truth.

2c What is your purpose?

As you think about requirements and audience, you will also want to ask yourself, "What is my purpose?" If your answer is, "to get a good grade," you will want to carefully consider the requirements of your assignment (2a). But even fulfilling the requirements of your assignment will make demands on your skills as a writer. It will be easier in the long run if you grapple with the underlying purpose, function, and intention of the assignment and what it is designed to get you to do as a writer. Answering the questions in the Key Points box below will help guide you to a preliminary answer.

The first three items listed in the Key Points box (on expository, persuasive, and scientific or technical writing) are generally the main purposes of college writing assignments. Among these categories, however, the overlap can be considerable. Some assignments may require you to explore and test concepts and opinions against what you already know. Other assignments may ask you to blend explanation with persuasion. Whatever you determine to be the main purpose or purposes of a given assignment should guide you as you write.

Your sense of purpose as a writer should come across to readers, quite apart from any separate purpose statement you may write. If you leave them scratching their heads and saying "So?" then you have not been clear in conveying what the readers are to think, feel, or do.

KEY POINTS
Asking about an Assignment's Purpose

1. Is the main purpose to explain an idea, analyze, or provide information? Writing with this purpose is called *expository writing*.

2. Is the main purpose to persuade readers to see things your way or to move readers to action? This aim leads to *persuasive writing* or *argumentation*.

3. Is the main purpose to describe an experiment or a detailed process or to report on laboratory results? Writing with this purpose is frequently referred to as *scientific* or *technical writing*.

4. Is the main purpose to record and express your own experience, observations, ideas, and feelings? In the humanities, such accounts are known as *expressive*, *autobiographical*, or *personal writing*.

5. Is the main purpose to create an original work of art, such as a poem, story, play, or novel? Writing with this purpose is called *creative writing*.

Purpose and planning Your purpose also relates to your planning (2e). If your purpose involves working with difficult or challenging texts and concepts for a research project, you will want to include extra time for getting acquainted with the most useful resources at your library. If your purpose is to write a job application letter, you will need to plan to consult business publications to find out more about the industry and the company. (See chapter 14, Writing for Employment.)

2d What is the right tone?

Choosing the right tone means fitting the structure and language you use to the type of writing you are doing, your purpose in doing the writing, and the expectations of your audience. Tone can also be explained as the attitude of the writer toward the subject and the audience. A casual e-mail message to a friend calls for a tone different from that of an informative business report for your supervisor. Use the chart in the Key Points box to check on how you convey tone within your draft.

KEY POINTS
Consistency of Tone

Look at each category and decide which option is most appropriate for your purpose and audience. Then check to see if your approach to tone is consistent. One instance of sarcasm, say, in an otherwise serious critical evaluation is out of place and likely to irritate readers.

Category	Which option is most appropriate?
Approach to topic	informative, humorous, serious, sarcastic, indignant, scathing, ironic, critical, judgmental, sentimental, praising
Level of formality	informal, chatty, slang, jargon, formal
Conventions	Standard English, dialect, other languages interspersed
Argument	rational, emotional, forceful, aggressive
Vocabulary	everyday, technical, community, literary, academic, ornate

Make sure your tone remains consistent throughout your piece of writing. Changes in tone can be jarring.

Your voice   Another way to think about tone is to consider your voice, which is closely connected to your purpose and audience. How do you want to come across to your readers? What impression do you want them to form of you as a person, of your values and opinions? One of the first considerations is whether you want to draw attention to your opinions as the writer by using the first person pronoun "I," or whether you will try the more objective-seeming approach of keeping that "I" at a distance. Even if you do the latter, though, as is often recommended for academic and especially for scientific writing, you know that readers will still see what you write as ultimately presenting you and your work.

Your instructor or work supervisor may have strong ideas about the voice, the level of formality, and the amount of authorial intervention expected, so ask him or her what is preferred.

EXERCISE 2.3

Match the tone of passages to the intended audience.

Read the following passages, and identify the tone of each passage (see the Key Points box preceding this exercise). Then match each passage with the audience or audiences you think the writer probably had in mind: readers or writers of personal journals, readers of newspapers, readers who want to be entertained as well as educated, or readers of medical or technical journals.

1. It's a bit oversimplified, but substantially true: A 30-minute walk a day helps keep the doctor away. That's the gist of the 278-page *Physical Activity and Health: A Report of the Surgeon General,* issued in 1996, which urged Americans to get 30 minutes of moderate activity on most days of the week. It's also the central finding of a Harvard University study, published last August in the *New England Journal of Medicine,* which concluded that walking can reduce the risk of heart attacks in women to the same degree as vigorous exercise.

   —Carol Krucoff, "A Walk a Day"

   Tone:_____   Audience:_____

2. The health benefits of physical activity have achieved international recognition following the publication of the 1996 US Surgeon General's report on physical activity and health. Given the high prevalence of inactivity, the promotion of physical

activity appears to be at least as important in coronary heart disease prevention as efforts to reduce high cholesterol or high blood pressure, and more important than these factors in contributing to the overall burden of disease. . . . Physical activity is also associated with aspects of injury prevention [and] positive mental health and reduces the risk of developing colon and probably breast and prostate cancer and possibly lung cancer. . . . Incidental [physical] activity can involve using stairs instead of lifts [elevators] or escalators, riding a bicycle rather than driving a car to do minor errands, or choosing not to use energy saving implements for domestic tasks.

> —Adrian Bauman, Neville Owen, and Eva Leslie, "Physical Activity and Health Outcomes: Epidemiological Evidence, National Guidelines and Public Health Initiatives"

Tone:_____ Audience:_____

3. There's a reason we're born with limbs. They're supposed to move. They *need* to move. And they need to move more than just three times a week when we put on special neon-colored clothes and stand on a machine that looks like the command cabin of the Space Shuttle Atlantis.

   The active use of our physical bodies has to be more a part of our everyday lives. We need to get into the habit of using our bodies every minute by engaging our bodies in work, in play, in our errands, in all our daily rituals.

> —Loretta LaRoche, *Life Is Not a Stress Rehearsal*

Tone:_____ Audience:_____

EXERCISE 2.4

Vary tone.

Pick an issue that is important to you as a college student. It could be making class sections smaller, creating an environmentally friendly campus, avoiding long lines during registration, improving the library, or any other topic you consider important. Write a persuasive e-mail (informal) to your classmates on this issue; then write a persuasive letter (formal) to your college president on the same issue. Discuss with classmates what changes you had to make.

2e What's the plan?

As soon as you know what the assignment is and when the final draft is due, work backward from that date to establish a work schedule that allows you to do what needs to be done. Here is a sample work plan for a short essay assignment in an English course with a six-day deadline. Section 46c provides detailed guidelines for setting up a schedule for a research paper.

Tuesday through Thursday	Find and narrow a topic, brainstorm ideas, make a scratch outline.
Friday	Write a first draft. Get feedback from a classmate, tutor, or study group.
Saturday	Read and analyze the draft and plan revisions.
Sunday	Find any necessary additional information. Revise, edit, and proofread.
Monday	Format, print, and hand in.

Adapt this plan to fit the requirements of the writing project, your study and work schedule, and the length of time available. If you have a heavy work and academic schedule, you may have to compress the activities into fewer segments and fewer days.

2f When is it due?

When instructors assign papers, they usually assign a due date. Note the date and make yourself a schedule of work to be done and steps to be accomplished, working backward from the due date to the date the paper is first assigned. Section 46c shows a sample schedule for writing a research paper. Adapt this schedule for shorter, less demanding papers.

If you don't even start a major paper until the evening before it is due, you are bound to feel helpless, desperate, and depressed about your dwindling GPA. In short, *get started early.* There is no better way to avoid panic. Then you will be able to say with a degree of confidence as you near the deadline, "The paper doesn't have to be perfect. It just has to be done." Work on finishing a draft to hand in—however rough or "drafty" it is. If you feel you still need additional time to revise, an instructor is likely to be more sympathetic to a request for an extension of the deadline if you show that you have made a genuine effort and have produced a solid draft.

Chapter **3**

Generate, Shape, and Focus Ideas.

Whether you have to generate your own idea for a topic or you already have a topic that you would like to explore in detail, you need strategies other than staring at the ceiling or waiting for inspiration to fly in through the window. Professional writers use a variety of techniques to generate ideas at various stages of the process. Diane Ackerman, in her article "Oh Muse! You Do Make Things Difficult!" reports that the poet Dame Edith Sitwell used to lie in an open coffin; French novelist Colette picked fleas from her cat; statesman Benjamin Franklin soaked in the bathtub; and German dramatist Friedrich Schiller sniffed rotten apples stored in his desk.

Perhaps you have developed your own original approach to generating ideas. Perhaps you were taught a more formal way to begin a writing project, such as constructing an outline. If what you do now doesn't seem to produce good results, or if you are ready for a change, try some of the methods described in 3a–3e and see how they work. Not every method works equally well for every project or for every writer. Experimenting is a good idea.

EXERCISE 3.1

Write about your own writing process.

Think about your most recent written assignment. Write an account of what the assignment was, how you generated ideas, how you wrote it, where you did your writing, and whether you wrote it with a word processing program. How much time was given between the assignment and the due date, and how did you use that time? How did you feel as you wrote the essay? Be complete and frank in describing your writing process. The point is to examine the way you write. Read your account aloud to a group of classmates. Then discuss any differences from their accounts.

3a Keep a journal or blog.

A *journal* is more than a personal diary. Many writers use journal entries for observations, references, quotations, questions for research, notes on events, and ideas about assigned texts or topics, as well as specific pieces of writing in progress. A journal can also serve as a review for final examinations or essay tests, reminding you of areas of special interest or subjects you did not understand.

The *double-entry* or *dialectical journal* provides a formalized way for you to think critically about readings and lectures. Two pages or two columns or open windows in your word processor provide the space for interaction. On the left side, write summaries, quotations, and accounts of readings, lectures, and class discussions—that is, record as exactly and concisely as you can what you read or heard. The left side, in short, is reserved for information about the material. On the right side, record your own comments, reactions, and questions about the material (see 1a on reading critically). The right side is the place to make your own connections between the reading or lecture and your own experience and knowledge.

Online Study Center Writing Process Double-entry journal

A *blog* also gives you the opportunity to think aloud—in public. Not only can others read your posting; they can respond to it as well. It is easy to set up a blog using an automated publishing system. Blogs are posted in reverse chronological order but otherwise function similarly to a writer's journal, except they get responses. The unedited blog entitled "The *Life* of a Salesman" demonstrates how Tiffany Brattina, a student at Seton Hill University, works out a personal, original, and critical point of view as she considers an alternative interpretation of the character Willie Loman in Arthur Miller's play *Death of a Salesman*. Brattina largely avoids the colloquial nature of instant messaging and informal e-mail and begins to move to the conventions of public discourse suitable for her academic audience. Knowing that other students in her English course will be reading her blog, Brattina openly asks what others think.

Online Study Center Writing Process Blogging

A Student's Blog on a Course Site

March 16, 2004
The *Life* of a Salesman
Ok. So, I'm sure during class today everyone talked about how crazy Willie was, and I am the first to agree. Willie was insane, in the end. However, what about his life?

In *Death of a Salesman* we see the end of Willie's life as a salesman. He went through his entire life working on the road selling things to buyers, he didn't know how to do anything else. Don't you think that would make you go crazy? If a company you worked for your entire life took you off of salary and put you on commission like you were just starting out wouldn't you feel like you were unworthy? Then there is the fact that Willie and his family didn't really have any money to their names at all. Willie kept borrowing money from Charley so that Linda wouldn't know that he wasn't getting paid anymore. Then the company he worked for fired him! I feel bad for Willie, I really do. His kids thought that he was insane and wanted nothing to do with him. The people he worked for his entire life turned him away. Willie was old, tired, and worn out and people including his family turned their backs on him.

Let me make this personal for a minute. My dad recently went through something very similar at his place of work. The company he worked for came into new management and they tried to put my dad on commission. My dad has major tenure where he works considering he is now 56 and has been working there for 40 years making him the longest member still working at the company. He took the new management to court and won his case. I know that while my dad was going through that time he was a total mess, so seeing my dad I can understand what Willie was going through.

What do you guys think? Do you feel bad for Willie or do you think he was just a jerk? Why or why not?

Posted by Tiffany Brattina at March 16, 2004 06:49 PM

Comments

Do you remember Greek Tragedy? I do, and let me say that Willie is the tragic hero. I kept wanting him to succeed, and he didn't. I really felt that there was a chance for him to make something of himself, and couldn't. I had the feeling that Willie was going to kill himself, but something kept telling me that he was going to get out of the severe skid that he was in.

Posted by: The Gentle Giant at March 16, 2004 08:58 pm

Never thought of that Jay . . . you are right though. I did feel like he was going to succeed, especially there at the end . . . Oh well.
Tiff

Posted by Tiffany at March 16, 2004 09:57 PM

3b Freewrite.

If you do not know what to write about or how to approach a broad subject, try doing from five to ten minutes of *freewriting* either on paper or on the computer. When you freewrite, you let one idea lead to another in free association, thinking only about ideas and what you can say on the topic. The important thing is to keep writing.

Zhe Chen selected the topic "name and identity" and did some exploratory work to find a focus and narrow the topic. She eventually decided to write an essay examining the effects of the Chinese Cultural Revolution on family identity. Here is the unedited freewriting that led her initially to that idea.

I have a unusual name, Zhe. My friends in China say it's a boys name. My friends in America think it has only one letter. Most of my American friends have difficulty pronouncing my name.

Some people ask me why don't I Americanize my name so it would be easier to pronounce. But I say if I change my name, it will not be me any more. What else can I write? When I was seven years old, I asked my mother what my name meant. "Ask your father," she said as she washed dishes. It was raining outside, and the room was so quiet that I could hear the rain puttering [?? Look this word up] on the #. My father's thoughts returned to another rainy day in 1967 when the Cultural Revolution just begun. Thousands of people had been banished to countryside and all the schools were closed. My grandparents fled to Hong Kong but my father and aunt stayed in China. Life was difficult. Gangs sent them to the countryside to work. It was here that my parents met.

Back to name again. My father named me Zhe. In Chinese my name means remember and hope. He wanted me remember the Cultural Revolution and he wanted me to finish college. He didn't have that chance.

KEY POINTS
Freewriting Tips

- Give yourself a time limit of five or ten minutes.
- Write as much as you can as quickly as you can on possible subjects or on a subject you have already determined.
- As you write, concentrate on getting some ideas on the page or screen. Don't pause to check or edit. This piece of writing is for your eyes only; no one else will ever read it, let alone judge it.
- If you get stuck, just keep repeating a promising idea or writing about why you get stuck or why the topic is difficult. Use slang, abbreviations, and the first words you think of—in any language. Try not to stop writing.
- At the end of the time limit, read through your freewriting, highlight the best idea that has emerged, and begin writing again with that idea as the focus.

ESL NOTE

Using Your First Language in Freewriting

Freewriting is writing for *you,* writing to discover ideas and get words down on a page or screen. If you can't think of a phrase or word, simply write it in your home language, or write a question in square brackets as Zhe Chen did, to remind yourself to get help from a dictionary or to ask a classmate or your instructor later.

EXERCISE 3.2

Freewrite on a topic.

Write down on a slip of paper two possible topics that you would like a classmate to freewrite on. Your instructor will distribute the slips. From the slip you receive, choose one of the topics and write as much as you can as quickly as you can for five minutes. Then read what you wrote. Is there an idea you could develop further? Discuss the ideas that came to mind with your classmates.

EXERCISE 3.3

Freewrite on a quotation.

Select a brief, interesting quotation from an article or book. Write it on a piece of paper. After collecting these quotations, your instructor will distribute one to you and each of your classmates. Write a timed five-minute freewrite on the quotation you receive. Circle any ideas that you feel you could develop into an essay. Discuss these with your classmates or group. If you feel comfortable, read your freewrite aloud.

3c Brainstorm, list, and map.

Another way to generate ideas is by *brainstorming*—making a free-wheeling list of ideas as you think of them. Brainstorming is enhanced if you do it collaboratively in a group, discussing and then listing or mapping your ideas. Alone or with the group, scrutinize the ideas, arrange them in lists or draw a map of them, and add to or eliminate them.

One group of students working collaboratively made the following brainstorming list on the topic "changing a name":

immigrants

Ellis Island

voluntary changes—hate name

George Eliot (Mary Ann Evans)

Woody Allen (Allen Stewart Konigsberg)

P. Diddy (Sean Combs aka Puff Daddy)

writers and their pseudonyms—who?

married women: some keep own name, some change, some use both names and hyphenate

Hillary Clinton/Hillary Rodham Clinton

forced name changes

political name changes

name changes because of racism or oppression

show business

criminals?

escape from family and parents

Once the students had made the list, they reviewed it, rejected some items, expanded on others, and grouped items. Thus, they developed a range of subcategories that led them to possibilities for new lists, further exploration, and essay organization:

Voluntary Name Changes

authors: George Eliot, Mark Twain, Isak Dinesen

show business and stage names: Woody Allen, Bob Dylan, Ringo Starr, P. Diddy, Ciara, Mos Def

ethnic and religious identification: Malcolm X, Muhammad Ali

Name Changes upon Marriage

reasons for changing or not changing

Hillary Clinton

problem of children's names

alternative: hyphenated name

Forced Name Changes

immigrants on Ellis Island

wartime oppression

slavery

Mapping, also called *clustering,* is a visual way of brainstorming and connecting ideas. It focuses your brainstorming, organizes the ideas as you generate them, and can be done individually or in a group. Write your topic in a circle at the center of a page, think of ideas related to the topic, and write those ideas on the page around the central topic. Draw lines from the topic to the related ideas. Then add details under each of the ideas you noted. For an assignment on "current issues in education," a student created the following map and saw that it indicated several possibilities for topics, such as school vouchers, home-schooling, and the social exclusivity of private schools.

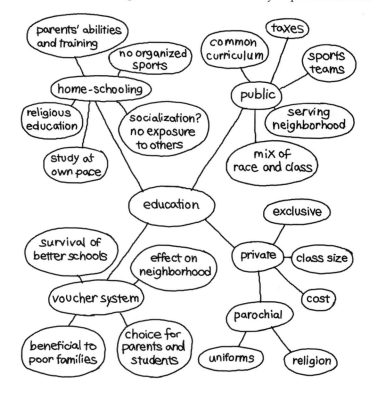

EXERCISE 3.4

Brainstorm in a group.

With four or five classmates, choose a topic you would like to brainstorm about. Select one student to be the recorder and another student to be the spokesperson. As you brainstorm ideas, the recorder will write everything that is said. All members of the group must contribute. Write down everything. Sometimes a seemingly silly or trivial idea can lead to an excellent idea.

After brainstorming, spend some time grouping ideas and filling in any gaps. Compare your brainstorming results with other students in the class. When it is your turn to share with the class, the spokesperson will report your findings.

EXERCISE 3.5

Make an ideas map.

Choose a broad topic such as the environment, politics, immigration, or aging and construct a map of ideas. Then look at your map. What ideas does it suggest about how you could develop and organize a piece of writing on that topic?

EXERCISE 3.6

Maintain a list of topics of interest.

Keep a list of topics you would like to learn more about. Any time you come across an idea or topic that interests you, jot it in your notebook. At this point, don't worry if the topic is too broad or too narrow. The point is to have access to a list of topics. Then, instead of asking yourself, "What will I write about?" you can ask, "How do I want to approach this topic?"

3d Learn what others think: electronic classroom conversations.

It is often useful in developing a topic to network with others on a course electronic bulletin board, in a chat room, or in a newsgroup (see 11c). Alternatively, you can set up your own group of students who want to work together to brainstorm online. Here are sample postings from students developing ideas for a research assignment on how their campus could be more environmentally sustainable. (See 12d for more on academic writing online.)

By <u>Wendy Talantzis</u> on Friday May 19, 2006, 12:35 PM:

Maybe one way to get started on this assignment is to research the ways our campus is already doing things like recycling, encouraging us to car pool, etc. etc. I know there are recycling bins in the student union and in the cafeteria but what happens to the stuff that gets thrown in there? And are the dorms, professor offices, etc. also practicing recycling or educating people in how to use the bins and what to recycle?

> **By** <u>Sedah Auerbach</u> **on Friday May 19, 2006, 12:47** PM:
>
> That's a great idea but where will we get all that information by Tuesday? I just did a quick Google search on "environment," "college," and "recycling" and found three Web sites from other campuses that have a list about their policies on sustainability.

> **By** <u>Jay Rajagopalan</u> **on Friday May 19, 2006, 1:05** PM:
>
> A friend of mine is doing an internship in the Human Resources Office here at school. Her supervisor said that there was a task-force this past semester that has set policies and goals for getting the campus "green" by 2008 and that there would be no problem using the memo outlining those goals. Sedah, can you send us the links to the sites you've found? We can begin by comparing the different goals of each campus.

EXERCISE 3.7

Initiate an e-mail discussion.

When you next have a writing assignment, arrange with three other students in your class to communicate about the topic via e-mail. Contribute at least two postings during the discussion. Print your results and bring them to class.

Alternatively, arrange with three other students to have an online chat. Set a time that is convenient to meet online and engage in an online dialogue about the assigned topic. Print your results and bring them to class.

3e Use journalists' questions and formal prompts.

Journalists check the coverage of their stories by making sure that they answer six questions—Who? What? When? Where? Why? How?—though not in any set order. A report on a public transit strike, for example, would include details about the union leaders (who they were), the issue of working conditions and benefits (what the situation was), the date and time of the confrontation (when the strike occurred), the place (where it occurred), what caused the confrontation (why it happened), and how the people involved behaved and resolved the strike (how it evolved and ended). If you are telling the story of an event, either as a complete essay or as an example in an essay, asking the journalists' six questions will help you think comprehensively about your topic.

Sometimes you might find it helpful to use a formal set of directions (known as *prompts*) to suggest new avenues of inquiry. Write down responses to any of the prompts that apply to your topic, and note possibilities for further exploration.

Define Your Terms

1. Look up key words in your topic in the dictionary, and write down the definition you want to use.
2. What synonyms (words with similar meaning) are possible?
3. Is a brief definition adequate, or do you need a detailed definition?
4. Should your definition be illustrated with an example?
5. Has the definition changed, or is it changing?

Include Descriptions

1. Whatever your topic, make your writing more vivid with details about color, light, location, movement, size, and shape.
2. Appeal to as many of the readers' senses as necessary or possible: tell readers not just what something looks like but also, if applicable, what it sounds, feels, smells, or tastes like.
3. Divide the object of your description into parts, and describe each part in detail.
4. Help your audience "see" your topic, such as a person, place, object, or scientific experiment, as exactly as you see it.
5. Collect visual images or sound recordings that could be integrated with the text of your assignment draft. (For more on using visuals, see 11d.)

Make Comparisons

1. Help your audience understand a topic by describing what it might be similar to. For example, is learning to write like learning to juggle?
2. Note what your topic is different from. For example, is learning to write different from learning to read?

Assess Cause and Effect

1. Will your audience need information on what causes or produces your topic? For example, what are the causes of dyslexia? inflation? acid rain? hurricanes? asthma?
2. What effects or results emerge from your topic?

Consider What Others Have Said

1. Can you give your audience information on what others say about your topic in interviews, surveys, reading, and research?
2. What facts and statistics can you find?
3. Who supports your views?
4. Who opposes them?

EXERCISE 3.8

Look for answers to the journalists' questions.

Go to a newsstand, library, or Web site and browse through current news headlines. Select a news article that grabs your attention and interest. Read the entire article. How does the journalist address the questions Who? What? When? Where? Why? How? Be specific. Then make a list of the main ideas in the article or make a map of the topic (putting the main concept the article deals with in the center).

EXERCISE 3.9

Use the formal prompts.

With a group of three or four classmates, select one of the following topics and explore it by using the sets of formal prompts on pages 36–37. Keep a list of your responses to each prompt. Report to the class about the experience and whether it stimulated any ideas that were unexpected.

study abroad	parenting styles
global warming	alternative energy sources
minimum wage	violent video games
immigration	genetically modified food
AIDS prevention	the placebo effect

EXERCISE 3.10

Explore a topic in several ways.

Work with a group of other students to select a broad topic (such as the environment, heroes, immigration, aging, or fast food). Each person in the group will explore the topic using two of the following methods:

- writing a blog to initiate an online discussion
- freewriting
- brainstorming and grouping ideas
- mapping
- writing answers to the journalists' questions

Read each other's explorations, and discuss which methods generated good ideas.

3f   Find and refine an essay topic.

Finding a topic   "What on earth am I going to write about?" is a question frequently voiced or at least thought in college classrooms, especially in those classrooms in which students are free to write about any topic that interests them.

Using the strategies in 3a–3e will help you find topics. In addition, think about what matters to you. Reflect on issues raised in your college courses; read newspapers and magazines for current issues; consider campus, community, city, state, and nationwide issues; and look at the Library of Congress Subject Headings to get ideas (see chapter 47). Sometimes browsing an online library catalog, a Web directory, or the site of an institution devoted to research can produce good ideas for choosing a topic, but it is usually better to begin with something that has caught your interest elsewhere and has some connection to your life.

TECH NOTE

Using Web Directories to Find a Topic

Academic Web directories assembled by librarians and academic institutions provide reliable sources for finding good academic subjects. For links to the Librarians' Index to the Internet, Academic Info, and Voice of the Shuttle, a University of California at Santa Barbara directory for humanities research, go to the Online Study Center. For more on using search engines and directories, see 47f; for evaluating online materials, see 48d.

Online Study Center   **Writing Process**   Finding a topic

General Internet search engines and directories such as Yahoo! and Google offer subject categories that you can explore and successively narrow down to find a topic suitable for an essay. For example, one Yahoo! search beginning with "Education" produced forty different categories with links to twenty-one site listings (such as *computers as tutors, National Clearinghouse for Comprehensive School Reform, Education Reform.net,* and *No Child Left Behind*).

Refining a topic you find or are assigned The strategies described in 3a–3e can help you find a topic and then generate ideas to include in an essay. While finding a topic is a necessary step, it is only a beginning. The topic then has to be tailored and adapted to make it appropriate for the length and type of essay you intend to write; then, for an opinion essay or an argument, you need to formulate what point of view you will express on the topic, in the form of a thesis (3g). You also need to generate specific and concrete details to use as evidence and support for the thesis (3h).

In college courses, you may be given any of the following types of assignments for an essay, arranged here from the broadest in scope to the narrowest:

- a free choice of subject
- a broad subject area, such as "genetic engineering" or "affirmative action"

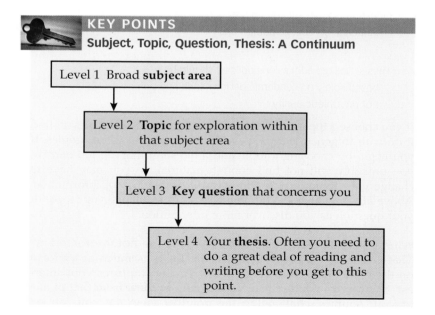

KEY POINTS

Subject, Topic, Question, Thesis: A Continuum

Level 1 Broad **subject area**

Level 2 **Topic** for exploration within that subject area

Level 3 **Key question** that concerns you

Level 4 Your **thesis**. Often you need to do a great deal of reading and writing before you get to this point.

- a focused and specific topic, such as "the city's plans to build apartments on landfill" or "the treatment of welfare recipients in California"
- an actual question to answer, such as "Is age an issue in cases of driving accidents?"

If you are given a free choice of subject, you will need to narrow your focus to a broad subject area, to a specific topic, and then to a specific question. After that, still more narrowing is necessary, eventually leading to a thesis. Your *thesis*, or *claim*, is your statement of opinion, main idea, or message that unifies your piece of writing, makes a connection between you and the subject area, lets readers know where you stand in relation to the topic, and answers the question posed. But you cannot move toward a good thesis if your topic is too broad or too narrow.

Here is one student's movement from subject to thesis over several days of reading, discussion, freewriting, and note-taking:

Subject: College admissions policies

↓

Narrowed Topic: College admissions for athletes

↓

Question: Should success in sports have any
    influence on college admissions?

↓

Thesis: College admissions policies should be
    based solely on academic performance and potential,
    not on athletic ability.

If you choose a topic and a question that are too broad, you will find it difficult to generate a thesis with focused ideas and examples. If you begin by choosing a topic and a question that are too narrow, you probably will not find enough material, so you may have to change your topic or question because of this lack of information. Above all, stay flexible: you may also want to change your topic or your question as you discover more information.

What if you are assigned a topic that you are not interested in?
That can happen, but do not despair. Read as much as you can on the topic until something strikes you and captures your interest. You can try taking the opposite point of view from that of one of your sources, challenging the point of view. Or you can set

yourself the task of showing readers exactly why the topic has not grabbed people's interest—maybe the literature and the research have been just too technical or inaccessible? If you can, find a human angle.

EXERCISE 3.11

Find and narrow a topic in a search directory.

Access an online library database such as *InfoTrac/Expanded Academic* or *EBSCO Host/Academic Search Premier.* In the Search box, start with a subject search of any broad category: for example, "family," "health," or "music." Look at the categories until you find one you are interested in. For example, a subject search of "family" yields "family and mass media" as one of the categories. Whatever broad category you decide to search, be sure to narrow the subject to a topic you could explore in a short paper.

Click on the category and access at least two sources. Then formulate a possible question that would focus your thinking and any research.

EXERCISE 3.12

Search the Web for a focused topic.

Work with a partner, and use a search directory such as Google, AltaVista, Librarians' Index to the Internet, or Yahoo! to work your way down the levels of a subject category in order to come up with some possible focused topics for writing. Then formulate for each topic a question that will yield a thesis statement.

EXERCISE 3.13

Narrow a topic.

In groups of two or three, discuss the ways in which one of the following broad subject areas could be narrowed to a topic and a question appropriate to a seven-page essay.

small businesses	women's rights	immigration
home-schooling	gambling	genetics
gun control	reality television	nature vs. nurture
learning disabilities	the film industry	birth order
	advertisements	the Olympics

3g Formulate a thesis.

Suppose someone were to ask you, "What is the main idea that you want to communicate to readers in your piece of writing?" The sentence you would give in reply is your *thesis*, also known as a *claim*. Your thesis tells readers what point you are going to make about your topic, what stand you are going to take. It is not enough to say, "I am writing about bilingual education." Are you going to address bilingual education in elementary, secondary, or higher education? Which readers do you regard as your primary audience? Which geographical areas will you discuss? Will you be concerned with the past or with the present? What do you intend to propose about the area of bilingual education you have selected? In short, what point do you want to make about which aspect of bilingual education—for which audience? It is also not enough to stop short with a question. Do not try to build an essay around a question such as "Do parents view bilingual education differently from school administrators?" You can certainly start with a question, but then you need to let your question lead you to the answer you provide, and that answer, in the form of a statement, will be your thesis.

You don't have to know where to put your thesis statement in your essay right away, nor do you need to settle immediately on the exact wording of your thesis. However, even a preliminary idea for a topic can generate a working thesis that you can then refine as you plan, read, and write. See 7d on the thesis in an argument paper.

How to write a good thesis statement A good thesis statement may be one or more of the following:

1. a generalization needing supporting evidence

   ▶ **Students benefit when they learn in two languages.**

2. a strong, thought-provoking, or controversial statement

   ▶ **Bilingual education has not fulfilled its early promise.**

3. a call to action

   ▶ **All inner-city schools should set up transitional bilingual programs.**

4. a question that will be answered by the thesis statement and then backed up with details in the essay

   ▶ **What can bilingual education accomplish for a child? It can lead to personal as well as academic development.**

5. an analytical statement that sets up the structure of the essay

> ▶ **Bilingual education suffers from two main problems: a shortage of trained teachers and a lack of parental involvement.**

> ▶ **Although bilingual education suffers from a shortage of teachers and lack of parental involvement, its theoretical principles are sound.**

KEY POINTS
Thesis Checklist

Use this list to help you work on the thesis statement of an essay. You should be able to put a checkmark next to each quality.

☐ Your thesis is worth saying.

☐ Your thesis narrows your topic to the one main idea that you want to communicate.

☐ Your thesis makes a claim or asserts an opinion about your topic.

☐ Your thesis can be supported by details, facts, and examples within the assigned limitations of time and space.

☐ Your thesis stimulates curiosity and interest in readers and prompts them to think, "Why do you say that?" and then read on.

☐ Your thesis uses exact language and concepts rather than vague generalizations.

☐ Your thesis does not include anything that you do not intend to discuss in your essay.

☐ Your thesis is one complete sentence, usually with only one independent clause (though you will come across many variations).

After you have formulated your working thesis, write it on a self-stick note or an index card, and keep it near you as you write. The note or card will remind you to stick to the point. If you still digress as you write, you may need to consider changing your thesis.

From working thesis to revision An initial working thesis may be a tentative opinion statement that you formulate soon after you formulate your question—but try to move beyond it to something focused as soon as you can. As you think more, read more, learn more, and discover more specific ideas, you will usually find that you rework your thesis several times to make it more informative, less general, and more precise. You may even indicate in your thesis what main points of support you will discuss in your essay. Here are some examples of a preliminary working thesis later revised as a final draft thesis for a two- to three-page essay:

Personal essay

Preliminary working thesis: Starting college at age thirty-four was difficult for me.

Revised thesis: Starting college at age thirty-four has involved reassessing my commitments to work and family.

Informative essay

Preliminary working thesis: There are many ways to handle credit responsibly.

Revised thesis: To handle credit responsibly, students need to stick to a budget and control their shopping. [Here the "many ways" have been limited to two, named specifically. In addition, the target population has been limited to students.]

Persuasive essay

Preliminary working thesis: Affirmative action is a controversial policy in college admissions.

Revised thesis: Affirmative action used in the college admissions process is a good way to ensure diversity of students and equality in society. [Here readers expect a twofold argument, one addressing the ability of affirmative action to create diversity in a student body, the other broadening the concept to the idea of affirmative action also having an equalizing effect on society.]

Persuasive essay

Preliminary working thesis: Cell phones have many advantages.

Revised thesis: Although cell phones may cause problems when they are misused, they are a boon to working parents wanting to keep track of their children's whereabouts after school hours. [This refined thesis statement limits discussion of the advantages of cell phones to the benefits they provide to working parents; it also indicates that the writer will acknowledge some disadvantages but will evaluate these as less important than the advantages.]

Recognizing a good thesis statement   A good thesis statement is a complete sentence (or, sometimes, more than one sentence), makes an interesting and debatable assertion, expresses an opinion that needs to be supported and explained, and does not simply state a fact or obvious truism. A good thesis statement also gives readers some sense of what main points will be used to support the thesis and how the essay will be organized.

INEFFECTIVE   **The desolation of shopping malls** [This phrase lacks a verb and so is not a sentence. It is more suitable as a title than a thesis. A thesis statement is a sentence that makes an assertion.]

INEFFECTIVE   **City life and its disadvantages.** [This phrase lacks a verb and so is not a sentence. A thesis statement is a sentence that makes an assertion.]

INEFFECTIVE   **There are many kinds of exercise machines.** [This statement is a sentence, but it does not make an interesting and debatable assertion. It does not express an opinion that needs to be supported and explained. Instead, it states a fact. The reader has no incentive to read on, no notion that by reading on he or she will find out useful or necessary information about exercise machines.]

INEFFECTIVE   ***Death of a Salesman* is a play by Arthur Miller.** [This sentence states a fact. It does not make an interesting and debatable assertion. Readers, especially those who know their literature, will nod and think, "Yes, I know that," and will not feel driven to read on to find out what makes you say that.]

INEFFECTIVE   **Murder is wrong.** [Almost nobody would disagree or find this an interesting statement. This sentence states a truism, a statement so obvious that it does not merit discussion or engage readers' interest.]

INEFFECTIVE   **Almost half of the students in college are adults with families and jobs.** [This sentence states a fact. It does not make an interesting comment or observation about this aspect of college life today.]

EFFECTIVE   **Because so many students are older adults, colleges should allow a longer time to get a degree, provide more day-care centers, and develop more online**

courses. [This thesis statement establishes a clear focus on a topic, asserts an opinion, and gives the reader some sense of what main points will be used to support the thesis and how the essay will be organized.]

ESL NOTE

Language, Identity, and the Thesis Statement

Often writers who have developed their writing skills in one language notice distinct differences in the conventions of writing in another, particularly with respect to the explicit statement of opinion in the thesis. It is difficult to determine how much of a role one's culture plays in the way one writes and to separate culture's role from the roles of gender, socioeconomic status, family background, and education. However, always consider what approaches your anticipated readers are likely to be familiar with and to value.

Stating your thesis in your paper   Even though it is useful to have a working thesis as you read and write drafts and to refine your thesis as you work, you will eventually need to decide if and where you will include a thesis statement in your essay. Ask your instructor about any special requirements for thesis location. In most academic writing in the humanities and social sciences, a thesis is stated clearly in the essay, usually near the beginning. See your thesis statement as a signpost—both for you as you write your draft and, later, for your readers as they read your essay. A clear thesis prepares readers well for the rest of the essay.

Sometimes, though, particularly in descriptive, narrative, and informative writing, you may choose to imply your thesis and not explicitly state it. In such a case, you make your thesis clear by the examples, details, and information you include. You may also choose to state your thesis at the end of your essay instead of the beginning. If so, you present all the evidence to build a case and then make the thesis act as a climax and logical statement about the outcome of the evidence. If you use key words from your thesis as you write, you will keep readers focused on your main idea.

On not falling in love with your working thesis   A good working thesis often takes so long to develop that you might be reluctant to change it. Be willing, however, to refine and change your thesis as you find more information and work with your material. Many writers begin with a tentative working thesis and then find that they come to a new conclusion at the end of the first draft. If that happens to you, start your second draft by focusing on the thesis that emerged during the writing of the first draft. Be flexible: it's easier to change a thesis statement to fit new ideas and newly discovered evidence than to find evidence to fit a thesis. Note that your final revised thesis statement should take a firm stand on the issue. Flexibility during the writing process is not the same as indecision in the final product.

EXERCISE 3.14

Evaluate thesis statements.

Which of the following statements work well as a thesis statement to focus an essay of three to five pages in length, and which do not? Give the reasons for your assessment.

1. Adding a sixth day of classes is more effective in helping students than extending the hours of the present five-day class schedule.

2. Although solar panels and wind farms offer promising energy alternatives, the economic relationships among countries using fuel oil make alternative energy sources highly unlikely to succeed.

3. Although art and music therapies differ in their approaches, there are compelling similarities between these methods.

4. In order to assist the increasing population of young homeless people, new policies are needed to improve the quality of shelters, create back-to-work employment programs, and fund medical and mental health treatment.

5. Although several studies reveal that placebos are effective in healing ill patients, physicians need to conduct more research into how and why placebos work.

6. Understanding personality types provides us with insights into ourselves and the world.

7. "Mindfulness" or "paying attention" to the world around us is a vital skill to develop because it enriches our lives, sharpens our memory skills, keeps us safe, and helps us become more aware eyewitnesses.

EXERCISE 3.15

Revise thesis statements.

The following thesis statements are too narrow, too broad, or too vague or are factual statements. Revise each one to make it an appropriate thesis statement for a three- to five-page essay.

1. Legalizing same-sex marriage is a controversial issue.
2. Literacy is an important issue that must be dealt with.
3. Plants enhance the beauty of a home.
4. People with disabilities can face employment discrimination in several ways.
5. Alcoholism affects children.
6. Advertisers of food products use color-enhanced images to entice consumers into purchasing their products.
7. The media are responsible for causing eating disorders, lowering self-esteem, and encouraging unrealistic ideals of beauty.

EXERCISE 3.16

Write thesis statements.

Read the following list of topics and, together with a group of classmates, refine the topics into thesis statements for a three- to four-page argumentative or persuasive essay. Use the four levels outlined in the Key Points box on page 39 and in the example below:

Example

Level 1:	Subject	Reality TV shows
Level 2:	Narrowed topic	Reality TV shows such as *The Amazing Race*
Level 3:	Key question	Why did they become popular?
Level 4:	Tentative thesis	Reality TV shows such as *The Amazing Race* enjoy widespread popularity and high ratings because of the perceived originality of the series, as well as interest in the contestants, challenging activities, and financial prizes.

1. Level 1: Subject   Your college's registration process
2. Level 1: Subject   America's system of movie ratings
   [Note: G (general audience, all ages admitted); PG (parental guidance suggested); PG-13 (parents strongly cautioned); R (restricted—under 17 requires accompanying parent or adult guardian); NC-17 (no one 17 or under admitted)]
3. Level 1: Subject   Women in combat
4. Level 1: Subject   Alternative energy sources for automobiles

3h Provide evidence and support.

Once you have come up with a good thesis for your essay, you then have to find ways to develop and support it. Readers expect to find out why you hold a certain point of view or why you regard your information as important: What are your reasons? What is your evidence? Where does the evidence come from? Your paragraphs will develop and support your thesis one point at a time.

Let's say you are writing a paper with the following thesis:

> College admissions policies should be based solely on academic performance and potential, not on athletic ability.

Your job in the paper is to show readers why you think that, to provide information that backs up your case, and to write a convincing argument. You may not be able to win over a scholarship football star to your side, but you should be able to make his team recognize that sound arguments exist. Here are some strategies you might use:

- Provide information about research studies showing the low academic success rate of athletes, and report statistics of class rank at graduation.
- Give an account of an interview with a college admissions officer and an athletics coach.
- Give examples of credentials of students who were rejected when athletes were admitted.
- Describe details of the athletic culture on a campus, showing how the athletic culture discourages academic study.
- Tell a story about an athlete's college applications.

- Compare and contrast two high school students—one athlete and one nonathlete—applying to the same college.
- Define the terms *academic performance* and *athletic ability.*
- Classify athletes into types of athlete (for example, athletes who have maintained a B, C, or D average; athletes who need to practice for 7 hours a week, 15 hours, or more than 15).
- Explain the problem facing admissions officers, and offer a solution.

KEY POINTS

Supporting a Point

The following methods can be used to support your thesis. In a paragraph, too, you can develop and support your controlling idea or topic sentence (see 5b) by using one or several of the following:

- facts and statistics
- examples
- stories
- descriptions
- definitions
- instructions on how to do something
- classifications or analysis
- comparisons and contrasts
- discussions of causes and effects
- analysis of problems and solutions
- expert testimony

See 5d for examples of the above types of supporting details that various writers have used within paragraphs and essays.

EXERCISE 3.17

Find details to use in support of a thesis.

For each of the following thesis statements, discuss with other students which types of supporting details you would choose to support the thesis and provide evidence to make a convincing case to readers (for example, facts and statistics, examples, stories, descriptions, definitions, instructions; see the Key Points box immediately preceding this exercise). Create a list of the types of supporting details that would be effective for each thesis statement, and include any specific details that would illustrate the point.

1. The current adoption systems must be reformed so that couples seeking to adopt a child avoid long delays, unnecessary extensive paperwork, and costly fees.

2. Community centers in ethnic neighborhoods play an important role in helping new immigrants assimilate into America by providing job assistance, English language instruction classes, and interaction with other immigrants who have successfully struck a balance between assimilation and preservation of heritage.

3. "Recycle, Reduce, and Reuse" are three activities citizens can do on a daily basis to help protect our environment from the hazards of pollution and solid waste.

4. Although law enforcement authorities claim that video surveillance of neighborhood streets protects residents from crime, video surveillance infringes on our civil liberties and should not be used.

5. Internships help students explore their intended careers, make important contacts, and gain valuable work experience.

3i Prepare an outline, a purpose statement, or a proposal.

Scratch outlines A *scratch outline* is a rough list of numbered points that you intend to cover in your essay. A scratch outline lets you see what ideas you already have, how they connect, what you can do to support and develop them, and what further planning or research you still need to do. One student in the group that made the brainstorming list on page 32 developed the following scratch outline and formulated a working thesis:

Topic: Changing a name
Question: Why do people change their names?
Tentative working thesis: People change their names because they either have to or want to.
Types of name changes:

1. Forced name changes in a new country or a new school

2. Name changes to avoid discrimination or persecution

3. Name changes upon marriage

4. Name changes in show business

5. Voluntary name changes to avoid recognition

   a. Criminals

   b. Writers

When this student began to write his draft, however, he changed direction and unified some of his points, developing a more focused thesis (see more on formal outlines, directly following).

Formal outlines A *formal outline* spells out, in order, what points and supportive details you will use to develop your thesis and arranges them to show the overall form and structure of the essay, moving from the general to the specific, using points you have generated in brainstorming, mapping (3c), or other methods. As you formulate an outline, keep an image of readers in mind. Imagine them asking when they read your thesis, "Why do you think that? What is the evidence?" If you have explored the question in enough depth and breadth, you should be able to identify several reasons or main points of support. These will form the structural backbone of the essay. Then for each main reason or piece of support, imagine readers again asking, "Why is this point important? What is the evidence?"

You may produce a formal outline before you begin to write, but you are likely to find that making an outline with a high level of detail is more feasible after you have written a draft. Done at this later point, the outline serves as a check on the logic and completeness of what you have written, revealing any gaps, repetition, or illogical steps in the development of your essay.

KEY POINTS
Writing an Outline

1. Write a formal outline only after you have done a great deal of thinking, reading, writing, and research. Sometimes it is better to delay writing an outline until after you have a rough draft on paper; then you can outline what you have written and see if it makes sense.

2. Decide on whether items in the outline will be words and phrases (with no end punctuation) or complete sentences. If

you can, go with complete sentences—you will find that doing that helps record or formulate your ideas more clearly. For a short essay, complete sentences written to indicate major points can then stand as the topic sentences of supporting paragraphs.

3. Use parallel structures for major headings—sentences or phrases, but not a mixture.

4. Organize your outline so that it moves from larger ideas to smaller, with all ideas under a similar letter or number equal in level of generality and importance.

5. Whenever you divide a point, always have at least two parts (just like dividing a cake). So whenever you have I, you must have II. Whenever you have A, you must have B, and so on.

6. Keep outline categories separate and distinct, without confusing overlap.

7. Do not include the introduction and the conclusion in your outline.

This is what a formal outline may look like:

Thesis statement
I. First major point of support
    A. First piece of evidence for first point of support
        1. First point of discussion, reason, or example
           a. First specific illustration or detail
           b. Second specific illustration or detail (and so on)
        2. Second point of discussion, reason, or example (and so on)
    B. Second piece of evidence for first point of support
        1. First point of discussion, reason, or example
        2. Second point of discussion, reason, or example
        3. Third point of discussion, reason, or example (and so on)
II. Second major point of support
    A. First piece of evidence for second point of support (and so on)

The student who worked with the group on brainstorming (3c) and made the scratch outline shown on pages 51–52 finally settled on a thesis and made this formal sentence outline of his essay draft.

Thesis: A voluntary name change is usually motivated by a desire to avoid or gain recognition.

I. The desire to avoid recognition by others is one motivation for a name change.
   A. Criminals change their names after serving a prison sentence.
   B. Writers often change their names.
      1. Women writers adopt men's names.
         a. Mary Ann Evans took on the name George Eliot.
         b. George Sand's real name was Amandine Aurore Lucie Dupin.
         c. The baroness Karen Blixen chose to write under the name Isak Dinesen.
      2. Writers adopt a pseudonym.
         a. Mark Twain's real name was Samuel Clemens.
         b. The writer of *Alice in Wonderland* was actually Charles Dodgson, but he hid behind the name Lewis Carroll.
         c. Crime novels by Amanda Cross are actually the work of a renowned scholar, Carolyn Heilbrun.
   C. People want to avoid ethnic identification.
II. Some people change a name to join a group and gain recognition.
   A. Married women mark membership in a family.
      1. They want to indicate married status.
      2. They want to have the same name as their children.
   B. Entertainers choose eye-catching names.
      1. Marilyn Monroe's given name was Norma Jean Baker.
      2. Woody Allen began life as Allen Stewart Konigsberg.
      3. Richard Starkey adopted the distinctively descriptive name Ringo Starr.
      4. Entertainers in the public eye often take extraordinary names: P. Diddy (Sean Combs) and Mos Def (Dante Smith).

Making this outline allowed the student to see some shortcomings in his draft. He saw that, on the whole, his draft was basically well structured, but he noticed gaps: for instance, he needed to find out more about criminals and their aliases (Point I.A. in the outline) and about people who change a name to avoid ethnic identification (Point I.C.). He was pleased that he had used complete sentences for the main divisions of the outline because he was then able to transfer these sentences directly into his next draft.

For an outline of an MLA research paper in 52f, see 50c.

>
> **TECH NOTE**
> **Using the Computer's Outline Function**
> Most word processing programs mark each paragraph of your draft with a symbol and mark levels of headings with a different symbol. (In Microsoft Word, go to the View menu and select Outline to see the outline view of your document.) You may find this feature helpful for seeing what shape your draft takes. Similarly, as you type, you can designate various levels of headings (1–9 in Word), and your program can format each heading for you. You can also print out an outline showing whichever levels of headings you select.

> **EXERCISE 3.18**
> **Write a scratch outline and a formal outline.**
> Choose one of the thesis statements you wrote in Exercise 3.15, and write a scratch outline. Bring your outline to class and, as a group, select one scratch outline to develop together into a formal outline.

> **EXERCISE 3.19**
> **Write a formal outline for an essay assignment.**
> Write a formal outline for an essay assignment you are currently working on. Alternatively, write a formal outline for a topic you are interested in using for your next essay assignment.

Purpose statements A purpose statement is useful to focus your ideas and give yourself something to work with. Write a simple statement of purpose after you have crafted a working thesis. This statement may become more developed or later even change completely, but it will serve to guide your first steps in the process. Here is an example of a purpose statement written by Nick Sakari for a short paper in his first-year writing course. (Purpose statements can often be expanded into full-scale proposals, like the one in 46g.)

> In this essay, I will try to persuade my professor and my classmates that historical novels blending fact and fiction—such as In the Time of the Butterflies by Julia Alvarez—should be included as required texts for history courses even though they go beyond historical fact. My thesis will be that history can never be the exact truth, and historical novels, along with memoirs and journals, offer valuable insight into how individual people are affected by historical events.

Proposals You may be asked to submit a proposal for a piece of writing to get approval for the topic, contents, and organization. A proposal is not necessarily as detailed or as precise as an outline, and in fact, you can view it as an exploration—something that tests whether a topic will work for you. A proposal should indicate your audience, your thesis, and your major points. It can be written as a narrative or a numbered list, whichever fits your topic. Here is an example of a proposal for a short paper in an expository writing course. (See 46e for a preliminary statement of purpose for a research paper; see 46g for a fuller research proposal.)

In this essay, I intend to persuade my classmates and my instructor that freedom of speech does not necessarily mean freedom from repercussions. While the Constitution guarantees the right to freedom of speech without imprisonment, it does not guarantee that people will not have to pay the price of being denounced or ostracized for expressing repugnant views. I will include the following points relating to reactions to the terrorist attack of September 11, 2001, and will provide specific examples to back up each one.

1. Television and news personalities should be able to express their views without the censorship of corporate sponsors stifling their freedom. However, they cannot expect viewers to agree with them; they should expect outrage if outrage is warranted. Discuss Bill O'Reilly on *The O'Reilly Factor.*

2. College professors should be able to express their views on controversial issues. However, students have the right to refuse to attend their classes, and taxpayers have the right to react strongly and even urge dismissal. Even so, the principle of academic freedom should stand to protect jobs. Discuss examples in Texas and Colorado.

3. Writers have the right to express their opinions in their works. Bookstore owners have the right not to stock their books, and readers have the right not to buy their books, thus denying them a living. Discuss Chris Hedges and *War Is a Force That Gives Us Meaning.*

Chapter **4**

Draft and Revise.

Drafting is a crucial part of the writing process, allowing you to develop and refine your ideas. Always allow time in your writing to put your draft away before looking at it with a critical eye.

Revising—making changes to improve a piece of writing—is another essential part of the writing process. It is not a punishment inflicted on inexperienced writers. Good finished products are the result of careful revision. Even Leo Tolstoy, author of the monumental Russian novel *War and Peace,* commented: "I cannot understand how anyone can write without rewriting everything over and over again."

As you revise and edit, you will address both "big-picture" and "little-picture" concerns. Big-picture revising involves making changes in content and organization. When you revise, you may add or delete details, sections, or paragraphs; alter your thesis statement; vary or strengthen your use of transitions; move material from one position to another; and improve clarity, logic, flow, and style. Little-picture editing involves making adjustments to improve sentence variety; vary sentence length; and correct errors in grammar, spelling, word choice, mechanics, and punctuation. Both are necessary, but most people like to focus first on the big picture and then turn to fixing up the details.

4a Get your drafts down.

Writing provides what speech can never provide: the opportunity to revise your ideas and the way you present them without your audience's realization. The drafting process lets you make substantive changes as you progress through drafts. You can add, delete, and reorganize sections of your paper. You can rethink your thesis and support. You can change your approach to parts or all of the paper. Writing drafts allows you to work on a piece of writing until you feel you have made it meet your goals.

KEY POINTS
Tips for a First Draft

1. Plan the steps and set a schedule. First set the deadline date; then, working backward, establish dates for completing drafts and getting feedback. See 2e and 46c for sample schedules.

2. Don't automatically begin at the beginning. Begin by writing the essay parts for which you already have some specific material.

3. Write in increments of twenty to thirty minutes to take advantage of momentum.

(Continued)

Online Study Center   This icon will direct you to quick reference tools, Web resources, and research guides on the Web site at http://college.hmco.com/keys.html.

(Continued)

4. Write your first draft as quickly and fluently as you can. Write notes to yourself in capitals or surrounded by asterisks to remind yourself to add or change something or do further research.

5. Print out your draft triple-spaced so that you can easily write in questions, comments, and changes.

6. Keep your topic, purpose, question, and thesis very much in mind.

7. Avoid the obvious (such as "All people have feelings"). Be specific, and include interesting supporting details.

8. Revise for ideas, interest, and logic; don't merely fix errors. It is often tempting just to correct errors in spelling and grammar and see the result as a new draft. Revising entails more than that. You need to look at what you have written, check for the logic and development of each paragraph (see 5d), imagine readers' reactions, and rethink your approach to the topic.

TECH NOTE

Using Comments and Auto Correct in a Word Document

Some word processing programs have a Comment function that allows you to type notes that can appear only on the screen, or on the screen and in a printout. These notes—to yourself or to your instructor—can be easily deleted from later drafts. In addition, if you use a term frequently (for example, "bilingual education"), abbreviate it (as *b.e.*, for example) and use a tool like Auto Correct to replace the whole phrase throughout your draft as you type.

Managing drafts and files Save all your notes and drafts until your writing is completed and the course is over. Print out a copy of each new draft so that if something happens to your disk, pen drive, or computer, you still have a copy of your work. In addition, save each new draft under a new file name, just in case you want to compare versions or return to ideas in a prior draft. If you cut out substantial passages, save them in a separate file labeled "Outtakes." Then you can easily retrieve the passages if you change your mind and want to use them. Above all, do remember to make back-up copies of all your draft files.

For a ten-page essay on athletic scholarships, a student kept eight computer documents in one "Athletic Scholarships Essay" folder to handle the recording of information from sources, as well as his own notes and drafts:

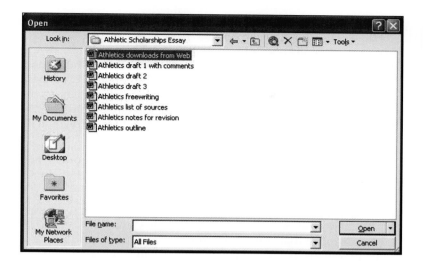

Consider the file structure you will use for every assignment you write.

EXERCISE 4.1
Use the tips; set a schedule.

Before you begin your next writing assignment, reread the Key Points box "Tips for Drafts" and use all or most of its first six tips. Then discuss with classmates what you did, how it was or was not a change from the way you usually write, and how well it worked. As you work on the first tip (to set a schedule), use or adapt the following template. Mark your calendar and use these dates as you complete your next writing assignment.

SCHEDULE FOR ASSIGNMENT #_____

Due Date (month and date)	Activity
Day 1 _____	Find a topic.
Day 2 _____	Brainstorm ideas.
Day 3 _____	Make scratch outline.
Day 4 _____	Write a first draft, get feedback (for example, from a tutor, study group, or classmate).
Day 5 _____	Revise and edit.
Day 6 _____	Proofread.
Day 7 _____	Format, print, and hand in.

4b Analyze and revise your drafts.

For college assignments and important business documents, always allow time in your writing schedule for at least a second draft—more if possible. Before writing a second draft, you should examine a printed copy of your first draft, assess how it measures up to the assignment, evaluate it as a response to the assignment, and plan the changes you need to make. Try any of the following to help you with your analysis:

- Create distance and space. Put a draft away for a day or two and then read it again with fresher, more critical eyes. Imagine readers' reactions to your title and your thesis.

- Highlight key words in the assignment. Mark passages in your draft that address the words. If you fail to find any, this could be a clear signal that you need to revise.

- Read your draft aloud. Mark any places where you hesitate and have to struggle to understand the point. Go back to them later. Alternatively, ask somebody else to read a copy of the draft; note where the reader hesitates or seems unclear about the meaning.

- Make an outline of what you have written (see 3i).

KEY POINTS
Triggers for Revision

The following should alert you to consider the need for revision:

1. a weak or boring introductory paragraph (see 5f)

2. any spot in your draft that causes a worried frown, a pause, or a thought of "Huh? Something is wrong here" as you read

3. a paragraph that never makes a point or offers support

4. a phrase, sentence, or passage that you cannot immediately and fully understand (if you have trouble grasping your own ideas, readers surely will have trouble, too)

5. excessive use of generalizations—*everyone, most people, all human beings, all students/lawyers/politicians,* and so on (it's better to use specific examples in their place: *the students in my political science course this semester*)

6. a feeling that you would have difficulty summarizing your draft (maybe it is too vague?)

7. an awareness that you have just read the same point earlier in the draft

8. a sense that you would like to turn beyond the last page in an attempt to find a definite conclusion

See 6d for a student's annotations on her first draft.

TECH NOTE

Copy and Paste First Sentences.

1. Select the first sentence of each paragraph, and use the Copy and Paste features to move the sequence of sentences into a new file. Then examine these first sentences. Do they provide a sense of a logical progression of ideas? Is there any repetition? What will readers of these first sentences expect the paragraph to contain?

2. Save all new drafts and old drafts under different file names so that you can retrieve older material if you need to. If you use Microsoft Word, use the Tools/Track Changes/Compare Documents features to highlight and examine the differences between drafts.

EXERCISE 4.2

Analyze a draft.

Select a paragraph from an essay you wrote earlier for this course or in another course. Read it aloud and then follow the guidelines on pages 60–61 to mark places where you would consider revising. For example, you may notice a paragraph that never makes a point, an excessive use of generalizations, a vague or confusing spot, and so on. Discuss with classmates what alerted you to the places that need revising.

4c Use feedback and peer review.

Sometimes another reader can spot things that we miss, especially when we have just finished a draft and feel flush with success. Ask a friend, colleague, or tutor to read your draft with a critical eye and a pencil in hand, placing a checkmark next to the passages that work well and a question mark next to those that do not. Ask your reader to tell you what main point you made and how you supported and developed it. This process might reveal any lack of clarity or indicate gaps in the logic of your draft. Your reader does not have to be an expert writing teacher to give you good feedback. If you notice worried frowns (or worse, yawns) as the person reads, you will know that something in your text is puzzling, disconcerting, or boring. Even that simple level of feedback can be valuable.

Here is a sample peer response form that a classmate can use to provide you with feedback.

 Online Study Center   Writing Process Peer response form

Draft by _____   Date _____

Response by _____ Date _____

1. What do you see as the writer's main point in this draft?

2. What part of the draft interests you the most? Why?

3. Where do you feel you would like more detail or explanation? Where do you need less?

4. Do you find any parts unclear, confusing, or undeveloped? Mark each spot with a pencil question mark in the margin and then write a note to the writer with questions and comments about the parts you have marked.

5. Give the writer one suggestion about one change that you think would improve the draft.

KEY POINTS
Giving Feedback to Others

1. When you are asked to give feedback to a classmate, don't think of yourself as a writing teacher armed with a red pen.

2. Read for positive reactions to ideas and clarity. Look for parts that make you think, "I agree," "I like this," or "This is well done."

3. As you read, put a light pencil mark next to one or two passages that make you pause and send you back to reread.

4. Try to avoid comments that sound like accusations ("You were too vague in paragraph 3"). Instead, use "I" to emphasize your reaction as a reader ("I had a hard time visualizing the scene in paragraph 3").

4d Write and revise collaboratively.

Writing, as well as providing feedback, is not necessarily a solitary process. In the academic or business world, you might be expected to work in formal collaborative structures. Groups, teams, or committees might be formed to draft a proposal or report, or you might be expected to produce documents reflecting the consensus of your section or group. You will always want to be sure, however, that you work collaboratively only when doing so is expected. An instructor who assigns an essay may not expect or want you to work on it with anyone else.

In such group settings, make sure that you work out a way for every member of the group to contribute. You can do this by assigning each person a set of specific tasks, such as making lists of ideas, drafting, analyzing the draft, revising, editing, assembling visuals, and preparing the final document. Schedule regular meetings, and expect everyone to come with a completed written assignment. Build on strengths within the group. For example, for a business report, ask the member skilled in document design and computer graphics to prepare the visual features of the final document (11).

TECH NOTE

Writing Collaboratively on the Computer

Microsoft Word provides useful tools for collaboration. You can work on a text, show additions and deletions, make and highlight changes, and attach the revised text to an e-mail message to a classmate or colleague, who can then click to Accept or Reject the changes. See 6b for more details.

4e The power of a title

A good title captures readers' attention, makes readers want to read on, and lets readers know what to expect in the essay. You probably have in mind a useful working title as you write, but after you finish writing, brainstorm several titles and pick the one you like best. If titles occur to you as you write, make a note of them. For information on correctly formatting a title for an academic paper, see 12a.

WORKING TITLE   **Problems in the Fashion Industry**

REVISED TITLE   **Thin and Thinner: How the Fashion Industry Denigrates Women**

WORKING TITLE   **The Benefits of Travel**

REVISED TITLE   **From Katmandu to Kuala Lumpur: A Real Education**

Let your title stand separately from your essay. Do not assume that readers know what your title is when you begin your essay. In the following example, the writer makes the first sentence refer to the title:

> What "The Red Convertible" Tells Us about War
> This story by Louise Erdrich tells us about a lot more than simply two brothers and their car.

She then revised the first sentence:

> What "The Red Convertible" Tells Us about War
> We learn about a lot more than the story of two brothers and their car from Louise Erdrich's atmospheric short story "The Red Convertible."

EXERCISE 4.3

Select a title.

From each of the following pairs of essay titles, choose the title that you think would be more effective. Explain the reasons for your choice.

1. (a) E-mails vs. Letter Writing
   (b) Reviving the Lost Art of Letter Writing in E-mails

2. (a) Chronic Fatigue Syndrome
   (b) Chronic Fatigue Syndrome: Misunderstood and Misdiagnosed?

3. (a) The Many Practical Uses of Fractions and Percents
   (b) The Benefits of Math

4. (a) Dangerous Music for the Mind
   (b) Rap Music Lyrics: Misogyny in the Name of Art

4f Turn writer's block into building blocks.

Most writers—however much they write or even profess to like writing—have at one time or another felt blocked. They know better than to sit and stare at a blank screen or take trips to the refrigerator for comfort. Experienced writers know how paralyzed they can feel at the beginning of a writing project, and even at the beginning of a writing session, in thinking about the end product. They know that the writing process involves breaking the project down into reasonable goals and sticking to them. This persistence helps turn writer's block into building blocks.

So it is quite likely that on occasion you too will feel overwhelmed with the task of organizing your research findings or frustrated because your writing doesn't seem to "sound right." If so, consider these questions and try the strategies.

KEY POINTS
Turning Writer's Block into Building Blocks

1. Do you have a set of rules that you follow in your writing process, such as "Always begin by writing a good introduction" or "Always have a complete outline before starting to write"? If you do, consider whether your rules are too rigid or even unhelpful. As you gather ideas and do your preparatory drafting, ignore any self-imposed rules that hinder you.

2. Do you edit as soon as you write, and do you edit often? Your desire to write correctly might be preventing you from thinking about ideas and moving forward. Try journal writing, freewriting, brainstorming, or mapping (3a–3c).

3. Do you feel anxious about writing, even though you have knowledge of and interest in your topic? Try using some freewriting and brainstorming strategies (3b, 3c) or begin writing as if you were talking about your topic with a friend.

4. Do you feel that you do not yet know enough about your topic to start writing, even though you may have done a great deal of research? Try freewriting or try drafting the sections you know most about. Writing will help show you what you know and what you need to know.

Chapter **5**

How Are You Going to Say It? Build Paragraphs to Build Essays.

It is not hard to signal the beginning of a new paragraph: indent the beginning of its first sentence five spaces from the left margin or, in business and online documents, add a blank line. However, a good paragraph needs more than the mark of indentation or a blank line above and below it. In the body of an academic essay, a new paragraph should signal a progression in your ideas.

5a Paragraph basics

A good paragraph advances your argument, supports your thesis, and has internal unity. Collectively, paragraphs are the building blocks of a piece of writing and should be shaped and arranged with care. They are, as Stephen King calls them, "maps of intent," letting readers know where you are heading.

Body paragraphs in an essay How do you know when to begin a new paragraph? Use these three points as a guide.

- Begin a new paragraph to introduce a new point in support of your thesis.
- Use a new paragraph to expand on a point already made by offering a further example or evidence.
- Use a paragraph to break up a long discussion or description into manageable chunks that readers can assimilate.

Therefore, both logic and aesthetics dictate when it is time to begin a new paragraph. Think of a paragraph as something that gathers together in one place ideas that connect to each other and to your main purpose for writing.

Transitional paragraphs Some paragraphs have more to do with function than with content. They serve to take readers from one point to another, making a connection and offering a smooth transition from one idea to the next. These *transitional paragraphs* are often short.

Online Study Center This icon will direct you to quick reference tools, Web resources, and research guides on the Web site at http://college.hmco.com/keys.html.

> ### KEY POINTS
> **Paragraph Basics**
>
> A good paragraph in the body of an academic essay should contain the following:
>
> - one clearly discernible main idea, either explicitly stated (in a topic sentence) or implied clearly in the content of the paragraph, with that idea clearly related to the thesis of the essay
> - unity of content, with no extraneous ideas or asides intruding or interrupting readers' attention to the main idea
> - development and support of its main idea with examples, reasons, definitions, and so on
> - coherence—that is, a logical flow of ideas from one sentence to the next, with the relationships between ideas clearly indicated.
>
> See 5b–5e for more on these features.

In her autobiography, *Dust Tracks on a Road,* Zora Neale Hurston tells about meeting the man she fell in love with. One paragraph is devoted to describing how she "made a parachute jump" into love, admiring his intellect, strength, good looks, and manly resolution. The next paragraph provides a transition to the story of how they met:

> To illustrate the point, I got into trouble with him for trying to loan him a quarter. It came about this way.

For introductory and concluding paragraphs, see 5f.

EXERCISE 5.1
Insert paragraph breaks.

Read the following passages, and mark where you think the writers should have inserted a paragraph break. Explain your reasons. For example, does the new paragraph introduce a new point, expand on a point, or break up a long discussion or description into manageable material?

1. Skill in reading is like skill in chess in many respects. Good reading, like good chess, requires rapid deployment of schemata that have already been acquired and do not have to be worked out on the spot. Good readers, like good chess players, quickly recognize typical patterns, and, since they can ignore many small-scale features of the text, they have space in short-term

memory to take in an overall structure of meaning. They are able to do all of this because, like expert chess players, they have ready access to a large number of relevant schemata. By contrast, unskilled readers lack this large store of relevant schemata and must therefore work out many small-scale meaning relationships while they are reading. These demanding tasks quickly overload their short-term memories, making their performance slow, arduous, and ineffective. How large is the "large number of schemata" that skilled persons have acquired? It has been estimated that a chess master can recognize about 50,000 positional patterns. Interestingly, that is the approximate number of words and idioms in the vocabulary of a literate person.

—E. D. Hirsch, Jr., *Cultural Literacy*

2. I was twenty-two. I was studying at the School of Fine Arts in Madrid. The desire constantly, systematically and at any cost to do just the opposite of what everybody else did pushed me to extravagances that soon became notorious in artistic circles. In painting class we had the assignment to paint a Gothic statue of the Virgin directly from a model. Before going out the professor had repeatedly emphasized that we were to paint exactly what we "saw." Immediately, in a dizzy frenzy of mystification, I went to work furtively painting, in the minutest detail, a pair of scales which I copied out of a catalogue. This time they really believed I was mad. At the end of the week the professor came to correct and comment on the progress of our work. He stopped in frozen silence before the picture of my scales, while all the students gathered around us. "Perhaps you see a Virgin like everyone else," I ventured, in a timid voice that was not without firmness. "But I see a pair of scales."

—Salvador Dalí, *The Secret Life of Salvador Dalí*

5b Focus and topic sentence

When you begin to write or revise a paragraph in an essay, keep in mind what the focus of the paragraph will be and how it will support your thesis. Imagine readers asking you, "What point are you making in this paragraph, and how does it relate to your thesis?" Write a sentence that makes a clear supporting point. You can include such a sentence (known as a *topic sentence*) to guide both the writing and the reading of the paragraph. Here are questions for you to consider:

- What point do you want to make in a paragraph? Make sure the main idea is clear. Your audience should be able to discern the point you want to make in a far more specific way than just noting that the paragraph is "about" a topic.

- Are you going to express that point in an actual topic sentence, or do you expect readers to infer the point from the details you provide? In academic writing, it is a common convention to express the point clearly in one sentence within the paragraph. Including such a topic sentence will help you stick to your point and limit a paragraph to discussion of that point. A topic sentence helps readers grasp the point of the paragraph.

- If you include a topic sentence, where will you position it in the paragraph? In academic writing, a topic sentence frequently begins a paragraph, letting readers know what to expect. Sometimes, though, a writer will prefer to lead up to the statement of the main idea and place it at the end of the paragraph.

KEY POINTS
Placement or Inclusion of a Topic Sentence

1. *Topic sentence at the beginning* If you state the main idea in the opening sentence, readers will then expect the rest of the paragraph to consist of specific details that illustrate and support that topic sentence. This is known as *deductive organization* (for an example, see the first paragraph example in 5d, item 1).

2. *Topic sentence at the end* You may prefer to begin with details and examples and draw more general conclusions from them in a topic sentence expressed at the end of the paragraph. This strategy is useful for building up to a climax and driving home the point you want to make. This is known as *inductive organization* (for an example, see the paragraph in 5d, item 2).

3. *Topic sentence implied* It may suit your content and purpose better to not state the main idea explicitly in a topic sentence but to use details vivid enough that readers can easily infer the main point you are making. Do this if your specific details are vivid and lead to an indisputable conclusion.

EXERCISE 5.2

Identify topic sentences in paragraphs.

Read each of the following paragraphs. Then determine whether the topic sentence is at the beginning, at the end, or implied.

1. Lisa wrote a list of all items they needed. She then went to the store, purchased essentials, and upon returning, packed the overnight bags for the family weekend getaway trip to upstate New York in the Catskills. Her husband, Charlie, confirmed the reservations at the resort and wrote down the directions. Their son Dave, who had recently received his driver's license, got the car washed and filled the tank with regular unleaded gas. Everyone in the family pitched in. Teamwork is essential in planning a trip.

2. On Wednesday, I ran for a bus and made it. The dentist said I had no cavities. The phone was ringing when I arrived home and even after I dropped my key a couple of times, I answered it and they were still on the line. The Avon lady refused me service saying I didn't need her as I already looked terrific. My husband asked me what kind of a day I had and didn't leave the room when I started to answer.

—Erma Bombeck, *If Life Is a Bowl of Cherries,*
What Am I Doing in the Pits?

3. There are only three ways to make money. One is to go out and work for it. However, few among us can work forever, and there will likely come a time in our lives when working for a paycheck may not be an option. The second way to make money is to inherit it or to win the lottery. Again, not something we all can count on. The third way, and the only one that is available to all of us for an unlimited amount of time, is to invest what we earn during our working years wisely, so that the money we work so hard for goes to work for us.

—Suze Orman, *The Courage to Be Rich*

5c Unity

When you write a body paragraph in an essay, you should be able to finish these two following sentences about it without hesitation—and so should your readers:

1. The paragraph is about . . . (What is the topic of the paragraph?)
2. The stated or implied topic sentence of this paragraph is . . . (What is the one main idea the paragraph expresses?)

You should also be able to look at a well-organized expository paragraph and note that the paragraph is unified—that is, that it contains only material that develops and supports the point of the paragraph.

In academic writing, a unified paragraph mirrors the structure of the whole essay: it includes one main idea that the rest of the piece of writing explains, supports, and develops. When you write a paragraph, imagine a reader saying, "Look, I don't have time to read all this. Just tell me in one sentence (or two) what point you are making here." Your reply would express your main point. Each paragraph in an academic essay generally contains a controlling idea expressed in one or two sentences, and all the other sentences in the paragraph relate to and develop and explain that controlling idea. It does not digress or switch topics in midstream. Its content is unified.

The following paragraph is indeed devoted to one topic—tennis—and the first sentence makes a promise to discuss the *trouble* the *backhand* causes *average* players (the key words are italicized). Some of the sentences in the paragraph do discuss that, but in the middle the writer, while still writing about tennis, loses sight of the announced focus in the topic sentence.

> The backhand in tennis causes average weekend players more trouble than other strokes. Even though the swing is natural and free flowing, many players feel intimidated and try to avoid it. Venus Williams, however, has a great backhand and she often wins difficult points with it. Her serve is a powerful weapon, too. When faced by a backhand coming at them across the net, mid-level players can't seem to get their feet and body in the best position. They tend to run around the ball or forget the swing and give the ball a little poke, praying that it will not only reach but also go over the net.

What is Grand Slam winner Venus Williams doing in a paragraph about average players? What relevance does her powerful serve have to the average player's problems with a backhand? The passage can be effectively revised by cutting out the two sentences about Venus Williams.

In academic essays, a paragraph in support of your essay's thesis will usually be unified and focused on one clear topic, whether or not you state it explicitly in one sentence.

5d Strategies for structuring paragraphs

Whether you are writing a paragraph or an essay, you would do well to keep in mind the image of critical readers always inclined to ask something challenging, such as "Why do you think that?" or "What leads you to that conclusion?" You have to show readers that your claim is well founded and supported by experience, knowledge, logical arguments, the work of experts, or reasoned examples. In addition, try to engage readers and provide vital, unique details. This section shows how some writers have used specific details to develop and support the thesis of an essay or the topic sentence (stated or implied) of a paragraph.

The following passages show a range of possibilities. While some writers may choose to use only one method of development in a paragraph (all statistics or all examples, for instance), others may combine methods to make their points in a varied and effective way. In fact, many published nonfiction writers write perfectly clear and acceptable paragraphs containing several methods of development, often with no explicit topic sentence, and sometimes even with more than one main idea.

However, the rule of thumb that has emerged for traditional academic writing is "One main idea per paragraph, with one method of development." Take that for what it is—a helpful guide rather than a straitjacket.

1. Give examples.   Examples make writing more interesting and informative. The paragraph that follows begins with a topic sentence that announces the controlling idea: "Ant queens . . . enjoy exceptionally long lives." The authors could have stopped there, expecting us to assume that they are right. As critical readers, we can't help wondering what "exceptionally long" means about the life of an ant (a month? a year? seven years?). Instead of letting us wonder, the authors develop and support the controlling idea with five examples organized to build to a convincing climax. Beginning with a generalization and supporting it with specific illustrative details (known as *deductive organization*) is a common method of organizing a paragraph. (See 7h to learn more about a deductive approach.)

> Ant queens, hidden in the fastness of well-built nests and protected by zealous daughters, enjoy exceptionally long lives. Barring accidents, those of most species last 5 years or longer. A few exceed in natural longevity anything known in the millions of species of other insects, including even the legendary 17-year-old cicadas. One mother queen of an Australian carpenter ant kept in a laboratory nest flourished for 23 years, producing thousands of offspring before she faltered in her reproduction and died, apparently of old age. Several queens of *Lasius flavus,* the little yellow mound-building ant of European meadows, have lived 18 to 22 years in captivity. The world record for ants, and hence for insects generally, is held by a queen of *Lasius niger,* the European black sidewalk ant, which also lives in forests. Lovingly attended in a laboratory nest by a Swiss entomologist, she lasted 29 years.
>
> —Bert Hölldobler and Edward O. Wilson, *Journey to the Ants*

2. Tell a story. A good way to make a point that will stick in readers' minds is through narration—telling a story. Readers like a good story, and the story will help reinforce the point you want to make. An abstract idea will come alive if you can illustrate it with a story. Organize the events in a story chronologically, from beginning to end, so that readers do not get lost. In the following paragraph, the writer tells a story and draws her point from it. Using *inductive organization,* she begins with background information and the specific details of the story in chronological order and ends with a topic sentence generalization that people with disabilities often experience insensitivity. (See 7h to learn more about an inductive—specific to general—approach.)

> Jonathan is an articulate, intelligent, thirty-five-year-old man who has used a wheelchair since he became a paraplegic when he was twenty years old. He recalls taking an ablebodied woman out to dinner at a nice restaurant. When the waitress came to take their order, she patronizingly asked his date, "And what would he like to eat for dinner?" At the end of the meal, the waitress presented Jonathan's date with the check and thanked her for her patronage. Although it may be hard to believe the insensitivity of the waitress, this incident is not an isolated one. Rather, such an experience is a common one for persons with disabilities.
>
> —Dawn O. Braithwaite, "Viewing Persons with Disabilities as a Culture"

3. Include descriptive details. If you read the sentence "She grew up in a pretty house," with no more details given, your own imagination would have to fill in the details. You may imagine a small white house in the country. Another reader may imagine an imposing seashore mansion, while yet another will envision a suburban ranch house with a rosebush at the front. Writers who provide details help their readers "see" a place just as they see it by clearly presenting details in an organized way. In the paragraph that follows, we learn about a farm: its location, the appearance of the front of the house, the vegetation at the front, the scent of the flowers, and the surroundings of the house. The author's inclusion of the sounds around the house completes the picture.

> The farm my father grew up on, where Grandpa Welty and Grandma lived, was in southern Ohio in the rolling hills of Hocking County, near the small town of Logan. It was one of the neat, narrow-porched, two-story farmhouses, painted white, of the Pennsylvania-German country. Across its front grew feathery cosmos and barrel-sized peony bushes with stripy heavy-scented

blooms pushing out of the leaves. There was a springhouse to one side, down a little walk only one brick in width, and an old apple orchard in front, the barn and the pasture and fields of corn and wheat behind. Periodically there came sounds from the barn, and you could hear the crows, but everything else was still.

—Eudora Welty, *One Writer's Beginnings*

4. Appeal to the senses.   To help readers see and experience what you see and experience, describe people, places, scenes, and objects by using sensory details that re-create those people, places, scenes, or objects for your readers. In the following paragraph from a memoir about growing up to love food, Ruth Reichl tells how she spent days working at a summer camp in France and thinking about eating. However, she does much more than say, "The food was always delicious." Reichl appeals to our senses of sight, smell, touch, and taste. We get a picture of the campers, we smell the baking bread, we see and almost taste the jam, we smell and taste the coffee, and we feel the crustiness of the rolls. We feel that we are there—and we wish we were.

When we woke up in the morning the smell of baking bread was wafting through the trees. By the time we had gotten our campers out of bed, their faces washed and their shirts tucked in, the aroma had become maddeningly seductive. We walked into the dining room to devour hot bread slathered with country butter and topped with homemade plum jam so filled with fruit it made each slice look like a tart. We stuck our faces into the bowls of café au lait, inhaling the sweet, bitter, peculiarly French fragrance, and Georges or Jean or one of the other male counselors would say, for the hundredth time, *"On mange pas comme ça à Paris."* Two hours later we had a *"gouter,"* a snack of chocolate bars stuffed into fresh, crusty rolls. And two hours later there was lunch. The eating went on all day.

—Ruth Reichl, *Tender at the Bone:*
Growing Up at the Table

 EXERCISE 5.3
Tell a story using descriptive details.

Write a paragraph on the distractions that you experience as a college student. In the paragraph, tell a story, use descriptive details, and include sensory details that have a specific appeal to at least one of the senses (sight, hearing, smell, touch, and taste). Be creative.

5. Provide an extended illustration. You saw in the paragraph on page 72 how a statement about the long life of ant queens is supported by a series of examples and facts. The author of the next paragraph uses one extended illustrative example to explain the point made in the opening sentence.

> Paper enables a certain kind of thinking. Picture, for instance, the top of your desk. Chances are that you have a keyboard and a computer screen off to one side, and a clear space roughly eighteen inches square in front of your chair. What covers the rest of the desktop is probably piles—piles of paper, journals, magazines, binders, postcards, videotapes, and all the other artifacts of the knowledge economy. The piles look like a mess, but they aren't. When a group at Apple Computer studied piling behavior several years ago, they found that even the most disorderly piles usually make perfect sense to the piler, and that office workers could hold forth in great detail about the precise history and meaning of their piles. The pile closest to the cleared, eighteen-inch square working area, for example, generally represents the most urgent business, and within that pile the most important document of all is likely to be at the top. Piles are living, breathing archives. Over time they get broken down and resorted, sometimes chronologically and sometimes thematically and sometimes chronologically and thematically; clues about certain documents may be physically embedded in the files by, say, stacking a certain piece of paper at an angle or inserting dividers into the stack.
>
> —Malcolm Gladwell, "The Social Life of Paper"

6. Provide facts and statistics. Facts and statistics provide convincing evidence to help persuade readers of your point. The following paragraph supports with facts and statistics the assertion made in its first sentence (the topic sentence) that the North grew more than the South in the years before the Civil War.

> While southerners tended their fields, the North grew. In 1800, half the nation's five million people lived in the South. By 1850, only a third lived there. Of the nine largest cities, only New Orleans was located in the lower South. Meanwhile, a tenth of the goods manufactured in America came from southern mills and factories. There were one hundred piano makers in New York alone in 1852. In 1846, there was not a single book publisher in New Orleans; even the city guidebook was printed in Manhattan.
>
> —Geoffrey C. Ward, *The Civil War: An Illustrated History*

7. Describe or give instructions for a process. Descriptions of the process of doing something usually either list the instructions in chronological order or provide a description of the steps in a sequence.

The following paragraph gives instructions for beginning the process of making a piñata. When you want to tell a reader how to do something, use the active voice and the imperative mood, as this writer does.

> Start making a piñata by covering an inflated beach ball with a thin layer of petroleum jelly. Dip newspaper strips into a prepared adhesive and apply them one at a time to the ball. Cover the entire surface of the ball, except for its mouthpiece, with about 10 layers of strips. Then let the paper dry, deflate the ball, and remove it through the mouthpiece opening. Poke two small holes through the surface of the papier-mâché and attach a long, sturdy string. Fill the sphere with candy and prizes. Seal the opening with masking tape.
>
> —Reader's Digest Association, *How to Do Just about Anything*

8. Define key terms. Sometimes writers clarify and develop a topic by defining a key term, even if it is not an unusual term. Often they will explain what class something fits into and how it differs from others in its class, such as "A duckbilled platypus is a mammal that has webbed feet and lays eggs." In his book on diaries, Thomas Mallon begins by providing an extended definition of his basic terms. He does not want readers to misunderstand him because they wonder about what the differences between a diary and a journal might be. He begins by immediately addressing the terms *diary* and *journal* and examining their use, and then he decides to treat them as having the same meaning.

> The first thing we should try to get straight is what to call them. "What's the difference between a diary and a journal?" is one of the questions people interested in these books ask. The two terms are in fact hopelessly muddled. They're both rooted in the idea of dailiness, but perhaps because of *journal*'s links to the newspaper trade and *diary*'s to *dear,* the latter seems more intimate than the former. (The French blur even this discrepancy by using no word recognizable like *diary;* they just say *journal intime,* which is sexy, but a bit of a mouthful.) One can go back as far as Dr. Johnson's *Dictionary* and find him making the two more or less equal. To him a diary was "an account of the transactions, accidents, and observations of every day; a journal." Well, if synonymity was good enough for Johnson, we'll let it be good enough for us.
>
> —Thomas Mallon, *A Book of One's Own: People and Their Diaries*

As necessary, define technical terms for readers, particularly if readers will need to understand the term to understand the rest of your essay. In the following paragraph, the authors establish the meaning of a filmmaking term that they will use in later discussion.

> In the original French, *mise-en-scène* (pronounced "meez-ahn-sen") means "staging an action," and it was first applied to the practice of directing plays. Film scholars, extending the term to film direction as well, use the term to signify the director's control over what appears in the film frame. As you would expect from the term's theatrical origins, mise-en-scène includes those aspects that overlap with the art of the theater: setting, lighting, costume, and the behavior of the figures. In controlling the mise-en-scène, the director *stages the event* for the camera.
>
> —David Bordwell and Kristin Thompson,
> *Film Art: An Introduction,* 3rd ed.

 EXERCISE 5.4

Experiment with different methods of development.

Choose a topic that interests you. First, write a paragraph about some aspect of your topic using one of the following methods of development:

1. one extended illustration
2. facts and statistics
3. an account of a process
4. definition of terms

Then write another paragraph on another aspect of your topic using a second method of development from the preceding list. In groups, discuss how different aspects of your topic worked with the two methods of development that you chose. Did one method of development work better or less well than the other, and if so, why?

9. Compare and contrast. When you compare people, objects, or concepts and examine similarities and differences, specific types of development achieve different purposes.

BLOCK ORGANIZATION You can deal with each subject one at a time in a block style of organization. This works well when each section is short and readers can easily remember the points made. A paragraph or an essay comparing and contrasting writing in college and writing at work could therefore be organized as follows:

Subject A: Writing in college

  Point 1: Audience   Instructor or classmates

  Point 2: Purpose   To fulfill an assignment

  Point 3: Outcomes   Need for revision, evaluation, grade

Subject B: Writing at work

  Point 1: Audience   Manager, colleagues, or customers

  Point 2: Purpose   To convey information

  Point 3: Outcomes   Action, follow-up, filing, evaluation by boss

POINT-BY-POINT ORGANIZATION   Alternatively, you can consider the important points of similarity or difference in a point-by-point style of organization, referring within each point to both subjects. The preceding material would then be presented as follows:

Point 1: Audience

  College: Instructor or classmates

  Work: Manager, colleagues, or customers

Point 2: Purpose

  College: To fulfill an assignment

  Work: To convey information or respond to a problem

Point 3: Outcomes

  College: Feedback, evaluation, grade

  Work: Follow-up action, filing, evaluation by supervisor

THE VOCABULARY OF COMPARING AND CONTRASTING   Helpful words and terms to use for comparing and contrasting are these:

although	on the contrary
both	on the other hand
however	similarly
in contrast	though
like	where (or whereas)
not . . . but rather	while

Note where these words and terms occur in the sample passages that follow.

The following passage uses a block organization to contrast how Aristotle and Galileo viewed a pendulum—first Aristotle and then Galileo.

When Aristotle looked at a pendulum, he saw a weight trying to head earthward but swinging violently back and forth because it was constrained by its rope. To the modern ear this sounds foolish. For someone bound by classical concepts of motion, inertia, and gravity, it is hard to appreciate the self-consistent world view that went with Aristotle's understanding of a pendulum. Physical motion, for Aristotle, was not a quantity or a force, but rather a kind of change, just as a person's growth is a kind of change. A falling weight is simply seeking its most natural state, the state it will reach if left to itself. Aristotle's view made sense. When Galileo looked at a pendulum, on the other hand, he saw a regularity that could be measured. To explain it required a revolutionary way of understanding objects in motion. Galileo's advantage over the ancient Greeks was not that he had better data. On the contrary, his idea of timing a pendulum precisely was to get some friends together to count the oscillations over a twenty-four-hour period—a labor-intensive experiment. Galileo saw the regularity because he already had a theory that predicted it. He understood what Aristotle could not: that a moving object tends to keep moving, that a change in speed or direction could only be explained by some external force, like friction.

—James Gleick, *Chaos*

The following passage compares John Stuart Mill, a British philosopher and economist, and Harriet Taylor, a woman with whom Mill had a close intellectual relationship. The author, Phyllis Rose, organizes the contrast point by point to emphasize the differences in their facial features, physical behavior, ways of thinking and speaking, and intellectual styles. (A block organization would have dealt first with all the characteristics of Taylor, followed by all the characteristics of Mill.)

You could see how they complemented each other by the way they looked. What people noticed first about Harriet were her eyes—flashing—and a suggestion in her body of mobility, whereas his features, variously described as chiseled and classical, expressed an inner rigidity. He shook hands from the shoulder.

John Stuart Mill

He spoke carefully. Give him facts, and he would sift them, weigh them, articulate possible interpretations, reach a conclusion. Where he was careful, she was daring. Where he was disinterested and balanced, she was intuitive, partial, and sure of herself. She concerned herself with goals and assumptions; he concerned himself with arguments. She was quick to judge and to generalize, and because he was not, he valued her intellectual style as bold and vigorous where another person, more like her, might have found her hasty and simplistic.

Harriet Taylor

—Phyllis Rose, *Parallel Lives: Five Victorian Marriages*

Similarly, Cheryl Mendelson contrasts two grandmothers on the basis of their housekeeping tradition, home decoration, music, ambience, and food tastes and smells, as well as their approaches to knitting.

My maternal grandmother was a fervent housekeeper in her ancestral Italian style, while my paternal grandmother was an equally fervent housekeeper in a style she inherited from England, Scotland, and Ireland. In one home I heard Puccini, slept on linen sheets with finely crocheted edging rolled up with lavender from the garden, and enjoyed airy, light rooms with flowers sprouting in porcelain pots on windowsills and the foreign scents of garlic and dark, strong coffee. The atmosphere was open and warmly hospitable. The other home felt like a fortress—secure against intruders and fitted with stores and tools for all emergencies. There were Gay Nineties tunes on the player piano and English hymns, rooms shaded almost to darkness against real and fancied harmful effects of air and light, hand-braided rag rugs, brightly colored patchwork quilts, and creamed lima beans from the garden. My Anglo-American grandmother taught me to knit American-style, looping the yarn around the needle with a whole-arm motion. My Italian grandmother winced at the sight of this tiring and inefficient method and insisted I do it the way she did, with a barely visible, lightning flick of the last joint on her index finger.

—Cheryl Mendelson, *Home Comforts*

DESCRIBING SIMILARITIES AND DIFFERENCES When you want to emphasize similarities as well as differences, you can deal with each in turn, following a point-by-point organization as you do so. This is what the writer of a *New York Times* article on U.S. presidents with sons who also became president chooses to do. He points out first the similarities between John Quincy Adams and George W. Bush and then the differences. Here is the paragraph that details the similarities.

> Both Adams and George W. Bush were born to privileged New England families, though Mr. Bush went with his father to Texas and adopted the persona and politics of a down-home Western oil man. Both followed fathers whose presidencies lasted just one term: John Adams, like the elder George Bush, was rejected by the electorate after four years in office. And like the younger Bush, the younger Adams was elected president with a disputed voter mandate and under controversial circumstances.
>
> —Sean Wilentz, "The Father-and-Son Presidencies"

EXERCISE 5.5

Compare or contrast two people.

Write a comparison or contrast essay on two people you know well. You can compare or contrast their work habits, attitudes, styles, appearances, approaches to life, reactions to stresses or crises, clothing, and so on. Use either a block or point-by-point organization.

10. Divide or analyze One way to approach a topic is to analyze and divide it into its component parts for purposes of discussion. This approach allows your audience to get a better understanding of the whole from a description of the parts. In the following example, the *Columbia Encyclopedia* online helps readers understand the vast concept of life itself by breaking it down into six component parts.

> Although there is no universal agreement as to a definition of life, its biological manifestations are generally considered to be organization, metabolism, growth, irritability, adaptation, and reproduction. . . . Organization is found in the basic living unit, the cell, and in the organized groupings of cells into organs and organisms. Metabolism includes the conversion of nonliving material into cellular components (synthesis) and the decomposition of organic matter (catalysis), producing energy. Growth in living matter is an increase in size of all parts, as

distinguished from simple addition of material; it results from a higher rate of synthesis than catalysis. Irritability, or response to stimuli, takes many forms, from the contraction of a unicellular organism when touched to complex reactions involving all the senses of higher animals; in plants response is usually much different than in animals but is nonetheless present. Adaptation, the accommodation of a living organism to its present or to a new environment, is fundamental to the process of evolution and is determined by the individual's heredity. The division of one cell to form two new cells is reproduction; usually the term is applied to the production of a new individual (either asexually, from a single parent organism, or sexually, from two differing parent organisms), although strictly speaking it also describes the production of new cells in the process of growth.

11. Classify   One way to examine people, objects, or concepts is to *classify* them, which means to split them up into groups that cover all the options. In the following paragraphs, Matthew Gilbert examines cell phone users by dividing them into three groups, each with a "different psychological need," and devoting one paragraph to each group in the classification. He assumes there are no other possible needs here, an assumption his readers might not agree with. However, he does qualify his classification by saying, "As I see it."

> Cell phone use has far exceeded practicality. For many, it's even a bit of an addiction, a prop—like a cigarette or a beer bottle—that you can hold up to your mouth. And each person is meeting a different psychological need by clinging to it.
>
> As I see it, the pack breaks down something like this: Some users can't tolerate being alone and have to register on someone, somewhere, all of the time. That walk down [the street] can be pretty lonely without a loved one shouting sweet nothings in your ear.
>
> Others are efficiency freaks and can't bear to lose 10 minutes standing in line at Starbucks. They have to conduct business while their milk is being steamed, or they will implode. The dividing line between work and home has already become permeable with the growth of telecommuting; cell phones contribute significantly to that boundary breakdown.
>
> Then there are those who like to believe they are so very important to the people in their personal and professional lives that they must be in constant touch. "Puffed up" is one way to describe them; "insecure" is another.
>
> —Matthew Gilbert, "All Talk, All the Time"

EXERCISE 5.6

Consider bases for classification.

Write down a number of different ways you could classify each of the following broad topics:

1. Students in your class
2. Restaurants in your neighborhood
3. Current movies showing in theaters
4. People and their pets

12. Identify cause and effect.   In writing about history, art history, or social movements, an examination of the causes and effects of events and trends can work well. In the following passage, Larry McMurtry begins by identifying a situation and devotes the next two paragraphs to discussing the cause that produced this effect.

> The American West has so far produced depressingly little in the way of literature. Out of it may have come a hundred or so good books, a dozen or so very good books; but it has not, as yet, yielded up a great book. In literature it still seems to be waiting its turn. At the beginning of the century the Midwest seemed dominant, in terms of literary gifts and literary energies; then, largely because of Faulkner, the South had a turn, after which the great concentration of American literary energy returned to where it had mainly always been, the East.
>
> Lately, looking through the various collections of photographs by the early photographers of the West—Alexander Gardner, John Hillers, Timothy O'Sullivan, William H. Jackson, and the others—it occurred to me that one reason the West hasn't quite got a literature was in part because the camera arrived just when it did. The first photographs were taken in the West only about forty years after Lewis and Clark made their memorable trek. By the 1850s there were cameras everywhere, and the romantic landscapes of Catlin, Bodmer, Miller, Moran, and the rest gave way to photography that was almost equally romantic—the photographers, quite naturally, gravitated to the beauty spots, to the grandeur of Yosemite, Grand Canyon, Canyon de Chelly.
>
> Writers weren't needed, in quite the same way, once the camera came. They didn't need to explain and describe the West to Easterners because the Easterners could, very soon, look at those pictures and see it for themselves. And what they saw was a West with the inconveniences—the dust, the heat, the distances—removed.
>
> —Larry McMurtry, *Walter Benjamin at the Dairy Queen*

13. Provide a solution to a problem. Many articles and many college writing assignments pose a problem and consider possible solutions, sometimes making a strong recommendation for one course of action. An article in the *New York Times* presents the problem of the considerable risks involved for a donor of an organ such as a kidney or part of a liver. After a discussion of the legal and ethical issues, the author devotes the following paragraph to proposing a solution to the problem.

> One way to ensure that the interests of prospective donors are recognized is to create a federal agency that would make certain that hospitals meet minimum standards when employing these new therapies and would monitor how hospital review boards screen potential donors. The boards also need to be able to shield potential donors from coercion. For example, in cases when an individual decides against becoming a donor, a board should simply inform the intended recipient that the potential donor is "not suitable" without further explanation.
>
> —Ronald Munson, "The Donor's Right to Take a Risk"

EXERCISE 5.7
Develop paragraphs using cause and effect or problem and solution.

Write two paragraphs, one analyzing the cause and the effect of excessive credit card use and the other focusing on the problem of and solutions for credit card debt.

14. Make an analogy. Making an analogy can be a powerful way to make a complicated topic clear to your readers. The psychiatrist and author David D. Burns, for example, uses an extended analogy in his discussion of how to defeat self-defeating perfectionism.

> Think of it this way—there are two doors to enlightenment. One is marked "Perfection," and the other is marked "Average." The "Perfection" door is ornate, fancy, and seductive. It tempts you. You want very much to go through. The "Average" door seems drab and plain. Ugh! Who wants it?
> So you try to go through the "Perfection" door and always discover a brick wall on the other side. As you insist on trying to break through, you only end up with a sore nose and a headache. On the other side of the "Average" door, in contrast, there's a magic garden. But it may never have occurred to you to open up this door and take a look.
>
> —David D. Burns, MD, *Feeling Good*

15. Provide expert testimony. Writers will often provide information from the opinions and research of others to develop a point. Such development strategies are common in college research papers. Here is a paragraph from a *Washington Post* article making the point that the varying prices of goods make shopping complicated, with historical background information provided from a noted historian.

> The historian Daniel Boorstin has written about how the industrial and commercial revolution of the 19th century brought standardized goods—such as clothes pre-made in various sizes rather than made-to-order—at standardized prices. Our current industrial and commercial revolution is reversing these developments. Computers are allowing clothiers from Levi's to Brooks Brothers to offer pants personalized for your personal rear end. On the Internet, you can fine-tune your appetites almost endlessly, and you rarely have to settle for cerise because taupe is out of stock.
>
> —Michael Kinsley, "Consuming Gets Complicated"

5e Strengthening coherence: Links, word repetitions, parallel structures, and transitions

However you develop your individual paragraphs, readers expect to move with ease from one sentence to the next and from one paragraph to the next, following a clear flow of argument and logic.

When you construct an essay or paragraph, do not cause readers to grapple with sudden jumps from one idea to another without clear links. Instead, a piece of writing needs to be coherent, with all the parts connecting clearly to one another—and to the thesis—with links and transitions.

Context links A new paragraph introduces a new topic, but that topic should not be entirely separate from what has gone before. Let readers know the context of the big picture. If you are writing about the expense of exploring Mars and then switch abruptly to the hazards of climbing Everest, readers will be puzzled. You need to state clearly the connection with the thesis: "Exploration on our own planet can be as hazardous and as financially risky as space exploration."

Word links and repetition You can also provide coherence by using repeated words, or connected words, such as pronouns linked to nouns; words with the same, similar, or opposite meaning; or words linked by context. The writer of the following paragraph maintains coherence by repeating words and phrases (*italicized*) and using pronouns (**bold**—**she** and **her** to refer to **wife**, and **they** to refer to **Greeks**) to provide a linking chain.

> Entire cultures operate on elaborate systems of *indirectness.* For example, I discovered in a small research project that most Greeks assumed that a wife who asked, "Would you like to go to the party?" was hinting that **she** *wanted to go.* **They** *felt* that **she** wouldn't bring it up if **she** didn't *want to go.* Furthermore, **they** *felt,* **she** would not state **her** *preference* outright because **that** would sound like a demand. *Indirectness* was the appropriate means for communicating **her** *preference.*
>
> —Deborah Tannen, *You Just Don't Understand*

In the following paragraph, Alice Walker, writing about the writer Zora Neale Hurston, uses the repetition of *without money* to drive her point home.

> *Without money,* an illness, even a simple one, can undermine the will. *Without money,* getting into a hospital is problematic, and getting out *without money* to pay for the treatment is nearly impossible. *Without money,* one becomes dependent on other people who are likely to be—even in their kindness—erratic in their support and despotic in their expectations of return. Zora was forced to rely, like Tennessee Williams's Blanche, "on the kindness of strangers." Can anything be more dangerous, if the strangers are forever in control? Zora, who worked so hard, was never able to make a living from her work.
>
> —Foreword to Robert E. Hemenway,
> *Zora Neale Hurston: A Literary Biography*

See also the Language and Culture box in 7f for another example of the effective use of repetition.

Parallel structures as a linking device   Parallel structures help readers see the connection between ideas:

> United, there is little we cannot do. Divided, there is little we can do.
>
> —John F. Kennedy, Inaugural Presidential Address

The structures can be clauses or phrases, as shown in the following passages, the first four of which are from "Maintenance" by Naomi Shihab Nye. See also 21e for more on clauses, 21d for more on phrases, and 25j for errors arising from faulty parallelism.

PARALLEL STRUCTURES: CLAUSES

> We saw one house *where walls and windows had been sheathed in various patterns of gloomy brocade.* We visited another *where the kitchen had been removed* because the owners only ate in restaurants.

PARALLEL STRUCTURES: VERB PHRASES

Sometimes I'd come home to find her *lounging* in the bamboo chair on the back porch, *eating* melon, or *lying* on the couch with a bowl of half-melted ice cream balanced on her chest.

PARALLEL STRUCTURES: ABSOLUTE PHRASES

One day she described having grown up in west Texas in a house of twelve children, *the air jammed* with voices, crosscurrents, *the floors piled* with grocery bags, mountains of tossed-off clothes, toys, blankets, the clutter of her sisters' shoes.

PARALLEL STRUCTURES: NOUN PHRASES

Barbara has the best taste of any person I've ever known—*the best khaki-colored linen clothing, the best books, the name of the best masseuse.*

PARALLEL STRUCTURES: PREPOSITIONAL PHRASES

Adolescence is a tough time for parent and child alike. It is a time between: *between childhood and maturity, between parental protection and personal responsibility, between life stage-managed by grown-ups and life privately held.*

—Anna Quindlen, "Parental Rites," *Thinking Out Loud*

Links signaling a transition Writers use transitional words and expressions to signal relationships between ideas. They can connect clauses within one sentence, one or more sentences in a paragraph, two or more paragraphs, and a paragraph and the thesis. Deborah Tannen, in the passage on page 86, uses "for example" and "furthermore" to indicate meaning connections. The Key Points box that follows here identifies the most common uses of transitional expressions and provides examples of each.

> ## KEY POINTS
> ### Transitional Expressions
>
> *Adding an idea:* also, in addition, further, furthermore, moreover
>
> *Contrasting:* however, nevertheless, nonetheless, on the other hand, in contrast, still, on the contrary, rather, conversely
>
> *Providing an alternative:* instead, alternatively, otherwise
>
> *Showing similarity:* similarly, likewise
>
> *Showing order of time or order of ideas:* first, second, third (and so on); then; next; later; subsequently; meanwhile; previously; finally
> (Continued)

(Continued)

Showing result: as a result, consequently, therefore, thus, hence, accordingly, for this reason

Affirming: of course, in fact, certainly, obviously, to be sure, undoubtedly, indeed

Giving examples: for example, for instance

Explaining: in other words, that is

Adding an aside: incidentally, by the way, besides

Summarizing: in short, generally, overall, all in all, in conclusion

For punctuation with transitional expressions, see 31e.

ESL NOTE

On Not Overusing Transitional Expressions

Transitional expressions are useful to reinforce meaning connections and connect one sentence to another or one paragraph to another. Make sure, though, that you do not overuse these expressions. Too many of them, used too often, give writing a heavy and mechanical flavor. To add an idea, point out a contrast, or show a result, *and, but,* or *so* may serve the purpose just as well.

EXERCISE 5.8

Identify the transitions in a paragraph.

In the following student paragraph, underline or highlight transitional words and expressions.

Although Julia is a returning college student, she blends in with the student population. She doesn't let the age difference interfere with her relationships with other students. Before she returned to school, she had concerns about whether or not she would fit in. However, after two semesters of interacting with other students, Julia has gained confidence. The younger students do not treat her differently. In fact, many of her classmates are interested in the reasons why Julia decided to return to school after her successful ten-year career as a nurse. Julia, likewise, shows interest in her classmates and enjoys the dialogue, debate, and controversies that arise during class discussion.

5f Drafting introductions and conclusions

Beginnings and endings are important. Try to give readers an idea of what to expect in your essay and make them eager to read more. And once they have read your explanations and arguments, your conclusion should make it clear that you have provided substantive information and covered the important points. Readers should leave your document feeling satisfied, not turning the page and looking for more or shrugging with a "So what?"

Introduction   Imagine a scene at a party. Someone you have never met before comes up to you and says, "Capital punishment should be abolished immediately." You're surprised. You wonder where this position came from and why you are being challenged with it. You probably think this person rather strange and pushy. Imagine now readers picking up a piece of your writing. Just like people at a party, readers would probably like to know something about the topic and its relevance before you pronounce on it. Think of your introduction as providing a social function between you and your audience.

Examine the following examples.

> On the day before Memorial Day, 1983, a poet called me to describe a city he had just visited. He said that one section included mosques, built by the Islamic people who dwelled there. Attending his reading, he said, were large numbers of Hispanic people, forty thousand of whom lived in the same city. He was not talking about a fabled city located in some mysterious region of the world. The city he'd visited was Detroit.
>
> —Ishmael Reed, "America: The Multinational Society,"
> *Writin' Is Fightin'*

Reed introduces the theme of multinationalism in the United States with the hook of an anecdote that leads readers to expect that the city he describes is in an unfamiliar part of the world. He then grabs readers with a surprise in the last sentence—the city is Detroit—and prepares readers for his discussion of a multinational continent.

> As the captain of the Yale swimming team stood beside the pool, still dripping after his laps, and listened to Bob Moses, the team's second-best freestyler, he didn't know what shocked him more—the suggestion or the fact that it was Moses who was making it.
>
> —Robert A. Caro, *The Power Broker:*
> *Robert Moses and the Fall of New York*

This sentence is the first in the introductory chapter of Caro's massive biography of Robert Moses, a powerful force in New York City construction and politics for four decades. He does not begin with where and when Moses was born. Instead, he draws us into the story by making us want to read on to find out what the suggestion was (Moses proposed misleading a donor into giving money to the swim team) and why it was shocking.

If you find it difficult to write an introduction because you are not yet clear about your thesis or how you will support it, wait until you have written the body of your essay. You will find something concrete easier to introduce than something you have not yet written.

When you write an introduction to an essay in the humanities, keep the following points in mind.

KEY POINTS
How to Write a Good Introduction

Options

- Make sure your first sentence stands alone and does not depend on readers' being aware of the essay title or an assigned question. For instance, avoid beginning with "This story has a complex plot."

- Provide context and background information to set up the thesis.

- Indicate what claim you will make in your essay, or at least indicate the issue on which you will state a claim (see 7d).

- Define key terms that are pertinent to the discussion.

- Establish the tone of the paper: informative, persuasive, serious, humorous, personal, impersonal, formal, informal.

- Engage the interest of your readers to make them want to explore your topic with you.

What to Avoid

- Avoid being overly general and telling readers the obvious, such as "Crime is a big problem" or "In this fast-paced world, TV is a popular form of entertainment" or "Since the beginning of time, the sexes have been in conflict."

- Do not refer to your writing intentions, such as "In this essay, I will . . . " Do not make extravagant claims, such as "This essay will prove that bilingual education works for every student."

- Do not restate the assigned essay question.

A good introduction might include any of the following:

surprising statistics

a challenging question

a pithy quotation

interesting background details

an unusual fact

an intriguing opinion statement

a relevant anecdote

EXERCISE 5.9

Evaluate introductory paragraphs.

Read the following three paragraphs and identify which method the author has chosen to introduce the topic. Consider whether the author's choice seems effective and why.

1. "If I die first and Papi ever gets remarried," Mami used to tease when we were kids, "don't you accept a new woman in my house. Make her life impossible, you hear?" My sisters and I nodded obediently, and a filial shudder would go through us. We were Catholics, so of course, the only kind of marriage we could imagine had to involve our mother's death. We were also Dominicans, recently arrived in Jamaica, Queens, in the early 60s before waves of other Latin Americans began arriving. So, when we imagined who exactly my father might possibly ever think of remarrying, only American women came to mind. It would be bad enough having a *madrastra,* but a "stepmother". . . .

—Julia Alvarez, "Hold the Mayonnaise"

2. How far can we go in exalting Newton's scientific achievements? Not far enough. Few minds in the intellectual history of humankind have left such an imprint as Newton's. His work represents the culmination of the Scientific Revolution, a grandiose solution to the problem of motion that had haunted philosophers since pre-Socratic times. In doing so, he laid the conceptual foundations that were to dominate not only physics but also our collective worldview until the dawn of the twentieth century.

—Marcelo Gleiser, *The Dancing Universe: From Creation Myths to the Big Bang*

3. Since 1970, the composition of households and families and the marital status and living arrangements of adults in the United States both experienced marked changes. For example, the proportion of the population made up by married couples with children decreased, and the proportion of single mothers increased, while the median age at first marriage grew over

time. Much of this variety has been regularly reported in two separate Census Bureau reports—*Household and Family Characteristics* and *Marital Status and Living Arrangements*. Beginning with the March 2001 Current Population Survey, these two reports are being replaced by this new publication, *America's Families and Living Arrangements*.

—*America's Families and Living Arrangements,* U.S. Census Bureau

Conclusion   Think of your conclusion as completing a circle. You have taken readers on a journey from the presentation of the topic in your introduction, to your thesis, to supporting evidence and discussion, with specific examples and illustrations. Remind readers of the purpose of the journey. Recall the main idea of the paper, and make a strong statement about it that will stick in their minds.

KEY POINTS
How to Write a Good Conclusion

Options

1. Include a summary of the points you have made, but keep it short and use fresh wording.

2. Frame your essay by reminding readers of both something you referred to in your introduction and your thesis.

3. End on a strong note: a quotation, a question, a suggestion, a reference to an anecdote in the introduction, a humorous insightful comment, a call to action, or a look to the future.

What to Avoid

4. Do not apologize for the inadequacy of your argument ("I do not know much about this problem") or for holding your opinions ("I am sorry if you do not agree with me, but . . . ").

5. Do not use the identical wording you used in your introduction.

6. Do not introduce a totally new idea. If you raise a new point at the end, readers might expect more details.

7. Do not contradict what you said previously.

8. Do not be too sweeping in your conclusions. Do not condemn the entire medical profession, for example, because one person you know had a bad experience in one hospital.

A long article on the health care system and insurance (or lack of it) in the United States concludes with a paragraph that summarizes the complex issues discussed in the article. The author condenses the issues to several rhetorical questions, ending by reiterating strongly his thesis concerning the assumptions made about health care both in the United States and in the rest of the world.

> The issue about what to do with the health-care system is sometimes presented as a technical argument about the merits of one kind of coverage over another or as an ideological argument about socialized versus private medicine. It is, instead, about a few very simple questions. Do you think that this kind of redistribution of risk is a good idea? Do you think that people whose genes predispose them to depression or cancer, or whose poverty complicates asthma or diabetes, or who get hit by a drunk driver, or who have to keep their mouths closed because their teeth are rotting ought to bear a greater share of the costs of their health care that those of us who are lucky enough to escape such misfortunes? In the rest of the industrialized world, it is assumed that the more equally and widely the burdens of illness are shared, the better off the population as a whole is likely to be. The reason the United States has forty-five million people without coverage is that its health-care policy is in the hands of people who disagree, and who regard health insurance not as the solution but as the problem.
>
> —Malcolm Gladwell, "The Moral-Hazard Myth"

EXERCISE 5.10

Improve an unsatisfactory conclusion.

Read the following concluding paragraph from a paper on protecting data from computer viruses. What suggestions would you give to the student writer about how to improve it? Be specific. Then revise the paragraph according to your suggestions.

> This concludes my paper on dangerous computer viruses. Each of the measures mentioned above, if practiced, will help you to avoid having your data destroyed. It's so easy to minimize danger. First, buy an antivirus program. Second, screen unknown data. Third, back up all your files. In doing so, one will, if not eliminate all potential danger, at the very least protect valuable data. Each day more viruses are created, since we can't know what's coming, we can, at the very least use "an ounce of prevention."

Chapter **6**

Edit and Proofread

6a Editing and proofreading

Always edit and proofread your final draft to make sure there are no errors. Examine your draft for grammar, punctuation, and spelling errors not caught by your word processor's checking programs. Often, reading your essay aloud will help you find sentences that are tangled, poorly constructed, or not connected. If you are unsure of a word or its function in a sentence, turn to chapters 21–29 for help with Standard English, common sentence problems, and methods for correcting errors.

As you become aware of the grammatical areas that cause you trouble, keep a list of your errors and corrections on a Sentence Problem Log Sheet, and analyze why you make these errors:

- Is your writing influenced by unedited speech?

- Do you speak a dialect and use the dialect forms in place of Standard English forms? In other words, do you use forms that sound familiar from conversations with friends?

- Do you speak a language other than English at home, and do you fall back on its linguistic forms when you grapple with new subject matter and complex ideas? For examples, see 40d.

- Are you trying to take on an "academic" voice that is new to you and makes you feel insecure?

Identify your main problems with editing, and for each writing assignment that you do, pay particular attention to these areas. Read the relevant sections in the handbook, do the exercises to flex your grammatical muscles, and then turn your attention to a close examination of your draft for each problem area, one at a time. Give your draft a separate reading as you check for each editing problem.

Prepare an edited draft. Familiarize yourself with common proofreading marks (inside back cover), and use them as you check this near-final draft of your document.

Online Study Center   This icon will direct you to quick reference tools, Web resources, and research guides on the Web site at http://college.hmco.com/keys.html.

Proofread   After you have edited your writing assignment and made the changes on your word processor, print out the document and proofread it.

KEY POINTS
Proofreading Tips

Try any or all of the following strategies:

1. Do not try to proofread a document on the computer screen. Always print out a hard copy to make it easier to find mistakes.

2. Make an additional copy, and ask a friend to read your document aloud while you note places where he or she stumbles over an error.

3. Use proofreading marks to mark typographical and other errors (see inside back cover).

4. Put a piece of paper under the first line of your text. As you read, move it down line by line to focus your attention on one line at a time. Touch each word with the end of a pencil as you either say the word aloud or mouth it silently to yourself.

5. Read the last sentence first, and work backward through your text. This strategy will not help you check for meaning, logic, pronoun reference, fragments, or consistency of verb tenses. Instead, it focuses your attention on the spelling, punctuation, and accuracy of each sentence.

6. If you have time, put your manuscript away for a day or two after you have finished it. Proofread it when the content is not so familiar.

EXERCISE 6.1
Mark up a passage with correction marks.

Proofread this paragraph for the writer who drafted it. Use correction marks (inside back cover) to indicate any problems or errors.

Insomnia is a sleep disorder that effects millions of people. Often they turn to over-the-counter pills to relieve their insomnia. Medication, especially self-medication, should not be the first course of action.   Patients should seek the advice of there physician. However, before taking any medication, they should seriously consider other options lifestyle changes can help including cutting back on caffeinated beverages, drinking herbal tea such as chamomile, reading a pleasant book, and writing a "to do" list before they go to bed.

6b Computer tools for checking (and their limitations)

Your word processor comes with useful tools to help you with editing and proofreading, but such tools have definite limitations. Electronic checking programs are only as good as their creators, and language is so complex that the programs cannot begin to approximate the power of the human brain.

Thesaurus feature The thesaurus feature is useful especially when you are writing a second draft and notice too much repetition of a word. In Microsoft Word, go to Tools/Language and then to Thesaurus. When you click on a word or expression, you will be prompted with synonyms and words close in meaning to the one you have highlighted. Before you use a recommended word, however, always check it in a dictionary to discover its nuances of meaning and its patterns of use. One of the options proposed as a substitute for *recommended* in the previous sentence is *suggested*, which would fit. Other suggested words are *optional* and *not compulsory*, which would not fit into the meaning or structure of the sentence. Always consider the context when you use a thesaurus. See also 20b.

Spelling-check feature Spelling-check programs are a boon, helping us catch and correct spelling errors we might otherwise miss. Always run the spelling checker in your word processor to check on spelling throughout your draft. The program will flag any word it does not recognize from its own dictionary. You then have the opportunity to look up the word in the dictionary or try it several ways until the program indicates you have gotten it right. The program may also automatically correct certain typographical or preentered common spelling errors, such as substituting *responsibility* if you happen to type *responsability*.

Be warned, however: the dictionaries of many spelling checkers are incomplete, and therefore you cannot rely on them to find and solve all spelling problems. In addition, a spelling checker will not identify grammatical errors that affect only spelling, such as missing plural or *-ed* endings. Nor will it find any omitted word or a misspelled word that forms another word such as *then* (for *than*), *their* (for *there*), *form* (for *from*), *coarse* (for *course*), or *affect* (for *effect*). Give your drafts a careful proofreading independent of the spelling checker and, if possible, have a peer reviewer do so as well.

Grammar-check feature   A grammar-check program, such as the program attached to Microsoft Word, analyzes your sentences and makes suggestions about what might need to be fixed, tightened, or polished. It provides a few helpful observations about simple mechanical matters, such as pointing out that commas and periods need to go inside quotation marks or that quotation marks have not been closed, drawing attention to passive verbs, labeling clichés, or indicating a problem with an easily identifiable error such as "Can the mayor wins?"

It may be worth activating a grammar-check program to catch these basic errors. But be aware that grammar-check programs cannot take content and varied syntax into account, so their capabilities are limited. They can't recognize some errors because they do not "understand" the context. For example, if you wrote "The actors were boring" but meant to write "The actors were bored," grammar-check programs would not reveal your mistake.

Many writers—including the authors of this handbook—deactivate the grammar-check feature while writing because its constant reminders not only interrupt their train of thought but are often wrong.

ESL NOTE

The Dangers of Grammar-Check Programs

Never make a change in your draft at the suggestion of a grammar-check program before verifying that the change is really necessary. A student from Ukraine wrote the grammatically acceptable sentence "What he has is pride." Then, at the suggestion of a grammar-check program, he changed the sentence to "What he has been pride." The program had not recognized the sequence "has is."

Find feature   Often more useful than a grammar-check program is the Edit/Find feature on your computer. Use it to search for problem areas throughout your document, such as the *its/it's* or *then/than* confusion. You can also use this feature to search for quotation marks—in order to make sure that each quotation has quotation marks at both beginning and end—or to find and delete "filler words" like *really* and *very*.

Word count feature   One tool that you can count on as being both accurate and useful is the Word Count tool. This feature lets you know how many words your document contains, useful information when you have a length limit. Beware, however, of using it too often in a desperate attempt to reach a prescribed number of words. Your writing will seem padded. Instead, concentrate on the ideas and content that you are conveying, keeping a rough sense of how many pages you have available. (Estimate that a double-spaced page will contain about 250 words.) Then, once you have finished a draft, do the word count, and expand or cut as necessary as you prepare your next draft.

For ways to use word processing software and other tools for formatting documents for college, online, or work presentation, see 11, 12, and 15.

EXERCISE 6.2

Try out spelling and grammar checkers.

Type these two sentences into your word processor:

> The economists spraedsheets were more simpler then the ones there competitors have prepared. "They was prepared quickly, said the manager.

Now run the spelling and grammar checkers. What do you find, and what conclusions can you draw? In Microsoft Word, go to Tools/Options/Spelling and Grammar and click on Settings to see what Word has been set to find. Do you think you need to change any of those settings? How would you correct the sentences?

6c   Computer tools for editing and collaborating

Revising and editing on the computer mean using the basic word processing features of Delete, Cut, Copy, and Paste. It also means becoming adept at saving as a new file any material you delete that might be useful to you later or even in another document. (See 4a for more on managing files.) Other useful features are AutoCorrect, Find, Replace, Comment, and Track Changes.

AutoCorrect   The AutoCorrect feature in Word allows you to take shortcuts and to save time. If, for example, you are writing about "housing preservation," you can simply write "hp" whenever you want to write "housing preservation." To set this feature, go to the

Tools menu, select AutoCorrect, and then select the AutoCorrect tab. In the Replace text box, type your shortcut (the text you wish to replace) and then in the With text box, type the text you want to take the place of the shortcut.

Find and Replace   The Find feature helps you find phrases that you tend to overuse. Use it to look for instances of "there is" or "there are," for example, and you will see if you are using either phrase too often. If you suspect you may have overused a key word or phrase in your essay ("pedagogy" or "addictive personality," for instance), you can find and check each instance of its use, substituting new words or cutting down on repetition.

Insert a Comment   The Comment feature on the Insert menu allows you, your classmates, or your instructor to ask questions or write a note in the middle of a draft. The place where a comment is inserted will be highlighted on your screen, and you can see the comment appear at the end of your document. You can then choose to print your document with or without the comments showing. This feature allows you to interact with your text as you write and helps remind you of leads to follow and points to check.

Here is a screenshot of student David Powers's summary (see 8a) and his own interpolated comments:

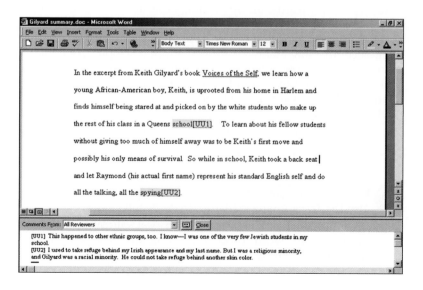

Track Changes The Track Changes feature on the Tools menu allows you to mark and highlight additions and changes to your own document or one you receive via e-mail that you have copied into your word processing program. This feature lets you see clearly on the screen and on the printed page the changes you have made. The Accept or Reject Changes option allows you to accept or reject all the changes or each change separately, and it will make the changes to your document automatically. You can also compare two drafts by using the Track Changes/Compare Documents feature. Simply load in a file containing a draft that you want to compare with the current draft, and the program will highlight the differences in the two drafts.

EXERCISE 6.3
Search and add comments to a document.

Imagine a long document beginning with the following passage. Which words might you search for throughout the document? Where might you add a comment, and what would the comment be?

> One of the most predominant battle cries of civilization, as we toddle into the twenty-first century, is "Look it up on the Internet!" Indeed, it is almost a cliché nowadays to say that the Internet has vastly affected the way the world works. Business transactions, market research, the distribution of music, pictures, and postcards; all these things can now be done in the unfathomable reaches of cyberspace. Of course, distribution and publication of literature is no exception, and cannot escape the all-encompassing embrace of the fiber-optic octopus. As if television hadn't done enough damage to books and booksellers, the Internet now gives people one less reason to leave the house, and one less reason to find a bookstore that has anything resembling character.
>
> —Benjamin Gould (student), "The Role of the Internet in Publishing: A Chilling Look at the Apocalypse"

EXERCISE 6.4
Use the Track Changes feature to work collaboratively.

Copy the following passage from the *Universal Keys* Web site, and paste it into your word processing program. Use the Track Changes feature to make changes to the text. Then work with another student. E-mail him or her the passage with your suggestions. Your partner will open the document in Word and decide whether to accept or reject each change. Print out the final version after you have accepted or rejected changes, and show it to your partner.

> Pablo Neruda, like so many great poets, had an immense reverence for things. From socks to cats to artichokes, from the sea to the word, Neruda was able to see a beauty not usually revealed to the common eye. His eyes took on a childlike quality, examining the world around him with intense curiosity and innocence, allowing him to see attributes overlooked, and at times not even imagined, by others. Not only in Neruda's subject matter, but also in his choice of wording in the descriptions of such things, do we see his gift for noticing beauty and connections. He often strikes those without his gift as odd or surreal. For Neruda, however, his vision was just that: his vision, his slant on reality. This perception of his gave him the insight that allowed him to find beauty all around, whereas others might search for it the world over.
>
> —Benjamin Gould (student), "Pablo Neruda"

6d A student's drafts

Elena Tate was assigned an essay on the topic of "communicating in a multilingual city." The instructor asked for a thesis supported by personal experience. Tate's first draft was an account of her own experiences with learning and using Spanish. She put her draft aside for a while and then, with feedback from classmates, turned her attention to reevaluating it and using her experiences to make a claim and present a thesis. She marked places where editing was needed and wrote comments to guide her revision. Here is her first draft, annotated with her comments after a peer review session.

Multilingual Communication   Find a better title.

I always thought that language was one of the most decisive   Move to end? Add new intro and thesis
divisions between people. But after learning Spanish and using it
in school and at work I see now that studying the gramatical
                                              m
structure of a new language is not nearly as hard as trying to
understand someone who leads an entirely different life.

frag me nt

Compare with other places

Big Jump in time

wordy

Choppy sentences — make connections

More about him. Connect to class discussions of motivation?

Better word?

comma splice

Cut? Off topic?

Fix Pronouns.

Good. Keep this.

I am what one might consider a voluntary bilingual. I could very well have turned out completely monolingual in the dominant language of the United States, like the majority of the United States population; among them, my entire family. Though I did come into contact with speakers of Haitian Creyole and Spanish starting at an early age, I grew up knowing only English in Cambridge, Massachusetts. I was like nearly every other kid who went through the mandatory two-year Spanish instruction program at my public elementary school, I could have forgotten even the little bit that I learned the summer after eighth grade. But I didn't. Now, attending Hunter College in New York City, one of the most multilingual cities in the world, I am proud to consider myself to be bilingual. I don't pretend to have near native control of two languages, but I can understand, speak, read, and even write well in a language other than my mother tongue and more importantly, I speak both languages for large parts of each day.

check sp.

as

I didn't learn another language during childhood, as it was perfectly acceptable to only speak English. I was taught to value other cultures and to hold them in high esteem as I held my own. I decided to learn another language, because this is the only way you can understand how other people experience life and you can learn from your experiences.

A Spanish teacher I had in high school was the first person to really inspire me to do the hard work necessary to really learn Spanish. He made me a promise: "If you can learn Spanish, you will be able to find work easier than if you only know English, and you will form beautiful friendships." At least for me, this worked. I did my homework and tried to absorb his lessons. But something was missing. I had nowhere to really use my Spanish, so it stuck somewhere between the past tense and the subjunctive.

The next year still in high school in Cambridge I decided to take a Spanish literature class and a U.S. history class in the bilingual department. These courses were taught entirely in Spanish. They were meant for Hispanic students still learning English. Anglo students who showed interest and ability were allowed to enroll as well. It was then that I understood what the political catchword "immersion" really meant.

Too choppy. Combine?

Luckily, it was one of the best experiences I have ever had. I was under no pressure to replace or reduce my first language, and a language and a positive self-concept have resulted from my study of a second language. I can see how it would have been one of the most traumatic experiences of my life if I ~~would have~~ *had* been in the opposite situation — if, instead of embarking on a journey to learn a new language, I was taking my first steps toward forgetting my native language.

Give detai[l]

Delete—this goes beyond the topic of communication.

Spanish is also linked in my mind to the real-world work experience. Once I worked at the Bush terminal industrial complex in Sunset Park, where thousands of (predominantly) Spanish-speaking workers produce clothing. I worked there over the summer to have the experience of a (job) in manufacturing. I wanted to know where the products I buy and use come from and to get a sense of what life is like for the people who produce them. The garment industry of Brooklyn employs women and men of all ages. Many (feel) that they (had) those jobs because they (have) limited English proficiency. Spanish was definitely the prevailing language on the (job.) Even the bosses spoke or shouted to everyone in their Russian-accented Spanish. Co-workers of mine listened to English tapes as they sewed, one attending English classes every evening after the ten-hour workday. Many felt that learning English would be their ticket to a more humane (job.)

Add details.

Make smoother + give details.

Make connection with communication, the essay topic

Repetition of word job

Of course, no one could understand why I was working there. "You speak English! You're American! You could be working at a clothing store! Or a waitress!" they would exclaim. <u>Lots</u> of my

Keep direct quotation. It works.

Many

co-workers had never carried on a conversation in English. One
girl who taught me how to use the button-hole machine got the
giggles when I spoke to her in English. They all understood that it   *But?*
was the language to know if you wanted to advance in the United
States. The segregation that takes place, however, is a question
that goes much deeper than language. It is a question of class, of
ethnicity, of legal status. Even though I could speak to my
coworkers in their native language, there was still so much I
couldn't understand.

Need better onclusion ∧ separate paragraph.

Tate then took her annotated draft and the notes she had taken
during a group peer session in class and during a conference with her
instructor and revised her draft. The annotations show her content
structure.

Beyond Language

Living in a multilingual city has proven to me that
communication can be reached among people who speak different
languages. But a multilingual experience also shows that even
among people speaking the same language, the ability to
communicate may be hindered by deeper rifts, including class and
culture. One's native language is simply not the single most
important consideration when it comes to relating to people.

Thesis

I am what one might consider a voluntary bilingual. I could
very well have turned out completely monolingual in the dominant
language of the United States, like the majority of the U.S.
population, among them my entire family. Though I did come into
contact with other languages starting at an early age, I never
learned a word of anything besides English. It was perfectly
acceptable to be monolingual (in English, of course) in Cambridge,
Massachusetts, as it is throughout the United States, in contrast to
parts of Africa, the Middle East, and Europe, where bilingualism is
seen as positive and necessary. Luckily, I did pick up the attitude
that to come in contact with other languages and the cultures they
reflected would expand my conception of humanity and the world.

The importance of early attitudes to language

I managed to hold on to the little Spanish I gained during the mandatory two-year program at my public elementary school, though I still had no real incentive to know Spanish. Nearly every other student in my class forgot everything the summer after eighth grade. A teacher I had in high school was the first person to inspire me to do the hard work necessary to really learn Spanish. Brent, as we called him, used a lure to focus his unmotivated class. He cleverly incorporated the two pillars of language-learning motivation, the instrumental and integrative, in a single promise: "If you can learn Spanish, you will be able to find work easier than if you know only English, and you will form beautiful friendships."

The importance of language instruction

At least for me, this worked. I did my homework and tried to absorb his lessons. But something was missing. I had nowhere to put my Spanish into practice, and so it stagnated somewhere between the past tense and the subjunctive. The next year, while still in high school in Cambridge, I decided to take a Spanish literature class and a U.S. history class in the bilingual department. These courses, taught entirely in Spanish, were meant for students with nascent English ability, but Anglo students who showed interest and ability were allowed to enroll as well. It was then that I got my first sense of what it means to be the only one in the room who is not fluent in the language being spoken and in the position of having to communicate in an unfamiliar language. It was then that I understood what the political catchword "immersion" really meant. Luckily, it was one of the best experiences I have ever had.

Advantages of having to communicate in a classroom

For one exhausting hour each day I had to pay perfect attention to each word or else quickly become confused and not understand again until the topic was changed and I could start over. I had to decipher a Madrid lisp, a Puerto Rican Spanish devoid of the -s sound, and a somersaulting Chilean accent. On top of all that, I actually had to participate and face a grade for my efforts.

Language and
communication
in the real
world of work

However, classrooms are still far from the real world of work. That initial appreciation of language and culture fueled my decision to get a job as a sewing machine operator in Brooklyn's garment industry over the summer. I wanted to get a sense of what it was like to use a language in everyday life, to work in manufacturing, to know who it was who powered the U.S. economy and produced the clothing that I wear every day. I knew that conditions in the plants were bad, and I knew that the work force was composed almost entirely of immigrant workers. I figured that since my Spanish was good, I would be able to get along on the job and get to know some of my coworkers. But it turned out that the language barrier was the least of the barriers between us.

Every morning, I would wake up and board the B35 bus to another world. At the Bush Terminal industrial complex in Sunset Park, thousands of women from Mexico, Ecuador, and other countries produce countless articles of clothing each day. Workers in their teens to their late sixties often work in nonunion shops

Connections
between
English
proficiency
and
opportunity

and are paid "piece rate," which in my factory was three cents a shirt label, far from any legislated "minimum wage." Many feel that their options are restricted because of their low level of English proficiency. Spanish was the prevailing language. Even the bosses spoke or shouted to everyone in their Russian-accented Spanish. However, several of my coworkers listened to English tapes as they sewed. One attended English classes every evening after the ten-hour workday. They all felt that learning English would be their ticket to a more humane job.

Of course, no one could understand why I was working there. "You speak English! You're American! You could be working at a clothing store! Or as a waitress!" they would exclaim. Lots of my coworkers had never carried on a conversation in English. One girl who taught me how to use the buttonhole machine would get the giggles when I spoke to her in English. But they all understood it is the language to know if you want to advance in the United States.

The segregation that takes place, however, in the workplace and in society at large is a question that goes much deeper than language. It is a question of class, of ethnicity, of legal status. Just by virtue of who I was, of where I had been born, questions that had never even crossed my mind plagued the lives of my coworkers. I didn't know what it was like to leave my native land and not know when I would ever be able to return. I didn't know what it was like to limp for months because I had a pain in my leg that went untreated. In fact, I had to quit my first garment job to go back to Boston to see my doctor, still covered by my mother's health insurance. And when the boss refused to pay anyone in my area the last payday before the end of the month, I knew I had somewhere to turn so that I could pay my rent.

What is mo[...] important than language?

I had always thought that language was one of the most decisive divisions between people. But after learning a second language, Spanish, and using it in the different contexts of school and work, it has become clear to me that studying the grammatical structure of a new language is not nearly as hard as trying to understand someone who leads an entirely different life, whose socioeconomic background differs dramatically from one's own. There are barriers and bonds beyond language that separate and connect people much more profoundly. A truly multicultural society needs to pay attention not only to language education but also to societal reforms that begin to break down the barriers of inequality.

Conclusion

Recapitulation of essay and of thesis

Ends with a recommendation

EXERCISE 6.5
Evaluate drafts.

Discuss with classmates the changes Tate made in her second draft. In what ways has she improved on her first draft? Are there further changes you would suggest if she were going to write a third draft?

6e Using a writing center

Find your college's writing or learning center by checking your college's Web site or asking at the student services office. Then you can call or e-mail to make an appointment with a peer or professional tutor. Go in with the right expectations—not to make your paper perfect but to develop stronger writing skills. The writing center resembles a gym more than a spa, and your tutor is more like a trainer than a massage therapist. The better prepared you are to work with your tutor, the stronger your paper will be.

KEY POINTS

How to Use Your Campus Writing Center

To get the most out of your visit to the writing center,

- **Make your appointment well before the due date of your paper.** You will need time to act on the points you and your tutor uncover while working on your draft.

- **Look at your instructor's comments on previous assignments.** Acting on your instructor's earlier comments can help you use your tutorial time efficiently and minimize your writing and revising workload.

- **Outline what you have written so far.** Outlining helps you to rethink the overall organization of your paper. Even a rough outline makes it easier to discuss your paper's structure with a tutor.

- **List your assignment goals.** List some of the features your paper should have to meet the goals of the assignment.

- **List your tutorial goals.** Mark sections of your draft that you want to discuss with your tutor. Write down your questions about these sections or sentences.

- **Collect your assignment, notes, and current draft.** Take your assignment description, relevant class notes, and your current draft to the writing center.

- **Bring *Universal Keys*.** Your tutor can help you to use your writing handbook to work on specific areas that you need to strengthen as a writer.

PART 2
Writing through College

ACADEMIC WRITING

We learn about a subject through writing about it. Part 2 alerts you to strategies for successfully addressing a variety of writing situations that you may meet during your college career. Many of these writing situations, such as arguments, for example, are frequently found outside college, too—in letters to the press or to government agencies or business organizations, in business proposals and reports, in Internet discussion groups, and in community service projects.

Chapter **7**

Writing an Argument

An argument in the academic or rhetorical sense is a reasoned, logical argument—supported by evidence—designed to persuade an audience to pay attention to significant points you raise. You can write an argument either on a controversial issue or simply on any issue on which you take a position and try to defend that position. For example, you could construct a reasoned, logical written exposition to argue that it is not only a passing fashion fad to pierce body parts but a potentially dangerous practice. Or you could write an argument paper to support your interpretation of a short story. Many writers of arguments will go a step further and try both to convince readers to adopt a certain position and to persuade readers to take some appropriate action or precaution.

Assignments to produce reasoned, logical written exposition occur frequently in courses in the humanities and social sciences, as well as in the work world. One way to become familiar with the techniques of writing arguments is to analyze the arguments you read: What makes a good argument? What types of argument do you find convincing? What types of argument fill you with scorn?

EXERCISE 7.1

Consider topics for arguments.

Consider and list what occasions you have had in recent months, in either conversation or writing, to argue a point. Think about, for example, your work situation, discussions with friends, opinions offered about movies, family issues, music, food, cars, and academic subjects. On your list, note which topics led to petty disagreements and which sparked fuller arguments in the rhetorical sense, arguments in which you could take a stand and support your view with evidence. Discuss your list with classmates.

7a What makes a good written argument?

Arguments are common not only in college essays but also in newspaper articles, letters, courts of law, daily discussions, and blogs. Some are responsible, well reasoned, and well constructed. Others lack these qualities. Whether or not you are convinced by the views of the speaker or writer, it is a good habit to step back and evaluate an argument critically, whether it is your own or somebody else's, in order to identify its merits and faults.

When you read an argument, use the same critical reading strategies discussed in 1a. Evaluate the writer's statements with care—and be aware that your readers will use the same care when they read an argument that *you* write. Here are questions to ask while you evaluate a written argument:

1. What am I reading? A statement of fact, an opinion, an exaggeration, an attack, or an emotional belief?

2. Where does the information come from? Do I trust the sources?

3. How reliable are the writer's statements? Are they measured, accurate, fair, and to the point? Do I feel the need to interject a challenge, using "But . . . "?

4. Can I ascertain the writer's background, audience, and purpose? What biases does the writer reveal?

5. What assumptions does the writer make? If a writer argues for a college education for everyone, would I accept the underlying assumption that a college education automatically leads to happiness and success? (For more on assumptions, see 7i.)

6. Does the writer present ideas in a convincing way, relying on a rational presentation of evidence rather than on extreme language or name-calling?

KEY POINTS

A Good Argument

A good argument

- deals with an arguable issue (7c)
- is based not on strong gut reactions or beliefs but on careful analysis of reliable information (7c)   *(Continued)*

Online Study Center   This icon will direct you to quick reference tools, Web resources, and research guides on the Web site at http://college.hmco.com/keys.html.

(Continued)

- takes a position on and makes a clear claim about the topic (7d)
- supports that position with detailed and specific evidence (such as reasons, facts, examples, descriptions, and stories) (7e)
- establishes common ground with listeners or readers and avoids confrontation (7f)
- takes opposing views into account and refutes them or shows why they may be unimportant or irrelevant (7g)
- presents reasons logically (7h, 7i, 7j)
- is engaged and vital, a reflection of your thinking rather than a marshalling of others' opinions

7b What makes a good visual argument?

We commonly think of arguments as being spoken or written. However, another type of argument is widespread—an argument that is presented visually. Think, for example, of arguments made in cartoons, advertisements, and works of art. Think of photographs of hurricane devastation or of starving children in Darfur in appeals for donations. The two visuals shown in 7e offer a strong visual argument to support a writer's thesis and make an emotional impact. For more on effective visual arguments, see 1b.

Pictures that tell a story You can supplement your written arguments with visual arguments: maps, superimposed images, photographs, charts and graphs, political cartoons—vivid images that will say more than many words to your readers.

An argument essay on the media, for example, would make a strong visual impact if its argument included this image from Adbusters.com, which itself makes an argument.

It says that children see what their parents watch, and it challenges us to consider how much the media dictate what we see.

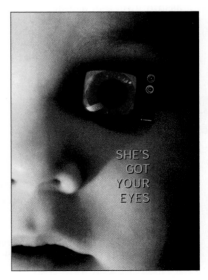

SHE'S
GOT
YOUR
EYES

Visual arguments make their appeals in ways similar to written arguments, appealing to logic, showcasing the character and credentials of the author, or appealing to viewers' emotions. When you write an argument, consider adding to the impact of your thesis by including a visual argument.

EXERCISE 7.2

Analyze a visual argument.

Write about one of the following images. What compelling argument could you make based on the image, and how effective it is as a visual?

a.   b.

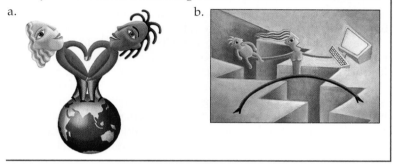

7c Select a topic.

If you are not assigned a topic from class discussion or reading, choose one that will be interesting for you to write about and for your audience to read about. The topic you choose should be one that is significant and can be debated, such as in what grade standardized testing should begin in schools rather than how many states require standardized tests. The former issue can lead to an arguable claim—"Standardized testing should not begin until the fifth grade"—rather than a truism (a statement that is obviously true and is not debatable) such as "Standardized testing is administered in many states."

You probably will want to persuade your readers to adopt your point of view. At the very least, you will want them to acknowledge that the claim you make about your topic rests on solid and reliable evidence (7e) and that you provide a fair and unbiased approach to this evidence. Let readers discover that you have good reasons for your position.

If the choice of topic for a written argument is up to you, choose one that is fresh. Unless personal involvement and experience drive you to explore topics such as the death penalty, prayer in schools, drug laws, and abortion, it is best to avoid such topics; they have been written about so often that original or interesting arguments are hard to find. In general, avoid issues that are gut reactions to matters of ideology or religion. Your views on these topics will tend to rest on belief rather than logical argument. Beware, also, of saying that you intend to write about "the importance of family," "the church and morality," or "racial prejudice." Such issues might mean a great deal to you personally, but unless you have a clear sense of a logical and debatable claim rather than just strong feelings, you will have difficulty structuring an argument around them and making a valid claim that you can support with evidence.

Brainstorming, reading (books, magazines, and newspapers), and browsing on the Internet in search directories, informational sites, or online discussion groups (3c, 1a, and 47f–47g) can help you discover novel and timely issues. When you find an interesting topic and your instructor has approved it (if necessary), begin by writing a question about it. Then make lists of the arguments on both (or all) sides.

Student Mara Lee Kornberg decided to tackle the issue of the health effects of a vegan diet. A vegan herself, she was interested in examining the facts of a case in which a child who had been fed a vegan diet had to be hospitalized. Envisioning her classmates, instructor, and a wider general audience as her audience, Kornberg began with a topic and a focused research question:

Topic: A vegan diet for children

Research question: Does a vegan diet supply adequate nutrition for children?

As she read and researched, took notes, and discussed her topic, she eventually developed her working thesis (7d), which guided her further research and the content and organization of her argument. (Her paper is in 7l.)

EXERCISE 7.3

Select good topics.

1. Which of the following would be good topics on which to base an argument? Explain your reasons for your choices.

Topics

genetic engineering of foodstuffs

the meaning of life

your grandmother

controlled hunting of deer in suburban areas

the love life of Paris Hilton (or your favorite celebrity)

abortion

bicycle lanes on all roads

preserving the ecosystem

the afterlife

2. Select one of the topics you earmarked as suitable, identify an interesting and debatable thesis within that topic, and make two lists, one of points that support the thesis and one of points that oppose (argue against) the thesis. Use extra paper as necessary.

Selected topic and thesis:_____

_____

_____

Points in support of the thesis: _____

_____

Points that oppose the thesis: _____

_____

_____

7d Formulate an arguable claim (thesis).

The position you take on a topic constitutes your thesis or claim. Mara Lee Kornberg knew that the claim in her argument paper should be debatable, so after some reading and research, she formulated a preliminary working thesis on her topic, though she remained prepared to change it if her research led her in a different direction. See her paper in 7l.

Working thesis: A vegan diet is a healthy diet for children.

Avoid using any of the following as claims, as they are not debatable:

- a neutral statement, which gives no hint of the writer's position
- an announcement of the paper's broad subject
- a fact, which is not arguable
- a truism (statement that is obviously true)
- a personal or religious conviction that cannot be logically debated
- an opinion based only on your own feelings
- a sweeping generalization

Here are some examples of nondebatable claims, each with a revision.

NEUTRAL STATEMENT	**There are unstated standards of beauty in the workplace.**
REVISED	**The way we look affects the way we are treated at work and the size of our paychecks.**

TOO BROAD	**This paper is about violence on TV.**
REVISED	**TV violence has to take its share of blame for the violence in our society.**

FACT	*Plessy v. Ferguson,* **a Supreme Court case that supported racial segregation, was overturned in 1954 by** *Brown v. Board of Education.*
REVISED	**The overturning of** *Plessy v. Ferguson* **by** *Brown v. Board of Education* **has not led to significant advances in integrated education.**

TRUISM	**Bilingual education has advantages and disadvantages.**
REVISED	**A bilingual program is more effective than an immersion program at helping students grasp the basics of science and mathematics.**

PERSONAL CONVICTION	**Racism is the worst kind of prejudice.**
REVISED	**The best weapon against racism is primary and secondary education.**

OPINION BASED ONLY ON FEELING	**I think water-skiing is a dumb sport.**
REVISED	**Water-skiing should be banned from public beaches.**

SWEEPING GENERALIZATION	**Women understand housework.**
REVISED	**The publication of a lengthy guide to housekeeping and its success among both men and women suggest a renewed interest in the domestic arts.**

Avoid loaded terms. In your claim, avoid sweeping and judgmental words—for instance, *bad, good, right, wrong, stupid, ridiculous, moral, immoral, dumb, smart*.

Revise your claim. Sometimes you will have an instant reaction to an issue and immediately decide which position you want to take. At other times, you will need to reflect and do research before you take a stand. Whenever you decide what your position is, formulate a position statement that will serve as your working thesis—for example, "Undocumented aliens should (or should not) have to pay higher college tuition fees than citizens or other immigrants." However, keep an open mind. Be prepared to find out more about an issue so that you can make an educated claim with concrete evidence (see 7c), and be prepared to modify, qualify, or even change your original claim as you do your research.

Mara Lee Kornberg began with a working thesis that guided her research. However, as she did more reading and research and as she examined her assumptions (see 7c) and got feedback on her ideas, she began to refine her thesis to take counterarguments into account. The following shows how she progressed in her planning:

> **Topic:** A vegan diet for children
>
> **Research question:** Does a vegan diet supply adequate nutrition for children?
>
> **Working thesis:** A vegan diet is a healthy diet for children.
>
> **Revised thesis:** A vegan diet can be healthy for children provided that it is supplemented with vitamins and minerals.

You can read a draft of her essay in 7l to see how Kornberg supports her claim with evidence, appeals to her readers, establishes common ground, and discusses opposing views.

Modify your claim. Even if you do not revise your position as Mara Lee Kornberg did, you will often find yourself modifying your claim as you read, think, and write, making it less all-embracing or less extreme. Here is how Ann Raimes, one of the authors of this book, modified her claim as she worked on writing an argument about a topic she cared deeply about. She took into account some opposing views, toned down the language, and set limits to her position—not arguing on all the issues raised by the proposed building of a cement factory but focusing specifically on environmental issues of pollution, wildlife, and nature.

Topic: Building a new cement plant

Audience: General audience

Initial question: What will be the effects of a Hudson River valley cement plant on jobs, the local economy, and the environment?

Initial claim (working thesis) after some research: A large new cement plant will irreparably damage the environment of the Hudson River valley.

Modified claim (seeking common ground with readers and acknowledging recognition of opposing views): Although we need to consider the increased demand for building materials and local economic development, a large cement plant on the Hudson River would not only pollute air and water but also threaten wildlife and natural beauty.

LANGUAGE AND CULTURE

Arguments across Cultures: Making a Claim and Staking a Position

The types of arguments described in this section are those common in academic and business settings in North America and the Western world. Writers state their views directly, arguing for their viewpoints. The success of their arguments lies in the credibility and strength of the evidence they produce in support. But such an approach is not universal. Other cultures may prefer a less direct approach, one that begins by exploring and evaluating all options rather than by issuing a direct claim. One of the basic principles of writing well—know your audience's expectations—is especially relevant to writing arguments in cultures different from your own.

7e Support the claim with reasons and concrete evidence.

Support your claim by telling your readers what reasons, statistics, facts, examples, and expert testimony bolster and explain your point of view. If a reader asks, "Why do you think that?" about your claim, the support you offer should answer that question in detail.

Reasons Imagine someone saying to you, "OK. I know your position on this issue, but I disagree with you. What led you to your position?" This is asking you to provide the reasons for your conviction. To begin to answer the question, add at least one "because clause" to your claim.

Claim: Colleges should stop using SAT scores to determine admissions.
Reason: (because) High school grades predict college success with more accuracy.

Claim: Organized hunting of deer is necessary in suburban areas.
Reason: (because) With a diminishing natural habitat, deer are becoming an otherwise uncontrollable hazard to people and property.

Claim: A large coal-fired cement factory in a rural scenic region could be an ecological disaster.
Reason: (because) Its operation would threaten water, wildlife, and the residents' health.

Once you have formulated a tentative claim, make a scratch outline listing the claim and developing and expanding your reasons for supporting it. As you work more on your argument, you will then need to find specific and concrete evidence to explain and support each reason. Here is an example of a scratch outline (see 3i) developed against building a cement factory in a rural scenic region. Note the revised, more detailed claim, the expanded list of reasons, and the inclusion of visual arguments to make a strong point.

Claim: Although a large, coal-fired cement factory on the Hudson River would satisfy the increased demand for building materials and might help boost the local economy, the danger is that it could not only pollute air and water but also threaten the wildlife and the natural beauty of the area.

Billboard (and poster on previous page) sponsored by Scenic Hudson, Inc. and Columbia Action Now to oppose the plans for a cement plant.

Reasons:

1. Drilling, blasting, and mining pose dangers to the local aquifer and to the nearby city's water supply.
2. Every year, a 1,800-acre coal-burning plant with a 406-foot stack would emit just under 20 million pounds of pollution, including arsenic, lead, and mercury.
3. Smokestack emissions could affect birds; barge traffic and discharge into the river could affect fish.
4. Views portrayed by the Hudson River school of painters would be spoiled.

Concrete evidence   You need reasons, but reasons are not enough. You also need to include specific evidence that supports, illustrates, and explains your reasons. Imagine a reader saying after you give one of your reasons, "Tell me even more about why you say that." The details you provide are what will make your argument vivid and persuasive.

Add to the outline any items of concrete evidence you will include to illustrate and explain your reasoning. What counts as evidence? Facts, statistics, stories, examples, and testimony from experts can all be used as evidence in support of your reasons.

 ESL NOTE

Evidence Used to Support an Argument

The way arguments are structured, the concept of *expertise,* and the nature of evidence regarded as convincing may vary from one culture to another. In some cultures, for example, the opinions of religious or political leaders may carry more weight than the opinions of a scholar in the field. Looking at newspaper editorials written in your home language and in English will help you discern what differences, if any, exist in the types of evidence used to support an argument. Be sure to consider the readers you will be writing for and the type of evidence they will expect.

EXERCISE 7.4

Generate ideas on an argument for improving your college.

With a group of classmates, decide on an argument for change you would like to present to the administrators of your college. List the specific and concrete details you would provide to show the nature and extent of the problem, the reasons change is necessary, and the ways in which change could be accomplished. List what the opposing views may be, and consider how you could answer or counter them.

7f Identify and appeal to the audience, and establish common ground.

Identify your audience. Consider the readers you are writing for. Assess what they might know, what assumptions they hold, what they need to know, how they can best be convinced to accept your position, and what strategies will persuade them to respect or accept your views.

When Ann Raimes, one of the authors of this book, wanted to argue that a huge new cement plant should not be built alongside a major river and next to a populated area, she needed to consider carefully who her readers would be. Cement company workers, the unemployed, and suppliers of industrial equipment and materials, on the one hand, and doctors, environmentalists, and homeowners, on the other, would bring their own assumptions and biases to the argument. All writers need to consider and address such biases.

If you are writing for readers with no specific prior knowledge of the topic, biases, or expertise—known as a *general audience*—remember to include background information: the place, the time, the context, the issues. Do not assume that general readers know a great deal more than you do. For more on audience, see 2b.

Appeal to the audience. Aristotle classified the ways that writers can appeal to their audiences in arguments. Identifying your audience will help you decide what types of appeal to use. Within one extended argument, you may find it necessary to use more than one type of appeal to reach all of your audience's needs. The examples of the appeals below, for example, were used by Nicholas Kristof in a *New York Times* op-ed argument for hunting to control the deer population ("For Environmental Balance, Pick Up a Rifle," 4 December, 2005: 4:12).

RATIONAL APPEAL (LOGOS)   A rational appeal bases an argument's conclusion on facts, examples, and authoritative evidence. Such an appeal is appropriate for an academic audience and useful when the audience is uninformed or hostile.

Examples: Kristof presents as evidence for his argument the fact that in the U.S., deer kill 150 people a year in car crashes and cause damage amounting to $1 billion (presumably to property and crops, though this is not specified). In addition, a square mile of New Jersey alone could be inhabited by up to 200 deer. To show the decline in hunting, he cites a report that gives figures for the decreasing numbers of hunters.

ETHICAL APPEAL (ETHOS)   You make an ethical appeal to an audience when you represent yourself or any sources you refer to as reliable, experienced, thoughtful, objective, and evenhanded, even when considering opposing views. Such an appeal is appropriate for formal situations in business and academic worlds. In advertising, too, ethical appeals often include testimony from famous people, whether they are experts or not—for example, American Express uses M. Night Shyamalan to promote its credit card.

Examples: Kristof presents himself as knowledgeable about country issues: he was raised on a farm and was even, as he says, "raised on Bambi," as well as on eating meat such as venison. He cites as a reliable source the New Jersey Audubon Society, which emphasizes the ecological need for deer hunting. He pays attention to counterarguments by granting that in the suburbs it is not feasible to hunt in backyards or to bring in wolves as natural predators, but he does advocate an increase in wilderness preservation and in hunting elsewhere to restore an ecological balance.

EMOTIONAL APPEAL   You make an emotional appeal when you try to gain the empathy and sympathy of your readers by assessing their values and to persuade them by using descriptions, anecdotes, case studies, and visuals in order to appeal to those values. Such an appeal is less common in academic writing than in journalism and the other media. It is appropriate when readers are regarded as either already favorable to particular ideas or apathetic toward them.

Examples: Kristof assesses his readers' values. He sees *New York Times* readers as being opposed to hunting, so when he proposes encouraging hunting, he speaks to readers head-on: "Now, you've probably just spilled your coffee." He ends his article with an anecdote aimed to gain his readers' empathy: a 200-pound man in Arkansas whose home was broken into by a buck fought with it for 40 minutes until he eventually had to kill it with his bare hands.

Within one extended argument, you will probably find it necessary to use all types of appeals to reach the maximum number of readers, each with individual expectations, preferences, and quirks. See 7l for examples of these appeals in a student's argument essay.

Establish common ground. Remember that readers turned off by exaggerations or extreme language have the ultimate power to stop reading and ignore what you have to say.

In Ann Raimes's discussion of the cement plant, for example, she wanted to acknowledge the importance of producing cement locally rather than importing it from other regions and to recognize the need for more local industry and jobs. One solution to the problem of finding common ground is to show how those goals could be achieved by upgrading an existing cement plant rather than building a huge new coal-fired plant.

KEY POINTS
Ways to Establish Common Ground with Readers

- Avoid extreme views or language. Do not label someone's views *ridiculous, ignorant, immoral, fascist,* or *crooked,* for example.

- Write to convince, not to confront. Recognize shared concerns, and consider the inclusive use of *we.*

- Steer clear of sarcastic remarks, such as "The company has come up with the amazingly splendid idea of building a gigantic cement factory right in the middle of a natural beauty spot."

- Use clear, everyday words that sound as if you are speaking directly to your readers.

- Acknowledge when your opponents' arguments are valid, and work to show why the arguments on your side carry more weight.

- If possible, propose a solution with long-term benefits for everyone.

EXERCISE 7.5

Add an emotional appeal.

The following passage presents a logical appeal. What could the writer add to include an emotional appeal, too?

> Hunger is not as serious here [in the United States] as in countries where children are so nutrient-deprived that brain growth is impeded. The moderate undernutrition found in the United States affects performance, but recovery is usually possible with adequate diet. Yet if dietary deficiencies persist, learning can suffer. Iron deficiency anemia, which is twice as common in poor as in better-off children, affects cognitive ability. In experiments where people got inexpensive vitamin and mineral supplements, test scores rose from that treatment alone.
>
> —Richard Rothstein, "Lessons: Food for Thought? In Many Cases, No"

7g Refute opposing views.

It is not enough to present your own reasons and evidence for your claim. When you take into account any opposing arguments and the reasons and evidence that support those arguments, you present yourself as objective and evenhanded, furthering your ethical argument. Examine opposing arguments; describe the most common or convincing ones; evaluate their validity, applicability, and limitations; and explain what motivates people to take those positions. Then discuss the ways in which you see your reasons and evidence as more pertinent and convincing than those in opposing arguments.

Be careful to argue logically and rationally without insulting your opponents—for instance, do not call opposing views *stupid* or *crazy*. Take pains to explain rationally why your views differ from opposing views. You might choose to do this by following each one of your own points with a discussion of an opposing view. Or you may prefer to devote an entire section of your essay to dealing with opposing views.

SUBJECTIVE AND INSULTING	The fools who want the company to build a cement plant think that it will provide jobs in the area. Get real! The company has publicly stated that there will be only five new jobs created.

OBJECTIVE
AND
EVENHANDED
One of the arguments used by many of those in favor of the proposed cement plant is that it will bring jobs to the area. But that particular argument has little basis in fact. The cement company officials have stated publicly that no more than five new jobs will be added if they build the plant.

7h Structure the argument.

Your material and your purposes will do a great deal to influence how you organize your argument to achieve the best results. Three common structures used in designing an argument are these: general to specific, specific to general, and problem and solution.

General to specific If you have not had much experience with writing arguments, you may find it useful to work with and adapt the following basic structure for an argument. Used frequently in the humanities and arts, this structure moves from the general to the specific, from thesis to support and evidence.

KEY POINTS
Basic Structure for a General-to-Specific Argument

1. *Introduction*   Provide background information on the issue, why it is an issue, and what the controversies are. After you have introduced your audience to the nature and importance of the issue, announce your position in a claim or thesis statement, perhaps at the end of the first paragraph or in a prominent position within the second paragraph, depending on the length and complexity of your essay.

2. *Body*   Provide evidence in the form of supporting points for your thesis, with concrete and specific details. For each new point, start a new paragraph.

3. *Refutation of opposing views*   Use evidence and specific details to describe and logically refute the opposing views. You could also deal with opposing views one by one as you deal with your own points of support.

4. *Conclusion*   Return to the issue and your claim. Without repeating whole phrases and sentences, reiterate the point you want to make. End on a strong note.

Specific to general   Alternatively, you might choose to begin with data and points of evidence and then draw a conclusion from that evidence. A basic specific-to-general argument looks like this:

Introduction: Background, statement of problem
Data:

1. Cell phone users admit to being distracted while driving.
2. Many accidents are attributable to cell phone use.
3. New York, New Jersey, and Connecticut have passed laws against using a handheld cell phone while driving.
4. AAA and insurance companies report that . . .

Conclusion: Discussion of data and presentation of thesis (generalization formed from analysis of the data): All states should prohibit the use of handheld cell phones while driving.

In an argument in the sciences or social sciences (see, for example, the APA-style sample paper in section 52f), writers often begin with a hypothesis that they can test: they list their findings from experimentation, surveys, facts, and statistics and then from the data they have collected they draw conclusions to support, modify, or reject the hypothesis. Here is an outline of an argument built around a hypothesis:

Introduction: Background, review of the literature
Hypothesis: Statins should be prescribed more widely than they are now to prevent heart attacks.
Data:

1. Decrease in heart failure for patients on statins
2. Need for women to be aware of heart disease and take preventive measures
3. What statins do that exercise and diet cannot do
4. Testimony from three heart-attack patients and six doctors

Conclusion: Analysis of data and confirmation of hypothesis

Problem and solution   If your topic offers solutions to a problem, you probably will find it useful to present the details of the problem first and then offer solutions. Consider whether the strongest position for the solution you consider the most desirable is at the beginning of your solutions section or at the end. Do you want to make your strong point early or lead up to it gradually? See 5d, item 13, for a passage from an argument providing a solution to a problem.

Cause and effect   Writers of arguments in history, art history, and social movements often examine the causes and effects of events and trends to enhance their points of view. The reasoning behind an analysis of causes and effects is far from simple, involving many variables and interpretations. Take care to not reduce your analysis to one simple cause, and avoid the logical fallacy of assuming that one event causes another when it merely precedes it (see 7k).

7i Ask Toulmin's four questions.

Keeping an open mind and asking probing questions are essential to both reading and writing arguments. As a reader of arguments, you will need to employ your critical thinking capabilities to examine the reasoning a writer uses and to ferret out the writer's assumptions, biases, and lapses in logic. (See chapter 48 for more on research and critical reading.) Remember that when you write an argument, your readers will be looking for your assumptions, biases, and lapses in logic too.

The four questions in the Key Points box, derived from Stephen Toulmin's *The Uses of Argument,* will provide you with a way to examine your own arguments critically.

KEY POINTS
Four Questions to Ask about Your Argument

1. What is your point? (What are you claiming?)

2. What do you have to go on? (What support do you have for your claim in the form of reasons, data, and evidence?)

3. How do you get there? (What assumptions—Toulmin calls them "warrants"—do you take for granted and expect the reader to take for granted, too?)

4. What could prevent you from getting there? (What qualifications do you need to include, using *but, unless,* or *if* or adding words like *usually, often, several, mostly,* or *sometimes* to provide exceptions to your assumptions?)

Here is an example showing how the Toulmin questions can be used to develop the claim and supporting reason introduced in 7d:

CLAIM **Colleges should stop using SAT scores in their admissions process.**

SUPPORT **(because) High school grades and recommendations predict college success with more accuracy.**

ASSUMPTION/ WARRANT	**Colleges use SAT scores to predict success in college.**
QUALIFIER	**. . . unless the colleges use the scores only to indicate the level of knowledge acquired in high school.**
REVISED CLAIM	**Colleges that use SAT scores to predict college success should use high school grades and recommendations instead.**

Examine your assumptions.　Pay special attention to examining assumptions that link a claim to the reasons and evidence you provide. Consider whether readers will share those assumptions or whether you need to explain, discuss, and defend them. For example, the claim "Telemarketing should be monitored because it preys on the elderly and the gullible" operates on the assumption that monitoring will catch and reduce abuses. The claim "Telemarketing should be encouraged because it benefits the economy" operates on the assumption that benefiting the economy is an important goal. These different assumptions will appeal to different readers, and some readers may need to be persuaded of the validity of your assumptions before they accept your claim or the reasons you give to support it.

Note that if your claim is "Telemarketing should be encouraged because it is useful," you are saying little more than "Telemarketing is good because it is good." Your reader is certain to object to and reject such circular reasoning. That is why it is important to ask question 3 from the Key Points box. That question leads you to examine how you get from your evidence to your claim and what assumptions your claim is based on.

EXERCISE 7.6
Analyze assumptions.

Examine the following arguments. What assumptions connect the claim to the data? Write a short analysis of the warrants (the assumptions). Then write a revised claim, suggesting any necessary qualifiers.

1. Claim: Steve is wealthy.

   Support/data: Steve wears designer clothing, drives a Mercedes, and has a summer home.

   Assumptions/warrants:_____

   Qualifier: _____

   Revised claim: _____

2. Claim: Rita Fiorella is probably of Italian descent.

Support/data: She has an Italian last name and dark hair.

Assumptions/warrants:_____

Qualifier: _____

Revised claim: _____

7j Check your logic.

Another way to check the logic of your arguments is to assess that they are valid examples of deductive or inductive reasoning.

Deductive reasoning The classical Aristotelian method of constructing an argument is based on a reasoning process (a *syllogism*) that moves from true premises to a certain and valid conclusion.
Here is an example:

MAJOR PREMISE — **Coal-fired factories can cause significant damage to the environment.**

MINOR PREMISE — **The proposed cement plant will use coal for fuel.**

CONCLUSION — **The proposed cement plant could cause significant damage to the environment.**

Even if the major premise is not stated, readers must nevertheless accept it as the truth: *Since the new proposed cement plant will be coal fired, it could cause significant damage to the environment.* The premises must be true for a conclusion to be valid.

Check the thoroughness of the evidence in inductive arguments.
While a deductive argument begins with a generalization and leads to a *certain* conclusion, an inductive argument begins with details that lead to a *probable* conclusion.

Inductive arguments are used often in the sciences and social sciences. Researchers begin with a tentative hypothesis. They conduct studies and perform experiments; they collect and tabulate data; they examine the evidence of other studies. Then they draw a conclusion to support, reject, or modify the hypothesis. The conclusion, however, is only probable and not necessarily certain. It is based on the circumstances of the evidence. Different evidence at a different time could lead to a different conclusion. Conclusions drawn in the medical field change with the experiments and the sophistication of the techniques—eggs are good for you one year, bad the next. That is not because researchers are wrong. It is that the nature of the evidence changes.

7k Avoid logical fallacies.

Faulty logic can make readers mistrust you as a writer. Watch out for some common flaws in logic (called *logical fallacies*) as you write and check your drafts.

Sweeping generalization Generalizations can sometimes be so broad that they fall into stereotyping. Avoid them.

▶ **All British people are stiff and formal.**

▶ **The only thing that concerns students is grades.**

The reader will be right to wonder what evidence has led to these conclusions. Without any explanation or evidence, such statements will simply be dismissed. Beware, then, of the trap of using words like *all, every, only, never,* and *always.*

Hasty conclusion with inadequate support To convince readers of the validity of a generalization, you need to offer enough evidence—usually more than just one personal observation. Thoughtful readers can easily spot a conclusion that is too hastily drawn from flimsy support.

▶ **My friend Arecelis had a terrible time in a bilingual school. It is clear that bilingual education has failed.**

▶ **Bilingual education is a success story, as the school in Chinatown has clearly shown.**

Non sequitur *Non sequitur* is Latin for "It does not follow." Supporting a claim with evidence that is illogical or irrelevant causes a non sequitur fallacy.

▶ **Maureen Dowd writes so well that she would make a good teacher.** [The writer does not establish a connection between good writing and good teaching.]

▶ **Studying economics is a waste of time. Money does not make people happy.** [Here the writer does not help us see any relationship between happiness and the study of a subject.]

Causal fallacy You are guilty of a causal fallacy if you assume that one event causes another merely because the second event happens after the first. (The Latin name for this logical flaw is *post hoc, ergo propter hoc:* "after this, therefore because of this.")

▶ **The economy collapsed because a new president was elected.** [Was the election the reason? Or did it simply occur before the economy collapsed?]

▶ **The number of A's given in college courses has increased. This clearly shows that faculty members are inflating grades.** [But does the number of A's clearly show any such thing? Or could the cause be that students are now better prepared in high school?]

Examine carefully any statements you make about cause and effect.

Ad hominem attack *Ad hominem* (Latin for "to the person") refers to unfair ethical appeals to personal considerations rather than to logic or reason. Avoid using arguments that seek to discredit an opinion by criticizing a person's character or lifestyle.

▶ **The new curriculum should not be adopted because the administrators who favor it have never even taught a college course.**

▶ **The student who is urging the increase in student fees for social events is a partygoer and a big drinker.**

Argue a point by showing either the logic of the argument or the lack of it, not by pointing to flaws in character. However, personal considerations may be valid if they pertain directly to the issue, as in "The two women who favor the abolition of the bar own property on the same block."

Circular reasoning In an argument based on circular reasoning, the evidence and the conclusion restate each other, thus proving nothing.

▶ **Credit card companies should be banned on campus because companies should not be allowed to solicit business from students.**

▶ **That rich man is smart because wealthy people are intelligent.**

Neither of these statements moves the argument forward. They both beg the question—that is, they argue in a circular way.

False dichotomy or false dilemma   Either/or arguments reduce complex problems to two simplistic alternatives without exploring them in depth or considering other alternatives.

▶ **After September 11, New York could do one of two things: increase airport security or screen immigrants.**

This proposal presents a false dichotomy. These are not the only two options for dealing with potential terrorism. Posing a false dilemma like this will annoy readers.

TECH NOTE

Logical Fallacies on the Web

Go to *Stephen's Guide to the Logical Fallacies* for lists of many more types of logical fallacies, all with explanations and examples. A link to this site and additional practices for identifying logical fallacies are at the Online Study Center.

Online Study Center   **Writing Process**   More logical fallacies

---

EXERCISE 7.7

Examine arguments.

For each of the following statements, determine whether the argument is logical or contains a logical fallacy. If it contains a logical fallacy, identify the logical fallacy and explain why it is a fallacy.

1. The new vice president of sales is untrustworthy because many years ago he was arrested for civil disobedience while in college.

2. Married couples without children often experience societal pressure to have or adopt children.

3. Mary can either matriculate as a full-time student in the fall or wait until the following fall to attend classes.

4. Keeping a diary is cathartic because writing on a daily basis releases bottled-up emotions.

5. All men like sports.

7l   Sample arguments: A student's essay and a persuasive letter in a community newspaper

Here is a draft of Mara Lee Kornberg's argument paper on a vegan diet, annotated to point out the strategies in her argument. Note how she presents her thesis, supports it, considers and refutes opposing views, and varies appeals to readers. See 51g for MLA format for a final draft.

Dispelling the Media Myth: Vegan Diet Is Safe for Children

In April 2003, a Queens couple was convicted of assault and related charges for nearly starving their young daughter to death by feeding her only vegan foods. Silva and Joseph Swinton placed their daughter on a strict, meat- and dairy-free diet shortly after her birth. By the time Ilce Swinton was fifteen months old, she weighed only ten pounds, had no teeth, had suffered broken bones and internal injuries, and was diagnosed as being severely malnourished. She was taken into foster care in 2001, and almost immediately the media swarmed, focusing not on the fact that this child had obviously been abused and neglected and never once given medical care, but on the fact that she had been fed—when she was fed at all—a vegan diet. Before long, the case was being referred to in newspapers as "the Vegan Baby Diet" (Retsinas).

Emotional appeal: story of a sick child

Definition of term

A vegan is, according to <u>Merriam-Webster Medical Dictionary</u>, a "strict vegetarian who consumes no animal food or dairy products." While it is not uncommon to be a vegetarian nowadays, "knowledge on adequacy and nutritional effects of vegan diets is still limited," according to the German Vegan Study (GVS) of 154 vegans, a scholarly study conducted in 2003, which has greatly helped in shedding light on this still widely unknown way of eating (Waldmann et al. 947). Because it is uncommon, the practice of veganism was not received well by the general public when the Swinton case became headline news last year. As is often the case, a way of life was perceived as problematic simply because it was not well understood, and this vegan diet was very quickly assumed to be the cause of the baby's medical problems. However, veganism can be a very healthful dietary choice for parents to make for their children, provided they see to it that the diet is properly employed and therefore sufficient in vitamins and minerals.

Claim—with qualifier (4h)

Scholarly research cited

While the mainstream media, in the wake of the Swinton case, has painted a portrait of veganism as a risky alternative lifestyle, it is for the most part simply a dietary decision a person makes, similar to the decision one may make to eat kosher. While the choice to observe a kosher diet is almost certainly a religious one, those who observe a vegan diet tend to fall into two schools of reasoning. Of the 154 vegans participating in the GVS, more than 90 percent of them admitted to becoming vegan for one of the following two reasons: ethics or health (Waldmann et al. 951).

Those who subscribe to the first set of reasons choose to eliminate animal by-products because of moral concerns. They feel that animals should not be used to feed human beings. Often, people who subscribe to this belief also choose to eliminate leather, wool, and other animal-based materials from their wardrobes. According to People for the Ethical Treatment of Animals (PETA), adhering to a vegan diet is one way of living a "cruelty-free" lifestyle ("Cruelty").

The second group of vegans excludes animal products for health reasons. Many people are lactose intolerant and therefore choose not to consume animal milk or similar products that may act as allergens upon their systems. Others eliminate foods such as red meat and cheese from their diets because of their high fat content. These vegans tend to regard veganism as a dietary option only and do not usually eliminate animal products from their wardrobes. Vegans who employ such a diet for their children tend to see the diet as a moral choice. Similar to those who encourage a kosher diet in their offspring because of their religious beliefs, these vegans attempt to pass down their set of beliefs and moral concerns to their children.

Veganism has gained exposure in recent years, especially after the details of the Swinton case brought it to the forefront of debates among nutritionists. This extends outside the medical field as well and has brought to society's attention both an opposition to and advocacy of veganism. Many celebrities, including singer

Ethical appeal: testimony from well-known people

Moby and Olympic gold-medal runner Carl Lewis, have claimed to be vegans. During the filming of the movie Gladiator, actor Joaquin Phoenix insisted that his costumes be made entirely of synthetic materials, as he not only excludes animals from his diet but from his wardrobe as well ("Joaquin Phoenix"). A crop of new vegan-friendly restaurants has popped up, offering both healthful vegetable dishes and more traditionally meaty fare in soy and grain-based forms. Moby's restaurant, Teany, specializes in sandwiches and desserts such as a soy "turkey" club and vanilla bean strawberry shortcake, among others, all of which once called for animal ingredients like eggs and milk (Pepe).

For children, the diet rightly comes under more scrutiny. For a child's diet to be a healthy one in the eyes of pediatric medicine, it should adhere to the recommendations made in the long-established food guide pyramid (U.S. Dept of Agriculture). According to medical journalist Karen Sullivan, the diet should be balanced and include at

Expert testimony to support thesis

the very least "the required number of fruits and vegetables" as well as "good sources of protein and carbohydrates" (76). Sullivan lists some of what she calls "good-quality protein" as including "fish, lean meat, chicken, turkey, cheese, milk, yogurt, tofu, nuts, nut butters, seeds, and legumes" (77). Perhaps most important in a child's diet is variety, which is precisely the problem that many nutritional experts express with the practice of veganism. "The keyword is balance," writes Sullivan (76). As long as a child eats a fair amount of foods from each group in the food guide pyramid and consumes a balanced group of nutrients and minerals, there should be no harm done to his or her general health. Almost half of the twelve items on Sullivan's list of proteins are appropriate for the very strictest vegan diet. Were a parent to eliminate meat, dairy, and fish from the sum of protein-rich foods he or she serves a child, there would still be a number of healthy proteins to choose from, as is shown in the legumes and nuts section of the vegan pyramid in Figure 1.

Use of image to make a visual argument

Figure 1   The vegan food pyramid
Source: Vegsource.com at <http://vegan.uchicago.edu/nutrition/01.html>.

While veganism is gaining some acceptance in today's society in spite of opposition, a stigma still attaches to those who choose to raise their children this way. This is evident in the way the media has focused on young IIce Swinton's vegan diet, despite the fact that she was obviously otherwise neglected and abused. Such a restrictive diet appears on the surface to be dangerous for young, developing bodies; however, if the diet is applied properly, a baby or toddler can live a perfectly healthy young life eating only vegan foods. Dr. Spock's Baby and Child Care, a text long regarded as the foremost authority on parenting and pediatric health, plainly states that "children can thrive on vegetarian and vegan diets" (Spock and Needleman 338), with the cautionary note that children should also receive vitamin and mineral supplements.

First opposing argument about diet

Authority to refute opposing view—with qualifier

In fact, adequate amounts of vitamins and minerals are a concern often associated with veganism. A mother's breast milk is allowed on even the strictest of vegan diets, but there have been cases in which babies fed breast milk of mothers on vegan diets suffered from malnutrition and/or vitamin B12 deficiency. Vitamin B12 "occurs naturally only in animal products" (Lawson). However, according to Maria Elena Jefferds, an epidemiologist who worked with the Centers for Disease Control in monitoring the babies involved in the aforementioned cases, vitamin B12 deficiency is a problem "that doesn't just affect vegetarians" (Lawson). Amy Joy Lanou, the nutrition director of Physicians for Responsible Medicine, who in fact testified during the 2003 Swinton case, warns that a vitamin B12 deficiency "is becoming more common among infants of vegan and vegetarians as well as meat-eating parents." She notes, however, that families who are vegetarians or vegans "generally take in much higher levels of important vitamins and minerals." And the GVS researchers found that only a few vitamins and minerals (calcium, iodine, and cobalamin) needed to be supplemented in the diets of the vegans they studied (Waldmann et al. 954).

2nd opposing argument about vitamin deficiency

Refutation of 2nd opposing argument

Logical appeal of facts from research

Those who oppose implementing vegan diets in children worry not only about what is lacking in the diet but also about the necessary additives that may interrupt a child's system. Soy milk, a staple of a vegan diet, may contain added sugar or artificial sweeteners, which can be disruptive to a child's body chemistry. Soy milk also contains phytoestrogens, hormonal compounds that, though helpful in preventing some cancers in adults, are unnecessary

3rd opposing argument about additives

for children and may adversely affect their hormones (Sullivan 350). In addition, just as a child can develop an allergy to cow's milk, too much soy milk can lead to similarly unfavorable reactions.

However, these problems that could potentially arise from a vegan diet are easily remedied. Sugar-free soy milks are available, and as long as they are not used as a child's sole source of protein and calcium, there is no problem with their inclusion in a pediatric diet plan. As to the lack of vitamin B12 and other important vitamins and minerals in a vegan diet, "parents need to take special care that their children are getting enough," advises Dr. Spock, which he thinks is easily achieved: "A multivitamin and mineral supplement can offer the needed insurance" (Spock and Needleman 338). Lucy Moll, author of The Vegetarian Child, agrees: "Including B12 in your diet is easy . . . the solution is as simple as a bowlful of fortified breakfast cereal" (18).

Solutions to counter 3rd opposing argument

Not only does a vegan diet satisfy a child's health needs; it also "offers significant protection from many health complications" (Lanou). Many sources of traditional proteins, the food group most often lacking in a vegetarian or vegan diet, are very high in saturated and trans fats, which can lead to obesity in children, which in turn can lead to a variety of other medical ailments. Soy proteins are generally lower in fat and cholesterol than their animal-based counterparts, and there is some evidence that soy proteins actually help lower levels of bad cholesterol, a substance in the blood that, in abundance, can lead to such medical conditions as heart disease (Sullivan 350).

Support for thesis: vegan diet is healthy

Dr. Spock has alerted parents to the dangers of animal milks: "Milk may actually pose health risks" (Spock and Needleman 340). Traditional animal milk is high in saturated fat and low in iron and essential fats. These healthy fats are more often found in vegetable sources, such as avocados, vegetable oils, and nut butters. Furthermore, cow milk is a common allergen in children, and just as many adults avoid animal milks because of lactose intolerance, it may be safest for children to avoid cow milk as well. Milk-based products can contribute to headaches and stomach ailments like diarrhea and constipation and can increase the risk of developing genetic diseases such as asthma, eczema, and juvenile onset diabetes (Spock and Needleman 341). Sullivan also addresses issues surrounding pediatric milk consumption. The recent use of genetically engineered bovine somatotrophin, a hormone naturally present in cow milk, to increase milk production in dairy cows has

Support: dangers of dairy products

led to concern about human consumption of such chemically enhanced milk (29). While the use of this hormone was banned in Canada and the United Kingdom ten years ago, it is still in use in the United States. Because children generally take in a much greater amount of milk than their parents, the youngest of Americans make up the group most at risk.

Although most of the blame for Ilce Swinton's poor health was laid on the vegan diet her mother and father fed her, it should be noted that although Silva Swinton admitted in court to feeding her daughter according to a vegan diet plan, she was not applying the diet properly. Because breast milk is not derived from animals, and none are harmed in its production, it is perfectly acceptable for a vegan baby to consume. Mrs. Swinton, however, chose not to feed Ilce with breast milk and chose instead to mix homemade soy formulas, which were obviously inadequately prepared. If a vegan diet is sensibly employed, it can be perfectly healthy, both for adults and children. In fact, vegans generally lead much healthier lifestyles than meat-eaters. The GVS reports that only three percent of the vegans studied were smokers (Waldmann et al. 949), and just one-quarter of participants regularly drank alcohol. The implication here is that vegans possess a greater awareness than the general population as to what are the building blocks of a healthy lifestyle. The GVS study concludes reassuringly with this: "Our data show that the participants of the GVS had an above average healthy lifestyle" (Waldmann et al. 955). Moreover, according to Dr. Spock, a meat-free diet, when set up with care, may be able to "offer even more long-term health benefits to you and your children" (Spock and Needleman 338). It is important that parents instill in their young children a sense of what is and what is not healthful so that they will make educated diet and lifestyle choices throughout their lives.

Lead-in to conclusion: a return to the introductory story

Strong logical appeal of data from research study

Conclusion

In light of the issues surrounding animal foods and the proven benefits of a meat-free diet, a viable dietary choice is to eliminate animal sources of nutrition from one's diet. This is especially true in the case of children, who are considerably more susceptible to the ills of poor nutrition and obesity. While there is still a great deal of opposition to veganism for children, much of it derived from society's general ignorance of the diet, raising a child as a vegan, with careful supplements of necessary vitamins and minerals, can be a safe and healthy choice.

Works Cited

"Cruelty-Free Living." People for the Ethical Treatment of Animals.
22 Nov. 2004 <http://peta.org/living/>.

"Joaquin Phoenix." Internet Movie Database. 20 Nov. 2004
<http://imdb.com/name/nm0001618/bio>.

Lanou, Amy Joy. "Vegan's Bad Wrap." Psychology Today Sept./Oct.
2003: 6. Academic Search Premier. EBSCO. Hunter College
Lib. 8 Nov. 2004 <http://search.epnet.com/login.aspx?
direct=true&db=aph&an=10602091>.

Lawson, Willow. "Brain Food." Psychology Today May/Jun. 2003:
22–. Academic Search Premier. EBSCO. Hunter College Lib. 8
Nov. 2004 <http://search.epnet.com/login.aspx?
direct=true&db=aph&an=9625534>.

Moll, Lucy. The Vegetarian Child. New York: Perigee, 1997.

Pepe, Michelle. "Teany: Moby's Tiny Tearoom." AOL City Guide.
2004. 30 Nov. 2004 <http://www.digitalicity.com/newyork/
dining/venue.adp?sbid=116500935>.

Retsinas, Greg. "Couple Guilty of Assault in Vegan Case." New York
Times. 5 Apr. 2003, late ed.: 1. Academic Universe: News.
LexisNexis. Hunter College Lib. 13 Nov. 2004
<http://web.lexis-nexis.com>.

Spock, Benjamin, and Robert Needleman. Dr. Spock's Baby and
Child Care. 8th ed. New York: Pocket, 2004.

Sullivan, Karen. The Parent's Guide to Natural Health Care in
Children. Boston: Shambala, 2004.

United States Dept. of Agriculture. Food Guide Pyramid. 5 Nov.
2004 <http://usda.gov/cnpp/images/pyramid.gif>.

"Vegan." Merriam-Webster Medical Dictionary. Medline Plus. 12
Nov. 2004 <http://www.nlm.nih.gov/medlineplus/
mplusdictionary.html>.

Waldmann, A., J. W. Koschizke, C. Leitzmann, and A. Hahn. "Dietary
Intakes and Lifestyle Factors of a Vegan Population in
Germany: Results from the German Vegan Study." European
Journal of Clinical Nutrition 2003: 947–955. Academic Search
Premier. EBSCO. Hunter College Lib. 8 Nov. 2004
<http://search.epnet.com/login.aspx?direct=true&db=
aph&an=10344856>.

List
includes
only works
actually
cited in the
paper

New page
for list of
works cited

Documented
in MLA style:
Chapter 51

A persuasive letter on a community issue   Here is an open letter to the governor of New York State, published as a letter to the editor in a local community newspaper. It presents an argument and attempts to persuade the governor to take action.

Calls on Pataki to Intervene in SLC (St. Lawrence Cement)

To the Editor:

> I wanted to share with readers this open letter I sent to Governor George Pataki:
>
> I am writing to make you aware of a proposal that has the potential to do great harm to the Hudson Valley and to ask for your help.
>
> This spring, I attended two dinners in New York City hosted by leading environmental organizations where you were rightly honored for your outstanding efforts to improve and preserve the environment of New York State. Listening to the list of accomplishments, even the most cautious judge would have to conclude that your interest is sincere and personal and that your efforts have been effective.
>
> It is for this reason that I write now in the belief that once you are fully aware of the harm that will result from the proposed project, you will use your political leadership to stop or modify it.
>
> My appeal to you is made particularly urgent by the fact that currently we are experiencing a complete breakdown in political leadership among the local elected officials in Columbia County. For reasons that are not now fully clear, the elected officials who should be protecting the interests of residents of Columbia County are paralyzed, mesmerized, or, in some cases (I fear), compromised by the efforts of a multinational corporation to build a 30-story facility topped by a 40-story smokestack sprawling over 1,800 acres.
>
> This coal-fired cement plant, virtually within the City of Hudson and within view of Claverack, Athens, and Olana, will release 20,000,000 pounds of regulated pollutants each year, according to the DEIS [Draft Environmental Impact Statement]. As proposed, this plant is so large and will produce so much pollution that even the residents of Berkshire County have asked their political leaders and the Massachusetts Department of Environmental Protection to become parties to the permitting process.
>
> Large, dirty, and noisy, this project will destroy southwestern Columbia County, covering a tranquil, economically sound, beautiful rural area of important agricultural lands in fine, gray dust. The riverfront of Hudson where we are working to build a public park will become a busy industrial dock where millions of tons of coal are off-loaded and millions of tons of cement are on-loaded into barges 800 feet in length in a 24-hour per day operation.

You are familiar with the damage caused by coal-burning power plants operating to the west of New York State. Ozone and acid rain are serious continuing problems for our state, yet this proposal would burn coal at huge rates on the edge of the Hudson River, while the profits are shipped out of the country.

St. Lawrence Cement, a subsidiary of the Swiss bank Holderbank, has attempted to argue that the project should be allowed because of economic benefits to the area. The record of DEC's [Department of Environmental Conservation] hearings held June 20 at Columbia-Greene Community College before Administrative Law Judge Helene Goldberger clearly refutes this notion.

I know you have supported sound economic development for New York State, and I support those efforts. I believe, however, that even a quick examination of the record will demonstrate to you that this project will bring economic destruction, not development.

I know there is a legal administrative process for these kinds of projects. I also know the process is not beyond the arena of political action. If this were not the case, St. Lawrence Cement would not have hired an established lobbyist long associated with the state Republican Party to represent its interests in Albany.

Governor Pataki, we desperately need your help and your leadership to save our homes, our health, and our peace of mind. All the people of Columbia, Greene, and northern Dutchess Counties will be deeply in your debt if you look into this proposal.

I am convinced that any fair-minded person examining the consequences of building this plant, as proposed, will have to conclude that the consequences are too grave to be ignored at the highest levels of state government.

Gerald Moore
Hudson

EXERCISE 7.8

Evaluate arguments.

Reread Gerald Moore's argument and respond to the following questions:

1. What strategies does Gerald Moore use to establish common ground with his audience, the readers of the newspaper, and the governor?

2. What arguments does he present to try to convince the governor (and the newspaper readers) of his point of view?

3. What comments can you make about the type and logic of the arguments he uses?

Chapter **8**

Writing about Literature

When the poet Ezra Pound describes literature as "news that stays news," he recognizes the enduring power of literature to entertain and instruct. In English and courses in other languages, you probably will be asked to read literature and write about it. Reading literature, with its insights into other worlds, other people, and other cultures, provides not only pleasure but knowledge. And writing about literature helps you distill that knowledge and apply it to your own world. A prerequisite to writing well about literature is reading literature thoroughly and analytically.

For examples of students' writing about literature, see 8j and 9b.

8a Reading literature critically

What is on a page is read and interpreted differently by different readers, depending on their age, gender, nationality, culture, socioeconomic level, experience, and educational background, as well as their personalities and preferences. Meaning is not fixed in the text and stable across place and time. Rather, it is fluid, depending on what is there on the page, who is doing the reading, and where and when that reader is reading. That is why interpretation and analysis have a large role to play in the appreciation of literature.

Writing about meaning in a literary work, then, involves argument. You argue for your interpretation, for the validity of your response and analysis, for your "take" on the work. The best evidence you can provide to bolster your case is either from the text in question in the form of summary, paraphrase, and quotation, or from other related texts.

When you read literature, it is important to read it thoroughly and critically in order to establish what the important issues are and how you respond to the work and to those issues.

KEY POINTS
Reading Critically

1. Read the work, especially a short work, as many times as you can. The first time, read to enjoy and appreciate the work and to form your first impressions. In later readings, read closely and critically.

2. If the work is short, and particularly if it is a poem, find time to read it aloud.

3. Read with a pencil in your hand. If you own the book or are working with a duplicated copy, underline or highlight significant passages, and write your own comments and questions in the margins. Mark only a few places on each page; otherwise, when rereading, you will not know what to pay attention to. If you do not own the book or article, do not mark the actual text; instead, use self-stick notes or make notes on index cards or in a computer file.

4. As you read, note any recurrent patterns, surprises, significant passages, and links to other parts of the text, and make connections to other works, people, or events.

5. Pay attention to the author's use of language, figures of speech, and symbolism.

6. For a long work such as a novel, keep a reading journal. In it, write a summary of each section or chapter and make notes. Add comments on significant passages in the text and record your responses to them. Using the double-entry notebook format (3a) is a good idea.

A sample reading journal   David Powers, a student in a first-year required writing course, read an excerpt from Keith Gilyard's *Voices of the Self* and wrote this summary and his own comments on it in his reading journal.

WHAT GILYARD WRITES

In the excerpt from Keith Gilyard's book Voices of the Self, we learn how a young African American boy, Keith, is uprooted from his home in Harlem and finds himself being stared at and picked on by the white students who make up the rest of his class in a Queens school. To learn about his fellow students without giving too much of himself away was to be Keith's first move and possibly his only means of survival. So while in school, Keith took a back seat and let Raymond (his actual first name) represent his standard English self and do all the talking, all the spying.

MY RESPONSE

I relate to Gilyard's struggle. From kindergarten to my senior year in a Bronx high school, I was either the only one or one of the very few Jewish students. I still remember the yellow "race-percentage" sheet we were given in my homeroom in my junior year. Seventy-seven percent of the school population was Hispanic, 13 percent black, 4 percent white, and 6 percent "other." I remember how many Jewish students there were in John F. Kennedy High School, too—I could count them on one hand!

I am not an African American male. I am an Irish American male whose mother brought him up to believe, follow, and take pride in his Jewish heritage. I, too, needed a mask to hide behind, and it was easier for me than for Gilyard. He could not take refuge behind another color of skin. But when I heard anti-Semitic comments and jokes, I would take refuge behind my Irish appearance and my last name. Even Gilyard shows insensitivity about those different from himself: "I began to wonder . . . about what these Jews were learning in those synagogues and those one-afternoon a week Hebrew School classes," he says. These Jews? Those synagogues? Do I detect a derogatory tone? Growing up as a minority makes one ultra-sensitive.

A sample annotated passage   Here is a poem about Rosa Parks, who in 1955 refused to give up her seat on a Montgomery, Alabama, bus to a white man and so helped inspire the civil rights movement. The poem is shown with a reader's annotations.

Rosa

How she sat there,
The time right inside a place
So wrong it was ready.

Stanzas of three lines: no rhyme
Everyday language
Is the place the bus?

That trim name with
Its dream of a bench
to rest on. Her sensible coat.

Her name: Parks—park bench

Nice touch of short fragment

Doing nothing was the doing:
the clean flame of her gaze
carved by a camera flash.

Repetition makes the point
that she was just there.
Metaphorical language

How she stood up
when they bent down to retrieve
Her purse. That courtesy.

Almost cinematic description
Who are "they"?

—Rita Dove, "Rosa," in *On the Bus with Rosa Parks*

Rita Dove

Rosa Parks

EXERCISE 8.1

Read and annotate a passage.

Give the following 1960 poem a critical reading and annotate it accordingly. See the example on page 144.

We Real Cool
Gwendolyn Brooks

The Pool Players.
Seven at the Golden Shovel.

We real cool. We
Left school. We

Lurk late. We
Strike straight. We

Sing sin. We
Thin gin. We

Jazz June. We
Die soon.

8b What do you need to say? Defining the assignment about literature

Always determine exactly what type of response the assignment calls for. You are not just writing "about" *Hamlet.* That is too general. Consider how you are expected to approach *Hamlet,* what aspects of the play you will address, and what points you want to make. Here are some common types of assignment situations and suggestions for handling them.

- *Book report/book review.* Include a brief summary of the contents of a book, if necessary, for the audience, along with an evaluation of the importance of the book and its intended audience (see 9b for an example).

- *Reaction/response.* Provide a summary of the work if necessary, but focus on the connections between the work and your own reading and experience (see 8j for an example).

- *Interpretation and analysis.* Discuss the meaning of the work from a close reading of the text itself—its theme, structure, universality, moral issues, or significance—addressing questions such as "Who is responsible for the crises in story X?" Give your view of how one or more of the elements of the work (plot, character, relationships, organization, point of view, language, imagery, symbolism, voice, and so on) contribute to the whole (see 8c for more details).

- *Comparison/contrast.* Compare elements within a work (for example, protagonists, points of view, acts in a play). Or compare several works to examine the treatment of a particular issue, such as "To what extent do the works studied support or refute William Faulkner's view that 'man has a spirit capable of compassion and sacrifice and endurance'?"). Or compare two or more works in terms of content or form (the *Odyssey* and James Joyce's *Ulysses,* for instance), perhaps comparing themes, characterization, or endings (see 8j for an example).

- *Cultural critique.* Take a specific point of view toward the work, such as examining it as a historical or cultural artifact, as a portrayal of gender roles or gender issues, or as a portrayal of issues of race and class.

- *Formal analysis.* Examine the structure of the text, or take a poststructural view, emphasizing ambiguities and unstated possibilities in the text.

For an explanation of terms often used in essay assignments, see 10c.

8c   What do you want to say? Guidelines for writing about literature

The type of assignment is just one consideration. As you plan to tackle your assignment, keep in mind these seven tips:

1. Identify your audience. Are you writing for readers who know the work you are writing about? If your instructor does not specify a reader and if you know that the instructor will be the only person to read the paper, assume a larger audience than this one expert. Think of your readers as people who have read the work but not considered the issues you have.

2. Determine the type of work. Determine the type of work you are examining (its *genre*). Is it a drama, a novel, a short story, a biography, a sonnet, or a polemical article? Ask yourself what you know about its features and what else you have read within that genre.

3. Ask questions about the work. Narrow your focus from the broad subject of the work to the specific questions you will ask and answer about it. Remember to phrase a question to focus your inquiry for the essay. (See 3f on finding a topic; see 8e for questions to ask in analyzing a work.)

- What does the work say and mean? This question may lead to a line-by-line explication, usually of a short work such as a poem or a significant passage from a longer work.

- What elements in the work are significant to understanding it, and what techniques has the writer used to develop those elements? These questions lead to an analysis of important points that relate to the theme of the whole work.

- How does this work compare or contrast with one or more other works? This type of question leads you to fit the work you have selected into a larger context. For this approach you probably will have to do more extensive research than would be necessary for explication or analysis of only one text. See 5d, item 9, for organizing a comparison and contrast.

4. Formulate a thesis. A thesis is as necessary when you write about literature as when you do other types of college writing. In your repeated readings and in your notes, interpret what you read in light of both other works you have read and your own experience. Use text annotations, notes, and a double-entry journal, as well as other methods of generating ideas, to help you formulate a claim (see 3a–3g). Your aim is to persuade readers to consider your interpretation. Here are several sample theses:

> Toni Morrison and Zora Neale Hurston present radically different perspectives on African American women's friendship.

Nicholson Baker's work has close stylistic links to the author he has written about so admiringly, John Updike.

The green light in *The Great Gatsby* is not necessarily the guiding image of the novel.

5. Avoid summarizing.   A brief summary of the work may be necessary to orient your audience. However, unless your instructor asks you to begin with a summary, devote your paper to an analysis and interpretation of the work, not simply a description or a summary. If, for instance, the work is *The Great Gatsby*, readers need to see clearly that the paper is not just a retelling of the story but is an explanation of your analysis and opinions of *The Great Gatsby*, organized around a thesis. They also need to understand why you advance this thesis. References to the text should help explain your interpretation.

6. Turn to the text for evidence—and do so often.   Offer support for your assertions, especially the debatable ones, by giving examples from the text. Text references are the most convincing evidence you can provide. Summarize, paraphrase, and when the exact words or tone are important, quote (49i–49j). Any quotation you include should support a point you are making in your essay. Quote only when the word, phrase, or sentence is absolutely necessary. Avoid stringing quotations together (49j).

7. Make a distinction between the author and the narrator.   As you read a short story, novel, or poem, consider who the narrator is (the narrator is the person represented as telling the story), what the narrator's background is, what happens, and why. Remember that the author is distinct from the narrator—the author has invented the narrator.

8d How are you going to say it? Conventions in writing about literature

For drafting and editing, be aware of the conventions that exist for writing about literature.

KEY POINTS
Common Conventions in Writing about Literature

- *Tense* Use the present tense to discuss works of literature even when the author is no longer alive (25f): "Polonius decides to eavesdrop, but the plan misfires tragically." "Edith Wharton presents Ethan Frome as a bitter man."

- *Authors' names* Use an author's full name the first time you mention it: "Stephen King." Thereafter, and always in parenthetical citations, use only the last name: "King," not "Stephen," and certainly not "Steve."

- *Titles of works* Underline or italicize the titles of books, plays, journals, films, and other works published as an entity and not as part of a larger work. Use quotation marks to enclose the title of a work forming part of a larger published work: short stories, essays, articles, songs, and short poems.

- *Quotations* Integrate quotations into your text, and use them for help in making your point (49h). Avoid a mere listing and stringing together: "Walker goes on to say. . . . Then Walker states. . . . " When quoting two or three lines of poetry, separate lines by a slash (/) (35d). When using long quotations (more than three lines of poetry or four typed lines of prose), indent one inch; do not add quotation marks; the indented format signals a quotation (50h).

- *Citations* Supply specific references to the literary text under discussion to support your opinions, and cite any references to the work or to secondary sources. (See 49d for advice on what to cite.) Cite author and page number within your essay for all quotations and references to the work of others; at the end of your paper, attach a list of works cited. Follow the MLA style of documentation (chapter 51).

TECH NOTE

Electronic Discussion Lists and Web Sites for Literature

Consider joining an electronic discussion list for literature. Consult a directory of lists to find one that fits your interests. For help with choosing topics and finding and writing about literature, try the Web sites *Voice of the Shuttle* and *Project Bartleby.*

Online Study Center **Across/Beyond College** Writing about literature

EXERCISE 8.2

Give advice for revising.

Read the following passage written by a student about Colette's "The Hand." What advice would you give the writer on how to improve this piece of writing?

In the short story *The Hand*, the main character described everything around her with her imagination. It is beautiful. The young girl's initial reaction to her husband is one of admiration and devotion. As she lies next to him in bed, she praises his mouth, full and likable, his skin the color of pink brick, and even his forehead. The young wife is swept up in the joy of being a newlywed. However, as the young girl perceives his well-manicured hands, she begins to perceive something dark and sinister. Her husband's hand takes on an animalistic appearance, "a vile, apelike appearance" (229). She went on to describe it in animalistic terms—"its claw," "a pliant beast" (229). The admiration and joy she experienced previously is replaced with disgust and fear. She stated with emotion and shock, "And I've kissed that hand! ... How horrible!" She cannot even touch the slice of toast he gives her in the morning. However, at the end she kisses the hand. This gesture, I believe, is demonstrative of the fact that she will settle for a life of submission, not a life of love.

8e Analyzing literature: Ten approaches

If your task is to analyze a feature of a work of literature, the questions that follow may be useful in determining which approach you want to take. You could focus on one or more of these features to examine their relationship to and effect on the work as a whole. For more specific details on analyses of prose fiction, poetry, and drama, see 8g, 8h, and 8i.

KEY POINTS
Ten Ways to Analyze a Work of Literature

1. *Plot or sequence of events* What happens? In what order? What stands out as important?

2. *Theme* What is the message of the work, the generalization that readers can draw from it? A work may focus, for example, on making a statement about romantic love, jealousy, sexual repression, ambition, revenge, failure, insanity, paranoia, political corruption, lust, greed, envy, or social inequality.

3. *Characters* Who are the people portrayed? What do you learn about them? What role does gender, ethnicity, or religion play? What effect would changing one of these have on the plot or theme?

4. *Genre* What type of writing does the work fit into—parody, tragedy, love story, epic, sonnet, haiku, melodrama, comedy of manners, or mystery novel, for example? How does this work compare with other works in the same genre? What conventions does the author observe, violate, or creatively vary?

5. *Structure* How is the work organized? What are its major parts? How do the parts relate to each other?

6. *Point of view* Whose voice speaks to readers and tells the story? Is the narrator involved in the action or an observer of it? How objective, truthful, and reliable is the narrator? What would be gained or lost if the point of view were changed?

7. *Setting* Where does the action take place? How are the details of the setting portrayed? What role, if any, does the setting play? What would happen if the setting were changed?

8. *Tone* From the way the work is written, what can you learn about the way the author feels about the subject matter and the theme? Can you, for example, detect a serious, informative tone, or is there evidence of humor, sarcasm, or irony?

9. *Language* What effects do the following have on the way you read and interpret the work: word choice, style, imagery, symbols, and figurative language?

10. *Author* What do you know or what can you discover through research about the author and the author's other works—and how do they illuminate this work?

8f Recognizing and analyzing figures of speech

The writers of literary works often use figures of speech to create images and intensify effects. When you analyze and interpret works of literature, look for the author's use of figurative language.

SIMILE A comparison of two basically dissimilar things, using the word *like* or *as* or a similar word; both sides of the comparison are stated

My love is like a red, red rose. —Robert Burns

Like as the waves make towards the pebbled shore,
So do our minutes hasten to their end.   —William Shakespeare

The weather is like the government, always in the wrong.

—Jerome K. Jerome

Harry picked [the letter] up and stared at it, his heart twanging
like a gigantic elastic band.   —J. K. Rowling

Playing for teams other than the Yankees is like having a crush on
Cinderella but dating her ugly stepsisters.

—David Wells (when Yankees pitcher)

A woman without a man is like a fish without a bicycle.

—Attributed to Gloria Steinem

METAPHOR   An implied comparison of two dissimilar things, with no
like or *as*

The still, sad music of humanity   —William Wordsworth

The quicksands of racial injustice   —Martin Luther King Jr.

All the world's a stage.   —William Shakespeare

ALLITERATION   Repetition of consonant sounds at the beginning of
stressed syllables

Peter Piper picked a peck of pickled peppers.   —Nursery rhyme

He bravely breach'd his boiling bloody breast.

—William Shakespeare

ASSONANCE   Repetition or resemblance of vowel sounds

And feed deep, deep upon her peerless eyes.   —John Keats

Blackish package   —Marie Ponsot

ONOMATOPOEIA   Sound of word associated with meaning (as in *growl*,
hiss)

Murmuring of innumerable bees   —Alfred, Lord Tennyson

PERSONIFICATION   Description or address of a thing as a person

Rosy-fingered dawn   —Homer

Death, be not proud.   —John Donne

The baby lamb chops demand to be eaten with the hands.

IRONY Saying the opposite of what is meant

> Enron, that company of great honesty and integrity, the darling of its stockholders . . .

ZEUGMA Use of a word with two or more other words, forming different and often humorous logical connections

> The art dealer departed in anger and a Mercedes.

For more on using figurative language in your own writing, see 20e.

EXERCISE 8.3
Experiment with figurative language.
In groups of two or three, write five sentences about your favorite food, object, activity, sport, or sports figure using at least four of the following stylistic devices: simile, metaphor, alliteration, personification, and irony.

8g Writing about prose fiction

As you read novels, short stories, and plays, remember to ask the journalists' questions (3e): Who? What? When? Where? Why? How? For instance, the following questions asked during the first reading will help establish the basic facts about the work: What happened? When and where did it happen? Who did what? How were things done? Why? Then, once you have decided on an approach to your analysis (see 8e), the list that follows may help draw your attention to issues you can explore in detail.

PLOT Sequence of events in the work, causes and effects, conflicts and resolutions

ORDER OF EVENTS Chronological, flashbacks, and flashforwards

CHARACTER AND CHARACTER DEVELOPMENT Main characters, who they are, how they interact, if and how they change, and if they reveal themselves through actions or words

THEME The author's main message in the work, a generalization that readers can derive from the work (*theme* is to prose fiction as *thesis* is to essay)

SETTING Time and place of the action and cultural/social context

POINT OF VIEW   Position from which the events are described, such as first- (*I/we*) or third-person (*he/she/they*) narrator

STANCE OF THE NARRATOR   Biased or reliable, trustworthy or untrustworthy, limited or omniscient (this stance might change from chapter to chapter or section to section)

AUTHOR   Relationship to narrator (can you tell how closely the author identifies with the narrator?) and to plot events; relevant facts of author's life

STRUCTURE   Shape of the work, chapters, crises, turning points

TONE   Attitudes expressed directly or indirectly by the author or narrator

STYLE   Word choice, sentence length and structure, significant features

LANGUAGE AND IMAGERY   Word choice, word order, images, sensory language, figures of speech such as similes and metaphors (see 8f and 20e)

SYMBOLS   Objects or events with special significance or with hidden meanings, such as a rose or a green light

NARRATIVE DEVICES   Foreshadowing, leitmotif (a recurring theme), alternating points of view, turning point, deus ex machina ("a god from a machine"—a sudden and unexpected resolution to a problem)—and dénouement (outcome of plot)

See 8j for sample student essays written about prose fiction.

8h   Writing about poetry

In addition to using some of the suggestions in 8g relating to prose, consider the following factors when you analyze a poem or provide a line-by-line interpretation or explication.

GENRE   Epic, pastoral, elegy, love poem, and so on

FORM   Sonnet, limerick, or other form, free form or not, rhymed or unrhymed, divided into stanzas or not, line length, meter

STANZA   Lines set off as a unit of a poem (like a paragraph in an essay)

RHYME SCHEME   System of end-of-line rhymes that you can identify by assigning letters to similar final sounds. For example, a rhyme scheme for couplets (two-line stanzas) would be *aa bb cc,* and a rhyme scheme for a sestet (a six-line stanza) would be *ababcc.*

FOOT   Unit (of meter) made up of a specific number of stressed and unstressed syllables

METER   Number and pattern of stressed and unstressed syllables (or *metric feet*) in a line. Common meters are trimeter, tetrameter, and pentameter (three, four, and five metric feet). The following line is written in iambic tetrameter (four metric feet, each with one unstressed and one stressed syllable):

> Whŏse woóds / thĕse aŕe / Ĭ thínk / Ĭ knów.   —Robert Frost

PUNCTUATION AND MECHANICS   Conventional punctuation or not, conventional capitalization or not

TONE   Approach to the topic, such as humor, anger, cynicism, or affection

SPEAKER   The person behind the poem, setting tone and attitude toward the topic

SOUND   Vowel and consonant sounds, harsh or soft effects (test these by reading aloud)

See 8j for a sample student essay written about poetry.

8i   Writing about drama, film, and video

As you prepare to write about a play, film, or video, use any of the relevant points listed in 8e, 8g, and 8h. In addition, focus on the following dramatic conventions.

STRUCTURE OF THE WORK   Acts and scenes

PLOT   Episodes, simultaneous events, chronological sequence, causality, climax, turning point

CHARACTERS   Analysis of psychology, social status, relationships

SCENES   The point and power of the scenes

SETTING   Time, place, and description

TIME   Real time depicted (all action takes place in two hours or so of the play) or passage of time

STAGE DIRECTIONS   Details about clothing, sets, actors' expressions and voices, information given to actors

SCENERY, COSTUMES, MUSIC, LIGHTING, PROPS, AND SPECIAL EFFECTS   Purpose and effectiveness

PRESENTATION OF INFORMATION   Recognition of whether the characters in the play know things that the audience does not or whether the audience is informed of plot developments that are kept from the characters

See 8j for a sample student essay written about a play, one that addresses the social status of the characters related to the social structure of the time.

8j   Students' essays on literature

On prose fiction: two assignments

1. SHORT RESPONSE TO A SHORT STORY: ANALYSIS OF MORAL POSITION   This essay was written by Kristi Livingston for an introductory course in critical reasoning at Metropolitan Community College, Omaha, Nebraska. Students were asked to read Richard Brautigan's short story "The Kool-Aid Wino" and discuss whether they perceived the boy who made the Kool-Aid as a positive or a negative character.

"The Kool-Aid Wino":
Positive Position

The boy in the story "The Kool-Aid Wino" has received a bad rap. He has been misunderstood and berated for his no-nonsense attitude. His normal need to enjoy life has been mistaken for laziness, and his passion for Kool-Aid has been described as an unnatural and unhealthy obsession.

I found his explanation of why he didn't change for bed to be humorous and refreshing. He said, "Why bother? You're only going to get up anyway. Be prepared for it. You're not fooling anyone by taking your clothes off." This boy has taken his own beliefs, stepped away from what society considers proper, and rejected what he sees as silly tradition. He has a fierce sense of individuality that shines through his no-nonsense attitude.

Also, it has been argued that the boy was lazy. Some people feel that because his physical condition made him unable to do hard, physical labor, he should assume all the household responsibilities. When the boy passed his younger brothers and sisters and didn't change their diapers, people immediately reacted with contempt. However, this was a young boy. Why was it his responsibility to take care of the babies? Isn't that a mother's job? I believe this is a normal child who is simply trying to enjoy his day, as all young children should.

Also, the boy never said that he wouldn't do the dishes; he just wouldn't do the dishes before he tended to his favorite part of the day . . . his Kool-Aid making.

Last, and most important, the boy had found a true passion for life through his Kool-Aid. It was during this ceremony that he was able to forget about his handicap and the intense poverty and chaos that surrounded him. It seemed as if he could devote himself fully to his task. This was the one thing that the boy could do without help from others. This was the one thing that the boy could do that gave him a true sense of independence from his family. Now tell me, what's unhealthy in that?

I think the Kool-Aid wino is a positive, rather than a negative, fellow. What was mistaken as a terrible "I-don't-care" attitude is actually a wonderful no-nonsense approach to life. What some people look at as laziness, I take for what it was . . . a boy with a handicap who lived his life in a way that made him happy. And finally, his obsession with his Kool-Aid was not unlike a swimmer's passion for the water. He had practiced and perfected his own art, and found his purpose and place in life through his Kool-Aid reality.

2. **COMPARING AND CONTRASTING WORKS OF TWO AUTHORS**   This essay was written by sophomore Brian Cortijo for a course on multicultural American literature. The assignment was to compare and contrast two collections of stories according to the way they present a concept of identity and to focus on the texts themselves without turning to secondary sources. Cortijo was writing for his instructor and class-mates, all of whom were familiar with the stories, so summary was unnecessary. He decided to focus on three of the ten areas in the Key Points box on pages 150–151: theme, setting, and language—specifi-cally, symbols. The paper is documented and formatted according to MLA style; for more on this, see chapter 51.

Identity and the Individual Self

While distinct in their subject matter, the collections of stories presented in Sherman Alexie's The Lone Ranger and Tonto Fistfight in Heaven and Edwidge Danticat's Krick? Krack! are strikingly similar in the responses they evoke and in their ability, through detached or seemingly detached narratives, to create a sense of collective selfhood for the peoples represented in those narratives. Through connected stories, repetition of themes and

Introduces the works with complete names of authors

States thesis, emphasizing similarity

Refers to setting and theme

events, shifting of narrative voice and honest, unapologetic discussion of the problems and the beauty of their personal experiences, Danticat and Alexie provide frank, cohesive portrayals of a Haitian and Native American peoplehood, respectively.

Now uses last names only

While it may not be the intention of these authors to address such a collective identity, it is clear that each is working from some conception of what that identity is, if not what it should be. Each author has symbols and characters that are used to display the identity in all its glory and shame, all its beauty and horror. For Alexie, both characters and objects are used, each for its own purpose. Most notable among these are Thomas Builds-the-Fire, a symbol of spirituality; Norma, who remains uncorrupted by the life imposed on the Indian peoples; and the seemingly ubiquitous drum, a symbol of religion that, if played, "might fill up the whole world" (23). Danticat, by contrast, concentrates more on objects than on characters to embody the ideals and the fears of the identity she is constructing through her narrative. The most prominent among these symbols are the bone soup, braids and, more generally, hair.

Points out how theme is addressed

Integrates quotation

Points to differences

Uses present tense

Danticat's use of the bone soup in her last story, "Caroline's Wedding," and of the braids in her "Epilogue: Women Like Us" is of paramount importance to any claim of Haitian peoplehood, or Haitian womanhood, that she might try to make. The use of these elements is indicative of the loving imposition and inclusion of past generations into one's own, as well as the attempt to pass down all that has gone before to those who will one day bear the burden of what that past means. Thus, Hermine's soup is her daughter Gracina's soup as well, not because she eats of it but because those bones—that ancestry— are a part of her and she will one day be responsible for passing them (and it) on. Likewise, Danticat's reader in the epilogue must know her history and her lineage, not only to know how to braid her daughter's hair but for whom those braids are tied.

Analyzes symbols

Provides specific references to the text and to characters

Not surprisingly, as both books deal greatly with ancestry, they also deal with the transition and maintenance of an identity over time. Both authors assert that the collective self represented by the past is part and parcel of that embodied by the future— bound to it and inseparable. The one serves to define the other. Likewise, there is a call to make the efforts and struggles of the past worthwhile—to do better, if simply for the sake of one's ancestors.

Returns to similarities in theme

In <u>Tonto</u>, Alexie goes as far as to suggest that time is unimportant, if even existent, with respect to reality. Watches and keeping track of time are of no consequence. One's past will always be present, and the future always ahead, so there is no need to dwell on either, but that does not mean that they do not matter. A person lives in the now, but every "now" was once the future and will become the past (22). Alexie make extensive use of the period of five hundred years, as though that is a length of time perceptible to the human consciousness, if appreciated more by the Indian.

Gives specific references

Danticat's twisting of time is less blatant than Alexie's, but that may be because it is not necessary to speak of things in terms of hundreds of years. A few generations suffice, and the connections between her characters rely so heavily on the similarities between their stories that their relations are obvious. The suicide of the new mother in the first story is mirrored perfectly in the last, though they might take place fifty years apart. The question and answer game played by the sisters forces one to wonder whether Caroline and Grace's mother went through an experience similar to Josephine's mother's. Then there is Marie, who finds and claims the dead baby Rose, who very well may be the daughter of Josephine, who is connected to at least two of the other tales. Beyond the characters themselves, the re-use of the symbols of hair and the bloody water is striking. The Massacre River, which took the lives of many who attempted to cross it, is named (44), but it is also implied in the bloody stream of Grace's dream with her father, even though the character may know nothing of it. After years, generations, and physical separation, the events at that river seem to pervade the collective consciousness of the Haitian people.

Focuses on structure of work

Provides specific details about characters

Points out relevance of symbols

Clearly, these authors make no attempt to glorify the identity that they are helping to define. What is vital to the presentation of these collective identities is that they are transcendent of both time and location and that they are honest, if not visceral, in their telling. As beautifully told as these pieces of fiction are, they aim for truth and are unapologetic in presenting the faults and difficulties inherent in that truth. By telling these tales honestly and without pretense, Alexie and Danticat help to reveal what many may not be willing to admit or acknowledge about others or about themselves—the importance, beauty, and complexity of a collective selfhood.

Draws threads together with term "collective identities"

Ends on a strong note, affirming thesis of "peoplehood"

Works Cited

Alexie, Sherman. <u>The Lone Ranger and Tonto Fistfight in Heaven</u>. New York: HarperCollins, 1994.

Danticat, Edwidge. <u>Krik? Krak!</u> New York: Vintage-Random, 1996.

Follow MLA for citing books (12a, 12c)

On poetry   This essay on a poem by Emily Dickinson was written by sophomore Kate Rudkin for an English course on American literature at Northeastern University. The assignment was to analyze the patterns of imagery in a poem. For reference, a copy of the poem appears after the essay.

An Exploration of Death through
Imperfect Structures

In her Poem #258, Emily Dickinson employs religious and political imagery to discuss personal and universal dilemmas. Words consistently associated with both spirituality and society are used throughout the poem. Through word choice, Dickinson is able to simultaneously discuss her two themes and explore the ways in which they are interrelated. In Poem #258, religious and political figurative language is used to examine the consequences of structure in Dickinson's life and the lives of humans as a whole. Structure is repeatedly associated with the concept of death and its elusive qualities. By intentionally providing multiple structures through which her poem can be interpreted, Dickinson forms a multifaceted view on death and its various degrees of imperceptibility.

In order to comprehend how Poem #258 can be read and how the various religious and political meanings within Poem #258 come together, one must first examine its individual elements. The religious aspects of the poem are more prominent and make a bold appearance in the figurative language of the first stanza. Dickinson's references to "a certain Slant of light" and of "Cathedral Tunes" conjure many church images associated with Christianity. Dickinson continues to use words like "heavenly," "affliction," and "death." She injects her poem with religiously charged words and images in order to establish resounding religious overtones.

While discussion of Poem #258 could be conducted only on its religious figurative language, the closely related political language cannot be ignored. By making political language a necessary part of the religious imagery, Dickinson implies that religion <u>is</u> political. The inevitable connection between the religious and the political shows a greater force at work, feeding the two from the same source. Amazingly, the very same poem that seemed to be discussing Dickinson's personal struggle to find her elusive faith or status of salvation also discusses British colonialism in North America. In a more abstract fashion, the poem also deals with the repercussions of socialization on an individual's freedom and on the freedom of humanity. The same words or phrases that were used to discuss religion can be used to discuss a political climate when read in a different context.

In Poem #258, Dickinson approaches and explores the meaning of death from as many angles as the poem has interpretations. Death is approached through various "imperfect" structures, such as religious and political structures and ultimately also the structure of the poem itself. Through limitations on form, Dickinson is able to express the limitations of herself and others in attempting to conceive of the notion and meaning of death. Although Dickinson never makes a direct reference to the act of death, everything within Poem #258 is deathlike. The imperceptibility of death is expressed through the failure of the poem's various structures, content and actual, to facilitate an understanding of death. In criticizing religion's and society's inability to illuminate the elusive topic of death, Dickinson is also demonstrating her inability to forge a clear conception.

There's a certain Slant of light,
Winter Afternoons—
That oppresses, like the Heft
Of Cathedral Tunes—

Heavenly Hurt, it gives us—
We can find no scar,
But internal difference,
Where the Meanings, are—

None may teach it—Any—
'Tis the Seal Despair—
An imperial affliction
Sent us of the Air—

Emily Dickinson

When it comes, the Landscape listens—
Shadows—hold their breath—
When it goes, 'tis like the Distance
On the look of Death—

On drama Sloan Laurits wrote the following essay in a course, Introduction to Literature, in his second semester in college. The assignment was to follow up on class discussion by writing a two-page essay analyzing *Twelfth Night* in terms of the characters' social roles.

Society in Shakespeare's Twelfth Night

The two houses in Shakespeare's Twelfth Night, Duke Orsino's and Lady Olivia's, are both examples of "the basic Elizabethan social unit" described in Peter Hyland's discussion of "Social Models" (34). All of the characters in the play fit into the social roles Hyland describes. Social class in fact is an essential element of the plot, and without a knowledge of its structure in Elizabethan times we could not make much sense of the complicated plot.

When we first meet the shipwrecked Viola in act 1, scene 2, we understand that she had been a member of the upper class. The Captain refers to her as "Lady," and politely answers all of her questions without asking any of his own. And when he tells her about Duke Orsino, she decides to go to him dressed as a boy and offer her skills as his servant because she can "sing and speak to him [Orsino] in many sorts of music." As Hyland points out, most commoners were illiterate, and only the children of upper class families were taught etiquette and the arts (35). Viola must be from a noble or very wealthy family.

Most of the characters in the play are actually connected to the house of Lady Olivia, so her house can be appropriately examined as an example of the social hierarchy of the time. Olivia, Sir Toby, and Sir Andrew Aguecheek represent the highest of the three levels; Malvolio, Maria, and Feste the middle class; and the unnamed attendants of the house the lower class. These class distinctions can be seen in the way the characters behave and interact. The relationship of Sir Toby and Sir Andrew reveals their social equality, as throughout the play they always treat each other in the same easy manner, making it obvious that they are comfortable in each other's presence as one would be with one's peers.

When Malvolio discovers the false love letter written by Maria and assumes that it comes from Olivia, he imagines ways to successfully approach her and overcome their class differences. He mentions the "Lady of Strachy [who] married the yeoman of the wardrobe" (2.5.36). Malvolio acknowledges the separation of the two by class status, but remains optimistic concerning their chances of a future together. Later, Malvolio attempts to charm Olivia by following the instructions written in the letter he found but is only seen by Olivia as acting "mad" (3.4.52). She asks Sir Toby to take care of him, and Sir Toby does what was the custom of the time and locks Malvolio in a dark room. The cruel joke played on Malvolio can be seen as a punishment for attempting to break the system of class, for he is the only character in the play who ends up as a victim in the twisting plot.

Malvolio's punishment for his actions can be looked at in two ways: as simply a reflection of the standards of Elizabethan society or as a satiric comment on the absurdity of its class divisions. Either way, the society displayed in Twelfth Night certainly represented the society of Shakespeare's time.

Work Cited

Hyland, Peter. An Introduction to Shakespeare: The Dramatist in His Context. New York: Macmillan, 1996.

EXERCISE 8.4

Evaluate the students' essays on literature.

Section 8j includes four essays written by students for a variety of college literature courses. Some are first drafts; some are revisions. Select two or more of the essays, read them closely, and evaluate them by responding to the following questions.

1. What assumptions do you think the writers make about their readers?

2. How do you as a reader respond to each piece of writing?

3. How would you assess the language: simple, direct, clear, informal, formal, literary, ornate, technical in terminology? How appropriate is the language for a college essay? Make three lists for each work: slang words, pretentious language, and technical literary terms that you find hard to understand.

4. What point is each writer making? Does the point come across clearly?

5. How do the writers begin? Do they make you want to read on?

6. What comments can you make about each writer's ability to write focused and unified paragraphs?

7. What advice do you have for each writer to improve the piece of writing?

8. Which part of each writer's essay do you like best? Why?

9. Do any of the essays inspire you to want to read the literature under discussion? Which?

Chapter **9**

Writing across the Curriculum

One semester you may be writing about *Hamlet,* and the next semester you may move to exploring the census, writing about Chopin's music, discussing geological formations, researching the history of the civil rights movement, or preparing a paper on Sigmund Freud and dreams. You may be expected to write scientific laboratory reports or to manipulate complex statistical data and to use a style of documentation different from one you learned in an English course. As you move from course to course in college, from discipline to discipline, the expectations and conventions of writing will change, along with the requirements for the documentation styles common in specific disciplines: MLA style in English and the humanities, *Chicago Manual* style in history and art, APA style in the social sciences, and CSE style (formerly CBE) in the sciences and mathematics. See 50f for more on writing research papers in the disciplines.

9a Different styles and conventions for different disciplines

The same topic can be treated in different ways in different disciplines. The style and conventions vary, as do the approaches to content, types of research, methods of documentation, and document design. The three passages that follow, all on the topic of sleep deprivation, illustrate some of the differences.

Science This excerpt is an abstract from a published scientific research article examining brain functions. Note the technical terminology and the use of the passive voice.

Online Study Center This icon will direct you to quick reference tools, Web resources, and research guides on the Web site at http://college.hmco.com/keys.html.

Abstract

There are complex and dynamic neural mechanisms affecting cognitive performance following sleep deprivation. These mechanisms are partly different from those used in the non-sleep deprived state. This research found that the prefrontal cortex was more responsive following one night of sleep deprivation than after normal sleep. Raised subjective tiredness in sleep-deprived subjects was strongly linked with activation of the prefrontal cortex. It is suggested that the impact of sleep deprivation on cognitive performance and related patterns of cerebral activation may be partly dependent on task-specific demands.

—Sean P. A. Drummond et al., "Altered Brain Response to Verbal Learning
Following Sleep Deprivation"

Social sciences   The following excerpt is also a published abstract, but an abstract of an article describing a sleep deprivation experiment involving groups of people. Note that the language is less technical than in the previous example.

Abstract

In two experiments, 64 male students worked almost continuously for 20 hours without sleep under varying social conditions. In Experiment 1, participants worked either individually or as a group. As hypothesized, performance deteriorated over time, especially in the group condition, which allowed participants to loaf. In Experiment 2, all participants worked in groups, but were instructed that public feedback would be provided either on the group result only or on the individual results of all group members. As expected, when individual results were made public, performance deteriorated less. Overall, the data suggest that fatigue increases social loafing. However, both individualizing the task and providing public individual feedback seem to counteract that effect.

—Claudia Y. D. Hoeksema–van Orden, Anthony W. K. Gaillard,
and Bram P. Buunk, "Social Loafing under Fatigue"

Humanities   The following passage is an excerpt from a personal essay describing a year of sleepless nights. The essay, written by a student, was published in *Newsweek*. In the personal essay, the first person narrator is naturally acceptable. In other types of writing for the humanities, such as documented essays and analysis of literature or art, use of the first person is usually avoided. Check with your instructor for guidelines.

Now a high-school senior, I still remember my freshman year with a shudder; it was the year my friends and I joked about as the Year of Sleepless Nights. It wasn't that I had contracted a rare sleeping disorder or suffered from a bad case of insomnia that particular year; in fact, nothing could have been farther from the truth. I had done what many diligent students do: sacrifice precious sleep for the sake of academic success.

Don't get me wrong; my parents never mandated that I take all the honors classes I could gain admission to. No one told me to take three honors classes. No one, that is, except the little voice in my head that convinced me scholarly success was based upon the number of H's on my high-school transcript. The counselors cautioned me not to do it, students who had fallen into the trap before warned me against it and my parents just left it up to me. Through it all, I just smiled and reassured them, Don't worry; I can handle it. The trouble was, I didn't have the slightest idea what lay ahead.

I soon found myself mired in work. For a person whose friends teased her about being a neat freak, I grew increasingly messy. My room and desk looked like my backpack had exploded. There was no time to talk to friends on the phone, not even on the weekends. Going to bed at midnight was a luxury, 1 a.m. was normal, 3 a.m. meant time to panic and 4 a.m. meant it was time to go to sleep defeated. Most days, I would shuffle clumsily from class to class with sleep-clouded eyes and nod off during classroom lectures. There was even a month in winter when I was so self-conscious of my raccoon eyes that I wore sunglasses to school.

—Jenny Hung, "Surviving a Year of Sleepless Nights"

LANGUAGE AND CULTURE
The Cultures of the Academic Disciplines

When you take a course in a new discipline, you are joining a new "discourse community" with its own established conventions and ways of thinking and writing. Use the following strategies to get acquainted with the discipline's conventions.

- Listen carefully to lectures and discussion; note the specialized vocabulary used in the discipline. Make lists of new terms and definitions.

- Read the assigned textbook, and note the conventions that apply in writing about the field.

- Use subject-specific dictionaries and encyclopedias to learn about the field. Examples include *Encyclopedia of Religion* and *Encyclopedia of Sociology.*

- When given a writing assignment, make sure you read samples of similar types of writing in that discipline.

- Talk with your instructor about the field, its literature, and readers' expectations.

Find out what way of writing and documenting is expected in each of your courses. Although each one may call for some adaptation of the writing process and for awareness of specific conventions, in general you will engage in familiar activities—planning, researching, drafting, revising, and editing. Sections 9b–9d discuss types of writing conventionally found in major academic disciplines. Section 50f provides more specific details on writing research papers in the disciplines.

Online Study Center **Across/Beyond College** Student papers in the humanities, sciences, and social sciences

TECH NOTE

Useful Sites for Writing across the Curriculum

Try these Web sites for useful advice on writing in all your courses and for more links to other sites:

- The Dartmouth College site with advice to nonmajors on writing in the humanities, sciences, and social sciences

- The George Mason University Writing Center site on writing in public affairs, management, psychology, biology, and history

Online Study Center **Across/Beyond College** Writing across the curriculum

9b Writing in the humanities and arts

The discipline of the humanities and arts is generally regarded as consisting of art, art history, communications and media, film, theater, history, languages, literature, music, philosophy, religion, and history, though some classify history as a social science. Writing in the humanities and arts is largely expository and interpretive. Only in creative writing courses will you be engaged in creating original works of literature. In many college courses, however, you will be asked to do a close reading or scrutiny of a variety of original works called *primary sources* (such as novels, philosophical works, poems, plays, speeches, performances, diaries, memoirs, photographs, films, and works of art) and also to study critical or evaluative books or articles, called *secondary sources*. See 46d for more on primary and secondary sources.

Your instructor will expect you to find your data and evidence in your own reactions, in primary sources, and frequently in secondary sources—what a critic has said about Toni Morrison, Samuel Coleridge, or Jackson Pollock, for example. Here are some points to consider as you write in the humanities and arts.

Guidelines for preparing to do expository writing in the humanities and arts

- Establish what the task entails and tailor your purpose statement accordingly. Some assignments, especially in first-year writing courses, may ask you to write about personal experience and express personal opinions on issues; others will ask you to begin with a text (a work of literature or art, an original document, or a media creation) and respond to, interpret, or analyze that text. A list of terms used in essay assignments is given in 10c.

- Read (or watch or listen to) and analyze primary sources: works of literature, letters, speeches, historical or philosophical documents, newspaper reports, or questionnaires.

- Closely scrutinize and analyze (and maybe compare) primary works of art: architecture, dance, theater, music, opera, or media communication, such as advertisements, films, TV shows, and Web sites.

- Form your own response to works before you consult appropriate secondary sources, such as works of literary criticism, biographies, commentaries, analyses, interpretations, and evaluations of research studies.

Interpretation In the humanities and arts, more than in the sciences and social sciences, your personal response to a work of art or a literary work is important. Every work under discussion needs interpretation; readers and observers play a crucial role in the process of understanding, interpreting, and explaining the meaning of a work of literature, a work of art, or a historical document. Base your interpretations on what you see and hear, referring to the source. Readers will look to the source text to make sure that your interpretations are within the bounds of possibility and good sense.

Appropriate support and expert testimony Whatever your claim, you should always support your conclusions by summarizing, paraphrasing, or quoting from both primary and secondary sources. If your claim is controversial, provide support from recognized expert testimony—for example, from Clement Greenberg if you are making a case for the timely brilliance of abstract expressionism in art or from Susan Sontag if you are arguing for the importance of "camp" in recent popular culture.

The terminology of the discipline   For any assignments, become familiar with terms used in the fields of literary analysis (such as *metaphor, persona, dramatic irony, omniscient narrator*), historical analysis (such as *historiography, imperialism, colonialism, carpetbagger, reconstruction, puppet state*), argument (such as *straw man, non sequitur*), and the analysis of works of art (such as *leitmotif, trompe l'oeil, chiaroscuro, tonal value*). Dictionaries in specific fields can be helpful here (47b).

The conventions of writing in the discipline   Always pay attention to any common conventions in the discipline. For example, two common conventions in writing in the humanities are these:

- Use the present tense to discuss literature and the arts, even for works produced in the past: "Van Gogh's letters show a man in deep distress." "Chaucer reveals his sense of humor in his tales." (See also 8d.)

- In philosophy papers, use the first person (*I*) less often than in other disciplines in the humanities. Especially avoid "I believe . . . " and "I feel. . . . " What counts more than personal feeling in philosophy and its search for the truth is rational argument and logic.

Types of college writing in the humanities and arts

ANALYTICAL/INTERPRETIVE ESSAY   A type of writing frequently assigned in college courses, the analytical or interpretive essay asks you to write about the meaning and the significance of the component parts of a work of literature, art, or media, or an event in history. Section 8e details approaches you can take to literary analysis. See 8j for sample papers about literature.

ANALYSIS/CRITIQUE OF VISUAL TEXTS: ART, PHOTOGRAPHS, ADVERTISEMENTS   Some of the general principles that apply to writing about literature also apply to writing about works of art: for example, the need for accurate use of specialized terms (*impressionism, abstract expressionism, cubism, encaustic, fresco, mezzotint, foreshortening, chiaroscuro, iconography,* and so on), the need for analysis rather than merely a description, and attention to biographical and cultural influences. Writing about art is similar to writing about works of literature in that writers frequently use the present tense to describe a work, even if the artist is no longer alive: "Berthe Morisot's short strokes of white paint fill the canvas with light and make her *Interior of a Cottage* glow with summer sunshine."   They also underline or use italics for the title of a work. In addition to these demands, writing about a work of art involves attention to formal principles of design, such as the characteristics of line, shape, color, light and dark, depth, balance, and proportion.

When you write about a work of art, you probably will find yourself focusing on one of the following:

- technique (print or painting, oil or watercolor, and so on)
- style (the way the artist depicts the world, such as realistic, conceptual, abstract, expressionistic)
- links between the work and social factors
- iconography (how subjects are represented in different times and by different artists)
- analysis of a work or works, concentrating on such aspects as the artist's purpose, audience reactions, sources, historical period of the work, how the work changed in process, or the symbolism of the work

It is a good idea to include an illustration of any artwork you discuss or to provide a direct link to the work as shown on a Web site.

Consult with your instructor about which style of documentation to use. MLA and *Chicago* are the styles commonly used in writing about art and art history.

The following sample essay was written for Professor Roberta Bernstein's course in modern art (at State University of New York at Albany) in response to this assignment, one of a series of assignments on a specified artist: "Write an analysis of an individual art work by your artist [this student's artist was Piet Mondrian], discussing craft, visual engagement, and meaning as they apply to that work. Document your sources of information with endnotes as needed." This is Lynn McCarthy's essay, documented in *Chicago* style (54) with endnotes.

Piet Mondrian's painting *Trafalgar Square* is dated 1939–43. Normally, an extended date on artwork indicates a continuous period of production until the work is completed. However, this is not the case with this painting or sixteen others, collectively known as the *transatlantic paintings*.[1]

Essentially these are the works Mondrian began in Paris and London. Some that he considered complete in the years 1935–40 were later finished or reworked in New York City after his October 1940 emigration to the United States.[2] So what viewers can see in *Trafalgar Square* in the bottom right corner, noted on the black grid line, are the numbers 39 and 43 (not visible in reproduction). The year 1939 is the first date that Mondrian records because at this time he felt it was finished. Later in New York City, he made revisions and adjustments that were completed in 1943, the second number he inscribed.

Trafalgar Square is an oil on canvas that measures 145.2 by 120 cm and today is housed in the Museum of Modern Art in New York City. It is interesting to discover that Mondrian planned out his compositions with colored tape before he applied any paint.[3] Some tape actually still remains on his *Victory Boogie Woogie* (1942–44), which is an unfinished work he was involved in at the time of his death. But what is even more interesting is that although Mondrian preplanned the compositions, we know from x-rays that he reworked the paint on his canvases over and over again.[4] So as methodical and mathematical as we may think Mondrian was, he still felt constant inspiration and intuitive urges to make changes along the way. It is interesting, too, to note that he worked on a flat, horizontal table rather than at an easel.[5] Maybe it was for practical or comfort reasons that he did this, but it also can be seen as a break from the conventional way artists created their works just as their subject matter broke from tradition. I think of how an artist like Jackson Pollock takes this even further by laying his canvas on the floor and walking on and around it, dropping and splattering the paint.

In *Trafalgar Square,* as with all of his work after 1917, Mondrian created a completely nonobjective image. There is no reference to natural forms or representational subject matter. The viewer is presented with just the two-dimensional space of the picture plane, and the forms are arranged on its flat surface. There is no illusion of depth, and the artist has rejected the convention that paintings are often windows to or mirrors of reality. And even

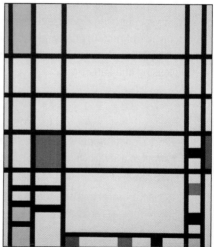

Trafalgar Square, 1939–43, by Piet Mondrian (1872–1944). Oil on canvas, 57 1/4" × 47 3/4", Gift of Mr. and Mrs. William A. M. Burden (510.1964). © 2002 Mondrian / Holtzman Trust, c/o Beeldrecht/Artists Rights Society, NY. Digital image © The Museum of Modern Art. Licensed by SCALA / Art Resource, NY.

though the title refers to a specific place, the painting is not meant to represent Trafalgar Square, but instead it reflects a more general interest Mondrian had in the culture of the metropolis.[6]

Mondrian focuses on pure, simple forms and the balance of the vertical and horizontal. He achieves simplicity by using only the three primary colors—red, blue, and yellow—along with black and white and by using basic rectangular shapes to create a grid layout. There are equal numbers of long vertical and horizontal black bands balancing the composition, which, along with the distribution on blocks of yellow, give the painting solidity and logic. The large red rectangle balanced by the two smaller ones is one element that charges the painting with energy. Otherwise it would seem static since the five large white rectangular areas account for more than half of the canvas space. All of these elements were central to Mondrian's Neo-Plasticism theory. He was intent on "'plastic expression' [which] meant simply the action of forms and colors" and a "new reality" or reality without the illusion or imitation of nature.[7]

This painting is visually engaging because the lines and scattered blocks of color keep one's eye moving around the composition. However, one can follow the elements in an orderly way; it is not at all chaotic. I can see Mondrian's interest in his urban surroundings in this grid work. Personally, I can interpret this composition in two ways. I see it as a type of map view seen from above the street blocks and buildings. But I can also visualize it as the side of a city skyscraper with its façade of rectangular windows and steel beams. So it is both horizontally and vertically balanced even in its interpretation, and offers a pleasing and satisfying image.

Notes

1. Harry Cooper and Ron Spronk, *Mondrian: The Transatlantic Paintings* (New Haven, Conn.: Yale University Press, 2001), 24.

2. Ibid., 24–25.

3. H. Harvard Arnason and Marla F. Prather, *History of Modern Art* (New York: Abrams, 1998), 393.

4. Cooper and Spronk, 237.

5. Arnason and Prather, 383.

6. Cooper and Spronk, 34.

7. Arnason and Prather, 233.

ANALYSIS/CRITIQUE OF FILM OR THEATRICAL PERFORMANCE An analysis of a theater production is similar to a literary analysis. It looks at plot, character, theme, setting, structure, form, or language in relation to the work as a whole. In addition, theatrical elements of acting, music, lyrics, direction, and staging will come into play.

In a 2003 essay titled "1969: How Broadway Reflected the Mood of a Nation," Elizabeth Drew draws on the history and politics of 1969; the audience's expectations; the role of tradition, lyrics, orchestration, and attitudes toward sex and religion to analyze, compare, and contrast the Broadway theatrical productions of *Hair* and *1776*. She posits that "*Hair* was revolutionary not only for its electric music qualities, nudity, and untraditional story line but also for its frank language regarding the taboo subjects of race and sex." Here is an excerpt from her essay supporting the first part of that statement:

> As one of the first musicals of the 1969 Tony season, Hair served to reinforce the notion that the world of 1968 was remarkably different from previous years. In the opening strains of the very first musical number, we hear an electric guitar. With the exception of one song, Hair was orchestrated in an electric rock style, a style new to the Broadway theater. And Act 1 ends with the random nudity of some cast members, symbolizing the characters' vulnerability and protestation of the Vietnam War and demonstrating that the world has changed.
>
>   The play's structure is traditional in the sense that it is written in two acts, discusses the pursuit of love, and finishes with a tremendous musical finale. But it departs from tradition in its storyline. Unlike many musicals that have an underlying plot, *Hair* is written in a style that places the audience in the role of observer. Authors and producers Gerome Ragni and James Rado present their story in an almost "day in the life" way, allowing the characters to communicate both individual emotions and group or "tribal" philosophies to audiences that otherwise relied only on the news media for insight into the younger generation's issues.

When you are writing about a film, it helps to watch it on a DVD so you can repeat the viewing of specific scenes and can freeze a frame to analyze it. In addition to analyzing the features of drama described in 8i, also consider features of film editing, casting, makeup, camera work, exposure, lighting, framing of shots, and cinematography.

BOOK REVIEW A book review focuses on providing information about the content of the work, perhaps including a summary, along with a critical evaluation of the content, style, language, and organization of the book. See also 8b. Here is an excerpt from student Jennifer Tang's prize-winning review of Paul Auster's memoir *The Invention of Solitude*.

> Auster shows how complex his father was by bringing in the perspective of the people his father worked with. Ironically, it was in his role as a landlord that his father showed the kind of paternal affection that Auster never received. The tenants who called his father "Mr. Sam" testify to his father's capacity to care about others, and it is a telling detail that his father was most kind to strangers, to those who had no personal association with him.
>
> He was obviously a man who sought to lose himself in his work and seemed to fade once he was forced to come back to his family when he retired. It was his personal life that Auster's father could not face.
>
> In presenting fragments of memory, Auster effectively conveys the fragile nature of his relationship with his father and offers the reader the opportunity to fill in the gaps between them. Unraveling the mystery of his father's remoteness keeps us in suspense, and we are firmly placed in Auster's shoes when the revelation of a murder of his father's father is presented. We can almost see the yellowed newspaper as he reads its lurid headlines. Auster doesn't tell the reader how the event affected his father's behavior; he trusts the reader's intelligence to put all the fragments together to create a full, if not complete, picture.
>
> Overall, I found the first part of the memoir to be much more compelling than the second. The second half was filled with literary allusions on the subject of father-and-son relationships that made me feel that Auster was trying to intellectualize what he had earlier approached with such human directness and feeling.

ANNOTATED BIBLIOGRAPHY   Your instructor may ask you to begin work on a research paper by preparing an annotated bibliography—a detailed bibliographical listing of the works you consult, each accompanied by a brief summary of the main points. Jared Whittemore was asked to prepare an annotated bibliography as part of his preparation for his MLA research paper on the community college system (see 51g for his final draft). The following entry is from his annotated bibliography. Note that full bibliographical details in MLA style are followed by an informative summary.

Significant Historical Events in the Development of the Public Community College. American Association of Community Colleges. 13 Feb. 2001 <http://www.aacc.nche.edu/allaboutcc/historicevents.htm>. This site provides a timeline charting the significant events in the history of community colleges, from 1862 to 2001. The timeline includes historical events, such as the founding of the first community college in 1901, and tracks important legislation and publications relating to the development and improvement of the community college system. It provides a historical perspective on the implementation and advancements made in the system in more than a century.

RESEARCH PAPER See chapters 46–50 for details on writing a research paper, and see examples of humanities research papers in 51f and 54f.

9c Writing in the social sciences

The social sciences include anthropology, business, economics, education, geography, political science, psychology, and sociology. (In the organization of college departments and divisions, history is sometimes grouped with the humanities, sometimes with the social sciences.) Social scientists try to understand why people do what they do. They examine how society and social institutions are constructed, how they work (or don't work), and what the ramifications of structures, organizations, and human behavior are. Two types of writing prevail in the social sciences. Some writers, for instance, use empirical scientific methods similar to those used in the natural sciences to gather, analyze, and report their data, with a focus on people, groups, and their behavior. These writers, who stress the "sciences" part of the term, concern themselves largely with data and statistics to draw their conclusions. Writers in the social sciences, especially in psychology, may conduct empirical laboratory research in the way that natural scientists do, but they also frequently rely on data collection by means of surveys and questionnaires, analyzing and reporting their results in tables, charts, and graphs. Numbers, percentages, averages, means, medians—all are important concepts in the social sciences.

Then there are writers in the social sciences who are more social philosophers than scientists. Scholars in fields such as public policy and international relations examine trends and events to draw their conclusions. Ethnographic studies are common too, with researchers taking detailed notes from observing a situation they want to analyze—the behavior of fans at a baseball game, for example, or the verbal reactions of constituents to a politician's tax cut proposals.

When you are given a writing assignment in the social sciences, it will be helpful if you can ascertain (from the approach in class—or just ask) whether your instructor leans toward the humanities or the sciences and whether an empirical study or a philosophical, interpretive essay is more appropriate.

Guidelines for writing in the social sciences

- Understand that the research method you choose will determine what kind of writing is necessary and how you should organize the writing.

- Decide whether your purpose is to describe accurately, measure, inform, analyze, or synthesize information.

- Decide on what kind of data you will use: figures and statistics from experimental research, surveys, the census, or questionnaires; observational data from case studies, interviews, and on-site observations; or reading.

- For an observational study, take careful field notes that describe accurately everything you see. Concentrate on the facts rather than interpretations. Save the interpretive possibilities for the sections of your paper devoted to discussion and recommendations.

- Back up your own observations and research with a review of the literature in the field.

- Use sections and headings in your paper. See the APA paper written for an undergraduate course in Interactive Media (communication department) (53f).

- Report facts and data. Add comments and expressions such as "I think" only when this is a specific requirement of the task.

- Use the passive voice when it is not important for readers to know the identity of the person performing the action: "The participants were timed. . . ."

- Present statistical data in the form of tables, charts, and graphs whenever possible.

- Follow the APA *Publication Manual* or whichever style manual is recommended.

Types of college writing in the social sciences Writing in the social sciences can follow much the same patterns and procedures as those of either the humanities or the sciences, depending on your purpose, orientation, and training.

DESCRIPTION OF EMPIRICAL RESEARCH   For a student essay written for a course in interactive media (communication department) and documented in APA style, see 52f.

ANALYTICAL REVIEW OF THE LITERATURE AVAILABLE IN A FIELD   For a student's review of the literature from 1950 to 2004 on the subject of standardized tests, go to the Online Study Center.

9d Writing in the sciences, medicine, and mathematics

Most writing in the natural sciences (astronomy, biology, chemistry, and physics), applied sciences (agriculture, engineering, environmental studies, computer science, and nursing), and medicine concerns itself with empirical data—that is, with the explanation and analysis of data gathered from a controlled laboratory experiment or from detailed observation of natural phenomena. Frequently, the study will be a replication of a previous experiment, with the new procedure expected to uphold or refute the hypothesis of that previous experiment. In mathematics, explorations of mathematical models occur, as do analyses of theorems and proofs, but writing is mostly of a specialized nature.

Experimental researchers generally do the following:

- review the literature, identify a problem, and propose a hypothesis about the problem
- review the literature describing relevant experiments and studies
- conduct a carefully controlled study or experiment to test the hypothesis
- collect, chart, analyze, and evaluate the data
- interpret the results
- draw conclusions about whether the results support the hypothesis
- explain the limitations of the study
- discuss the implications of the results and suggest further research

Writers in the sciences are much more likely to generate their own data and evidence from their empirical experiments than they are to base a paper on a logical argument or an analysis of another work in the field. Reviews of the literature relating to a topic are common, but they serve as background material to the writer's own work and to the writer's involvement in the issue at hand.

In science courses, you may be asked to post your papers online for your instructor and classmates. Section 12c provides detailed instructions.

KEY POINTS

A Model for the Organization of an Experimental Paper in the Sciences

1. Title page: running head, title, author's name, institution

2. Table of contents: necessary for a long paper or for a paper posted online

3. Abstract: a summary of your research and your conclusions (about 100–175 words)

4. Title, followed by background information: why the study is necessary, your hypothesis, review of other studies

5. Method: with headed subsections on participants, apparatus, procedures

6. Results: backed up by statistics or survey data, with tables, charts, and graphs, where appropriate

7. Discussion: evaluation of the results from the perspective of your hypothesis

8. Conclusion and recommendations: implications of the results of the study and suggestions for further research

9. References: a list of the works cited in the paper

10. Tables and figures: check with your instructor about placing these at the end or within your text.

Guidelines for scientific writing

- Establish a hypothesis and procedures.

- Include an abstract (see examples on pp. 180–181, and in section 53f).

- Divide your paper into sections, with headings. See the example of a lab report on page 182 and a student paper for a communication course in 52f.

- Whenever possible, illustrate your methods with illustrations and your findings with statistical tables, charts, or graphs (see also 11c). Give each visual a number and refer to it by that number (for example, Figure 1, Table 2). If you are using the CSE style of documentation, place any figures (charts, tables, photographs, graphs, and so on) in your text close to the point where you first mention them; in APA style, place figures at the end of the paper, after the list of references.

- Introduce a survey of the literature by using the present perfect tense: "Several studies have shown that the mutation may prevent degradation of unknown substrates."

- Give details of specific studies in the past tense: "Cocchi et al. isolated the protein fraction secreted by CD8+ T cells."

- Summarize other research studies rather than directly quoting from researchers.

- Avoid personal reflection and the pronoun *I*.

- Use the passive voice to describe the steps of a procedure: "The muscle was stimulated. . . ."

- Become familiar with technical terms and use them judiciously when writing for an audience who will understand them (that is, readers within the scientific discourse community).

- Follow a recommended style manual.

Types of college writing in the sciences

THE TABLE OF CONTENTS If your paper is long or if you are posting your paper online, provide a table of contents. Jennifer Richards provided one for a paper posted online for the Intelligent Machines Design Lab course in the Department of Electrical and Computer Engineering at the University of Florida. In this course, students have to plan and design a robot. Here is her table

Leroy

of contents for her paper on "Leroy, the 'Go Fishin' Robot." You can find the paper online at <http://www.mil.ufl.edu/5666/papers/IMDLFall2000.html>.

THE ABSTRACT   Most scientific papers begin with an abstract that summarizes the study and its results. An abstract is intended to give readers enough information about the sections of the paper, the results of the study, and its significance so that they need to turn to the full article only for the details. Many databases publish abstracts: *Chemical Abstracts* and *Biological Abstracts,* for example.

Here is the abstract Jennifer Richards wrote for her paper on Leroy, the robot she designed. Note that in an online posting, a heading is not centered.

ABSTRACT

This report outlines the complete design of Leroy and describes the desired behaviors and actions necessary for him to complete the set objectives. These objectives include the ability to accept and manage a hand of cards to play a game of "Go Fish" with human counterparts. In order to interact, Leroy and the players must communicate using pushbuttons and LEDs. Figures detailing the construction and arrangement of these critical components are included in this report. Other key parts include the recirculation mechanism where Leroy's cards are kept, the "fishpond" that holds the deck, and the "body" platform that encompasses all moving parts. This report also describes a model test of

Leroy's desired behaviors and functions. This test involves a real time investigation into the ability of Leroy to perform a set of critical tasks.

The sample CSE paper in 53f includes an abstract.

LAB REPORT Students write laboratory reports to describe their controlled experiments in science courses and in experimental psychology courses. Some instructors provide detailed directions on the format they expect for a lab report. If yours does not, follow the guidelines of the *Publication Manual of the American Psychological Association* (APA). This manual describes a report format that generally is acceptable to college instructors in the sciences as well as the social sciences, especially since the APA author/year style closely resembles the author/year style described in the CSE manual as one of its recommended styles of documentation.

For an APA-style lab report, include a title page, a page header on every page, and an abstract (see 52f). Divide the report into headed sections.

Include a list of references (52c and 52f) and any notes on separate pages. Finally, attach any tables and figures, such as graphs, drawings, and photographs, on separate pages at the end of your report.

KEY POINTS
Headed Sections of a Lab Report

1. *Introduction*   Include the purpose and background of the experiment, your hypothesis, and a review of similar experiments.
2. *Materials and methods*   Include subsections with headings such as Apparatus (or Equipment), Participants, and Procedure.
3. *Results*   Include observations, statistical data, and mathematical formulae, accompanied when appropriate by tables, charts, and graphs.
4. *Discussion of results*   Discuss whether the results bear out the hypothesis and offer explanations for unexpected results.
5. *Conclusion(s)*   Fit the results into the larger context of other studies, explain implications, and comment on directions for further study.

The following passage is from Natasha Williams's lab report on microbial genetics conjugation, written for a college cell biology course. This excerpt shows part of the Discussion section, annotated to point out various conventions of science writing.

Major section heading is centered.

Discussion

Conjugation involves transfer by appropriate mating types. F+ and Hfr are donor cells with respectively low and high rates of genetic transfer. F- cells are recipients. Contact between the cell types is made by a conjugation bridge called an F pilus extending from the Hfr cell. The donor chromosome appears to be linearly passed through the connecting bridge. Sometimes this transfer is interrupted. The higher the frequency of recombination, the closer the gene is to the beginning of the circular DNA. In this way one can determine the sequence of genes on the chromosome.

Passive instruction, common in lab reports

Note the use of *one* for general reference

Researcher places Table 1 at end of report and here dicusses its details.

Table 1 shows consistently that histidine is the last amino acid coded with the smallest number of recombinants, and arginine is the second to last coded with the next smallest number of recombinants. However, the results obtained for proline and leucine/threonine vary.

9e Community service learning courses

Often defined as "experiential learning," service learning projects link college students to the community. For such projects, students volunteer for 20–30 hours of community service in a research laboratory, nursing home, hospice, homeless shelter, AIDS clinic, poor neighborhood school, and so on; they relate their work there to the content of a discipline or a particular course. Courses and coursework are oriented to problems in society that students engage with at a personal level in order to attempt to find some solutions. They also are asked to reflect on their service experiences and demonstrate to the college instructor what they learned. These are the three main types of writing in community service projects:

1. writing done initially with the site supervisor to outline the goals, activities, and desired outcomes of the service project

2. writing done during the service work, such as reports to a supervisor, daily records, and summaries of work completed

3. writing done for the college course—usually reflective reports describing the service objectives and the writer's experiences and evaluating the success of the project.

To reflect fully on the work you do, keep an ongoing journal of your activities so that you can provide background about the setting and the work and give specific details about the problems you encounter and their solutions. Link your comments to the goals of the project.

The following paragraph is from the reflective journal of a student in a community service course. While enrolled in a microbiology course at Kapi'olani Community College in Hawaii, Joanne L. Soriano worked at an arboretum (a place to study trees) propagating endangered plant species.

> Through Service Learning, I am able to contribute to the Lyon Arboretum's efforts. I made my first visit on February 5th, and was taken to their micropropagation lab. In it, my supervisor, Greg Koob, showed me racks and racks of test tubes filled with plantlets. They were either endangered or native Hawaiian, or both. The endangered ones were clones; in some cases they were derived from only a few remaining individuals. A major function of the lab is to perpetuate these species by growing them in the test tubes and then splitting each individual into more test tubes as it grows. Thus one specimen can become hundreds, under the right conditions. They can be planted on the Arboretum's grounds, or sent to various labs to be studied. I am thrilled to be given the opportunity to participate in the process.

Online Study Center   **Across/Beyond College** Student service learning projects

For an example of a Web site designed by a student in a course devoted to community service, see 13d.

  TECH NOTE
Students' Writing in Service Learning Courses
For samples of student community service writing, go to *The Writing Center: Michigan State University* site.

9f Oral reports and presentations

You may be asked to give oral reports or oral presentations in writing courses, in other college courses, and in the work world. Usually you will do some writing as you prepare your talk, and you will deliver your oral report either from notes or from a manuscript text written especially for oral presentation.

Situation, purpose, and audience Consider the background and expectations of your audience. Jot down what you know about your listeners and what stance and tone will best convince them of the validity of your views. For example, what effect do you want to have on the members of your audience? Do you want to inform, persuade, move, or entertain them? What do you know about each listener's age, gender, background, education, occupation, political affiliation, beliefs, and knowledge of your subject? What do listeners need to know? In a college class, your audience will be your classmates and instructor. It is often desirable to build a sense of community with your audience by asking questions and using the inclusive pronoun *we*.

Preparation   Making an effective oral presentation is largely a matter of having control over your material, deciding what you want to say, and knowing your subject matter well. Preparation and planning are essential.

KEY POINTS
Guidelines for Preparing an Oral Report

1. Find an aspect of the topic you feel committed to, and decide on a clear focus.

2. Make a few strong points. Back them up with specific details. Have a few points that you can expand on and develop with interesting examples, quotations, and stories.

3. Include signposts and signal phrases to help your audience follow your ideas (*first, next, finally; the most important point is . . .*).

4. Structure your report clearly. Present the organizational framework of your talk along with visual materials in handouts, flipcharts, transparencies, PowerPoint slides, posters, charts, or other visuals (12b, 15c).

5. Use short sentences, accessible words, memorable phrases, and natural language. In writing, you can use long sentences with one clause embedded in another, but these are difficult for listeners to follow.

6. You can effectively use repetition much more in an oral report than in a written report. Your audience will appreciate being reminded of the structure of the talk and points you referred to previously.

7. Meet the requirements set for the presentation in terms of time available for preparation, length of presentation (most people read a page of double-spaced text in just over two minutes), and possible questions from the audience.

8. Prepare a strong ending that will have an impact on the audience. Make sure that you conclude. Do not simply stop or trail off.

You can make your presentation from notes that you memorize or consult as you talk, or you can prepare a special manuscript.

Speaking from notes Speaking from notes is the best way. It allows you to be more spontaneous and to look directly at your audience. Think of your presentation as a conversation. For this method, notes or a key-word outline must be clear and organized, so that you feel secure about which points you will discuss and in what order you will discuss them. Here are a speaker's notes for a presentation of her views on the granting of paternity leave.

1. Children's needs
   Benefits
   Bonding

2. Issue of equity
   Equal treatment for men and women
   Cost

Your notes or outline should make reference to specific illustrations and quotations and contain structural signals so that the audience knows when you begin to address a new point. You can also use slides prepared with your word processor or PowerPoint slides to guide the direction and structure of your presentation (12c). For a short presentation on a topic that you know well, use notes with or without the visual aid of slides. Do not read aloud, especially in front of a small audience.

Speaking from a manuscript Writing out a complete speech may be necessary for a long formal presentation, but even if you do this, you should practice and prepare so that you do not have to labor over every word. Remember, too, to build in places to pause and make spontaneous comments. The advantages of speaking from a prepared manuscript are that you can time the presentation exactly and that you will never dry up and wonder what to say next. The disadvantages are that you have to read the text and that reading aloud is not easy, especially if you want to maintain eye contact with your audience. If you prefer to speak from a complete manuscript text, prepare the text for oral presentation as follows:

- Triple-space your text and use a large font.
- When you reach the bottom of a page, begin a new sentence on the next page. Do not start a sentence on one page and finish it on the next.
- Highlight key words in each paragraph so that your eye can pick them out easily.
- Underline words and phrases that you want to stress.
- Use slash marks (/ or //) to remind yourself to pause. Read in sense groups (parts of a sentence that are read as a unit—a phrase or clause, for example—often indicated by a pause when spoken and by punctuation when read). Mark your text at the end of a sense group.
- Number your pages so that you can keep them in the proper sequence.

The following excerpt from a student's text prepared for an oral report shows some distinctive features.

1

Short and direct
Signpost to structure

Should men get and take paternity leave? Of course they

should. Here's why. / First, everyone benefits if fathers have a

chance to bond with their children—the father, the mother, and

most of all, the infant. The literature we have read in this class

tells us that <u>crucial bonding</u> takes place between mother and

child in the early days after birth. // But the issue is not only one

of personal need for bonding. It's an issue of <u>social and gender</u>

<u>equity</u>. If women are granted time off from work and often take

Direct quotation

it, men should take time off, too. "But business and industry can't

afford it," I hear you say. Let's look at what it would cost. . . .

Question used to draw the audience in

Pause mark

Informal language

Practice, practice, practice Whether you speak from notes or a manuscript, practice is essential.

- Practice not just once but many times. Try tape-recording yourself, listening to the tape, and asking a friend for comments.

- Speak at a normal speed and at a good volume. Speaking too quickly and too softly is a common mistake.

- Imagine a full audience; use gestures and practice looking up to make eye contact with people in the audience.

- Beware of filler words and phrases like *OK, well, you know,* and *like.* Such repeated verbal tics annoy and distract an audience.

- Do not punctuate pauses with *er* or *uhm.*

ESL NOTE

Dealing with Nerves

If you have only recently moved to speaking and writing in English, having to speak in front of others may seem intimidating. Make sure you know your material thoroughly. Practice and make sure you know when to pause and how to pronounce all the words. Ask someone to listen to you practice and give you helpful hints. Then relax. You'll be surprised at how sympathetic and understanding an audience can be—a "foreign" accent can often charm away the perception of errors.

Visual and multimedia aids If you use multimedia aids to outline your talk and provide essential information, check your equipment and practice with it. If you use an overhead projector or PowerPoint slides (see 12b), the font size must be large enough for people at the back of the room to read, and the colors you choose should be clear—black on white is best. Use headings and bulleted lists (11c) to make your material clear. When you speak, remember to face the audience, not the projector or screen. Do not provide lengthy or complicated visual aids; otherwise, your audience will be reading them instead of listening to you. (See 15c for more on multimedia presentations.)

Presentation and performance It is natural to feel some anxiety before the actual presentation, but most people find that their jitters disappear as soon as they begin talking, especially when they are well prepared.

Look frequently at your listeners. Work the room so that you gaze directly at people in all sections of the audience. In *Secrets of Successful Speakers,* Lilly Walters points out that when you look at one person, all the people in a V behind that person will think you are looking at them. Bear in mind that no matter how well prepared a report is, listeners will not respond well if the presenter reads it too rapidly or in a monotone or without looking up and engaging the audience. Remember to smile.

9g Preparing a portfolio/e-portfolio

Portfolios are used by artists, writers, and job hunters. In a college writing course, selecting work to include in a portfolio gives you an opportunity to review your progress over time and to assess which pieces of writing best reflect your abilities and interests. Choose pieces that indicate both the range of topics covered in the course (or in your course of study) and the types of writing you have done. To show readers that you are able to produce more than one type of writing, include pieces on different topics, written for different purposes. If your instructor does not issue specific guidelines for presenting your portfolio, use those in the Key Points box.

KEY POINTS

Presenting a Portfolio

1. Number and date drafts; clip or staple all drafts and the final copy together.

2. To each separate package in your portfolio add a cover sheet describing the contents of the package (for example, "In-class essay" or "Documented paper with three prior drafts").

3. Include a brief cover letter to introduce the material and yourself.

4. Pay special attention to accuracy and mechanics. Your semester grade may depend on the few pieces of writing that you select to be evaluated, so make sure that the ones you include are carefully edited and well presented.

Sample cover letter   This cover letter introduces readers to the writer and to the material in the portfolio they are about to read.

Dear Reader:

In this portfolio you will find the results of my hard work in my Expository Writing class during the last semester. Throughout this time, under the guidance of my professor, I learned to write essays, do research, critique others' papers by working in groups, and edit my work "with great care," as my professor kept reminding me.

When I first came to Hunter College, I was not sure I would make it through since this was the first time I had had to learn in English. But after taking this course in my second semester, I feel more confident about my writing and better prepared for future courses.

Reading this portfolio, you will find out about my identity as a newly married woman, children's dreams, and the moral dilemmas in shooting an elephant (not my experience but a George Orwell work). I tried to choose a variety of topics and types of writing to include here so that you get a sense of what I can do. In addition, my research paper on the role of women in Virginia Woolf's time, which I began with fear but ended with pride, makes the point that the glass ceiling has not broken in the last sixty or seventy years, though it may show a few cracks.

I hope you will enjoy reading my work because that would mean that Professor Raimes succeeded in getting this Polish student to write well in English.

Sincerely,
Magdalena Wisniewska

Preparing an e-portfolio Increasingly, individual instructors, as well as college-wide programs, require or strongly encourage students to construct an e-portfolio. They provide space on a server where students can store writing samples and/or documents they have retrieved from the Web. The specific charges or tasks vary with the course. While an English instructor will probably focus on writing samples, a social science instructor may ask students to locate primary sources about a specific research topic (like the environmental movement or laws and court cases related to civil unions). In education, e-portfolios have become quite common to document a student's progress through a course of study—for example, to file lesson plans, lesson evaluations, and so on.

Whatever software your school may use to support e-portfolios, typically you will have control over the material that goes onto your pages of the (Web) server. In your private storage area, you'll be able to make material available to your instructors and/or other students for review so that these "reviewers" can add their comments to the material. Also, you may have the option of making a document (without the reviewer comments) available to a wider audience ("publish it to the Web") so that future employers or friends and family can also see the work. You can make different documents—aimed at different audiences—available for viewing at any time. One advantage to e-portfolios is that you have the flexibility to remix the materials for different purposes. In addition, you can include a variety of materials that you produce, such as HTML documents, graphics, images, sound, and film clips, rather than simply printed college essays that make up more conventional portfolios.

ePortfolio

Welcome   About me   Classes and Projects   Educational goals   Resume   Contact Info   My Links

About Me

The photo above was taken in fall 2004 by Gary Vollo, when I was interning in the Visual Arts Department at LaGuardia Community College. At the time I was ambushed by Gary with a camera while carrying a manikin from the drawing studio to be placed in storage. My pure smile shown in this photograph represents my personality.

I am Charles Mak, a current student at LaGuardia Community college. This is my senior year, and I am proud to be graduating in the fall. I was born in the United States; my parents are from Hong Kong. Besides speaking English, I speak Cantonese fluently.

I am currently majoring in Fine Arts at LaGuardia and transferring to Hunter College in fall 2005 for my Bachelors. I chose Fine Arts as my major because I always believed that art is prominent in society; we see it everywhere we go. Also, I've always been involved with art. In my early adolescence I spent a lot of time in arts and craft activities. I also copied comic book images out of interest. In my teenage years, I finally understood that art is a form of communication. Like words in a poem, elements of art transmit messages and they differ in their effect upon the receiver.

Entering this college was a major step for me; it introduced me to a whole different environment. Studying and working among diverse students with different backgrounds has improved my interpersonal skills. It has enlightened me and changed my perspective. Each culture has different ideals and approaches in thought. To experience how others feel about issues and approach problems is important in self-development. Attending LaGuardia Community College has given me the opportunity to develop myself and work on my weaknesses.

LaGuardia Community College
31-10 Thomson Avenue, Long Island City, NY 11101

A student's e-portfolio   Charles Mak prepared an e-portfolio over the course of one semester when he was a student at LaGuardia Community College, City University of New York. Then a fine arts major, he is now majoring in studio art at Hunter College. The seven-part structure of the portfolio was provided by templates offered by his college; the actual appearance of the template, with its unifying color scheme throughout the site, is his own design. The screenshots show an excerpt from two pages—About Me and Classes and

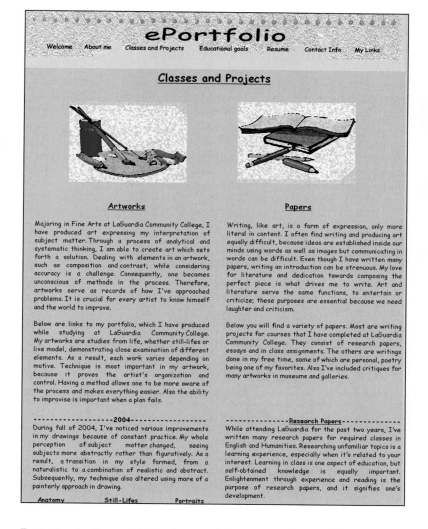

ePortfolio

Welcome   About me   Classes and Projects   Educational goals   Resume   Contact Info   My Links

Classes and Projects

Artworks

Majoring in Fine Arts at LaGuardia Community College, I have produced art expressing my interpretation of subject matter. Through a process of analytical and systematic thinking, I am able to create art which sets forth a solution. Dealing with elements in an artwork, such as composition and contrast, while considering accuracy is a challenge. Consequently, one becomes unconscious of methods in the process. Therefore, artworks serve as records of how I've approached problems. It is crucial for every artist to know himself and the world to improve.

Below are links to my portfolio, which I have produced while studying at LaGuardia Community College. My artworks are studies from life, whether still-lifes or live model, demonstrating close examination of different elements. As a result, each work varies depending on motive. Technique is most important in my artwork, because it proves the artist's organization and control. Having a method allows one to be more aware of the process and makes everything easier. Also the ability to improvise is important when a plan fails.

-------------------2004-------------------
During fall of 2004, I've noticed various improvements in my drawings because of constant practice. My whole perception of subject matter changed, seeing subjects more abstractly rather than figuratively. As a result, a transition in my style formed, from a naturalistic to a combination of realistic and abstract. Subsequently, my technique also altered using more of a painterly approach in drawing.

  Anatomy   Still-Lifes   Portraits

Papers

Writing, like art, is a form of expression, only more literal in content. I often find writing and producing art equally difficult, because ideas are established inside our minds using words as well as images but communicating in words can be difficult. Even though I have written many papers, writing an introduction can be strenuous. My love for literature and dedication towards composing the perfect piece is what drives me to write. Art and literature serve the same functions, to entertain or criticize; these purposes are essential because we need laughter and criticism.

Below you will find a variety of papers. Most are writing projects for courses that I have completed at LaGuardia Community College. These consist of research papers, essays and in class assignments. The others are writings done in my free time, some of which are personal, poetry being one of my favorites. Also I've included critiques for many artworks in museums and galleries.

--------------Research Papers--------------
While attending LaGuardia for the past two years, I've written many research papers for required classes in English and Humanities. Researching unfamiliar topics is a learning experience, especially when it's related to your interest. Learning in class is one aspect of education, but self-obtained knowledge is equally important. Enlightenment through experience and reading is the purpose of research papers, and it signifies one's development.

Projects—both combining text and images and providing internal links to his research papers (on literature, biological sciences, and psychology) and art projects (anatomy, still-life works, and portraits). Note that the links to the home page and all the other pages appear across the top of each screen, allowing easy access to all parts of the site at all times.

Online Study Center **Across/Beyond College** Student e-portfolios

Chapter **10**

Writing under Pressure

Pressure is a fact of life in college. Papers are due, exams are looming, you are working, and you have a family crisis. You stay up late night after night trying to get it all done. Unfortunately, this book can't produce a magic formula to make the pressure go away. Remember, though, that most instructors are sympathetic about genuine emergencies (even though they won't accept the "fact" that a grandmother dies three times in one semester). This section offers advice that you might find useful in pressured moments.

10a Essay exams

Essay exams are an important part of your life as a student. In an examination setting, you have to write quickly on an assigned topic. Learn how to cope with these tests so that you don't dread them. The advantage of an essay exam over a multiple-choice test is that you can include in your answer more of the information you have learned. Knowing the material of the course thoroughly will give you a distinct advantage, allowing you to choose the facts and ideas you need and to present them clearly.

KEY POINTS
Guidelines for Essay Exams

1. Go into the exam knowing that you are well prepared with necessary information. For a content-based essay test, review assigned materials and notes; assemble facts; underline, annotate, and summarize significant information; predict questions on the basis of the material your instructor has covered in detail in class; and draft some answers.

2. Highlight or underline key terms in the assigned questions (see 10c and the sample essay exam that follows). Ask for clarification if necessary.

Online Study Center   This icon will direct you to quick reference tools, Web resources, and research guides on the Web site at http://college.hmco.com/keys.html.

3. Think positively about what you know. Work out a way to highlight the details you know most about. Stretch and relax.

4. Make a scratch outline (see 3i) to organize your thoughts. Jot down specific details as evidence for your thesis.

5. Focus on providing detailed support for your thesis. In an exam essay, this is more important than an elaborate introduction or conclusion.

6. Check your essay's content, logic, and clarity. Make sure you answered the question.

A sample essay exam   Here is Professor Barbara Apstein's essay exam question (Bridgewater State College, Massachusetts), along with student Alexander Thompson's highlighting of key words, scratch outline, and completed essay.

> In her book *A Distant Mirror: The Calamitous Fourteenth Century,* historian Barbara Tuchman makes the following observation: "The conflict between the reach for the divine and the lure of earthly things was to be the central problem of the Middle Ages" (New York: Knopf, 1978: 6).
>
>   To what extent does this statement apply to the *Canterbury Tales?* In other words, does the conflict between the "reach for the divine" and the "lure of earthly things" seem to you to be very important in Chaucer's poem, somewhat important, or not important at all? Explain your point of view, using specific details and examples from at least three of the prologues and/or tales. (2 typed pages: 20 points)

Alexander Thompson's scratch outline:

> Issue: Earthly (pleasures of the world, material riches) vs. divine (religious life, spiritual leadership of church, serving God)
>
> Thesis: Conflict is very important.
>
> Support:
>
>> Prioress
>>
>>> coy smile
>>>
>>> eating
>>>
>>> anti-Semitism

Monk

likes hunting

not humble—hypocritical

Friar

enjoys life

earns profit from penances—also hypocritical

Exam Essay

The conflict between the "reach for the divine" and "the lure of earthly things" is an idea that Chaucer displays in several characters in The Canterbury Tales, but particularly the members of the church. This is shown in the General Prologue with his descriptions of the Prioress, the Monk, and the Friar. These are figures who would have been well respected for their standing in the church and the community, and yet all three are described as not completely dedicated to the church because of their inability to give up the everyday pleasures in life.

Not even two full lines into the Prioress's description in the General Prologue we see a hint that this nun may have other concerns in her life besides her devotion to God. The line describing her smile as "ful simple and coy" (C. 7) would not be what we would expect for a nun, especially an older nun who should be a role model for the younger ones. It suggests that she may be flirtatious and enjoys or craves attention. "In curteisie was set ful muchel hir lest" (C. 7), which describes the elegance of her eating, again is not how we would expect her to be described. Instead we would expect a nun to be humble in the way she looked at people and the way she ate. To go one step further, the tale, which deals with themes of anti-Semitism, would not be something we would expect from a nun. Chaucer is not necessarily criticizing nuns or even this nun in particular but is reminding us that members of the church are still people who are not perfect. Even though they are held to a higher standard than the rest of us, they still share many of the habits that are common to everyone.

The very next description in the General Prologue is that of the Monk, and he shares in this conflict as well. We think of monks as being close spiritually to God, people who should be held to a higher standard than the rest of the common people. However, like the Prioress he has much in common with the common people. Again the opening lines of his description tell us something about him that we would not necessarily associate with a monk. The line "An outridere, that lovede venerie" (C. 8) describes him as a hunter, someone who enjoys the outdoors and sport. Hunting seems to go against the Christian belief of loving all God's creatures, and we would expect a monk to spend nearly all of his time studying or teaching scriptures, but again we are shown a member of the church who does not give up the everyday things that regular people enjoy. Also he is described as "ful fat" (C. 8), indicating that he is not humble and is not really concerned with how a clergy member should present himself but rather lives his life to please himself rather than others. Ironically his tale is almost an instruction manual in how a person should behave in the eyes of God. Chaucer is either making fun of a clergy member to point to hypocrisy in the church or he is simply showing that these people are no different from us.

The Friar has much in common with the Monk in that he has pledged to live a humble life and yet he lives life to the fullest, enjoying every minute. He is described as being "wantowne and merry" (C. 8), telling us from the opening lines that he is also far from humble and more of an everyday person who enjoys life. This character is said to earn a profit from hearing penances, which suggests again that Chaucer is pointing out hypocrisy in the church by giving him characteristics of the common man such as a love of fun and having a good time.

All of these members of the church are on a higher pedestal than the rest of us, but they never give up the everyday pleasures of life such as good food, social gatherings, and sport. They are clearly conflicted in the "reach for the divine" and "the lure of earthly things."

EXERCISE 10.1

Evaluate essay exam questions.

Describe what makes a fair and successful essay exam question and what makes a poor and frustrating one. Then, using the reading material you have done for this class, construct a good essay exam question. Bring it to class, and discuss it with classmates.

10b Short-answer tests

In short-answer tests, use your time wisely. So that you know how long you should spend on each question, count the number of questions and divide the number of minutes you have for taking the test by the number of questions (add 1 or 2 to the number you divide by, to give yourself time for editing and proofreading). Then for each answer decide which points are the most important ones to cover in the time you have available. You cannot afford to ramble or waffle in short-answer tests. Get to the point fast and show what you know. To increase your confidence, answer the easiest question first.

Make sure you do not miss a class before the test; instructors will often review material that will appear on the test, and if you pay careful attention, you will pick up hints as to the type of questions that will be asked and the material that will be covered. For both essay exams and short-answer tests, always read the questions carefully, underline the key terms used, and make sure you understand what each question asks you to do. Before a test, familiarize yourself with the terms in essay exams and short-answer tests (10c).

Short answers to an exam question in a sociology course   The following questions and short answers were posted on a Web site for a philosophy course at California State University, Dominguez Hills. They are accompanied by the commentaries of the instructor, Professor Jeanne Curran. The letters and words within square brackets are her corrections of the student's text.

> Question: How does the tension of which Habermas speaks fit into the individual versus the structural control of society?
>
> [Student 1:] Structural control of society is use[d] to protect the individual right[s] of a society or people who must live together. Each citizen has a right in the U.S. to freedom of choice, according to Habermas; the tension occurs due to society limiting the freedom of choice of the individual.
>
> [Instructor:] *This is a good example of someone struggling with the concept. The answer is short, leaving out much of the elaboration I would like, but it is on point, considers both structural and individual, as requested, and links the idea to Habermas's system of law.*
>
> [Student 2:] The tension [comes from] an individual's right to make free choices within the limits or norms that have been set by society, as a

whole. The limits were set to maintain moral freedom for all of us who are a part of it. Though our constitution dictates that all within our society are free, there are limits that have been set. These limits are there to protect the whole society so that others have the right to choose within those same limits. Obedience to self-imposed law is true freedom, our willingness to accept and adhere.

[Instructor:] *Well stated. Follows the text answer closely, but gives a clear sense that you have grasped the concept. Good last sentence links the idea to Habermas's requirements for social integration, "self-imposed," and "willingness to adhere."*

[Student 3:] The tension is that of the individual and the limits they place on their own freedom for the good of the rest of society. The society ensures the freedom of individuals by limiting the rights of the individual freedom. The individual and society then have a collective agreement, which in turn brings legitimacy to the system.

[Instructor:] *Good statement of tension between individual freedom and good of social community. Good link to Habermas in emphasis on "collective agreement" and "legitimacy." More concise than I would have liked. I would have liked you to spell out how important the collective nature of agreement is to Habermas, and more precisely how he defines legitimacy. But that was our fault for leaving too little space.*

EXERCISE 10.2

Identify key terms in essay exam questions.

Underline key terms that writers should address when they respond to the following essay exam questions from various courses.

1. In Chapter 10, we explored the controversial issues surrounding the death penalty. Write a 350-word essay arguing for or against the death penalty, making reference to some or all of these issues. You have the entire class period.

2. Define *coup d'état.*

3. Compare and/or contrast the major characteristics of the Romantic period in Britain with the Augustan period in Britain. Be sure to refer to at least two writers who you believe are representative of each period.

4. What are the various ways rocks can be classified?

5. Discuss the key issues presented by both candidates during the last mayoral election.

6. Evaluate the significance of Maslow's "Hierarchy of Needs."

7. Explain the effects of current immigration policies on families and children.

10c Terms used in essay assignments and short-answer tests

For essay exams, short-answer tests, and any assigned writing tasks, always read the question carefully and make sure you understand what you are being asked to do. Essay questions often contain the following verbs:

analyze Divide into parts and discuss each part

argue Make a claim and point out your reasons

classify Organize people, objects, or concepts into groups

compare Point out similarities

contrast Point out differences

define Give the meaning of

discuss State important characteristics and main points

evaluate Define criteria for judgment and examine good and bad points, strengths and weaknesses

explain Give reasons or make clear by analyzing, defining, contrasting, illustrating, and so on

illustrate Give examples from experience and reading

relate Point out and discuss connections

PART 3
Writing with Technology for Academic and Professional Purposes

Your audience will have expectations as to what a particular type of document will look like. Think, for example, of what you would expect in the following: a college essay on paper or on a computer screen, a business letter, an e-mail message, a memo, an advertisement, a Web site or blog, a brochure, a résumé, or information displayed on presentation software.

With ongoing technological expansion, the design of documents and the presentation of information have become more complex as well as more visual. Just consider the expectations of text that readers who have grown up with the Internet hold compared with those of their older family members. It has become increasingly common to find printed text supplemented by multimedia displays. Straight text (in words) has been joined by pictures, photographs, tables, graphs, music, and film to convey information and emotion, often more immediately and dramatically than words alone.

Online readers have the complex task of analyzing and evaluating new media. They also use the texts of the new media interactively—changing photographs, adding or deleting illustration or sound, and inserting their own contributions to a Web site, as in wikis. To the ancient art of rhetoric (the art of effective communication and persuasion in words) we now add the component of visual rhetoric, in daily life and increasingly in college and the workplace. An important question to ask when you consider how to present your project to your readers, therefore, is this: What is the best way to meet my audience's expectations, engage their attention, and make my points with the most impact?

As a college student in the twenty-first century, you're probably quite at ease with using the functions of a word processing program to add, delete, and move material and to check your spelling. You have probably worked with presentation software for in-class reports and may very well have your own Web site or blog. But you may not know how masterfully you can apply your technology skills to the conventions of academic writing and the work world.

Part 3 details useful technology applications for document design, presentations, Web sites, and employment-related writing.

Chapter **11**

Designing Documents

11a Document design

Word processing programs Word processing programs include features to ease the process of writing, revising, editing, collaborating with others, and formatting your finished document. They allow you to perform the following operations:

- check the spelling of the document
- delete text and save it as a separate file
- copy a section of text and paste it into another draft or into a totally different document
- number pages automatically
- insert a header or footer without having to type it over and over again on each individual page
- automatically count the number of words
- access an online thesaurus to avoid overusing the same words
- search for words and punctuation that you often use incorrectly, evaluate them, and replace them if warranted
- design the format of your finished document (font, spacing, margins, text features, color, visuals, and the like)
- insert comments and revisions in your own document or someone else's

For details on the specifics of formatting for college essays, see 12a.

Computer software programs to help with writing and editing As you look for a topic to write about or as you generate ideas about an assigned topic, you may wish to use software programs or Web sites for help. These tools can supplement brainstorming, freewriting, mapping, journal writing, and other approaches (see 3a–3e). Software such as Inspiration can help with developing ideas and organizing thinking. Software such as Writer's Helper can also help with responding to writing and with revising and editing. And soft-

Online Study Center   This icon will direct you to quick reference tools, Web resources, and research guides on the Web site at http://college.hmco.com/keys.html.

ware such as Writer's Workbench and MLA Editor can help with analyzing a document, pointing out possible trouble spots, and suggesting revisions. For editing, too, grammar-checking software and online advice sites are available, though see 6b on the limitations of grammar-checking programs. Your college computer lab may offer some of the software on its network. Always check to see what tools are available for you to use.

EXERCISE 11.1
Use a style- or grammar-checking program.

A. The passage that follows is also available on the *Universal Keys* Web site. Copy and paste the passage into a document on your own computer and run it through any style- or grammar-checking program your college computer lab offers. What suggestions does the program make? Discuss with classmates how useful (or not useful) those suggestions are.

> If I had a boat, I'd sleep on it every once in a while, moored out on the open ocean, but not too terribly far out, because though I hate the city I'd like the comfort of house lights twinkling on the shore as the waves would rock me to sleep. If a storm would come I would jump up and immediately bustle about the ship. Battening hatches that wouldn't need battening, tying down things already nailed, and basically making a great wet fool out of myself. All the while I would be shouting challenges at the whether to try it's worst, because by God, me and the ship weren't giving up without a fight! And I'd probably get tremendously wet and catch a whale of a cold. But it would still be wonderful because it would be the boat and me, just the boat and me, alive against the Sea.

B. Now take a passage from a paper you have written for one of your classes and run it through the same program. How helpful are the suggestions it makes? Does it catch every mistake? Does it suggest any incorrect "corrections"?

11b Features of Microsoft Word for college writing

Writing college essays or business documents is very different from writing e-mail messages. Editing and formatting are important. Fortunately, word processors make most of the basic operations available at the click of a mouse.

1. Setting up the page and previewing it before printing
Before you start your document, go to File/Page Setup to set page
size, paper orientation, margins, and layout for headers and footers,
and so on. When you have written your document, Print Preview
shows what each page will look like before you actually print. The
screenshot shows Word 2003; other versions of Word may vary, as
will individual settings.

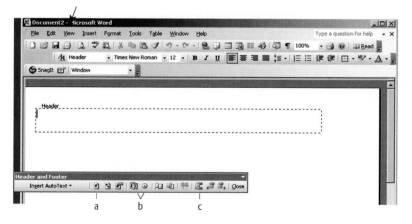

2. Adding a header or footer on every page   When you open the
View menu, you will see the Header and Footer option. The toolbar
allows you to (a) include a page number along with any text, such
as your name or a short running head; (b) include the date and time;
(c) toggle between the choice of headers or footers. Headers and footers
will adjust automatically to any changes in the pagination of your
document. You type the information once only, and it appears in the
place you specify on every page, however much material you add or
delete.

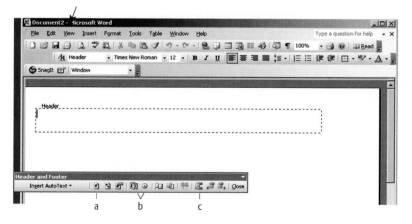

In addition, use the View menu to add toolbars to your screen. The Drawing and Reviewing toolbars are useful for college and business writing.

3. Inserting text features and visuals The Insert menu provides access to useful functions. Here you can insert into your text a page number, a footnote, or a hyperlink to a URL, though you can also set up Word to hyperlink all the URLs automatically (Tools/AutoFormat). You can insert Comments into your own or someone else's document, a useful feature for writing collaboratively and giving feedback. It is also possible to insert into your text a picture, caption, diagram, or chart. For presentation of data, the chart feature is particularly useful and easy to use: simply type your data into a data grid and then choose from a wide variety of charts, such as bar, line, pie, doughnut, scatter, and pyramid. One click, and your chart appears (see 11c; Figures 2 and 5 show a graph and a chart made in Word).

4. Formatting a document The Format menu takes you to the following features:

- Font: for changing typeface, style, and size, as well as using superscripts, useful for *Chicago Manual of Style* citations.
- Paragraph: options for line spacing and indenting (see the screen capture below for how to set the special command for the hanging indents used in an MLA list of works cited)
- Bullets and Numbering for lists, Borders and Shading, Columns, Tabs, Dropped Capitals (just highlight the text to be formatted)
- Change Case: for changing text from capital letters to lowercase or vice versa

5. Using Word tools for checking, correcting, and changing
The Tools menu gives you access to a word count, to spelling and grammar checkers and a thesaurus, and to AutoCorrect and AutoFormat functions (such as turning off the automatic hyperlinks when you do not need them underlined for an MLA list of works cited). Note that you can set a grammar checker to look for specific features, such as "Punctuation with quotes" and "Passive sentences": from the Tools menu, go to Options/Spelling and Grammar/Check Grammar with Spelling/Settings. In the Tools menu you will also find the Track Changes feature, a useful tool for adding editing suggestions to your own or somebody else's text.

6. Inserting a table   When you click on Table/Insert Table, you can then select the numbers of columns and rows you want.

Insert Table

Table size
Number of columns: 3
Number of rows: 2

AutoFit behavior
◉ Fixed column width: Auto
○ AutoFit to contents
○ AutoFit to window
Table style: Table Grid   AutoFormat...

☐ Remember dimensions for new tables
OK   Cancel

11c Typefaces, color, headings, columns, and lists

Typefaces (fonts)   What's in a typeface? A lot. It's not just what you write but how it looks when it's read. Fitting the typeface to the content of a public document can be seen as an aesthetic challenge, as it was for the choice of the simple and legible Gotham typeface for the Freedom Tower cornerstone at the site of the former World Trade Center. The silver-leaf letters, with strokes of uniform width with no decorative touches, have been described by David Dunlap in the *New York Times* as conjuring "the exuberant, modernist, midcentury optimism of New York even as they augur the glass and stainless-steel tower to come." That's what's in a typeface. The cornerstone, according to Dunlap, looks "neutral enough so that viewers could impose their own meanings" on a site of profound historical and emotional impact.

Of course, you are designing the presentation of an essay, not of a historic monument. However, you can still make a choice that emphasizes simplicity and legibility.

The business text *Contemporary Business Communication*, 6th edition, by Scot Ober (Boston: Houghton, 2006) recommends the following typefaces in business correspondence, and the advice extends to college essays in hard copy:

Times Roman for the body of the text (This is a *serif* font, with little strokes—serifs—at the top and bottom of individual characters: Times Roman.)

Arial or some other *sans serif* font for captions and headings (The word *sans* is French for "without"; a sans serif font does not have the little strokes at the tops and bottoms of the characters.)

Avoid ornamental fonts such as **Dom Casual** and *Brush Script*. They are distracting and hard to read.

Note that if you are designing a Web page or an online communication, your readers' computer settings determine which fonts can be displayed. The simpler the font you choose, the more likely readers are to see the font of your choice.

For the body of your text in a college essay or a business communication, stick to 10- to 12-point type. Use larger type only for headings and subheadings in business, technical, or Web documents (chapters 12, 13, and 15). Never increase or decrease font size in order to achieve a required page length. You will convey desperation, and you will certainly not fool your instructor.

Note: MLA and APA guidelines do not recommend typeface changes or bold type for titles and headings.

Color   Color printers and online publication have made the production of documents an exciting enterprise for both writers and readers. You can include graphs and illustrations in color, and you can highlight headings or parts of your text by using a different color typeface. However, simplicity and readability should prevail. Use color only when its use will enhance your message. Certainly, in the design of business reports, newsletters, brochures, and Web pages, color can play an important and eye-catching role. But for college essays, the leading style manuals ignore and implicitly discourage the use of color. Also keep in mind that many people may not have a color printer, and printing color charts on a black-and-white printer may lead to parts that are difficult to distinguish.

Headings   Headings divide text into helpful chunks and give readers a sense of your document's structure. Main divisions are marked by first-level headings, subdivisions by second- and third-level headings.
  For headings, bear in mind the following recommendations:

- If you use subheadings, use at least two—not just one.
- Whenever possible, use the Style feature from the Format menu to determine the level of heading you need: heading 1, 2, 3, and so on.
- Style manuals, such as the one for APA style, recommend specific formats for typeface and position on the page for levels of headings. Follow these recommended formats. See chapter 52 for an APA paper with headings.
- Keep headings clear, brief, and parallel in grammatical form (for instance, all commands: "Set Up Sales Strategies"; all beginning with *-ing* words: "Setting Up Sales Strategies"; or all noun-plus-modifier phrases: "Sales Strategies").

Columns   Columns, as well as headings, are useful for preparing newsletters and brochures (see the example in 11d). In Word, go to Format/Columns to choose the number of columns and the width. Your text will be automatically formatted.

Lists   Lists are particularly useful in business reports, proposals, and memos. They direct readers' attention to the outlined points or steps. Decide whether to use numbers, dashes, or bullets to set off the items in a list. Introduce the list with a sentence ending in a colon; for an example, see the sentence introducing the bulleted list in the previous section on "Headings." Items in the list should be parallel in grammatical form (all commands, all *-ing* phrases, all noun phrases, for example) and should not end with a period unless the listed items are complete sentences. See 5e and 24j.

11d Visuals: Tables, graphs, charts, and images

The technology of scanners, photocopiers, digital cameras, and downloaded Web images provides the means of making documents more functional and more attractive by allowing the inclusion of visual material. Frequently, when you are dealing with arguments using complicated data, the best way to get information across to readers is to display it visually.

Computer software and word processing programs make it easy for you to create your own visuals to accompany your written text. For a college paper, you can download visuals from the Web to strengthen an argument or to present data clearly and efficiently. Alternatively, computers make it easy for you to take data from a source or from your own research and present it as a table, graph, or chart (11a).

KEY POINTS
On Using Visuals

1. Decide which type of visual presentation best fits your data, and determine where to place your visuals; these are usually best within your text. However, APA style for papers to be printed requires visuals in an appendix. See 12b and 15c on using PowerPoint for an oral presentation.

2. Whenever you place a visual in your text, introduce it and discuss it fully before readers come across it. Do not just make a perfunctory comment like "The results are significant, as seen in Figure 1." Rather, say something like "Figure 1 shows an increase in the number of accidents since 1997." In your discussion, indicate where the visual appears ("In the table below" or "In the pie chart on page 8"), and carefully interpret or analyze the visual for readers, using it as an aid that supports your points, not as something that can stand alone.

3. When you include a visual in your online document, make sure the image file is not so large that it will take a long time for readers to download.

4. Give each visual a title, number each visual if you use more than one of the same type, and credit the source.

5. Do not include visuals simply to fill space or make your document look colorful. Every visual addition should enhance your content and provide an interesting and relevant illustration.

Tables   Tables are useful for presenting data in columns and rows. They can be created easily with word processing programs using figures from large sets of data, as the table below was.

TABLE 1   **Internet Use from Any Location by Individuals Age 3 and Older, September 2001 and October 2003, and Living in a Home with Internet Broadband, Age 3 and Older, October 2003**

Educational Attainment	Internet Users (Percent)		Lives in a Broadband Household (Percent)
	Sept. 2001	Oct. 2003	Oct. 2003
Less than high school	13.7	15.5	5.9
High school diploma/GED	41.1	44.5	14.5
Some college	63.5	68.6	23.7
Bachelor's degree	82.2	84.9	34.9
Beyond bachelor's degree	85.0	88.0	38.0

Source: *A Nation Online: Entering the Broadband Age*, September 2004. From Appendix, Table 1. U.S. Dept. of Commerce, National Telecommunications and Information Administration. Data from *U.S. Bureau of the Census, Current Population Survey* supplements, September 2001 and October 2003, based on a survey of 57,000 households.

Graphs and charts   Graphs and charts are useful for presenting data and comparisons of data. Many software products allow you to produce graphs easily, and even standard word processing software gives you several ways to present your numbers in visual form. In Microsoft Office you can create graphs and charts in Word or Excel. In Word, for example, go to Insert/Picture/Chart, and in the Chart screen go to Chart/Chart Type. You will be able to select a type of chart, such as a pie chart or a bar chart, and enter your own details, such as title, labels for the vertical and horizontal axes of a bar graph, numbers, and data labels.

SIMPLE LINE GRAPH   Use a line graph to show changes over time. Figure 1 has a clear caption and is self-explanatory.

FIGURE 1 **Freshmen Keeping Up-to-Date with Political Affairs**

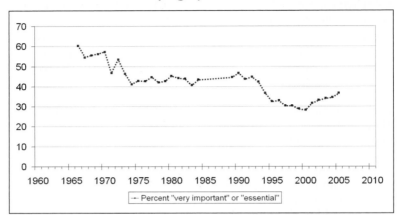

Source: Data are excerpted from Sylvia Hurtado and John H. Pryor, *The American Freshman: National Norms for Fall 2005,* Los Angeles, Higher Education Research Institute, University of California, 2006, <http://www.gseis.ucla.edu/heri/heri/html>, slide 14; sample size varies over the years; for 2005 data are based on the responses of 26,710 first-time, full-time freshmen at 385 4-year colleges and universities.

COMPARATIVE LINE GRAPH Line graphs such as Figure 2 are especially useful for comparing data over time.

FIGURE 2 **Changes in Childbearing in Five Nations**

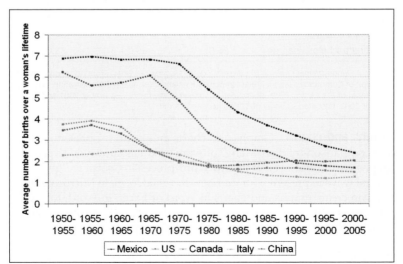

Source: Data from the Population Division of the Department of Economic and Social Affairs of the United Nations Secretariat, World Population Prospects: The 2004 Revision and World Urbanization Prospects: The 2003 Revision, <http://esa.un.org/unpp>

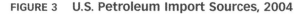

KEY POINTS

Using Graphs and Charts

- Use a graph or chart only to help make a point.
- Set up a graph or chart so that it is self-contained and self-explanatory.
- Make sure that the items on the time axis of a line graph are proportionately spaced.
- Always provide a clear caption.
- Use precise wording for labels.
- Always give details about the source of the data or the chart itself if you download it from the Web.
- Choose a value range for the axes of a graph that does not exaggerate or downplay change (11e).

PIE CHART Use a pie chart to show how fractions and percentages relate to one another and make up a whole. Figure 3 shows petroleum imports in the United States in 2004.

FIGURE 3 **U.S. Petroleum Import Sources, 2004**

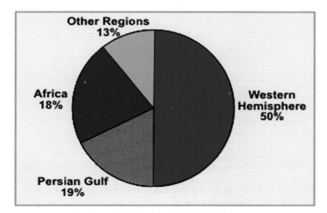

Source: United States, National Energy Information Center, Department of Energy, June 2005, <http://www.eia.doe.gov/neic/brochure/gas04/gasoline.htm>

BAR CHART A bar chart (or graph) is useful to show comparisons and correlations and to highlight differences among groups. The bar chart in Figure 4 presents clear data for grade inflation over time at a variety of institutions.

FIGURE 4   **Grade Inflation among Students Entering Different Types of Institutions (Percentage Earning A Averages)**

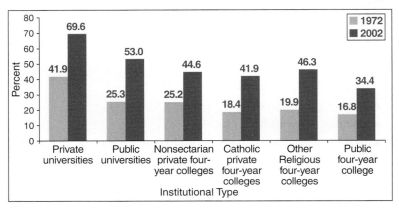

Source: L. J. Sax et al., *The American Freshman: National Norms for Fall 2002,* Los Angeles, Higher Education Research Institute, UCLA, 2003, <http://www.gseis.ucla.edu/heri/norms.charts.pdf>. Data are from 282,549 students at 437 higher education institutions.

See also the bar charts that student Emily Luo included in her PowerPoint presentation on genetically modified crops (12b).

A bar chart can also be presented horizontally, which makes it easier to attach labels to the bars. Figure 5 was produced in MS Office using the data from Table 1.

FIGURE 5   **Internet Use from Any Location by Individuals Age 3 and Older, September 2001 and October 2003, and Living in a Home with Internet Broadband, Age 3 and Older, October 2003**

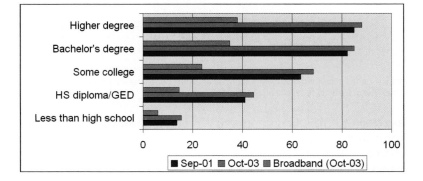

Images Your computer software provides many standard images (clip art) and photographs that you can use free in your documents, without any copyright concerns. Web sites offer images to download, either free or at a small cost.

Online Study Center **Design/Media** Finding images online

Note that if your document is to be posted on the Web, readers who have slow Internet connections may find it time-consuming or even impossible to download images with a large file size. Use a lower-quality setting for .jpg files or the .gif or .png format instead (resave if necessary).

Sophisticated and original graphics are usually copyrighted, so if you intend to use an image in a document that you post on the Web or make widely available in print, you need not only to download the image and cite the source but also to get permission from the creator to use and disseminate it. For a college paper, you may want to include an illustration you find on the Web, such as a map, a photograph of an author, a work of art, or an illustration from an online encyclopedia. You can do so without getting permission, but you must cite the source.

Exercise the same caution with photographs and other graphics as you do with clip art. Do not include illustrations just because you find them and like them. An illustration should add to and supplement your text, not merely provide a decorative touch. If your document is to be posted on the Web, readers who have slow Internet connections or videocards may find it time-consuming or even impossible to download elaborate images, so keep images small and simple.

EXERCISE 11.2
Use clip art.
Your word processing program probably has many clip art files. Browse through the categories (Insert/Picture/Clip Art) and practice inserting them into a word document. How effective are the pictures? Are there some you would or would not use in your papers for other classes? Give reasons.

11e Honesty in visuals

With the ability to use software programs such as Photoshop to crop, combine, juxtapose, erase, and enhance images come attendant dangers and innumerable opportunities for comedy. Late-night talk show hosts show edited photos and video clips from the day's news to hilarious effect. Image manipulation can also be used for political effect (such as Josef Stalin's order to delete Leon Trotsky from photographs that included Vladimir Lenin). In academic work, the changing of images is never acceptable. Falsifying data can reach the level of fraud, as in the case of the disgraced scientist who passed off manipulated images of stem cells for the results of his research. Scientific journals are beginning to check photos that are submitted with research studies to ensure that they have not been manipulated by removing images, changing the contrast, or combining images from several slides into one.

The lesson here is a simple one: **Be ethical in your use of visuals**.

Charts and graphs can also be manipulated—not by changing the original data, but simply by selectively plotting the axes of a graph. Take care when choosing the value range for the axes to avoid exaggerating or downplaying changes over time. For example, for comparative data on population projections ranging between a 50 and a 60 % increase, a vertical axis of 0 to 100 % will show the lines as almost flat, indicating little change over time, whereas a vertical axis of 40 to 70 % will emphasize and maybe exaggerate the small projected increase—one that could be attributed solely to a sampling fluctuation.

11f Design principles: brochures, newsletters, and flyers

When you are producing material that will be printed or photocopied and then distributed to many people, you will want to take extra care to create a document that is attractive and effective. Attention to design increases the chance that your brochure, newsletter, or flyer will be read and have the effect that you intend. While there is never a single "right" way to arrange information and images on a page, some basic principles can help you design a successful print communication in academic, community, or business settings.

1. *Plan.* Consider the audience and the purpose of your document: Who will read the document? How and when will people see the document? What is the most important message you are communicating? Does the document need to relate to any other documents in a series from your school or organization?

2. *Experiment.* Leave time to try out variations in the document format: to experiment with type sizes and fonts, to add more or less

white space at different places, to test various colors or arrangements—in short, to play with the design and get feedback from sample audience members. This way you can see what surprises and delights people and what puzzles or bores them.

3. *Value readability and clarity.* Consider the proportion of one element to another within your piece so that important information is highlighted or given priority and nothing appears overly crowded or illegibly small.

4. *Keep consistency and coherence* from page to page in matters of margins, typefaces, headings, captions, borders, column widths, and so forth. While you do not want the document to be dull, you also do not want it to be a distracting, shifting jumble of formats and type styles. *Note:* If you are using a desktop publishing program, set up a grid or template to block out the consistent placement of headings, columns, margins, and boxed features for each document you are designing. The lines of a grid appear on your computer but will not appear when the document is printed; they become like an empty vessel into which you "pour" your content.

5. *Give careful consideration to the following design variables:*

   ■ *Type size and font* For the main text of your document, choose a readable type size, not one that is uncomfortably small or that has letters that are hard to decipher. Serif fonts (the ones with little protruding edges on all the letters) are more readable and thus the best choice for the main body of a print document. For headlines and headings, use a limited number of other larger type sizes. Headings should help to organize material for the reader and establish a hierarchy of importance among different sections of the document.

   ■ *Use of white space* Cut and condense your text as necessary to allow for a generous amount of white space in your margins and borders and above and below headings. Adequate line spacing is important, too, to make the text easy to read.

   ■ *End-of-line alignment* Lines of type can be justified—spaced out uniformly to be all the same length—or set with a "ragged right" margin. Justified lines appear more formal, have a greater type density, and can create a lot of hyphenated words; lines that are ragged right create a less formal and more open look.

   ■ *Column width and line length* In general, the wider the column or line of type, the easier it is for a reader to lose his or her place. Shorter columns and shorter lines of type are easier to read.

- *Rules (printed lines)* Horizontal and vertical rules of various thicknesses can be effective in setting off columns, headings, pull-out quotations, photos, and captions.
- *Boxes and sidebars* These elements separate smaller segments of material from the larger flow of text. Boxing a part of your document can give it extra emphasis or attention.
- *Reversed type* With this technique, type appears white against a black or other colored background. *Note:* Reversed type becomes hard to read when the type is very small.
- *Screened backgrounds* or images If your document is to be printed with black ink and you want a certain section of your document to have a gray background, printers can create that effect by "screening" the section at a certain percentage, which you specify. Ink of any color can be screened.
- *Bleed images or bleed type* This effect makes an image or word appear as if it is running off the side of the page. It can be used to create a sense of an expanded design space.

In college and community life, much information is shared through brochures, newsletters, and flyers. The following sample documents demonstrate some principles of effective design.

MODEL DOCUMENT 1 · **Community Brochure Offering Services (Front)**

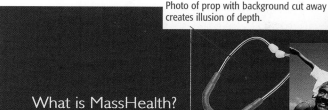

Photo of prop with background cut away creates illusion of depth.

Use of two colors creates fields within whole and highlights main heading.

What is MassHealth?

MassHealth is a state program that pays for health care for qualified people living in Massachusetts with low and medium incomes.

Even some people who have private health insurance can get MassHealth. If you qualify, MassHealth can give you health-care benefits directly or by paying part or all of your health-insurance premiums.

Blank space left throughout so information is not crowded.

What does MassHealth offer?

MassHealth offers a broad range of health-care services by paying for part or all of a MassHealth member's health insurance, or paying medical providers for services given to MassHealth members. MassHealth covers doctor visits, prescription drugs, hospital stays, and many other important services.

Who can get MassHealth?

MassHealth offers benefits to a wide range of people who meet eligibility rules. We look at your family size and income to decide if you or your family can get MassHealth. If you are aged 65 or older, we also count some of your assets. Income levels are shown on the back page. All uninsured children who cannot get MassHealth are eligible for preventive health-care coverage from another state program called the Children's Medical Security Plan (CMSP).

See the next page for the reverse side of this brochure.

MODEL DOCUMENT 2 **Community Brochure Offering Services (Back)**

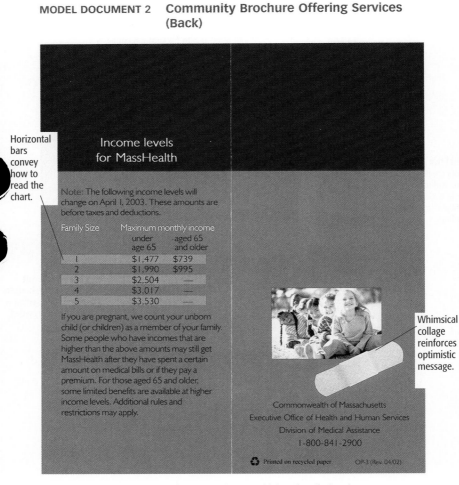

Horizontal bars convey how to read the chart.

Income levels for MassHealth

Note: The following income levels will change on April 1, 2003. These amounts are before taxes and deductions.

Family Size	Maximum monthly income under age 65	aged 65 and older
1	$1,477	$739
2	$1,990	$995
3	$2,504	—
4	$3,017	—
5	$3,530	—

If you are pregnant, we count your unborn child (or children) as a member of your family. Some people who have incomes that are higher than the above amounts may still get MassHealth after they have spent a certain amount on medical bills or if they pay a premium. For those aged 65 and older, some limited benefits are available at higher income levels. Additional rules and restrictions may apply.

Whimsical collage reinforces optimistic message.

Commonwealth of Massachusetts
Executive Office of Health and Human Services
Division of Medical Assistance
1-800-841-2900

♻ Printed on recycled paper   OP-3 (Rev. 04/02)

Illustration reproduced courtesy of the Massachusetts Division of Medical Assistance.

Overall, this brochure creates a friendly, welcoming, problem-solving mood. It sends its reassuring message visually as well as through its words and numbers.

MODEL DOCUMENT 3 **Community Brochure Offering Volunteer Opportunities (Front)**

The type has a handlettered look, adding a personal touch to the message.

The number of words is limited for maximum effect.

Effective logo captures the concept of the organization—adults helping children.

A CUTE KID ON TV CAN GET YOU TO SPEND $900 ON TIRES.

CAN THIS ONE GET YOU TO SPEND TWO HOURS WITH HOMELESS KIDS?

The Horizons Initiative
90 Cushing Avenue
Dorchester, MA 02125

Volunteer For The Horizons Initiative
Helping Hands For Homeless Children

See the next page for the reverse side of this brochure.

MODEL DOCUMENT 4 **Community Brochure Offering Volunteer Opportunities (Back)**

Tan background sets off introduction.

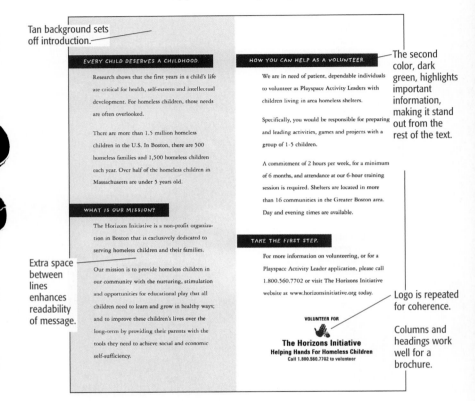

The second color, dark green, highlights important information, making it stand out from the rest of the text.

Extra space between lines enhances readability of message.

Logo is repeated for coherence.

Columns and headings work well for a brochure.

EVERY CHILD DESERVES A CHILDHOOD.

Research shows that the first years in a child's life are critical for health, self-esteem and intellectual development. For homeless children, those needs are often overlooked.

There are more than 1.5 million homeless children in the U.S. In Boston, there are 500 homeless families and 1,500 homeless children each year. Over half of the homeless children in Massachusetts are under 5 years old.

WHAT IS OUR MISSION?

The Horizons Initiative is a non-profit organization in Boston that is exclusively dedicated to serving homeless children and their families.

Our mission is to provide homeless children in our community with the nurturing, stimulation and opportunities for educational play that all children need to learn and grow in healthy ways; and to improve these children's lives over the long-term by providing their parents with the tools they need to achieve social and economic self-sufficiency.

HOW YOU CAN HELP AS A VOLUNTEER.

We are in need of patient, dependable individuals to volunteer as Playspace Activity Leaders with children living in area homeless shelters.

Specifically, you would be responsible for preparing and leading activities, games and projects with a group of 1-5 children.

A commitment of 2 hours per week, for a minimum of 6 months, and attendance at our 6-hour training session is required. Shelters are located in more than 16 communities in the Greater Boston area. Day and evening times are available.

TAKE THE FIRST STEP.

For more information on volunteering, or for a Playspace Activity Leader application, please call 1.800.560.7702 or visit The Horizons Initiative website at www.horizonsinitiative.org today.

VOLUNTEER FOR

The Horizons Initiative
Helping Hands For Homeless Children
Call 1.800.560.7702 to volunteer

Courtesy of Horizons for Homeless Children, Dorchester, Massachusetts.

Overall, this brochure makes a clear, direct appeal, with no excess clutter.

MODEL DOCUMENT 5 **Nonprofit Organization's Newsletter**

Top banner uses summery colors and a seasonal graphic image.

The white letters of the newsletter's title stand out well. They are "dropped out" or "reversed out" of the background color.

The photos bring to life this article on summer interns.

Stylish, compact logo conveys the group's identity in a memorable way.

Large initial capital letters emphasize or announce the beginning of each article.

A three-column arrangement organizes material well.

Courtesy Bookbuilders of Boston.

This newsletter's function is to link members of an organization. Its design effectively accommodates the needs for photos, a preview panel, a masthead, and news articles.

MODEL DOCUMENT 6 **Flyer Announcing Classes**

Black bars anchor the design, framing the images and message.

The photo images are placed off-center, creating a dynamic and interesting effect.

The pale ("screened back") type adds depth and interest to the page without cluttering it.

Creative placing of the captions here makes the information clear but not in the way.

Design by Marlies Gielissen. Courtesy Impulse Dance, Boston, Massachusetts.

This design captures the vibrant and energetic spirit of the place being presented.

Chapter **12**

Presentation for Academic Purposes

A document written for presentation on paper has very different requirements from those of a document designed to be posted online. You need to recognize the online culture of hypertext in order to make your online postings appropriate for the medium, useful, and attractive.

12a College essay formats

Perhaps you are wondering why this section refers to *formats* and not just to *a format* for college essays. The plural is necessary because the various organizations that offer guidelines for manuscript preparation (as found in the MLA, APA, and CSE manuals and the *Chicago Manual of Style*) provide different sets of recommendations and because various disciplines and individual instructors have their own preferences. Whichever format you choose, use your word processor's functions to help with your design.

A major format consideration is the destination of your document. Will you be presenting your essay on paper (hard copy), e-mailing it (to your instructor, your classmates, or both), or posting it on the Web? You will need to think of a hard-copy document in a linear way because readers will progress methodically from beginning to end and information must fit logically within the whole. For a Web posting, in contrast, electronic links (to other Web sites or other sections of your essay) in your essay can do the work of descriptive and substantive footnotes, references to sources, and examples of external evidence. An essay prepared for Web posting also needs internal divisions, each with an internal link so readers can go directly to a specific section. For details on posting a college essay online, see 12c.

Formatting guidelines   Here are basic guidelines for preparing your essay on paper, whichever style guide you follow. See 11a, 11b, and 11c for more on the formatting tools on your word processor.

Online Study Center   This icon will direct you to quick reference tools, Web resources, and research guides on the Web site at http://college.hmco.com/keys.html.

Title and identification of essay Your instructor may prefer a separate title page or ask you to include the identification material on the first page of the essay.

TITLE AND IDENTIFICATION ON THE FIRST PAGE The following sample shows one format for identifying a paper and giving its title. The MLA recommends this format for papers in the humanities.

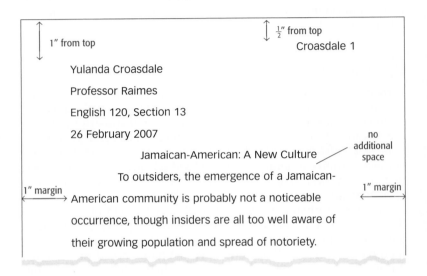

1" from top

$\frac{1}{2}$" from top
Croasdale 1

Yulanda Croasdale

Professor Raimes

English 120, Section 13

26 February 2007

no additional space

Jamaican-American: A New Culture

To outsiders, the emergence of a Jamaican-

1" margin

American community is probably not a noticeable

1" margin

occurrence, though insiders are all too well aware of

their growing population and spread of notoriety.

At the top of subsequent pages, write the page number in the upper right corner, preceded by your last name. No period or parentheses accompany the page number. See 11a on creating the page header with word processing program commands.

TITLE AND IDENTIFICATION ON A SEPARATE TITLE PAGE In the humanities, include a title page only if your instructor requires one or if you include an outline. On the title page include the following, all double-spaced:

- *Title:* Centered, about one-third of the way down the page. Do not enclose the title in quotation marks, do not underline it, and do not put a period at the end.
- *Name:* Centered, after the word *by,* on a separate line.

- *Course information:* Course and section, instructor, and date, each centered on a new line, either directly below your name or at the bottom of the title page.

If you include a title page, you do not need to also include the title and identification on your first page.

Title centered, about 1/3 of way down page
No quotation marks, no underlining, no period

Jamaican-American: A New Culture

Name, centered   By Yulanda Croasdale

Course information, centered

English 120, Section 13

Professor Ann Raimes

Date, centered   26 February 2007

> ### KEY POINTS
> ### Guidelines for College Essay Format
>
> 1. *Paper* White bond, unlined, $8\frac{1}{2}$" $\times$ 11"; not erasable or onionskin paper. Clip or staple the pages.
>
> 2. *Print* Always use dark black printing ink.
>
> 3. *Margins* 1" all around for MLA style. For other styles, $1\frac{1}{2}$" may be acceptable. Lines should not be justified (should not align on right).
>
> 4. *Space between lines* Uniformly double-spaced.
>
> 5. *Spaces after a period, question mark, or exclamation point* Most style manuals suggest one space. Your instructor may prefer two in the text of your essay.
>
> 6. *Type font and size* Use a standard type font (such as Times New Roman or Courier), not a font that looks like handwriting. Select a regular size of 10 to 12 points.
>
> 7. *Page numbers* Put in the top right margin (in MLA style, put your last name before the page number). Use arabic numerals with no period.
>
> 8. *Paragraphing* Indent $\frac{1}{2}$" (5 spaces) from the left.
>
> 9. *Title and identification* On the first page or on a separate title page.
>
> 10. *Parentheses for sources cited* In MLA and APA styles, for any written source you refer to or quote, including the textbook for your course (for an electronic source, give author only); then add at the end a list of works cited (see 51 and 52).

12b Academic presentations: PowerPoint and other tools

Today presenters are not limited to using handouts or visuals printed on a page. Thanks to multimedia technology, they can use screens to present an interaction of words, drawings, photographs, animation, film, video, and audio to make a point.

TECH NOTE

Finding Images Online

This comprehensiv e Web site, constructed by librarian Heidi Abbey of the University of Connecticut Libraries, provides demystifying information on digital image formats; a primer on basic copyright issues; links to search engines; and, best of all, links to several annotated image Web sites, including image resources for specific subjects.

Online Study Center **Design/Media** Finding images online

In preparing a live or online multimedia presentation, consider the effectiveness of positioning images near your words and of conveying emotion and meaning through pictures. Imagine, for instance, how you might present an argument against genetic engineering of food crops to classmates or colleagues. In addition to your well-formed argument, you could show graphs of public opinion data on the issue, pictures of chemicals that are used on crops and of the way they are applied, and a movie clip of interviews with shoppers as they read labels and buy produce. If you use media imaginatively, you can do what writing teachers have long advised for printed essays: Show; don't just tell.

TECH NOTE

A Multimedia Project

"The City of Troy" is a multimedia project created by undergraduates at the University of Southern California for a course in Near Eastern and Mediterranean archeology.

Online Study Center **Design/Media** Student multimedia projects

Using PowerPoint   Using a multimedia tool such as PowerPoint to prepare a presentation gives you access to organizing tools. As the name suggests, PowerPoint forces you to think of your main points and organize them. Preparing slides that illustrate the logic of your presentation helps you separate the main points from the supporting details, and the slides keep you focused as you give your presentation. Your audience follows your ideas not only because you have established a clear principle of organization but also because the slide on the presentation screen reminds people of where you are in your talk, what point you are addressing, and how that point fits into your total scheme. Presentation software also allows you to include sound, music, and movie clips to illustrate and drive home the points you want to make. However, be careful not to overdo these effects. PowerPoint features can easily become distracting "bells and whistles" to make up for lack of content. They should enhance your work, not dominate it. (For more on presentation, see 9f and 15c.)

A PowerPoint specialist has advised, "If you have something to show, use PowerPoint." *Show* is the important word. Do not expect your audience to read a lot of text. PowerPoint is not for writing paragraphs and essays for readers to digest. It's for getting and keeping the audience's attention with the main points and illustrative details. Outlines, bulleted lists, tables, pie charts, and graphs are what PowerPoint does well.

Peter Norvig, a computer scientist and director of search quality at Google, cautions PowerPoint users to "use visual aids to convey visual information: photographs, charts, or diagrams. But do not use them to give the impression that the matter is solved, wrapped up in a few bullet points." For a wonderful object lesson of PowerPoint gone wrong, see Norvig's Web site showing the Gettysburg Address in PowerPoint.

Online Study Center Design/Media PowerPoint slides

A student's PowerPoint slides The PowerPoint slides shown here were prepared in 2003 by student Emily Luo for a project in a course called "Empirical Research Using the Internet." The assignment was to find public-opinion data and documents to present a "fact-based and balanced summary of the public debate" surrounding an issue. The students each wrote a paper to be posted on the course Web site, with links to all sources. Each student also prepared a classroom presentation of his or her research, using PowerPoint slides. Luo chose an assigned topic, "genetic engineering," and narrowed the focus to "genetically modified crops." For her classroom presentation, she prepared several slides. Shown here are her outline slide and a slide illustrating public-opinion data. She prepared the bar charts herself with Microsoft Word (see 11a), using data from three polling organizations.

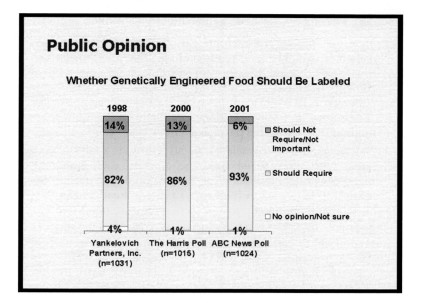

12c   Posting academic writing online

You may be required to submit an essay for a course online rather than in hard copy. Your instructor may ask you to e-mail him or her an attachment, or in a hybrid or a synchronous distance-learning course, you may be required to submit your essays in a dropbox or post them on a class online discussion board for the instructor and other students to read and comment on. Alternatively, you may have your own e-portfolio or Web site where you display your work. In all of these cases, keep in mind the following general guidelines, and ask your instructor for instructions specific to the course, format, and type of posting.

Recent versions of word processing programs can automatically convert a document and save it as an HTML file for the Web. In Word, for example, you simply produce your document in the usual way but then, when you save it, go to "Save As" and change "Save as type" from "Word" to "Web page." The HTML commands are done for you, automatically. In addition, Netscape Composer provides an HTML editor that tends to be more efficient in display speed.

KEY POINTS
Posting an Essay or a Research Paper Online

1. *Structure*   Set up a structure with sections and subsections (called "fragments"), all with headings, that allows each section to be accessed directly—for example, from your table of contents (see item 2 below) and from any other part of your paper as well. So instead of saying diffusely, "See above" or "See below," you can provide a specific link allowing readers to jump directly to this part (see item 3).

2. *Links to sections from a table of contents*   Provide a table of contents, with an internal link anchored to each fragment, marked with a "bookmark" or "target," and give each bookmark (MS IE) or target (Netscape) a name. Readers can then click on and go directly to any section they are interested in.

3. *Internal hyperlinks*   Use internal hyperlinks (Insert/Hyperlink) to connect readers directly to relevant sections of your text, content notes, and visuals. Also provide a link from a source cited in the body of your paper to the entry in your list of works cited.

4. *External hyperlinks*   Use external hyperlinks to connect to Web documents from references in the body of your paper and from your list of works cited. Useful for the works-cited

list, Word has a function that will automatically convert any string starting with <http://> into a hyperlink (go to Tools/AutoCorrect/AutoFormat, and AutoFormat As You Type, and then check Replace Internet and Network Paths with Hyperlinks).

5. *No paragraph indentation*   Do not indent for a new paragraph. Instead, leave a line space between paragraphs.

6. *Attribution of sources*   Make sure that the link you give to an online article in a database is a persistent link, not a link that works for only a few hours or days. It is often difficult to determine at first glance whether a link is persistent or not. Some databases are explicit; others are not. Double-check your links after a few days to see whether the links are still working. Some sites (such as Thomas at Library of Congress and EBSCO databases) provide persistent links.

7. *List of works cited or list of references*   Give a complete list, with visible hyperlinked URLs, even if you provide some external links to the sources from the body of your paper. If a reader prints your paper, the exact references will then still be available.

Online Study Center   **Design/Media**   Student online research paper

12d E-mailing in an academic environment (netiquette)

Communicating online to professors in academic contexts is different from writing personal e-mail. Observe the following conventions.

Length and readability   Be brief, and state your main points clearly at the start. One screen holds about 250 words, and online readers do not want to scroll repeatedly to find out what you are saying. Keep paragraphs short and manageable so that readers can take in the information at a glance. Use numbered or bulleted lists to present a sequence of points as brief items that can be readily seen and absorbed. Avoid multiple colors, fonts, and graphics unless you are certain your readers can receive and read these features.

Capitals   Avoid using all capital letters in an e-mail message. To readers, it looks as if you are SHOUTING. But do use capitals when appropriate, especially for *I*.

URLS Pay attention to accuracy of punctuation and capital letters. Both matter; one slip can invalidate an address and cause you great frustration. Whenever possible, to avoid having to write out a long URL, simply copy that URL from a document and paste it into your own document (Select/Copy/Paste). If you need to spread an address over two lines, break it after a slash (MLA style) or before a dot, and do not insert any spaces or line breaks.

Accuracy Use a spelling checker and edit your e-mail before sending it if you are writing to people you do not know well and if you want them to take your ideas seriously.

Subject heading Subscribers to a list and regular e-mail correspondents are likely to receive a great deal of mail every day. Be clear and concise when composing a subject heading so that readers will know at a glance what your message is about.

Quoting a whole message or part of a message Do not include an entire message with your reply unless you find it necessary for clarity or if you refer to it point by point. Include only parts of a message that you respond to directly.

Forwarding messages Never forward a message indiscriminately. Consider first whether the recipient will need or appreciate the forwarded message. In addition, make sure that forwarding does not violate rules established by your college or business organization. If necessary, ask the original sender for permission to forward the message. He or she can then veto the idea if anyone is likely to be offended or harmed.

Signing off Always put your actual name (not just <cutiepie3@aol.com>) at the end of your online message. You can also construct a "signature file," which will appear automatically at the end of every message you send. Find out how to do this from the Help or Tools menu of your e-mail program.

The danger of attachments Attachments can harbor computer viruses, so always be cautious about opening any attachments to an e-mail message. Open attachments only from known senders, and keep your own antivirus software up-to-date so that you will not spread a virus.

Spam Make sure you add your instructors or business associates to your safe list so that their messages are not classified as spam.

> ## KEY POINTS
> ### A Checklist for E-Mail Netiquette

1. What will your reader expect?
   - formal language
   - standard but informal English
   - colloquialisms, slang, and abbreviations

   How does your document measure up to those expectations?

2. What is a reader likely to think or say after reading your e-mail communication?
   - This e-mail was written quickly and was not checked.
   - This makes just the right assumptions about me as a reader.
   - I hate all these abbreviations and slang words.
   - I could send this to my manager.

   Is that what you want a reader to think?

3. Have you checked your grammar and spelling? Should you do so for this reader? Will this reader judge your abilities according to what he or she reads?

4. Which of the following can you find in your e-mail? How appropriate are they for your readers?
   - emoticons
   - abbreviations such as LOL ("laughing out loud") or IMHO ("in my humble opinion")
   - contractions
   - technical words (jargon)
   - pretentious language (trying to sound important and academic)
   - typographical, spelling, or punctuation errors
   - familiar and colloquial phrases (*OK; cool dude; yeah; ugh*)

12e Writing a personal statement for graduate school admission

Your personal statement may be one of the most important things you ever write. Graduate school admissions committees read hundreds of such statements, and your aim is to get yours to stand out so that the program of your choice offers you admission. Some basic rules apply:

- Read the instructions carefully, and do specifically what you are asked to do.
- Do not write one statement and send it to several schools.
- Do not send a first draft. Revise until you get it right.
- Show your interest in your field of study, and describe your specific interests and accomplishments.
- Make sure you demonstrate why the admissions committee should admit you: What makes you a good fit for that particular school? What makes you better than other candidates?
- Pay special attention to your first paragraph, where you can attract or lose a reader.
- Have someone else check your work, and proofread, proofread, proofread. Mistakes will immediately put off a reader.

TECH NOTE

Online Advice on Personal Statements

The Online Writing Lab at Purdue University includes a useful twelve-point bulleted list of questions to ask yourself before you write, as well as general advice, examples of successful statements, and advice from admissions representatives at six institutions.

Chapter **13**

Designing a Web Site

A great deal of online help is available for the mechanics of finding a server for a site (many schools offer space for student Web pages, as do many Internet service providers) and for the actual creation of a site (use MS Word and save a file as "Web page," for instance). With so much technical help accessible, you don't need to worry too much about HTML and coding. Instead, you can focus on adapting what you know about writing for the page: the important rhetorical considerations of purpose, audience, voice, structure, interaction of text and images, and the design of your document.

13a Planning and organizing a Web site

Purpose Determine the message you want your site to convey and what you want your audience to learn from your site or do as a result of viewing it. Do you want to inform, persuade, entertain—or all three?

Audience   Try to form a clear idea of the main audience you want to reach: friends and family, fellow students, colleagues, members of a club or community, or the general public? Consider what their expectations will be. For a professional or academic audience, choose fonts and colors that are sober rather than flashy. If you know that many of your readers do not have broadband access, that factor will affect the speed of downloading any video or audio clips you decide to include on the site.

Voice and tone   Visitors to your Web site take away an impression of you or the institution you represent, so make sure that the content, language, and images keep any visitors to your site interested and engaged. Some sites and some audiences enjoy extremes, but for a professional site, play it safe and avoid rants, insults, jargon, terminal cuteness, and flat attempts at humor.

Structure   Web sites typically consist of several pages and many internal and external links. Your viewers need directions on finding their way and not getting lost. On each page, include a link to the home page on a navigational bar—at the top or bottom or in a sidebar. Also consider including an "About" page to explain the purpose of the site. Refer to the structure of sites you like and find easy to navigate to help you devise the structure for your site. Make a site map.

Interaction of text and images   Plan the look of each page so that images supplement and complement text and the site's purpose, and draw the audience into the content. In other than personal sites designed for family and friends, avoid using images and animation that add peripheral glitz and clutter. Remember the need to acknowledge text or images from another source, and request permission to use them; the Web is a highly public forum.

Design and presentation   The design and presentation of your work are extremely important in a Web site as it is open to so many more potential readers than a paper text, even one widely distributed. See 13b for tips on Web site design.

Making a site map   Draw a flowchart that shows how the different parts of your site will relate to each other. In the *Refugee Resettlement*

Program Web site (shown in 13d), the structure is simple. The home page clearly links to the other pages within the site. Here is a map of that site:

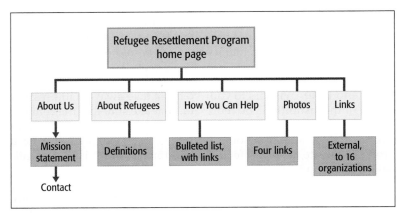

13b Tips for Web site design

KEY POINTS
Web Site Design Guidelines

- Keep pages short and simple—as a general rule, no more than two to three screens, with no fancy fonts.
- To test your page, set your own monitor to a resolution not higher than 800 × 600, and make sure all the text is visible on your screen without horizontal scrolling.
- Keep sentences short and direct.
- Break text into short passages. Use lists to help readers scan quickly.
- Use headings, and provide internal links to the headings. Use a larger point size for the type in headings.
- Use visuals—such as pictures, diagrams, photographs, graphs, clip art, or animation—to enhance and illustrate ideas. Save photos as .jpeg and graphs as .gif files. Pay attention to the file size of such add-ons. It is often possible to reduce the file size significantly with only a minimal loss of image quality. Position visuals so that they relate clearly to the written text.

- Choose descriptive text or images as "anchors" for hyperlinks (not just "Click here."). Check on their reliability and keep them up-to-date.

- Use color and background patterns judiciously and consistently. Choose colors to complement the subject matter: dramatic? subdued? Blue type on a black swirling background may look interesting, but it can be difficult to read.

- Be sensitive to issues of accessibility for people with disabilities, such as using descriptive text as well as images and offering alternatives to visual and auditory material. Refer to the Bobby site at the Center for Applied Special Technology for guidelines.

- Keep the site uncluttered for ease of navigation.

- Include relevant navigational links from each page of your site to other pages, such as the home page. Consider the use of a navigation bar that appears on each page of your site. Update your site regularly to maintain the links to external URLs.

- Include your own e-mail address for comments and questions about your site. State the date of the last page update.

- For text and graphics that you download to use in your own site, ask for permission and acknowledge the fact that you received permission to use the material. Be aware that you may have to pay a fee to use copyrighted material. Also, provide full documentation for your sources (see 50d).

13c Getting feedback

Before you launch the site, get as much feedback as you can from classmates or colleagues. Ask for their responses to the following:

- the ease of navigating to individual pages and back to the home page
- the length of time it takes for graphics to load
- page length and width (no horizontal scrolling and little vertical scrolling)
- the legibility and relevance of images (no animation or flashing icons just for effect)
- the sense that everything on the site serves a purpose
- the grammar and mechanics (no errors or inconsistencies).

After you launch the site, continue to invite feedback from those who visit your Web site by creating a guest book or a feedback form, or simply by including contact information. Guest books and feedback forms are readily found on the Internet by using a search engine such as Google and are free to download onto your Web site. Guestbooks are appropriate for a personal Web site; feedback forms are used for business and commercial Web sites. Based on feedback from your Web site visitors, you should be able to assess how well you are getting your message across.

TECH NOTE

Getting Help with Web Site Design

A useful resource is Jennifer Niederst, *Learning Web Design: A Beginner's Guide to HTML, Graphics, and Beyond*, 2nd edition (Cambridge, O'Reilly & Associates, 2003).

Online Study Center   **Design/Media** Web site design

13d Sample student Web site

The Soling Program at Syracuse University focuses on experiential learning and community involvement (for more on community service writing, see 9e). The program offers a course, "Web Design for Novices," in which students work with community organizations to design Web sites. In fall 2005, Daniel Sauve worked with the Refugee Resettlement Program cosponsored by the Interreligious Council of Central New York and United Way to develop an informational site containing an appeal for help. Two pages from the site shown here illustrate features of good Web site design.

- The purpose of the site is clear, and the content is succinct and accessible.
- The home page provides a good introduction to the whole site, with no distractions and no vertical scrolling necessary.
- Text does not fill the width of the screen, and no horizontal scrolling is necessary.
- The navigation bar appears on the left side of each page.
- Clicking on the title (Refugee Resettlement Program) on each page takes one back to the home page.

Home Page of Site

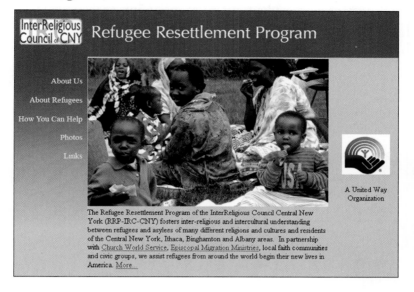

How You Can Help

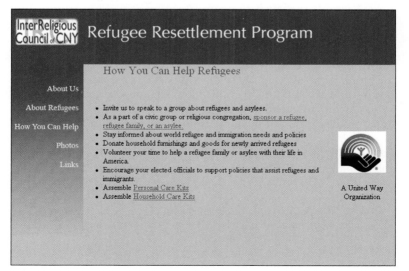

- The logos of the two sponsors, linked to their sites, appear on each page, providing instant access to information about the organizations and their purpose.

- The tone is objective, direct, and clear throughout, avoiding hype.

- The content of a hyperlink is made clear in the wording of the text for the link.

- The consistent use of color and heading format unifies the whole site.

EXERCISE 13.1

Search for students' Web sites.

Use a search engine to find students' Web sites. Select one that is particularly clear and attractive and report on it to your classmates.

Chapter **14**

Writing for Employment*

14a Preparing your résumé: Length and format

Although recruiters sometimes refer to the résumé as a *wilawid* ("What I've learned and what I've done"), the emphasis in the résumé should be on the future rather than on the past: you must show how your education and work experience have prepared you for future jobs—specifically, the job for which you are applying. The résumé and accompanying application letter (cover letter) are crucial in advancing you beyond the mass of initial applicants and into the much smaller group of potential candidates invited to an interview.

Résumé length How much is too much? Surveys of employment and human resources executives consistently show that most managers

Online Study Center   This icon will direct you to quick reference tools, Web resources, and research guides on the Web site at http://college.hmco.com/keys.html.

---

* This section has been adapted from Scot Ober, *Contemporary Business Communication*, 6th ed. (Boston: Houghton, 2006). Used with permission.

prefer a one-page résumé for the entry-level positions typically sought by recent college graduates; a two-page résumé may be appropriate for unusual circumstances or for higher-level positions.

A one-page résumé is *not* the same as a two-page résumé crammed onto one page by means of small type and narrow margins. Your résumé must be attractive and easy to read. Shorten your résumé by making judicious decisions about what to include and then by using concise language to communicate what is important. Do not, on the other hand, make your résumé *too* short. A résumé that does not fill one page may tell the prospective employer that you have little to offer.

TECH NOTE

Online Résumé, Cover Letter, and Job Search Assistance

Major national newspapers such as the *New York Times* and the *Chicago Tribune* offer free online courses and support groups for job seekers, providing everything from using strategic keywords for your field to getting a background check on yourself before you submit a résumé. If you want to relocate, search the "classifieds" or "help wanted" sections of online newspapers from other areas of the country where you might be interested in working. They can help you begin your planning long before you make your move. Other online job search sites, such as Monster.com, offer an even wider range of career support services, including advice for new college graduates, as well as for experienced workers seeking to make transitions.

Résumé format   Choose a simple, easy-to-read typeface, and avoid the temptation to use a lot of "special effects" just because they're available on your computer. One or two typefaces in one or two different sizes should be enough. Use a simple format, with white space, short paragraphs, and a logical organization. Through the use of type size and style, indentation, bullets, and the like, make clear which parts are subordinate to main features. One of your word processor's built-in résumé templates is a good place to start.

Format your résumé on standard-size paper ($8\frac{1}{2}$" $\times$ 11") so that it can be filed easily. Also, avoid brightly colored papers: they will get attention but perhaps the wrong kind. Dark colors do not photocopy well, and you want photocopies of your résumé (whether made by you or by the potential employer) to look professional. Choose white or an off-white (cream or ivory) paper of good quality—at least 20-pound bond.

Finally, your résumé and application letter must be 100 percent free of error—in content, spelling, grammar, and format. Ninety-nine percent accuracy is not good enough when you are seeking a job.

One survey of large-company executives showed that fully 80 percent of them had decided against interviewing a job seeker because of poor grammar, spelling, or punctuation in his or her résumé. Don't write, as one job applicant did, "Education: Advanced Curses in Accounting," or as another did, "I have an obsession for detail; I make sure that I cross my i's and dot my t's." Show right from the start that you take pride in your work.

14b Preparing your résumé: Content

Fortunately, perhaps, there is no such thing as a standard résumé; each is as individual as the person it represents. There are, however, standard parts of the résumé—those parts recruiters expect and need to see to make valid judgments.

Identifying information It doesn't do any good to impress a recruiter if he or she cannot locate you easily to schedule an interview; therefore, your name and complete address (including phone number and e-mail address) are crucial.

Your name should be the very first item on the résumé, arranged attractively at the top. Use whatever form you typically use for signing your name (for example, with or without initials). Give your complete name, avoiding nicknames, and do not use a personal title such as *Mr.* or *Ms.*

If you will soon be changing your address (as from a college address to a home address), include both, along with the relevant dates for each. If you are away from your telephone most of the day and no one is at home to answer it and take a message, you would be wise to secure phone company voice mail, invest in an answering machine, or get permission to use the telephone number where you work as an alternate phone listing. The important point is to be available for contact.

KEY POINTS
Résumé Content

Include on your résumé

1. Name, address, phone number, and e-mail address
2. Job objective
3. College major, degree, name of college, and graduation date
4. Jobs held, employers, dates, and duties
5. Special aptitudes and skills

Do not include on your résumé
1. Bases for discrimination
   - Religion
   - Ethnicity
   - Age
   - Gender
   - Photograph
   - Marital status
2. High school activities

Job objective   The job objective is a short summary of your area of expertise and career interest. Most recruiters want the objective stated so that they will know where you might fit into their organization. Don't force the employer to guess about your career goals. Furthermore, don't waste the objective's prominent spot at the top of your résumé by giving a weak, overly general goal:

WEAK   **Challenging position in a progressive organization**

For your objective to help you, it must be personalized—both for you and for the position you are seeking. Also, it must be specific enough to be useful to the prospective employer but not so specific as to exclude you from many types of similar positions. The following job objective meets these criteria:

STRONG   **Position in personal sales in a medium-size manufacturing firm**

If your goals are so broad that you have difficulty specifying a job objective, either eliminate this section of your résumé or develop several résumés, each with a different job objective and emphasis.

Be aware that an increasing number of large corporations have begun scanning the résumés they receive into their computer systems and then searching this computerized database by keyword. Be certain, therefore, that the title of the actual position you desire and other relevant terms are included somewhere in your résumé.

Education   Unless your work experience has been extensive, fairly high level, and directly related to your job objective, your education is probably a stronger job qualification than your work experience and should therefore be listed first on the résumé.

List the title of your degree, the name of your college and its location if needed, your major and (if applicable) minor, and your expected date of graduation (month and year).

List your grade-point average if it will set you apart from the competition (generally, at least a 3.0 on a 4.0 scale). If you have made the dean's list or have financed a substantial portion of your college expenses through part-time work, savings, or scholarships, mention that. Unless your course of study provided distinctive experiences that uniquely qualify you for the job, avoid listing college courses.

Work experience   Work experience—*any* work experience—is a definite plus. It shows the employer that you have had experience in satisfying a supervisor, following directions, accomplishing objectives through team effort, and being rewarded for your labors. If your work experience has been directly related to your job objectives, consider putting it ahead of the education section, for emphasis.

KEY POINTS
Use Career Development Services at Your College

Take advantage of the free career development services and programs that most colleges offer their students. Career advisors can help you translate your marketable skills and experiences into language that employers value and seek on résumés.

Campus career services and programs typically include the following:

- *Career exploration* provides guides and road maps to connect a college major with a career; two-year and four-year plans can help you think about how your academic trajectory can dovetail with your career aspirations.

- *Job search tools* help you prepare résumés, brush up on interview etiquette, participate in mock interview appointments, explore job search ethics, and negotiate job offers.

- *Employment opportunities* are often listed on your college's Web site. You can easily register, browse, and apply for part-time and full-time employment and internships. Or visit your campus career development office for listings.

- *Career days and internship fairs* are excellent ways for companies to meet students on campus, and they provide good opportunities for you to practice preliminary interviews, network with companies, and learn more about companies you might be interested in joining.

In relating your work experience, use either a chronological or a functional organizational pattern.

In a *chronological* arrangement, you organize your experience by date, describing your most recent job first and working backward. This format is most appropriate when you have had a strong continuing work history and much of your work has been related to your job objective (see p. 243). About 95 percent of all résumés are chronological, beginning with the most recent information and working backward.

KEY POINTS
Writing a Résumé

1. Decide how to present your résumé, or follow a prospective employer's instructions: on paper, on the Web, in the body of an e-mail message, as an e-mail attachment—or all of these. Start with a paper version and save it as .rtf or .doc. Convert it to HTML or to PDF to show it on the Web.

2. For a hard-copy version, print on standard-size paper of good quality, white or off-white.

3. Use headings to indicate the main sections.

4. For a hard-copy version, highlight section headings and important information with boldface, italics, bullets, indentation, or different fonts. Use a clear, simple design. Do not use overly elaborate fonts, colors, or design features.

5. Keep a print résumé to one page, if possible. Do not include extraneous information to add length, but do not cram by using single-spacing between sections, a small font, or a tiny margin.

6. Include information and experience relevant to the job you are applying for. Use reverse chronological order (begin with your most recent work experience and education).

7. Proofread your résumé several times, and ask someone else to examine it carefully as well. Make sure it contains no errors. Avoid howlers such as "rabid typist" and "responsible for ruining a five-store chain."

8. Accompany your print résumé with a cover letter (14d), also carefully checked to avoid an error such as "Thank you for considering me. I look forward to hearing from you shorty."

Note: Microsoft Word provides résumé templates that set up headings for you—a useful guide.

Sample print or Web page résumé Notice how Aurelia Gomez organized her résumé into clear divisions, using bold headings and a space between sections. This résumé presents the most recent job experience and education first and works backward.*

<table>
<tr><td></td><td colspan="2" align="right">225 West 70th Street
New York, NY 10023
Phone: 212-555-3821
E-mail: agomez@nyu.edu</td><td></td></tr>
<tr><td></td><td colspan="2">**Aurelia Gomez**</td><td></td></tr>
</table>

Objective:	Entry-level staff accounting position with a public accounting firm	Provides specific enough objective to be useful
Experience:	Summer 2005 — **Accounting Intern:** Coopers & Lybrand, NYC • Assisted in preparing corporate tax returns • Attended meetings with clients • Conducted research in corporate tax library and wrote research reports	Places work experience before education because applicant considers it to be her stronger qualification
	Sept. 2001–Nov. 2003 — **Payroll Specialist:** City of New York • Worked full-time in a civil service position in the Department of Administration • Used payroll and other accounting software on both DEC 1034 minicomputer and Pentium III • Represented 28-person work unit on the department's management-labor committee • Left job to pursue college degree full-time	Uses action words such as *assisted* and *conducted*; uses incomplete sentences to emphasize the action words and to conserve space
Education:	Jan. 2000–Present — Pursuing a 5-year bachelor of business administration degree (major in accounting) from the Stern School of Business, NYU • Expected graduation date: June 2006 • Attended part-time from 2001 until 2003 while holding down a full-time job • Have financed 100% of all college expenses through savings, work, and student loans • Plan to sit for the CPA exam in May 2007	Provides degree, institution, major, and graduation date Makes the major section headings parallel in format and in wording
Personal Data:	• Helped start the Minority Business Student Association at NYU and served as program director for two years; secured the publisher of *Black Enterprise* magazine as a banquet speaker • Have traveled extensively throughout South America • Am a member of the Accounting Society • Am willing to relocate	Formats the side headings for the dates in a column for ease of reading Provides additional data to enhance her credentials
References:	Available on request	Omits actual names and addresses of references

*Sample documents in 14b–15 are adapted from Scot Ober, *Contemporary Business Communication*, 6th ed. (Boston: Houghton, 2006). Used with permission.

14c Electronic résumés

Companies often scan the print résumés they receive in order to establish a database of prospective employees. They can then use a keyword search to find suitable candidates from those in the database. You may also need to e-mail your résumé to a prospective employer. In either case, you need to be able to adapt a print or formatted résumé to make it easy for users to read and scan. You do not need to limit the length of either a scannable or an e-mail résumé.

KEY POINTS
Preparing a Scannable or an E-mail Résumé

- Check any prospective employer's Web site to find its emphasis and important keywords.
- Use nouns as résumé keywords to enable prospective employers to do effective keyword searches (use "educational programmer," for example, rather than "designed educational programs").
- To transform a formatted MS Word document, such as a résumé, into a plain text format suitable for scannable and electronic résumés, copy your document into Notepad (go to Start, then Accessories). Documents created or pasted into Notepad are automatically stripped of formatting.
- Use a standard typeface (Times New Roman or Arial) and 10- to 12-point type, and for an e-mail document, use "plain text" or ASCII (a file name with a .txt extension).
- Avoid italics, underlining, and graphics.
- Avoid marked lists, or change bullets to + (plus signs) or to * (asterisks).
- Begin each major heading line at the left margin.
- Do not include any decorative vertical or horizontal lines or borders.
- E-mail yourself or a friend a copy of your résumé (both as an attachment and within the body of a message) before you send one to an employer so that you can verify the formatting.
- If you feel that it is necessary, attach a note saying that a formatted version is available in hard copy, and send one as a backup.

Sample electronic résumé Here is Aurelia Gomez's résumé adapted for e-mailing and scanning.

AURELIA GOMEZ

225 West 70 Street
New York, NY 10023
Phone: 212-555-3821
E-mail: agomez@nyu.edu

OBJECTIVE

Entry-level staff accounting position with a public accounting firm

EXPERIENCE

Summer 2005
Accounting Intern: Coopers & Lybrand, NYC
* Assisted in preparing corporate tax returns
* Attended meetings with clients
* Conducted research in corporate tax library and wrote
  research papers

Sept. 2001–Nov. 2003
Payroll Specialist: City of New York
* Full-time civil service position in the Department of
  administration
* Proficiency in payroll and other accounting software on DEC 1034
  minicomputer and Pentium III
* Representative for a 28-person work unit on the department's
  management-labor committee
* Reason for leaving job: To pursue college degree full-time

EDUCATION

Jan. 2000–Present
Pursuing a 5-year bachelor of business administration degree (major
in accounting) from the Stern School of Business, NYU
* Expected graduation date: June 2006
* Attended part-time from 2001 until 2003 while holding down a full-
  time job
* Have financed 100% of all college expenses through savings,
  work, and student loans
* Plan to sit for the CPA exam in May 2007

PERSONAL DATA

* Helped start the Minority Business Student Association at New
  York University and served as program director for two years;
  secured the publisher of BLACK ENTERPRISE magazine as a
  banquet speaker
* Have traveled extensively throughout South America
* Am a member of the Accounting Society
* Am willing to relocate

REFERENCES

Available upon request

NOTE

An attractive and fully formatted hard-copy version of this resume
is available upon request.

Annotations:

Begins with name at the top, followed immediately by address

Emphasizes, where possible, nouns as keywords

Uses only ASCII characters—one size with no special formatting; no rules, graphics, columns, or tables are used

Uses vertical line spaces (Enter key) and horizontal spacing (space bar) to show relationship of parts

Formats lists with asterisks instead of bullets

Runs longer than one page (acceptable for electronic résumés)

Includes notice of availability of a fully formatted version

14d Cover letter: Print or electronic

Accompany your print or e-mail résumé with a cover letter that explains what position you are applying for and why you are a good candidate. Find out as much as you can about the potential employer and type of work; then, in your letter, emphasize the connections between your experience and the job requirements. (On the next page is an example of a solicited application letter; it accompanies the résumé on page 246.) Let the employer see that you understand what type of person he or she is looking for. State when, where, and how you can be contacted. As you do with the résumé itself, proofread the letter carefully.

KEY POINTS
Checklist for Job Application Letters

- Use your job application letter to show how the qualifications listed in your résumé have prepared you for the specific job for which you're applying.
- If possible, address your letter to the individual in the organization who will interview you if you're successful.
- When applying for an advertised opening, begin by stating the reason for the letter, identify the position for which you're applying, and tell how you learned about the opening.
- When writing an unsolicited application letter, first gain the reader's attention by showing that you are familiar with the company and can make a unique contribution to its efforts.
- In one or two paragraphs, highlight your strongest qualifications and relate them directly to the needs of the specific position for which you're applying. Refer the reader to the enclosed résumé.
- Treat your letter as a persuasive sales letter: provide specific evidence, stress benefits you could provide, avoid exaggeration, and show confidence in the quality of your product.
- Close by tactfully asking for an interview.
- Maintain an air of formality throughout the letter. Avoid cuteness.
- Make sure that the finished document has a professional, attractive, and conservative appearance and that it is 100 percent error-free.

March 13, 2006

Mr. David Norman, Partner
Ross, Russell & Weston
452 Fifth Avenue
New York, NY 10018

Dear Mr. Norman:

Subject: EDP Specialist Position (Reference No. 103-G)

My varied work experience in accounting and payroll services, coupled with my accounting degree, has prepared me for the position of EDP specialist that you advertised in the February 9 *New York Times*.

In addition to taking required courses in accounting and management information systems as part of my accounting major at New York University, I took an elective course in EDP auditing and control. The training I received in this course in applications, software, systems, and service-center records would enable me to immediately become a productive member of your EDP consulting staff.

My college training has been supplemented by an internship in a large accounting firm. In addition, my two years of experience as a payroll specialist for the city of New York have given me firsthand knowledge of the operation and needs of nonprofit agencies. This experience should help me to contribute to your large consulting practice with government agencies.

After you have reviewed my enclosed résumé, I would appreciate having the opportunity to discuss with you why I believe I have the right qualifications and personality to serve you and your clients. I can be reached by e-mail or phone after 3 p.m. daily.

Sincerely,

Aurelia Gomez

Aurelia Gomez
225 West 70th Street
New York, NY 10023
Phone: 212-555-3821
E-mail: agomez@nyu.edu

Enclosure

Addresses the letter to a specific person

Identifies the job position and source of advertising

Emphasizes a qualification that might distinguish her from other applicants

Relates her work experience to the specific needs of the employer

Provides a telephone number (may be done either in the body of the letter or in the last line of the address block)

Online Study Center **Across/Beyond College** Cover letters and résumés

14e After the interview

After you have had an interview with a prospective employer, follow up with an immediate thank-you note. (For a sample, see p. 252.) Send or fax a prompt, brief business letter to the interviewer (and anyone else you spoke to). Thank the person for his or her time, review your qualifications, and express your interest in the position and in further communication. Richard Nelson Bolles, author of the famous job-search manual *What Color Is Your Parachute?*, stresses the importance of writing a postinterview thank-you note, citing seven reasons:

1. It indicates that you have good people skills.
2. It reminds the busy employer that you were there and who you are.
3. It can be circulated to other people in the organization who were not at the interview.
4. It allows you to say that you would be interested in talking further.
5. It gives you a chance to relay any point you may have forgotten to mention or to correct any miscommunication.
6. It can give you an advantage over other applicants for the same position who have not followed up with a thank-you note.
7. It makes it easier, later, to ask the person who interviewed you for additional job leads, even if you do not get the job.

Taking the time to write a brief thank-you note conveys that you are an organized, personable, and efficient person with good communication skills—often the very qualities that a potential employer is looking for.

Interview follow-up letter The interview follow-up letter should be written within a day or two of the job interview.

April 15, 2006

ddresses the
person in the
salutation as he or
she was addressed
during the interview

Mr. David Norman, Partner
Ross, Russell & Weston
452 Fifth Avenue
New York, NY 10018

Dear Mr. Norman:

Begins directly with
an expression of
appreciation

Thank you for the opportunity to interview for the position of EDP specialist yesterday. I very much enjoyed meeting you and Arlene Worthington and learning more about the position and about Ross, Russell & Weston.

Mentions an incident
that occurred and
relates it to the
writer's background

I especially appreciated the opportunity to observe the long-range planning meeting yesterday afternoon and to learn of your firm's plans for increasing your consulting practice with nonprofit agencies. My experience working in city government leads me to believe that nonprofit agencies can benefit greatly from your expertise.

Closes on a
confident,
forward-looking
note

Again, thank you for taking the time to visit with me yesterday. I look forward to hearing from you.

Sincerely,

Aurelia Gomez
225 West 70 Street
New York, NY 10023
Phone: 212-555-3821
Email: agomez@nyu.edu

Chapter **15**

Writing in the Professional World

As you move from the academic to the professional world, you will continually call on many of the skills and strategies you have practiced while writing essays, conducting research, documenting sources, creating visuals, and designing documents. Whether you plan to produce business reports, grant proposals, press releases, newsletters, or advertisements, you will need to consider carefully the purpose, the audience, and the conventions of the genre you are writing in. You will want to check carefully your grammar, mechanics, and punctuation. You will also want to make sure that you have properly acknowledged your sources. In the professional world, just as in the academic world, you will always benefit from asking questions when you are not entirely sure what is expected of you.

15a Writing business letters

Basic features of a business letter   A good business letter usually has the following six qualities:

1. It is brief.
2. It clearly conveys to the reader information and expectations for action or response.
3. It lets the reader know how he or she will benefit from or be affected by the proposal or suggestion.
4. It is polite.
5. It is written in relatively formal language.
6. It contains no errors.

LANGUAGE AND CULTURE
Business Letters across Cultures

Basic features of business letters vary from culture to culture. Business letters in English avoid flowery language and references to religion, elements that are viewed favorably in some other

(Continued)

Online Study Center   This icon will direct you to quick reference tools, Web resources, and research guides on the Web site at http://college.hmco.com/keys.html.

(Continued)

cultures. Do not assume that there are universal conventions. When writing cross-cultural business letters, follow these suggestions:

1. Use a formal style; address correspondents by title and family name.
2. If possible, learn about the writing conventions of your correspondent's culture.
3. Use clear language and summary to get your point across.
4. Avoid humor; it may fall flat and could offend.

Technical requirements of a business letter

PAPER AND PAGE NUMBERING Use $8\frac{1}{2}$" × 11" white unlined paper. If your letter is longer than one page, number the pages beginning with page 2 in the top right margin.

SPACING Type single-spaced, on one side of the page only, and double-space between paragraphs. Double-space below the date, the inside address, and the salutation. Double-space between the last line of the letter and the closing. Quadruple-space between the closing and the typed name of the writer, and then double-space to *Enc.* (enclosing materials) or *cc:* (when sending a copy to another person). (See also page 255.)

LEFT AND RIGHT MARGINS The sample letter in 14d uses a block format: the return address, inside address, salutation, paragraphs, closing, and signature begin at the left margin. The right margin should not be justified; it should be ragged (with lines of unequal length) to avoid awkward gaps in the spacing between words. The modified block format places the return address and date, closing, and signature on the right.

RETURN ADDRESS If you are not using business letterhead, give your address as the return address, followed by the date. Do not include your name with the address. If you are using business stationery on which an address is printed, you do not have to write a return address.

INSIDE ADDRESS The inside address gives the name, title, and complete address of the person you are writing to. With a word processing program and certain printers, you can use this part of the letter for addressing the envelope.

SALUTATION   In the salutation, mention the recipient's name if you know it, with the appropriate title (*Dr., Professor, Mr., Ms.*), or just the recipient's title (*Dear Sales Manager*). If you are writing to a company or institution, use a more general term of address (*Dear Sir or Madam*) or the name of the company or institution (*Dear Gateway 2000*). Use a colon after the salutation in a business letter.

CLOSING PHRASE AND SIGNATURE   Capitalize only the first word of a closing phrase, such as *Yours truly* or *Sincerely yours*. Type your name four lines below the closing phrase (omitting *Mr.* or *Ms.*). If you have a title (*Supervisor, Manager*), type it underneath your name. Between the closing phrase and your typed name, sign your name in ink.

OTHER INFORMATION   Indicate whether you have enclosed materials with the letter (*Enc.*) and to whom you have sent copies (*cc: Ms. Amy Ray*). The abbreviation *cc:* used to refer to *carbon copy* but now refers to *courtesy copy* or *computer copy*. You may, however, use a single *c:* followed by a name or names, to indicate who besides your addressee is receiving the letter.

ENVELOPE   Choose an envelope that fits your letter folded from bottom to top in thirds. Use your computer's addressing capability to place the name, title, and full address of the recipient in the middle of the envelope, and your own name and address in the top left-hand corner. Include ZIP codes. Word processing programs include a function (Tools) that allows you to create labels for envelopes.

Sample business letter The sample letter below uses a block format, with all parts aligned at the left. This format is commonly used with business stationery.

All Natural
BEN & JERRY'S
VERMONT'S FINEST

November 1, 2006 ↓ 4

The arrows indicate how many lines to space down before typing the next part. For example, ↓ 4 after the date means to press Enter four times before typing the recipient's name.

Ms. Ella Shore, Professor
Department of Journalism
Burlington College
North Canyon Drive
South Burlington, VT 05403 ↓ 2

Dear Ms. Shore: ↓ 2

Subject: Newspaper Advertising

Thank you for thinking of Ben & Jerry's when you were planning the advertising for the back-to-school edition of your campus newspaper at Burlington College. We appreciate the wide acceptance your students and faculty give our products, and we are proud to be represented in the *Mountain Lark.* We are happy to purchase a quarter-page ad, as follows.

• The ad should include our standard logo and the words "Welcome to Ben & Jerry's." Please note the use of the ampersand instead of the word "and" in our name. Note also that "Jerry's" contains an apostrophe.

• We would prefer that our ad appear in the top right corner of a right-facing page, if possible.

Our logo is enclosed for you to duplicate. I am also enclosing a check for $375 to cover the cost of the ad. Best wishes as you publish this special edition of your newspaper. ↓ 2

Sincerely, ↓ 4

Joseph W. Dye

Joseph W. Dye
Sales Manager ↓ 2

rmt
Enclosures
c: Advertising Supervisor

Reference initials: initials of the person who typed the letter (if other than the signer)
Notations: indications of items being enclosed with the letter, copies of the letter being sent to another person, special-delivery instructions, and the like

30 Community Drive • South Burlington, Vermont • 05403-6828 • Tel: 802/846-1500 • www.benjerry.com

15b Business memos and e-mail

A memo (from the Latin *memorandum*, meaning "to be remembered") is a message from one person to someone else within an organization. It can be sent on paper or by e-mail. A memo usually reports briefly on an action, raises a question, or asks permission to follow a course of action. It addresses a specific question or issue in a quick, focused way, conveying information in clear paragraphs or numbered points.

Begin a memo with headings such as *To, From, Date,* and *Subject*; such headings are frequently capitalized and in boldface type. In the first sentence, tell readers what your point is. Then briefly explain, giving reasons or details. Single-space the memo. If your message is long, divide it into short paragraphs, or include numbered or bulleted lists and headings (see 11b) to organize and draw attention to essential points. Many computer programs provide a standard template for memo format. The design and headings are provided; you just fill in what you want to say.

KEY POINTS
Online Professional Behavior

Business E-Mails Are Company Property

Be sure to check with your company's human resources department about the appropriate use of your business e-mail account. Many companies have rules about employee use of e-mail. Unlike personal e-mail or even that from your college e-mail account, all e-mail sent from your business's computer or e-mail server is the legal property of that business. Always keep in mind that any e-mail you write can be read by your supervisor or your colleagues. Never use your business e-mail for personal correspondence, to discuss or share confidential business information, or to send jokes or photographs that might be offensive. (To read about e-mail netiquette, see 12d.)

Social Networking Sites and Your Career

A *New York Times* article entitled "For Some, Online Persona Undermines a Résumé" describes how a presence on the Internet can ruin employment opportunities. Prospective employers, corporate recruiters, and educational consulting firms often check job applicants through search engines and social networking sites. Many are turned off when they see unprofessional sides of otherwise promising candidates. Do you have a profile on a

(Continued)

(Continued)

social networking site? Have you offered opinions or statements on a blog or Web site that might be construed as controversial or in bad taste? If so, you may want to weigh your freedom of speech against your career ambitions. At the very least, reconfigure your privacy settings on social networking sites and create an alias on blogs and Web sites.

Sample memo

Barnes & Noble Inc.
Booksellers Since 1873
122 Fifth Avenue New York, NY 10011
(212) 633-3300

→ TAB

Heading

MEMO TO: Max Dillon, Sales Manager ↓ 2

FROM: Andrea J. Hayes ↓ 2 *ajh*

DATE: February 23, 2006 ↓ 2

SUBJECT: New-Venture Proposal ↓ 3

The arrows indicate how many lines to space down before typing the next part. For example, ↓ 2 after the date means to press Enter twice before typing the recipient's name.

Body

I propose the purchase or lease of a van to be used as a mobile bookstore. We could then use this van to generate sales in the outlying towns and villages throughout the state.

We have been aware for quite some time that many small towns around the state do not have adequate bookstore facilities, but the economics of the situation are such that we would not be able to open a comprehensive branch and operate it profitably. However, we could afford to stock a van with books and operate it for a few days at a time in various small towns throughout the state. As you are probably aware, the laws of this state would permit us to acquire a statewide business license fairly easily and inexpensively.

With the proper advance advertising (see attached sample), we should be able to generate much interest in this endeavor. It seems to me that this idea has much merit because of the flexibility it offers us. For example, we could tailor the length of our stay to the size of the town and the amount of business generated. Also, we could customize our inventory to the needs and interests of the particular locales.

The driver of the van would act as the salesperson, and we would, of course, have copies of our complete catalog so that mail orders could be taken as well. Please let me have your reactions to this proposal. If you wish, I can explore the matter further and generate cost and sales estimates in time for your next manager's meeting. ↓ 2

Reference initials
Attachment notation

jmc
Attachments

Barnes & Noble Bookstores ■ B. Dalton Bookseller ■ Doubleday Book Shops ■ Scribner's Bookstores ■ Bookstop

---

15c Business presentations and multimedia*

When you give an oral presentation, you consider many of the same issues you do with written communications: you determine the purpose of the presentation, analyze the audience, consider the length of the presentation, and assess the best way to deliver it. As with written communications, you organize oral presentations by collecting the data and arranging it in a logical order so that it will effectively and persuasively convey your message to your audience. For general guidelines on oral presentations, see 9f.

Tips for Presentation Visuals

Font Tips

Use UPPERCASE sparingly

Avoid using more than 2 fonts

Use Helvetica, Arial or Times Roman

Use 24 point size or larger

Color Tips

Choose legible colors

Use bright colors to highlight

Use light backgrounds with dark text

Avoid red/green combinations

Design Tips

Use warm colors (orange/reds) to excite

Use cool colors (greens/blues) to calm

Use ample spacing

Use colors to organize slide elements

Consistency Tips

Group related data or points

Keep slide transitions consistent

Keep background consistent

Maintain a consistent color scheme

Maintain consistent fonts

---

* This section has been adapted from Scot Ober, *Contemporary Business Communication*, 6th ed. (Boston: Houghton, 2006). Used with permission.

The value of a multimedia presentation Today's visually oriented audience is accustomed to some visual element, whether it is a
flipchart, an overhead transparency, slides, a film, a videotape, a
model, or audience handouts. Visual aids can be simple to create and
help audiences understand your presentation, especially if it
includes complex or statistical data. In a review of Al Gore's *An
Inconvenient Truth,* film critic A. O. Scott writes, "I can't think of
another movie in which the display of a graph elicited gasps of horror, but when the red lines showing the increasing rates of carbon-
dioxide emissions and the corresponding rise in temperatures come
on screen, the effect is jolting and chilling."

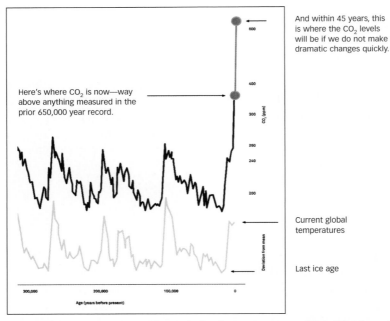

Line graph from Al Gore, *An Inconvenient Truth: The Planetary Emergency of Global Warming and
What We Can Do about It* (Emmaus, PA: Rodale, 2006), 66–67. By arrangement with Rodale, Inc.

KEY POINTS
Common Types of Multimedia Visual Aids

- *Electronic presentations* consist of slides or video shown directly from a computer and projected onto a screen by a projector. Because the slides come directly from the computer and do not have to be made, they are easy to prepare and update. On the other hand, you are limited by your equipment and the facility where you will be presenting.

- *Transparencies* are easy to use with an overhead projector. You do not need to darken the room, and you can face the audience while you speak. They are easy to prepare and update. Thanks to presentation software such as PowerPoint, overhead transparencies easily use to advantage color, interesting fonts, charts, artwork, and templates (see 12b).

- *Slides* provide high-quality visuals to a presentation. Slides are particularly effective when the focus of your presentation is specifically visual—for example, when you want to show reproductions of fine art or architecture. However, they do not provide the flexibility of an electronic presentation and can be relatively expensive to produce.

- *Film, videotape, and DVDs* require a moderate amount of production but can be particularly effective for orientations and other training purposes. Because of their relatively low reproduction cost, DVDs are increasingly being handed out to audience members so they can review the presentation long after it is over.

- *Flipcharts* are best used in informal presentations with a smaller audience. They are easy to prepare and update and require no equipment.

- *Handouts* provide the audience with printed copies of notes, tables, or illustrations used in your presentation. They can also give the audience a permanent record of the major points of a presentation. So not only do they help the audience follow your presentation; they can provide a review and new information for the audience after the presentation is over.

Preparing a multimedia presentation   When you prepare an oral presentation, think about which multimedia would be appropriate and effective for your purpose, your audience, the length of your presentation, and the media you have available. The goal of your presentation is to effectively communicate to the members of your audience. You want them to leave thinking about *what* you said, not *how* you said it. Use visual aids only when they will help your audience grasp an important point, and remove them when they are no longer needed.

Using multimedia equipment smoothly does not come naturally, so be sure to practice your presentation before you give it. And because bulbs can burn out, cords can be forgotten, and computers can crash, always be prepared to give your presentation without visuals, if necessary.

Language

Style and Accuracy

Science fiction writer and editor Teresa Neilson Hayden, in *Making Book,* characterizes English as "a generous, expansive, and flexible language," but adds, "a less charitable description would characterize it as drunk and disorderly." The task of editing, she claims, is to try to impose "a degree of regularity on something that is inherently irregular." What exists to help you move away from irregularities that appear in your writing is a set of conventions that go under the label of "Standard English" (1d).

Its practices are what readers expect in the academic and business worlds. Writing instructors often hear students complain that making changes in their writing to conform to Standard English hinders their creativity. But in fact, being creative and meeting readers' expectations are not mutually exclusive aims.

Whether you write in a college course, a business setting, or your local community, and whether you present your ideas on paper or on the screen, paying close attention to the clarity, style, and accuracy of your work always pays off.

A recent study of 120 corporations found that one third of the employees of major companies had poor writing skills, leading an executive to say, "It's not that companies want to hire Tolstoy. But they need people who can write clearly."

In chapters 16–38, you will find answers to common questions about correct style, usage, grammar, and punctuation. You will also find passages labeled "Variation" that recognize language change and writers' flexibility in the face of so-called *rules* of language.

Chapters 40–46 provide additional editing assistance for students who grew up surrounded by languages or dialects other than Standard English.

PART 4
The 5 C's of Style

What is style? William Strunk, Jr., and E. B. White in their classic book *The Elements of Style,* 4th edition, define it as the sound "words make on paper." That sound is important to readers and affects their response to a piece of writing and their willingness to continue reading. Sometimes, even when ideas are well organized, readers can suffer from the so-called MEGO reaction to a piece of writing—"My Eyes Glaze Over." Readers are bored by wordiness, flatness, inappropriate word choice, clichés, and sentences constructed without interesting variations. Working on sentence structure and style can help prevent that glazing over.

With acknowledgment to Joseph Williams's *Style: Ten Lessons in Clarity and Grace,* 7th edition, chapters 16–20 examine five anti-MEGO strategies, called here the "Five C's of Style."

LANGUAGE AND CULTURE
Style across Cultures

It is impossible to identify one style as the best. What is considered good (or appropriate) style varies according to the writer's purpose and the expectations of the anticipated readers. Country, culture, region, ethnic heritage, language, gender, class—all can play a role in writing and in influencing what readers define as *style.* What may please readers in one language and culture in one setting in one part of the world may seem too flat or too adorned in another. The Japanese novelist Junichuro Tanizaki, for example, gives writers this advice: "Do not try to be too clear; leave some gaps in the meaning." He illustrates this approach by comparing it to keeping "a thin sheet of paper between the fact or the object and the words that give expression to it" (in Edward G. Seidensticker's introduction to *Some Prefer Nettles*). Strunk and White give different advice: "The approach to style is by way of plainness, simplicity, orderliness, sincerity." Good style is relative.

Follow these guidelines for determining an appropriate style for each document you write.

1. Consider context and readers' expectations.   Assess where you are writing, what your purpose is, and what readers will expect in the part of the world you reside in and in the context you inhabit (such as an academic, business, or community setting).

What are readers' stylistic preferences in terms of organization and format of the document?

What elements should be included and excluded?

How direct or indirect do readers expect you to be in stating opinions and making recommendations?

What formulaic expressions are commonly in use (such as "Sincerely yours" or "In conclusion")?

What language will readers be comfortable with: short or long sentences, plain or ornate language and sentence structure, everyday words or technical vocabulary?

2. Address the underlying structure of your piece of writing. Work first on generating ideas and organizing them clearly and logically. Once you have organized your content and found a clear structure for expressing your ideas, then you can turn your attention to conscious presentation of the ideas, fine-tuning your style so that it appeals to specific readers.

3. Be adaptable. Choose a style as you choose your clothes: the right outfit for the occasion. One style will not fit all. If you develop an effective figurative style for short stories, do not continue to use it in business communications or e-mail.

4. Favor a plain style rather than writing to impress readers. Focusing on style does not mean focusing on ornate or stuffy language. For many writing situations in North America, the best style is often what is known as a "plain style"—something that is clear and easy for readers to follow. The following sentences, part of an e-mail message, are not in the plain style. They are overdressed and stuffed with bureaucratic nothings: "It has been a pleasure assisting you. It is my hope that the information provided would be of great help with regards to your concern." The same message can be conveyed more directly: "I hope I have helped you solve your problem."

5. Less is often more. In most types of college and business writing, a good style is writing that does not draw attention to itself with flourishes and flowery language. Avoid trying to dazzle readers with big words and obscure turns of phrase or overloading your writing with adjectives and adverbs: *The perky little red-haired twin sat* *languidly in the comfortable, overstuffed green-striped armchair and bit enthusiastically into a red and yellow, fleshy, overripe peach.* Such prose is as overripe as the peach.

6. Keep the presence of a "self."   Think of formal, academic style as something that makes readers realize that a real person has written the document—a person with a strong sense of self and a conviction that the ideas in the piece of writing are interesting, credible, and well presented. Do not fade into insignificance behind bland overgeneralities.

KEY POINTS
Style in College Essays: A Checklist for Revision

- ☐ Do any parts seem wordy or repetitive? Make your writing concise. Cut what you can. (See 16.)

- ☐ Are any sentences flat because of an unnecessary *there is* or *there are,* too many prepositional phrases (21d), or passive voice verbs? If so, ask, "Who's doing what?" and revise. (See 17.)

- ☐ Do any passages seem jumpy, disconnected, and not easy to follow? Have you used coordination and subordination effectively? Aim for coherence and make clear connections. (See 20.)

- ☐ Do any passages seem weak, apologetic, and flat? Commit to a point of view, to an appropriate tone, to confident language, and to sentence variety. (See 19.)

- ☐ Could any of your words baffle, bore, or offend a reader? Choose exact, concrete words, and eliminate clichés and language that is biased, inappropriate, or stuffy. (See 20.)

- ☐ Have you used a style-check/grammar-check program and exercised caution in taking its suggestions (see 6b)? Computer style-check programs alert you to such problems as possibly wordy phrases, repetition, clichés, sexist language, and colloquial usage. However, often they are not attuned to the subtleties of language and grammar. Never simply accept a suggestion as accurate.

Chapter **16**

The First C: Cut

You can improve most of your writing if you focus on stating your ideas succinctly. Examine your writing for unnecessary ideas, sentences, phrases, and individual words. Don't be tempted to pad your work to fill an assigned number of pages. Work on filling pages with substantive information and commentary, not with empty words.

16a Cut repetition and wordiness.

Say something only once and in the best place.

▶ The Lilly Library ~~contains many rare books. The books in~~

~~the library are~~ carefully preserved, ~~The library also houses~~
s
many rare books and manuscripts.
~~a manuscript collection.~~

director of
▶ Steven Spielberg, ~~who has directed~~ the movie ~~that has been~~
described as the best war movie ever made, ~~is someone who~~
knows many politicians.

▶ California residents voted to abolish bilingual education,
~~The main reason for their voting to abolish bilingual~~
because
~~education was that~~ many children were being placed

indiscriminately into programs and kept there too long.

If your draft says something like "As the first paragraph states" or "As previously stated," beware. Such phrases probably indicate that you have repeated yourself.

16b **Cut formulaic phrases.**

Writers sometimes use formulaic phrases in a first draft to keep the writing process going. In revision, these wordy phrases should come out or be replaced with shorter or more concise expressions.

Formulaic	Concise
at the present time	now
at this point in time	
in this day and age	
in today's society	
are of the opinion that	believe
have the ability to	can
is dependent upon	depends on
last but not least	finally
prior to	before
concerning the matter of	about
because of the fact that	because
due to the fact that	
in spite of the fact that	although

In *The Elements of Style*, William Strunk, Jr., and E. B. White rail against any use of the phrase "the fact that," seeing it as "especially debilitating." Their advice? Cut it out.

▶ Few people realize ~~the fact~~ that the computer controlling the *Eagle* lunar module in 1969 had less memory than a cheap wristwatch does today.

▶ A 1999 Gallup poll revealed ~~the fact~~ that almost six percent of Americans believe the moon landing in 1969 was a hoax.

EXERCISE 16.1
Cut wordiness and formulaic phrases.
Edit the following sentences to eliminate wordiness and formulaic phrases.

EXAMPLE:

> Although
> ~~In spite of the fact that~~ Michael Jordan has decided to play basketball again, fans are not likely to see incredible ~~and unbelievable~~ athletic feats from their hero ~~again.~~

1. Michael Jordan first retired from basketball in 1993 and tried to begin a career in the game of baseball, but he returned to the Chicago Bulls in the spring of 1995 because of the fact that he had not been successful enough in baseball to reach the major leagues.

2. When Jordan retired again in 1999, he told reporters that he was "99.9 percent" sure that he would never return to basketball, but basketball fans who loved the game were of the opinion that he had meant to leave himself a loophole.

3. At the point in time when Jordan began working out on a basketball court again, many people thought he was planning a comeback, but Jordan insisted that he was simply and solely trying to lose weight.

4. Finally, in the fall of 2001, Jordan, who at the time was then thirty-eight years old, revealed that he would play with the Washington Wizards and donate his first year's salary to victims of the September 11 attacks.

5. Jordan had owned a part of the Washington Wizards, a team with a poor record in the 2000–2001 season, prior to making the decision to sell his stake in the team and come in as a player.

16c As appropriate, cut references to your intentions.

In writing for the social sciences or sciences, the main goal is usually to provide information. In those disciplines, therefore, you may acceptably state how you intend to structure your argument (for example, *This paper describes three approaches to classifying germs*) and then summarize that structure again at the end of the essay—thus presenting a plan of your organization at both the beginning and the end of the essay.

In the humanities, readers usually are not interested in explanations of your thinking process and plan of organization. Eliminate references to the organization of your text and your own planning, such as *In this essay, I intend to prove . . .* or *In the next few paragraphs, I hope to show . . .* or *In conclusion, I have demonstrated . . .* or *What I want to say here is. . . .*

16d   Cut redundant words and phrases.

Trim words that simply repeat an idea expressed by another word in the same phrase: *basic* essentials, *true* facts, *circle* around, cooperate *together*, *final* completion, return *again*, refer *back*, *advance* planning, consensus *of opinion*, *free* gift. Also edit redundant pairs: *various and sundry, hopes and desires, each and every,* and any redundant phrases.

▶ The task took ~~diligence and~~ perseverance.

▶ His surgeon ~~is a doctor with~~ a great deal of clinical experience. _has_

EXERCISE 16.2

Cut redundant words and phrases.

Edit to eliminate redundant words and phrases.

EXAMPLE:

The Strangler cases terrified ~~and unnerved~~ Bostonians until 1965, when Albert DeSalvo confessed to the eleven murders.

1. The nephew of one of the Boston Strangler's murder victims began to investigate his aunt's case in 1999 to prove to his own mother that the Strangler had been caught, but he eventually became mentally certain that Albert DeSalvo, the confessed killer of the victims, was not guilty.

2. In the 1960s, the public was told that DeSalvo had admitted details in his confession that only the murderer or killer would have known.

3. DeSalvo was never convicted of the Strangler murders, but he went to prison, where he was jailed for another crime and was fatally stabbed there in 1973.

4. DeSalvo seemed to have exclusive and inside knowledge of the murders, but others have since noted that he had heard many details from lawyers and police officials, and DeSalvo was

known for his complete and total recall of each and every thing he had been told.

5. Since the victim's nephew got involved, lawyers and forensic specialists have been cooperating together to investigate new leads and DNA evidence that could either exonerate DeSalvo or finally prove him guilty at last.

16e Cut material quoted unnecessarily.

Quote only as much material from a source as is needed to support your point. Often a phrase or clause will be enough; quoting a whole sentence or more than one sentence is usually unnecessary.

NO   **Film critic Elvis Mitchell says of *Harry Potter and the Sorcerer's Stone:* "The most awaited movie of the year has a dreary, literal-minded competence, following the letter of the law as laid down by the author" in its close portrayal of the book.**

YES   **Film critic Elvis Mitchell says that the long-anticipated *Harry Potter and the Sorcerer's Stone* suffers from "a dreary, literal-minded competence" in its close portrayal of the book.**

REVIEW EXERCISE FOR CHAPTER 16

Make appropriate cuts.

Edit the following passage to eliminate any unnecessary material.

> With computer graphics imaging becoming more lifelike and realistic in today's society, filmmakers in the motion picture industry are now able to create animated characters who could conceivably take the place of human beings or people in leading roles onscreen. Nonliving stars are not a completely and totally unknown quantity, of course. Mickey Mouse and Bugs Bunny are cartoon characters who earned millions of fans in spite of the fact that they did not exist in the real world outside of an animation studio. King Kong, who was the first stop-motion animation star, thrilled and delighted audiences beginning in the decade of the 1930s because of the fact that he was believably realistic at that point in time. However, modern innovations in computer graphics make cartoons and stop-motion characters look quaint and dated. At the present time, filmmakers are

resolved and determined to create "synthespians" who will look, move, speak, and talk in such a realistic manner that audiences will be awed, and studios are enlisting animators with expertise and experience in computer graphics rather than traditional old-fashioned cartoonists to model the new breed of cyber-actors. Some film and movie critics are of the opinion that filmmakers are failing to grasp something vital and important, which is that audiences want genuine and honest emotion and creative storytelling rather than whiz-bang special effects and computer graphics. They argue that no computer-generated synthespian will ever really matter or be important to filmgoers unless his or her films are well written and well directed.

Chapter **17**

The Second C: Check for Action

"Check for action" means to convey to readers a clear sense of who (or what) is doing what. As a general rule, use vigorous sentences with vivid, expressive verbs. Avoid bland forms of the verb *be* (*be, am, is, are, was, were, being, been*) or verbs in the passive voice (see 25l).

17a Ask, "Who's doing what?" about subject and verb.

Wherever possible, let the subject of your sentence perform the action, and use expressive verbs. Ask these questions:

Who or what is doing the action?

Is it the subject of the clause?

If not, could it be and should it be?

Online Study Center This icon will direct you to quick reference tools, Web resources, and research guides on the Web site at http://college.hmco.com/keys.html.

WORDY

subject   verb
The mayor's approval of the new law was due to the voters' suspicion of concealment of campaign funds by his deputy.

This dull thud of a sentence uses the verb *was*, which conveys no sense of action. The subject of the verb is an abstract noun, *approval*—not exactly informative or interest-grabbing. The use of the weak verb *to be* leads to an excess of abstract nominalizations (nouns formed from verbs) and of prepositional phrases. The sentence contains three abstract nouns formed from verbs (*approval/approve, suspicion/suspect, and concealment/conceal*), as well as five prepositional phrases: *of the new law, due to voters' suspicion, of the concealment, of campaign funds,* and *by his deputy.* Asking "Who's doing what?" helps unpack the dense mass:

Who's Doing What?

Subject	Verb
the mayor	approved
the voters	suspected
his deputy	had concealed

REVISED

The mayor approved the new law because voters suspected that his deputy had concealed campaign funds.

Always put verbs to work to make a sentence strong.

celebrates
▶ **In Nicholson Baker's *The Mezzanine*, a long footnote** ~~is about~~ **the concept of perforation.**

See page 276 for an exercise on 17a.

17b Use caution in beginning a sentence with *there* or *it*.

For a lean, direct style, rewrite sentences in which *there* or *it* occupies the subject position (as in *there is, there were, it is, it was*). Revise by using verbs that describe an action and subjects that perform the action. Asking "Who's doing what?" helps here, too.

EXERCISE 17.1

Ask, "Who's doing what?"

Rewrite each of the following sentences using vivid, expressive verbs.

EXAMPLE:

    Can   *solve*

~~Are~~ genetically engineered pigs ~~a solution to~~ pressing environmental problems?

1. Factory hog farms are problematic due to the small quarters and their housing of thousands of pigs, with the resulting excretion of many tons of manure.

2. Contents of the manure include phosphorus and other chemicals that are pollutants of water supplies and cause harm to humans, fish, and wildlife.

3. Canadian researchers are the developers of a new strain of genetically engineered pig with lower phosphorus content in its manure.

4. The "Enviropig" is a delight to industrial pork producers but not to environmental groups, which are against genetic modification of foods.

5. The reduction of industrial hog-farming pollution is necessary, but the Enviropig is a technical solution while environmental groups are hoping for the end of the raising of hogs in small, enclosed areas by farmers.

WORDY	**There was a discussion of the health care system by the politicians.** [Who's doing what?]
REVISED	**The politicians discussed the health care system.**
WORDY	**There is a big gate guarding the entrance to the park.**
REVISED	**A big gate guards the entrance to the park.**
WORDY	**It is a fact that Arnold is proudly displaying a new tattoo.**
REVISED	**Arnold is proudly displaying a new tattoo.**

> **TECH NOTE**
>
> **Searching for Uses of *It* and *There***
>
> Use the Find function of your word processing program to find all instances in your draft of *it is/was*, *there is/are*, and *there was/were*. If you find a filler subject with little purpose, revise.

> **EXERCISE 17.2**
>
> **Revise sentences beginning with *there* or *it*.**
>
> Rewrite each sentence to eliminate *there* or *it* wherever possible.
>
> **EXAMPLE:**
>
> Families
> ~~There are families~~ known as "travelers" ~~who~~ live in mobile homes in̂ Ireland and lead nomadic lives.
>
> 1. It is traditional for some families in Ireland to travel from place to place instead of settling permanently in one location.
>
> 2. There are deep-seated prejudices among many Irish people against the traveler families.
>
> 3. Although most travelers share the Catholic faith and the Celtic background of the majority of Irish people, it is not unusual for travelers to face discrimination and accusations of thievery.
>
> 4. There have been instances in which parents have removed children from local schools after traveler children arrived.
>
> 5. There was a law instituted in Ireland requiring communities to begin providing water and other basic services to traveler populations by 2004, but few districts made plans to comply.

17c Avoid unnecessary passive voice constructions.

The *passive voice* tells what is done to the grammatical subject of a clause ("The turkey *was cooked* too long"). Extensive use of the passive voice makes your style dull and wordy. When you can, replace it with active voice verbs.

PASSIVE   **The problem will be discussed thoroughly by the committee.**

ACTIVE   **The committee will discuss the problem thoroughly.**

If you are studying in the social sciences or sciences, disciplines in which readers are primarily interested in procedures and results rather than who developed or produced them, you will find passive voice constructions are more common and more acceptable than in the humanities. For example, in lab reports and experiments, you will read *The rats were fed* instead of *The researchers fed the rats*. For acceptable uses of the passive voice, see 25l and 18a.

TECH NOTE

Using Grammar-Check Software

Grammar checkers will point out passive voice constructions. If you have a tendency to overuse the passive voice, use a grammar checker to alert yourself to the places that you can check. However, use the grammar checker only as a guide; programs sometimes identify structures wrongly. Use the grammar checker simply to send you back to your sentence to reread and check it.

EXERCISE 17.3

Avoid unnecessary passive voice constructions.

Rewrite any passive voice constructions in the active voice.

EXAMPLE:

     Poachers   wild animals
~~Wild animals~~ have ~~been~~ hunted ~~by poachers~~ in national parks all over the world.

1. In some wildlife preserves abroad, a radical new strategy has been adopted by conservationists.

2. Even in preserves that are supposed to be safe, many threatened wild species are either captured by poachers for the thriving black market in exotic pets or killed for their valuable body parts.

3. Poachers have been asked by wildlife organizations to use their knowledge of animals and animal habitats to contribute to wildlife preservation.

4. Many poachers have agreed to stop hunting endangered animals in exchange for a living wage and health benefits for themselves and their families; instead, information about the animals in the preserves is now collected by former poachers.

5. Local economies in poor areas near the preserves have long been supported by poaching, but with this new approach, local young people can see that working to support wildlife conservation is a better and safer way to earn a living than illegal poaching.

REVIEW EXERCISE FOR CHAPTER 17

Check for action.

Revise any sentences that could be made more vigorous.

Alzheimer's disease is a terrible affliction of the elderly in the United States and around the world. People are robbed by the disease of a lifetime of memories, and family members often care for patients who no longer recognize them. There can be years of round-the-clock care required to help an Alzheimer's patient, and such care is expensive. A heavy toll is taken on any stricken family by this disease.

However, there is hope offered by new research to those who fear that they may develop this illness. The rate of people affected by Alzheimer's in India is the lowest in the world, and scientists have been investigating possible reasons. The Indian diet is considered by some scientists to be an answer. There is a spice called curcumin that is common in Indian curries, and it is being tested by researchers as a possible preventive medicine. In one intriguing study, a diet rich in curcumin was fed to laboratory mice bred to develop brain defects similar to those produced by Alzheimer's, and the result was the development of fewer brain defects in the mice during the aging process. It is not yet known whether curcumin or other spices will help reduce the number of people developing Alzheimer's; if curcumin does prove to be effective, it will take some time for scientists to discover the reasons. Someday, perhaps, there will be a currently unknown property of curcumin found by researchers that will reveal a solution to the puzzle of Alzheimer's.

Chapter **18**

The Third C: Connect

In coherent pieces of writing, information that has been mentioned before is linked to new information in a smooth flow, not in a series of grasshopper-like jumps. Connect ideas clearly for maximum coherence.

Online Study Center   This icon will direct you to quick reference tools, Web resources, and research guides on the Web site at http://college.hmco.com/keys.html.

18a Use consistent subjects and topic chains for coherence.

Readers expect to be able to connect the ideas beginning a sentence with what they have already read. From one sentence to the next, avoid jarring and unnecessary shifts from one subject to another. Let your subjects form a topic chain.

JARRING SHIFT *Memoirs* **frequently top the bestseller list.** *Readers* **of all ages are finding them appealing.**

TOPIC CHAIN *Memoirs* **frequently top the bestseller list.** *They* **appeal to readers of all ages.**

In the revised version, the subject of the second sentence, *they*, refers to the subject of the previous sentence, *memoirs*; the new information about "readers of all ages" comes at the end, where it receives more emphasis (18b).

Examine your writing for awkward topic switches. Note that constructing a topic chain may mean using the passive voice, as in the last sentence of the revision that follows:

FREQUENT TOPIC SWITCHES *I* **have lived all my life in Brooklyn, New York.** *Park Slope* **is a neighborhood that has many different ethnic cultures.** *Harmony* **exists among the people there, even though it does not in many other Brooklyn neighborhoods.** *Several articles in the press* **have praised the Slope for its ethnic variety.**

REVISED WITH TOPIC CHAIN *Many different ethnic cultures* **flourish in Park Slope, Brooklyn, where I have lived all my life.** *These different cultures* **live together harmoniously there, even though they do not in many other Brooklyn neighborhoods. In fact,** *the ethnic variety* **of the Slope has often been praised in the press.**

EXERCISE 18.1
Use consistent subjects and topic chains.
Revise the following passage to avoid jarring and unnecessary shifts from one subject to another.

EXAMPLE:

Meiyuan Ding won the heavyweight division of the first Olympic

She competed in the summer 2000 Olympic Games in

women's weightlifting competition. Sydney, Australia hosted the

Olympic Games where this event took place in the summer of 2000.

Weightlifter Cheryl Haworth hails from Savannah, Georgia. The bronze medal in the 75-kilograms-and-up class in women's weightlifting at the 2000 summer Olympics went to Haworth. Many people were surprised that the sixteen-year-old Haworth, who weighs 290 pounds and stands five feet nine inches tall, could be an Olympic medalist. Weighing more makes lifting heavier weights possible, so in this sport, size is actually an asset. The former American women's record fell when Haworth lifted 125 kilograms over her head, a weight she had never attempted to lift before the Olympic games. The combined total of the weights lifted for the bronze medal in the snatch and the clean and jerk competitions was 270 kilograms, nearly 600 pounds. Having a large body may not be every person's dream, but Haworth's being the third-strongest woman in the world is proof that bigger is sometimes better.

18b Place information at the end of a sentence for emphasis.

If you form a topic chain of old information, new information will come at the end of a sentence. Make your sentences end on a strong and interesting note, one that you want to emphasize. This technique helps keep your ideas flowing smoothly. Don't let a sentence trail off weakly.

WEAK ENDING	**Women often feel silenced by men, according to one researcher.**
REVISED	**According to one researcher, women often feel silenced by men.**

WEAK ENDING	**Odysseus encounters Calypso, who tempts him with immortality, after he has resisted the Sirens.**
REVISED	**After resisting the Sirens, Odysseus encounters Calypso, who tempts him with immortality.**

Cumulative and periodic sentences Cumulative (or loose) sentences begin with the independent clause and add on to it. Periodic sentences begin with words and phrases that lead to the independent clause, giving it more impact. The cumulative sentence is the norm in English prose. Use a periodic sentence to make a specific impact.

CUMULATIVE *The experienced hunter stood stock-still for at least five minutes,* **sweat pouring from his brow, all senses alert, waiting to hear a twig snap.**

PERIODIC **Sweat pouring from his brow, all senses alert, waiting to hear a twig snap,** *the experienced hunter stood stock-still for at least five minutes.*

EXERCISE 18.2

Emphasize information.

Revise the following sentences as needed to emphasize the important information.

EXAMPLE:

According to a 1997 study, the
~~The~~ human sleep cycle can be disrupted after many weeks in
⊙
space, ~~according to a 1997 study.~~

1. Human beings follow circadian rhythms that regulate the body according to a twenty-four-hour schedule under normal circumstances.

2. In 1997, an American astronaut at the Mir space station measured his own body temperature and recorded his level of alertness and the amount and quality of his sleep in order to research the effect on the body of months in space.

3. The temperature of the human body normally falls when a person sleeps and rises again just before the person wakes, as sleep researchers have known for years.

4. However, after four months in space, the American astronaut's body temperature remained the same at all times, he was not sleepy at bedtime, and he woke often and rarely dreamed, the astronaut found.

5. Space travelers may need to find a way to trick their bodies into retaining circadian rhythms, say the creators of the astronaut study.

18c Explore options for connecting ideas: Coordination, subordination, and transitions.

When you write sentences containing two or more clauses (21e), consider where you want to place the emphasis. Decide whether to give each clause equal weight or to subordinate one or more ideas in a complex sentence (see 21f).

Coordination   You are giving two or more clauses equal emphasis when you connect them with a coordinating conjunction—*and, but, or, nor, so, for,* or *yet* (see 21a). (For more on clauses, see 21e and 21f.)

┌── independent clause ──┐ ┌── independent clause ──
▶ **The bus trip was long, and the seats seemed more**

uncomfortable with every mile.

┌── independent clause ──┐ ┌── independent clause ──┐
▶ **The bus trip was long, but we managed to enjoy it.**

Subordination   When you use subordinating conjunctions (21e) such as *when, if,* or *because* to connect clauses, you give one idea more importance by putting it in the independent clause.

▶ **Brillo pads work well. I don't give them as gifts.** [Two independent clauses: equal importance]

┌────── dependent clause ──────┐ ┌── independent clause ──┐
▶ **Although Brillo pads work well, I don't give them as gifts.**

[The focus is on the notion of what makes a suitable gift.]

Note how subordinating a different idea can change meaning and emphasis: *Although I don't give Brillo pads as gifts, they work well.*

▶ **We cannot now end our differences. At least we can help make the world safe for diversity.** [Two independent clauses: statements of equal importance]

▶ **If we cannot now end our differences, at least we can help**
┌────── independent clause ──────┐
make the world safe for diversity.   —John F. Kennedy

[Dependent clause begins with *If,* setting up a condition under which the independent clause holds true]

Transitional expressions Use words such as *however, therefore,* and *nevertheless* (known as *conjunctive adverbs;* see 21a) and phrases such as *as a result, in addition,* and *on the other hand* after a semicolon to signal the logical connection between independent clauses (for a list of transitional expressions, see 5e). A transitional expression also can move around in its own clause—yet another stylistic option for you to consider.

▶ He made a lot of money; however, his humble roots were always evident.

▶ He made a lot of money; his humble roots, however, were always evident.

▶ He made a lot of money; his humble roots were always evident, however.

The Key Points box summarizes the available connecting options.

KEY POINTS

Options for Connecting Clauses

Purpose	Coordinating Conjunction	Transitional Expression	Subordinating Conjunction
addition	and	also, further, furthermore, moreover, in addition	
contrast	but, yet	however, nevertheless, on the other hand	although, even though, whereas, while
alternative	or, nor	instead, otherwise, alternatively	unless
result	so, for	therefore, as a result, hence, consequently, thus, accordingly, then	because, as, since, so/such that, now that, once

The following examples illustrate how the options may work.

▶ I often use parking meters. I have never seen the Department of Transportation emptying them.

▶ I often use parking meters, but I have never seen the Department of Transportation emptying them.

▶ Although I often use parking meters, I have never seen the Department of Transportation emptying them.

▶ I often use parking meters; however, I have never seen the Department of Transportation emptying them.

▶ I often use parking meters; I have, however, never seen the Department of Transportation emptying them.

Make your choice by deciding what you want to emphasize and seeing what structures you used in nearby sentences. If, for example, you used *however* in the immediately preceding sentence, choose some other option for expressing contrasting ideas.

Avoiding excessive coordination or subordination   Too much of any one stylistic feature will become tedious to readers.

EXCESSIVE COORDINATION WITH *AND*	I grew up in a large family, and we lived on a small farm, and every day I had to get up early and do farm work, and I would spend a lot of time cleaning out the stables, and then I would be exhausted in the evening, and I never had the energy to read.
REVISED	Because I grew up in a large family on a small farm, every day I had to get up early to do farm work, mostly cleaning out the stables. I would be so exhausted in the evening that I never had the energy to read.
EXCESSIVE SUBORDINATION	Because the report was weak and poorly written, our boss, who wanted to impress the company president by showing her how efficient his division was, to gain prestige in the company, decided, despite the fact that work projects were piling up, that he would rewrite the report over the weekend.
REVISED	Because the report was weak and poorly written, our boss decided to rewrite it over the weekend, even though work projects were piling up. He wanted to impress the company president by showing her how efficient his division was; that was his way of gaining prestige.

EXERCISE 18.3

Use different options for connecting ideas.

In each of the following sentences, rewrite the two independent clauses as a single sentence, giving the information appropriate emphasis by using coordination, subordination, or a transitional expression. Then identify the method that you used.

EXAMPLE:

Environmental groups have often portrayed American Indians

as conservationists. ~~Some~~ *, but some* tribes feel that such portrayals are simplistic and culturally insensitive. [coordination]

1. Environmentalists believe that drilling for oil in the Arctic National Wildlife Refuge would damage a wilderness area. They have also cast drilling for oil as a human rights issue.
2. The Gwich'in Indians rely on a caribou herd in the wildlife refuge. Drilling for oil on the caribou's calving ground could disrupt the herd and the tribe's way of life.
3. The Gwich'in are not categorically opposed to oil drilling on tribal lands. They have permitted an oil company to drill on their lands in Canada.
4. Many tribes around the United States have turned to allowing drilling for oil and gas, gambling, and even nuclear waste storage on their reservations in an effort to achieve economic independence. The Gwich'in are not alone in trying to use their land to make money.
5. The view of American Indians as stewards of the land may be based more on myth than on fact. Some feel that this view denies natives a place in the modern world.

EXERCISE 18.4

Avoid excessive coordination or subordination.

Eliminate excessive coordination or subordination.

EXAMPLE:

Isadora Duncan may have been one of the most riveting dancers

in the world, but she never allowed anyone to film ~~her, so~~ *her. Therefore,* dance historians must rely on still photographs of her dancing~~, and~~

these can only offer tantalizing hints of what it must have been like to see her perform.

1. Isadora Duncan developed modern dance and inspired early-twentieth-century audiences around the world with her riveting performances, and she continues to be an iconic figure.

2. Duncan came from a poor San Francisco family, but everyone in it was apparently convinced of Isadora's genius from her girlhood on, so when she was eighteen, she and her mother traveled east, and she worked briefly in theater before deciding that her talents lay in dance; by the time she was twenty-one, she had achieved some fame in New York and in New England by performing before wealthy and influential people, but after a hotel fire, the Duncans decided to travel to Europe, where Isadora soon achieved a reputation as one of the most exciting and charismatic figures on the stage.

3. Photographs of Duncan's performances indicate that she maintained an expressionless face so that audiences would pay attention to the movement of her hands, arms, legs, and feet, which she usually kept bare, and she did not leap high in the air, as a ballet dancer might, but instead used the floor a great deal, and her costumes were usually scanty and sometimes even shocking, although in general, audiences adored her.

4. Duncan had no love for ballet, which she once described as "living death," yet her arrival in St. Petersburg in 1904 greatly influenced the young Russian ballet choreographer Michel Fokine, and Russian ballet audiences loved Duncan as much as European dance fans had.

5. Many people who know little and care less about modern dance have still heard of Duncan, who lived a flamboyant life, having many passionate affairs with great and near-great men, in addition to losing her two children in a tragic automobile accident, and her bizarre death remains one of the most noteworthy facts about her since she was strangled when the long scarf she was wearing became entangled in the wheel of the sports car in which she was riding.

18d Perhaps begin a sentence with *and* or *but*.

Sometimes writers choose to start a sentence with *and* or *but*, either for stylistic effect or to make a close connection to a previous, already long sentence:

> ▶ **You can have wealth concentrated in the hands of a few, or democracy. But you cannot have both.**
>
> —Justice Louis Brandeis

People who consider *and* and *but* conjunctions to be used to join two or more independent clauses within a sentence may frown when they see these words starting a sentence. Nevertheless, examples of this usage can be found in literature from the tenth century onward, and sentences of this type occur in formal and academic writing. As with any stylistic device, it is wise not to use *and* or *but* too often at the beginning of sentences. And, given the difference of opinion on this usage, checking with your instructor may be a good idea, too.

18e Connect paragraphs.

Just as readers appreciate a smooth flow of information from sentence to sentence, they also look for transitions—word bridges—to move them from paragraph to paragraph. A new paragraph signals a shift in topic, but careful readers will look for transitional words and phrases that tell them *how* a new paragraph relates to the paragraph that precedes it. Provide readers with steppingstones; don't ask them to leap over chasms.

KEY POINTS
A Checklist for Connecting Paragraphs

- ☐ Read your draft aloud. When you finish a paragraph, make a note of the point you made in the paragraph. Then, check your notes for the flow of ideas and logic.

- ☐ Refer to the main idea of the previous paragraph as you begin a new paragraph. After a paragraph on retirement, the next paragraph could begin like this, moving from the idea of retirement to saving: *Retirement is not the only reason for saving. Saving also provides a nest egg for the unexpected and the pleasurable.*

- ☐ Use adjectives like *this* and *these* to provide a link. After a paragraph discussing urban planning proposals, the next paragraph might begin like this: *These proposals will help. However, . . .*

- ☐ Use transition words such as *also, too, in addition, however, therefore,* and *as a result* to signal the logical connection between ideas (5e).

REVIEW EXERCISE FOR CHAPTER 18

Make connections.

Revise the following passage to improve connections between ideas. As necessary, improve topic chains; add emphasis; include coordination, subordination, and transitions; eliminate excessive use of coordination and subordination; and connect paragraphs.

The Taliban rulers of Afghanistan fell from power in the fall of 2001. An interim government was formed to rule the war-torn country, and under the Taliban, the law had forbidden women to hold jobs, reveal their faces in public, or speak to men other than their relatives, and the interim government included a department devoted to women's affairs in a sign that times had changed in Afghanistan. Dr. Sima Samar was chosen as the minister for women's affairs. Dr. Samar earned a medical degree from Kabul University. Dr. Samar had spent years working from exile and from within Afghanistan to improve the conditions for women in her native country.

Dr. Samar had practiced medicine in refugee camps in Pakistan. She had helped to set up clinics and schools for women and girls inside Afghanistan, traveling frequently between Pakistan and her homeland. She was breaking Taliban law by giving women access to medical services and education. She believed that her work was worth the risk. "I've always been in danger, but I don't mind," she said in a BBC interview in December 2001.

Dr. Samar did not anticipate problems with any of the men who would work under her as she took her new post in the ministry for women's affairs. She told a reporter for the *New York Times* that she had goals for the ministry, and she expected the men working for her to help achieve the goals, and those goals included making sure that each woman in Afghanistan had "access to education, the right to vote, the right to go to work, to choose her spouse. All those things are the basic rights of human beings." Offering Afghan women even those basic rights after decades of war would be a difficult task for anyone. Dr. Samar did not turn away from the responsibility of ensuring women those rights when she was asked to serve her country through its interim government.

Chapter **19**

The Fourth C: Commit

Readers of academic prose in English usually expect writers to commit to an informed and interesting point of view (not necessarily to the dominant view) and to provide convincing reasons why that view is valid. For writers, commitment means researching and considering an issue, taking a position, and persuasively supporting that position (7a–7g). It means committing to a point of view and using an appropriate tone so that readers feel they know what the writer's views are and where they come from. Readers want to feel they are in reliable hands.

According to E. B. White, his coauthor on *The Elements of Style,* William Strunk, Jr., "scorned the vague, the tame, the colorless, the irresolute. He felt it was worse to be irresolute than to be wrong." This chapter focuses on ways to be bold and resolute.

19a Commit to a point of view.

Your background reading, critical thinking, and drafting will help you discover and decide upon a perspective and thesis that seem correct to you (3g). Once you have made those decisions, commit to that point of view in your essay. When you are trying to persuade readers to accept your point of view, avoid the ambivalence and indecisiveness evident in words and phrases like *maybe, perhaps, it could be, it might seem,* and *it would appear.* Aim for language that reflects accountability and commitment: *as a result, consequently, believe, need, must.* Use the language of commitment, however, only after thoroughly researching your topic and satisfying yourself that your evidence is reliable and thorough and its presentation is convincing.

19b Commit to an appropriate tone.

Readers will expect the tone of your document to fit its purpose. The tone of your piece of writing reflects your attitude toward your subject matter and is closely connected to your audience's expectations and your purpose in writing. If you were, for example, writing about a topic such as compensation for posttraumatic stress disorder suffered by families of victims of the World Trade Center attack on September 11, 2001, a serious, respectful tone would be appropriate.

For most academic writing, commit to an objective, serious tone, one that does not intrude upon the reader and take attention away from the ideas you are presenting. Avoid sarcasm, colloquial language, name-calling, or pedantic words and structures, even in the name of variety. Make sure you assign a special reading of a draft to the task of examining your tone; if you are reading along and a word or sentence strikes you as being unexpected and out of place, flag it for later. Since tone is really a function of how you anticipate readers' expectations, ask a tutor or friend to read your document and note for you any lapses in consistency of tone.

19c Commit to a confident stance.

Convey to readers an attitude of confidence in your own abilities and judgment. Readers will not be impressed by apologies. One student ended an essay draft this way:

TOO
APOLOGETIC
I hope I have conveyed something about our cultural differences. I would like my reader to note that this is just my view, even if a unique one. Room for errors and prejudices should be provided. The lack of a total overview, which would take more time and expertise, should also be taken into account.

If you really have not done an adequate job of making and supporting a point, try to gather more information to improve the draft instead of adding apologetic notes. The student writer revised the ending after reading 5f, on conclusions.

REVISED
VERSION
The stories I have told and the examples I have given come from my own experience; however, my multicultural background has emphasized that cultural differences do not have to separate people but can instead bring them closer together. A diverse, multicultural society holds many potential benefits for all its members.

EXERCISE 19.1

Commit to a point of view and a confident stance.

In the following passage, underline places where you would advise the writer to consider revising to reflect a clear point of view, an appropriate tone, and a confident stance. Revise any of the sentences that seem too ambivalent or apologetic.

EXAMPLE:

EBay ~~seems to provide~~ *provides* the kind of online community many

people want~~; of course, this is only one option.~~ ⊙

1. The end of the dot-com boom drove many online companies out of business, but I believe that eBay, the online auction service, continued to thrive.

2. Although there may not be any concrete evidence to prove this, it could be that online shoppers could still feel that they were getting a bargain when they bid on eBay's merchandise.

3. Tough economic times did not stop me from bidding for items on eBay, but others might have had different experiences.

4. As a way of explaining eBay's popularity, writer Verlyn Klinkenborg argues that it would seem that eBay buyers and sellers love the idea of giving and getting feedback about transactions.

5. EBay's feedback system helps to make the transactions safe, but the real thrill of eBay, at least in some cases such as my own, might perhaps be the feeling shared by buyer and seller that each has gotten the best deal.

19d Commit to sentence variety.

Length   Readers appreciate variety, so revise for a mix of long and short sentences. If your word processing program can print out your text in a series of single numbered sentences, you will easily be able to examine the length and structure of each sentence. Academic writing need not consist solely of long, heavyweight sentences. Short sentences interspersed among longer ones can have a dramatic effect.

This passage from a student memoir demonstrates the use of short sentences to great effect:

> When I started high school and Afros became the rage, I immediately decided to get one. Now at that time, I had a head full of long, thick, kinky hair, which my mother had cultivated for years. When she said to me, "Cut it or perm it," she never for one minute believed I would do either. I cut it. She fainted.
>
> —Denise Dejean, student

Inverted word order   Sometimes, inverted word order—switching from the usual subject (S) + verb (V) order to verb + subject—will help you stylistically to achieve coherence, consistent subjects, emphasis, or a smooth transition:

► Next to the river runs a superhighway.

► Never have I been so tired.

► Not only does the novel entertain, but it also raises our awareness of poverty.

► So eager was I to win that I set off before the starter's gun.

► Rarely has a poem achieved such a grasp on the times.

Using an occasional rhetorical question will also help drive a point home:

► How could anyone have thought that war was the answer?

Sentence beginnings   Consider using some of the following variations to begin a sentence, but remember that beginning with the subject will always be clear and direct for readers. Any of these beginnings repeated too often will seem like a stylistic tic and will annoy or bore readers.

Begin with a *dependent clause* or a *condensed clause.*

dependent clause

► While my friends were waiting for the movie to begin, they ate three tubs of popcorn.

clause condensed to a phrase

► While waiting for the movie to begin, my friends ate three tubs of popcorn.

Begin with a *participle* or an *adjective*. A sentence can begin with a participle or an adjective only if the word is in a phrase that refers to the subject of the independent clause. If the word does not refer to the subject, the result is a *dangling modifier* error (24c).

-ing present participle
▶ **Waiting for the movie to begin, my friends ate popcorn.**

past participle
▶ **Forced to work late, they ordered a pepperoni pizza.**

adjective
▶ **Aware of the problems, they nevertheless decided to continue.**

Begin with a *prepositional phrase*.

┌ prepositional phrase ┐
▶ **With immense joy, we watched our team win the pennant.**

You can also occasionally use inverted word order after a prepositional phrase for stylistic flow.

┌── prepositional phrase ──┐   verb   ┌─── subject ───┐
▶ **At the end of my block stands a deserted building.**

For more on sentences, see chapter 21.

EXERCISE 19.2
Commit to sentence variety.

Select a piece of your own writing. Using your word processing program, print out your text in a series of single numbered sentences. Examine the length, word order, and sentence beginnings, and consider how they might be revised for greater effect.

Chapter **20**

The Fifth C: Choose the Best Words

Word choice, or *diction*, contributes a great deal to the effect your writing has on readers. Do not give readers puzzles to solve.

20a Word choice checklist

KEY POINTS
Word Choice: A Checklist for Revision

☐ Underline words whose meaning or spelling you want to check and words that you might want to replace. Then spend some time with a dictionary and a thesaurus. (20b)

☐ Look for words that might not convey exactly what you mean (*thrifty* versus *stingy*, for example) or fit your audience's expectations, and look for vague words. (20c)

☐ Check for the appropriateness of any colloquial, regional, ethnic, or specialized work terms. (20d)

☐ Check figurative language for appropriateness, think about where a simile (a comparison) might help convey your meaning, and find original substitutes for any clichés. (20e, 20g)

☐ Check for gender bias in your use of *he* and *she* and other words that show gender. (20f)

☐ Look for language that might exclude or offend (such as *normal* to mean people similar to you). Build community with readers by eliminating disrespectful or stereotyping terms referring to race, place, age, politics, religion, abilities, or sexual orientation. (20f)

20b Use a dictionary and a thesaurus.

A good dictionary contains a wealth of information—spelling and definitions, syllable breaks, pronunciation, grammatical functions and features, word forms, etymology (word origins and historical development), usage, synonyms (words of similar meaning), and antonyms (words of opposite meaning). The following dictionary entry from *The American Heritage Dictionary of the English Language,* 4th edition, shows how much information is available. A "Usage Note" after this entry endorses using "She graduated from Yale in 1998" but notes that "She graduated Yale in 1998" was unacceptable to 77 percent of a usage panel.

Online Study Center   This icon will direct you to quick reference tools, Web resources, and research guides on the Web site at http://college.hmco.com/keys.html.

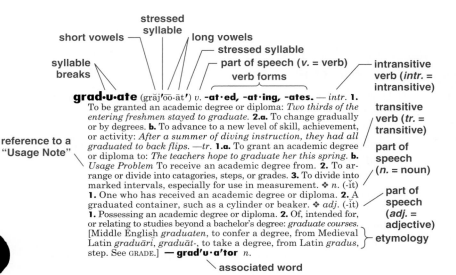

short vowels
stressed syllable
long vowels
stressed syllable
part of speech (*v.* = verb)
verb forms
syllable breaks
intransitive verb (*intr.* = intransitive)

grad•u•ate (grăj′oo-āt′) *v.* **-at·ed, -at·ing, -ates.** — *intr.* **1.** To be granted an academic degree or diploma: *Two thirds of the entering freshmen stayed to graduate.* **2.a.** To change gradually or by degrees. **b.** To advance to a new level of skill, achievement, or activity: *After a summer of diving instruction, they had all graduated to back flips.* —*tr.* **1.a.** To grant an academic degree or diploma to: *The teachers hope to graduate her this spring.* **b.** *Usage Problem* To receive an academic degree from. **2.** To arrange or divide into catagories, steps, or grades. **3.** To divide into marked intervals, especially for use in measurement. ❖ *n.* (-ĭt) **1.** One who has received an academic degree or diploma. **2.** A graduated container, such as a cylinder or beaker. ❖ *adj.* (-ĭt) **1.** Possessing an academic degree or diploma. **2.** Of, intended for, or relating to studies beyond a bachelor's degree: *graduate courses.* [Middle English *graduaten*, to confer a degree, from Medieval Latin *graduāri*, *graduāt-*, to take a degree, from Latin *gradus*, step. See GRADE.] — **grad′u·a′tor** *n.*

reference to a "Usage Note"

transitive verb (*tr.* = transitive)
part of speech (*n.* = noun)
part of speech (*adj.* = adjective)
etymology
associated word

Use a dictionary to learn or confirm the *denotation*—the basic meaning—of a word. Some words that appear similar are not interchangeable. For example, *respectable* has a meaning very different from *respectful; emigrant* and *immigrant* have different meanings; and so do *defuse* and *diffuse, uninterested* and *disinterested,* and *principal* and *principle.* Also see section 38g on words frequently misspelled.

A thesaurus is useful when you want to find alternatives to words that you know. Exercise caution, however, to make sure that the word you choose fits your context. Suppose you use the word *privacy* a few times and want an alternative in the sentence "She values the privacy of her own home." You could consult a thesaurus. The following entry, from Barbara Ann Kipfer, *Roget's Twenty-first Century Thesaurus,* provides synonyms listed alphabetically:

> **privacy** *n.* aloofness, clandestineness, concealment, confidentiality, isolation, one's space, penetralia, privateness, quiet, retirement, retreat, seclusion, separateness, separation, sequestration, solitude.

The word *aloofness* would not work as a replacement for *privacy* in the example sentence. *Seclusion* would probably be the best choice, but the thesaurus has no way of letting you know that. Using a thesaurus along with a dictionary allows you to find the exact word or words you need. You might, in the end, want to use two words to convey your meaning: "She values the *safety* and *seclusion* of her own home."

Thesaurus programs attached to word processing programs typically offer lists of synonyms but little guidance on *connotation*—the meaning associated with a word beyond its literal definition.

 EXERCISE 20.1
Use the dictionary.

Look up one of the following pairs of words in a comprehensive dictionary and in a thesaurus. Write a paragraph about what you learn. Report results to classmates.

uninterested, disinterested	proceed, precede
beside, besides	denote, connote
comprise, compose	carry, convey

20c Use exact words and connotations.

When you write, use words that convey exactly the meaning you intend at the appropriate level of specificity and that meet readers' expectations of tone and level of formality.

Check for connotation. Two words that have similar dictionary definitions (*denotation*) can also have additional positive or negative implications and emotional overtones (*connotation*). Readers will not get the impression you intend if you describe a person as *lazy* when you mean *relaxed*. Select words with appropriate connotations. Hurricanes *devastate* neighborhoods; construction workers *demolish* buildings. Writing "Construction workers devastated the building" would be inappropriate. Note how word choice can affect meaning:

VERSION 1   **The crowd consisted of young couples holding their children's hands, students in well-worn clothes, and activist politicians, all voicing support of their cause.**

VERSION 2   **The mob consisted of hard-faced workers dragging children by the hand, students in leather jackets and ragged jeans, and militant politicians, all howling about their cause.**

Make sure words convey specific meaning. Notice the increasing concreteness and specificity in this list: *tool, cutting instrument, knife, penknife. Tool* is a general term; *penknife* is a specific term. Some words do little more than fill space because they are so abstract, general, and vague. Words such as the following signal the need for revision: *area, aspect, certain, circumstance, factor, kind, manner, nature, situation, thing.*

VAGUE
> Our perceptions of women's roles differ as we enter new *areas*. The girl in Kincaid's story did many *things* that are commonly seen as women's work.

REVISED
> Our perceptions of women's roles differ as we learn more from what we *see, hear, read, and experience*. The girl in Kincaid's story did many *household chores* that are commonly seen as women's work. She *washed the clothes, cooked, swept the floor, and set the table.*

If you do not move away from the general and abstract, you will give readers too much imaginative leeway. "Her grandmother was shocked by the clothing she bought" leaves a great deal to readers' imaginations. What kind of clothing do you mean: a low-necked dress, high-heeled platform

shoes, and black fishnet stockings, or a conservative navy blue wool suit? Choose words that convey exact images and precise information.

Check that your words fit the tone of your document. Word choice conveys tone (see also 2d and 19c) as well as connotation and specificity. Note how the synonyms listed here convey different attitudes and varying degrees of formality:

child: kid, offspring, progeny

friend: dog, peeps, buddy, brother/sister, comrade

jail: slammer, cooler, prison, correctional institution

angry: ticked off, furious, mad, fuming, wrathful

computer expert: geek, hacker, techie, programmer

threatening: spooky, scary, eerie, menacing

fine: rad, phat, dope, fly, cool, first-rate, excellent

Some of these words—*kid, peeps, slammer, ticked off, geek, spooky, cool*—are so informal that they would rarely if ever be appropriate in formal academic writing or business letters, though they would raise few eyebrows in journalism, advertising, or e-mail. Overuse of formal words—*progeny, comrade, wrathful*—on the other hand, could produce a tone that suggests a stuffy, pedantic attitude (see 20g).

EXERCISE 20.2

Use exact words and connotations.

Write revisions of the following sentences, changing any words that are inexact or that have inappropriate connotations.

EXAMPLE:

American adults today are more likely than their parents were at

the same age to have their own ~~choppers~~.
                                     teeth

1. Better tooth care and fluoridated water are two of the reasons for falling rates of toothlessness among old people in North America.

2. Nutrition also plays a part in whether people hang on to their own teeth as they age.

3. The rate of toothlessness deviates from state to state, with Hawaii having the lowest rate of toothlessness among the elderly and West Virginia having the highest.

4. Rates of indigence—which can affect nutrition and dental care—and of smoking are probable reasons for these state-by-state variations in toothlessness.

5. Those who are better educated are also more likely to have their own teeth later in life, probably because education influences things like earnings.

20d Monitor the language of speech, region, and workplace.

The language of speech   In a formal college essay, avoid colloquial language and slang. Do not enclose a slang expression in quotation marks to signal to readers that you know it is inappropriate. Instead, revise to reach an appropriate level of formality.

> *inhumane.*
> ▶ The working conditions were "~~gross.~~"

> *affects me powerfully*
> ▶ The sound of sirens ~~gets to me.~~

> *defendant*
> ▶ The jury returned the verdict that the ~~guy~~ was guilty.

In formal writing, avoid colloquial words and expressions such as *folks, guy, OK or okay, pretty good, cool, hassle, kind of interesting/nice, too serious of a problem* (*of* here is nonstandard), *a lot of, lots of, a ways away,* and *no-brainer.*

Regional and ethnic language   Use regional and ethnic dialects in your writing only when you are quoting someone directly (*"Your car needs fixed," the mechanic muttered.*) or you know that readers will understand why you are using a nonstandard phrase.

> *myself*
> ▶ I bought ~~me~~ a camcorder.

> *any attention*
> ▶ He vowed that he wouldn't pay them ~~no never mind.~~

> *have been*
> ▶ They'~~re~~ here three years already.

> *be able to*
> ▶ She used to ~~could~~ run two miles, but now she's out of shape.

The language of the workplace   People engaged in most areas of specialized work and study use technical words that outsiders perceive as jargon. A sportswriter writing about baseball will refer to *balks, twi-night double-headers, ERA, brushbacks,* and *sliders.* A linguist writing about language for an audience of linguists will use terms like *phonemics, sociolinguistics, semantics, kinesics,* and *suprasegmentals.* If you know that your audience is familiar with the technical vocabulary of a field, specialized language is acceptable. Avoid jargon when writing for a more general audience; if you must use technical terms, provide definitions that will make sense to your audience.

LANGUAGE AND CULTURE
Dialect and Dialogue in Formal Writing

Note how Paule Marshall uses Standard English for the narrative thread of her story while reproducing the father's Barbadian dialect and idioms in the dialogue, thus combining the formal and the informal, the academic and the personal into a rich whole:

> She should have leaped up and pirouetted and joined his happiness. But a strange uneasiness kept her seated with her knees drawn tight against her chest. She asked cautiously, "You mean we're rich?"
> "We ain rich but we got land."
> "Is it a lot?"
> "Two acres almost. I know the piece of ground good. You could throw down I-don-know-what on it and it would grow. And we gon have a house there—just like the white people own. A house to end all house!"
> "Are you gonna tell Mother?"
> His smile faltered and failed; his eyes closed in a kind of weariness. "How you mean? I got to tell she, nuh."
> "Whaddya think she's gonna say?"
> "How I could know? Years back I could tell but not any more."
> She turned away from the pain darkening his eyes.
>
> —Paule Marshall, *Brown Girl, Brownstones*

EXERCISE 20.3
Monitor word choices.

Revise the following sentences to eliminate inappropriately colloquial language, regional or community dialect, non-Standard English, or workplace jargon. Some sentences may not need revision.

EXAMPLE:

Organic farmers have ~~a rough time~~ difficulty protecting their corn crops from genetic contamination by corn ~~produced through bioengineering~~ that has been genetically modified because corn is open-pollinating, wind and insects carry pollen from one plant to other plants that can be miles away.

1. A common agricultural genetic modification introduces *Bacillus thurengensis* into corn plants.

2. These bacteria bump off caterpillars; the bacteria, also called *Bt*, are sometimes spread on organic corn plants to rid them of corn borers and other destructive insects.

3. Organic farmers have been testing their corn crops for the presence of genetic modifications, and many of these guys are discovering that their crops have been contaminated by genetically modified corn grown up the road.

4. Some farmers are getting stuck with unsold corn, and others are selling it on the open market for less than half the price they would have gotten for a purely organic crop.

5. The problem of cross-pollination of genetically modified corn with organic corn—known as "genetic drift"—troubles many nonfarmers as well.

6. A lot of other countries buy organic produce from the United States, and few of them countries allow genetically modified foods to cross their borders.

7. If genetically modified corn can contaminate organic corn naturally, pretty soon there won't be hardly any corn without genetic modifications, and exports of American corn will be greatly reduced.

8. Genetic drift also bugs people who believe that maintaining crops' genetic diversity is important to avoid massive crop failures caused by disease and pests.

9. Most of the dozens of unique corn types found in the world come from Central America.

10. Genetic drift has gotten to lots of the unique corn types in parts of Mexico that scientists have studied, and some folks fear that eventually there will be no untainted corn.

20e Use figurative language for effect, but use it sparingly.

Figures of speech can enhance your writing and add to imaginative descriptions, as in the following examples:

▶ [Tiger] Woods protects three-stroke leads like a miser protecting the combination to his safe.

—Clifton Brown, "A Challenge Becomes a Coronation"

Particularly useful are similes, analogies, and metaphors. A *simile* is a comparison in which both sides are stated explicitly and linked by the word *like* or *as*. A *metaphor* is an implied comparison in which the two sides are indirectly compared.

Simile: an explicit comparison with both sides stated

▶ America is *not like a blanket*—one piece of unbroken cloth, the same color, the same texture, the same size. America is more *like a quilt*—many pieces, many colors, many sizes, all woven and held together by a common thread.

—Rev. Jesse Jackson

▶ [Matt Drudge] is *like a kind of digital Robin Hood* among a corrupt and venal press.

—Joshua Quittner

▶ I hate and mistrust pronouns, every one of them *as slippery as a fly-by-night personal-injury lawyer*.

—Stephen King

Metaphor: an implied comparison, without *like* or *as*

▶ A foolish consistency is the hobgoblin of little minds.

—Ralph Waldo Emerson

▶ Some television programs are so much chewing gum for the eyes.

—John Mason Brown

Mixed metaphors   Take care not to mix metaphors.

▶ As she walked onto the tennis court, she was ready to sink or swim. [Swimming on a tennis court?]

▶ He is a snake in the grass with his head in the clouds. [The two metaphors clash.]

▶ **He was a whirlwind of activity, trumpeting defiance whenever anyone crossed swords with any of his ideas.** [The three metaphors—*whirlwind, trumpet, crossed swords*—obscure rather than illuminate.]

Be careful not to overdo figurative language so that it becomes tedious and contrived. For more on figurative language in literature, see 8e.

EXERCISE 20.4

Use figurative language appropriately.

Revise any of the following items that contain mixed metaphors or other inappropriate figurative language. Some sentences may not need revision.

EXAMPLE:

Grade inflation may have begun as a ~~salve to~~ students' self-esteem, but some professors believe that it has now become ~~a~~ ~~tidal wave.~~

[above "salve to":] way to promote

[below:] a self-perpetuating force.

1. Dr. Harvey C. Mansfield, a professor at Harvard University, argued that college students are too often allowed to coast easily along in the sea of courses and arrive in a harbor protected by unrealistically high grade point averages.

2. According to Mansfield's article in the *Chronicle of Higher Education,* half of the grades given at Harvard are either A's or A-minuses, so some professors, and even students, complain that there is no way to distinguish the cream from the chaff or to tell where students stand in relation to one another.

3. Faculty members who lack tenure are often handicapped in their grading because they know that good student evaluations can help them in the ceaseless competition for scarce teaching appointments.

4. Instructors who do not offer the carrot of A's and B's to students whose work is below par are likely to be bludgeoned with poor evaluations.

5. Mansfield wards off the minefield of grade inflation by keeping two grades for each student, an official inflated one that appears on the transcript and a privately communicated one that tells the student how well his or her work compared with that of other students in the class and with Dr. Mansfield's standards.

20f Avoid biased and exclusionary language.

You cannot avoid writing from perspectives and backgrounds that you know about, but you can avoid divisive terms that reinforce stereotypes or belittle other people. Be sensitive to differences. Consider the feelings of members of the opposite sex, minorities (perhaps more correctly labeled as "world majorities"), and special-interest groups. Do not emphasize differences by separating society into *we* (people like you) and *they* or *these people* (people different from you). Use *we* only to be truly inclusive of yourself and all readers. Be aware, too, of terms that are likely to offend. You don't have to be excessive in your zeal to be PC ("politically correct"), using *underachieve* for *fail,* or *vertically challenged* for *short,* but do your best to avoid alienating readers.

Gender   The writer of the following sentence edited it after a reader alerted him to gender bias in the perception of women's roles.

> Andrea
> ► ~~Mrs. John~~ Harrison, ~~married to a real estate tycoon and herself the bubbly, blonde~~ chief executive of a successful computer company, has expanded the business overseas.

Choice of words can reveal gender bias, too.

Avoid	Use
actress	actor
authoress	author
chairman	chair *or* chairperson
female astronaut	astronaut
forefathers	ancestors
foreman	supervisor
mailman	mail carrier
male nurse	nurse
man, mankind (meaning any human being)	person, people, our species, human beings, humanity
manmade	synthetic, artificial
policeman, policewoman	police officer

Avoid	Use
salesman	sales representative, salesclerk
veterans and their wives	veterans and their spouses

When using pronouns, too, avoid the stereotyping that occurs by assigning gender roles to professions.

                                                           or she

▶ **Before a surgeon can operate, he must know every detail of the patient's history.**

Often it is best to avoid *he or she* by recasting the sentence or using plural nouns and pronouns.

▶ **Before operating, a surgeon must know every detail of the patient's history.**

▶ **Before surgeons can operate, they must know every detail of the patient's history.**

At times when the singular form is preferable, consider using *he* in one chapter of your manuscript and *she* in another, as long as you do not alternate within a paragraph. See 27e for more on pronouns, gender, and the use of *he or she.*

Race   Mention a person's race only when it is relevant. If you write "Attending the meeting were three doctors and an Asian computer programmer," you reveal more about your own stereotypes than you do about the participants in the meeting. In general, use the names that people prefer for their racial or ethnic affiliation. *The Columbia Guide to Standard American English* advises: "It is good manners (and therefore good usage) to call people only by the names they wish to be called." Consider, for example, that currently *African American* or *black* are preferred terms; *American Indian,* or better still, the particular tribe (Sioux, etc.) is sometimes preferred to *Native American; Asian* is preferred to *Oriental.*

Place   Avoid stereotyping people according to where they come from. Some British people may be stiff and formal, but not all are, and they certainly do not all play cricket, drink tea all day, and wear derbies (called "bowler hats" in England). Not all Germans eat sausage and drink beer; not all North Americans wear Spandex and talk loudly. Be careful, too, with the way you refer to countries and continents. The Americas include both North and South America, so you need to make the distinction. England, Scotland, Wales, and Northern Ireland make up the United Kingdom. In addition, shifts in world politics and national borders have resulted in the renaming of countries and cities: *Ceylon* became *Sri Lanka; Rhodesia* is now *Zimbabwe; Czechoslovakia* has been divided into the *Czech Republic* and *Slovakia*. The *Democratic Republic of the Congo* was *Zaire* between 1971 and 1997. *Beijing* used to be called *Peking*. *Mumbai* was formerly called *Bombay*. Always consult a current atlas, almanac, or Web site.

Age Avoid derogatory or condescending terms associated with age. Refer to a person's age or condition neutrally, if at all: not "a well-preserved little old lady" but "a woman in her eighties"; not "an immature sixteen-year-old" but simply "a teenager"; not "a middle-aged spinster" but "an unmarried woman."

Politics Words referring to politics are full of connotations. Consider the positive and negative connotations of *liberal* and *conservative* in various election campaigns. Take care when you use words like *radical, left-wing, right-wing,* and *moderate.* How do you want readers to interpret them? Are you identifying with one group and implicitly criticizing other groups?

Religion An old edition of an encyclopedia referred to "devout Catholics" and "fanatical Muslims." The new edition refers to both Catholics and Muslims as "devout," thus eliminating the bias of a sweeping generalization. Examine your use of the following: words that sound derogatory or exclusionary, such as *cult* or *fundamentalist;* expressions, such as *these people,* that emphasize difference; and even the word *we* when it implies that all readers share your beliefs.

Health and abilities Avoid expressions such as *confined to a wheelchair* and *AIDS victim* so as not to focus on difference and disability. Instead, write *someone who uses a wheelchair* and *person with AIDS,* but only if the context makes it necessary to include the information. Do not unnecessarily draw attention to a disability or an illness. If the CEO of a huge fashion chain has Parkinson's disease, how relevant is that information to your account of the rise of the company in the stock market?

Sexual orientation   Mention a person's sexual orientation only if the information is relevant in context. To write that someone accused of stock market fraud was "defended by a homosexual lawyer" would be to provide gratuitous information. The sexual orientation of the attorney might be more relevant in a case involving discrimination against homosexuals. Since you may not know the sexual orientations of readers, do not assume it is the same as your own.

The word *normal*   Be especially careful about using the word *normal* when referring to your own health, ability, or sexual orientation. Some readers might justifiably find that usage offensive.

EXERCISE 20.5
Avoid biased language.

In each of the following sentences, revise any biased or exclusionary language.

EXAMPLE:

~~The radical leftist~~ Aaron McGruder's comic strip offended some readers with its claim that the United States had helped to arm and train Osama bin Laden.

1. Some comic strips, such as *Doonesbury*, written by Garry Trudeau, and *The Boondocks*, created by the African American Aaron McGruder, can be considered political satires.

2. Many normal people have found *Doonesbury* offensive throughout its long history, for Trudeau has depicted premarital sex and drug use, championed women's libbers and peaceniks, and criticized politicians from Richard Nixon to George W. Bush.

3. In the fall of 2001, the main character in McGruder's comic strip argued that the ultra-conservative Reagan administration had aided Osama bin Laden and other fanatical Muslims fighting against the Soviet Union.

4. Many newspapers refused to carry McGruder's comic that day, and one female editor who claimed to be a fan of *The Boondocks* argued that the strip was inappropriate.

5. As newspaper comics have become more modern, comic strips feature single girls and dysfunctional families, but political issues that upset Midwestern readers are apparently still out of bounds.

20g Avoid pretentious language, tired expressions (clichés), and euphemisms.

Be aware that even formal academic writing should be clear. Don't think that a formal college essay has to be filled with big words and long complicated sentences. It certainly does not. In fact, the journal *Philosophy and Literature* sponsors an annual Bad Writing Contest, often "won" by renowned college professors. Convoluted writing is not necessarily a sign of brilliance or of an astonishingly powerful mind. It is usually a sign of bad writing. This passage from an essay on mimicry written by Professor Homi K. Bhabha, an academic now teaching at Harvard University, won second prize in the Bad Writing Contest in 1998:

> If, for a while, the ruse of desire is calculable for the uses of discipline soon the repetition of guilt, justification, pseudo-scientific theories, superstition, spurious authorities and classifications can be seen as the desperate effort to "normalize" formally the disturbance of a discourse of splitting that violates the rational, enlightened claims of its enunciatory modality.

Emily Eakin, a *New York Times* writer, calls this "indecipherable jargon" ("Harvard's Prize Catch, a Delphic Postcolonialist"). It is. Don't emulate it.

Distinguish the formal from the stuffy. *Formal* does not mean stuffy and pretentious. Writing in a formal situation does not require you to use obscure words and long sentences. Clear, direct expression works well in formal prose. Pretentious language makes reading difficult, as the following example shows.

> When a female of the species ascertains that a male with whom she is acquainted exhibits considerable desire to extend their acquaintance, that female customarily will first engage in protracted discussion with her close confidantes.

Simplify your writing if you find sentences like that in your draft. Here are some words to watch out for:

Stuffy	Direct	Stuffy	Direct
ascertain	find out	optimal	best
commence	begin	prior to	before
deceased	dead	purchase	buy

(Continued)

Stuffy	Direct	Stuffy	Direct
endeavor	try	reside	live
finalize	finish	terminate	end
implement	carry out	utilize	use

Avoid clichés.   *Clichés* are tired, overly familiar expressions such as *hit the nail on the head*, *crystal clear*, *better late than never*, and *easier said than done*. They never contribute anything fresh or original. Avoid or eliminate them as you revise your early drafts.

▶ ~~Last but not least,~~ Finally, the article recommends the TeleZapper.

▶ My main ambition in life is not to make a fortune since I

know that / ~~as they say, "money is the root of all evil."~~
having
~~Having~~ money does not lead automatically to a good life.

arose
▶ For Baldwin, the problem never ~~reared its ugly head~~ until

one dreadful night in New Jersey.

Joseph Epstein quotes a definition of a *cliché* and comments on the definition in a humorous way by using five clichés himself in his commentary (boldface added):

In *On Clichés*, a Dutch sociologist named Anton C. Zijderveld defines a cliché thus:
     "A cliché is a traditional form of human expression (in words, thoughts, emotions, gestures, acts) which—due to repetitive use in social life—has lost its original, often ingenious heuristic power. Although it thus fails positively to contribute meaning to social interactions and communication, it does function socially, since it manages to stimulate behavior (cognition, emotion, volition, action), while it avoids reflection on meanings."
     This is a definition that doesn't, you might say, **throw the baby out with the bathwater;** it **leaves no stone unturned** while offering several **blessings in disguise,** and **in the final analysis** provides **an acid test.** You might say all this, that is, if you have an ear dead to the grossest of clichés.

—Joseph Epstein, "The Ephemeral Verities," in *The Middle of My Tether*

Avoid euphemisms. *Euphemisms* are expressions that try to conceal a forthright meaning and make the concept seem more delicate, such as *change of life* for *menopause* or *passed away* for *died*. Because euphemisms often sound evasive or are unclear, avoid them in favor of direct language. Similarly, avoid *doublespeak* (evasive expressions that seek to conceal the truth, such as *downsized* for *fired*). Examples of such language are easy to find in advertising, business, politics, and some reporting. Do not equate formality with these roundabout expressions.

REVIEW EXERCISE FOR CHAPTER 20

Choose the best words.

Revise the following passage as needed to correct inappropriate word choice.

Although Columbus is often cited as the first person to have landed in America, people of Norse descent on voyages from Iceland and Greenland must get the credit, for they came to this continent around the year 1000. Hale and hearty Viking seamen, whose methods of navigation were primitive, were sometimes blown off course as they sailed the North Atlantic, and on one such voyage a Viking named Bjarni Herjulfsson saw land even though he was far from his destination of Greenland. A few years later, Greenlander Leif Eriksson sailed west from his home so that he might ascertain the truth about Bjarni's stories. He found him a rocky island—probably Baffin Island—and named it Helluland, which means "Land of Stone." Leif also stopped at places he called Markland ("Land of Forest"), probably Labrador, and Vinland ("Land of Wine"), a still-unidentified island liberal with grapes. At the closure of his voyage, Leif established a camp in what is now Newfoundland; he collected timber there to take home to Greenland, where trees were scarce.

The Icelandic sagas, written two or three hundred years after these voyages, may not contain the truth, the whole truth, and nothing but the truth of the western explorations of these Vikings, but they yield tantalizing clues. Until 1960, however, there wasn't nobody knew for sure that Leif Eriksson had actually visited North America, let alone set up a camp there. In that year, a Norwegian explorer named Helge Ingstad sailed around the coast of western Canada looking for possible sites of Norse settlements. Ingstad talked to local yokels in Newfoundland, who directed him to L'Anse aux Meadows. For eight years, a noted female archaeologist, Anne Stine, led digs there, and L'Anse aux Meadows is now recognized as the only authenticated Viking site on the North American continent—the settlement founded by Leif Eriksson and used for a few years by other Vikings as a summer timber-gathering and trading site.

PART 5
Common Sentence Problems

SENTENCES

Chapter **21**

How a Sentence Works

When you write, you use words to form sentences, sentences to form paragraphs, and paragraphs to give shape and logic to a document. Knowing how sentences work helps you edit those that don't work well.

21a Parts of speech

To think about and discuss how sentences work and how to edit them, a shared vocabulary is useful. Words are traditionally classified into eight categories called *parts of speech*. Note that the part of speech refers not to the word itself but to its function in a sentence. Some words can function as different parts of speech.

▶ They re~~spect~~ the orchestra manager.
     verb

▶ Re~~spect~~ is a large part of a business relationship.
  noun

Nouns   Words that name a person, place, thing, or concept are called *nouns*.

Types of Nouns

Type of noun	Function	Examples
COMMON		
Countable (42a)	Names people, places, objects, concepts; can be counted; has a plural form, usually with *-s* or *-es*, though some are irregular	teacher/teachers, party/parties, leaf/leaves, proposal/proposals, dish/dishes, man/men, goose/geese
Uncountable (42b)	Names a mass or an abstraction; cannot be counted; has no plural form	furniture, money, rice, advice, information, happiness
Collective (26g)	Names a group	family, society, clergy
Compound (26h)	Names a person or thing by using several parts of speech in combination	toothbrush, mother-in-law, passerby, cover-up
Noun derived from verb, with *-ing* (26e) *Gerund*	Names an action; used as subject or object of a verb or preposition	*Swimming* is healthy. She likes *swimming*. She bought flippers for *swimming*. But not: He is swimming across the lake. [Here *swimming* is part of the verb.]
PROPER		
Name (42f)	Names a specific person, place, or thing; needs capital letters for main words	Harry Potter, the Empire State Building, Hinduism, Shakespeare, Italy, Italians

Online Study Center   This icon will direct you to quick reference tools, Web resources, and research guides on the Web site at http://college.hmco.com/keys.html.

A noun is often used with other words to form a noun phrase. These other words include an article (*a, an, the*), a possessive pronoun (*my, your, his, her, its, our, their*), a demonstrative (*this, that, these, those*), numbers, quantity words, adjectives, and adjective phrases. The following are noun phrases: *a difficult problem, his aged parents, six broken computers, these impossibly dilapidated barns, complex information.*

Pronouns   A *pronoun* is a word that stands in for and refers to a noun, a noun phrase, or another pronoun. Examples include *it, she, his, those, themselves, whom, whoever, anyone.*

In writing, a pronoun usually refers to a noun phrase stated just before it in the text (its antecedent—see 27d).

noun phrase antecedent   pronoun
▶ **My sister loves shoes. She bought three pairs last week.**

Pronouns are of several types. Illustrations follow.

Personal Pronouns

Type of personal pronoun	Function	Examples
Subject form (27a) *I, you, he, she, it, we, they*	Refers to a specific person, place, or thing known to the reader; forms the subject of the verb	The director is leaving. *She* promises to return.
Object form (27a) *me, you, him, her, it, us, them*	Refers to a specific person, place, or thing known to the reader; forms the object of the verb or preposition	Maria knows Michalis well. She likes *him.*
Possessive form (27b) Adjective (used with a noun): *my, your, his, her, its, our, their*	Answers the question "Whose?" and tells to whom something belongs or is attached	The accident is *their* fault.
Stand-alone pronoun: *mine, yours, his, hers, ours, theirs*	Also tells to whom something belongs	The twins paid for the skateboard. It is clearly *theirs.*
Intensive (27h) *myself, yourself, himself, herself, oneself, itself, ourselves, yourselves, themselves*	Emphasizes stated noun or pronoun	The mayor *himself* was at the scene immediately.
Reflexive (27h) *myself, yourself, himself, herself, oneself, itself, ourselves, yourselves, themselves*	Refers to person or thing receiving the action, the same person or thing who performs the action	The president incriminated *himself* in his testimony. Cells reproduce *themselves.*

See the Key Points box on page 446 for the forms of personal pronouns.

Other Pronouns

Type of pronoun	Function	Examples
Demonstrative (26j) Singular: *this, that* Plural: *these, those*	Identifies and refers to a noun phrase or a clause nearby in the text	The firm offers free computer training. We advise you to sign up for *this.*
Relative (29a) *who, whom, whose, which, that*	Introduces a dependent relative clause by making reference to a stated noun or pronoun	People *who* live in the city can walk their dogs in the park.
Pronoun beginning a noun clause (21e) *whoever, whomever, whichever, what, whatever*	Makes a reference to something or someone	*Whoever* guesses accurately wins the prize. She praises *whatever* her students write.
Interrogative (27i) *who, whom, what, whose, which, whoever, whomever*	Introduces a question	*Who* wrote that article? *What* can we deduce?
Indefinite *anyone, somebody, everyone, nobody, anything, none, some* (for a full list, see 26i)	Makes a nonspecific reference; some indefinite pronouns are singular and some are plural.	*Something* is about to happen. Most students know the rules; *some* do not. *Everyone* is celebrating.
Reciprocal *each other, one another*	Refers to one part of a plural antecedent	The sisters look after *each other.*

Verbs   A *verb* is a word that tells about actions or states of being, often with the help of auxiliary verbs (forms of *do, be,* and *have;* and *will, would, can, could, shall, should, may, might,* and *must*):

- An *active verb* tells what a subject (a person, place, thing, or concept) does. It tells about an action: The puppy *is barking.* The proposal *created* unusual possibilities.

- A *passive verb* tells what is done to a subject: The proposal *was contested.* The cake *has been eaten.*

- A *linking verb* tells what a subject is, seems, becomes, looks, or appears to be. It tells about a state of being. It links the subject to a word or idea that describes or renames it: They *are* happy. He *seems* efficient. Julia *became* captain of the team.

A verb is a necessary part of a sentence. A complete verb is made up of a main verb along with any auxiliaries necessary to indicate person, number, tense, mood, and voice. Forms such as *to see, seeing,* and *seen* are not complete (or *finite*) forms; they cannot function as the complete verb of a clause.

THE COMPLETE VERB AND THE MAIN VERB

■ Every complete verb phrase ends with the main verb.

		Predicate	
		Complete verb phrase	
Subject		***Main verb***	**Rest of predicate**
The athletes		*practiced*	every day last week.
They	have been	*practicing*	all day today.
He	should	*practice*	this week.
She	is	*practicing*	in the gym.

■ Auxiliary verbs often are needed with a main verb to form a complete verb phrase:

	Predicate		
	Complete verb phrase		
Subject	***Auxiliary verb***	**Main verb**	**Rest of predicate**
They	*have been*	recognized.	
She	*did*	recognize	him.
He	*was*	wearing	a disguise.

■ Modal auxiliary verbs provide nuances of meaning, such as intention, ability, permission, advisability, necessity, and expectation (see 43b). The modal auxiliaries, which can be used with other auxiliaries, are *will, would, can, could, shall, should, may, might,* and *must.* Note that a modal is always immediately followed by a base form (*have, be,* and *take* in the following examples):

	Predicate			
	Complete verb phrase			
Subject	***Modal auxiliary***	**Auxiliary verb**	**Main verb**	**Rest of predicate**
They	*might*	have been	driving	too fast.
The car	*should*	be	repaired	right away.
You	*must*		take	driving lessons.

FEATURES OF VERBS

1. The base form (the form found in the dictionary) of a verb fills the slot in sentences like this: They will _____. It might _____.

2. A verb has five forms (25b):
   - a base (no -s) form (*sing*)
   - an -s form (*sings*)
   - an -ing form (*singing*)
   - a past tense form (*sang*)
   - a past participle form (*sung*)

3. Both the past tense and the past participle forms of regular verbs, such as *decide, watch, talk,* and *play,* end in -d or -ed: *decided, watched, talked, played.* The past tense and past participle of irregular verbs, such as *bring, ride, write,* and *quit,* are formed in different ways: *brought, brought; rode, ridden; wrote, written; quit, quit.*

4. A complete verb—a main verb with any necessary auxiliaries—indicates tense (present, past, and future) and aspect (progressive or perfect):
   - Present, past, and future: *walk, walked, will walk; sing, sang, will sing*
   - Progressive aspect: *was running, will be traveling, are working*
   - Perfect aspect: *has watched, should have examined*
   - Perfect progressive aspect: *has been considering, will have been writing, might have been complaining*

5. In the present tense, a main or auxiliary verb generally changes form to reflect person (*I, you, he/she/it, we, they*) and number (singular and plural) (26a): I *am*, you *are*, he *is*; the children *walk*, the child *walks*.

6. A verb that can be followed by a direct object can show active or passive voice (25l):
   - Active: The dog bit the intruder. [The dog does the action—biting.]
   - Passive: The intruder *was bitten* by the dog. [The subject of the sentence, *the intruder*, had something done to him—he did not do the biting.]

7. A verb indicates mood:
   - Indicative mood in a statement or question: He *goes* to church every week. *Do* they *go* to church every week?
   - Imperative mood in a command: *Go* away!
   - Subjunctive mood expressing a speculation about a hypothetical condition, a wish, a request, a demand, or a recommendation (25k): If they *went* on vacation, they would feel better.

8. A verb is either transitive (it is followed by a direct object) or intransitive (with no direct object):

> direct object
> ► Their generosity *surprises* us every day. [Transitive verb]

> ► Accidents *happen*. [Intransitive verb]

9. A verb has forms that cannot function as a complete main verb. These forms, known as **verbals,** are the infinitive form (*to go, to see,* and so on), the *-ing* form used as a noun or an adjective, and the *-ed* form used as an adjective. For more on these forms, see 43c–43f.

Adjectives *Adjectives* are words that provide information about nouns and pronouns. They do not take a plural *-s* ending, though some have a different plural form—for example, *this* car; *these* cars.

FEATURES OF ADJECTIVES

1. Adjectives describe (*purple* boots), point to (*those* boots), or tell the quantity of (*some* boots) nouns and pronouns.

2. Adjectives precede nouns or follow linking verbs: He is wearing *purple* boots. His boots are *purple*.

3. Descriptive adjectives have comparative and superlative forms: *big, bigger, biggest; helpful, less helpful, least helpful*.

4. Some adjectives function as limiting adjectives or determiners:

   - Articles: *a, an,* and *the: a* scarred old elm tree
   - Demonstratives: *this, that, these,* and *those: this* tickly red feather boa
   - Numerical determiners: *one, two, first, second,* and so on: the *Fifth* Amendment
   - Interrogative: *who, which, what, whose: Which* chapter did you read?
   - Possessive: *my, your, his, her, its, our, their: His* day will come.
   - Quantity: *each, few, other, some, many, much: Much* time has elapsed.

Some words can function as adjectives in one context and as pronouns in other contexts.

> adjective
> ► Many cars have been sold.

> pronoun (no following noun)
> ► The cars are on sale. Many were sold last week.

For more on adjectives, see chapter 28.

Adverbs *Adverbs* provide information about verbs, adjectives, other adverbs, and some kinds of clauses. They answer one of the following questions: *When? Where? Why? How? Under what conditions?* and *To what extent?*

FEATURES OF ADVERBS

1. Many adverbs end in *-ly: quickly, immediately, intelligently.*
2. Some common adverbs do not end in *-ly: not, very, well,* and "time" adverbs such as *always, soon, often, sometimes, first,* and *never.*
3. Adverbs modify verbs, adjectives, adverbs, and clauses.

   modifies verb
   ▶ **Lisa Leslie dunked** *brilliantly.*

   modifies adjective
   ▶ **Leslie is an** *extremely* **energetic player.**

   modifies adverb
   ▶ **Leslie played** *spectacularly* **well.**

   ———— modifies whole clause ————
   ▶ *Undoubtedly,* **Leslie is a player with promise.**

4. Adverbs usually use *more* and *most* and *less* and *least* to form comparisons: *more efficiently, less eagerly, most aggressively, least confidently.*
5. Adverbs that modify a whole clause and signify its relationship to the previous clause are known as *conjunctive adverbs.* (See the accompanying chart.) They are used as transitional expressions to connect ideas within a sentence or among sentences. For the punctuation to use with conjunctive adverbs, see 31e.

Conjunctive Adverbs

Conjunctive adverbs	Function
also, besides, furthermore, incidentally, moreover	To add an idea
however, nevertheless, nonetheless, conversely, rather	To point out a contrast
alternatively, instead, otherwise	To provide an alternative
similarly, likewise	To show similarity
first, second (and so on), *next, then, subsequently, meanwhile, previously, finally*	To show time, order, and sequence

Conjunctive adverbs	Function
therefore, consequently, accordingly, thus, hence	To show result
certainly, indeed	To affirm with emphasis

See also 5e for a Key Points box showing transitional expressions, including conjunctive adverbs.

Conjunctions   *Conjunctions* are words that "join together." They connect two or more similar parts of a sentence—that is, words, phrases, or clauses.

WHAT CONJUNCTIONS DO

1. *Coordinating conjunctions* connect two sentence elements of similar type and equal weight:

   Two words: ham *and* eggs

   Two phrases: She cannot decide whether to fly to Florida *or* to take the train.

   Two clauses: He tore a ligament, *so* he dropped out of the race.

   The coordinating conjunctions are *and, but, or, nor, so, for,* and *yet.*

2. *Subordinating conjunctions* connect two clauses of unequal weight—that is, one is an independent clause, and the other is dependent on and subordinate to that clause. The conjunction specifies the logical relationship between the two clauses, answering questions such as the following:

   WHEN? *Before* they left, they changed dollars to euros.

   After they arrived, they went straight to bed.

   When they saw their hotel, they were ecstatic.

   Until they saw Venice, they had been car fanatics.

   WHY? *Because* they had enough money, they had one meal at the best restaurant in town.

   UNDER WHAT CONDITIONS? *If* they can, they will return next year.

   See 21e for a list of subordinating conjunctions.

3. *Correlative conjunctions* work in pairs to connect equivalent grammatical elements: *either/or, neither/nor, both/and, not only/but also:*

   Neither whales *nor* dolphins are fish.

   His firm has moved, so *either* he will have to change jobs *or* commuting will become a big part of his life.

Prepositions   *Prepositions*—often little words—convey details about relationships. A preposition connects a noun, pronoun, or other noun equivalent to another noun, pronoun, or noun equivalent, such as a noun clause or an *-ing* form. Every preposition is part of a prepositional phrase that serves as an adjective or adverb.

> preposition   preposition   preposition
> ► At dawn, a bird with a red crest flew into the open doorway.

Some common prepositions are

about	before	from	regarding
above	behind	in	through
across	below	into	to
after	beneath	like	toward
against	between	off	under
among	by	on	until
around	during	outside	without
as	except	over	
at	for	past	

Prepositional phrases are often idiomatic: *on occasion, in love.* To understand their use and meaning, consult a good dictionary. See also chapter 45 ESL.

Interjections   Words that express emotion and can stand alone— *Ha! Wow! Ugh! Ouch! Say!*—are called *interjections*. Interjections are not used frequently in academic writing. The more formal ones (such as *alas, oh*) are sometimes used in poetry:

> But she is in her grave, and, oh,
> The difference to me!   —William Wordsworth

EXERCISE 21.1

Identify parts of speech.

On the lines after each sentence, identify the two parts of speech that are underlined in the sentence.

EXAMPLE:

Nelson Mandela, the former president of South Africa, spent nearly thirty years in prison for his work to end apartheid.

Mandela _____noun_____

for _____preposition_____

1. He <u>wrote</u> an autobiography called *Long Walk to Freedom.*

   He   _____

   wrote   _____

2. In his book, Mandela says, "I am not <u>truly</u> free if I am taking away someone else's freedom, just as surely as I am not free when my freedom is taken away from <u>me</u>."

   truly   _____

   me   _____

3. <u>Many</u> additional writers have also used their talents to fight for <u>freedom</u> for themselves and others.

   many   _____

   freedom   _____

4. Writers such as Frederick Douglass, Aleksandr Solzhenitsyn, <u>and</u> Mary Wollstonecraft called attention <u>to</u> injustices that they saw around them.

   and   _____

   to   _____

5. The Lithuanian poet Czeslaw Milosz <u>once</u> asked, "What <u>is</u> poetry which does not save nations and peoples?"

   once   _____

   is   _____

Segregated beach

Nelson Mandela

21b What a sentence is, needs, and does

What a sentence is   You have probably heard various definitions of a *sentence*, the common one being that a "a sentence is a complete thought." Sometimes it is. Sometimes it is not, depending on what one expects by "complete." In fact, that definition is not particularly helpful. How complete is this thought?

▶ **He did not.**

You probably do not regard it as complete because it relies on text around it, on other sentences, to tell what it was he did not do.

▶ **She always made an effort to be punctual. He did not.**

Still, it is a grammatically correct sentence.

KEY POINTS

Features of a Written English Sentence

1. It begins with a capital letter.
2. It ends with a period (a "full stop" in British English), question mark, or exclamation point. A semicolon can provide a partial ending, taking readers on to the next idea without a full stop.
3. It must contain at the very least a subject (or an implied *you* subject, as in "Run!") and a predicate (12e) that provides information about the subject; and both must form an independent clause. The predicate must contain a complete verb, as indicated here in italics:

Independent Clause

Subject	Verb + Rest of Predicate
Birds	*sing.*
Max	*was* tired.
Everyone	*wants* security.
The driver	*had forgotten* to signal.
His three sisters	*sent* him a hammock.
Bills and mortgage payments	*must have consumed* most of his salary.
Skating	*can be* wonderful exercise.
What you wrote	*should have been edited.*

Sentences like these, with no attachments to the basic subject + predicate framework, are called *simple sentences* (see 8d, item 3).

(Continued)

(Continued)

4. Words, phrases, and clauses can be attached to the framework of the simple sentence.

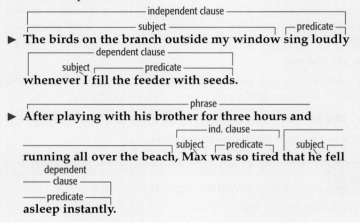

▶ The birds on the branch outside my window sing loudly
whenever I fill the feeder with seeds.

▶ After playing with his brother for three hours and
running all over the beach, Max was so tired that he fell
asleep instantly.

Read more about writing complete sentences and avoiding sentence fragments in chapter 23. For more on adding words, phrases, and clauses to a simple sentence, turn to 21d, 21e, and 21g.

What a sentence does   A sentence can function as a statement, question, command, or exclamation.

Sentence Functions

Sentence function	What it does	Example
Declarative	Makes a statement	Lower interest rates help home buyers.
Interrogative	Asks a question	Who can afford to buy a house on the beach?
Imperative	Gives a command	Watch this space.
Exclamatory	Expresses surprise or emotion	This expensive restaurant has had no fewer than fifteen violations!

Most of the sentences in expository and academic writing are declarative statements, though an occasional question is useful to draw readers into thinking about a topic. An occasional exclamatory sentence can be powerful, too, but bear in mind that, according to *The*

New York Times Manual of Style and Usage, "When overused, the exclamation point loses impact, as advertising demonstrates continually."

ESL NOTE

Language and Sentence Structure

The shape of a sentence varies from language to language—in German, for instance, the verb does not necessarily follow the subject (*Gestern habe ich ihm einen Brief geschrieben* is literally translated as *Yesterday have I him a letter written*). In other words, the structure of a sentence is not fixed across languages. If English is not your native language, keep its basic structures in mind as you write and revise. Use your first language to help you with ideas, but avoid transferring sentences from one language to another without first reminding yourself of the features of words and sentences in English.

21c The basis of a sentence: Subject and predicate

A sentence in English minimally consists of a *subject* (person, place, thing, or concept) that is doing an action, is being something, or is being acted upon in the *predicate*. The predicate makes a comment or assertion about the subject.

▶ **A huge storm rattled the windows.** [A thing doing the action]

▶ **Physics is a challenging subject.** [A concept being something]

▶ **The president was impeached.** [A person being acted upon; somebody else did the impeaching]

A simple subject is one word (*storm, physics, president*); a complete subject includes the simple subject and all its modifiers (*a huge storm, the president*). A predicate must always include a main verb or auxiliaries with a main verb, such as *sit, sat, will sit, persuades, persuaded, might persuade, should be working, must have been built,* along with any modifiers and any objects or complements.

Finding the subject To test what the subject of a sentence is, ask a question about the verb. This questioning is easy with a short simple sentence:

▶ **Henry smiled.** [Who smiled? Henry. *Henry* is the subject of the sentence.]

▶ **Laura is pregnant.** [Who is pregnant? Laura. *Laura* is the subject of the sentence.]

▶ **The ball was thrown.** [What was thrown? The ball. *The ball* is the complete subject.]

verb (over "was thrown")

These sentences have simple subjects, just one or two words. Often, though, a subject consists of more than just the simple subject of one word. Again, to determine what the simple subject is, ask a question about the verb and shrink the answer down to one word.

▶ **His new boss left.** [Who left? His new *boss.* The complete subject is *His new boss.*]

When you ask the same question about the much longer simple sentence that follows, the answer is still the same simple subject:

simple subject — *complete subject* — *verb*

▶ **The *boss* of the successful new computer company *left* the elegantly furnished conference room.**

predicate

Compound subjects and compound predicates   A subject may consist of two or more nouns, pronouns, or other noun substitutes (infinitives, *-ing* forms, noun clauses) usually joined by *and.*

┌ compound subject ┐
▶ *Juan and Rafael* **fell asleep.**

┌ compound subject ┐
▶ *Li Chen and I* **waded in the ocean.**

Similarly, a predicate may consist of two or more verbs, known as a **compound predicate**:

┌─ compound predicate ─┐
▶ **Li Chen and I** *waded in the ocean and collected shells.*

EXERCISE 21.2

Identify the subject and predicate in a simple sentence.

In each of the following sentences, underline the complete subject once and underline the predicate twice. Then write *S* over the simple subject and *V* over the verb. Remember that the verb may consist of more than one word and that sentences can have more than one subject or verb.

EXAMPLE:

S   V
Many people in the United States carry too much credit-card debt.

1. Most experts consider some types of debt, such as a mortgage, financially necessary.

2. However, credit-card debt never benefits an individual's long-term financial goals.

3. Today even college students without jobs or credit records can usually acquire credit cards easily.

4. Unfortunately, many students charge expensive purchases and pay only the minimum balance on their cards every month.

5. Graduating from college with a large credit-card debt can severely limit a person's opportunities.

Seven basic predicate patterns Here are seven common predicate patterns (the components of the predicate appear in brackets).

1. **SUBJECT + PREDICATE [VERB]** The basic pattern for a simple statement in English is a simple subject followed by a predicate consisting only of a verb.

    S   V
▶ **Babies cry.**

    S   V
▶ **The book was published.**

Even when elements are added to the simple sentence, the subject and verb maintain their key positions.

       simple subject   S   V
▶ **All the *babies* in the hospital nursery *are crying*.**

              complete subject
          simple subject
▶ **The sensational book about Hollywood in its heyday**

       verb
was published by the multinational company.

ESL NOTE
Subject and Verb across Languages
Not all languages require a subject and a verb. English requires both, except in a command. See 44a.

2. **SUBJECT + PREDICATE [VERB + DIRECT OBJECT]** A transitive verb in the active voice needs a direct object to complete its meaning.

```
    ┌──── S ────┐   V      DO
```
▶ **Many people wear glasses.**

In this sentence, the direct object (DO) completes the meaning of the verb by telling what many people wear. Verbs that take a direct object are known as transitive verbs. To identify a direct object, ask *Who[m]?* or *What?* about the verb:

```
┌─────────────────────── S ───────────────────────┐
```
▶ **The *artist* who lives in the large apartment on the sixth floor**

```
  V       ┌──────────── DO ────────────┐
```
owns **five cute Weimaraner *puppies.*** [What does he own? *Five cute Weimaraner puppies* is the direct object.]

Intransitive verbs, such as *lie* (meaning "recline"), *sit,* and *rise,* do not take a direct object.

3. SUBJECT + PREDICATE [VERB + SUBJECT COMPLEMENT] Some verbs, such as *be, seem, become, look,* and *appear,* are linking verbs. They are followed by a noun or an adjective phrase that refers to and renames or describes the subject. This noun or adjective phrase is known as a subject complement (SC).

```
  S    V        SC
```
▶ **George is the president of the club.**

```
  S                    V    SC
```
▶ **The president of the club is George.**

```
┌──────────── S ────────────┐  V   SC
```
▶ **The *players* on the visiting team look fit.**

4. SUBJECT + PREDICATE [VERB + INDIRECT OBJECT + DIRECT OBJECT] Some transitive verbs, such as *give, send,* and *offer,* can be followed by an indirect object (IO), naming the person or thing to whom or for whom the action of the verb takes place, and by a direct object (DO). You can test for an indirect object by asking *To whom?* or *For whom?*

```
┌────────── S ──────────┐   V    ┌───── IO ─────┐  ┌──── DO ────┐
```
▶ **The *director* of the play *gave* his leading *lady* one exquisite**

```
┌──┐
```
rose.

See ESL Note on page 331.

5. SUBJECT + PREDICATE [VERB + DIRECT OBJECT + OBJECT COMPLEMENT] The object complement (OC) refers to and renames or describes the direct object.

```
  S    V     ┌──── DO ────┐  ┌──── OC ────┐
```
▶ **They named the football *star* Rookie of the Year.**

ESL NOTE

No *to* before an Indirect Object

Do not add the word *to* in front of an indirect object that precedes the direct object.

NO   **I gave to the driver a tip.**

         I gave to her a tip.

YES   **I gave the driver a tip.**

         I gave her a tip.

Use the word *to* or *for* only when the verb is followed directly by the direct object. Then use a prepositional phrase with *to* or *for* in place of an indirect object.

▶ **I gave a tip to the driver.**

See also 43c.

6. (SUBJECT IMPLIED) + PREDICATE [VERB +] A command is the only type of sentence that has only a predicate and an implied rather than a stated subject. The unstated, implied subject of a command is always *you.*

            V

▶ **[You] Leave me alone!**

7. VERB + SUBJECT + REST OF PREDICATE In Standard English sentences, the verb precedes the subject in inverted order in specific contexts— such as in questions; after adverbs such as *here, there, never, seldom,* and *rarely;* and after phrases used for emphasis at the beginning of a sentence. Here are some of the patterns that you are likely to read or use in your writing:

                V
                S

▶ **Did the committee finish its work?**

             V   ⌐——— S——— ⌐

▶ **Next to the river runs a superhighway.**

      V   S   V

▶ **Never have I been so tired.**

        V   ⌐— S—— ⌐   V

▶ **Not only does the novel entertain, but it also raises our awareness of poverty.**

         V   S

▶ **So eager was I to win that I set off before the starter's gun.**

        V   ⌐—S—⌐   V

▶ **Rarely has a poem achieved such a grasp on the times.**

Modifiers added to subjects or predicates Descriptive words (adjectives, adverbs, and phrases) included in the subject or predicate to expand the meaning are known as *modifiers*. In the examples that follow, the simple subject + predicate structures are *computer + whirred* and *It + was*. The words in italics expand the meaning of the subject and predicate.

▶ *The powerful new* **computer whirred** *disconcertingly.* **It was** *decidedly distracting.*

EXERCISE 21.3

Identify direct and indirect objects.

In each of the following sentences, first circle the active verb or verbs. Remember that a verb can consist of more than one word. Then underline the complete direct object. If there is an indirect object, underline the complete indirect object twice.

EXAMPLE:

A government-sponsored breeding program (is giving) endangered California condors a chance to survive.

1. The federal California condor reintroduction program encountered some obstacles in 2001.

2. In June, a captive condor had laid an egg.

3. Biologists then gave a now-wild female condor the unhatched egg.

4. She subsequently hatched it and was raising the chick.

5. Unfortunately, the surrogate mother briefly left the chick alone in the nest.

6. Another condor entered the nest, attacked the chick, and killed it.

7. This chick's death brought the condor reintroduction program its first setback.

8. Then a few days later a year-old condor in flight hit a power line and died.

9. Nevertheless, the reintroduction program still offers the condors their best hope for survival.

10. Wildlife conservationists still regard surrogate-mother condors as potentially good mothers.

EXERCISE 21.4

Find subjects and verbs in your own writing.

Look at piece of your own writing. Underline the complete verbs. Circle the subject of each verb.

21d Phrases

A *phrase* is a group of related words that lacks a subject, a verb, or both. A phrase cannot function as a sentence; it must be part of the subject or predicate of an independent or a dependent clause. Phrases perform a number of grammatical functions.

Noun phrase   A noun phrase can function as a subject, an object, or an appositive phrase defining or renaming a preceding noun or pronoun.

    ┌─────── noun phrase as subject ───────┐
▶ **An elegant sequined evening gown was on sale.**

        ┌─────── noun phrase as object ───────┐
▶ **She bought an elegant sequined evening gown.**

         ┌──── appositive noun phrase (31d) ────┐
▶ **Her latest purchase, an elegant sequined evening gown, now hangs in her closet.**

Verb phrase   A verb phrase consists of all the words that together make up the complete verb of a clause. (A *complete* verb indicates time— when the action mentioned in the clause takes place; see 21a and 20e.)

            ┌── verb phrase (complete verb) ──┐
▶ **That embarrassing letter should have been destroyed years ago.**

Verbal phrase   Some phrases begin with parts of verbs. These parts of verbs (called *verbals* or *nonfinite verbs*) can never function alone as a complete verb; they do not tell about person, number, tense, mood, or voice.

         ┌──────── S ────────┐ Verbal
NO   ▶ **The children on the beach building sandcastles.**

         [Fragment: *building* is a verbal, not a complete verb]

         ┌──────── S ────────┐ ┌── V ──┐
YES   ▶ **The children on the beach were building sandcastles.**

         ┌──────────── S ────────────┐
YES   ▶ **The children on the beach building sandcastles**
         V
         are all in the same family.

Verbals are the present participle (*-ing*) form used as an adjective, the past participle (*-ed*) form used as an adjective, the *-ing* form used as a noun (a *gerund*), and the infinitive form (*to* + base form) used as a noun, adjective, or adverb. A verbal phrase consists of one of these verbals and any words that modify it. Examples follow.

Participle phrase   A participle phrase can never stand alone as a sentence.

> ┌──────── past participle phrase ────────┐   S   V
> ► **Frightened by her own loud heartbeat, she tried to stay calm.**

>   S   past participle phrase   V
>   ┌───────────────────┐
> ► **Noises heard from afar seem louder at night.**

>   ┌──── *-ing* participle phrase ────┐ S   V
> ► **Hurrying across the grass, she heard a loud crash.**

   A participle phrase at the beginning of a sentence must always describe the subject; otherwise, it is a misplaced or dangling modifier (24b, 24c), as in *Hurrying across the grass, a loud crash startled her.* (The *crash* was not hurrying; *she* was.)

-ing phrase used as a noun (gerund)   An *-ing* verbal can function as a noun. When it does, it is known as a *gerund.*

>   ┌── *-ing* noun phrase (subject) ──┐
> ► **The blaring of a car horn made her angry.**

>   *-ing* noun phrase
>   ┌────── (object) ──────┐
> ► **He enjoys singing in the rain.**

Infinitive phrase   An infinitive phrase (*to* + base form of verb) can function as a noun, adverb, or adjective.

>   ┌──── (noun subject) ────┐
> ► **To return to Beijing was her dream.**

>   ┌── (noun direct object) ──┐
> ► **She planned to return to Beijing.**

>   ┌────── (adverb) ──────┐
> ► **To return to Beijing, she took a job as an English teacher.**

>   ┌───── (adjective) ─────┐
> ► **She had a plan to return to Beijing.**

Prepositional phrase   A prepositional phrase consists of a preposition and a noun or pronoun called the *object* of the preposition. A prepositional phrase functions as an adjective or adverb.

prepositional phrase   prepositional phrase   prepositional phrase
┌── (adverb) ──┐   ┌── (adjective) ──┐   ┌── (adverb) ──┐

▶ **Without fail, the eerie music from the park began at midnight.**

Absolute phrase   An absolute phrase begins with a noun phrase followed by a verbal or a prepositional phrase. It contains no verb form that indicates tense. An absolute phrase modifies a whole sentence and is set off from the rest of the sentence by a comma.

┌─ absolute phrase, modifying the whole sentence ─┐
▶ **She stood in suspense, the clanging noises growing louder.**

absolute phrase,
┌─ modifying the whole sentence ─┐
▶ **Her thoughts in turmoil, she decided to consult a lawyer.**

Adjective phrase   An adjective phrase contains an adjective and may include other words and phrases. It modifies a noun or pronoun.

phrase used as an adjective after a noun, not before
┌───────────────────────────────┐
▶ **The person responsible for the profits refused to take credit.**

adjective phrase
┌──────────┐
▶ **Sad to leave, Mohammed stalled and brushed some lint from his hat.**

For more on word order with adjective phrases, see 43b.

EXERCISE 21.5

Identify phrases.

In the following sentences, identify the underlined phrases as one of the following types: noun phrase, verb phrase, participle phrase, gerund phrase, infinitive phrase, prepositional phrase, absolute phrase, or adjective phrase. Then identify its function in the sentence.

EXAMPLE:

In the Middle Ages, most advances in science occurred in <u>the Arab world</u>.

     type of phrase: *prepositional phrase*

     function in sentence: *adverb modifying the verb occurred*

  1. The astronomer and philosopher <u>Nasir al-Din al-Tusi</u> spent many years in the Persian city of Alamut.

     type of phrase: _____

     function in sentence: _____

2. Using Alamut's well-known library, al-Tusi researched and wrote about scientific topics.

type of phrase: _____

function in sentence: _____

3. According to al-Tusi's later claims, he had been kept in Alamut against his will.

type of phrase: _____

function in sentence: _____

4. Nevertheless, to work in the library there must have been the fulfillment of a dream for a brilliant scholar such as al-Tusi.

type of phrase: _____

function in sentence: _____

5. Among the works completed by al-Tusi in Alamut were treatises on mathematics, ethics, and astronomy.

type of phrase: _____

function in sentence: _____

6. In the mid-thirteenth century, Alamut was surrounded by the armies of the warrior Hulagu, the grandson of Genghis Khan.

type of phrase: _____

function in sentence: _____

7. His reputation as a scholar ensuring his safety, al-Tusi was transported to Baghdad in 1256 by the conqueror Hulagu.

type of phrase: _____

function in sentence: _____

8. Knowing of al-Tusi's reputation as a genius, Hulagu appointed the astronomer to serve as one of his ministers.

type of phrase: _____

function in sentence: _____

9. Hulagu built an observatory for al-Tusi's use in what is now Iran.

type of phrase: _____

function in sentence: _____

10. Al-Tusi and his followers' work at the observatory is now credited with establishing the basis of modern astronomy.

type of phrase: _____

function in sentence: _____

21e Independent and dependent clauses

A *clause* contains a subject and a predicate. A clause can either stand alone (*independent*) or be attached to and dependent on another clause to complete its meaning. A *dependent clause* must be attached to an independent clause to form a complete sentence.

Independent clause   An independent clause is a group of related words that contains at least a subject and a verb and does not begin with a subordinating word. It can be punctuated as a sentence when standing alone. In each sentence you write, the predicate should include a complete verb and make a comment or assertion about the subject (except in commands, p. 331).

Subject	*Verb*/Predicate
Eyesight	*deteriorates.*
Many people	*wear* glasses.
Audre Lorde	*was* a poet.
Lorde's poems and essays	*make* one think.

A subject can also be a noun formed from a verb (an *-ing* participle [gerund] or an infinitive) or a noun clause, as in the following examples.

Subject	*Verb*/Predicate
-ing form (gerund) Winning	*is* not everything.
infinitive phrase To do one's best	*is* more important.
noun clause How the players train	*makes* all the difference.

CONNECTING INDEPENDENT CLAUSES: COORDINATION   Use a coordinating conjunction—*and, but, or, nor, so, for, yet*—usually preceded by a comma, to connect two independent clauses in one sentence. For more on the stylistic options of choosing coordination or subordination, see 18c.

▶ **Thomas Wolfe's manuscript was originally eleven hundred pages, but his editor cut it substantially.**

Dependent clause   A dependent clause contains a subject and a predicate but cannot stand alone. A clause beginning with a subordinating conjunction, such as *if, when, because, although,* or *since,* or with a relative pronoun, such as *who, which,* or *that,* needs to be attached to an independent clause. The idea in a dependent clause is subordinate to the idea in the independent clause.

A sentence can contain any number of independent and dependent clauses, but it must always contain at least one independent clause. Never punctuate a dependent clause alone as a sentence (see chapter 23).

Dependent clauses fall into three types, according to their role in a sentence, functioning as adverbs, adjectives, or nouns.

Adverb Clauses   Adverb clauses provide information about the verbs, adjectives, or adverbs in an independent clause. They answer questions such as *when, how, where, why, for what purpose or reason, under what conditions,* and *to what extent,* and they express logical relationships between the ideas of the independent and dependent clauses. Adverb clauses begin with subordinating conjunctions.

Relationships that Subordinating Conjunctions Express

time: when, whenever, until, till, before, after, while, once, since, as soon as, as long as

place: where, wherever

reason/cause: because, as, since

condition: if, even if, unless, provided that

contrast: although, though, even though, whereas, while

comparison: than, as, as if, as though

purpose: so that, in order that

result: so . . . that, such . . . that

By attaching a dependent clause to an independent clause—using *subordination*—you provide information about the relationship between clauses.

INDEPENDENT CLAUSES   **The two-way radio had rechargeable batteries and no usage fees. She decided to buy it.**

COMBINED BY SUBORDINATION

—— dependent clause, showing reason ——
Because the two-way radio had rechargeable batteries
—— independent clause ——
and no usage fees, she decided to buy it.

INDEPENDENT
CLAUSES

The pitcher hurled the broken bat at the running batter. The crowd jeered.

COMBINED BY
SUBORDINATION

┌──────── dependent clause, showing time ────────┐
When the pitcher hurled the broken bat at the
──────────────────── ┌ independent clause ┐
running batter, the crowd jeered.

INDEPENDENT
CLAUSES

The quiz show host immediately moved on to the next question. He could see one of the contestants trying to shout out an answer.

COMBINED BY
SUBORDINATION

┌──────────── independent clause ────────────┐
The quiz show host immediately moved on to
──────────────── ┌ dependent clause, showing contrast ─
the next question although he could see one of

┌──────────────────────────────────────┐
the contestants trying to shout out an answer.

ADVERB CLAUSE BEFORE INDEPENDENT CLAUSE   As a general rule, if an adverb clause precedes the independent clause, use a comma to separate the two clauses. See also 31c.

┌──── dependent clause ────┐ ┌ comma ─ independent clause ────┐
▶ **If you send that memo, the columnist will be angry.**

Some writers do omit the comma, but if you adopt the general rule of always choosing to use a comma, you will avoid errors and ambiguities that can occur if you inadvertently leave out a necessary comma, as in the following example.

NO

While the anthropologists were eating bears were circling their tent. [Leaving out the comma could make a reader read the sentence as "While the anthropologists were eating bears"—not what the writer intended.]

YES

While the anthropologists were eating, bears were circling their tent.

ADVERB CLAUSE AFTER INDEPENDENT CLAUSE   Ordinarily, no comma is needed when the dependent clause follows the independent clause.

▶ **The columnist will be angry if you send that memo.**

However, when the adverb clause is nonrestrictive (that is, adds information that contrasts rather than modifies and limits), set it off with a comma (31d).

▶ **My boss prefers phone calls, whereas I like e-mail.**

Adjective clauses   Adjective clauses (also called *relative clauses*) provide information about nouns or pronouns.

INDEPENDENT   **The contestant quickly claimed the prize. The**
CLAUSES   **contestant knew the correct answer.**

COMBINED BY   **The contestant who knew the correct answer quickly**
ADJECTIVE   **claimed the prize.**
(RELATIVE)
CLAUSE

The subordinating words that introduce adjective clauses are relative pronouns, such as *who, whom, whose, which,* and *that.* For more on relative pronouns and relative clauses, see chapter 29.

       ——— adjective (relative) clause ———
▶ **The kick that brought the crowd to its feet broke the impasse.**

       ⌐ adjective (relative) clause ¬
▶ **The soccer player whose head is bowed missed a kick.**

NOUN CLAUSES   A noun clause functions like a noun in a sentence. Noun clauses are introduced by subordinating words such as *what, that* (or omitted *that*), *when, why, how, whatever, who, whom, whoever,* and *whomever.* (A clause that you can replace with the pronoun *something* or *someone* is a noun clause.)

               noun clause
           ⌐——— = *something* ———
▶ **He wants to know what he should do.**

           ⌐——— noun clause = *something* ———¬
▶ **The fans wish that the match could be replayed.**

    ⌐ noun clause = *someone* ¬
▶ **Whoever scores a goal will be a hero.**

EXERCISE 21.6

Identify dependent clauses.

In the following sentences, underline any dependent clauses. Note that some sentences may contain only independent clauses.

EXAMPLE:

Scientists who study the brain disagree about the nature of dreams. Because dreams cannot be examined by direct observation, scientists have to rely on the dreamers' descriptions of their dreams.

1. In 1900, Sigmund Freud, a former neurologist, published a book called *The Interpretation of Dreams,* which discussed the purpose of dreams. *pron.*

2. Freud believed that dreams reveal the sleeper's unconscious desires in a disguised form.

3. Today modern psychoanalysts are less interested in dream interpretation, and some disagree with Freud's theories.

4. One of these is Dr. J. Allan Hobson, a psychiatrist at Harvard Medical School, who considers dreams simply a byproduct of the sleeping brain.

5. The activity of the brain stem produces dream images, but according to Dr. Hobson, this activity is random.

6. However, Mark Solms of the Royal London School of Medicine, a neuropsychologist, holds a different view and maintains that dreams help to motivate people to pursue goals.

7. Dr. Solms's opinion is more in line with Freud's century-old theory because Freud saw providing motivation as one purpose of dreams.

8. Although everyone without brain damage appears to dream, dreams may serve different functions for people in different societies. *signal that indept. clause is coming*

9. For example, according to a Finnish researcher, when people in hunter-gatherer societies dream about threatening events, they apparently unconsciously use those dreams to prepare responses to the threats.

10. Freud abandoned the physical study of the brain, neurology, to study the workings of the mind, but neurologists today use dreams to understand how the brain and the mind work together.

EXERCISE 21.7

Identify independent clauses.

Underline the independent clauses in the passage by Ruth Reichl on page 74.

EXAMPLE:

When we woke up in the morning, <u>the smell of baking bread was wafting through the trees.</u>

Note: The subordinating word *that* can sometimes be omitted from an adjective clause or a noun clause (p. 340).

EXERCISE 21.8

Identify clauses.

In the following passage by Calvin Trillin, which type of clause dominates: independent or dependent? How many clauses make up the second sentence? Find an example in the passage of coordinate independent clauses.

> In fact, most people find us rather traditional. My wife and I have a marriage certificate, although I can't say I know exactly where to put my hands on it right at the moment. We have two children. We have a big meal on Christmas. We put on costumes at Halloween. (What about the fact that I always wear an ax-murderer's mask on Halloween? This happens to be one of the peculiarities.) We make family decisions in the traditional American family way, which is to say that the father is manipulated by the wife and the children. We lose a lot of socks in the wash. At our house, the dishes are done and the garbage is taken out regularly—after the glass, cans and other recyclable materials have been separated out. We're not talking about a commune here.
>
> —Calvin Trillin, "A Traditional Family"

EXERCISE 21.9

Find clauses in your own writing.

Look at a recent piece of your own writing. Underline in pencil all the independent clauses. Underline subordinate dependent clauses in another color pen or pencil.

21f Sentence types

You saw several examples of simple sentences in 21c, sentences with a subject and a predicate in only one independent clause. But as you know, writing is much more varied. When you review a draft of your writing, check to see whether your sentences connect well to each other and flow gracefully. A string of simple sentences may seem to readers like a grade school primer—*See Spot run; Jane saw Spot*—sentences not exactly guaranteed to excite your readers. If you examine and revise how the sentence before and the sentence after are related to the sentence under consideration, then you should be able to vary your sentences and include a mix of the four sentence types: simple, compound, complex, and compound-complex sentences.

1. A *simple sentence* contains one independent clause.

   ▶ **Kara raised her hand.**

2. A *compound sentence* contains two or more independent clauses connected with one or more coordinating conjunctions (*and, but, or, nor, so, for, yet*), or with a semicolon alone, or with a semicolon and a transitional expression (5e).

   ┌── independent clause ──┐   ┌────── independent clause ──────┐
   ▶ **She raised her hand, and the whole class was surprised.**

   ┌── independent clause ──┐   ┌──── independent clause ────┐
   ▶ **She raised her hand, but nobody else responded.**

   ┌── independent clause ──┐ ┌──── independent clause ────┐
   ▶ **She raised her hand; the whole class was surprised.**

   ┌── independent clause ──┐   ┌── independent clause ──┐
   ▶ **She raised her hand; as a result, the whole class was**

   ┌──────┐
   surprised.   *comes first + so is punctuated*

3. A *complex sentence* contains an independent clause and one or more dependent clauses (21e).

   ┌──────── dependent clause ────────┐   ┌ independent clause ┐
   ▶ **Because she had never volunteered before, the whole class**

   ┌──────┐ ┌──── dependent clause ────┐
   was surprised when she raised her hand.   *comes after, so no punct.*

   ┌ independent clause ┐
   ┌────── ┌──── dependent clause ────┐
   ▶ **The student who had never volunteered before decided to**

   ┌──────┐
   raise her hand.

   ┌ independent clause ┐   ┌──── dependent clause ────┐
   ▶ **Kara wondered what the response would be.**

4. A *compound-complex sentence* contains at least two independent clauses and at least one dependent clause.

   ┌──── dependent clause ────┐ ┌──── independent clause ────┐
   ▶ **When she raised her hand, the whole class was surprised,**

   ┌────── independent clause ──────┐ ┌── dependent clause ──┐
   and the professor waited eagerly as she began to speak.

EXERCISE 21.10

Identify sentence functions and sentence types.

In each of the following sentences, first underline any dependent clause once and any independent clause twice. Then identify each sentence by function (declarative, interrogative, imperative, or exclamatory) and by type (simple, compound, complex, or compound-complex) on the line following each sentence.

EXAMPLE:

<u><u>Oscar Wilde may be best known as a playwright</u></u>, but <u><u>he was</u></u>

<u><u>also a poet, novelist, journalist, essayist, and writer of children's</u></u>

<u><u>stories</u></u>. *declarative, compound*

1. As Oscar Wilde predicted in his youth, his writings have become his "great monument." _____

2. Wilde was famous in his twenties for his quick wit and clever retorts, and he was celebrated for his plays, particularly *The Importance of Being Earnest,* which has been called "one of the greatest English comedies of all time." _____

3. Has anyone ever seen the play without laughing out loud? _____

4. At the end of the twentieth century, Wilde's plays were again being performed on Broadway, and movie versions of them were being filmed. _____

5. See the original film of *The Importance of Being Earnest* if you possibly can, since it is a perfect comedy of manners. _____

6. Another successful play in New York at the end of the millennium was based on the transcripts of Wilde's sensational trial. _____

7. Wilde, married and the father of two children, became notorious later in life when he was arrested and jailed for having a homosexual relationship. _____

8. When the father of Wilde's young lover accused him of sodomy, Wilde retaliated by suing for libel, but he lost his case. _____

9. Was Wilde out of his mind to sue for libel, or did he expect his great popularity to protect him? _____

10. Wilde died a pauper in Paris at the age of forty-six, but his works continue to be read and performed, so his lost reputation has been restored. _____

EXERCISE 21.11
Identify types of sentences.

In the passage by Malcolm Gladwell on page 75, identify and label (1) a simple sentence, (2) a compound sentence, (3) a complex sentence, and (4) a compound-complex sentence. Compare your findings with those of your classmates, and discuss why you think Gladwell used those sentence types. Discuss what you think the effect would be if all the sentences were simple sentences.

21g Building up sentences

A sentence can be made up of many parts and still be a correctly structured sentence. The following examples show some of the many types of possible additions to a simple sentence. A note of caution, though: Although complicated structures can be technically correct, they may not be effective, as some of the following sentences illustrate.

┌ independent clause ┐
► **The lawyer roared.**

modifier (adjective)
► **The brilliant lawyer roared.**

modifier (adverb)
► **The brilliant lawyer roared loudly.**

prepositional
┌── phrase ──┐
► **The brilliant lawyer roared loudly with laughter.**

┌────── compound subject ──────┐
► **The brilliant lawyer and his client roared loudly with laughter.**

modifier (adverb)
► **Finally, the brilliant lawyer and his client roared loudly with laughter.**

▶ Finally, while they listened to the tapes on the bugging _____ adverb clause (time) _____

device, the brilliant lawyer and his client roared loudly with laughter.

▶ Finally, while they listened to the tapes on the bugging

compound
_____ predicate _____

device, the brilliant lawyer and his client roared loudly

with laughter and gave each other high-fives.

▶ Finally, while they listened to the tapes on the bugging device, the brilliant lawyer and his client roared loudly with

_ adverb clause (reason) _

laughter and gave each other high-fives because they knew

they had found a way to win the case.

_____ absolute phrase _____

▶ Finally, their hearts beating fast while they listened to the tapes on the bugging device, the brilliant lawyer and his client roared loudly with laughter and gave each other high-fives because they knew they had found a way to win the case.

▶ Finally, their hearts beating fast while they listened to the tapes on the bugging device, the brilliant lawyer and his client roared loudly with laughter and gave each other high-fives because they knew they had found a way to win

_____ adjective clause (relative) _____

the case that had once seemed unwinnable.

▶ Finally, their hearts beating fast while they listened to the tapes on the bugging device, the brilliant lawyer and his client roared loudly with laughter and gave each other high-fives because they knew they had found a way to win

the case that had once seemed unwinnable, but each of them

_____ coordinate independent clause _____

was smart enough to realize the opposition's strength.

▶ Finally, their hearts beating fast while they listened to the tapes on the bugging device, the brilliant lawyer and his client roared loudly with laughter and gave each other high-fives because they knew they had found a way to win the case that had once seemed unwinnable, but each of them was smart enough to realize the opposition's strength and

noun clause as direct object

what pitfalls lay ahead.

By the end, the sentence is getting unwieldy. But it is still structured accurately as a compound-complex sentence.

EXERCISE 21.12

Build up sentences from a simple sentence.

Build up two of the following simple sentences by adding modifiers, phrases, and clauses correctly connected to the basic subject + predicate.

The girl sang.   The novel is romantic.

The instructor gave a lesson.   My computer froze.

The dog ate my homework.   The architects decided.

The reviewer panned the restaurant.   People sweat.

REVIEW EXERCISE FOR CHAPTER 21

Identify sentence elements.

In the following passage, identify each of the numbered sentence elements. Choices include dependent clause, independent clause, simple subject, complete subject, active verb, passive verb, linking verb, subject complement, direct object, indirect object, object complement, adjective, adverb, prepositional phrase, participle phrase, gerund phrase, infinitive phrase, or conjunction.

EXAMPLE:

Toussaint L'Ouverture's successes gave Haitian revolutionaries a reason to continue their struggle.

indirect object

     (1) After the American Revolution had ended, other countries responded to the idea that a tyrannical government (2) could be

overthrown. A revolution began in France in 1789, and soon French colonial rulers also faced trouble. (3) A group of slaves and former slaves on the island of Saint-Domingue, now called *Haiti*, rebelled against the French government there in 1791. A former slave named François Dominique Toussaint became an able leader of the slave rebellion and insisted that every human had a (4) universal right to freedom and citizenship. When a French (5) governor of the island noted that Toussaint's soldiers could (6) always find an opening through enemy lines, Toussaint adopted the surname *L'Ouverture*, (7) which means "the opening." The slave rebellion was successful, and the French rulers abolished (8) slavery on Saint-Domingue in 1793. Toussaint L'Ouverture's continuing calls for independence for his homeland (9) met with sympathy from President John Adams, who had also been a (10) revolutionary. Adams appointed a consul to the island in 1799 and hinted that the United States would not be opposed to (11) recognizing an independent Saint-Domingue. However, in 1800 the United States had elected (12) Thomas Jefferson the new (13) president. Jefferson was less (14) enthusiastic about supporting the new country. Since he (15) had been a firm believer in the necessity of both the American Revolution (16) and the French Revolution, Jefferson did not approve of a nation (17) made up of Afro-Caribbean slaves who had won their own freedom. (18) Although the nation did become independent, acquiring the name *Haiti* in 1804, Toussaint L'Ouverture did not live to see that event. (19) He was betrayed and captured by Napoleon's troops in 1802, and he died the following year (20) in a French prison. He is still honored as a freedom fighter and the father of Haitian independence.

Chapter **22**

Top Ten Sentence Problems

This chapter introduces you to ten of the most common problems facing all writers of Standard English sentences, drawn from classrooms over more than thirty years.

Online Study Center   This icon will direct you to quick reference tools, Web resources, and research guides on the Web site at http://college.hmco.com/keys.html.

Common Problems

1. Phrase fragments, p. 349
2. Clause fragments, p. 350
3. Run-on sentences and comma splices, p. 350
4. Mixed constructions, p. 350
5. Wrong verb forms, p. 351
6. Inappropriate tense shifts, p. 351
7. Lack of subject-verb agreement, p. 351
8. Wrong pronoun case and reference, p. 352
9. Adjective/adverb confusion, p. 352
10. Double negatives, p. 352

The purpose of this list is to make you aware of common errors. To learn more about any of the sentence problems—for more definitions, details, and examples—turn to the sections mentioned in the cross-references.

Online Study Center **Sentence Problems** Sentence problem checklist

1. Phrase fragments To be complete, a sentence must have both a subject and a complete verb. A phrase fragment lacks a subject, a complete verb, or both. Identify phrase fragments and edit to attach them to a sentence that contains a subject and a complete verb (23b).

NO
: **Whoever wrote, "Not a creature was stirring, not even a mouse," never had mice in the wall.** *Creating a terrible racket at night.* [Lacks a subject and a complete verb]

YES
: **Whoever wrote, "Not a creature was stirring, not even a mouse," never had mice in the wall. They create a terrible racket at night.**

: **Whoever wrote, "Not a creature was stirring, not even a mouse," never had mice in the wall creating a terrible racket at night.**

NO
: **She never talks about her inner feelings.** *Her feelings of fear or joy.* [Lacks a verb]

YES
: **She never talks about her inner feelings of fear or joy.**

NO   **She is looking for new acting parts.** *The more varied,*
         the better. [Lacks a subject and a verb]

YES   **She is looking for new acting parts, the more varied,**
         the better.

2. Clause fragments   A dependent clause must always be connected to an independent clause. If you begin a sentence with *when,*
because, if, although, whereas, or some other subordinating conjunction, or with a relative pronoun such as *who, which,* or *that,* connect
that clause to an independent clause (23c).

▶ The play failed/ ~~Because~~ it received three bad reviews.
  ^{because}

▶ Fog can interfere with film projection at a drive-in movie
  theater/ ~~Whereas~~ power outages sometimes interrupt the
  ^{, whereas}

  show at a mall cinema.

▶ The manager reprimanded all the slackers/ ~~Who~~ had been
  spending too much time at the water cooler.
  ^{who}

3. Run-on sentences and comma splices   A sentence should not
run on into another sentence without appropriate end punctuation.
Separate or revise independent clauses that are connected incorrectly
(see 23g and 23h).

▶ He trained hard, ~~he~~ never considered the strain.
  ^{He}

▶ The city is lively, the restaurants and clubs are open late.

▶ The film has been released, however, it has not come to
  our theater.

4. Mixed constructions   Look for sentences that might make readers say "Huh?"—sentences that begin in one way but end in another,
resulting in fuzzy syntax (24a). Readers should be able to tell clearly
who (or what) is doing what (17a).

▶ In ~~the~~ essay "Notes of a Native Son" ~~by~~ James Baldwin
  ^{his}

  discusses growing up in Harlem with his strict father.

The cat the scientists cloned
▶ ~~Scientists cloned a cat~~ has some resemblance to its
biological mother.

                                                          we
▶ Because movies don't show history accurately ~~makes us~~ all
wonder about the truth.

5. Wrong verb forms   Be sure to use standard verb forms. Avoid
nonstandard forms, such as *brung, has went, should of, have being
noticed, have drank* (25a, 25b, 25c).

                                    come
▶ The cloned kitten could have ~~came~~ out with anomalies.

                      have
▶ The parents should ~~of~~ supported the teacher in her decision
to fail the students.

6. Inappropriate tense shifts   Avoid flip-flopping between past
and present time without reason (25i).

               writes
▶ Foote ~~wrote~~ about Shiloh and describes its aftermath.

▶ We lived without furniture for six weeks this fall while the
            were   was
movers ~~are~~ all busy, the bank ~~is~~ processing a loan, and

school began.

7. Lack of subject-verb agreement   In the present tense, use the
same form of the verb for each person except third person singular.
For the verb *be*, see 25d.

| I, you, we, they | walk |
| he, she, it | walks |

                has
▶ the owner ~~have~~   ▶ the author suggest_s_
            doesn't
▶ she ~~don't~~   ▶ It pose_s_ a problem.

▶ The students in the class likes͞ peer response.

However, determining what is a singular subject can be difficult:
see chapter 26 for detailed explanations and examples.

8. Wrong pronoun case and reference Check that subject and object pronouns are correct (27a), and avoid ambiguous or unclear pronoun references (27c).

My sister and I
▶ ~~Me and my sister~~ went to Florida.
              ^

                                                         me
▶ The incident in the story reminds him of my mother and ~~I~~.
                                                        ^

▶ When Dean and George crossed the border with two

   customs officers
   friends, ~~they~~ searched all the luggage.
            ^

9. Adjective/adverb confusion Use the appropriate forms of adjectives and adverbs in the right places (28a–28c).

        well
▶ They did ~~good~~ in the playoffs.
          ^

                      really
▶ They managed to compete ~~real~~ well in the playoffs.
                         ^

Well is an adverb and needs an adverb as a modifier, not an adjective.

10. Double negatives Double negatives can be vibrant in speech and are customary in some dialects, but avoid them in formal writing (28g).

       any
▶ They don't have ~~no~~ problems with the proposal.
                 ^

    can
▶ He ~~can't~~ hardly wait.
     ^

KEY POINTS
Keep a Sentence Problem Log

1. Keep a written log of any of the top ten sentence problems you or your tutor, instructor, or classmates identify in your writing.

2. Write down each problematic sentence and one way to revise it.

3. Identify the nature of each problem.

4. Write down which handbook sections may help you deal with those problems and how you intend to work on identifying and correcting those types of errors. As time goes on, you should find yourself adding fewer and fewer examples to the list.

Online Study Center **Sentence Problems** Sentence Problem Log

EXERCISE 22.1

Identify problems.

Each of the following items contains one of the ten most common sentence problems. Find and correct the problem in each sentence. Then write the type of problem on the line following the sentence.

EXAMPLE:

When an ecosystem becomes less diverse, Aᵃdisease that strikes one kind of plant or animal can affect every creature in the food chain.
clause fragment _____

1. In 1983, a mysterious disease attacks sea urchins in the Caribbean and killed most of the species known as *Diadema.*

   _____

2. According to the Smithsonian Tropical Research Institute. The sea urchin plague caused the biggest die-off ever reported for a marine animal. _____

3. In a 3.5-million-square-kilometer area of the Caribbean had once been home to millions of *Diadema* sea urchins.

   _____

4. Algae began to spread quickly in this vast ocean area. After 97 percent of the *Diadema* urchins that had once controlled the algae's growth by eating them died. _____

5. Soon, the algae had grew over many of the coral reefs, preventing young coral from attaching and building on top of older coral. _____

6. Consequently, the coral reefs of the Caribbean have been dying off since 1983 scientists now know that their survival depends on the algae-eating services of the *Diadema* sea urchins.

   _____

7. *Diadema* sea urchins had not always been the only algae-controlling species in this part of the Caribbean; several species of fish and them had once competed to eat the aquatic plants.

   _____

8. Then overfishing removed most of the other algae eaters of the coral reefs so that for a time the sea urchins could dine real well on the algae until they, too, began to disappear.

   _____

9. Scientists from a Florida laboratory has a plan to reintroduce *Diadema* sea urchins to the algae-choked waters.

   _____

10. Marine biologists do not have no illusions that simply bringing sea urchins back to the Caribbean can save the reefs, but the experiment is a hopeful start. _____

Chapter **23**

Sentence Fragments, Run-Ons, and Comma Splices

The boundaries of a sentence are important in Standard English. Readers expect the beginnings and endings of sentences to occur at anticipated points and with appropriate signals in the form of punctuation marks. Misleading signals mislead readers. Do not use a comma to mark the end of a sentence, and never use a period if a group of words is not a complete sentence. Indicate the end of a sentence with a period, question mark, or exclamation point (chapter 31).

23a What is a fragment?

Speech is filled with fragments, and nobody expects otherwise.

> Done your essay?
> 'Fraid not.
> Again?
> Not my fault this time.
> Where were you yesterday?
> At the beach.
> Who with?
> Joe and Tom.
> Cool.

Online Study Center   This icon will direct you to quick reference tools, Web resources, and research guides on the Web site at http://college.hmco.com/keys.html.

But writing is different from speech. Writers do not have intonation, face-to-face contact, gestures, and facial expressions at their disposal to help them communicate. They have to rely on structure and punctuation—the look of words and sentences on the page or screen. Readers of formal, academic writing will expect only a complete sentence to be punctuated as a complete sentence. They always expect complete sentences, not fragments.

KEY POINTS

What Is a Sentence Fragment?

A sentence fragment is a string of words punctuated as a sentence but missing one or more crucial elements. See 21b for the necessary features of a sentence. Identify your own sentence fragments by asking these three questions about a series of words you punctuate as a sentence:

1. Does the "sentence" have a complete verb?

   were
   ▶ We watched the rehearsal. The jugglers‸practicing for four hours. [The verb is not complete. "The jugglers practicing for four hours" is a fragment.]

2. Does the verb have a subject?

   They argued
   ▶ They drove for six days. ~~Argued~~‸all the way.

3. Is there an independent clause—a subject + predicate not introduced with a subordinating word (a subordinating conjunction, a relative pronoun, or a word introducing a noun clause)?

   because
   ▶ The spectators shrieked/ ~~Because~~‸the race was so close.
   ["Because the race was so close" is an adverb clause not attached to an independent clause. It is a fragment.]

A phrase not attached to an independent clause, a dependent clause not attached to an independent clause, and an independent clause with no subject or complete verb are all sentence fragments. You need to watch out for them and edit them. Often you can fix a fragment by connecting it to a closely related sentence in your text.

23b Identifying and correcting a phrase fragment

A phrase is a group of words that lacks a subject, a verb, or both (21d). A phrase fragment is a phrase incorrectly punctuated as if it were a complete sentence.

▶ He wanted to make a point. **To prove his competence.**
　　　　　　　　　　　　　⌐— fragment: infinitive phrase —⌐

▶ Althea works every evening. **Just trying to keep up with her boss's demands.**
　　　　　　　　　　⌐— fragment: -*ing* participle phrase —⌐

▶ Ralph talked for hours. **Elated by the company's success.**
　　　　　　　⌐— fragment: past participle phrase —⌐

▶ They kept dialing the boss's phone number. **With no luck.**
　　　　　　　　　　　fragment: prepositional phrase

▶ A prize was awarded to Ed. **The best worker in the company.**
　　　　　　　⌐— fragment: noun phrase (appositive) —⌐

▶ The family set out for the new country. **A country with freedom of religion.**
　　　　　　　fragment: noun phrase
　　　　　　　⌐— (appositive) —⌐

▶ Nature held many attractions for Thoreau. **First, the solitude.**
　　　　　　　　　　fragment: noun phrase

Methods of correcting a phrase fragment

1. Attach the phrase to a nearby independent clause.

▶ He wanted to make a point, ~~To~~ **to** prove his competence.
[Simply remove the period and capital letter.]

▶ A prize was awarded to Ed, ~~The~~ **the** best worker in the company. [Use a comma before an appositive phrase, and remove the capital letter.]

▶ The family set out for a new country, ~~A country~~ with freedom of religion.

Or change the period to a dash for emphasis:

▶ The family set out for a new country—a country with freedom of religion.

2. Change the phrase to an independent clause.

> *She is just*
> ▶ **Althea works every evening.** ~~Just~~ **trying to keep up with her boss's demands.** [Add a subject and a complete verb.]

> *he valued*
> ▶ **Nature held many attractions for Thoreau. First, the solitude**. [Add a subject and a verb.]

3. Rewrite the whole passage.

> *was so*   *elated*   *that he talked for hours.*
> ▶ **Ralph** ~~talked for hours. Elated~~ **by the company's success.**
> [Make the fragments into a clause, and connect it to another clause with a subordinating word—in this case, one showing a result.]

EXERCISE 23.1

Identify and correct phrase fragments.

In each of the following items, identify any phrase fragment, and correct it either by attaching it to a nearby independent clause or by changing it to an independent clause. Some sentences may be correct.

EXAMPLE:

American popular music has had an enthusiastic following

since
around the world. ~~Since~~ the early days of rock and roll.

1. Every country has its own musical styles. Based on the traditional music of its people.

2. Having its own tradition as the birthplace of jazz, blues, and rock music. The United States has long been one of the world's leading exporters of popular music.

3. In spite of enjoying enormous popularity in their own countries. Many performers from Europe, South America, Africa, and Asia have had a hard time attracting American fans.

4. Some American musicians have championed their favorite artists from abroad. Examples include the hip-hop artist Jay-Z's collaboration with South Asian artist Punjabi MC on the hit song "Beware of the Boys" and Beck's tribute to the late French singer-songwriter Serge Gainsbourg.

5. Although some U.S. music fans pay attention to foreign musical styles, most Americans buy the music they know from

American top-40 radio and MTV. Songs also loved by fans around the world for sounding typically American.

6. However, not all Americans are native English speakers. Listening exclusively to English-language music.

7. Latin music has had some crossover success in the United States. Propelled, at least at first, by the high percentage of Spanish-speaking people in this country.

8. On American radio and television today, some of the most popular male acts are Latin pop stars. Singing sensations such as Marc Anthony, Ricky Martin, and Enrique Iglesias.

9. These singers are considered crossover artists because they have achieved mainstream success by singing in English. After making earlier recordings in Spanish.

10. Perhaps there will be a time when artists can have big hits with songs sung in a foreign language. At present, however, singing in English is almost always required for being successful in America.

23c Identifying and correcting a dependent clause fragment

A dependent clause cannot stand alone. The subordinating words that introduce dependent adverb clauses include, for example, *because, if, unless, when, whenever, while, although,* and *after* (see p. 338 in 21e for a list); *that, which, who, whom,* or *whose* introduce adjective clauses; and words such as *what, when, why,* or *whatever* introduce noun clauses (p. 340). A clause introduced with any subordinating word must be attached to an independent clause.

▶ **The family set out for a new country. A country in which** ⌐ fragment ⌐

they could practice their culture and religion.

▶ **Lars had always wanted to be a stand-up comic. Because he** ⌐ fragment ⌐
liked to make people laugh.

▶ **Rosa often talks about her relationship with her parents.** ⌐ fragment ⌐
How she grew up following her family's values.

Note: Some "time" words (such as *after, before, since,* and *until*) can function as prepositions, adverbs, or subordinating conjunctions:

adverb
▶ **We ate dinner. After, I left.**

subordinating conjunction
▶ **After we ate dinner, I left.**

Methods of correcting a dependent clause fragment

1. Connect the dependent clause to an independent clause.

   ▶ **The family set out for a new country in which they could practice their culture and religion.**

   ▶ **Rosa often talks about her relationship with her parents,**
   and how
   ~~How~~ she grew up following her family's values.

2. Delete the subordinating conjunction (see the list on p. 336). The dependent clause then becomes an independent clause, which can stand alone.

   He
   ▶ **Lars had always wanted to be a stand-up comic. ~~Because he~~ liked to make people laugh.**

Beginning a sentence with a dependent clause   A subordinating conjunction (such as *because, when,* or *although*) at the beginning of a sentence does not automatically signal a fragment. A correctly punctuated sentence may begin with a subordinating conjunction introducing a dependent clause, as long as the sentence also contains an independent clause.

As you edit your own work, if you begin your sentence with an adverb clause, always make sure you put a comma rather than a period at the end of that clause. A period at the end of an adverb clause at the beginning of a sentence creates a sentence fragment—as in *Because he liked to make people laugh.*

Look for the following pattern whenever you begin a sentence with a capitalized subordinating conjunction:

Because (When, Although, Since, etc.)…**,** subject + predicate.

subject
comma
▶ **Because Lars had always wanted to make people laugh, he**
├────── predicate ──────┤
decided to be a stand-up comedian.

subordinating conjunction   comma
     ⌐┼——— dependent clause ————┐ ││ ┌——— independent clause ———
▶ **When the circus arrives in town, the elephants parade along**

       ⌐——————————┐

the main street.

EXERCISE 23.2
Identify and correct dependent clause fragments.

The following sentences may contain dependent clause fragments. Identify and correct any such fragments either by connecting the dependent clause to an independent clause (deleting any unnecessary repetition) or by deleting the subordinating conjunction. Some sentences may be correct.

EXAMPLE:

A study by psychologists at the University of Kentucky in

                     that
Lexington offers interesting results, ~~That~~ support a relationship
                          ^

between thinking positively and living a long life.

1. A group of nuns wrote autobiographies sixty years ago. When they were young women.

2. Because the nuns all had similar lifestyles and social status. Psychologists have looked closely at the autobiographies and compared the lives of the writers.

3. Not surprisingly, few nuns reported negative emotions. Since they knew that their Mother Superior would read the autobiographies.

4. However, some reported having "very happy" experiences and a positive attitude about the future. Others were more neutral.

5. Psychologists discovered that the nuns who had expressed positive views lived an average of seven years longer than the other nuns. A conclusion that indicates that looking on the bright side may be good for a person's health.

6. The nuns' autobiographies have also been studied by experts in Alzheimer's disease. Who were hoping to discover clues about the illness.

7. Researchers examined the autobiographies to find out. If the nuns who later developed the disorder had provided hints in their writing.

8. After they had analyzed the autobiographies. The researchers found an interesting difference between the nuns who had developed Alzheimer's disease and the nuns who had not.

9. The nuns whose memories had remained intact throughout their lives had used more complicated syntax. When they had written about their experiences.

10. Although the research findings are fascinating, no one knows how syntax and Alzheimer's are linked. Using complicated syntax may not cause any changes in a person's brain.

23d Identifying and correcting a fragment resulting from a missing subject, verb, or verb part

Every sentence must contain a subject and a complete verb in an independent clause. A word group that is punctuated like a sentence but lacks a subject or a verb or has an incomplete verb that does not show tense (25a and 25d) is a fragment.

▶ **The commuters were staring hopefully down the track. Just**
———— fragment: missing subject ————
wanted to get to work on time.

—— fragment: incomplete verb ——
▶ **Overcrowding is a problem. Too many people living in**

one area.

—— fragment: missing verb ——
▶ **The candidate explained his proposal. A plan for off-street**

parking.

Methods of correcting Add a subject to the fragment, add a complete verb, or recast the word group.

They just
▶ **The commuters were staring hopefully down the track. ~~Just~~ wanted to get to work on time.**

▶ **The commuters were staring hopefully down the**
just wanting
track. ~~Just wanted~~ to get to work on time.

▶ Overcrowding is a problem. Too many people ^are^ living in one area.

▶ Overcrowding is a problem, ^with too^ ~~Too~~ many people living in one area.

▶ The candidate explained his ~~proposal. A~~ plan for off-street parking.

▶ The candidate explained his proposal. ^He emphasized a^ A plan for off-street parking.

ESL NOTE

Subject *it* Required

Never omit an *it* subject, even in a dependent clause. Remember that every clause needs both a subject and a predicate.

▶ The essay won a prize because ^it^ was so well researched.

EXERCISE 23.3

Identify and correct fragments resulting from missing subjects, verbs, or verb parts.

In each of the following items, identify and correct any fragment resulting from a missing subject, verb, or verb part either by adding the necessary subject, verb, or verb part or by rewriting. Some items may be correct.

EXAMPLE:

Many parts of the United States now face a shortage of teachers.

^Few people are^
~~People~~ willing to put up with evening and weekend work,

unruly classes, and a smaller paycheck than other professions

offer.

1. Teachers were once regarded as committed, admirable professionals. People earning more respect than money.

2. Today, many teachers feel that they do not even command respect. Just seem to get blamed when students do not do well in class.

3. Most people enter teaching with high ideals. Young graduates hoping to make a difference in a child's life.

4. To many young people today, however, teaching seems less attractive than ever. Trying to remain idealistic is difficult in the face of low pay, large classes, and disrespect from politicians and parents who accuse teachers of performing their jobs badly.

5. Better training, higher pay, and more respect from political figures might help attract bright, motivated young people to the teaching profession. Might make them choose the classroom over a business or legal career.

23e Identifying and correcting a fragment consisting of one part of a compound predicate

A predicate with two parts joined by *and, but, or,* or *nor* (known as a *compound predicate*) should not be split into two sentences. Both parts of the predicate must appear in the same sentence.

┌── fragment ──┐
▶ **After an hour, the dancers changed partners. And adapted**

────────────────────────

to a different type of music. [The compound predicate is *"changed* partners and *adapted* to a different type of music."]

Method of correcting   Correct the fragment by removing the period and capital letter.

and
▶ **After an hour, the dancers changed partners, ~~And~~ adapted to a different type of music.**
                                              ^

EXERCISE 23.4
Identify and correct fragments consisting of part of a compound predicate.

In each of the following items, identify and correct any fragment containing part of a compound predicate by joining it to the independent clause containing the rest of the predicate. Some items may be correct.

EXAMPLE:

Carl Linnaeus, an eighteenth-century Swedish botanist, placed

all living things into carefully defined categories/ ~~And~~ created a
                                                    and

system for naming every creature and plant.

1. Entomologists, scientists who study insects, often discover new species. And get the opportunity to name the creatures that they find.

2. Most people who name a new species either choose a name in honor of someone who assisted with the discovery. Or describe the species—often in Latin—with the new name.

3. However, the discoverer of a new wasp in the genus *Heerz* wanted to add humor to the new discovery. And called the wasp *Heerz tooya.*

4. One entomologist wanted to compliment *Far Side* cartoonist Gary Larson. And named a newly discovered owl louse *Strigiphilus garylarsoni* in 1989.

5. Entomologists do serious work with insects, but many of them also appear to have a sense of humor about their discoveries.

23f Using fragments intentionally

Advertisers and writers occasionally use fragments deliberately for a crisp, immediate effect: "What a luxury car should be." "Sleek lines." "Efficient in rain, sleet, and snow." "A magnificent film." Novelists and short story writers use fragments in dialogue to simulate the immediacy and fragmentary nature of colloquial speech. Journalists and nonfiction writers often use a fragment for a stylistic effect, to make an emphatic point:

> Maybe we are looking backward because we are unable to live in the future anymore, because the future comes so fast that we can't look forward to it. Or because one can feel happier in the past by being selective about it.
>
> —Roger Rosenblatt, "The Downside of Talking to the Dead"

I've sat in the spider-haunted remains of the living room where Evelyn wrote her letter, and looked out at the view she described, which doesn't look in the least like Argyllshire, or Kent, or Sussex. Not even little bits of it. Not even *slightly*.

—Jonathan Raban, *Bad Land: An American Romance*

In academic writing, too, writers sometimes use a fragment intentionally to make an emphatic point.

He [Dylan Thomas] lived twenty-four years after he began to be a poet. Twenty-four years of poetry, dwindling rapidly in the last decade.

—Donald Hall, *Remembering Poets*

You will also find fragments used intentionally in question form. This use is quite common in academic writing.

The point of the expedition is to bring them back alive. But what then?

—Carl Sagan, *Cosmos*

By all means, use fragments when you are writing dialogue or when you need to achieve a specific emphatic effect. However, when you are writing expository papers in college or business reports, use intentional fragments sparingly.

23g Identifying run-on (or fused) sentences and comma splices

If you run two independent clauses together without any punctuation or any coordinating conjunction between them, readers may not know where one idea ends and the next one begins.

RUN-ON ERROR **The lion cubs were fighting the elephants were snoozing.**

This error is called a *run-on* (or *fused*) *sentence*. If you use only a comma to connect independent clauses, the meaning may be clear, but the sentence is a *comma splice*—a sentence in which the clauses are improperly joined together (spliced) only with a comma.

COMMA SPLICE ERROR **The lion cubs were fighting, the elephants were snoozing.**

Here a reader seeing the comma would anticipate a series: *The lion cubs were fighting, the elephants were snoozing, and the seals were splashing.*

REVISED **The lion cubs were fighting, and the elephants were snoozing.**

Here are more examples (for ways to correct these, see 23h):

RUN-ON (FUSED) SENTENCES

┌──── independent clause ────┐ ┌──── independent clause ────┐
▶ **My mother's name is Marta my father's name is George.**

┌─ independent clause ─┐ ┌──── independent clause ────┐
▶ **Success is their goal happiness comes a close second.**

COMMA SPLICES

┌──── independent clause ────┐ ┌─ independent clause ─┐
▶ **The train picked up speed, the scenery flashed by.**

┌──── independent clause ─┐ ┌──── independent clause ────┐
▶ **Salmon swim upstream, they leap over huge dams to reach**

┌────────────┐
their destination.

┌──────── independent clause ────────┐ ┌──
▶ **Some parents support bilingual education, however, many**
                                           transitional expression
┌── independent clause ──┐
oppose it vociferously.

VARIATION Comma splices and run-ons are used in advertising, journalism, and other writing for stylistic effect.

                              comma splice emphasizing contrast
▶ **W. [George W. Bush] and Hillary [Clinton] took radically different paths. She clutched her husband's coattails, he**

clutched his father's.   —Maureen Dowd, *From A to Y at Yale*

                    comma splice emphasizing contrast
▶ **It's not that I'm afraid to die, I just don't want to be there when it happens.**   —Woody Allen, *Without Feathers*

Readers of academic expository writing may prefer a period or semicolon or a recasting of the sentence. Take the stylistic risk of an intentional comma splice only if you are sure what effect you want to achieve and you are sure readers will realize your intentions. See also 31b, Variations.

EXERCISE 23.5

Identify run-on sentences and comma splices.

For each of the following items, write *CS* on the line before the sentence if it is a comma splice, *RO* if it is a run-on sentence, and *OK* if the sentence is correctly written.

EXAMPLE:

_____CS_____ Many consumers want to buy American cars, unfortunately, choosing an American car is not as easy as it sounds.

1. _____ Often a car's parts are made in one country and assembled in another, can the car be considered American if the whole thing is not manufactured in this country?

2. _____ Sometimes car companies manufacture parts in the United States and also put cars together here however, these companies may have their headquarters in Japan.

3. _____ People who buy cars sold by Ford, an automaker whose name implies "made in the United States" to many Americans, may not know that the vehicles may have been assembled in Mexico.

4. _____ On the other hand, most Honda Accords are made in Ohio in fact, the Honda Corporation now manufactures more cars in the United States than in Japan.

5. _____ As several American auto manufacturers have become part of multinational corporations, globalization has made "buying American" increasingly difficult, consumers can no longer simply rely on the make of a car to determine its country of origin.

23h Correcting run-on sentences and comma splices

You can correct run-on sentences and comma splices in the following five ways. Select the one that works best for the sentence you are editing.

Method 1 Separate the independent clauses into individual sentences with a period (or question mark or exclamation point, if required).

▶ Success is their goal ⊙ ̂Happiness ~~happiness~~ comes a close second.

> They
> ► Beavers cut down trees with their teeth, ~~they~~ use the trees for
> food and shelter.

Method 2 Separate the independent clauses with a semicolon if one of the clauses begins with a transitional expression (which is followed by a comma) or if their ideas are closely related.

> ;
> ► Some parents support bilingual education however, many
> oppose it vociferously.
> ;
> ► The hummingbird is amazing its wings beat fifty to seventy-
> five times per second.

Method 3 Separate the independent clauses with a comma and a coordinating conjunction (*and, but, or, nor, so, for, yet*).

> , and
> ► My mother's name is Marta my father's name is George.
> but
> ► Woodpeckers look for insects in trees, they do not
> intentionally destroy live trees.

Method 4 Make one clause dependent by adding a subordinating conjunction (see the list on p. 336).

> When the
> ► ~~The~~ beavers dammed up the river, the rise in the water level
> destroyed the trees.
> whenever
> ► The scenery flashed by the train picked up speed.

Method 5 Make one clause a phrase beginning with an *-ing* participle and attach the phrase to the remaining independent clause.

> leaping
> ► Salmon swim upstream, ~~they leap~~ over huge dams to reach
> their destination.

EXERCISE 23.6

Correct run-on sentences and comma splices.

For each of the following items, write *CS* on the line if it is a comma splice, or write *RO* if it is a run-on sentence. Then correct the error by using one of the five methods described in 23h.

EXAMPLE:

_____CS_____ Pierre de Fermat, who was a brilliant mathematician,

but
left a puzzle in the margin of a book, he died without providing
                                    ^

its solution.

1. _____ Pierre de Fermat was a lawyer by trade his passion was mathematics.

2. _____ Fermat discussed his ideas in correspondence with other mathematicians nevertheless, as a modest man, he refused to have his name attached to any published work on mathematics.

3. _____ Fermat regarded prime numbers with a special fascination, he formulated a theory about prime numbers in 1640 that later became famous as Fermat's Last Theorem.

4. _____ In his notes, Fermat said that the theorem had a "marvelous" proof however, he claimed that he did not have enough room in the margin to write it down.

5. _____ Some mathematicians believed that a short, elegant answer existed, they struggled to find the proof of Fermat's Last Theorem.

6. _____ No one has ever found a short proof of the theorem most mathematicians now think that Fermat did not have one, either.

7. _____ Mathematician Andrew Wiles, who had been intrigued by Fermat's theorem since childhood, spent seven years working on the problem, in 1993, he announced that he had solved it.

8. _____ His proof was 150 pages long, a month after his announcement, other mathematicians discovered an error in Wiles's calculations.

9. _____ Wiles worked with another mathematician, Richard Taylor, he repaired the proof a year later.

10. _____ The proof of Fermat's Last Theorem was finally complete Wiles now says that successfully solving the problem that had occupied his mind for so many years was a bittersweet experience.

23i Correcting run-ons and comma splices occurring with transitional expressions

Run-ons and comma splices often occur with transitional expressions such as *in addition, however, therefore, for example,* and *moreover* (see the list in 5e). When one of these expressions precedes the subject of its own clause, end the previous independent clause with a period or a semicolon. Put a comma after the transitional expression, not before it.

CORRECTED
RUN-ON
ERROR

Martha cleaned her closets ~~in~~ addition she reorganized the kitchen.

CORRECTED
COMMA
SPLICE
ERROR

The doctor prescribed some medicine, however she did not alert the patient to the side effects.

Note: You can use the coordinating conjunctions *and, but,* and *so* after a comma to connect two independent clauses, but *in addition, however,* and *therefore* do not follow the same punctuation pattern.

▶ The stock market was rising, so he decided to invest most of his savings.

▶ The stock market was rising; therefore, he decided to invest most of his savings.

Commas should both precede and follow a transitional expression that does not appear at the beginning of its own clause:

▶ The doctor prescribed some medicine. She did not,

however, alert the patient to the side effects.

REVIEW EXERCISE FOR CHAPTER 23
Revise a passage.

Rewrite the following passage, revising any fragments, run-on sentences, and comma splices. Identify each type of error in the margin. Some sentences may be correct.

Millions of Americans express a belief in extrasensory perception, or ESP, they believe that certain people have psychic abilities. Movies like *The Sixth Sense* and commercials for telephone psychics add to the common perception. That psychic abilities are real.

Newspapers and television news shows are frequently too ready to provide a forum for self-proclaimed psychics. And too quick to dismiss the skeptical viewpoint—if the writers even bother to find out what skeptics believe. People who believe in ESP claim that skeptics are curmudgeons. Who automatically reject any claim about paranormal abilities, no matter how compelling the evidence. The truth is that no psychic has ever been able to demonstrate his or her abilities under controlled laboratory conditions, even though a skeptical organization, the James Randi Educational Foundation, has offered a million-dollar prize as an incentive for genuine psychics to step forward. People trained as magicians scoff at the performances of television psychics. Insisting that the techniques used are nothing more than "cold reading" tactics long favored by fortunetellers. Which any competent actor can learn. Although skeptics are often accused of belittling the feelings of grieving people, many would respond that the bereaved do not need to be cheated into thinking that their lost loved ones are in contact with television psychics. If there are "psychic" frauds preying on human grief. They should be exposed before any more innocent sufferers become pawns in their con games.

Chapter **24**

Sentence Snarls

Snarls, tangles, and knots are as difficult to deal with on a bad writing day as on a bad hair day, though they may not be as painful. Sentences with structural inconsistencies give readers trouble. They make readers do the work of untangling. This chapter points out how to avoid or edit common snarls.

24a Avoid fuzzy syntax.

Revise sentences that begin in one way and then veer off the track, departing from the original structure. When you mix constructions, make faulty comparisons, or tangle your syntax (the structure of a sentence), you confuse readers.

Online Study Center   This icon will direct you to quick reference tools, Web resources, and research guides on the Web site at http://college.hmco.com/keys.html.

Some

▶ ~~With some~~ professors who never give grades like to write comments. [Who are the people who "like to write comments"? The prepositional phrase *with some professors* cannot serve as the subject of the sentence.]

Pay special attention to sentences beginning with *with, by -ing,* or *when -ing.*

MIXED CONSTRUCTION | **When wanting to take on a greater role in business might lead a woman to adopt new personality traits.** [Readers get to the verb *might lead* without knowing what the subject is.]

POSSIBLE REVISIONS | **When wanting to take on a greater role in business, a woman might adopt new personality traits.** [This version provides a grammatical subject—*woman*—for the independent clause.]

Wanting to take on a greater role in business might lead a woman to adopt new personality traits. [This version deletes the subordinating conjunction *When.* Now the *-ing* phrase functions as the subject of *might lead.*]

When you make comparisons, be sure to tell readers clearly what you are comparing. (See also 27a, 27b, and 28i.)

FAULTY COMPARISON | **Like Wallace Stevens, her job strikes readers as unexpected for a poet.** [It is not her job that is like the poet Wallace Stevens; her job is like his job.]

REVISED | **Like Wallace Stevens, she holds a job that strikes readers as unexpected for a poet.**

Revise sentences that ramble on to such an extent that they become tangled. Make sure your sentences have clear subjects and verbs, and use coordination or subordination effectively. For a concise style, cut and check for action (chapters 16 and 17).

TANGLED | **The way I feel about getting what you want is that when there is a particular position or item that you want to try to get to do your best and not give up because if you give up you have probably missed your chance of succeeding.**

POSSIBLE REVISION | **To get what you want, keep trying.**

Note, though, that a sentence can be long and filled with phrases and clauses but still be grammatically accurate and stylistically acceptable, as in the examples in 21g. Tailor the length and complexity of your sentences to what you want to express and to readers' preferences.

EXERCISE 24.1

Correct fuzzy syntax: Mixed constructions and faulty comparisons.

In each of the following items, suggest corrections for any mixed constructions or faulty comparisons.

EXAMPLE:

Adopting
~~By adopting~~ the poetic techniques popular in colonial America enabled Phillis Wheatley to find an audience for her writings.

1. Phillis Wheatley's education, which was remarkable mainly because she received one, a rare luxury for a slave girl in the American colonies.

2. Wheatley, kidnapped from her homeland and sold into slavery when she was about seven, an experience that must have been traumatic.

3. By learning to read and write gave Phillis an opportunity to demonstrate her aptitude for poetry.

Book of poems by Phillis Wheatley, 1773

4. Like Alexander Pope, iambic pentameter couplets were Phillis Wheatley's preferred poetic form.

5. Publishing a book of poems, Phillis Wheatley, becoming famous partly because she was an African slave who could compete as a poet with well-educated white men.

6. Her work, poems in a very formal eighteenth-century style that found aristocratic admirers in America and England.

7. With the deaths of Mr. and Mrs. Wheatley, when Phillis was in her twenties, left her free but also penniless.

8. Like Zora Neale Hurston in the twentieth century, an impoverished, lonely death followed a loss of public interest in Wheatley's writings, but scholars discovered her work posthumously and realized her contribution to American literature.

24b Position modifiers appropriately.

A *modifier* is a word or phrase that describes or limits another word or phrase. Put modifiers in the right place. Keep single words, phrases, and clauses next to or close to the sentence elements that they modify.

Place a phrase or clause close to the word or words it modifies.

MISPLACED   **Sidel argues that young women's dreams will not always come true in her essay.** [Will the dreams come true in Sidel's essay, or does Sidel argue this point in her essay?]

REVISED   **In her essay, Sidel argues that young women's dreams will not always come true.**

Keep subject, verb, and object in close connection.   Sentences are clearer for a reader when all the parts are clearly connected. Once you have announced the subject, don't make readers wait too long for a verb.

NO   **The main *character* in the play, because the director in a rash moment had given the part to his inexperienced brother, *turned out* to be the weakest portrayal.**

YES   **Because the director in a rash moment had given the part to his inexperienced brother, the main *character* in the play *turned out* to be the weakest portrayal.** [Putting the adverb clause first creates expectation and keeps the subject and verb of the independent clause together.]

Similarly, do not delay a direct object to the end of a sentence.

NO   **The actors *had to rehearse* over a period of two days without a break *all the dramatic scenes*.**

YES   **The actors *had to rehearse all the dramatic scenes* over a period of two days without a break.**

Place modifiers (*only, even,* and so on) carefully.   Place a modifier such as *only, even, just, nearly, merely,* or *simply* immediately before the word it modifies. Consider the differences in meaning in the following sentences:

▶ She *only* likes Tom. [She doesn't love him.]

▶ She likes *only* Tom. [Does she like Juan?]

▶ *Only* she likes Tom. [Does anyone else like Tom?]

The meaning of a sentence changes significantly as the position of the word *only* changes, so careful placement is important.

▶ *Only* the journalist began to investigate the forgery. [and nobody else]

▶ The journalist *only* began to investigate the forgery. [but did not finish]

▶ The journalist began to investigate *only* the forgery. [and nothing else]

Make sure the modifier's position does not produce ambiguity. Don't make readers guess which part of a sentence a modifier refers to. A modifier that is ambiguous is often called a *squinting modifier* because it looks two ways at once.

NO   ▶ The writer who was being interviewed *aggressively* defended the violent scenes in

his novel. [Who was being aggressive here—the interviewer in his approach to the interview or the writer in his own defense?]

YES   ▶ The writer who was being *aggressively* interviewed defended the violent scenes in his novel.

▶ The writer who was being interviewed defended the violent scenes in his novel *aggressively.*

Consider the case for splitting an infinitive.   You split an infinitive when you place a word or phrase between *to* and the verb:

He tried to *immediately* answer *the question.* At one time, a split infinitive was regarded as an error—if not in grammar, at least in grace—and the general advice was always to avoid splitting an infinitive.

VARIATION   For current usage, *The New Oxford Dictionary of English* finds the use of split infinitives "both normal and useful," as in "To boldly go where no man has gone before" (*Star Trek*). However, such splitting may still irritate some readers, especially when a clumsy sentence is the result, as in the following:

———————— clumsy split infinitive (to inform) ————————

▶ **We want to sincerely, honestly, and in confidence inform you of our plans for expansion.**

Use common sense. Read a sentence aloud. If you think your readers may fret over a split infinitive and if the sentence works just as well without splitting the infinitive, then revise the sentence. If the sentence is clear and effective with the split and the split helps to avoid ambiguity or clumsy syntax (*She saw it as a necessity to always achieve perfection in her work*), then keep it—but get ready *to boldly face* any criticism.

EXERCISE 24.2

Correct misplaced modifiers.

Revise any of the following sentences in which the placement of modifiers could be improved. Some sentences may not need revision.

EXAMPLE:

only

By July 2002, two sisters had ~~only~~ competed against each other four times in the finals of a Grand Slam tennis tournament.

1. In 1884, the sisters Maud and Lilian Watson, years before women's tennis was a professional sport, played against each other in the first Wimbledon ladies' championship final.

2. More than a century later, two young California sisters who played tennis seriously began to hope that they would someday rule the tennis world.

3. In September 2001, those sisters, Venus and Serena Williams, faced each other after demolishing their semifinals opponents in the final match of the U.S. Open.

4. Millions of viewers watched as the first Grand Slam tennis championship was shown on prime-time television to feature two African American players.

5. With a serve that has been measured at 127 miles per hour, most fans anticipated that the winner would be Venus.

6. Venus Williams won in two sets, who had won four of the five professional matches against her younger sister before the U.S. Open.

7. However, in 2002, Serena was able to powerfully and skillfully win against her older sister in the French Open, Wimbledon, and U.S. Open finals.

8. Richard Williams, the father of Venus and Serena, who has only been their coach and manager, refuses to watch the matches.

9. Richard Williams taught all five of his daughters to play tennis when they were preschoolers on the public courts in South Central Los Angeles.

10. Many fans wondered if Venus and Serena Williams could sustain their reign, but as Serena came back from a slump to win the Australian Open in 2005, both sisters seemed likely to continue as major players in the tennis world.

EXERCISE 24.3

Change meaning by changing the position of a modifier.

How many meanings can you get from the following sentence about a bus accident by placing the word *only* in a variety of positions? What are the positions, and what are the meanings that result from each position?

The passenger hurt his arm.

24c Avoid dangling modifiers.

A modifier that is not grammatically linked to the noun or phrase it is intended to describe is said to be *dangling*. A sentence must contain a word or phrase that the modifier is intended to modify, as the following examples illustrate.

DANGLING

Walking into the house, the telephone rang.

[The sentence says the telephone was walking.]

DANGLING Delighted with the team's victory, the parade route was decorated by the fans.

[The sentence says the parade route was delighted.]

Fix a dangling modifier in one of the following ways.

Method 1   Retain the modifier, but make the subject of the independent clause the person or thing modified.

REVISED Walking into the house, we heard the telephone ring.

REVISED Delighted with the team's victory, the fans decorated the parade route.

Method 2   Change the modifier phrase into a clause with its own subject and verb.

REVISED While we were walking into the house, the telephone rang.

REVISED Because the fans were delighted with the team's victory, they decorated the parade route.

VARIATION   Not all dangling modifiers are equal. Some are awkward and may make readers laugh (*After boiling for five hours, Granny May turned off the cabbage*), while others, particularly those with *it* used as a filler subject, are barely noticeable. *Looking at the house, it occurred to me that I had seen it before.* Readers can easily adjust to that usage and will not always feel confused. Still, it ultimately may please readers more (especially English instructors) if you are consistent and do not let your modifiers dangle.

EXERCISE 24.4

Identify dangling modifiers.

Classify each of the following sentences as *A* (if the sentence contains no dangling modifier), *B* (if the sentence contains a dangling modifier that is a clear error), or *C* (if the sentence contains a dangling modifier that might not offend the average reader). Then revise any sentences classified as *B* or *C*.

EXAMPLE:

I spotted

_____B_____ Browsing at the bookstore, a copy of the new translation of the *Iliad* caught my eye.

1. _____ Translating literature from one language into another, it is important to strive for both literal accuracy and a similar effect to that of the original work.

2. _____ Turning the Greek of the *Iliad* into English in 1997, Robert Fagles managed to translate the words accurately while keeping the poetry lyrical and muscular.

3. _____ Awarded several prizes for his translation of the *Iliad*, many educators delighted in using Fagles's book to show their students the difference that a good translation can make.

4. _____ Turning a lively, intelligent book from another culture into a dry, dull, or inaccurate English-language text, a reader's perspective can be distorted by a bad translation.

5. _____ Helping people everywhere appreciate the beauty and power of literature from around the world, cultural awareness improves with every great translation.

24d Avoid shifts in mood, pronoun person and number, and direct/indirect quotation.

Sudden shifts in your sentences can disconcert readers. (See also 25i on avoiding unnecessary shifts in verb tense.)

Do not make an abrupt shift in mood, especially between statement and command or between subjunctive and indicative. If you are writing declarative statements, use the indicative mood (see 21a) consistently.

▶ The students in this university should do more to keep the

They should pick
place clean. ~~Pick~~ up the litter and treat the dorms like home.

Keep the mood consistent. Do not begin in the indicative mood and then switch to the imperative. Choose one mood or the other, not both.

NO   **College administrators have issued several directions: Students should use only the south parking lots and do not park on the grass.**

YES   **College administrators have issued several directions: Students should use only the south parking lots and should not park on the grass.**

YES   **College administrators have issued several directions: Use only the south parking lots and do not park on the grass.**

Be careful with conditional sentences (begining with *if* or *unless*), and avoid a shift in mood (25k).

were
▶ He would be able to make significant changes if only he ~~is~~ more organized.

Do not shift person, number, or point of view. To make generalizations about people, use *they, we, you,* or *one,* and use it consistently. Be consistent in using first, second, or third person pronouns. For example, if you begin by referring to *one,* do not switch to *you* or *we.* Also avoid shifting unnecessarily between third person singular and plural forms. Note, though, that long passages devoted to discussing what "one" does become vague and pretentious for readers.

SHIFT   *One* **needs a high salary to live in a city because** *you* **have to spend so much on rent and transportation.**

POSSIBLE   *One* **needs a high salary to live in a city because** *one*
REVISIONS   **has to spend so much on rent and transportation.**

         People **need a high salary to live in a city because** *they* **have to spend so much on rent and transportation.**

         A high salary is necessary in a city because rent and transportation cost so much.

See also 27g on when to use and when to avoid using *you.*

Do not shift between direct and indirect quotation, with or without quotation marks. See 25j and 43d for more on quotations.

SHIFT   The client told us that he wanted to sign the lease and would we prepare the papers.

REVISED   The client told us that he wanted to sign the lease and asked us to prepare the papers.

SHIFT   She wanted to find out whether any interest had accumulated on her account and was she receiving any money.

REVISED   She wanted to find out whether any interest had accumulated on her account and whether she was receiving any money.

EXERCISE 24.5
Correct inappropriate shifts: Mood, pronoun person and number, direct and indirect quotations.

On the line after each of the following sentences, identify inappropriate shifts in mood by writing *M*, inappropriate shifts in pronoun person by writing *PP*, inappropriate shifts in pronoun number by writing *PN*, and inappropriate shifts in direct and indirect quotations by writing *Q*. Then revise each inappropriate shift.

EXAMPLE:

                                                              people
Sharks do occasionally attack swimmers, but ~~you~~ are more
likely to be killed by a falling television than by a shark bite.
   _PP___

1. When a tourist in Florida wants an underwater adventure, you can swim in the ocean with sharks. _____

2. In 2001, a series of shark attacks on the east coast of the United States made Florida Fish and Wildlife Conservation commissioners ask whether swimmers were being too careless or were tourist attractions that feature swimming with sharks the cause of the problem? _____

3. When a tour operator puts bait in the water before a shark swim, they may be teaching sharks to associate people with food. _____

4. If sharks were fed too frequently by human beings, the commissioners wondered, will the big fish be more likely to endanger swimmers? _____

5. The curator of the International Shark Attack File told commissioners that the feeding probably didn't contribute to the attacks and would they tell people more about the good behavior of sharks. _____

6. The shark attacks shocked people around the country, and you heard about the attacks constantly in the late summer of 2001. _____

7. A shark can seem ferocious, but they are often in more danger from humans than humans are from the sharks. _____

8. People should not be frightened by the shark's torpedo-like body, scaly skin, and sharp teeth. Try to learn about the shark's habits instead. _____

9. Some scientists believe that if a person studies sharks, they will understand ocean ecosystems better. _____

10. Some species of sharks have become endangered because so many people like the taste of it. _____

24e Make subject and predicate a logical match: Avoid faulty predication.

To avoid confusing readers, never use a subject and predicate that do not make logical sense together (see 21c).

>   Building
> ► ~~The decision to build~~ an elaborate extension onto the train station made all the trains arrive late. [The decision did not delay the trains; building the extension did.]

>   Finding the
> ► ~~The~~ solution to the problem is a hard task. [A solution is not a task.]

EXERCISE 24.6

Avoid faulty predication.

In each of the following items, revise any sentence containing a subject and predicate that do not make logical sense together. Some sentences may be correct.

EXAMPLE:

> The
> ~~The coverage of the~~ Watergate scandal destroyed many
> Americans' faith in government.
> ^

1. The home of the Democratic National Committee was occupying a suite at the Watergate Hotel in Washington, D.C., in 1972.

2. A call to the police from a Watergate employee caught five men with eavesdropping equipment breaking into the suite.

3. The Nixon White House's attempts to cover up the involvement of senior officials led to the downfall of the Nixon presidency.

4. The reason the public became aware of crimes by high officials in the Nixon White House was because of reporting done by *Washington Post* journalists in the early 1970s.

Journalists Bob Woodward and Carl Bernstein

5. The determination of Bob Woodward and Carl Bernstein, two young *Post* reporters, traced a cover-up all the way to President Nixon.

6. Courageous action by the *Post*'s publisher, Katharine Graham, made the decision to continue running Woodward and Bernstein's Watergate reports when other papers feared to print the information.

7. At that time, the position of Katharine Graham was the only woman heading a major news organization.

8. The scorn of one official targeted by Woodward and Bernstein's investigation treated Graham with contempt; he apparently believed that she could be intimidated.

9. Katharine Graham instead personally telling Woodward and Bernstein and their editor, Ben Bradlee, not only to stick with the story but also to forge ahead with the investigation.

Transforming a newspaper's reputation: publisher Katharine Graham

10. Creating the *Post*'s reputation as one of the country's top news sources began with its coverage of Watergate.

24f Avoid faulty predication with definitions and reasons.

When you write a definition of a term, use parallel structures on either side of the verb *be*. In formal writing, avoid defining a term by using *is when* or *is where* (or *was when, was where*).

NO   **A tiebreaker in tennis is *where* they play one final game to decide the set.**

YES   **A tiebreaker in tennis is the final deciding game of a tied set.**

Writing about reasons, like writing definitions, has pitfalls. Avoid *the reason is because* in Standard English. Grammatically, an adverb clause beginning with *because* cannot follow the verb *be*. Instead, use *the reason is that*, or recast the sentence.

NO   *The reason* **Tiger Woods lost** *is because* **he could not handle the weather in Scotland.**

YES   *The reason* **Tiger Woods lost** *is that* **he could not handle the weather in Scotland.**

YES   **Tiger Woods lost *because* he could not handle the weather in Scotland.**

VARIATION   In speech, *the reason is because* is common and would probably hardly be noticed or tagged as an error. In writing, though, consider the audience and your writing situation. If formality and correctness are important to readers, avoid using *the reason is because*. Similarly, you may hear and see in print *the reason why*. Use *the reason that* in its place.

                                                                that
▶ **The TV commentator explained the reason ~~why~~ Tiger Woods lost.**

Another possibility is to omit *that* if the meaning is clear without it.

▶ **The TV commentator explained the reason Tiger Woods lost.**

EXERCISE 24.7

Avoid faulty predication with definitions and reasons.

In each of the following sentences, identify and revise any faulty predication. Some sentences may be correct.

EXAMPLE:

                cash grants
Farm subsidies are ~~where~~ the government gives farmers ~~money~~ to help them grow certain crops.

1. One reason for farmers to receive subsidies is because they set aside part of their land for wildlife conservation.

2. Conservation, which is where the land is preserved in the most natural state possible, accounts for about 9 percent of farm subsidies in the United States.

3. Wetland preservation is when farmers stop draining swampy land and allow it to remain as a habitat for ducks and other waterfowl.

4. The main reason why the duck population is rebounding after ten years of decline is that a large percentage of farmers in North Dakota accepted subsidies to preserve wetlands on their property.

5. Providing federal subsidies for conservation was originally proposed by environmental groups but are now supported enthusiastically by organizations such as the National Rifle Association because the subsidies also benefit hunters.

24g Avoid using an adverb clause as the subject of a sentence.

An adverb clause cannot function as the subject of a sentence. (See 21e on adverb clauses.)

▶ ~~Because she swims~~ every day does not guarantee she is
Swimming
healthy. [The subject is now a noun (gerund) phrase,
Swimming every day, instead of a clause, *Because she swims every day*.]

▶ When beavers eat trees destroys the woods. [The dependent
, they
clause *When beavers eat trees* is now attached to an independent
clause with its own subject, *they*.]

24h Include all necessary words and apostrophes.

Include necessary words in compound structures. If you omit a verb form from a compound verb, the main verb form must fit into each part of the compound; otherwise, you must use the complete verb form (see 24j on parallel structures).

▶ He has always and will always try to preserve his father's
tried
good name in the community. [*Try* fits only with *will*, not with *has*.]

Include necessary words in comparisons. See also 28i.

▶ The volleyball captain is as competitive or even more
as
competitive than her teammates.

Sometimes you create ambiguity if you omit the verb in the second part of a comparison.

▶ He liked baseball more than his son. [Omitting *did* implies
did
that he liked baseball more than he liked his son.]

Include apostrophes with words that need them. Include an apostrophe to indicate possession or a contraction.

▶ My mother's expectations differed from Jing-Mei's mother.
's

▶ He can't understand her reasoning.

See also 28i and 33c.

EXERCISE 24.8

Identify omitted words and apostrophes.

In the following sentences, find and correct any errors of missing words or apostrophes.

EXAMPLE:

                                                  at
Quantum mechanics inspires new ways of looking and thinking about the universe.

1. One physicist seriously claims that there are as many universes or even more universes than the human mind can imagine.

2. This theory, known as the Many Worlds Interpretation, has always and may always be considered by many other physicists to be nothing more than a poetic way of thinking about quantum mechanics.

3. However, their basically metaphorical view of the Many Worlds Interpretation differs from David Deutsch.

4. Deutsch, an Oxford physicist, regards the Many Worlds Interpretation as more realistic than, for example, Stephen Hawking.

5. Deutsch's book *The Fabric of Reality* argues for the existence of infinite parallel universes populated by people who are similar but not quite the same as the individuals existing in our own universe.

24i State the grammatical subject only once.

Even when a phrase or clause separates the subject and verb of a clause, do not restate the subject, either with the same word or in pronoun form. (See also 43f.)

                                                        restated subject
▶ The nurse who took care of my father for many years she gave him comfort and advice.

When the subject is a whole clause, do not add an *it* subject.

▶ What may seem moral to some it is immoral to others.

EXERCISE 24.9

Avoid restating subjects.

In the following passage, cross out any restated subjects.

EXAMPLE:

Mother Ann Lee, who was an extremely unusual eighteenth-century woman, ~~she~~ founded the United Society of Believers in Christ's Second Appearing, a group that was also called the *Shakers*.

The Shakers, a religious sect that was founded in England in 1747 by Mother Ann Lee, were an offshoot of the Quakers. The Shaker belief in gender equality and the surprising fact that the Shaker leader was female they were viewed with suspicion in eighteenth-century England, and the Shakers faced persecution there. The group emigrated to the United States in search of religious freedom in 1774. Mother Lee's followers, who lived celibate lives in gender-segregated houses, they worked and prayed communally and replenished their numbers by recruiting. The Shakers were never a large group, but their numbers grew steadily until the twentieth century. The idea of choosing celibacy it now seems peculiar to many Americans, and the Shakers, indeed, have nearly died out since the group stopped accepting new members decades ago. However, some of the Shakers' beliefs have found modern admirers: their view that "beauty rests on utility" and the exquisitely crafted furniture designs they created to embody that view they are more popular than ever.

EXERCISE 24.10

Write sentence completions.

Make the following items into complete sentences, making sure you name only one grammatical subject in each independent clause.

EXAMPLE:

The book I read on my summer vacation __told a story of World War II__ .

1. The student who is the head of student government

2. Whatever you can do to help

3. Why a writer would want to avoid using the letter *e*

4. The big oak trunk sitting in the corner of the little girl's room

5. Computer programs aiming to identify grammar errors

24j Use parallel structures.

Structures are parallel when they have the same form. Use parallel structures to help readers see connections between the ideas in a sentence and to bring stylistic cohesion and emphasis to your writing. Section 5e gives examples of parallel structures used to help produce cohesion in a text. Be consistent and keep connected structures, however long and complicated, parallel in form. The following sentence contains parallel *-ing* phrases as direct objects:

▶ **When on vacation, they enjoy *playing* volleyball,**
 **   *bicycling* on country roads, and**
 **   *snorkeling* in the Gulf waters.**

Use similar grammatical structures in parts of the sentence with a similar function.

NOT PARALLEL **He wants a new girlfriend, to buy a house, and find a good job.**

PARALLEL **He wants a new girlfriend, a house, and a good job.**

PARALLEL **He wants to have a new girlfriend, to buy a house, and to find a good job.**

Parallel structures with paired (correlative) conjunctions   When your sentence contains correlative conjunctions, pairs such as *either . . . or, neither . . . nor, not only . . . but also, both . . . and, whether . . . or,* and *as . . . as,* the structure after the second part of the pair should be exactly parallel in form to the structure after the first part.

▶ **He made up his mind *either* to paint the van *or* ^to^ sell it to another buyer.** [*To paint* follows *either*; therefore, *to sell* should follow *or.*]

▶ **She loves *both* swimming competitively *and* ^playing^ ~~to play~~ golf.** [An *-ing* form follows *both*; therefore, an *-ing* form should also follow *and.*]

▶ **He made up his mind *either* to paint the van *or* ^to^ sell it to another buyer.** [*To paint* follows *either*; therefore, *to sell* should follow *or.*]

Parallel structures in comparisons   When making comparisons with *as* or *than*, use parallel structures. In the following examples, the revisions could have used either the infinitive form (*to drive, to take*) in both parts of the sentence, or the *-ing* form.

To drive
► ~~Driving~~ to Cuernavaca is *as* expensive *as* to take the bus.

Taking
► ~~To take~~ the bus is less comfortable *than* driving.

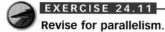

EXERCISE 24.11

Revise for parallelism.

Revise the following sentences to make structures parallel. Some sentences may be correct.

EXAMPLE:

Evangelist Aimee Semple McPherson made news in 1926 for

running a successful radio ministry, preaching in a Los Angeles

disappearing
temple, and ~~her disappearance~~ during an ocean swim.

1. Aimee Semple McPherson was not only the founder of a phenomenally successful ministry but became the first female evangelist to preach on the radio.

2. McPherson's thousands of followers reacted with shock and horror in May 1926 when the evangelist either staged her own disappearance or kidnappers captured her.

3. Resurfacing in Mexico, McPherson claimed to have escaped from kidnappers by walking through the desert for seventeen hours, but she showed no signs of dehydration, heavy sweating, or that she had been sunburned.

4. Was McPherson having an affair with her married radio engineer, telling the truth about the kidnapping, or did she simply need a break from the pressures of celebrity?

5. Not knowing the truth about her disappearance is perhaps more fascinating than to be sure of what happened to Aimee Semple McPherson.

REVIEW EXERCISE FOR CHAPTER 24

Identify and revise sentence snarls.

Identify and revise any sentence snarls in the following passage. Some sentences may not contain any errors.

Many people think that electroshock therapy was only used to treat mental illness until the middle of the twentieth century.

You may be surprised to learn that this radical therapy is still used as a treatment of last resort for certain diseases. The reason is because electroshock therapy, which triggers a grand mal epileptic seizure in the patient, somehow alleviates symptoms of such mental illnesses as depression. No one knows why the convulsions are effective, but they do seem to help many patients.

Because the treatment works is no excuse for torturing people who are already suffering, however, and electroshock in the 1930s was undoubtedly a hideous procedure. Placed on a gurney with electrodes applied to the temples, doctors simply sent a strong electric current into the patient's brain. The resulting convulsions sometimes caused patients either to dislocate a joint or bones were broken. Eventually, advances in medical research made the decision to provide patients with anesthetics and muscle relaxants before electroshock therapy was administered. By changing the procedure dramatically reduced injuries to patients.

Electroshock therapy continues to strike many people as barbaric. Many doctors who have and continue to claim success from electroshock therapy believe, however, that it can be a better treatment for major depression than drugs. Nevertheless, sending electric current into a patient's brain it still seems extreme, and no one today would suggest that a patient undergo the procedure if any other treatment seems likely to work.

Chapter 25

Verbs

A verb tells what a person, thing, or concept does or is.

▶ **The community college in my county *provides* opportunities for disadvantaged students.**

Ask the following question about a clause to determine the verb:

Who (or what) does (or is) what?

[Answer: The community college *provides* opportunities.]

The base form of a verb (the form with no endings or vowel changes) will fit into one or both of the following slots:

Online Study Center   This icon will direct you to quick reference tools, Web resources, and research guides on the Web site at http://college.hmco.com/keys.html.

▶ **They will** _____. [They will provide.]

▶ **It might** _____. [It might provide.]

See also 25d for modal auxiliary verbs, such as *can* and *should*, which do not fit this pattern. For more on verbs and verb functions, see 21a.

25a Verb basics

The verb phrase of a clause provides the following information:

Tense: present, past, future	They *decide*. They *decided*. They *will decide*.
Aspect: simple, progressive, perfect, perfect progressive	He *works*. He *is working*. He *has worked*. He *has been working*.
Person: the person speaking, being spoken to, being spoken about	We *try*. You *try*. She *tries*.
Number: singular, plural	The room *is* gloomy. The rooms *are* gloomy.
Voice: active, passive	The city *has demolished* the building. The *building has been* demolished by the city.
Mood: indicative (makes a statement or asks a question), imperative (gives a command), subjunctive (expresses a hypothetical condition, recommendation, and so on)	She *cleaned* her room. *Clean* your room right now. The boss suggested that she *clean* her office.

KEY POINTS
Verb Types

1. **Complete verb**   All the words of a verb phrase make up the complete verb of a clause: She *might have been promoted*. An *-ing* verb form by itself cannot be a complete verb.

   is
   ▶ She ^ preparing a report.

2. **Main verb**   The main verb is the part of a complete verb phrase that occurs after any auxiliaries: She might have been *promoted*.

3. **Auxiliary verb**   An auxiliary verb is a helping verb (see 25d). It helps provide information to complete the meaning of the main verb of a clause. It provides information about the following:

   - tense and aspect (They *have* left. She *did* not leave.)
   - voice (The suspects *are being* questioned. The police *are* questioning them now.)
   - mood (*Do* not make a mistake. If she *were* mayor, she would build more housing.)

   The auxiliary verbs are *am, is, are, was, were, has, have, had, do, does, did.* The forms *be, being,* and *been* also occur in auxiliary verb phrases, after another auxiliary or modal auxiliary: has *been* trying; might *be* performing; were *being* written.

4. **Modal auxiliary verb**   A modal auxiliary verb provides information about future time (*will*), intention, possibility, ability, advisability, and necessity (see also 25d and 42b). The modal auxiliaries are *will, would, can, could, shall, should, may, might,* and *must.*

5. **Transitive verb**   A transitive verb is followed by a noun phrase, pronoun, *-ing* noun form, or noun clause as its direct object:

   - My friends *painted the door.*
   - He *invited her* to the party.
   - They *enjoy skiing.*
   - We *do* not *know what he intended.*

   A transitive verb can be used in the passive voice: The door *was painted* by my friends. The dictionary indicates whether a verb is transitive (*tr.* or *vt*) or intransitive (*intr.* or *vi*). See 25c and 25l.

6. **Intransitive verb**   An intransitive verb is not followed by a direct object: The tornado *occurred* at night. It cannot be used in the passive voice. See 25c and 25l.

7. **Linking verb**   A linking verb provides information about the subject: They *are* actors. He *looks* happy. The steak *smells* good.

25b Forms of regular and irregular verbs

Although you might use a variety of verb forms when you speak, readers generally expect formal writing to conform to Standard English usage. All verbs except *be* have five forms.

Regular verbs The five forms of regular verbs follow a predictable pattern. Once you know the base form, you can construct all the others:

1. base form (no -*s*): the form listed in a dictionary
2. -*s* form: the third person singular form of the present tense
3. -*ing* form (the *present participle*): needs auxiliary verbs to function as a complete verb
4. past tense form: functions as a complete verb, without auxiliary verbs
5. past participle: also called the -*ed* form; needs auxiliary verbs to function as a complete verb (*has selected, was selected*).

Regular Verbs

Base	-*s*	-*ing* Present Participle	Past Tense	Past Participle
paint	paints	painting	painted	painted
smile	smiles	smiling	smiled	smiled
watch	watches	watching	watched	watched

Irregular verbs In contrast, irregular verbs do not use -*ed* to form the past tense and the past participle. (See 25d for the forms of irregular verbs *be, do,* and *have.*)

Irregular Verbs

Base	-*s*	-*ing* Present Participle	Past Tense	Past Participle
take	takes	taking	took	taken
go	goes	going	went	gone
swim	swims	swimming	swam	swum

The following list shows common irregular verbs. Notice the past tense form and past participle of each one.

Base Form	Past Tense	Past Participle
arise	arose	arisen
bear	bore	born
beat	beat	beaten
become	became	become
begin	began	begun

Base Form	Past Tense	Past Participle
bend	bent	bent
bet	bet	bet, betted
bind	bound	bound
bite	bit	bitten
bleed	bled	bled
blow	blew	blown
break	broke	broken
bring	brought	brought
build	built	built
burst	burst	burst
buy	bought	bought
catch	caught	caught
choose	chose	chosen
cling	clung	clung
come	came	come
cost	cost	cost
creep	crept	crept
cut	cut	cut
deal	dealt	dealt
dig	dug	dug
do	did	done
draw	drew	drawn
drink	drank	drunk
drive	drove	driven
eat	ate	eaten
fall	fell	fallen
feed	fed	fed
feel	felt	felt
fight	fought	fought
find	found	found
flee	fled	fled
fly	flew	flown
forbid	forbad(e)	forbidden
forget	forgot	forgotten
forgive	forgave	forgiven
freeze	froze	frozen
get	got	gotten, got
give	gave	given
go	went	gone

Base Form	Past Tense	Past Participle
grind	ground	ground
grow	grew	grown
hang*	hung	hung
have	had	had
hear	heard	heard
hide	hid	hidden
hit	hit	hit
hold	held	held
hurt	hurt	hurt
keep	kept	kept
know	knew	known
lay	laid	laid (see also 25c)
lead	led	led
leave	left	left
lend	lent	lent
let	let	let
lie	lay	lain (see also 25c)
light	lit, lighted	lit, lighted
lose	lost	lost
make	made	made
mean	meant	meant
meet	met	met
put	put	put
quit	quit	quit
read	read	read
ride	rode	ridden
ring	rang	rung
rise	rose	risen (see also 25c)
run	ran	run
say	said	said
see	saw	seen
seek	sought	sought
sell	sold	sold
send	sent	sent
set	set	set (see also 25c)
shake	shook	shaken

Hang meaning "put to death" is regular: *hang, hanged, hanged.*

Base Form	Past Tense	Past Participle
shine (intr.)	shone	shone
shoot	shot	shot
shrink	shrank	shrunk
shut	shut	shut
sing	sang	sung
sink	sank	sunk
sit	sat	sat (see also 25c)
sleep	slept	slept
slide	slid	slid
slit	slit	slit
speak	spoke	spoken
spend	spent	spent
spin	spun	spun
spit	spit, spat	spit
split	split	split
spread	spread	spread
spring	sprang	sprung
stand	stood	stood
steal	stole	stolen
stick	stuck	stuck
sting	stung	stung
stink	stank, stunk	stunk
strike	struck	struck, stricken
swear	swore	sworn
sweep	swept	swept
swim	swam	swum
swing	swung	swung
take	took	taken
teach	taught	taught
tear	tore	torn
tell	told	told
think	thought	thought
throw	threw	thrown
tread	trod	trodden, trod
understand	understood	understood
upset	upset	upset
wake	woke	waked, woken
wear	wore	worn

Base Form	Past Tense	Past Participle
weave	wove	woven
weep	wept	wept
win	won	won
wind	wound	wound
wring	wrung	wrung
write	wrote	written

25c Verbs commonly confused

You may need to give special attention to certain verbs that are similar in form but differ in meaning. Some of them can take a direct object; these are called *transitive verbs*. Others never take a direct object; these are called *intransitive verbs*. (See also 21c, pp. 329–330 and 43c.)

1. *rise, arise:* to get up, to ascend (intransitive)

   raise: to lift, to cause to rise (transitive)

Base	-s	-ing	Past Tense	Past Participle
rise	rises	rising	rose	risen
raise	raises	raising	raised	raised

   ▶ Sarah *rose* early to fix breakfast for the family.

   ▶ The bread *rose* as soon as she put it in the oven.

   ▶ She *raised* her daughter by herself.

2. *sit:* to occupy a seat (intransitive)

   set: to put or place (transitive)

Base	-s	-ing	Past Tense	Past Participle
sit	sits	sitting	sat	sat
set	sets	setting	set	set

   ▶ He has been ~~setting~~ *sitting* on the bench and staring for half an hour.

   ▶ She ~~sat~~ *set* the vase on the middle shelf.

3. *lie:* to recline (intransitive; not followed by a direct object)
   lay: to put or place (transitive; followed by a direct object)

Base	-s	-ing	Past Tense	Past Participle
lie	lies	lying	lay	lain
lay	lays	laying	laid	laid

Note the possibility for confusion especially with the form *lay* being both the base form of the transitive verb and the past tense form of the intransitive verb. (But then, whoever said language was logical?)

> lay
> ▶ I ~~laid~~ down for half an hour.
> ^

> lying
> ▶ I was ~~laying~~ down when you called.
> ^

> Lay
> ▶ ~~Lie~~ the map on the floor.
> ^

VARIATION You are likely to come across many variations of the *lie/lay* distinction. Confusion is commonplace. You will certainly hear people say things like "Grandma laid down for a nap" or "She lay the dress out on the bed." You will also come across confusion of the forms in (presumably) edited writing: "Do you want a comfortable mattress to lay down on?" and "He just laid there, asking for help." Yes, people will understand you, but they may also notice that you do not seem to be aware of the difference between the two forms and regard that negatively. So avoid falling into the common trap. Make a point of showing you *are* aware of the distinction between *lie* and *lay*.

In addition, note the verb *lie* ("to say something untrue"), which is intransitive.

Base	-s	-ing	Past Tense	Past Participle
lie	lies	lying	lied	lied

▶ He *lied* when he said he had won three trophies.

EXERCISE 25.1

Use commonly confused verbs correctly.

In each of the following sentences, choose the verb needed in the sentence from the choices in parentheses and underline it. Then write the correct form of the verb in the blank.

EXAMPLE:

Most children who are ____*raised*____ (<u>raise</u> / rise) in the United States learn the Pledge of Allegiance in elementary school.

1. Francis Bellamy, the author of the Pledge of Allegiance, wanted to add the word *equality* when he _____ (set / sit) down the line *with liberty and justice for all* in 1892.

2. He knew, however, that many Americans would _____ (raise / rise) objections because equality for women and African Americans was not a widely accepted idea at that time.

3. Although Bellamy was a Baptist minister, he did not _____ (set / sit) down to write a prayer; the original version of the Pledge of Allegiance does not contain the phrase *under God*.

4. Responsibility for adding *under God* to the Pledge must _____ (lay / lie) with Congress, which voted to include those words in 1954.

5. Bellamy _____ (lay / lie) plans to incorporate the Pledge into a flag-raising ceremony in honor of the 400th anniversary of the discovery of America, and since then, his pledge has been a popular addition to American ceremonies of all kinds.

25d *Do, have, be,* and the modal auxiliaries

The verb and auxiliary *do* *Do* can serve as a main verb, with or without auxiliaries. Forms of *do* can serve as either main verbs or auxiliaries:

> Present: (I, you, we, they) *do*
> (he, she, it) *does*

> Past: *did*

> *-ing* form: *doing*

> Past participle: *done*

Use a *do* auxiliary to form a negative, a question, or an emphatic statement.

DO AS A MAIN VERB	She *did* the job quickly. They have *done* well. He is *doing* his best.
DO AS AN AUXILIARY	She *did* not *quit.* He *does* not *approve. Do* you *agree?* He *does,* indeed, *trust* their promises.

The verb and auxiliary *have*   *Have* can serve as a main verb, with its own auxiliaries if necessary; or you can use *have, has,* or *had* as an auxiliary verb with another main verb.

Present: (I, you, we, they) *have*
          (he, she, it) *has*

Past: *had*

-ing: having

Past participle: *had*

      main verb   main verb (base form)
▶ They *have* a huge apartment. They should *have* a house-warming party soon.

      auxiliary   auxiliary
▶ They *have* furnished the room beautifully. The table *has* been painted maroon.

      auxiliary   main verb
▶ He *has* never *had* a raise.

Use *have* or *has* as an auxiliary to form the present perfect tense (see 25f). Use *had* as an auxiliary to form the past perfect tense (see 25g). The forms of *have* can be used as auxiliaries in both the active and the passive voices:

▶ The sun *has* set. [Active]

▶ The paintings *have* been stolen. [Passive]

The verb and auxiliary *be*   The verb *be* has eight forms, including three present tense forms (*am, is, are*) and two past tense forms (*was, were*).

Present: (I) *am*
          (you, we, they) *are*
          (he, she, it) *is*

Past: (I, he, she, it) *was*
      (you, we, they) *were*

-ing: *being*

Past participle: *been*

You can use the appropriate forms of *be* as main verbs or as auxiliaries. The auxiliary *be* is used in both the active and the passive voices:

▶ **My uncle** *was winning.* [Active]

▶ **However, he** *was overtaken* **at the finish line.** [Passive]

For more on the use of *be, being* and *been,* see page 405.

▶ **The tigers** *are* **hungry. The antelope** *is* **afraid.**
   main verb / main verb

▶ **The jungle** *was* **quiet.**
   main verb

▶ **She** *is* **jogging. I have** *been* **dreaming. They** *were* **arrested.**
   auxiliary / auxiliary / auxiliary

▶ **He will** *be* **rewarded.**
   auxiliary

LANGUAGE AND CULTURE

Language and Dialect Variation with *Be*

In some languages (Chinese and Russian, for example), forms of *be* used as auxiliaries ("She *is* singing") or as linking verbs ("He *is* happy") can be omitted. In some spoken dialects of English (African American Vernacular, for example), subtle linguistic distinctions not possible in Standard English can be achieved; for instance, the omission of a form of *be* and the use of the base form in place of an inflected form (a form that shows number, person, mood, or tense) signal entirely different meanings.

Vernacular	Standard
He busy.	[temporarily] He is busy [now].
She be busy. [habitually]	She is busy [all the time].

Standard English always requires the inclusion of an inflected form of *be.*

      are
▶ **Latecomers ˄ always at a disadvantage.**

Auxiliaries and modal auxiliaries   Both an independent clause and a dependent clause need a complete verb. The *-ing* form and the past participle are not complete verbs because they do not show tense. They need auxiliary or modal auxiliary verbs to complete their meaning in a clause. (See 42b for the meanings of modal auxiliary verbs.)

Auxiliary Verbs	Modal Auxiliary Verbs	
do: do, does, did	will, would	shall, should
be: be, am, is, are, was, were, being, been	can, could	may, might, must
have: have, has, had		

Auxiliary verbs and modal auxiliary verbs can be used in combination. Whatever the combination, the form of the main verb is determined by the auxiliary that precedes it.

Auxiliary Verb	Followed by	Example
do, does, did	Base form	Does she *travel* much?
will, would, can, could, shall, should, may, might, must	Base form	She will *send* him an angry letter.
have, has had	Past participle	The song has *ended.*
am, is, are, was, were, be, been	*-ing* (for active voice only)	They are still *applauding.*
am, is, are, was, were, be, been, being	Past participle (for passive voice only)	The singer was *applauded* loudly.

Which form should I use?

1. Immediately after *do, does, did,* and the nine modal auxiliaries— *will, would, can, could, shall, should, may, might,* and *must*—use the base form.

   ▶ The singer *did*n't *smile* once.

   ▶ *Did* the audience *leave*?

   ▶ He *should* stay longer.

   ▶ Time *will pass.*

   ▶ They *must* try to find a parking space.

ESL NOTE

Form of Modal Auxiliary and Verb Form Following a Modal

A modal auxiliary never changes form or takes an *-s* ending. The form of the verb after a modal auxiliary is always the base form, never a verb with an *-s* or *-ed* ending.

▶ They should~~s~~ offer to help.

▶ Everyone can enjoy~~s~~ the view.

▶ The band might ~~has~~ *have* finished playing.

2. Immediately after *has, have,* and *had,* use the past participle.

▶ It *has snowed.*

▶ They *had eaten* when I arrived.

▶ It *has been* snowing for five hours.

▶ They should *have gone.* [Not: They should *have went.*]

In informal speech, we run sounds together, and the pronunciation may be mistakenly carried over into writing.

▶ She should ~~of~~ *have* left that job last year.

The pronunciation of the contraction *should've* is probably responsible for the nonstandard form *should of.* Edit carefully to catch misuse of the word *of* in place of *have* in verb phrases.

3. Immediately after *am, is, are, was, were, be* and *been,* use the *-ing* form for active voice verbs.

▶ She *is taking* her driving test.

▶ You *were watching.*

▶ He might have *been driving.*

▶ They could *be jogging.*

ESL NOTE

The *-ing* Form

To form a complete verb, always use a *be* auxiliary before the *-ing* form. The *-ing* form alone can never be a complete verb in a clause.

> *are*
> ► The poets and the novelists on the faculty planning to
> give a public reading.
>   ^
>
> See 43a ESL.

4. Immediately after *am, is, are, was, were, be, been,* and *being,* use the past participle for the passive voice (see 25l).

   ► They *were taken* to a tropical island for their anniversary.

   ► The faucet should *be fixed.*

   ► The pie might have *been eaten.*

   ► The suspects are *being watched.*

ESL NOTE

What Comes before *Be, Been,* and *Being*

1. Modal auxiliary + *be*

    ► *might be* **late,** *could be* **jogging** (active), *will be* **presented**
    (passive)

2. *have, has, had* + *been*

    ► *have been* **driving** (active), *has been* **eaten** (passive)

3. *am, is, are, was, were* + *being*

    ► You *are being* **silly.** (active)

    ► He *was being* **followed.** (passive)

EXERCISE 25.2

Use verb forms correctly.

In the following passage, correct any errors in the use of verbs and auxiliaries.

EXAMPLE:

is
Cladistics ~~be~~ the science of determining evolutionary
         ^
relationships by examining the shared physical characteristics
of organisms.

Scientists have always try to analyze which organisms are related to each other and to place them into family trees. Paleontologists interested in determining the descendants of an ancient creature must to rely on the fossil record. By comparing the creature's body structure and bones with those of living organisms, these scientists can making educated guesses about the relationship between a fossilized animal and a modern-day one. Today, the science of DNA analysis is offering new clues into how creatures be related to one another; many of the answers so far surprising. One recent DNA discovery convinced many scientists that the grebe—a small, stocky diving bird—should of been classified as a cousin of the flamingo rather than as a relative of the loon and other diving birds. Flamingo fossils more than fifty million years old have been discover, but nothing in the flamingo ancestors' body type suggested this relationship with the grebe. Fossils have no DNA, so using this valuable new technique will not solves many questions about classifications of ancient organisms. However, many scientists already wondering what other surprises DNA testing might bring.

25e Time and verb tenses

Tenses indicate time as perceived by the speaker or writer. Verbs change form to indicate present or past time: *We play. We played.* To indicate future time, English uses the modal auxiliary *will* (*We will play*) as well as expressions such as *be + going to* (*We are going to play when our work is finished*). For each time (present, past, and future), we can use auxiliary verbs with the main verb to convey completed actions (perfect forms), actions in progress (progressive forms), and actions that are completed by some specified time or event and also emphasize the length of time in progress (perfect progressive forms).

The following examples illustrate aspects of active voice verbs referring to past, present, and future time. For passive voice verbs, see 25l.

Past Time

Simple past	They *arrived* yesterday. They *did* not *arrive* today.
Past progressive	They *were leaving* when the phone rang.
Past perfect	Everyone *had left* when I called.
Past perfect progressive	We *had been sleeping* for an hour before you arrived.

Present Time

Simple present	He *eats* Wheaties every morning. He *does* not *eat* eggs.
Present progressive	They *are working* today.
Present perfect	She *has* never *read* Melville.
Present perfect progressive	He *has been living* here for five years.

Future Time (Using *Will*)

Simple future	She *will arrive* soon. She *will not (won't) be* late.
Future progressive	They *will be playing* baseball at noon tomorrow.
Future perfect	He *will have finished* the project by Friday.
Future perfect progressive	By the year 2010, they *will have been running* the company for twenty-five years.

Other modal auxiliaries can substitute for *will* and thus change the meaning: *must arrive, might be playing, may have finished, should have been running* (see 43b).

ESL NOTE

Verbs Not Used in Progressive Form

Use simple tenses but not progressive forms with verbs expressing ideas related to the senses, preference, emotion, or thought (for example, *smell, taste, prefer, want, need, appreciate, know, understand*), as well as with verbs of possession, appearance, and inclusion (for example, *own, possess, seem, resemble, contain*).

smells
▶ The fish in that showcase ~~is smelling~~ bad.
                              ^

possess
▶ They ~~are possessing~~ different behavior patterns.
         ^

25f Present tenses

Simple present   Use the simple present tense for the following purposes:

1. To make a generalization

   ▶ Babies *sleep* a lot.

   ▶ A baseball player *dreads* the words "blown save."

2. To indicate an activity that happens habitually or repeatedly

▶ We *turn* the clocks ahead every April.

▶ He *works* for Sony.

▶ They *take* vacations in Puerto Rico.

3. To discuss literature and the arts even if the work was written in the past or the author is no longer alive

▶ In *Zami,* Audre Lorde *describes* how a librarian *introduces* her to the joys of reading.

When used in this way, the present tense is called the *literary present.* However, when you write a narrative of your own, use past tenses to tell about past actions.

walked   kissed

▶ Then the candidate ~~walks~~ up to the crowd and ~~kisses~~ all the babies.

4. To express future time in a dependent clause beginning with a conjunction such as *if, when, before, after, until,* or *as soon as*

▶ When they ~~will~~ arrive, the meeting will begin. [Use *will* only in the independent clause. Use the simple present in the subordinate clause.]

Present progressive   Use the present progressive to indicate an action in progress at the moment of speaking or writing.

▶ It's spring and the grass *is growing.*

▶ Publishers *are getting* nervous about plagiarism.

Present perfect and present perfect progressive   Use the present perfect in the following instances:

1. To indicate that an action that occurred at some unstated time in the past is related to present time

▶ They *have worked* in New Mexico, so they know its laws.

2. To indicate that an action that began in the past continues to the present

▶ They *have worked* for the same company ever since I have known them.

If you state a time in the past when something occurred and ended, use the simple past tense, not the present perfect.

▶ They ~~have worked~~ in Arizona three years ago.
                      ^worked

Use the present perfect progressive when you indicate the length of time an action has been in progress up to the present time.

▶ They *have been dancing* **for three hours.** [This implies that they are still dancing.]

25g Past tenses

Use the past tenses consistently. Do not switch to present or future for no reason (see 25i).

Simple past Use the simple past tense when you specify exactly when an event occurred or when you write about a past time.

▶ She *married* **him last month.**

▶ **World War I soldiers** *suffered* **in the trenches.**

When the sequence of past events is indicated with words such as *before* or *after*, use the simple past for both events.

▶ **She** *knew* **how to write her name before she** *went* **to school.**

Past progressive Use the past progressive for an activity in progress over time or at a specified point in the past.

▶ **They** *were working* **all day yesterday.**

▶ **He** *was lifting* **weights when I called.**

Past perfect Use the past perfect or the past perfect progressive only when one past event was completed before another past event or stated past time.

▶ **Ben** *had cooked* **the whole meal by the time Sam arrived.** [Two events occurred: Ben cooked the meal; then Sam arrived.]

▶ **He** *had been cooking* **for three hours when his sister finally offered to help.** [An event in progress—cooking—was interrupted in the past.]

Make sure that the past tense form you choose expresses your exact meaning.

▶ **When the student protesters marched into the building at noon, the administrators** *were leaving.* [The administrators were in the process of leaving. They began to leave at, say, 11:57 a.m.]

▶ **When the student protesters marched into the building at noon, the administrators** *had left.* [There was no sign of the administrators. They had left at 11 a.m.]

▶ **When the student protesters marched into the building at noon, the administrators** *left.* [The administrators saw the protesters and then left at 12:01 p.m.]

EXERCISE 25.3
Identify verb tenses.

In each of the following sentences, identify the tense of the under-lined verb.

EXAMPLE:

A monument in Fort Greene Park in Brooklyn, New York, <u>honors</u> the memory of the prisoners of war during the American Revolution who died on prison ships anchored in New York Harbor.
 <u>simple present</u>

1. Between 1776 and 1783, the British <u>sent</u> most captured American soldiers to New York City, which was occupied by the British throughout the Revolutionary War. _____

2. More than eleven thousand American prisoners <u>had died</u> on New York's British prison ships before the war ended. _____

3. On the most notorious ship, the *Jersey,* work parties of prisoners <u>were</u> routinely <u>removing</u> six or eight corpses each day during the war. _____

4. Most Americans <u>have</u> never <u>heard</u> about the prison ships, so they are unaware that nearly twice as many people died on them as died in combat during the entire Revolutionary War.

   _____

5. Public funding paid for a monument to the prisoners, which <u>has been standing</u> in Fort Greene Park since 1907. _____

EXERCISE 25.4
Use present tenses correctly.

In each of the following sentences, correct any errors in the use of present tense verb forms. Some sentences may be correct.

EXAMPLE:

<pre>   do   observe</pre>
What ~~did~~ babies ~~observed~~ when they look at faces?

1. Within a few hours of birth, newborn babies are showing a preference for looking at human faces.

2. Cognitive psychologists determine what has interested babies by measuring how long they look at certain patterns or objects.

3. Recent studies have shown that babies' brains have been forming the ability to differentiate faces by the time the babies are a few months old.

4. Scientists have not yet come to an agreement on whether babies are born with the ability to recognize faces or whether they are simply born with a preference for certain shapes and contours.

5. Scientific debate on the subject is raging, but as further studies will be completed, our understanding of how humans learn face recognition will continue to grow.

EXERCISE 25.5
Use past tenses correctly.

In the following passage, correct any errors in the use of past tense forms. Some sentences may be correct.

EXAMPLE:

<pre>   have been</pre>
Since the late 1970s, teenagers ~~were~~ buying every hip-hop record they can find.

In 1973, Clive Campbell, a Jamaican immigrant who was living in the Bronx, New York, since 1967, christened himself "DJ Kool Herc" and began to work as a neighborhood disc jockey. During his childhood in Jamaica, Campbell saw performers known as *toasters* talking rhythmically over reggae music. At dance parties in the Bronx, DJ Kool Herc had chanted rhymes while he played popular records. His favorite parts of the records, the parts that had made the crowds dance, were the instrumental breaks, some of which were lasting only fifteen seconds. Kool Herc began buying two copies of the records with the best breaks and performing with two turntables, which he manipulated by hand so that the fifteen-second break could last as long as the crowd enjoyed it. DJ Kool Herc's innovation had been creating the music now known as *hip-hop*.

DJ Kool Herc

25h *-ed* endings: Past tense and past participle forms

Both the past tense form and the past participle of regular verbs end in *-ed*. This ending causes writers trouble because in speech the ending is often dropped—particularly when it blends into the next sound.

>   *ed*
> ▶ They wash two baskets of laundry last night.

Standard English requires the *-ed* ending in the following instances:

1. To form the past tense of a regular verb

>   *ed*
> ▶ He ask to leave early.

2. To form the expression *used to*, indicating past habit

>   *d*
> ▶ They use to smoke.

3. To form the past participle of a regular verb after the auxiliary *has, have,* or *had* in the active voice or after a form of *be* (*am, is, are, was, were, be, being, been*) in the passive voice (see 25l)

>   *ed*
> ▶ She has work there for a long time. [Active]
>   *ed*
> ▶ The work will be finish tomorrow. [Passive]

4. To form a past participle for use as an adjective

               ped   ed

▶ **Put in some chop meat.**   ▶ **The frighten boy ran away.**

Note: The following *-ed* forms are used with verbs such as *be* and *get*. Some can also be used with *seem, appear,* and *look.*

concerned	embarrassed	scared
confused	married	surprised
depressed	prejudiced	used (to)
divorced	satisfied	worried

Do not omit the *-d* ending. In addition, note also the form *supposed to* (not *suppose to*).

                   d

▶ **I was surprise to see how many awards they won.**

                   ied   ed

▶ **Parents get worry when their children are depress.**

                       d

▶ **The general was suppose to be in charge.**

Do not confuse the past tense form and the past participle of an irregular verb. A past tense form stands alone as a complete verb, but a past participle does not.

          did

▶ **They ~~done~~ well.**

EXERCISE 25.6

Use *-ed* endings correctly.

In each of the following sentences, edit errors in using *-ed* forms of verbs. Some sentences may be correct.

EXAMPLE:

              changed

Technology has ~~change~~ the classroom experience for many students.

1. College classrooms use to be seen as places where professors lectured to passive students, with only the most verbal students participating in discussions of the material. *(Continued)*

2. Today, however, many professors have noticed the difference computers can make in their students' ability to join in class discussions.

3. For some courses, students are expose to Web sites filled with multimedia materials as well as to more typical readings on a given subject.

4. Before attending class, students are often ask to participate in e-mail discussions on a topic related to what they are studying; the discussions usually continue in the classroom.

5. Professors who once notice the same students doing all the talking in every class maintain that starting discussions in writing on a listserv is more likely to enable all students to participate.

25i   Avoiding unnecessary tense shifts

If you use tenses consistently throughout a piece of writing, you help readers understand what is happening and when. Check that your verbs consistently express present or past time, both within a sentence and from one sentence to the next.

TENSE SHIFTS   **Selecting a jury *was* difficult. The lawyers *ask* many questions to discover bias and prejudice; sometimes the prospective jurors *had* the idea they *are acting* in a play.**

REVISED   **Selecting a jury *was* difficult. The lawyers *asked* many questions to discover bias and prejudice; sometimes the prospective jurors *had* the idea they *were acting* in a play.**

When you write about events or ideas presented by another writer, use the literary present (see 25f).

▶ **The author illustrate̶d̶ the images of women in two ways, using advertisements and dramas on TV. One way shows women who advance̶d̶ their careers by themselves, and the other shows those who use̶d̶ beauty to gain recognition.**

Tense shifts are appropriate in the following instances:

1. When you signal a time change with a time word or phrase

signal for switch from past to present

▶ **Harold *was* my late grandfather's name, and *now* it *is* mine.**

2. When you follow a generalization (present tense) with a specific
   example of a past incident

   ┌──────────────── generalization ────────────────┐
   ▶ **Some bilingual schools** *offer* **intensive instruction in**

   ┌────────┐ ┌──────────── specific example ────────────────┐
   English. My sister, for example, *went* **to a bilingual school**
   where she *studied* **English for two hours every day.**

EXERCISE 25.7

Correct tense shifts.

In the following passage, correct any unnecessary tense shifts.

EXAMPLE:

Anthropologist Cai Hua's book *A Society without Fathers*

describes
or Husbands: The Na of China ~~described~~ a tribe in Yunnan
                                    ^
                              marry
province whose members rarely ~~married~~.
                               ^

> The Na tribe of southern China are an isolated people with an
> unusual social system. A typical Na household did not consist of
> a nuclear or extended family made up of a husband and wife and
> their relatives; Na households are made up of mothers, children,
> sisters, and brothers, but no fathers. The Na did not marry, and
> women conceived children when the men make secret midnight
> visits to their homes. Such visits happened frequently. Cai Hua
> explained that either a man or a woman can propose such a visit,
> and the person who receives the proposition is free to accept or
> reject it. Women and men appeared to have equal power in Na
> society. Unlike most other social groups known to anthropolo-
> gists, the Na had no words for infidelity or promiscuity, and there
> was apparently no stigma attached to men or women who have
> many lovers.

25j Tenses in indirect quotations

An indirect quotation reports what someone said. It does not use
quotation marks. When the verb introducing an indirect quotation is
in a present tense, the indirect quotation should preserve the tense of
the original direct quotation. See also 24d and 43d.

DIRECT   **"The client *has signed* the contract."**

                        present   ┌────── indirect quotation ──────
INDIRECT   **The lawyer *tells* us that the client *has signed* the**
           ┌──────┐
           contract.

When the introductory verb is in a past tense, use forms that express past time in the indirect quotation.

DIRECT   **"The meetings are over, and the buyer has signed the contract."**

                        past   ┌────── indirect quotation ──────
INDIRECT   **Our lawyer *told* us that the meetings *were* over and**
           ───
           the buyer *had signed* the contract.

In longer passages, preserve the sequence of tenses showing past time throughout the whole indirect quotation.

▶ **Our lawyer, Larraine, told us that the meetings *were* over and the buyer *had signed* the contract. Larraine's firm h*ad reassigned* her to another case, so she *was leaving* the next day.**

Note: Use a present tense after a past tense introductory verb only if the statement is a general statement that holds true in present time.

▶ **Our lawyer *told* us she *is* happy with the progress of the case.**

EXERCISE 25.8
Use the correct tense in indirect quotations.

In each of the following sentences, correct any errors in verb tense. Some sentences may be correct.

EXAMPLE:

                                    had
In 1996, two sportsmen reported that they ~~have~~ found a
human skeleton in a riverbank in Kennewick, Washington.

1. James Chatters, the forensic anthropologist who examined the bones, at first believed that the skeleton is that of a modern murder victim.

2. He then told authorities that he had noticed a prehistoric arrowhead embedded in the skeleton's pelvic bone.

3. After the skeleton had been determined to be more than 9,000 years old, Native American groups announced that they want to rebury the bones.

4. Tribal leaders claim that the bones were those of an ancient tribal ancestor.

5. Many scientists argue that the skull's features did not resemble a Native American's face and that researchers needed to study the bones to find out all they could about the history of ancient peoples in this country.

25k Verbs in conditional sentences, wishes, requests, demands, and recommendations

Conditions   When *if* or *unless* is used to introduce a dependent clause, the sentence expresses a condition. Four types of conditional sentences are used in English: two refer to actual or possible situations, and two refer to speculative or hypothetical situations. The Key Points box summarizes the four types. Each one is also explained and illustrated in more detail.

1. Conditions of fact   Sentences expressing conditions of fact refer to actual situations or make generalizations. They state what may be real and true. (The word *when* can also introduce clauses in sentences expressing conditions of fact.) Use the same tense, usually the present simple, in both the dependent and the independent clauses. (See 21e on clauses.)

▶ If the sun's rays *are* strong, our skin *burns.*

▶ House sales *increase* if mortgage rates *go* down.

▶ Prices *fluctuate* unless the government *intervenes.*

2. Conditions of prediction/possibility   Sentences expressing conditions of prediction look to the future and predict what will happen if certain circumstances prevail. Use the present tense in the dependent clause and *will* (or another modal auxiliary) plus the base form of the verb in the independent clause to express future time.

▶ If it *rains* this afternoon, I *will stay* home.

▶ If I *get* married, I *might wait* a few years before I have children.

▶ They *will* not *drive* to Kansas unless their car *has* a new muffler.

▶ Housing sales *will decline* unless mortgage rates *decrease*.

KEY POINTS

Summary: Verb Tenses in Conditional Sentences

Meaning Expressed	*If* Clause	Independent Clause
1. Fact	Simple present	Simple present

▶ If people *earn* more, they *spend* more.

2. Prediction/ possibility	Simple present	*will, can, should, might* + base form

▶ If you *turn* left here, you *will end up* in Mississippi.

3. Speculation about present or future	Simple past *or* subjunctive *were*	*would, could, should, might* + base form

▶ If he *had* a cell phone, he *would use* it. [But he does not have one.]

▶ If she *were* my lawyer, I *might* win the case. [But she is not.]

4. Speculation about past	Past perfect (*had* + past participle)	*would have could have should have might have* ⎫ + past ⎬ participle ⎭

▶ If they *had saved* the diaries, they *could have sold* them. [But they did not save them.]

---

3. Conditions of speculation about present or future time

Sentences expressing conditions of speculation consider hypothetical situations in the present or the future. Use the simple past tense in the dependent clause and *would* (or another modal auxiliary verb) plus the base form of the verb in the independent clause.

▶ If they *worked* harder on the job, they *might get* a promotion. [They may or may not work harder.]

▶ If we *had* a million dollars, we *would make* a donation to the museum. [We don't have a million dollars.]

THE USE OF SUBJUNCTIVE *WERE* IN PLACE OF *WAS* With speculative conditions about the present and future using the verb *be*, *were* is used in place of *was* in the dependent *if* clause. This use of *were* to indicate hypothetical situations involves what is called the *subjunctive mood*.

▶ If I *were* an Alaskan, I *would* probably *choose* to live in Anchorage. [I am not an Alaskan.]

▶ If my aunt *were* sixty-five, she *could get* a discount air fare. [My aunt is sixty.]

4. Conditions of speculation about the past Sentences that look back to past events and speculate about an entirely different outcome also express hypothetical conditions. Use the past perfect tense in the dependent clause and *would have* (or another modal auxiliary verb) plus the past participle in the independent clause to speculate about past time.

▶ If they *had saved* more money, they *would have moved* to a bigger apartment. [The opposite is true: they didn't save, so they didn't move.]

BLENDING Some blending of conditional meaning and tenses can occur, as in the case of a condition that speculates about the past in relation to the effect on the present.

▶ If I *had bought* a new car instead of this old wreck, I *would feel* a lot safer today.

THE USE OF *WOULD* When writing Standard English, use *would* only in the independent clause, not in the conditional clause. However, *would* occurs frequently in the conditional clause in speech and in informal writing.

> showed
▶ If the fish fry committee ~~would show~~ more initiative, people might attend their events more^ regularly.

> had
▶ If I ~~would have~~ heard him say that, I would have been angry.
^

WOULD, COULD, AND MIGHT WITH CONDITIONAL CLAUSE UNDERSTOOD *Would, could,* and *might* are used in independent clauses when no conditional clause is present. These are situations that are contrary to fact, and the conditional clause is understood.

▶ I *would* never *advise* her to leave college without a degree. She *might come back* later and blame me for her lack of direction.

WISHES Like some conditions, wishes deal with speculation. For a present wish—about something that has not happened and is therefore hypothetical and imaginary—use the past tense or subjunctive *were* in the dependent clause. For a wish about the past, use the past perfect: *had* + past participle.

A WISH ABOUT THE PRESENT

▶ I wish I *had* your attitude.

▶ I wish that Shakespeare *were* still alive.

A WISH ABOUT THE PAST

▶ Some union members wish that the strike *had* never *occurred*.

▶ He wishes that he *had bought* a lottery ticket.

Requests, demands, and recommendations The subjunctive also appears after certain verbs, such as *request, command, insist, demand, move* (meaning "propose"), *propose,* and *urge.* In these cases, the verb in the dependent clause is the base form, regardless of the person and number of the subject.

▶ The dean suggested that students *be* allowed to vote.

▶ He insisted that she *submit* the report.

▶ I move that the treasurer *revise* the budget.

Some idiomatic expressions preserve the subjunctive in Standard English—for example, *far* be *it from me, if need* be, *as it* were.

EXERCISE 25.9

Use correct verb tenses in conditional sentences.

In each of the following sentences, correct any errors in the use of verb tenses. Then identify which of the four types of conditional sentences the item represents.

EXAMPLE:

       ate
If domestic dogs ~~would eat~~ the same diet that their wild ancestors ate, they might not have tooth and gum problems.
#3 *Speculation about the present (hypothetical situation)*

1. If prehistoric canines would have eaten crunchy, bite-sized food, they would probably have lost most of their teeth at an early age.

2. If dogs eat commercial dog food, plaque will tend to collect on their teeth.

3. If people would allow their pet dogs to forage for their own food, the canines might develop stronger teeth.

4. Unless pet owners managed to brush their dogs' teeth daily— which is difficult to do, even with a cooperative dog—their pets will develop gum diseases and lose their teeth, just as humans do.

5. Veterinarians believe that if commercial kibble was made with larger pieces and a chewier texture, it could clean dogs' teeth effectively.

251 Passive voice

In the active voice, the grammatical subject is the doer of the action, and the sentence tells "who's doing what." The passive voice, on the other hand, tells "what is done to" the subject of the sentence. The person or thing doing the action may or may not be mentioned but is always implied: "My car has been repaired [by somebody at the garage]."

ACTIVE

┌── subject ──┐ active voice verb ┌── direct object ──┐
▶ **Alice Walker** **wrote** *The Color Purple.*

PASSIVE

                                  passive voice
┌──── subject ────┐ ┌── verb ──┐ ┌── doer or agent ──┐
▶ *The Color Purple* **was written** by Alice Walker

When to use the passive voice   Use the passive voice sparingly. However, do use it specifically in two cases.

1. Use the passive voice when the doer or agent in your sentence (the person or thing acting) is unknown or is unimportant.

   ▶ **The pandas are rare. Two of them will be returned to the wild.** [It is not important to mention who will return the pandas to the wild.]

2. Use the passive voice to establish a topic chain from one clause or sentence to another.

> He had a lot of people working for him, maybe sixty, and most of them liked him most of the time. Three of them *will be* seriously *considered* for his job.

—Ellen Goodman, "The Company Man"

[The idea of *people* in the first sentence sets up the need for *three of them,* which necessitates the passive voice verb.]

> I remember to start with that day in Sacramento . . . when I first entered a classroom, able to understand some fifty stray English words. The third of four children, I *had been preceded* to a Roman Catholic school by an older brother and sister.

—Richard Rodriguez, *Hunger of Memory*

[The passive voice preserves the chain of *I* subjects.]

For more on using the passive voice to make old and new information connect well, see 18b.

Verbs to use with the passive voice Use the passive voice only with verbs that are transitive in English. Intransitive verbs such as *happen, occur,* and *try (to)* are not used in the passive voice.

> The ceremony ~~was~~ happened yesterday.
>
> have
> Morality is an issue that ~~was~~ tried to explain ~~by~~ (many philosophers).

How to form the passive voice The complete verb of a passive voice sentence consists of a form of the verb *be* followed by a past participle.

receiver
— as subject —

verb: *be* +
past participle

doer omitted or named after *by*

> The windows are cleaned (by someone) every month.

With different tenses, note the forms of the verb in the passive transformations:

Tense and Aspect	Active Voice	Passive Voice
Simple present	Someone *cleans* the windows every month.	The windows *are cleaned* every month.
Present progressive	Someone *is cleaning* the windows right now.	The windows *are being cleaned* right now.
Present perfect	Someone *has* just *cleaned* the windows.	The windows *have* just *been cleaned.*

Tense and Aspect	Active Voice	Passive Voice
Present perfect progressive	Someone *has been cleaning* the windows for hours now.	[rare]
Simple past	Someone *cleaned* the windows yesterday.	The windows *were cleaned* yesterday.
Past progressive	Someone *was cleaning* the windows all yesterday afternoon.	The windows *were being cleaned* all yesterday afternoon.
Past perfect	Someone *had cleaned* the windows before the family moved in.	The windows *had been cleaned* before the family moved in.
Past perfect progressive	Someone *had been cleaning* the windows for several hours when the wedding began.	[rare]
Simple future	Someone *will clean* the windows tomorrow.	The windows *will be cleaned* tomorrow.
Future progressive	Someone *will be cleaning* the windows during the meeting this afternoon.	[rare]
Future perfect	Someone *will have cleaned* the windows by the end of the workday.	The windows *will have been cleaned* by the end of the workday.
Future perfect progressive	Someone *will have been cleaning* the windows for eight hours by the time the caterers arrive.	[rare]

Auxiliaries such as *would, can, could, should, may, might,* and *must* can also replace *will* when the meaning demands it.

▶ The windows *might be cleaned* next month.

▶ The windows *should have been cleaned* already.

The passive voice in scientific writing   In scientific writing, the passive voice is often preferred to indicate objective procedures. Scientists and engineers are interested in analyzing data and in performing studies that other researchers can replicate. The individual doing the experiment is therefore relatively unimportant and usually is not the subject of the sentence.

▶ The experiment *was conducted* in a classroom. Participants *were instructed* to remove their watches prior to the experiment.

Caution with the passive voice Generally your writing will be clearer and stronger if you name the subject and use verbs in the active voice to tell "who's doing what." If you overuse the passive voice, the effect will be heavy and impersonal (see also 17c).

UNNECESSARY **He** *was alerted* **to the danger of drugs by his**
PASSIVE **doctor and** *was persuaded* **by her to enroll in a**
treatment program.

REVISED **His doctor** *alerted* **him to the danger of drugs**
and *persuaded* **him to enroll in a treatment**
program.

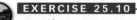

EXERCISE 25.10
Identify active and passive voices.
In each of the following sentences, write *P* on the line before each sentence that is in the passive voice and *A* before each sentence that is in the active voice. Then rewrite each passive voice sentence as active whenever it is possible or advisable to do so, and underline the verb that you changed.

EXAMPLE:

Each acre of the fertile rice fields of southern China yields more
___P___ ~~More~~ than a thousand pounds of rice ~~is yielded by each~~
~~acre of fertile rice fields of southern China.~~

1. _____ The sticky rice that brings the highest prices in China is often attacked by rice blast, a fungus that destroys the rice crop.

2. _____ A farmer in Yunnan province discovered that he could nearly eliminate rice blast by planting alternating rows of sticky rice and long-grain rice.

3. _____ The technique of alternating rows of rice was then adopted widely.

4. _____ The application of expensive and toxic fungicides that had been used to fight the rice blast was discontinued by most farmers.

5. _____ Healthier fields, bigger rice yields, and more money for the farmers were subsequently produced by this low-tech, environmentally sound agricultural method.

REVIEW EXERCISE FOR CHAPTER 25

Correct verb errors.

Edit the following passage by correcting any verb errors, including the use of unnecessary passive voice. Underline any verbs that you change.

The legend of Prester John was a fable that had circulated throughout most Christian countries of Europe for several centuries during the Middle Ages. The legend first appears in the twelfth century, and it continued to reappear until at least the sixteenth century. Stories about an immensely wealthy Christian ruler of a vast land somewhere in Asia were brought back to Europe by people who had claimed to have traveled to the then-mysterious East, and a large audience was entertained by these stories.

Some stories attach to Prester John are typical medieval marvel tales—travelers' tall tales about unusual people and creatures in exotic foreign lands. Through a popular letter supposedly written by Prester John himself, credulous Europeans learned that John's country has a province full of horned men with one eye in the front of their heads and three or four in the back. The letter also describes "wild bulls of seven horns, white bears, and the strangest lions of red, green, black, and blue color."

In many other stories, the life of Prester John resembled the life of Alexander the Great, which also circulated regularly in legends during the Middle Ages. Like Alexander, Prester John was suppose to have acquire his massive kingdom by defeating armies in Asia. Christian crusaders in medieval Europe, who feared the growing power of Islam, must of found the idea of a Christian conqueror in Asia comforting, even if it never proved to be true. Then, after Europeans became aware of the Christian kingdom of Abyssinia (now Ethiopia), many stories stated that the kingdom of Prester John laid in Africa.

Although scholars are now knowing that many of the travelogues disseminated in medieval Europe were pure fiction, many people of the time had believed the story of Prester John, perhaps simply because they wanted it to be true. In the media-saturated world of the twenty-first century, sophisticated readers may find it easy to laugh at those who were believing in the existence of Prester John. However, the tall tales, urban legends, and Internet hoaxes that have been circulating today demonstrate that modern life produced its own unstoppable legends.

Chapter **26**

Subject-Verb Agreement

26a   What is agreement?

A subject can be first, second, or third person. A third person subject, in some tenses, will need to agree with a specific third-person form of the verb.

KEY POINTS
Person and Number

Person	Singular	Plural
First	I like ice cream.	We like yogurt, too.
Second	You like spinach.	You like cake.
Third	My brother likes clams.	My cousins like shrimp.
	He likes clams.	They like shrimp.
	My sister likes garlic.	My parents hate garlic.
	She likes garlic.	They hate garlic.

You need to be concerned about agreement when using the simple present tense (*like/likes*) and when using *am, is, are, do, does, have, has, was,* or *were* as an auxiliary verb.

26b   The -*s* ending

In the simple present tense in Standard English, a third person singular subject always takes a singular verb (with -*s*), and a plural subject always takes a plural verb (with no -*s*).

Singular Subject	Plural Subject
A baby *cries*.	Babies *cry*.
He *lose*s.	They *lose*.
His brother *plays* baseball.	Her brothers *play* soccer.

Online Study Center   This icon will direct you to quick reference tools, Web resources, and research guides on the Web site at http://college.hmco.com/keys.html.

Difficulties arise because the ending -s serves two functions. It is added to both nouns and verbs, but for different reasons.

1. An -s ending on a noun is a plural signal: *Her brothers always wear black.* [She has more than one brother.]
2. An -s ending on a verb is a singular signal; -s is added to a third person singular verb in the present tense: *Her plumber wears gold jewelry.*

Most simple present verbs show agreement with an -s ending. Note the irregular forms of the auxiliary verbs in the following table: *has, is,* and *does.* Note, too, that the verb *be* has three instead of two present tense forms, so the person of the subject determines whether you use *am, are,* or *is.* In addition, *be* is the only verb to show agreement in the past tense, where it has two forms: *were* for second and third person plural, and *was* for the first and third person singular.

Subject-Verb Agreement

Base Form	like	have	be	do
Simple Present: Singular				
First person: I	like	have	am	do
Second person: you	like	have	are	do
Third person: he, she, it	likes	has	is	does
Simple Present: Plural				
First person: we	like	have	are	do
Second person: you	like	have	are	do
Third person: they	like	have	are	do

KEY POINTS
Two Key Points about Agreement

1. Follow the "one -s rule." Generally, you can put an -s on a noun to make it plural, or you can put an -s on a verb to make it singular. (But see the irregular forms *is* and *has,* above.) An -s on both subject (as plural ending) and verb (as singular ending) is not Standard English.

   NO   **My friends comes over every Saturday.** [Violates the "one -s rule"]

   (Continued)

(Continued)

YES   **My friend comes over every Saturday.**

My friends come over every Saturday.

2. Do not omit a necessary -*s*.

s
His supervisor want͜ him to work the night shift.
͜

s
The book͜ on my desk describe life in Tahiti.
͜

s
She *uses* her experience, *speaks* to the crowds, and *win͜*
͜
their confidence.

ESL NOTE
Modal Auxiliaries and Agreement

Modal auxiliaries never add an -*s* ending, and the verb form following them is always the base form of the verb, even with a third person singular subject: I *can sing;* she *should go;* he *might be* leaving; she *must have* been promoted (25d and 42b).

LANGUAGE AND CULTURE
Issues of Subject-Verb Agreement

Many languages make no change in the verb form to indicate number and person, and several spoken versions of English, such as London Cockney, Caribbean Creole, and African American Vernacular (AAV), do not observe the standard rules of agreement.

▶ **Cockney: He *don't* never wear that brown whistle.**

[The standard form is *doesn't;* other nonstandard forms in this sentence are *don't never* (a double negative) and *whistle*—short for *whistle and flute,* rhyming slang for *suit.*]

▶ **AAV: She *have* a lot of work experience.**

Use authentic forms like these when freewriting or quoting direct speech; for your formal academic writing, though, follow the subject-verb agreement conventions of Standard English.

EXERCISE 26.1

Correct basic subject-verb agreement.

In each of the following sentences, correct any errors in subject-verb agreement. Some sentences may contain more than one error, and some sentences may be correct.

EXAMPLE:

divide
Psychologists ~~divides~~ risks into categories: risk may be
known or unknown, controllable or uncontrollable.

1. Every day, a person have to evaluate risks and make choices based on those evaluations, such as whether to get a flu shot, whether to eat meat, and whether to stop smoking.

2. People sometimes makes irrational choices in attempts to avoid uncontrollable risks.

3. Even experts in risk assessment are not immune to making a riskier choice that seems more controllable, like driving to a distant destination instead of flying.

4. The average person fear unknown dangers—nuclear attack, for instance—more than known ones, even if the evidence show that everyday risks cause more harm.

5. After a disaster, when people's nerves is on edge, unknown and uncontrollable risks seem more frightening than they does in normal, everyday life.

26c Words between the subject and the verb

When words separate the subject and verb, find the verb and ask, "Who?" or "What?" about it to determine the simple subject. Ignore any intervening words. See 21c, page 328.

▶ **The child picking flowers looks tired.** [Who looks tired? The subject, *child*, is singular.]

▶ **Her collection of baseball cards is valuable.** [What is valuable? The subject, *collection*, is singular.]

▶ **The government's proposals about preserving the environment cause controversy.** [What things cause controversy? The subject, *proposals*, is plural.]

Do not be confused by intervening words ending in -s, such as *always* and *sometimes*. The -s ending still must appear on a present tense verb if the subject is singular.

▶ His assistant always make ˢ mistakes.

Phrases introduced by *as well as, along with,* and *in addition to* that come between the subject and the verb do not change the number of the verb.

▶ His daughter, as well as his two sons, want ˢ him to move nearby.

EXERCISE 26.2

Ignore words between the subject and verb.

In each of the following sentences, underline the simple subject. Then correct any errors in subject-verb agreement.

EXAMPLE:

Environmentalists in the United States and Canada finally

have

~~has~~ some good news about the pollution in the Great Lakes.

1. An international agency monitoring the air and water quality around the Great Lakes have discovered a previously unknown ecological process.
2. Toxic chemicals banned for at least a quarter of a century is dispersing from the lakes into the air.
3. Since 1992, Lake Ontario, along with the other lakes, have released tons of PCBs and other dangerous chemicals in a self-cleaning process.
4. Massive pollution in the enormous lakes were first brought to public attention several decades ago, and pollution remains a serious problem there.
5. The lakes' "exhaling," according to researchers, help to clean the water without posing any danger to human beings.

26d Agreement after a linking verb

Linking verbs such as *be, seem, look,* and *appear* are followed by a complement, and a subject complement should not be confused with a subject (see 21c). Make the verb agree with the subject stated before the linking verb, not with the noun complement that follows the verb.

> plural   singular
> ┌── subject ──┐   ┌ complement ┐
> ▶ **Rare books are her passion.**
>   plural verb

> singular   plural
> ┌── subject ──┐   ┌ complement ┐
> ▶ **Her passion is rare books.**
>   singular verb

▶ **My favorite part of city life *is* the parties.**

▶ **Parties *are* my favorite part of city life.**

EXERCISE 26.3

Make subjects and verbs agree and identify linking verbs.

In the following passage, underline the subject in each independent clause. Then correct any errors in subject-verb agreement. Write *LV* over any linking verbs.

EXAMPLE:

> LV
>
> *are*
> There is~~ many security <u>questions</u> involved in cryptography.

Do the government have the right to keep certain kinds of information out of the hands of the public? There is no easy answers to this question. When the science of cryptography was being developed, the National Security Agency wanted to restrict access to powerful, unbreakable codes. After all, using codes are one way that a government keeps information from its enemies, and breaking codes allows a government to find out what its enemies are planning. N.S.A. agents worried that unbreakable codes would allow enemies of the United States to conceal their activities from U.S. intelligence. Cryptographers won the right to develop and distribute their new codes to the general public, and unbreakable codes have certainly been a boon to the computer science and communications industries. Does these codes also hamper efforts to discover what terrorists are doing? Probably, say cryptographers. However, technologies that scientists decide not to develop out of fear of the results is a potential danger: if someone else develops these technologies, they can be used against anyone who has not considered their potential. There is dangers in cryptography, but perhaps there is even more problems in avoiding the issue. Somewhere in the future is the answers to these and other urgent security questions.

26e   When the subject follows the verb

When the subject follows the verb in the sentence, make the subject and verb agree.

1. Questions   In a question, the auxiliary verb agrees with the subject.

singular
┌─subject─┐
▶ *Does* **the editor agree to the changes?**

plural
┌─subject─┐
▶ *Do* **the editors approve?**

┌──────────── plural subject ────────────┐
▶ *Do* **the editor and the production manager agree to them?**

2. Initial *here* or *there*   When a sentence begins with *here* or *there*, the verb agrees with the subject.

singular
┌─subject─┐
▶ **There** *is* **a reason to rejoice.**

┌─ plural subject ─┐
▶ **There** *are* **many reasons to rejoice.**

However, avoid excessive use of initial *there* (see 17b): *We have a reason to rejoice.*

ESL NOTE

Agreement with Subject *It*

It does not follow the same pattern as *here* and *there*. The verb in a sentence beginning with *it* is always singular.

▶ **It** *looks* **like a good match.**

▶ **It** *is* **hundreds of miles away.**

3. Inverted word order   When a sentence begins not with the subject but with a phrase preceding the verb, the verb still agrees with the subject (see also 21c).

plural
┌─ prepositional phrase ─┐ verb ┌─ plural subject ─┐
▶ **In front of the library sit two stone lions.**   Who or what performs the action of the verb? Two stone lions do.]

26f Tricky subjects

1. *Each* and *every* *Each* and *every* may seem to indicate more than one, but grammatically they are singular words. Use them with a singular verb.

▶ Each of the cakes *has* a different frosting.

▶ Every change in procedures *causes* problems.

2. *-ing* verb form as subject With a subject beginning with the *-ing* verb form used as a noun (called a *gerund*, see 21d), always use a singular verb form.

singular
┌ subject ┐
▶ Playing the piano in front of a crowd *causes* anxiety.

3. Singular nouns ending in *-s* Some nouns that end in *-s* (*news, economics, physics, politics, mathematics, statistics*) are not plural. Use them with a singular verb.

▶ The news *has* been bad lately. ▶ Politics *is* dirty business.

4. Phrases of time, money, and weight When the subject is regarded as one unit, use a singular verb.

▶ Five hundred dollars *seems* too much to pay.

▶ Seven years *was* a long time to spend at college.

But

▶ Seven years have passed.

5. Uncountable nouns An uncountable noun (*furniture, jewelry, equipment, advice, happiness, honesty, information, knowledge*) encompasses all the items in its class. An uncountable noun does not have a plural form and is always followed by a singular verb (41b).

▶ That advice *makes* me nervous.

▶ The information found in the press *is* not always accurate.

6. *One of*   *One of* is followed by a plural noun (the object of the preposition *of*) and a singular verb form. The verb agrees with the subject *one*, not with the object of the preposition.

▶ *One* of her friends *loves* to tango.

▶ *One* of the reasons for his difficulties *is* that he spends too much money.

For agreement with *one of* and *the only one of* followed by a relative clause, see 29c.

7. *The number of / a number of*   The phrase *the number of* is followed by a plural noun (the object of the preposition *of*) and a singular verb form.

▶ The number of reasons *is* growing.

With the phrase *a number of,* meaning "several," use a plural verb.

▶ A number of reasons *are* listed in the letter.

8. Percent   Use a singular or plural verb, according to how the quantity is perceived.

▶ Forty percent of available housing *is* owned by the city.

▶ Polls report that 10 percent of the voters *are* undecided.

9. The title of a work or a word referred to as the word itself
Use a singular verb with the title of a work or a word referred to as the word itself. Use a singular verb even if the title or word is plural in form. See also 36a and 36d.

▶ *Cats has* finally ended its long run on Broadway.

▶ In her story, the word *dudes appears* five times.

26g Collective nouns

Generally, use a singular verb with a collective noun (*class, government, family, jury, committee, group, couple, team*) if you are referring to the group as a whole.

▶ My family *goes* on vacation every year.

Use a plural verb if you wish to emphasize differences among individuals or if members of the group are thought of as individuals.

▶ His family *are* mostly artists and musicians.

▶ The jury *are* from every walk of life.

If that usage seems awkward, revise the sentence.

▶ His close relatives *are* mostly artists and musicians.

▶ The members of the jury *are* from every walk of life.

Some collective nouns, such as *police, poor, elderly,* and *young,* always take plural verbs.

▶ The elderly *deserve* our respect.

EXERCISE 26.4

Make verbs agree with tricky subjects and collective nouns.
In each of the following sentences, underline the simple subject of each independent clause and correct any errors in subject-verb agreement.

EXAMPLE:

Every possible <u>complaint</u> about the violence of soccer players

        has
and their fans ~~have~~ been made at one time or another since the
        ^

sport began around 1100 C.E.

1. To play soccer, a team need few things other than a ball, a field, and a group of opponents.

2. When medieval British warriors defeated a Danish chieftain on the battlefield a millennium ago, their kicking the loser's head around the bloody fields were the origin of soccer, according to a hard-to-prove legend.

3. There was still violent aspects of the game in the 1100s when whole towns, each with hundreds of players, competed against each other on fields several miles long.

4. One of the signs that soccer would eventually be the world's most popular sport were that soccer was banned repeatedly in

fourteenth- and fifteenth-century England; a number of kings was worried that soldiers who played soccer would not spend enough time at archery practice.

5. Modern soccer follows rules drawn up at Cambridge University in 1863, but the sport's following among some devoted but aggressive fans have ensured that soccer's bloody reputation does not disappear entirely.

26h Compound subjects with *and, or,* and *nor*

With *and* When a subject consists of two or more parts joined by *and,* treat the subject as plural and use a plural verb.

┌─────────── plural subject ──────╱➔ plural verb
► His instructor and his advisor *want* him to change his major.

However, if the parts of the compound subject refer to a single person or thing, use a singular verb.

┌─────── singular subject (one person) ──╱➔ singular verb
► The restaurant's chef and owner *makes* good fajitas.

┌─singular subject ╱➔ singular verb
► Fish and chips *is* a popular dish in England, but it is no longer served wrapped in newspaper.

With *each* or *every* When *each* or *every* is part of a compound subject, the verb is singular.

► Every toy and game *has* to be put away.

► Each plate and glass *looks* new.

With *or* or *nor* When the parts of a compound subject are joined by *or* or *nor,* the verb agrees with the part nearer to it.

► Her sister or her parents *plan* to visit her next week.

► Neither her parents nor her sister *drives* a station wagon.

EXERCISE 26.5

Use correct subject-verb agreement with compound subjects.

In each of the following sentences, underline the subject or subjects of each independent clause, and correct any errors in subject-verb agreement. Some sentences may be correct.

EXAMPLE:

<u>Every statue, painting, and photograph</u> of human beings ~~are~~ **is** forbidden by fundamentalist factions of Islam.

1. In the Bamiyan valley of eastern Afghanistan, a 150-foot Buddha, believed to have been the largest standing Buddha in the world, and a 120-foot Buddha was carved out of sandstone cliffs in the fourth or fifth century.

2. During that period, when the Silk Route wound through the mountains of Afghanistan, wandering Buddhist monks or a caravan of silk or ivory merchants was a common sight in the Bamiyan valley, which was home to Buddhist monasteries until the arrival of Islam in the ninth century.

3. The Buddhas of Bamiyan and other art from Afghanistan's non-Islamic past was destroyed by order of Taliban leaders in March 2001.

4. A Taliban commander and leader of the operation to destroy the statues were reported to have said that the statues represented a woman and her husband.

5. Neither the protests before the destruction of the Buddhas nor the global outrage expressed afterward were enough to convince Taliban leaders that the Buddhas had been an important part of Afghan history.

26i   Agreement with indefinite pronouns and quantity words

Words that refer to nonspecific people or things are known as *indefinite pronouns*. These indefinite pronouns, as well as words and phrases that refer to quantity, pose interesting questions of agreement. Some take a singular verb (even the word *everyone*, which may seem to be plural); some take a plural verb; and some take a singular or a plural verb, depending on what they refer to. Some are used alone as a pronoun; others are used with a countable or uncountable noun in a noun phrase (for more on this, see 41a and 41b). In addition, usage may differ in speech and writing. What is the best way to deal with these questions of agreement? Look at the following examples, learn the lists, try out your own sentences, and make a note of sentences you read that use the words.

INDEFINITE PRONOUNS USED WITH A SINGULAR VERB

anybody	everyone	nothing
anyone	everything	somebody
anything	nobody	someone
everybody	no one	something

► **Nobody** *knows* **the answer.**

► **Someone** *has* **been sitting on my chair.**

► **Everyone** *agrees* **on the author's intention.**

► **Everything about the results** *was* **questioned in the review.**

QUANTITY WORDS REFERRING TO A COUNTABLE NOUN AND USED WITH A SINGULAR VERB

another	every
each	neither (see p. 440)
either	none (see p. 440)

► **Another company** *has* **bought the land.**

► **Each of the chairs** *costs* **more than $300.**

► **Of the two options, neither** *was* **acceptable.**

► **Every poem** *contains* **a stark image.**

QUANTITY WORDS REFERRING TO AN UNCOUNTABLE NOUN AND USED WITH A SINGULAR VERB

a great deal (of)	much (of)
(a) little	less (see p. 440)
a(n) _____ amount (of)	

▶ Less *has* been accomplished than we expected.

▶ A great deal of information *is* being released.

▶ Much of the machinery *needs* to be repaired.

▶ An enormous amount of equipment *was* needed to clean up the spilled oil.

QUANTITY WORDS REFERRING TO A PLURAL COUNTABLE NOUN AND USED WITH A PLURAL VERB

both	many
a couple/number of	other/others
(a) few (see 45)	several
fewer (see p. 440)	

▶ She has written two novels. Both *receive* praise.

▶ Many *have* gained from the recent stock market fluctuations.

▶ Few of his fans *are* buying his recent book.

▶ A number of articles *refer* to the same statistics.

QUANTITY WORDS USED WITH A SINGULAR OR PLURAL VERB

all	half	most	some
any	more	no	

▶ **All the students** *look* **healthy.** [The plural countable noun *students* takes a plural verb.]

▶ **All the furniture** *looks* **old.** [The uncountable noun *furniture* takes a singular verb.]

▶ **You gave me some information. More** *is* **necessary.** [*More* refers to the uncountable noun *information*.]

▶ **You gave me some facts. More** *are* **needed.** [*More* refers to the countable noun *facts*.]

▶ **Some of the jewelry** *was* **recovered.** [The uncountable noun *jewelry* takes a singular verb.]

▶ **Some of the windows** *were* **open.** [The plural countable noun *windows* takes a plural verb.]

A note on *none, neither, less,* and *fewer*

NONE Some writers prefer to use a singular verb after *none* (*of*), because *none* means "not one": *None of the contestants has smiled.* However, as *The American Heritage Dictionary* (4th ed.) points out about *none,* "The word has been used as both a singular and a plural noun from old English onward." In formal academic writing, a singular or a plural verb is therefore technically acceptable: *None of the authorities has* (or *have*) *greater tolerance on this point than H. W. Fowler.* As with many issues of usage, however, readers form preferences. Check to see if your instructor prefers the literal singular usage.

NEITHER The pronoun *neither* is, like *none,* technically singular: *The partners have made a decision; neither wants to change the product.* In informal writing, however, you will see it used with a plural verb, especially when it is followed by an *of* phrase: *Neither of the novels reveal a polished style.* Ask your instructor about his or her preferences.

LESS AND FEWER Technically, *less* refers to a singular uncountable noun (*less spinach*), *fewer* to a plural countable noun (*fewer beans*). In journalism and advertising, and especially on supermarket signs (*12 items or less*), *less* is often used in place of *fewer.* In formal writing, however, use *fewer* to refer to a plural word: *In the last decade, fewer Olympic medalists have been using steroids.*

For agreement with *one of,* see page 434. For agreement with *one of* and *the only one of* followed by a relative clause, see 29c.

EXERCISE 26.6

Use correct subject-verb agreement with indefinite pronouns and quantity words.

In each of the following sentences, choose the verb that agrees with the subject, and underline the subject.

EXAMPLE:

<u>Nothing</u> (was / ~~were~~) dearer to Edward Gorey than the New York City Ballet, except perhaps his six cats.

1. Many of the small, hand-lettered, meticulously illustrated books by Edward Gorey (concerns / concern) macabre events, yet most of Gorey's stories (is / are) hilarious.
2. In the story "The Wuggly Ump," for example, every human character (ends up / end up) being eaten by the title monster, yet the tale itself looks and sounds like a Victorian nursery rhyme.

3. Anyone who saw Gorey in person (is / are) sure to remember the tall, bearded man in a floor-length fur coat and sneakers, dressed like one of the odd characters that he drew.

4. A number of interviewers and critics (was / were) able to talk to the eccentric writer, illustrator, and designer before his death in 2000, and a great deal (has been / have been) written about the intersections of his life and his art.

It would carry off objects of which it grew fond,
And protect them by dropping them into the pond.

Illustration from *The Doubtful Guest* © 1957 Edward Gorey.
Used with permission of the Estate of Edward Gorey.

5. Gorey admitted that some of his eccentricity (was / were) genuine although some of his behaviors (was / were) deliberately cultivated for shock value.

26j Demonstrative pronouns and adjectives (*this, that, these, those*) as subject

A *demonstrative adjective* must agree in number with the noun it modifies. Ask, "Is the noun singular or plural?"

Singular	Plural
this	these
that	those
this solution	these solutions
that problem	those problems

A *demonstrative pronoun* must agree in number with its antecedent (see 27d).

▶ **The mayor is planning changes. These will be controversial.**

EXERCISE 26.7

Use correct subject-verb agreement with demonstrative pronouns and adjectives.

In the following sentences, correct any errors in the use of demonstrative pronouns and adjectives and the verbs that follow them. Some sentences may be correct.

EXAMPLE:

This
Australia's Antarctic base has begun a cleanup. ~~These~~ will remove more than three thousand tons of garbage.

1. Since the exploration and experimentation began in Antarctica, people from more than forty nations have come to the icy continent to establish research bases. This is home to researchers year-round.

2. Unfortunately, humans create waste, and these are beginning to contaminate Antarctica's environment.

3. Experts believe that Antarctic explorers and scientists have abandoned more than 330,000 tons of waste. These waste include building materials, chemicals, batteries, and other residue of human presence.

4. Australia has contracted with a French environmental services company for 240 cargo containers. These giant bins will be filled with garbage from the Australian base camp in Antarctica, known as *Casey*, and shipped back to Australia for disposal.

5. Once the cleanup at *Casey* has been completed, Australia plans to share the containers. This could be used by other nations' research bases to remove additional garbage before Antarctica's pristine ecosystem is harmed.

26k Possessive pronouns as subject

To determine whether the verb after a one-word subject such as *mine* or *hers* should be singular or plural, find the word or phrase the possessive pronoun refers to. That antecedent determines whether the verb is singular or plural. Possessive pronouns such as *mine, his, hers, ours, yours,* and *theirs* can refer to both singular and plural antecedents (see 27d).

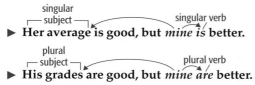

▶ **Her average is good, but *mine is* better.**

▶ **His grades are good, but *mine are* better.**

26I Agreement with a *what* clause as the subject

When a clause introduced by *what* functions as the subject of an independent clause, use a third person singular verb in the independent clause.

▶ **What they are proposing *concerns* us all.**

When the verb is followed by the linking verb *be* and a plural complement, some writers use a plural verb. However, some readers may object.

▶ **What I need *are* black pants and an orange shirt.**

You can avoid the issue by revising the sentence to eliminate the *what* clause.

▶ **I need black pants and an orange shirt.**

EXERCISE 26.8

Use the correct verb with possessive pronouns as subject and with subject clauses beginning with *what*.

In the following sentences, correct any problems with agreement between possessive pronoun subjects and their verbs or with agreement between subject clauses beginning with *what* and their verbs. Some sentences may be correct.

EXAMPLE:

Eighteenth-century society did not even have a word for the

state of boredom, but ours ~~do.~~ *does*

1. What boredom means in modern American culture is the subject of a new book by Patricia Meyer Spacks.

2. Like Robert Burton's book *The Anatomy of Melancholy*, hers are a study of a common mental state.

3. According to Spacks, what people really feel when they say they are bored are often dislike or confusion.

4. Medieval people's lives did not allow for boredom because they spent so much time simply trying to survive; ours permits us to be bored because we have the luxury of free time.

5. What is ironic about modern boredom are the enormous number of diversions people have invented to avoid it at all costs.

REVIEW EXERCISE FOR CHAPTER 26
Use correct subject-verb agreement.

In the following passage, correct any errors in subject-verb agreement.

There is more people of African descent living in Brazil than in any other country outside of Africa. Although only about 10 million of Brazil's 170 million people identifies themselves as black, according to a recent survey, an additional 40% of the population call themselves *pardo*, meaning "dark," or *mulato* or *mestiço*, indicating mixed European and African ancestry. There are more than three hundred Brazilian words for skin color, so racial categories in the country is difficult to define. Brazil is a multiracial society that prides itself on avoiding racial divisions like that found in the United States. However, what is clear are that economic and social problems trouble many black Brazilians. Some argue that poor self-image and discrimination based on skin color has contributed to keeping Brazilians from claiming their African ancestry.

The problems of black Brazilians are hard to ignore. Brazil was the last country in the western hemisphere to outlaw slavery. The average income of white-skinned Brazilians are twice the average earnings of blacks. Only 2% of Brazilian college students are black. Brazilian newspaper advertisements for jobs in the private sector often requires applicants to have a "good appearance," a phrase most Brazilians agree is a code for "whites only." Even on television, soap operas and commercials rarely offers roles for black actors. As a solution, the Brazilian Congress have suggested a system of quotas that would require 30% of political candidates, 25% of actors on every television show, 20% of civil service employees, and 20% of college students to be black or of mixed race. Some Brazilians insist that quotas will fail in Brazil, but many hopes that such a quota system will increase opportunity for blacks in the country. Politics do not always provide good solutions for difficult social problems. However, the future of a great number of Brazilians looks bleak unless the country find a way to reduce the problem of racial discrimination.

Chapter **27**

Pronouns

A *pronoun* is a word that substitutes for a noun, a noun phrase, or another pronoun (see 21a).

▶ Jack's hair is so long that *it* hangs over *his* collar.

▶ Philip Larkin, *who* worked as a librarian,

   did not directly refer to *his* work in *his* poems.

27a Use the correct forms of personal pronouns.

Personal pronouns change form to indicate person (first, second, or third), number (singular or plural), and function in a clause.

After a linking verb   In formal academic writing, use the subject form of a personal pronoun after a linking verb. (See 21c on linking verbs.)

▶ Was that Gwyneth Paltrow? It was *she*. [Informal: "It was her."]

▶ It was *she* who sent the flowers. [Many writers would revise this sentence to sound less formal: "She was the one who sent the flowers."]

Online Study Center   This icon will direct you to quick reference tools, Web resources, and research guides on the Web site at http://college.hmco.com/keys.html.

After a verb and before an infinitive   Use the object form of a personal pronoun after a verb and before an infinitive. When a sentence has only one object, this principle is easy to apply

▶ The dean wanted *him* to lead the procession.

KEY POINTS

Summary of Forms of Personal Pronouns

PERSON	SUBJECT	OBJECT	POSSESSIVE (+ NOUN)	POSSESSIVE (STANDS ALONE)	INTENSIVE AND REFLEXIVE
1st person singular	I	me	my	mine	myself
2nd person singular and plural	you	you	your	yours	yourself/ yourselves
3rd person singular	he	him	his	his	himself
	she	her	her	hers	herself
	it	it	its	its [rare]	itself
1st person plural	we	us	our	ours	ourselves
3rd person plural	they	them	their	theirs	themselves

Difficulties occur with compound objects.

> him and me
▶ The dean wanted ~~he and I~~ to lead the procession.
>   ^

In a compound subject or compound object with *and* (I *or* me? he *or* him?)   To decide which pronoun form to use with a compound subject or compound object, mentally recast the sentence with only the pronoun in the subject or object position.

┌── subject ──┐   ┌── object ──┐
▶ He and his sister invited my cousin and me to their party. [He invited me.]

                    I
▶ Jenny and ~~me~~ went to the movies. [If *Jenny* is dropped, you would say *I went to the movies,* not *me went to the movies.* Here you need the subject form, *I*.]

>   me
> ▶ **They told my brother and I to wait in line.** [If *my brother* is
> dropped from the sentence, you would say, *They told me to wait
> in line.* Here you need the object form, *me.*]

After a preposition   After a preposition, you need an object form.

> ▶ **I started off rapping for people just like myself, people who
> were in awe of wealth and flash. It was a conversation
> *between me* and *them*.**   —Ice-T, *Observer*, 27 Oct. 1991

>   He   me
> ▶ ~~Him~~ **and his brother waved to my colleague and I.** [*He* waved
> to my colleague. They waved to *me.*]

>   me
> ▶ **Between you and I, the company is in serious trouble.**

In appositive phrases and with *we* or *us* before a noun   When
using a personal pronoun in an appositive phrase (a phrase that
gives additional information about a preceding noun), determine
whether the noun that the pronoun refers to functions as subject or
as object in its own clause.

>   appositive
>   ┌─ direct object ─◄─┐   phrase
> ▶ **The supervisor praised only two employees, Ramon and me.**

>   ┌─ subject ─◄─┐   appositive phrase
> ▶ **Only two employees, Ramon and I, received a bonus.**

Similarly, when you consider whether to use *we* or *us* before a
noun, use *us* when the pronoun is the direct object of a verb or preposition, *we* when it is the subject.

>   object of preposition
> ▶ **LL Cool J waved to us fans.**
>   subject
> ▶ **We fans have decided to form a club.**

In comparisons   When writing comparisons with *than* and *as,*
decide on the subject or object form of the personal pronoun by mentally completing the meaning of the comparison. (See also 28i.)

> ▶ **She is certainly not more intelligent than I.** [. . . than I am.]

> ▶ **Andres and Marcylene work in the same office; Andres criti-
> cizes his boss more than she.** [. . . more than Marcylene does.]

▶ **Andres and Marcylene work in the same office; Andres criticizes his boss more than her.** [. . . more than he criticizes Marcylene.]

EXERCISE 27.1

Use the correct form of personal pronouns.

In the following passage, correct any errors in the form of personal pronouns.

EXAMPLE:

Although Marie and Pierre Curie made important scientific

discoveries, both ~~her~~ and ~~him~~ spent years being unable to
        she   *he*

afford a decent laboratory to work in.

Marie Curie, born Maria Sklodowska in Poland in 1867, devoted her life to pure science in the hope that humans would benefit from what she discovered. Her parents, poor teachers, wanted she and her siblings to get an education. Marie went to Paris to study at the Sorbonne when she was twenty-four; her work as a governess had earned her enough money to educate she and her older sister. Marie struggled to learn French and overcome her deficient early education in physics and mathematics—subjects that girls in Poland such as her and her sister had not been allowed to study. When she completed her master's degree in physics in 1894, she placed first in her class. Pierre Curie, who was doing research on magnetism, and her met when Marie was searching for a laboratory she could use. Although Pierre did not have space for Marie in his lab, him and her fell in love and married.

Marie and Pierre Curie

The Curies did much of their innovative research in a small lab set up in an abandoned shed because both she and him believed that scientists should not waste valuable research time trying to make money. Marie did work on uranium and thorium, and it was her who invented the term *radioactivity*. In 1903, three scientists, Pierre and her, along with Henri Becquerel, shared the Nobel Prize in Physics. At around the same time, Pierre and Marie discovered the elements polonium (named after Marie's homeland) and radium. In 1911, after her husband's death, an unprecedented second Nobel Prize, this time in chemistry, was awarded to she alone. Marie Curie died in 1934 as a result of years of exposure to radiation, but her legacy continued. The Curies' daughter Irene, who had learned physics and chemistry from Marie and was nearly as skilled in scientific research as her, shared a Nobel Prize in Chemistry with her husband, Frederic Joliot-Curie, in 1935.

27b Use appropriate possessive forms of pronouns.

Distinguish between the adjective form of the possessive personal pronoun and the pronoun itself, standing alone.

▶ **The large room with three windows is *her* office.** [*Her* is an adjective.]

▶ **The office is *hers*.** [*Hers*, the possessive pronoun, can stand alone.]

Note: The word *mine* does not follow the pattern of *hers, theirs, yours,* and *ours*. The form *mines* is not Standard English.

mine
▶ **The little room on the left is ~~mines~~.**

When a possessive pronoun functions as a subject, its antecedent determines singular or plural agreement for the verb. (See 26k.)

▶ **My shirt is cotton; hers *is* silk.** [Singular antecedent and singular verb]

▶ **My gloves are black; hers *are* yellow.** [Plural antecedent and plural verb]

Possessive pronoun before an *-ing* form Generally, use a possessive personal pronoun before an *-ing* verb form used as a noun (a *gerund*).

▶ We would appreciate *your* participating in the auction.

▶ We were surprised at *their* winning the marathon.

VARIATION Sometimes the *-ing* form is a participle functioning as an adjective. In that case, the pronoun preceding the *-ing* form should be the object form.

▶ We saw *them* giving the runners foil wraps.

No apostrophe with possessive personal pronouns Even though possessive in meaning, the pronouns *yours, ours, theirs, his,* and *hers* should never be spelled with an apostrophe. Use an apostrophe only with the possessive form of a noun.

▶ That coat is *Maria's*.

▶ That is *her* coat.

▶ That coat is *hers*.

▶ These books are the *twins'*. **(33c)**

▶ These are *their* books.

▶ These books are *theirs*.

No apostrophe with *its* as a possessive pronoun The word *it's* is not a pronoun; it is the contraction of *it is* or *it has*. An apostrophe is never used with *its,* the possessive form of the pronoun *it* (33f).

▶ The paint has lost *its* gloss.

▶ *It's* not as glossy as it used to be. [It is not as glossy . . .]

Comparisons using possessive forms Note how using *them* in place of *theirs* in the following sentence would change the meaning by comparing suitcases to roommates, not suitcases to suitcases.

▶ It's really hard to be roommates with people if your suitcases are much better than *theirs*.

—J. D. Salinger, *The Catcher in the Rye*

Forgetting to use the appropriate possessive form in the next example, too, could create a misunderstanding: are you comparing a house to a person, or his house to her house?

▶ I like his house better than I like her. ^s

EXERCISE 27.2
Use the correct possessive pronoun form.

In the following sentences, correct any errors in the use of possessive forms of pronouns. Some sentences may be correct.

EXAMPLE:

Bonhoeffer tried to convince other Germans to oppose Nazi
views of racial purity, and ~~him~~ *his* playing gospel records in
Nazi Germany required courage.

1. When Dietrich Bonhoeffer was a visiting pastor at Harlem's Abyssinian Baptist Church in 1931, the congregation was pleased with him learning to love gospel music.

2. As a white German Protestant among African American worshippers, Bonhoeffer at first worried that his life was too different from them.

3. When Bonhoeffer returned to Germany, something of their's went with him: members of the church gave him several gospel records.

4. Dietrich Bonhoeffer's opposition to the Nazi regime led to him putting his life on the line by participating in the plot to assassinate Hitler in 1944; it's failure resulted in his imprisonment and execution.

5. Bonhoeffer's influence still appears in today's Germany, where the popularity of gospel music is still growing as a result of his championing of it decades ago.

27c **Make a pronoun refer to a clear antecedent.**

A pronoun substitutes for a noun, a noun phrase, or a pronoun already mentioned. The word or phrase that a pronoun refers to is known as the pronoun's *antecedent*. Antecedents should always be clear and explicit.

▶ Although the Canadian skater practiced daily with *her* trainers,

she didn't win the championship.

State a specific antecedent. Be sure to give a pronoun such as *they* or *it* an explicit antecedent.

▶ When Mr. Rivera applied for a loan, thèy outlined the procedures for him. [The pronoun *they* lacks an explicit antecedent.]

When Mr. Rivera applied to bank officials for a loan, *they* outlined the procedures for him.

When you use a pronoun, make sure it does not refer to a possessive modifier. You may need to revise to make your reference clear.

George Orwell
▶ In ~~George Orwell's~~ "Shooting an Elephant," ~~he~~ reports an incident that shows the evil effects of imperialism. [The pronoun *he* cannot refer to the possessive noun *Orwell's*.]

Make sure, too, that you revise a sentence in which *it* is left hanging, making a vague reference to a word in a phrase, such as "in the essay" or "in the article":

Lance Morrow's essay
▶ ~~In the essay by Lance Morrow, it~~ points out the problems of choosing a name.

Or In his article, Lance Morrow points out the problems of choosing a name.

Avoid ambiguous pronoun reference. Readers should never wonder what your pronouns refer to.

AMBIGUOUS   My husband told my father that hè should choose the baby's name. [Does *he* refer to *husband* or *father*?]

REVISED   My husband told my father to choose the baby's name.

REVISED   My husband wanted to choose the baby's name and told my father so.

AMBIGUOUS   **He had to decide whether to move to California.**

This was not what he wanted to do. [Does *This* refer to making the decision or to moving to California?]

REVISED   **He had to decide whether to move to California. The decision was not one he wanted to make.**

REVISED   **He had to decide whether to move to California. Moving there was not something he wanted to do.**

AMBIGUOUS   **Briggs noticed Mellersh as he passed by the fountain and ducked behind a hedge, and, thinking himself unobserved, took out binoculars.**

REVISED   **Briggs noticed Mellersh passing by the fountain and ducking behind a hedge. Briggs, thinking himself unobserved, took out binoculars.**

EXERCISE 27.3

Use clear antecedents with pronouns.

In each of the following sentences, rewrite any sentence in which a pronoun lacks a clear antecedent.

EXAMPLE:

officials
At the U.S. Patent and Trademark Office, ~~they~~ do not
endorse health claims made by any product.

1. Any food supplement or vitamin can obtain a patent, but it may not be effective.

2. The U.S. Patent Office's purpose is to help inventors lay claim to their unique creations, but it does not investigate whether a creation actually does what its inventor claims.

3. Consumers want products to perform miracles, but they are frequently disappointing.

4. If a food supplement or vitamin has questionable value, they may try to sell the product by advertising the fact that it is patented.

5. When a product label implies that its being patented proves a health claim, consumer advocates advise buyers to beware.

27d Make a pronoun agree in number with its antecedent.

A plural antecedent needs a plural pronoun; a singular antecedent needs a singular pronoun.

> plural antecedent   plural pronoun
> ▶ The *investigators* intercepted a phone call. *They* found the proof they needed.

> singular antecedent   singular pronoun
> ▶ The *detective* questioned several witnesses, but *she* was not able to determine who the accomplices were.

Make a demonstrative pronoun agree with its antecedent. The demonstrative pronouns *this* and *that* refer to singular nouns; *these* and *those* refer to plural nouns: *this house/that house, these houses/those houses* (26j).

> singular antecedent
> ▶ He published his autobiography two years ago. This was his first book.

> ———— plural antecedent ————
> ▶ One reviewer praised his honesty and directness. Those were qualities he had worked hard to develop.

Make a pronoun agree with a generalized (generic) antecedent. Generic nouns name a class or type of person or object, such as *a student* meaning "all students" or *a company* meaning "any company" or "all companies." Do not use *they* to refer to a singular generic noun.

FAULTY AGREEMENT

singular antecedent   plural pronoun

When a student is educated, they can go far in the world.

REVISED

singular antecedent   singular pronoun

When a student is educated, he or she can go far in the world.

REVISED

plural antecedent   plural pronoun

When students are educated, they can go far in the world.

Increasingly, you see in advertising, journalism, and informal writing a plural pronoun referring to a singular antecedent, as in the following car advertisement:

faulty agreement
► One day *your child* turns sixteen and you let *them* borrow the keys to the wagon.

However, many readers still expect a pronoun to agree with its antecedent in formal academic writing. Often the best solution is to make the antecedent plural.

people
► We should judge ~~a person~~ by who they are, not by the color of their skin.

Make a pronoun agree with an indefinite pronoun or quantity word.   Indefinite pronouns, such as *everyone, somebody*, and *nothing* (p. 437), are singular in form, so they occur with a singular verb. Some quantity words, such as *each, either, every*, and *neither*, are also singular in form (p. 437). A singular antecedent needs a singular pronoun to refer to it. But which singular pronoun should you use— *he, she*, or both? To avoid gender bias (27e and 20f) and possible clumsiness, writers often use the plural *they* to refer to a singular indefinite pronoun. Some readers, however, may object to this usage, so revising the sentence is a good idea.

SINGULAR PRONOUN WITH GENDER BIAS	**Everyone picked up** *his* **marbles and ran home to do his homework.**
REVISED BUT CLUMSY	**Everyone picked up** *his* **or** *her* **marbles and ran home to do** *his* **or** *her* **homework.**
REVISED BUT INFORMAL	**Everyone picked up** *their* **marbles and ran home to do** *their* **homework.** [The plural pronoun *their* refers to a singular antecedent.]
	VARIATION: You will probably often hear and read sentences like this one, but readers of formal academic prose may object to the fact that grammatically the plural pronoun *their* refers to a singular antecedent. Unless you know your audience well, play it safe and revise.
PROBABLY BEST	**The** *children* **all picked up their marbles and ran home to do** *their* **homework.**

Make a pronoun agree with the nearer antecedent when the parts of a compound antecedent are joined by *or* **or** *nor*.   When the elements of a compound antecedent are connected by *or* or *nor*, a pronoun agrees with the element that is nearer to it. If one part of the compound is singular and the other part is plural, put the plural antecedent closer to the pronoun and have the pronoun agree with it.

▶ **Either my friend or my brother has left *his* bag in the hall.**

▶ **Neither Bill nor the campers could find *their* soap.**

Make a pronoun agree with a collective noun. Use a singular pronoun to refer to a collective noun (*class, family, jury, committee, couple, team*) if you are referring to the group as a whole.

▶ **The class revised *its* examination schedule.**

▶ **The committee has not yet completed *its* report.**

Use a plural pronoun if members of the group named by the collective noun are considered to be acting individually.

▶ **The committee began to cast *their* ballots in a formal vote.**

EXERCISE 27.4

Use correct pronoun-antecedent agreement.

In each of the following sentences, correct any errors in pronoun-antecedent agreement, revising sentences as necessary. Some sentences may be correct.

EXAMPLE:

 the work of
 In wartime, a country's intelligence community ~~finds that their work~~ has tremendous importance and urgency.

1. If a historian studies World War II, they will learn how important intelligence was for the Allied victory.

2. At first, however, U.S. intelligence was unable to identify the risk of a Japanese attack, and their failure brought the country into the war.

3. Neither the head of the F.B.I. nor his counterparts at the State Department, Army, and Navy allowed other government officials access to secrets their agents had discovered, and the result was American unpreparedness for the attack on Pearl Harbor.

4. In December 1941, an American could easily have felt that his country might lose the war against the Japanese military and the still-undefeated German army.

5. Everyone involved in decoding German and Japanese messages deserves their share of the credit for the ultimate defeat of the Axis powers in 1945.

27e Avoid gender bias in pronouns.

Personal pronouns   For many years, the pronoun *he* was used routinely in generic references to unspecified individuals in certain roles or professions, such as student, doctor, lawyer, and banker; and *she* was used routinely in generic references to individuals in roles such as nurse, teacher, secretary, or typist. This usage is now considered biased language.

NOT **When an accountant learns a foreign language,** *he*
APPROPRIATE **gains access to an expanded job market.**

To revise such sentences that make general statements about people, roles, and professions, use one of the following methods:

1. Use a plural antecedent plus *they* (see also 27d and 20f).

   ▶ **When accountants learn a foreign language,** *they* **gain access to an expanded job market.**

2. Rewrite the sentence to eliminate the pronoun.

   ▶ **An accountant who learns a foreign language gains access to an expanded job market.**

3. Use a singular antecedent plus *he or she*.

   ▶ **When an accountant learns a foreign language,** *he or she* **gains access to an expanded job market.**

The problem with option 3 is that awkward and repetitive structures can result when such a sentence is continued.

   ▶ **When an accountant learns a foreign language,** *he or she* **gains access to an expanded job market once** *he or she* **has decided on** *his or her* **specialty.**

Use the *he or she* option only when a sentence is relatively short and does not repeat the pronouns. See also agreement with indefinite pronouns (26h and 27d).

EXERCISE 27.5

Avoid gender bias.

Rewrite the following sentences as necessary to remove any gender-biased pronouns. Some sentences may not need revision.

EXAMPLE:

All   parents want their
~~Every~~ concerned ~~parent wants her~~ children to have the best
possible education.

1. In the past, a first grade teacher might teach her students to read by asking them to sound out letters.

2. In the last two decades of the twentieth century, many a principal asked his school to teach reading using new theories.

3. Advocates of whole language theory hoped that a student who might otherwise have fallen behind his peers in reading would be encouraged by a method that eliminated lesson-based primers and spelling tests.

4. However, many parents were concerned to discover that their children were not reading or spelling well by the third grade.

5. By the end of the century, any lawmaker who advocated whole language theory in schools in his constituency was likely to face angry parents who wanted a return to spelling and reading basics.

27f Be consistent in your perspective.

It is important to be consistent with the perspective from which you are writing. Pronouns can help maintain consistency. Consider the person and number of the pronouns you use:

- Are you emphasizing the perspective of the first person (*I* or *we*)?
- Are you primarily addressing the reader as the second person (*you*)?
- Are you, as is more common in formal academic writing, writing about the third person (*he, she, it, one,* or *they*)?

Avoid confusing readers by switching from one perspective to another.

INCONSISTENT **We are all born with some of *our* personality already established in *us*. However, *I* believe that experiences also help shape who *you* are.**

REVISED *We* are all born with some of *our* personality already established in *us*. However, experiences also help shape who *we* are.

INCONSISTENT *The company* decided to promote only three mid-level managers. *You* had to have worked there for ten years to qualify.

REVISED *The company* decided to promote only three mid-level managers. *The employees* had to have worked there for ten years to qualify.

EXERCISE 27.6

Maintain a consistent point of view.

Revise the following passage as needed so that it maintains a consistent point of view.

EXAMPLE:

Residents
~~People~~ do not always see eye to eye with others in their

communities; talking about a novel might be a way to bring

people
~~us~~ together.

> Several municipalities around the United States—from small towns to the city of Chicago—are trying a new method to establish a sense of community: all residents are being encouraged to read the same book at the same time. When we read a book that we can discuss with our neighbors, we have a common ground for discussion. In the summer of 2001, ten thousand or more Chicagoans were reading Harper Lee's classic novel, *To Kill a Mockingbird*. You did not have to be a promoter of the reading program to hope that the novel's powerful portrayal of racism in the rural South could inspire discussions among all facets of the city's diverse population. Can reading books help us unite? Many around the country hope that book discussion groups held on a large scale can prove to people that they really are part of a community. Even if you don't agree with other readers about a book, the fact that you have read it means that you have something in common.

27g Use the pronoun *you* appropriately.

In formal writing, do not use the pronoun *you* when you mean "people generally." Use *you* only to address readers directly and to give instructions.

NO | **Credit card companies should educate students about how to handle credit. *You* should not have to find out the problems the hard way.** [This usage assumes readers are all students and addresses them directly. Some readers will not feel included in the group addressed as "you." A reader addressed directly in this way might think, "Who, me? I don't need to be educated about credit and I have no problems."]

YES | **Turn to the next page, where *you* will find an excerpt from Edith Wharton's novel that will help *you* appreciate the accuracy of the details in this film.**

Edit uses of *you* if you are making a generalization about a group or if using *you* entails a switch from the third person.

▶ While growing up, ~~you~~ face arguments with ~~your~~ parents.
               teenagers   their

▶ It doesn't matter if young professionals are avid music
  admirers or comedy fans; ~~you~~ can find anything ~~you~~ want
             they   they
  in the city.

EXERCISE 27.7
Use the pronoun *you* appropriately.

In the following sentences, decide if the pronoun *you* is used appropriately. If the use is inappropriate, revise the sentence. Some sentences may be correct.

EXAMPLE:

Nutritionists know how valuable deep-green vegetables are
      a person's
in ~~your~~ diet.

1. If you are like most Americans, you do not eat enough green, red, orange, and yellow fruits and vegetables.

2. Scientists have discovered that deeply colored vegetables and fruits provide you with important phytochemicals that inhibit cancer, regulate cholesterol, and offer other health benefits.

3. The average American eats more white potatoes than any other vegetable, but you get fewer healthy antioxidants from such white or pale-colored vegetables.

4. Studies have shown that eating more colorful fruits and vegetables can help you lose weight more effectively than concentrating on a low-fat diet.

5. To improve your chances of living a long and healthy life, you should choose two servings of fruit or vegetables a day from each of the four color groups.

27h Use standard forms of intensive and reflexive pronouns.

Intensive pronouns emphasize a previously mentioned noun or pronoun. Reflexive pronouns identify a previously mentioned noun or pronoun as the person or thing receiving the action.

INTENSIVE   **The president *himself* appeared at the gates.**

REFLEXIVE   **He introduced *himself*.**

Intensive and Reflective Pronouns

	Singular	Plural
First person	myself	ourselves
Second person	yourself	yourselves
Third person	himself	themselves
	herself	
	itself	

Note: Do not use an intensive pronoun in place of a personal pronoun in a compound subject.

           I

▶ Joe and ~~myself~~ will take care of the design of the newsletter.

Forms such as *hisself, theirself,* and *theirselves* occur in spoken dialects but are not Standard English.

EXERCISE 27.8

Correct intensive and reflexive pronouns.

In the following sentences, correct any errors in intensive and reflexive pronouns. Some sentences may be correct.

EXAMPLE:

Scientists who have successfully cloned animals such as sheep

have not cloned ~~theirselves~~ —or at least not yet.
themselves
                                    ^

1. The process of cloning is not complicated: a cloned cell gets a nucleus from the animal to be cloned, and a jolt of electricity convinces the cell to begin replicating it as if it had been fertilized.

2. The famous cloned sheep, Dolly, who died at age six, was the mother of healthy lambs, but her cloner hisself has expressed concerns about potential problems with cloning humans.

3. After the death of a second cloned sheep whose lungs had not developed properly, Ian Wilmut, director of the group that cloned Dolly, convinced himself that human cloning could result in children with terrible medical problems.

4. Of course, since cloning began to appear possible, both scientists and nonscientists have debated among theirselves about the ethics of cloning a human being.

5. Some argue that any people who cloned themselves would believe they owned their cloned human, but others point out that a clone himself is simply a genetic copy, just as identical twins are.

27i **Use *who* and *whom* and *whoever* and *whomever* correctly.**

In all formal writing situations, distinguish between the subject and object forms of the pronouns used to pose questions (interrogative pronouns) or to introduce a dependent noun clause (21e).

Subject	Object
who	whom (or, informally, who)
whoever	whomever

In questions   In a question, ask yourself whether the pronoun is the subject of its clause or the object of the verb. Test the pronoun's function by rephrasing the question as a statement, substituting a personal pronoun for *who* or *whom*.

▶ **Who wrote that enthusiastic letter?** [*He* wrote that enthusiastic letter. Subject: use *who*.]

▶ **Whoever could have written it?** [*She* could have written it. Subject: use *whoever*.]

▶ **Whom were they describing?** [They were describing *him*. Object: use *whom*.]

VARIATION   In speech and informal writing, *who* frequently replaces *whom* as a question word for the direct object, probably because to some people *whom* tends to sound overly correct and formal, verging on the pompous. *The Columbia Quiz Book* goes with *who* when it labels its first set of questions "Who Did Romeo Love?" The humorist Calvin Trillin sums up the views of many writers: "As far as I'm concerned, *whom* is a word that was invented to make everyone sound like a butler" (in "Whom Says So?"). Assess which form your readers are likely to expect.

In dependent noun clauses   When introducing a dependent clause with a pronoun, determine whether to use the subject or object form by examining the pronoun's function in the clause. Ignore expressions such as *I think* or *I know* when they follow the pronoun; they have no effect on the form of the pronoun.

                       subject of clause
▶ **They want to know who runs the business.**
                       subject of clause (who runs the business)
▶ **They want to know who I think runs the business.**
                       object of *to* [the manager reports to him or her]
▶ **They want to know whom the manager reports to.**
                       subject of clause
▶ **I will hire whoever is qualified.**
                       object of *recommends*
▶ **I will hire whomever my boss recommends.**

For uses of *who* and *whom* in relative clauses, see 29a.

EXERCISE 27.9

Use *who, whom, whoever,* and *whomever* correctly.

In each of the following sentences, cross out the incorrect pronoun contained within the parentheses.

EXAMPLE:

The writer V. S. Naipaul, (who / ~~whom~~) claims that he does not "stand for any country," won the Nobel Prize for Literature in 2001.

1. V. S. Naipaul, (who / whom) was raised in Trinidad by Indian parents, now lives in England.

2. Naipaul, (who / whom) one of the Nobel jury members called "the first global Nobelist," has written frequently about the problems of people in former colonies of England.

V. S. Naipaul

3. The author has targeted (whoever / whomever) expresses religious intolerance, and he has been denounced by fundamentalists in the Islamic world, (who / whom) he has written about recently.

4. Naipaul, (who / whom) is married to a Pakistani Muslim, has never shied away from criticizing, irritating, or infuriating readers of any religious or ethnic background.

5. His keen eye sees through (whoever / whomever) he describes in his books.

REVIEW EXERCISE FOR CHAPTER 27

Correct errors in pronoun use.

In the following passage, revise any errors in pronoun use. Remember to make all necessary changes to the sentence if you change a pronoun.

By some estimates, 70 percent of all of the antibiotics produced in the United States are used to promote growth in healthy livestock. In 1998, in a report by the National Research Council and the Institute of Medicine, they said that feeding antibiotics to farm animals contributed to the rise of some antibiotic-resistant bacteria and that this could make human beings sick. Papers published in a 2001 issue of the *New England Journal of Medicine* also concluded that you should be concerned about the use of antibiotics to make livestock grow more quickly and about the bacteria that are becoming harder to kill as a result.

When David G. White and a team of researchers from the Food and Drug Administration tested two hundred packages of supermarket chicken for salmonella, his researchers and himself discovered thirty-five samples of bacteria that were resistant to at least one antibiotic. L. Clifford McDonald and other scientists from the Centers for Disease Control and Prevention also tested supermarket chicken for an even more frightening study; their's found that 350 of 407 samples contained *Enterococcus faecium*, 250 samples of which were resistant to a potent new antibiotic cocktail called Synercid. You carry *E. faecium* in your intestines naturally, but it can cause illness if you get sick from something else. Today, a doctor usually prescribes Synercid if his patient's illness is caused by *E. faecium* because the bacteria have grown resistant to the antibiotic that was previously used. McDonald believes that the use of an antibiotic related to Synercid as a growth promoter in farm animals has led to bacteria's increasing resistance to Synercid.

Everyone should be concerned about the rise in antibiotic-resistant bacteria; whether or not they eat meat, they could someday be infected with a bug that is difficult to defeat. If antibiotics continue to be used simply to make livestock bigger, humans will have a harder time protecting theirselves against bacteria that were once easy to kill. Antibiotics have contributed greatly to improved human health in the past century, and no one whom understands the power of these miracle drugs should support its misuse.

Chapter **28**

Adjectives and Adverbs

Adjectives describe, or modify, nouns or pronouns. They do not add -*s* or change form to reflect number or gender.

Online Study Center   This icon will direct you to quick reference tools, Web resources, and research guides on the Web site at http://college.hmco.com/keys.html.

▶ Analysts acknowledge the *beneficial* effects of TV.

▶ He tried a *different* approach.

▶ The depiction of rural life is *accurate*.

▶ She keeps her desk *tidy*.

▶ The policy serves to keep the taxpayers *happy*.

ESL NOTE

No Plural Form of an Adjective

Never add a plural *-s* ending to an adjective that modifies a plural noun.

▶ He tried three *differents* approaches.

Adverbs modify verbs, adjectives, and other adverbs, as well as whole clauses.

▶ She settled down *comfortably*.

▶ The patient is demanding a *theoretically* impossible treatment.

▶ *Apparently*, the experiment was a success.

28a Use correct forms of adjectives and adverbs.

No single rule indicates the correct form of all adjectives and adverbs.

Adverb: adjective + -ly   Many adverbs are formed by adding *-ly* to an adjective: *soft/softly; intelligent/intelligently.* Sometimes when *-ly* is added, a spelling change occurs: *easy/easily; terrible/terribly.*

Adjectives ending in -ic   To form an adverb from an adjective ending in *-ic*, add *-ally* (*basic/basically; artistic/artistically*), except for *public*, whose adverb form is *publicly*.

Adjectives ending in -ly Some adjectives, such as *friendly, lovely, timely,* and *masterly,* already end in *-ly* and have no distinctive adverb form.

                adjective
▶ **She is a friendly person.**

                 ┌─ adverbial phrase ─┐
▶ **She spoke to me in a friendly way.**
                         adjective

Irregular adverb forms Certain adjectives do not add *-ly* to form an adverb.

Adjective	Adverb
good	well
fast	fast
hard	hard

    adjective   adverb
▶ **He is a good cook.**   ▶ **He cooks well.**
    adjective   adverb
▶ **She is a hard worker.**   ▶ **She works hard.**

    [*Hardly* is not the adverb form of *hard.* Rather, it means "barely," "scarcely," or "almost not at all": *I could* hardly *breathe in that stuffy room.*]

Note: Well can also function as an adjective, meaning "healthy" or "satisfactory": *A well baby smiles often. She feels well.*

EXERCISE 28.1
    Use correct forms of adjectives and adverbs.
In each of the following sentences, correct any errors in adjective or adverb forms. Some sentences may be correct.

EXAMPLE:

Amish adolescents face issues of independence and
                    basically
conformity that are ~~basicly~~ the same as those confronting
other young Americans.

1. People in Amish communities live without electricity or cars, in isolation from the modern world, where technology makes activities such as work and travel go swift.

2. Members of the church live strict by its rules, but a young person in an Amish household does not join the church until adulthood.

3. Amish teenagers are allowed to break church rules and experiment with the outside world; many non-Amish are shocked to learn how widely accepted such behavior is in the Amish community.

4. The great majority of young Amish do eventually join the church, and those who feel that they are not suited good to a highly regulated life may decide to join a more tolerant Amish group in another area.

5. A church member who breaks the rules faces excommunication and shunning by others in the community, so Amish groups try hardly to encourage young people to get over their interest in experimentation before they join the church.

28b Know when to use adjectives and adverbs.

In speech, adjectives (particularly *good, bad,* and *real*) are often used to modify verbs, adjectives, or adverbs. This is nonstandard usage. Use an adverb to modify a verb or an adverb.

▶ They fixed the latch ~~good~~. *(well)* ▶ I sing ~~real good~~. *(really well)*

▶ She speaks very ~~clear~~. *(clearly)* ▶ They sing ~~bad~~. *(badly)*

EXERCISE 28.2

Use adjectives and adverbs appropriately.

In the following passage, correct any errors in adjective or adverb use.

EXAMPLE:

                  really
High school sports are ~~real~~ important to many communities.

    Participating in a team sport can teach many good lessons to high school students. They can learn sportsmanship, the value of practicing to improve skills, and the strength that comes from working good together. However, many administrators, teachers, alumni, and students take high school athletics too serious. When students are forced to practice football in full uniforms in real hot weather at the beginning of the school year, the coaches' priorities are misplaced. When communities rally around champion high school athletes who have behaved extremely bad or even committed crimes, the communities are sending a terrible message to both athletes and nonathletes about the importance of a winning team. Sports should be fun, and although winning is important, playing good and honorable should be the most important goal of a high school team.

28c Use adjectives after linking verbs.

After linking verbs (*be, seem, appear, become*), use an adjective to modify the subject. (See 21c on subject complements.)

▶ That steak is good.

▶ Her new coat seems tight.

▶ She feels bad because she sings so badly.

Some verbs (*appear, look, feel, smell, taste*) are sometimes used as linking verbs, sometimes as action verbs. If the modifier describes the subject, use an adjective. If the modifier tells about the action of the verb, use an adverb.

ADJECTIVE   She looks *confident* in her new job.

ADVERB   She looks *confidently* at all the assembled partners.

ADJECTIVE   The waiter feels *bad*.

The steak smells *bad*.

ADVERB   The chef smelled the lobster *appreciatively*.

Note: Use a hyphen to connect two words used as an adjective when they appear before a noun. Do not use a hyphen when the words follow a linking verb with no noun complement.

▶ Sonny Rollins is a well-known saxophonist.

▶ Sonny Rollins is well known.

EXERCISE 28.3

Use adjectives and adverbs correctly after linking verbs.

In each of the following sentences, correct any errors in adjective and adverb use. Some sentences may be correct.

EXAMPLE:

suddenly

The aurora borealis appeared ~~sudden~~ in the sky.

1. The Norwegian scientist Kristian Birkeland felt certainly about the cause of the aurora borealis (or northern lights).

2. The lights, which hang like a brightly colored curtain in the night sky, look spookily to most observers.

3. Birkeland looked careful at the lights from a Norwegian mountaintop in midwinter during his 1899 expedition to study the phenomenon.

4. His two expeditions to observe the northern lights appeared successful, but some members of his scientific teams were badly injured or killed in the severe winter conditions.

Northern Lights

5. He appeared madly to some colleagues, but Birkeland finally determined that sunspots caused the aurora borealis.

28d Use correct forms of compound adjectives.

A compound adjective consists of two or more words used as a unit to describe a noun. Many compound adjectives contain the past participle *-ed* verb form: *flat-footed, barrel-chested, broad-shouldered, old-fashioned, well-dressed, left-handed*. Note the forms when a compound adjective is used before a noun: hyphens, past participle (*-ed*) forms where necessary, and no noun plural (*-s*) endings.

▶ They have a *five-year-old* **daughter.** [Their daughter is five years old.]

▶ She gave me a *five-dollar* **bill.** [She gave me five dollars.]

▶ He is a *left-handed* **pitcher.** [He pitches with his left hand.]

For more on hyphenation with compound adjectives, see 38j.

EXERCISE 28.4
Use compound adjectives correctly.

In each of the following sentences, correct any errors in the use of compound adjectives.

EXAMPLE:

Augusta Persse was twenty-eight years old when she
married her ~~sixty three years old~~ neighbor, Sir William
          sixty-three-year-old
Gregory, owner of Coole Park in Galway, Ireland.

1. Lady Gregory's twelve years marriage ended with her husband's death, and afterward she began to finish her husband's incomplete autobiography.

2. Her friendship with the well known poet W. B. Yeats was profitable for both of them: they inspired each other and collaborated on one act plays.

3. One play, *Cathleen ni Houlihan,* was an enormous success; although Yeats took credit for it, the manuscript contains pencil written notes that prove how much Lady Gregory had contributed.

4. Lady Gregory became the director of Dublin's famous Abbey Theatre; she won several hard fought battles over the theater's right to present plays such as John Millington Synge's *The Playboy of the Western World* and Sean O'Casey's *The Plough and the Stars.*

5. Many of the hand-pick plays that Lady Gregory championed are still considered masterpieces of Irish literature.

28e **Know where to position adverbs.**

An adverb can be placed in various positions in a sentence.

▶ *Enthusiastically,* **she ate the sushi.**

▶ **She** *enthusiastically* **ate the sushi.**

▶ **She ate the sushi** *enthusiastically.*

Do not place an adverb between a verb and a short direct object (43b).

▶ **She ate** *enthusiastically* **the sushi.**

Put adverbs that show frequency (*always, usually, frequently, often, sometimes, seldom, rarely, never*) in one of four positions:

1. At the beginning of a sentence

▶ *Sometimes* **I just sit and daydream instead of writing.**

When *never, seldom,* or *rarely* occurs at the beginning of the sentence, word order is inverted (see also 21c).

▶ *Never will* **I let that happen.**

2. Between the subject and the main verb

▶ **They** *always* **arrive half an hour late.**

3. After a form of *be* or any auxiliary verb (such as *do, have, can, will, must*)

▶ **They are** *always* **unpunctual.**

▶ **She is** *seldom* **depressed.**

▶ **He has** *never* **lost a game.**

4. In the final position

▶ **He goes to the movies** *frequently.*

Note: Never place the adverb *never* in the final position.

EXERCISE 28.5

Position adverbs correctly.

In the following passage, revise any sentence containing a misplaced adverb.

EXAMPLE:

He has read ~~often~~ the century-old diaries of Antarctic explorers.

often (inserted with caret after "read")

> In the nineteenth and twentieth centuries, polar exploration attracted usually courageous and foolhardy explorers. Many of these explorers kept journals or wrote books, and even today their writings are popular. Why would modern people want to read them? Perhaps the charm of these tales for modern readers lies in the strangeness of the quests. Seldom the early polar explorers gave satisfying reasons for their journeys: on one British expedition to the South Pole, biologists endured weeks of the coldest weather ever recorded in order to collect specimens that scientists at home did not want. Another fascinating feature of polar exploration adventures is that they frequently were fatal: the most celebrated heroes of polar exploration have been those often who failed. Captain Robert Scott, who lost the race to the South Pole and then died in the attempt to return home, is always almost portrayed sympathetically. Rarely Roald Amundsen, the man who beat Scott to the Pole, is mentioned unless his name comes up in discussions of Scott's doomed journey. The romance of failure and of fool's errands entices readers today; modern writers about polar exploration try to find frequently explanations of why these people took such risks. Never the answers can be known with certainty. However, generations of readers will be grateful always that the explorers preserved records of their astonishing journeys to the Poles.

28f　Know the usual order of adjectives.

When two or more adjectives modify a noun, they usually occur in the order listed in the Key Points box. Commas separate coordinate adjectives that offer subjective evaluation; their order can be reversed, and the word *and* can be inserted between them (31g). No commas separate adjectives in the other categories listed in the box.

KEY POINTS
Guide to the Order of Adjectives

1. Determiner: articles (*a, an, the*), demonstrative adjectives (*this, that, these, those*), possessives (*its, our*), quantity words (*many, some*), numerals (*five, nineteen*)　*(Continued)*

(Continued)

2. Coordinate adjective (subjective evaluation): *interesting, delicious, comfortable, inexpensive, heavy, tedious*
3. Adjective describing size: *little, big, huge, tiny*
4. Adjective describing shape: *round, square, rectangular*
5. Adjective describing age: *new, young, old*
6. Adjective describing color: *white, red, blue*
7. Adjective describing national origin: *Italian, American*
8. Adjective describing architectural style or religious faith: *Gothic, Romanesque, Catholic, Buddhist*
9. Adjective describing material: *oak, ivory, wood(en)*
10. Noun used as an adjective: *kitchen* cabinet, *writing* desk

    1   2   5   9   10
▶ **the lovely old oak writing desk**

    1   3   6   9
▶ **many little white ivory buttons**

    1   2   4   10
▶ **that beautiful square kitchen table**

    1   2   7   9
▶ **his efficient European wood stove**

    1   2   2
▶ **her efficient, hardworking assistant** [Commas occur only between coordinate adjectives of subjective evaluation.]

As a general rule, avoid long strings of adjectives. Two or three adjectives of evaluation, size, shape, age, color, national origin, faith, or material should be the limit.

EXERCISE 28.6

Use adjectives in the correct order.

In each of the following sentences, make any necessary changes in the order of adjectives and use of commas.

EXAMPLE:

    Short, dark winter
~~Dark, winter, short~~ days can cause some people to become depressed. ^

1. In northern states in wintertime, many office workers spend most of the daylight hours indoors.

2. Architects are beginning to design some new big buildings to admit as much natural light as possible.

3. A building with features such as skylights, large windows, or an atrium reduces the need for artificial light, but the most money-saving one benefit of outside light is its effect on many workers.

4. A recent architectural study demonstrated that workers in buildings with natural light were happier, more productive employees than workers in dark or artificially lighted offices.

5. Concerned employers can help their office workers maintain a positive outlook through winter dreary months by ensuring that workplaces are brightly lit, preferably with natural light.

28g Avoid double negatives.

Adverbs like *hardly, scarcely,* and *barely* are considered negatives, and the contraction *-n't* stands for the adverb *not*. Some languages and dialects allow the use of more than one negative to emphasize an idea, but Standard English allows only one negative in a clause. Avoid double negatives.

NO **We do*n't* have *no* excuses.**

YES **We do*n't* have *any* excuses.** [Or] We have *no* excuses.

NO **She did*n't* say *nothing*.**

YES **She did*n't* say *anything*.** [Or] She said *nothing*.

NO **They ca*n't hardly* pay the rent.**

YES **They can *hardly* pay the rent.**

EXERCISE 28.7
Avoid double negatives.

Rewrite the following sentences as necessary to correct any double negatives.

EXAMPLE:

People with age-related deafness ~~don't~~ rarely hear high-pitched sounds as well as low-pitched ones.

1. People speaking to a hearing-impaired elderly person often pitch their voices higher to make themselves heard, but studies have shown that using a higher pitch doesn't help the person's perception none.

2. In an elderly person, perception of higher-frequency sounds, such as high-pitched voices, isn't no better than perception of lower-frequency sounds; in fact, perception of higher-frequency sounds is often much worse.

3. Usually, a person with age-related hearing loss doesn't hear no distortion in low-frequency sounds—these may actually sound louder to older people than they do to younger ones.

4. In one study, elderly people exposed to rock music, with its low-frequency bass and drum sounds, consistently rated it as louder than young people did; however, the study didn't necessarily demonstrate nothing about whether elderly or youthful people hear better.

5. Psychologists point out that people exposed to music that they can't hardly bear always think it is louder than fans of the music think it is.

28h Know the comparative and superlative forms of adjectives and adverbs.

The *comparative* and *superlative* forms of adjectives and adverbs are used for comparisons. Use the comparative form to compare two people, places, things, or ideas; use the superlative to compare more than two.

Regular forms Add the ending *-er* to form the comparative and *-est* to form the superlative of both short adjectives (those that have one syllable or those that have two syllables and end in *-y* or *-le*) and one-syllable adverbs. (Change *-y* to *-i* if *-y* is preceded by a consonant: *icy, icier, iciest.*) Generally, a superlative form is preceded by *the* (*the shortest distance*).

Positive	Comparative (comparing two)	Superlative (comparing more than two)
short	shorter	shortest
pretty	prettier	prettiest
simple	simpler	simplest
fast	faster	fastest

With longer adjectives and with adverbs ending in *-ly,* use *more* (for the comparative) and *most* (for the superlative). Note that *less* (comparative) and *least* (superlative) are used with adjectives of any length (*less bright, least bright; less effective, least effective*).

Positive	Comparative	Superlative
intelligent	more intelligent	most intelligent
carefully	more carefully	most carefully
dangerous	less dangerous	least dangerous

If you cannot decide whether to use *-er/-est* or *more/most,* consult a dictionary. If there is an *-er/-est* form, the dictionary will say so.

Note: Do not use the *-er* form with *more* or the *-est* form with *most.*

▶ The first poem was ~~more~~ better than the second.

▶ Boris is the ~~most~~ fittest person I know.

Irregular forms   The following common adjectives and adverbs have irregular comparative and superlative forms:

Positive	Comparative	Superlative
good	better	best
bad	worse	worst
much/many	more	most
little	less	least
well	better	best
badly	worse	worst

***Than* with comparative forms**   To compare two people, places, things, or ideas, use the comparative form and the word *than.* If you use a comparative form in your sentence, you need *than* to let readers know what you are comparing with what.

▶ This course of action is more efficient. than the previous one
                                          ^

Comparative forms are also used without *than* in an idiomatic way

▶ The *harder* he tries, the *more satisfied* he feels.

▶ The *more,* the *merrier.*

Absolute adjectives   Do not use comparative and superlative forms of adjectives that imply absolutes: *complete, empty, full, equal,* *perfect, priceless,* or *unique.* In addition, do not add intensifying adverbs such as *very, totally, completely,* or *absolutely* to these adjectives. To say that something is "perfect" implies an absolute, rather than something measured in degrees.

▶ He has ~~the most~~ *a* perfect view of the ocean.

▶ They bought a ~~totally~~ unique quilt at an auction.

EXERCISE 28.8

Use comparative and superlative forms correctly.

In the following passage, correct any errors in comparative and superlative forms of adjectives and adverbs.

EXAMPLE:

Before farmers and fishermen in India had access to cell

phones, they fared ~~worst~~ *worse* when marketing their goods than

they do today.

In the United States, the first people to have cellular telephones were the most rich members of the population. In India, in contrast, many poor and working-class people have been among the people who have adopted cell phone technology the quickest. Many of these people live and work in areas that are not served by traditional land telephones, and they are finding that cell phones are one of the usefullest inventions for improving a small business. Fishermen in western India, for example, have no other access to telephones from their boats, and calling the markets before heading to shore with the day's catch allows them to find the most high prices. Growers of produce in rural areas are also beginning to rely on cell phones to find the most high prices for their wares.

Indian cellular companies are responding to a real need in the country—there are far more few telephones per household in India than in the industrialized world—but they are also creating more greater demand. The cell phone marketers have made a tremendous effort to increase the numbers of cellular telephones in the country, offering new customers efficienter service than land lines provide while also making cell phone calls widelier available and most affordable. For the time being, at least, the introduction of cell phone technology has created totally unique opportunities for both cell phone marketers and consumers in India.

28i Avoid faulty or incomplete comparisons.

Make sure that you state clearly what items you are comparing. Some faulty comparisons can give readers the wrong idea. See 24h, 27a, 27b.

INCOMPLETE **He likes the parrot better than his wife.**

To avoid suggesting that he prefers the parrot to his wife, clarify the comparison by completing the second clause.

REVISED **He likes the parrot better *than his wife does*.**

Edit sentences like the following:

▶ **My essay got a higher grade than Maria.** 's
  [Compare the two essays, not your essay and Maria.]

▶ **Williams's poem gives a more objective depiction of the painting than Auden.** 's [To compare Williams's poem with Auden's poem, you need to include an apostrophe; otherwise, you compare a poem to the poet W. H. Auden.]

Comparisons must also be complete. If you say that something is "more efficient," your reader wonders, "More efficient than what?"

▶ **Didion shows us a home that makes her feel more tied to her roots.** than her home in Los Angeles does [Include the other part of the comparison.]

EXERCISE 28.9

Correct faulty or incomplete comparisons.

In each of the following sentences, correct any faulty or incomplete comparisons. Some sentences may be correct.

EXAMPLE:

Two Stanford University linguists think that the click languages are older than some linguists. think they are

1. Khoisan, or click, languages, whose vocabularies include click-ing sounds, are more prevalent in southwestern Africa.

2. The members of the Hadzabe tribe in the East African country of Tanzania speak a Khoisan language similar to the San and !Kung tribes of West Africa.

3. Genetic comparisons between the San people and the Hadzabe people prove that their genes differ more than any other two populations in the world.

4. To some linguists, including Alec Knight and Joanna Mountain of Stanford University, these genetic differences prove that the San and Hadzabe populations diverged very early in the development of human beings; Knight and Mountain believe this clue means that Khoisan languages are older.

5. Was the original human language a click language? Knight and Mountain are more convinced of that possibility than they were before learning of the genetic comparisons, but they admit that there are other possible explanations for the fact that two geographically distant tribes both speak Khoisan languages.

REVIEW EXERCISE FOR CHAPTER 28

Correct errors in adjective and adverb use.

In the following passage, correct any errors in adjective and adverb use.

Recently, paleontologists have discovered the complete fossils of five 110 million years old ancestors of modern crocodiles. The fossils of *Sarcosuchus imperator,* which means "emperor of the flesh eating crocodiles," were found in an African ancient riverbed. The skull of one adult animal measures four and a half feet long, and scientists estimate that the creature's length would have been more than thirty-five feet; modern crocodiles don't rarely reach half that size. In a photograph released by scientists at the University of Chicago, the skull of the *Sarcosuchus* looks enormously next to the skull of a modern crocodile.

The skeletons of juvenile *Sarcosuchus* found in Africa provide fortunately clues to the lives and habits of the giant prehistoric crocodiles. They did not grow especially quick: at forty years of age, the creatures were not yet adults, and they may not have reached maturity until they were fifty or sixty. They were covered with stiff bony plates that were similarly to armor, so they did not move lively. The *Sarcosuchus* had smooth, stout teeth that worked good for grabbing and crushing its prey.

Like its present day descendants, *Sarcosuchus* had eyes and nostrils on top of its skull, so it was built totally perfect for lurking underwater and grabbing prey on the riverbank. Other ancient reptiles may have been more larger, but the prehistoric crocodile's great similarity to its modern descendants allows humans today to imagine the fearsome ancient creatures vividly. Most people who see the *Sarcosuchus* skull are certain to feel relievedly that this prehistoric creature no longer roams the rivers of the earth.

Chapter **29**

Relative Clauses and Relative Pronouns

Relative clauses are introduced by relative pronouns: *who, whom, whose, which,* and *that.* Relative clauses are also called *adjective clauses* because they modify nouns and noun phrases in the same way as adjectives do. Relative clauses follow the nouns to which they refer. A dependent relative clause refers to a word or words (its *antecedent*) in an independent clause. See 21e for more on clauses.

┌── relative clause ──┐
▶ **The girl *who* can't dance says the band can't play.**

—Yiddish proverb

29a   Use an appropriate relative pronoun: *Who, whom, whose, which,* or *that*.

The forms of relative pronouns vary in speech and writing and in informal and formal usage. In academic writing, use the relative pronouns designated *formal* in the discussion that follows.

Human antecedents   In formal writing, use *who, whom,* and *whose* to refer to people.

Online Study Center   This icon will direct you to quick reference tools, Web resources, and research guides on the Web site at http://college.hmco.com/keys.html.

Relative Pronouns: Human Antecedents

Subject	Object	Possessive
who	whom (sometimes omitted)	whose
	that (informal)	

For *who* and *whom* as question words, see 27i.

The form of the relative pronoun depends on the pronoun's grammatical function in its own clause. To identify the correct form, restate the clause, using a personal pronoun.

subject of clause

▶ **The teachers who challenge us are the ones we remember.**

[*They* challenge us.]

object of clause

▶ **The teachers whom the students honored felt proud.**

[The students honored *them*. (*Whom* may be omitted.)]

possessive

▶ **The teachers whose student evaluations were high won an award.** [*Their* student evaluations were high.]

VARIATION *Whom* is the grammatically correct form of the relative pronoun in the direct object position in its own clause. However, in speech and informal writing, it often tends to be replaced by *who*. When in doubt as to whether to use *who* or *whom,* and if you cannot work out which is grammatically appropriate, opt for *who*. Readers are far less likely to accept *whom* in place of *who* than the other way around. See also 27i

Phrases such as *I know, he thinks,* and *they realize* inserted into a relative clause do not affect the form of the pronoun.

subject of clause

▶ **We should help children *who* we realize *cannot defend***

***themselves*.** [*They* cannot defend themselves.]

Nonhuman antecedents: animals, things, and concepts
Standard English, unlike languages such as Spanish, Arabic, and

Thai, uses different relative pronouns for human and for nonhuman antecedents. Use *that* or *which* to refer to only nonhuman antecedents.

> *who*
> ► The teacher ~~which~~ taught me math in high school was strict.
>   ^

Relative Pronouns: Nonhuman Antecedents

Subject	Object	Possessive
that	that (sometimes omitted)	of which (formal)
which	which (sometimes omitted)	whose (informal)
(see 29d)		

Use the relative pronoun *that* to refer to an antecedent naming an animal, a thing, or a concept (such as *success* or *information*). When the relative pronoun *that* functions as the direct object in its clause, it can be omitted.

► They stayed at a hotel *that* had two pools and a sauna. [*That* is the subject of the relative clause.]

► They stayed at a hotel *that* their friends had recommended. [*That* is the direct object in the relative clause.]

► They stayed at a hotel their friends had recommended. [*That* as direct object in the relative clause can be omitted.]

► They stayed at a hotel the name *of which* I can't remember. [Formal]

► They stayed at a hotel *whose* name I can't remember. [Informal]

EXERCISE 29.1

Use relative pronouns correctly.

In the following passage, revise any incorrect or informal use of relative pronouns, and supply any missing pronouns.

EXAMPLE:

who
No one could dispute the fact that George Lucas, ~~which~~
                                                  ^
created the *Star Wars* films, is a marketing genius.

When George Lucas made the movie *Star Wars* in 1977, he told people whom asked about the film's box-office prospects that it would make sixteen million dollars. In fact, the original *Star Wars*, whose story was based on old movie serials and comic book adventures, went on to become the second-highest-grossing film of all time. However, the real money-making potential of the *Star Wars* films lies in the merchandise accompanies them. Lucas, that owns the licenses for all of the merchandise, was said to have earned about four billion dollars from sales of those products even before the release of *Star Wars: Episode I— The Phantom Menace* in 1999. Before that film appeared, reporters who newspapers assigned to write *Phantom Menace* stories were typically business journalists rather than film reviewers. Many of the stories they wrote estimated that *The Phantom Menace* would make a profit even if no tickets to the film were ever sold. Not surprisingly, some film reviewers and moviegoers that saw *The Phantom Menace* were disappointed; even less surprisingly, the film was a hit, and fans continue to buy the merchandise.

When to use *that* In Standard English, for a nonhuman antecedent, use *that* rather than *which* in the subject position and use *that* (or omit *that*) as an object in a restrictive relative clause. Never use *what* as if it were a relative pronoun.

>   that
> ▶ The book ~~which~~ won the prize is a love story.
>   ^
>   [that]
> ▶ The deal ~~what~~ she was trying to make fell through.
>   [that]
> ▶ Everything ~~which~~ she does for United Way is appreciated.

Use *that* rather than *who* when referring to groups of people.

>   that
> ▶ The class ~~who~~ meets here is late.
>   ^

When not to use *that* In the following instances, use *which* or *whom* instead of *that*.

1. In nonrestrictive clauses supplying extra information (see 29d)

> ▶ **Ellsvere Shopping Center, *which* was sold last month, has changed the whole area.**

2. Directly following a preposition

▶ **The woman to** *whom* **they gave the award is a famous physicist.**

In informal contexts, however, the preposition is likely to occur at the end of the clause; in this case, *that* can be used or omitted.

▶ **The woman [that] I was talking to is a famous physicist.**

EXERCISE 29.2

Use *that* correctly as a relative pronoun.

In each of the following sentences, correct any errors in the use of relative pronouns. Some sentences may be correct.

EXAMPLE:

Methamphetamine is a drug ~~what~~ that is becoming a serious problem in some rural states.

1. Methamphetamine laboratories, that are illegal and consequently unregulated by the government, produce large amounts of toxic waste.

2. For every pound of methamphetamine which is made in these drug labs, six pounds of poisonous chemicals are created.

3. The use of a drug what was once rare in this country has increased dramatically since the 1990s, and waste from the illegal meth-amphetamine labs is becoming a serious environmental problem.

4. The toxic byproducts, which can include acids, benzene, and other lethal chemicals, are often dumped on the ground by the drug manufacturers, and from there the toxins can seep into water supplies.

5. In many cases, even when the labs are discovered and closed down, no one cleans up the sites; agencies who deal with criminal activities rarely notify environmental agencies or any other groups that might take responsibility for removing the toxic waste.

29b Distinguish between restrictive and nonrestrictive relative clauses.

The two types of relative clauses, restrictive and nonrestrictive, fulfill different functions and need different punctuation (31d).

RESTRICTIVE	**The people** *who live in the apartment above mine* **make a lot of noise at night.**
	The writers *who lived in Harlem in the 1940s* **started a great tradition.**
NONRESTRICTIVE	**The Sullivans,** *who live in the apartment above mine,* **make a lot of noise at night.**
	Zora Neale Hurston, *who was a leading writer of the Harlem Renaissance,* **was greatly influenced by her mother.**

Restrictive relative clause   A restrictive relative clause provides information essential for identifying the antecedent and restricting its scope.

FEATURES

1. The clause is not set off with commas.
2. An object relative pronoun can be omitted.
3. *That* (not *which*) is preferred for reference to nonhuman antecedents.

▶ **The teachers** *who challenge us* **are the ones we remember.** [The independent clause—"The teachers are the ones"—leads us to ask, "Which teachers?" The relative clause provides information that is essential to completing the meaning of the subject; it restricts the meaning from "all teachers" to "the teachers who challenge us."]

▶ **The book** [*that*] *you gave me* **was fascinating.** [The relative pronoun *that* is the direct object in its clause ("You gave me the book") and can be omitted.]

Nonrestrictive relative clause   A nonrestrictive relative clause provides information that is not essential for understanding the antecedent. It refers to and describes a proper noun (which names a specific person, place, or thing and begins with a capital letter) or a noun that is identified and unique.

FEATURES

1. The antecedent is a unique, designated person or thing.
2. The clause is set off by commas.

3. *Which* (not *that*) is used to refer to a nonhuman antecedent.
4. An object relative pronoun cannot be omitted.

> ▶ *War and Peace,* **which you gave me, is a fascinating novel.**
> [The independent clause—"*War and Peace* is a fascinating novel"—does not promote further questions, such as "Which *War and Peace* do you mean?" The information in the relative clause ("which you gave me") is almost an aside and not essential for understanding the independent clause.]

EXERCISE 29.3

Identify restrictive and nonrestrictive clauses.

In the following sentences, underline each relative clause and write *R* (restrictive) or *NR* (nonrestrictive) on the line before the sentence. There may be more than one relative clause in a sentence. Then edit to make sure that each clause is punctuated correctly and that the correct form of the relative pronoun is used.

EXAMPLE:

__R__ People/who speak a pidgin language/are finding a way to bridge the communication gap.

1. _____ When a person who speaks only English and a person, who speaks only Spanish, must communicate, they will find common ground by using the simple grammar and vocabulary of pidgin.

2. _____ Pidgin which is not spoken as a native tongue by anyone is different from creolized language.

3. _____ When a language, that started out as pidgin, becomes the common speech of a community, that language has been creolized.

4. _____ For example, Haitian Creole that is a language with its own complex grammar and vocabulary came from the pidgin speech created by slaves from many cultures, who were forced to live and work together.

5. _____ Creolized languages which often develop when pidgin speakers raise children in a multicultural community demonstrate both the creativity of human beings—even in terrible hardship—and the depth of the human need to communicate with other people.

Nonrestrictive clauses with quantity words Relative clauses beginning with a quantity word such as *some, none, many, much, most,* or *one* followed by *of which* or *of whom* are always nonrestrictive. Use a comma to set off such a clause.

▶ **They selected five candidates, one of whom would get the job.**

▶ **The report mentioned five names, none of which I recognized.**

You need only the relative pronoun, not a personal pronoun in addition.

most of whom

▶ **I tutored some students, ~~which most of them~~ were my classmates.**

EXERCISE 29.4

Use relative clauses with quantity words correctly.

In each of the following sentences, correct any errors in relative pronouns or punctuation. Some sentences may be correct.

EXAMPLE:

whom

Previous Nobel Prize winners in economics, ~~who~~ many of ~~them~~ have advocated free-market capitalization, were not surprised when Amartya Sen won in 1998.

1. As early as the beginning of the 1960s, the economist Amartya Sen was writing arguments, most of which were ignored by other social scientists, that women suffered terrible inequalities in the developing world and that these inequalities harmed local economies.

2. Sen continues to advocate gender-specific aid programs to help poor women in developing countries, who many of them lack even basic education.

Amartya Sen

3. Economists around the world have begun to acknowledge the accuracy of Sen's economic theories some of which focus on the advantages of treating women as full members of a society.

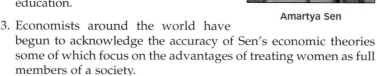

4. New groups of social scientists many of whom have been inspired by Sen's groundbreaking work are investigating the ways that improving women's status in developing countries can also lead to improvements in family income, education, nutrition, and life expectancy.

5. Sen has now set up two foundations, which both of them aim to reduce illiteracy and gender inequality in India and Bangladesh, to put his theoretical views into practice in the developing world.

29c Make the verb agree with the antecedent of a subject relative pronoun.

Determine subject-verb agreement within a relative clause by asking whether the antecedent of a subject relative pronoun is singular or plural.

▶ **The book that *is* at the top of the bestseller list gives advice about health.** [The singular noun *book* is the antecedent of *that*, the subject of the singular verb *is* in the relative clause.]

▶ **The books that *are* at the top of the bestseller list give advice about health, success, and making money.** [The plural noun *books* is the antecedent of *that*, the subject of the plural verb *are* in the relative clause.]

Agreement with *one of* and *the only one of*   The phrase *one of* is followed by a plural noun phrase. However, the verb can be singular or plural, depending on the meaning.

▶ **Juan is one of the employees who *work* long hours.** [Several employees work long hours. Juan is one of them. The plural word *employees* is the antecedent of *who*, the subject of the plural verb *work* in the relative clause.]

▶ **Juan is the only one of the employees who *works* long hours.** [Only Juan works long hours.]

EXERCISE 29.5

Make verb and antecedent of subject relative pronoun agree.

In each of the following sentences, correct any subject-verb agreement errors within the relative clauses. Then draw an arrow from any subject relative pronoun to its antecedent. Some sentences may be correct.

EXAMPLE:

make
Keeping costs down is one of the reasons that ~~makes~~ most health maintenance organizations require approval for certain treatments.

1. Most people who participate in group insurance plans now use some form of managed care.

2. Many insurance companies require any patients who participates in managed care plans to get a referral from their primary care physician before seeing an expensive specialist.

3. This practice, which are known as "gatekeeping," often infuriates both patients and physicians.

4. In some cases, patients may believe that a particular specialist is the only one of the doctors in the group who know how to treat a particular condition.

5. Everyone in the plan who need to see a specialist must first make an appointment with a primary care physician to get his or her referral; many patients resent having to make this extra visit.

6. In addition, many insurance companies pay lower fees to any doctor in a managed care plan who refer patients to a specialist for treatment, so doctors are often reluctant to make referrals.

7. Any patients in managed care who sees a specialist without a referral usually have to pay for the full cost of the visit.

8. According to some analysts, feeling angry about being forced to get a primary care physician's permission to see a specialist is one of the situations that causes patients to sue their doctors.

9. One of the surprises that has come from a recent study of health maintenance organizations is the finding that few

patients made unnecessary visits to specialists when referrals were not required.

10. In spite of this finding, many experts still support some version of gatekeeping because they think that patients who get a specialist's care should nevertheless let the primary care physicians who knows them best participate in decisions about treatment.

29d Take care when a relative clause contains a preposition.

When a relative clause contains a relative pronoun within a prepositional phrase, do not omit the preposition. Keep in mind these three points:

1. Directly after the preposition, use *whom* or *which*, never *that*.

   ┌────── relative clause ──────┐
   ▶ **The man *for whom* we worked last year has just retired.**

2. If you place the preposition after the verb, use *that* (or you can omit *that*), but do not use *whom* or *which*.

   [that]
   ▶ **The man ~~whom~~ we worked for was efficient.**

   [that]
   ▶ **The security measures ~~which~~ the mayor had insisted on made him unpopular.**

3. Do not add an extra personal pronoun object after the preposition at the end of the relative clause.

   ▶ **The company [that] I worked for ~~it~~ last summer has gone bankrupt.**

   ▶ **The director [whom] they are devoted to ~~her~~ has produced six new plays this season.**

EXERCISE 29.6
Use relative clauses with prepositions correctly.

In the following passage, correct any errors in relative clauses containing prepositions.

EXAMPLE:

                                which
A terrible day on ~~that~~ few airplanes were in U.S. airspace
proved to have some benefits for climatologists.

> Jet airplanes leave trails in the sky called *contrails,* which are made of frozen exhaust fumes. Eventually, the contrails become cirrus clouds. Scientists which weather is part of a research question for have often wondered how these contrails affect climate. Is some warming of which people call it the *greenhouse effect* caused by these clouds? Climatologists had long known that the best way to measure the effect of contrails would be to conduct a controlled study: data should be collected, some of that should be from periods of heavy air traffic and some from periods when no planes were flying. The problem was that planes were always flying. However, when nearly all flights over the United States were suspended after the terrorist attacks on New York and Washington, D.C., on September 11, 2001, climatologists had a brief opportunity to collect data from skies which no airplanes were flying in. These scientists hope to use the data that was gathered on September 12 to learn whether contrails affect global warming.

29e Position a relative clause close to its antecedent.

To avoid ambiguity, place a relative clause as close as possible to its antecedent. (See also 24b on misplaced modifiers.)

AMBIGUOUS   **He searched for the notebook all over the house that his friend had forgotten.**

[Had his friend forgotten the house?]

REVISED   **He searched all over the house for the notebook that his friend had forgotten.**

29f Avoid using a pronoun after a relative clause to rename the antecedent.

Although this kind of usage occurs in informal speech and in many other languages, avoid it in formal writing. (See also 43.)

▶ My colleague who moved to Italy three years ago and has his own apartment in Milan ~~he~~ has a good life.

EXERCISE 29.7

Position relative clauses correctly and delete unnecessary pronouns.

In the following sentences, correct any ambiguity caused by the position of the relative clause and remove any repetitive pronouns.

EXAMPLE:

that is being decoded

The fish genome will reveal information useful to genetic researchers ~~that is being decoded.~~

1. Fugu is considered a delicacy in Japan, but only the most adventurous eaters are willing to order a meal when dining at a restaurant that might contain a deadly poison.

2. A chef must train for many months before being legally allowed to serve the potentially deadly puffer fish who wants a license to prepare fugu.

3. Although many people who have heard about daredevil restaurant-goers ordering fugu they wonder why anyone would be interested in the ugly and possibly toxic fish, geneticists have long been fascinated by the puffer fish known as *Fugu rubripes*.

4. The fugu's genome, which is shorter than that of any other vertebrate on earth, it has now been almost completely deciphered by an international team of scientists.

5. Geneticists hope that their analysis of the puffer fish genome will speed scientists' identification of human gene functions, which is like a condensed version of the complex human genome.

29g Use *where* and *when* as relative pronouns when appropriate.

When you refer to actual or metaphoric places and times, you can use *where* to replace *in which, at which,* or *to which,* and you can use *when* to replace *at which, in which,* or *on which.* Do not use a preposition with *where* or *when.*

▶ The morning on which she graduated was warm and sunny.

▶ The morning *when* she graduated was warm and sunny.

▶ The village in which he was born honored him last year.

▶ The village *where* he was born honored him last year.

However, use *where* or *when* only if actual time or physical location is involved.

                                              according to which
▶ The influence of the Sapir-Whorf hypothesis, ~~where~~ behavior
   is regarded as influenced by language, has declined.

EXERCISE 29.8

Use *where* and *when* appropriately.

In each of the following sentences, revise any inappropriate uses of *where* and *when* as relative pronouns. Some sentences may be correct.

EXAMPLE:

                                                  in which
Spelunking is one name for the profession or hobby ~~where~~
people explore caves, but most cave explorers prefer the
term *caving.*

1. In 1838, Stephen Bishop, a seventeen-year-old slave, arrived at Kentucky's Mammoth Cave, to where he had been sent to work as a guide.

2. Bishop was a popular guide, but he was also a great and fearless explorer, squeezing through tight passages in which no humans had been for centuries.

3. In a single year where Bishop explored previously unknown parts of the cave, he doubled the explored portion of Mammoth Cave, earning fame—but not freedom—and attracting hundreds of tourists to the site.

4. Bishop discovered the underground river in Mammoth Cave, in which blind fish and crustaceans live, and in 1842 he drew a careful map of the cave that was used by explorers for the next forty years.

5. In 1972, cave explorers found a passage called Hanson's Lost River that led from another Kentucky cave system into Mammoth Cave; the explorers later discovered that the passage through where they had crawled to make the connection was marked on Bishop's 130-year-old map.

REVIEW EXERCISE FOR CHAPTER 29

Correct errors in relative clauses and relative pronoun clauses.

In the following passage, correct any errors in relative pronouns and relative clauses.

The QWERTY typewriter and computer keyboard, that is named for the first six letters on the left-hand side, was invented in the late nineteenth century. That keyboard came into common use precisely because it prevented typists which used it from typing fast. The typewriter keys which were used in those days became tangled if they moved too quickly, so slow typing was actually beneficial. However, the situation soon changed. The typewriters which were more mechanically sophisticated and faster that were in use by the 1920s, so the QWERTY system was holding typists back instead of allowing them to type their fastest. At that time Dr. August Dvorak, whom taught at the University of Washington, began to research keyboard layouts.

Dr. Dvorak, of which his original plan was to create a keyboard that could be used by a one-handed typist, studied both the most common letters used in several languages and the physiology of the human hand. He applied this research to create a new layout for the keyboard. The Dvorak keyboard, which it has all of the most frequently used letters in the home row, increased typing speeds for experienced typists and was easy for beginners to learn. The time at when Dr. Dvorak completed his design was shortly before World War II, and a planned change from the QWERTY system to the Dvorak was put aside during the war. In the meantime, the QWERTY keyboard had become a tradition. However, users who the QWERTY system is troublesome for today have an option if they use modern computers, most of that allow users to shift to the Dvorak system if they prefer it. Some Dvorak keyboard advocates believe that beginning typists should learn the Dvorak system, where common words are learned quickly, instead of the QWERTY system. Perhaps Dr. Dvorak's keyboard may yet become the standard of the future.

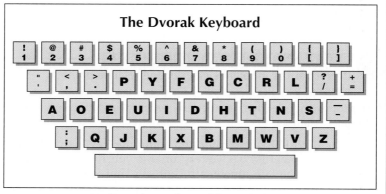

The Dvorak Keyboard

An alternative to the traditional keyboard.

Adapted from *The Dvorak Keyboard* by Randy Cassingham (1986), <www.Dvorak-keyboard.com>. Used with permission of the author.

PART 6

Punctuation, Mechanics, and Spelling

PUNCTUATION

Punctuation serves to regulate the flow of information through a sentence, showing readers how to read your ideas: how to separate, anticipate, and emphasize individual words, phrases, clauses, and sentences. The following headline from the *New York Times*, "Stock Fraud Is Easier, and Easier to Spot," says that stock fraud is not only easy to engage in but also easy to detect. Without the comma, however, the sentence would send a different message: it would say that detecting stock fraud is becoming increasingly easy.

Why do punctuation and mechanics matter? They matter because they chunk words into meaningful groups for readers. Try reading the following without the benefit of the signals a reader usually expects.

When active viruses especially those transmitted by contact can spread easily within the world health organization hard working doctors are

Online Study Center This icon will direct you to quick reference tools, Web resources, and research guides on the Web site at http://college.hmco.com/keys.html.

continually collaborating to find treatments for several infectious diseases sars avian flu and hepatitis.

Conventional punctuation and mechanics clarify the meaning:

When active, viruses—especially those transmitted by contact—can spread easily; within the World Health Organization, hard-working doctors are continually collaborating to find treatments for several infectious diseases: SARS, avian flu, and hepatitis.

Chapter 30

Periods, Question Marks, and Exclamation Points

Periods, question marks, and exclamation points often function to signal the end of a sentence.

▶ **I have lost my pencil.**

▶ **Have you taken it?**

▶ **It's behind your ear!**

By convention, one or two spaces then follow the end punctuation and another sentence begins. The Web site of the Modern Language Association (MLA), in its list of Frequently Asked Questions, recommends leaving one space after a punctuation mark at the end of a sentence but sees "nothing wrong with using two spaces after concluding punctuation marks." Ask your instructor for her or his preference.

30a Period (.)

A period in British English is descriptively called a "full stop." The stop at the end of a sentence is indeed full—much more of a stop than a comma provides. Periods are also used, though, with abbreviations, decimals, and amounts of money, as in the following examples.

1. Use a period to end a declarative sentence—a sentence that makes a statement.

▶ **The interviewer asked the CEO about the company's finances.**

2. Use a period to end a sentence concluding with an indirect question.

NO   The interviewer asked the CEO how much did
        the company make last year?

NO   The interviewer asked the CEO how much the
        company made last year?

YES   The interviewer asked the CEO how much the
        company made last year. [For more on verbs and
        word order in indirect questions, see also 24d, 25j,
        and 44d.]

3. Use a period to end an imperative sentence—a command—that does not express strong emotion.

▶ Note the use of metaphor in the last paragraph.

▶ Turn left at the iron sculpture.

4. Use a period to signal an abbreviation. In these instances, use only one space after the period:

▶ Mr. Mrs. Dr. Rev. Tues. etc. [*etc.* is short for *et cetera,*
Latin for "and so on," "and the others"]

Some abbreviations contain internal periods. Do not include a space
after these internal periods:

▶ a.m. p.m. *or* A.M. P.M. i.e. e.g. [*i.e.* is short for
id est, Latin for "that is"; *e.g.* is short for *exempla gratia,* Latin
for "for example"]

See also 37b.

5. For some abbreviations with capital letters, use or omit periods. Just be consistent.

▶ A.M. or AM

▶ P.M. or PM

▶ U.S.A. or USA

When ending a sentence with an abbreviation, do not use two periods:

▶ The plane left at 7 a.m. [not 7 a.m..]

Note: In MLA style, do not use periods in uppercase initials of names
of government agencies or other organizations, acronyms (abbrevia-

tions pronounced as words), Internet abbreviations, or common time indicators. See 37b.

ACLU	BC	HUD	NAACP	NPR
AD	FAQ	IBM	NASA	URL
AIDS	HTML	IRS	NOW	USC

6. Use a period followed by one space at the end of each entry in a list of works cited. Note, though, that an APA entry ending with a URL does not conclude with a period. See page 784.

7. Use a period in writing figures with decimals and amounts of money greater than a dollar.

▶ 3.7 $7.50

30b Question mark (?)

Questions are useful devices to engage readers' attention. A question will draw readers into thinking about an issue, to which you can then provide the answer. Such questions are known as *rhetorical questions*.

▶ **Many cooks nowadays are making healthier dishes. How do they do this? For the most part, they use unsaturated oil.**

Use the following guidelines with questions.

1. Use a question mark at the end of a sentence to signal a direct question. Do not use a period in addition to a question mark.

NO   **What is he writing?.**

YES   **What is he writing?**

2. Use a question mark at the end of each question in a series of questions.

▶ **In "A Rose for Emily," how does Emily relate to the town? How does the town relate to her?**

If the questions in a series are not complete sentences, you still need question marks. A question fragment may begin with a capital letter or not. Just make your usage consistent.

▶ **Are the characters in the play involved in the disaster? Indifferent to it? Unaware of it?**

▶ **Are the characters in the play involved in the disaster? indifferent to it? unaware of it?**

3. Use a question mark at the end of a direct question but not at the end of an indirect question (24d, 25j, and 44d).

DIRECT   The interviewer asked, "When is the recession going to end?"

INDIRECT   The interviewer asked when the recession was going to end.

4. In MLA style, do not use a comma with a question mark.

▶ "What is the meaning of life?" the writer asks.

VARIATION   Many writers do use both a comma and a question mark. The following example is from a book review by Elizabeth Spires in the *New York Times Book Review*.

▶ In answer to "Who is the most important one?," Sonja declares it is "those who are closest to heaven. . . ."

Such usage may help make it clear to readers that the sentence continues after the question mark.

5. Avoid using a question mark or an exclamation point enclosed in parentheses to convey irony or sarcasm.

NO   The principal, that great historian (?), has proposed a new plan for the history curriculum.

YES   The principal, who admits he is no historian, has proposed a new plan for the history curriculum.

Note: You may occasionally come across a question mark used to express uncertainty in a statement or used within parentheses to express uncertainty about the information offered.

▶ "She jumped in?" he wondered.

▶ Plato (427?–347 BC) founded the Academy at Athens.

Use the question mark with a date only if the date is generally not established, and even then it is often better to rephrase the sentence using *about* or *approximately*. In addition, if the uncertainty is a result of your not knowing an exact date, find it out. Don't announce that you do not know by using a question mark.

REVISED   **He wondered if she had jumped in.**

REVISED   **Plato, who lived from approximately 427 to 347 BC, founded the Academy at Athens.**

See 37b, page 559, for more on the use of BC and its alternative, BCE.

30c Exclamation point (!)

An exclamation point at the end of a sentence indicates that the writer considers the statement amazing, surprising, or extraordinary. In general, follow the advice given by the novelist F. Scott Fitzgerald, who in 1958 urged : "Cut out all these exclamation points. An exclamation point is like laughing at your own joke." Try to avoid exclamation points. Let your words and ideas carry the force of any emphasis you want to communicate.

NO   **The last act of her play is really impressive!**

YES   **The last act resolves the crisis in an unexpected and dramatic way.**

If you feel you absolutely have to include an exclamation point to get your point across in dialogue or with an emphatic command or statement, do not use it along with a comma, a question mark, or a period indicating the end of a sentence.

▶ **"Just watch the ball!" the coach yelled.**

Note: An exclamation point (or a question mark) can be used with a period that signals an abbreviation:

▶ **The match didn't end until 1 a.m.!**

REVIEW EXERCISE FOR CHAPTER 30

Use end punctuation correctly.

Mark with "X" the sentence (A or B) that uses more appropriate end punctuation. Explain your choice to your classmates.

EXAMPLE:

_____ A. The Web site asks users whether they are so afraid of flying that they avoid airplanes in all circumstances?

___X___ B. The Web site asks users whether they are so afraid of flying that they avoid airplanes in all circumstances.

1. _____ A. With modern technology come modern fears, and thousands of people in industrial societies are terrified of air travel.

_____ B. With modern technology come modern fears, and thousands of people in industrial societies are terrified of air travel!

2. _____ A. If people who must fly for business or family reasons are too frightened to board an airplane, where can they turn for help.

_____ B. If people who must fly for business or family reasons are too frightened to board an airplane, where can they turn for help?

3. _____ A. Although most fearful fliers know that flying is statistically safer than driving a car, many of them cannot overcome the part of the mind that says, "What if the plane crashes?"

_____ B. Although most fearful fliers know that flying is statistically safer than driving a car, many of them cannot overcome the part of the mind that says, "What if the plane crashes?".

4. _____ A. Self-help classes and Web sites help fearful fliers to become more familiar with airplanes; the idea is that familiar things are less frightening.

_____ B. Self-help classes and Web sites help fearful fliers to become more familiar with airplanes; the idea is that familiar things are less frightening!

5. _____ A. After a plane crash has been in the news, enrollment in self-help classes for fearful fliers tends to decline; psychologists believe that such events convince people that their irrational fears are based in reality, so they say to themselves, "See. I was right to avoid airplanes at all costs."

_____ B. After a plane crash has been in the news, enrollment in self-help classes for fearful fliers tends to decline; psychologists believe that such events convince people that their irrational fears are based in reality, so they say to themselves, "See? I was right to avoid airplanes at all costs!"

Chapter 31

Commas

A comma separates parts of a sentence; a comma alone does not separate one sentence from another. When readers see a comma, they think, "These parts of the sentence are being separated for a reason."

Readers have expectations as to how a sentence will progress, and a misplaced or missing comma can throw off their understanding. Look at the following sentence, which misuses the comma:

▶ **The rain fell, the roof fell in.**

Here the comma is an error, forming a comma splice (see 23g). Readers reading this and seeing the comma would then expect a third item in a series, something like the following:

▶ **The rain fell, the roof fell in, and Jake fell into a depression.**

But when the sentence does not continue in the expected way because a comma is misused, readers feel thwarted and have to back-track to make sense of the writer's intention. Readers would have no difficulties with any of the following revisions:

▶ **The rain fell. The roof fell in.**

▶ **The rain fell; the roof fell in.**

▶ **The rain fell, and the roof fell in.**

Use the guidelines in this section to determine when to use a comma. If you absolutely cannot decide whether commas are appropriate, follow this general principle: *When in doubt, leave them out.* Readers find excessive use of commas more distracting than a few missing ones.

31a Two checklists—comma: yes, comma: no

The two checklists provide general rules of thumb. Details and more examples of each rule follow in the rest of chapter 31.

KEY POINTS

Comma: Yes

1. Before a coordinating conjunction (*and, but, or, nor, so, for, yet*) to connect independent clauses, including commands, but optional if the clauses are short (*Wharton entertained and James visited*) and optional in British English usage (31b).
   (Continued)

Online Study Center   This icon will direct you to quick reference tools, Web resources, and research guides on the Web site at http://college.hmco.com/keys.html.

(Continued)

▶ The producer of the drama wanted to change the ending, but the author refused.

▶ Accept your fate, and learn to accept it cheerfully.

2. After most introductory words, phrases, or clauses (31c)

▶ During the noisy party, the neighbors complained.

3. To set off any extra (nonrestrictive) information included in a sentence ("extra commas with extra information") (31d)

▶ My father, a computer programmer, works late at night.

▶ The Federalists sought help from their leader, the diminutive James Madison.

4. To set off transitional expressions and explanatory inserts (31e)

▶ The ending, however, is disappointing.

▶ On the other hand, little girls talk to maintain community and contact.

▶ And girls, I hasten to add, will often emulate their mothers.

5. To separate three or more items in a series (31f)

▶ They ordered eggs, bacon, and potatoes.

▶ Kazan used music ingeniously, let his actors interpret crucial scenes, and constantly choreographed scenes with geometric precision.

See also 32c for the use of semicolons in a series.

6. Between coordinate evaluative adjectives that can be reversed and connected by *and* (28f and 31g)

▶ We ate a delicious, well-prepared, and inexpensive meal.

7. After a verb that introduces a quotation (31h)

▶ She gasped, "We haven't a moment to lose!"

KEY POINTS
Comma: No

See 31j for additional details and examples.

1. Not between subject and verb

   ▶ **The actor we saw in *Get Shorty* plays Tony in *The Sopranos*.**

   However, use two commas to set off any extra information inserted between subject and verb (see 31d):

   ▶ **The actor we saw in *Get Shorty*, directed by Barry Sonnenfeld, plays Tony in *The Sopranos*.**

2. Not before part of a compound structure that is not an independent clause

   ▶ **She won the trophy and accepted it graciously.**

   ▶ **Poet Marie Ponsot has published only five books of poetry but has discarded many poems in her eighty-one years.**

3. Not *after* a coordinating conjunction connecting two independent clauses, but *before* it

   ▶ **The movie tried to be engaging, but it failed miserably.**

4. Not between two independent clauses without a coordinating conjunction (use either a period and a capital letter or a semicolon instead)

   ▶ **He won; she was delighted.**

5. Not between an independent clause and a following dependent clause introduced by *after, before, because, if, since, unless, until*, or *when* (neither before nor after the subordinating conjunction)

   ▶ **She will continue working for the city until she has saved enough for graduate school.**

   ▶ **His prose comes alive when he describes the battle**

6. Not before a clause beginning with *that*

   ▶ **They warned us that the meeting would be difficult.**

(Continued)

(Continued)

7. Not before and after essential, restrictive information (see also 31d)

   ▶ The player who scored the goal became a hero.

8. Not between a verb and its object or complement

   ▶ The best gifts are food and clothes.

   ▶ The task was to feed and clothe all the survivors.

9. Not after *such as*

   ▶ Popular fast-food items, such as hamburgers and hot dogs, tend to be high in fat.

EXERCISE 31.1
Identify commas: yes or no.

In the passage, identify commas that are used correctly with a checkmark and commas that are used incorrectly with an X. For those marked as correct, give the number of the item in the *Comma: Yes* Key Points box that explains why the comma is correct.

EXAMPLE:

√(2)

Since the first computers were invented, people have tried to find

×

out if computers, can actually learn to think.

The notion of artificial intelligence, is one of the most intriguing, controversial ideas in computer programming today. Anyone, who studies computers, has probably wondered whether modern computers are learning to think. Alan Turing, who helped to develop computers during and after World War II, believed that the only way to tell if a computer could think was to ask it questions. According to him, if the computer gave answers that were indistinguishable from those of a human, the computer could be considered intelligent. John Searle, a philosopher at the University of California at Berkeley, argued that a computer that was able to create intelligent-sounding answers to questions need not actually understand anything, it might simply be popping out replies based on the rules it had absorbed. Does a machine such as, the chess-playing computer Big Blue qualify as a thinking mechanism, or, has it simply learned the rules of chess well enough to simulate thought? One reason, that this question is difficult to answer is that human thought is difficult to define and quantify. No one, apparently, has yet figured out exactly what causes consciousness, and no one understands exactly how human brains think. As Searle points out, "I think we could build a thinking machine; it's just that we don't have the faintest idea how to go about it, because we don't know how the brain goes about it."

31b Comma before a coordinating conjunction connecting independent clauses

To connect independent clauses with a coordinating conjunction (*and, but, or, nor, so, for,* or *yet*), place a comma before the conjunction. Your sentence should look like this:

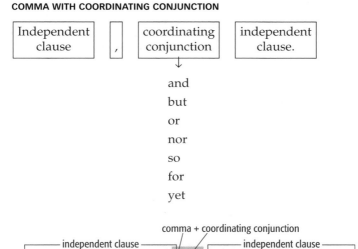

COMMA WITH COORDINATING CONJUNCTION

| Independent clause | , | coordinating conjunction | independent clause. |

and
but
or
nor
so
for
yet

comma + coordinating conjunction

independent clause / independent clause

▶ The managers are efficient, but personnel turnover is high.

▶ The juggler juggled seven plates, and we all cheered.

▶ Teachers can ask for a specific assignment, or their supervisors can make plans for the whole school.

► The novel did not sell well, nor was it favorably reviewed.

► The soldiers had been well trained, so they knew exactly what to do.

► The Monarch butterflies are heading south, for winter is clearly on the way.

► Drugs are available for heart disease, yet many have unpleasant side effects.

VARIATION

1. If the two independent clauses are short, some writers omit the comma before the conjunction.

   ► He offered to help and he meant it.

   But if you always include it, you will never be wrong.

   ► He offered to help, and he meant it.

2. If the second clause presents a contrast, particularly after a negative, some writers use just a comma without a coordinating conjunction. See 23g.

   ► Chicano Spanish is not correct, it is a living language.
   —Gloria Anzaldúa, "How to Tame a Wild Tongue"

   ► His dog doesn't just bark, it bites.

   Readers of academic prose, however, may regard this as a comma splice error and may prefer a semicolon, a period, or a dash in place of the comma.

   ► His dog doesn't just bark—it bites.

3. If one or both of the independent clauses contain internal commas, you can use a semicolon in place of a comma between the two clauses.

   ► When he was awarded the prize, the actor praised his director, who had first offered him the part; but he refused to acknowledge the author.

EXERCISE 31.2

Use commas before coordinating conjunctions connecting independent clauses.

Combine each of the sentence pairs into a single sentence by using a coordinating conjunction and a comma.

EXAMPLE:

Patrick O'Brian wrote twenty novels about the voyages of a sea

captain and a naval doctor during the Napoleonic ~~Wars.~~ Wars, but O'Brian

~~O'Brian~~ died after beginning to write their twenty-first

adventure.

1. Patrick O'Brian once said that he was a derivative writer. All of his information came from "log books, dispatches, letters, memoirs, and contemporary reports" from two centuries ago.

2. O'Brian wrote about adventure on the high seas and naval battles. He also brought the manners and customs of naval society to life.

3. O'Brian's books are filled with obscure naval terminology. Many readers who have little interest in sailing ships have become devoted fans of Jack Aubrey and Stephen Maturin, the main characters in his twenty-volume series.

4. A *New York Times* book review once called O'Brian's books "the best historical novels ever written." Readers recognize that the characters are every bit as realistic as the descriptions of life on a British naval ship.

5. O'Brian's fans can simply keep rereading the twenty novels about Aubrey and Maturin. They can help support the cookbooks, glossaries, and Web sites devoted to exploring every detail of O'Brian's texts.

31c Comma after an introductory word, phrase, or dependent clause

1. Use a comma to signal to readers that the introductory part of the sentence has ended. It says, in effect, "Now wait for the independent clause."

The sentence pattern looks like this:

COMMA AFTER INTRODUCTORY ELEMENT

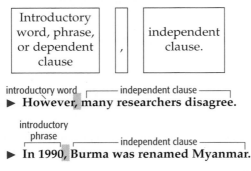

introductory word ┌─── independent clause ───┐
► However, many researchers disagree.

introductory phrase ┌─── independent clause ───┐
► In 1990, Burma was renamed Myanmar.

┌─── dependent clause ───┐ ┌─── independent clause ───┐
► If you blow out all the candles, your wishes will come true.

VARIATION If the introductory element is only one word or a short phrase establishing the time frame, many writers omit the comma.

► Soon the climate will change.

► In a few months children learn to crawl, walk, and talk.

However, if you want to apply a rule consistently, it will never be wrong to include a comma:

► Soon, the climate will change.

► In a few months, children learn to crawl, walk, and talk.

2. Never omit the comma after an introductory phrase or clause if a misreading could result.

MISREADING POSSIBLE   When active viruses can spread easily.

REVISED   When active, viruses can spread easily.

POSSIBLE	**While she was cooking her cat ran off with a lamb chop.**
REVISED	**While she was cooking, her cat ran off with a lamb chop.**

MISREADING POSSIBLE	**Until this spring fever was the most serious symptom treated at the health center.**
REVISED	**Until this spring, fever was the most serious symptom treated at the health center.**

3. Take special care with an *-ing* phrase at the beginning of a sentence. An *-ing* word can begin an introductory phrase (and the phrase will end with a comma), or it can be the subject of the sentence, in which case use no comma between the subject and the verb.

INTRODUCTORY PHRASE	**Investigating the DNA evidence, the** subject verb **detectives found the attacker.**
SUBJECT	┌──────── subject ────────┐ verb **Investigating the DNA evidence led detectives to the attacker.**

31d Commas to set off an extra (nonrestrictive) phrase or clause

The sentence patterns for the use of commas with nonrestrictive elements look like this:

COMMAS WITH NONRESTRICTIVE ELEMENTS

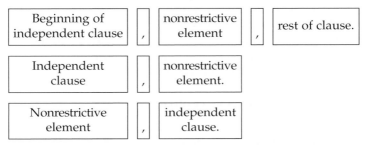

| Beginning of independent clause | , | nonrestrictive element | , | rest of clause. |

| Independent clause | , | nonrestrictive element. |

| Nonrestrictive element | , | independent clause. |

Commas signal that the extra, nonessential information they set off (useful and interesting as it may be) can be removed without radically altering or limiting the meaning of the independent clause (21e). Think of paired commas as handles that can lift the enclosed information out of the sentence without making the sentence's meaning confusing.

┌──────── nonrestrictive element ────────┐
▶ **The Colosseum, Rome's most famous landmark, once held crowds of more than fifty thousand people.**

┌──────────── nonrestrictive element ────────────┐
▶ **The American diner, a narrow restaurant with booths and a**
┌────────┐
counter, frequently features wall-mounted juke boxes.

┌──────── nonrestrictive element ────────┐
▶ **We will attend, even though we would rather not.**

nonrestrictive element
┌──────── (used as introductory phrase) ────────┐
▶ **The brainchild of forester Benton MacKaye, the Appalachian Trail stretches from Georgia to Maine.**

Two nonrestrictive elements can follow each other, separated by a comma.

nonrestrictive
┌── element ──┐
▶ **The elevator opened into an imposing foyer, a dim and**
┌──────────────┐ ┌──────── nonrestrictive element ────────┐
drafty space, old-fashioned from its marble floor to its high
┌──┐
ceiling and furnished only with an ornate umbrella stand.

DO NOT USE COMMAS TO SET OFF RESTRICTIVE INFORMATION. A phrase or clause that limits or restricts the meaning of the independent clause is said to be *restrictive* (essential). A restrictive phrase or clause cannot be removed without changing the meaning of the sentence. Do not use commas to set off restrictive information.

┌ restrictive element ┐
▶ **We will attend if we have time.**

[The phrase "if we have time" is essential to the meaning of this sentence. If it were removed, the sentence would convey a different message, "We will attend" instead of "We might attend."]

┌──────── restrictive element ────────┐
▶ **The players who practice often and keep fit are usually the ones who succeed.**

The restrictive element is essential. If it were removed, the sentence would be "The players are usually the ones who succeed." A reader would wonder, "Which players?" The clause "who practice often and keep fit" restricts the meaning of "the players" to a subgroup.

In the following example, the same clause "who practice often and keep fit" does not restrict the subject to a subgroup of teammates. Readers can grasp fully the meaning of "His daughter's Little League teammates win every game." Rather, the clause adds additional, nonessential information, which is nonrestrictive and therefore set off with commas.

> ┌nonrestrictive element ─
> ▶ **His daughter's Little League teammates, who practice often**
> └─────────────┐
> **and keep fit, win every game.**

See 29d for more on restrictive and nonrestrictive relative clauses.

USE COMMAS TO SET OFF THE FOLLOWING NONRESTRICTIVE ELEMENTS:

1. An appositive phrase   An appositive phrase renames or gives additional information about a noun or pronoun. If the phrase were omitted, readers might lose some interesting details but would still be able to understand the message.

> ┌──── appositive phrase ────┐
> ▶ **A collector since childhood, the gallery owner decided to leave his sculptures to a museum.**

> appositive
> ┌── phrase ──┐
> ▶ **She loves her car, a red Toyota.**

> ┌──── appositive phrase ────┐
> ▶ **His dog, a big Labrador retriever, is afraid of mice.** [If you read "His dog is afraid of mice," you would not necessarily need to know what type of dog he owns.]

> ▶ **Salinger's first novel, *The Catcher in the Rye,* captures the language and thoughts of teenagers.** [The commas are used because Salinger obviously wrote only one *first* novel, and the title provides supplementary information, not information that identifies which novel the writer means.]

2. A participle or prepositional phrase   Nonrestrictive participle and prepositional phrases add extra descriptive, but not essential, information.

> ▶ **My boss, wearing a red tie and a green shirt, radiated the holiday spirit.**

> ▶ **The poet's study, in which she spent her final months, is now a shrine.**

3. Extra information in a relative clause   When you give nonessential information in a relative clause introduced by *who, whom,* or *which* (never *that*), set off the clause with commas.

▶ **My boss, who wears bright colors, is a cheerful person.** [The independent clause "My boss is a cheerful person" does not lead readers to ask "Which boss?" The relative clause does not restrict the meaning of *boss.*]

▶ **His recent paintings, which are hanging in our local restaurant, show dogs in various disguises.** [The relative clause, introduced by *which,* merely provides the additional fact that his recent paintings are on display in the restaurant.]

Do not use commas with relative clauses providing essential, restrictive information (29d and 31j).

              ┌ restricts *people* to a subgroup ┐
▶ **People who wear bright colors send an optimistic message.** [The relative clause, beginning with *who,* restricts "people" to a subgroup: not all people send an optimistic message; those who wear bright colors do.]

EXERCISE 31.3

Use commas after introductory material or with nonrestrictive elements.

Add any necessary commas. Some sentences may be correct.

EXAMPLE:

Working for a major chemical manufacturer ˏ Charles Baldwin ˏ

an engineer ˏ helped to develop the symbol that identifies

biohazards.

1. Realizing that laboratories and medical facilities around the world all needed to dispose of biohazards researchers wanted a symbol that would indicate to everyone which material was infectious.
2. Designers who create symbols want them to be memorable.
3. However the biohazard symbol needed to be unlike any other symbol.
4. In 1966 the symbol which is three-sided so that it looks the same if seen upside-down or sideways was chosen.

> 5. With its vivid orange color, a shade determined to be the most visible of all colors under most conditions the symbol was soon accepted by the Centers for Disease Control, the Occupational Safety and Health Administration, and the National Institutes of Health.

31e Commas with transitional expressions and explanatory insertions

1. Transitional expressions   Transitional expressions such as *on the other hand* and words such as *therefore* and *however* (conjunctive adverbs) connect or weave together the ideas in your writing and act as signposts for readers. (See 5e for a list of these expressions.) Use commas to set off a transitional expression from the rest of the sentence. If the transitional expression is at the end of a sentence, introduce it with a comma and follow it with a period. Note the following patterns:

COMMAS TO SET OFF TRANSITIONAL EXPRESSIONS

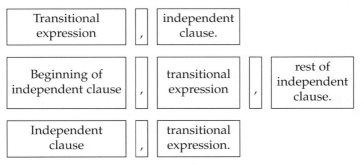

▶ **My dog is afraid of mice. However, most Labrador retrievers are courageous.**

▶ **Most Labrador retrievers, however, are courageous.**

▶ **Most Labrador retrievers are courageous, however.**

Note: When you use a transitional word or expression such as *however, therefore, nevertheless, above all, of course,* or *in fact* at the beginning of an independent clause, end the previous clause with a period or a semicolon. Then place a comma after the transitional expression.

| Independent clause | ; | transitional expression | , | independent clause. |

▶ **My dog is afraid of mice; however, most Labrador retrievers are courageous.**

▶ **The party was a success. In fact, it was still going on at 2 a.m.**

See also 31c.

2. Explanatory insertions   Sometimes writers insert a phrase or a clause to make a comment, to offer an example, or to point out a contrast. Insertions used for these purposes are set off by commas.

▶ **The consequences will be dire, I think.**

▶ **Seasonal allergies, such as those caused by ragweed, are a common affliction.**

▶ **The best, if not the only, solution is to apologize and start over.**

▶ **His assets, not his earnings, are being scrutinized.**

31f   Commas separating three or more items in a series

Readers see commas between items in a series (words, phrases, or clauses) and think, "This is a list." If you said a series aloud, you would probably pause between items; in writing, you use commas to separate them. Here is a common sentence pattern:

COMMAS WITH ITEMS IN A SERIES

| item 1 | , | item 2 | , | and | item 3 |

The item can be a word, phrase, or clause.

WORDS   **The performance was tasteful, emotional, and dramatic.**

However, do not insert a comma between the last adjective of a series and the noun the adjectives modify (31g):

▶ **The long, thorough, tireless/ investigation yielded the expected results.**

PHRASES   **Searching through the drawer, the detective found a key, a stamp, three coins, and a photograph.**

CLAUSES   **The report questioned why the collapse occurred, what could have been done to prevent it, and who was responsible.**

VARIATIONS   For stylistic effect, a writer may not include the word *and* before the last item in the series of words or phrases.

▶ **Etiquette books provide guidance on celebrations, travel customs, polite communications, weddings, funerals.**

In a series of words or phrases, some writers, particularly journalists or those using British English, will omit the comma separating the last item from the one before it—*snow, sleet and freezing rain.* Though you will see this usage, it is better to use a comma between each item in a list so that your meaning is always clear.

▶ **The director achieved a romantic atmosphere with soft music, soothing dialogue about love, and happy couples.**
   [Without the comma after *love,* readers could think that the dialogue was about happy couples.]

Note: Use commas only between each of the items in a series. Do not insert a comma to signify the beginning or end of the series.

▶ **Some basic terms in economics are / supply, demand, and consumption.**

▶ **France, Dorset, and the Lake District / exerted a significant influence on Wordsworth's poems.**

31g Commas between coordinate evaluative adjectives

Adjectives are *coordinate* when their order can be reversed and the word *and* can be inserted between them without any change in meaning. Coordinate adjectives (such as *beautiful, delicious, exciting, noisy*) make subjective and evaluative judgments. Separate coordinate adjectives with commas. See 28f.

▶ **Energetic, efficient people are the ones he likes to hire.**

▶ **Efficient, energetic people are the ones he likes to hire.**

Do not, however, put a comma between the final adjective of a series and the noun it modifies.

▶ **Energetic, efficient, and polite salespeople are in demand.**

When each adjective in a series modifies all the adjectives that follow it and gives objectively verifiable information about, for instance, number, size, shape, color, or nationality, the adjectives are said to be *cumulative,* not coordinate.

▶ **Entering the little old stone house brought back memories of her childhood.** [The house is made of stone. The stone house is old. The old stone house is little.]

Do not separate cumulative adjectives with commas.

31h Comma with a direct quotation

Use a comma to separate the verb from the direct quotation. The verb may come either before or after the quotation.

▶ **When asked what she wanted to be later in life, she replied, "An Olympic swimmer."**

▶ **"I want to be an Olympic swimmer," she announced confidently.** [The comma is inside the quotation marks.]

However, do not add a comma to a quotation that ends with a question mark or an exclamation point (but see p. 502 for a variation).

NO   **"What do you want to be?," she asked.**

YES   **"What do you want to be?" she asked.**

In addition, do not insert a comma before a quotation that is integrated into your sentence:

NO   **The advertisers are promoting, "a healthier lifestyle."**

YES   **The advertisers are promoting "a healthier lifestyle."**

EXERCISE 31.4

Use commas with transitional expressions, items in a series, coordinate adjectives, and direct quotations.

Add any necessary commas; delete any that are unnecessary.

EXAMPLE:

A surprising perplexing proposal from the U.S. Department of Energy would allow the recycling of steel that is slightly radioactive.

The Department of Energy has proposed recycling scrap metal from weapons and research plants that are going to be demolished in Tennessee, Kentucky, Ohio, South Carolina and Colorado. Radiation has, unfortunately contaminated the surface of the metals that the DOE plans to recycle. Over a million tons of the contaminated metal will be available for recycling if the proposal is accepted.

First however, the DOE is, funding an environmental study of the plan analyzing the feasibility of recycling and reusing only those metals that meet lower radiation standards, and scheduling public hearings around the country. On one side scrap metal dealers have expressed preliminary support for the proposal. Citizens who live near steel-recycling plants on the other hand have asked the DOE to reject the proposal as an irresponsible environmentally unsound, idea. In Minnesota, which has steel-recycling plants, a public hearing drew many concerned, outspoken, citizens who testified that they did not want radioactive material trucked through their neighborhoods. In addition many noted that they would not want the government to allow scrap metal plants to add radioactive steel to the items that the plants manufacture, such as, snow shovels eyeglasses forks, and, cars. One woman announced "I propose that our federal government have a zero tolerance for any release of radioactive materials because I'm scared." Minnesota's largest steel-recycling plant has in fact already announced that it has rejected the DOE plan. The manager of the DOE environmental study said that the department would abide by the study's results.

31i Special uses of commas

1. To make the meaning clear and prevent misreading Use a comma to separate elements in a sentence that may otherwise be confusing.

▶ **He who can, does. He who cannot, teaches.**

—George Bernard Shaw, *Man and Superman*

[Usually a comma is not used to separate a subject from the verb. Here the comma is necessary to prevent confusing the readers.]

2. With an absolute phrase   Use a comma to set off a phrase that modifies the whole sentence (an absolute phrase).

⌐—————————— absolute phrase ——————————⌐

▶ **The audience looking on in amusement, the valedictorian blew kisses to all her favorite instructors.**

3. With a date   Use a comma to separate the date from the year and the day from the date:

▶ **On May 14, 1998, the legendary singer Frank Sinatra died.**

▶ **The poet laureate is reading in San Francisco on Wednesday, May 1.**

Do not use a comma when you mention only the month and date (*May 14*) or month and year (*May 1998*).

4. With numbers   Use a comma (never a period) to divide numbers into thousands.

▶ **1,200**   ▶ **515,000**   ▶ **34,000,000**

No commas are necessary in years (*2007*), numbers in addresses (*3501 East 10th Street*), or page numbers (*page 1008*).

5. With scene or line references   In the body of your text (not in a parenthetical reference) use a comma between act and scene and between page and line: act 3, scene 4; page 14, line 9.

6. With titles   Use commas to set off a person's title or degree.

▶ **Stephen L. Carter, PhD, gave the commencement speech.**

7. With an inverted name   Use a comma between the last name and the first:

▶ **Dillard, Annie**

8. With the parts of an address

▶ **Alice Walker was born in Eatonton, Georgia, in 1944.**

However, do not use a comma before a ZIP code: Newton, MA 02459.

9. **With a conversational tag or tag question**

▶ Yes, Salinger's daughter, like others before her, has produced a memoir.

▶ She has not won a Pulitzer Prize, has she?

10. **With a direct address or salutation**

▶ Whatever you build next, Mr. Trump, will cause controversy.

31j When not to use commas: Nine rules of thumb

1. Do not use a comma to separate a verb from its subject.

▶ The gifts she received from her colleagues made her realize her value to the company.

▶ Interviewing so many women in the United States helped the researcher understand the "American dream."

Between a subject and verb, you may need to put two commas around inserted material, but never use just one comma.

▶ The engraved plaque, given to her by her colleagues on her

subject

verb

last day of work, made her feel respected.

2. Do not use a comma within a compound structure when the second part of the compound is not an independent clause.

▶ Amy Tan has written novels and adapted them for the screen.

▶ Tan has written about her mother and the rest of her family.

3. Do not use a comma after a coordinating conjunction that connects two sentences. The comma goes before the conjunction, not after it.

▶ *Mad Hot Ballroom* is supposed to be good, but I missed it when it came to my local movie theater.

4. Do not use a comma to join two independent clauses when no coordinating conjunction is present. Instead, end the first clause with a period and make the second clause a new sentence, or insert a semicolon between the clauses. Use a comma only if you connect the clauses with a coordinating conjunction. (See 23h for ways to correct a comma splice, the error that results when two independent clauses are incorrectly joined with a comma.)

▶ **Amy Tan has written novels; they have been adapted for the screen.**

VARIATION Some writers, however, do use a comma between two independent clauses when the clauses use parallel structures to point out a contrast (see also 23g and 31b, variation 2).

▶ **She never insults, she just criticizes.**

If you do not know readers' expectations on this point, play it safe and separate the clauses with a period or a semicolon.

5. Do not use a comma to separate an independent clause from a following dependent clause introduced by *after, before, because, if, since, unless, until,* **or** *when.*

▶ **The test results were good because all the students had studied in groups.**

▶ **The audience broke into a wild applause when the young poet finished his reading.**

6. Do not use a comma to separate a clause beginning with *that* **from the rest of the sentence.**

▶ **The girl in Tan's story tried to convey to her mother that she did not have to be a child prodigy.**

Note: A comma can appear before a *that* clause when it is the second comma of a pair before and after extra information inserted as a nonrestrictive phrase.

▶ **He skates so fast, despite his size, that he will probably break the world record.**

7. Do not use commas around a phrase or clause that provides essential, restrictive information.

> ▶ Alice Walker's essay "Beauty: When the Other Dancer Is the Self" discusses coping with a physical disfigurement.
> [Walker has written more than one essay. The title restricts the noun *essay* to one specific essay.]

Similarly, a restrictive relative clause introduced by *who, whom, whose, which,* or *that* is never set off by commas. The clause provides essential identifying information (see also 29d and 31d).

> ▶ The teachers praised the children who finished on time. [The teachers didn't praise all the children; they praised only the ones who finished on time.]

8. Do not use a comma to separate a verb from its object or complement.

> ▶ The qualities required for the job are punctuality, efficiency, and the ability to work long hours.

9. Do not use a comma after *such as.*

> ▶ They bought kitchen supplies such as detergent, paper towels, and garbage bags.

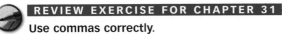

REVIEW EXERCISE FOR CHAPTER 31

Use commas correctly.

Add any necessary commas, delete any that are unnecessary, and replace commas with periods or semicolons as needed.

"All men are created equal" wrote Thomas Jefferson but his deeds did not always match his eloquent words. Like most of the other aristocratic landowners in Virginia, Jefferson the author of the Declaration of Independence founder of the University of Virginia and third president of the United States, owned slaves. One of them was a woman named, Sally Hemings who was one-quarter African, and was probably the daughter of Jefferson's father-in-law and a half-African slave, if this genealogy is correct Hemings was the half-sister of Jefferson's late wife, Martha. Indeed observers at the time noted that, Hemings looked remarkably like Martha Jefferson, who had died on September 6 1782, when Jefferson was thirty-nine.

In 1802 a disgruntled former employee reported that President Jefferson, was the father of Hemings's three children. Jefferson never responded publicly to the charge but, many people noticed the resemblance between him and the Hemings children. The believable scandalous rumors continued to circulate for years after Jefferson's death in 1826. A few historians speculated, that Jefferson's nephews might have fathered the Hemings children but, most ignored the story altogether. Yes it was true that slaveholders had often been known to impregnate slave women, yet such an act was difficult for many white Americans to reconcile with their views of one of the country's founders.

In the 1990s DNA tests were used to determine whether Jefferson could have been the father of Sally Hemings's children. The tests showed a match between the DNA of Jefferson's closest male relative's descendants, and the descendants of Hemings's youngest son, Eston. Clearly either Jefferson or a close relative was Eston's father. Most historians are now convinced that, Jefferson did father at least one of the Hemings children. A recent biography of Jefferson was called *American Sphinx* and the third president does, indeed seem to have hidden many secrets. Whether the revelations about his relationship with Hemings will change the way Americans feel about this Founding Father, remains to be seen.

Chapter **32**

Semicolons and Colons

A colon (:) may look like a semicolon (;)—one is two dots, the other a dot above a comma—but they are used in different ways, and they are not interchangeable. Note the use of the semicolon and colon in the following passage discussing the musical number "Cheek to Cheek" in the Fred Astaire and Ginger Rogers film *Top Hat:*

Online Study Center   This icon will direct you to quick reference tools, Web resources, and research guides on the Web site at http://college.hmco.com/keys.html.

[Ginger] Rogers is perhaps never more beautiful than when she's just listening; she never takes her eyes off him and throughout this scene I don't think she changes her expression once. The modesty of the effect makes her look like an angel: such a compliant, unasking attitude, handsome beyond expectation in such a fierce woman.

—Arlene Croce, *The Fred Astaire and Ginger Rogers Book*

Ginger Rogers and Fred Astaire

32a When to use a semicolon (;)

A period separates independent clauses with finality; a semicolon (such as the one you have just seen in this sentence) provides a less distinct separation and indicates that an additional related thought or item will follow immediately. As essayist Lewis Thomas comments in "Notes on Punctuation": "The period tells you that that is that; if you didn't get all the meaning you wanted or expected, anyway you got all the writer intended to parcel out and now you have to move along. But with a semicolon there you get a pleasant little feeling of expectancy; there is more to come." Use a semicolon instead of a period when the ideas in two independent clauses are closely connected and you want readers to expect more.

Here are the patterns for semicolons used between independent clauses:

SEMICOLONS

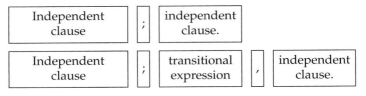

32b   Semicolon between independent clauses

Use a semicolon to separate—and connect—two closely related independent clauses that are not joined by a coordinating conjunction (21f).

▶ **Biography tells us about the subject; biographers also tell us about themselves.**

A comma between the two independent clauses would produce a comma splice, and no punctuation at all would produce a run-on sentence (see 23g). Do not use a capital letter to begin a clause after a semicolon. Semicolons are often used when the second independent clause contains a transitional expression, such as a conjunctive adverb—*however, therefore, nevertheless, moreover*—or a phrase—*in fact, as a result, above all, on the other hand*. (See 5e and 18c for more on transitional expressions.)

▶ **The results of the study support the hypothesis; however, further research with a variety of tasks is necessary.**

32c   Semicolons between clauses or items in a series containing internal commas

Generally, you will use a comma to separate two independent clauses connected by a coordinating conjunction:

▶ **Our dependence on foreign oil supplies is economically problematic, yet SUVs are dominating our roads.**

However, use a semicolon in place of a comma if the independent clauses themselves contain commas.

▶ **Our dependence on foreign oil supplies, constantly discussed in the press, is economically problematic; yet SUVs, those gas-guzzling monsters, are dominating our roads.**

Items in a series are usually separated by commas (see 31f). However, to avoid ambiguity, use semicolons to separate long listed items when internal commas are present.

▶ **When I cleaned out the refrigerator, I found a chocolate cake half-eaten; some canned tomato paste, which had a blue fungus growing on the top; and some possibly edible meat loaf.**

In addition, use semicolons to separate a series of long independent clauses that contain internal commas, even if a coordinating conjunction is present before the last item in the series.

▶ **Some students planned to do library research; those who were working on controversial, debatable issues turned to databases; and several, among them the best writer in the class, decided to use interviews and a questionnaire.**

32d When not to use a semicolon

1. Do not use semicolons interchangeably with colons. Do not use a semicolon to introduce a list or explanation. Use a colon instead (32e).

▶ **They contributed a great deal of food; salad, chili, and dessert.**

2. Do not use a semicolon after an introductory phrase or dependent clause, even if the phrase or clause is long. Using a semicolon will produce a fragment. Use a comma instead.

▶ **With the advent of sound in the world of Hollywood movies; the whole nature of stardom changed.**

▶ **Because the training period was so long and arduous for all the players; the manager allowed one visit by family and friends.**

3. Do not overuse semicolons. Use a semicolon in place of a period only when the link between two independent clauses is strong. If you are in doubt as to whether a semicolon is appropriate, using a period will probably be a safe course.

EXERCISE 32.1
Know when to use and when not to use a semicolon.
Add semicolons and change commas to semicolons as needed.

EXAMPLE:

Jan Harold Brunvald is the man who coined the term *urban legend;* he once said that the truth never stands in the way of a good story.

> Many urban legends are the kinds of stories that people use to frighten one another around a campfire. Some of the best-known ones are about escaped lunatics and murderers such as the man with a hook for a hand who terrorizes a young couple who, while parked on a deserted road, hear a radio broadcast about him, the man who telephones a babysitter with dire warnings, finally revealing that he is calling from another extension in the same house, and the killer who hides in the back seat of a woman's car or under the bed in her dorm room. These stories are chilling but faintly unbelievable, we all realize, eventually, that they are not true.

32e When to use a colon (:)

A colon (:) signals anticipation. It follows an independent clause and introduces information that readers will need. A colon tells readers, "What comes next will define, illustrate, or rename what you have just read." Use one space after a colon.

Here are the colon patterns:

COLONS

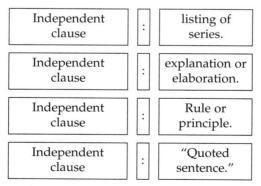

Use a colon in the following situations.

1. Use a colon after an independent clause to illustrate a concept by providing a listing of a series of examples.

> ► The students included three pieces of writing in their portfolios: a narrative, an argument, and a documented paper.

2. Use a colon after an independent clause to introduce an explanation, expansion, or elaboration.

▶ [Galileo] understood what Aristotle could not: that a moving object tends to keep moving. —James Gleick, *Chaos*

▶ After an alarming cancer diagnosis and years of treatment, Lance Armstrong was victorious: he won the Tour de France seven times and had a son.

▶ The author has performed a remarkable feat: she has maintained suspense to the last page.

VARIATION Some writers prefer to use a capital letter after a colon introducing an independent clause. Be consistent in your usage.

3. Use a colon followed by a capital letter to introduce a rule or principle.

▶ The main principle of public speaking is simple: Look at the audience.

4. Use a colon in salutations, precise time notations, titles, and biblical citations.

Letters and memos	**Dear Chancellor Witkin:**
	To: The Chancellor
Hours and minutes	**7:20 p.m.**
Titles and subtitles	*Backlash: The Undeclared War against American Women*
Biblical citations	**Genesis 37:31–35.** [Here, a period could be used in place of the colon.]

5. Use a colon to introduce a quotation that is not integrated into the structure of your sentence and is not introduced by a verb like *say*.

▶ Emily Post has provided an acceptable alternative to our always trying to outdo others: "To do *exactly as your neighbors do* is the only sensible rule."

6. Use a colon to introduce a long quotation that you set off from your own text. See 50h for an example.

32f When not to use a colon

1. Do not use a colon directly after a verb (such as a form of *be,* *consist of,* **or** *include***).**

▶ The two main effects were the improvement of registration and an increase in the numbers of advisers.

▶ The book includes a preface, an introduction, an appendix, and an index.

2. Do not use a colon after a preposition (such as *except* **and** *regarding***) or** *such as.*

▶ The novel will please all readers except academics, linguists, and lawyers.

▶ They packed many different items for the picnic, such as tortilla chips, salsa, bean salad, pita bread, and egg rolls.

3. Do not use a colon after *for example, especially,* **or** *including.*

▶ His taste is so varied that his living room includes, for example, antiques, modern art, and art deco lighting fixtures.

EXERCISE 32.2

Know when to use and when not to use a colon.

Make any changes so that colons are used correctly.

EXAMPLE:

Turtles are a unique life form $\overset{:}{\wedge}$ no other creature has a rigid shell made up of vertebrae and ribs.

1. The professor required each student to have a copy of *Herpetology An Introductory Biology of Amphibians and Reptiles.*

2. Turtles are divided into two main branches according to the way they retract their necks into their bodies, the cryptodire branch, which means *hidden neck,* can pull their heads completely into their shells, but the pleurodire branch, which means *side neck,* can only partially retract their heads.

3. Turtles are different from other reptiles because: their chest cavities cannot expand when they inhale.

4. Turtles can survive without air much longer than other reptiles, some turtles have lived for as long as thirty-three hours without oxygen.

5. Many species of turtles can take in oxygen through sacs which emerge from the turtle's digestive and urogenital cavity; turtles share this unusual method of breathing with life forms such as: dragonfly nymphs and sea cucumbers.

REVIEW EXERCISE FOR CHAPTER 32
Use semicolons and colons correctly.

Correct any errors in the use of semicolons and colons.

Japan has long been one of the most homogeneous of the modern industrial nations, many Japanese protect their cultural identity so strongly that foreigners are rarely allowed to feel a part of Japan, no matter how long they and their families remain in the country. Foreign nationals who make Japan their home are not required to send their children to school as Japanese parents must, in addition, non-Japanese are not covered by Japan's national health insurance. Many foreign nationals, consequently; consider Japan only a temporary home. However, the Japanese population is: getting older, with more retirees than new babies throughout the country, currently, the Japanese birthrate is one of the lowest in the world. To keep the economy alive and pay for pensions for retired workers and their families; Japan must find more workers. The United Nations now recommends that Japan begin to encourage immigration.

Many Japanese emigrants in the early nineteenth century went to Brazil to work. In the 1990s, Japan began to allow Brazilians of Japanese descent to return to Japan on temporary work visas today, there are a quarter of a million Brazilians in Japan, and many of them now hold permanent visas. Japan has: two Brazilian television channels, four Brazilian newspapers, and forty-one Brazilian schools. Although many of these Brazilians have Japanese ancestors; they are culturally Brazilian, and the Brazilian and Japanese cultures occasionally clash. Some Japanese in cities with large Brazilian populations complain that Brazilians do not comply with Japanese regulations, some Brazilians say that the Japanese make them feel unwelcome. Accepting cultural diversity is rarely easy; and it may be more difficult in Japan, where a single culture has been dominant for centuries. One thing, however, is certain; Japan must accommodate foreign workers if the nation's economy is to survive the population slump.

Chapter **33**

Apostrophes

Apostrophes indicate ownership or possession (*Fred's books, the government's plans*). They can also signal omitted letters (*who's, can't*).

33a Two checklists—apostrophe: yes, apostrophe: no

The two checklists provide general rules of thumb. Details and more examples of each rule follow in the rest of chapter 33.

KEY POINTS
Apostrophe: Yes

1. Use -'s for the possessive form of all nouns except plural nouns that end with -s: *the hero's misfortune, the journalist's sources.*
2. Use an apostrophe alone for the possessive form of plural nouns that end with -s: *journalists' sources, the heroes' misfortunes.*
3. Use an apostrophe to indicate the omission of letters in contracted forms such as *didn't* and *they're.*
4. Use *it's* only for "it is" or "it has": *It's a good idea; it's been a long time.* (The possessive form of the pronoun *it* is spelled with no apostrophe: *The house lost its roof.*)

KEY POINTS
Apostrophe: No

1. Generally, do not use an apostrophe to form the plurals of nouns. (See 33e for rare exceptions.)

Online Study Center   This icon will direct you to quick reference tools, Web resources, and research guides on the Web site at http://college.hmco.com/keys.html.

▶ Flock*'s of sheep dot the hillsides in Scotland.

▶ Scholarship students* need to maintain a high grade point average.

2. Never use an apostrophe before an -s ending on a verb. (Note that *let's* is short for *let us*; the -s is not a third person singular present tense ending.)

▶ The author let's his characters take over.

~~implies~~
▶ The word ~~imply's~~ that the mood is somber.
  ^

~~tries~~
▶ He ~~try's~~ hard to correct his spelling.
  ^

3. Do not write possessive pronouns (*hers, its, ours, yours, theirs*) with an apostrophe.

4. Do not use an apostrophe to form the plural of names: *the Browns.*

5. Do not use an apostrophe to indicate possession by inanimate objects such as buildings and items of furniture; instead, use *of: the roof of the hotel, the back of the desk.*

33b -'s to signal possession

As a general rule, to signal possession, use -'s with singular nouns, with indefinite pronouns, and with plural nouns that do not form the plural with -s.

the child's books	anybody's opinion
the children's toys	today's world
this month's budget	Mr. Jackson's voice
someone else's idea	their money's worth
the author's voice	this year's curriculum

1. Individual and joint ownership   To indicate individual ownership, use the possessive form with each person you mention.

▶ Updike's and Roth's recent works received glowing reviews.

▶ Teachers' and students' ideas about good teaching often differ.

To show joint ownership, use the possessive form only with the last person you mention.

▶ **Sam, Sue, and Pat's house has just been sold to a single buyer.** [Sam, Sue, and Pat own the house jointly.]

2. Compound nouns   Add -'s to the last word in a compound noun.

▶ **my brother-in-law's car**

3. Singular nouns ending in -*s*   When a singular noun ends in -*s*, add -'s as usual for the possessive.

▶ **Thomas's toys**   ▶ **his boss's instructions**

33c Apostrophe with a plural noun ending in -*s*

When a plural noun already ends in -*s*, add only an apostrophe.

▶ **the students' suggestions**   ▶ **my friends' ambitions**
  [more than one student]   [more than one friend]

Remember to include an apostrophe in comparisons with a noun understood (24h and 28i):

▶ **His views are different from other professors'.**

  [… from other professors' views]

EXERCISE 33.1

Use apostrophes to signal possession.

Correct any errors in the use of apostrophes.

EXAMPLE:

In parts of Africa that have been devastated by AIDS, doctors who practice Western-style medicine are looking at traditional
                                                 healers'
~~healer's~~ roles in treating the sick.
         ^

1. Doctors and healers' ideas about useful treatments for people infected with the AIDS virus sometimes conflict with each other.
2. For example, traditional healers often prescribe emetics to cause vomiting, and if a patients' treatment also includes retroviral drugs, the patient may expel the drugs before they take effect.

3. Because many doctors in Africa understand their patients faith in traditional healing, some doctors are trying to work with healers rather than fighting them.

4. Some healers have agreed to attend conferences' at hospitals, where they learn to wear latex gloves when treating patients and to use alcohol to clean razor blades' edges and porcupine quills that have contacted any patients' body fluids.

5. Many patients trust healer's more than they trust doctor's, so hospitals in some areas have deputized traditional healers to monitor their patients intake of AIDS drugs and their mental well-being.

33d Apostrophe with contractions

1. Use contractions to represent informal speech.

▶ **Let's roll!**

In a contraction (*shouldn't, don't, let's, we're, I'm, they've, should've*), the apostrophe appears where letters have been omitted. To test whether an apostrophe is in the correct place, mentally replace the missing letters. The replacement test, however, will not help with *won't*, which is the contraction for *will not*.

Note: Some readers may object to contractions in formal academic writing, especially scientific writing, because they view them as colloquial and informal. It is safer not to use contractions unless you know the conventions of the genre and readers' preferences.

can't	cannot	they'd	they had *or* they would
didn't	did not	they're	they are
he's	he is *or* he has	it's	it is *or* it has
's	is, has, *or* does (How's it taste?)	let's	let us (Let's go.)

2. Use an apostrophe to take the place of the first part of a year or decade.

▶ **the greed of the '80s**
[the 1980s]

▶ **the Spirit of '76**
[the year 1776]

Note: Fixed forms spelled with an apostrophe, such as *o'clock* and the poetic *o'er*, are contractions ("of the clock," "over").

33e -'s for plurals only in special instances

The general rule is that -'s is not used to form a plural. However, there are a few exceptions. Use the following four guidelines.

1. Use -'s for the plural form of letters of the alphabet.
Italicize or underline only the letter, not the plural ending (36d).

▶ Maria picked all the *M*'s out of her alphabet soup.

▶ Georges Perec's novel called *A Void* has no *e*'s in it at all.

2. Use -'s for the plural form of a word referred to as the word itself. Italicize or underline the word named as a word, but do not italicize or underline the -'s ending (see 36d).

▶ You have too many *but*'s in that sentence.

3. Be consistent with the plural forms of numbers, acronyms, and abbreviations (see 37b). MLA and APA styles prefer no apostrophe in the plural form of numbers, acronyms, and abbreviations.

▶ the 1900s　　▶ CDs　　▶ FAQs　　▶ VCRs

VARIATION You will frequently see such plurals spelled with -'s: the 1900's, CD's. Just be consistent in your usage.

4. Never use an apostrophe to signal the plural of common nouns or personal names.

NO　　　　big bargain's, the Jackson's

YES　　　　big bargains, the Jacksons

33f The difference between *it's* and *its*

When deciding whether to use *its* or *it's*, think about meaning. *It's* is a contraction meaning "it is" or "it has." *Its* is the possessive form of the pronoun *it* and means "belonging to it." See also 27b.

　　　It is
▶ It's a good idea.　　▶ The committee took its time.

EXERCISE 33.2

Use apostrophes correctly with contractions in special instances and with *it's*.

Correct any errors in the use of apostrophes.

EXAMPLE:

Trainspotting has ~~it's~~ fans in Great Britain, and airplane spotters aren't ~~are'nt~~ unusual either.

1. Although theyre often regarded as geek's by people who do'nt share their passion, trainspotters are devoted to their hobby of watching trains and noting engine numbers.
2. Planespotting, a variation of trainspotting, resulted in legal difficulties for a group of vacationing Briton's who were arrested and accused of spying on airfields in Greece.
3. The arrests led to a diplomatic rift between Great Britain and Greece, with the Britons claiming that theyd merely been enjoying the Greek Air Force celebrations and the Greeks claiming that the spotters were illegally monitoring pilots conversations and observing high-security military installations.
4. Its not surprising that the Greek police were unfamiliar with planespotting, since the hobby attracts few people outside of it's British birthplace.
5. "Its an embarrassment," said one Greek official; the detained Britons may have been accustomed to seeing their passions ridiculed at home, but they probably were'nt expecting to meet such a reception abroad.

REVIEW EXERCISE FOR CHAPTER 33

Use apostrophes correctly.

Correct any errors in the use of apostrophes in the following passage.

Vermonts legislature passed a law in 2000 that recognizes gay and lesbian civil unions in its state as the equivalent of marriage. Since it's passage, the law has attracted gay tourists to Vermont, which along with Massachusetts is currently one of the few states that grant's gay and lesbian couples the right to all of the benefits of marriage. In the first year of the new laws' existence in Vermont, two thousand gay and lesbian couples got civil-union licenses (in the same period, about five thousand heterosexual couples got traditional marriage licenses). Eighty percent of the gay and lesbian couples werent Vermont residents; the great majority of them celebrated civil unions' and then went home to states that didn't recognize their new status under the law. Most took vows for symbolic reasons, aware that they probably would'nt gain any legal rights' from the civil union. However, many of the gay and lesbian couple's trips to Vermont and now to Massachusetts seem to them, at least, to be rewarding. Most feel that its important to have official recognition of the two partners commitment to each other.

Chapter **34**

Quotation Marks

Quotation marks indicate where a quotation begins and ends. The text between the quotation marks repeats the exact words that someone said, thought, or wrote. For omitting words in a quotation, see 35e.

34a Guidelines for using quotation marks

> **KEY POINTS**
> **Quotation Marks: Basic Guidelines**
> 1. Quote exactly the words used by the original speaker or writer.
> 2. Pair opening quotation marks with closing quotation marks to indicate where the quotation ends and your ideas begin.
> 3. Use correct punctuation to introduce and end a quotation, and place other marks of punctuation carefully in relation to the quotation marks.
> 4. Enclose the titles of short works such as short stories and poems in quotation marks.
> 5. Enclose short definitions and translations in quotation marks.

Details and more examples of each guideline follow.

Online Study Center   This icon will direct you to quick reference tools, Web resources, and research guides on the Web site at http://college.hmco.com/keys.html.

34b Introducing and ending a quotation

1. After an introductory verb such as *said, stated,* or *wrote,* use a comma followed by quotation marks and a capital letter to introduce a direct quotation.

> ▶ It was Erma Bombeck who said, "Families aren't dying. They're merging into conglomerates."
>
> —"Empty Fridge, Empty Nest"

For British English variations on double quotation marks and the punctuation used with quotation marks, see the Variation note in item 4.

2. Use a colon after a complete sentence introducing a quotation that is not integrated into your text, and begin the quotation with a capital letter.

> ▶ Woody Allen always tries to make us laugh even about serious issues like wealth and poverty: "Money is better than poverty, if only for financial reasons."   —*Without Feathers*

3. When a quotation is integrated into the structure of your own sentence, use no special introductory punctuation other than the quotation marks.

> ▶ Phyllis Grosskurth comments that "anxiety over money was driving him over the brink."   —*Byron: The Flawed Angel*

4. Put periods and commas inside quotation marks, even if these punctuation marks do not appear in the original quotation.

> ▶ When Henry Rosovsky characterizes Bloom's ideas as "mind-boggling," he is not offering praise.
>
> —*The University: An Owner's Manual*

LANGUAGE AND CULTURE
Quotations Using British Style

In British English, and noticeably in older texts, usage varies and can be significantly different from American English usage. In some British English publications, you will find single quotation marks used for quotations (and double quotation marks for a quotation inside a quotation), and commas and periods placed outside the closing quotation mark.

(Continued)

(Continued)

BRITISH   His reaction was one of stupefied amazement: 'Our father never called you a "genius", and I'm certain he never even thought it'.

AMERICAN   His reaction was one of stupefied amazement: "Our father never called you a 'genius,' and I'm certain he never even thought it."

Note that in a documented paper, when you use a parenthetical citation after a short quotation at the end of a sentence, you put the period at the end of the citation, not within the quotation. (But see 34f for long quotations.)

▶ **Geoffrey Wolff observes that when his father died, there was nothing to indicate "that he had ever known another human being" (11).**   *—The Duke of Deception*

5. Put question marks and exclamation points inside the quotation marks if they are part of the original source, with no additional period.   When your sentence is a statement, do not use a comma or period in addition to a question mark or exclamation point.

▶ **She asked, "Where's my mama?"**

6. Put an added question mark, exclamation point, semicolon, or colon outside the closing quotation marks.   If your sentence contains punctuation that is your own, not part of the original quotation, do not include it within the quotation marks.

▶ **The chapter focuses on this question: Who are "the new American dreamers"?**

34c Quotation marks in dialogue

Do not add closing quotation marks until the speaker changes or you interrupt the quotation. Begin each new speaker's words with a new paragraph.

interruption
┌ of quotation ┐
▶   **"I'm not going to work today," he announced. "Why should I? I worked all weekend. My boss is away on vacation. And I have a headache."**

┌─────────── change of speaker ───────────┐
"Honey, your boss is on the phone," his wife called from the bedroom.

If a quotation from one speaker continues for more than one paragraph, place *closing* quotation marks at the end of only the final paragraph of the quotation. However, place *opening* quotation marks at the beginning of every paragraph so readers realize that the quotation is continuing.

34d Double and single quotation marks

Enclose quotations in double quotation marks. Enclose a quotation that occurs within another quotation in single quotation marks.

▶ **Margaret announced, "I have read 'The Lottery' already."**

VARIATION   British usage can be different: *Margaret announced, 'I have read "The Lottery" already'*. See the Language and Culture box in 34b for more on the differences between British and American usage in quotations. Always use the conventions your readers will expect.

34e Quotation marks around titles of short works, definitions, and translations

In your writing, enclose in quotation marks the title of any short works you mention, such as a short story, a poem published with other poems, an article, a song, or a chapter.

▶ **Ishmael Reed's essay "America: The Multinational Society" begins with an illuminating quotation.**

▶ **"Everything That Rises Must Converge"** [short story]

▶ **"Kubla Khan"** [poem]

For long poems published independently, use italics or underlining.

▶ <u>The Wasteland</u>

▶ *Leaves of Grass*

Use quotation marks to enclose a translation or a definition.

▶ **The abbreviation *p.m.* means "post meridiem."**

34f When not to use quotation marks

1. Do not put quotation marks around indirect quotations.

▶ One woman I interviewed said that her husband argued like a lawyer.

2. Do not put quotation marks around clichés, slang, or trite or ironic expressions. Instead, revise to eliminate the cliché, slang, or trite expression. See also 20d and 20g.

involvement.
▶ All they want is ~~"a piece of the action."~~

3. Do not put quotation marks at the beginning and end of a long indented quotation. When you use MLA style to quote more than three lines of poetry or four typed lines of prose, indent the whole passage one inch (or ten spaces) from the left margin. Do not enclose the quoted passage in quotation marks, but retain any internal quotation marks. See 50h for an illustration.

4. Do not put quotation marks around the names of parts of long works or unpublished works.

▶ Peter Conrad's introduction to *Pride and Prejudice* discusses Austen as ironist.

5. On the title page of your own essay, do not put quotation marks around your essay title. Use quotation marks in your title only when it contains a quotation or the title of a short work.

▶ The Advantages of Bilingual Education

▶ Charles Baxter's "Gryphon" as an Educational Warning

EXERCISE 34.1

Use quotation marks correctly.

Correct any errors in the use of quotation marks and related punctuation.

EXAMPLE:

W. H. Auden did not like the line that reads, "We must love
die."
one another or ~~die".~~
                ^

1. Auden's poem *September 1, 1939,* in which the poet prays to: "Show an affirming flame", was widely circulated on the Internet

and reprinted in newspapers and magazines after the events of September 11, 2001.

2. Auden did not want the poem included in his collected works because he felt that it was, "infected with an incurable dishonesty.

3. Peter Steinfels wondered if a 2001 version of Auden's poem would "be found guilty of what has come to be labeled "moral equivalence"."

4. "There is a new demand," Steinfels wrote in the *"New York Times"* that ideas and language, especially about war and peace but also about religion and moral obligation, be precise and explicit."

5. The poem, which was written after the Nazi invasion of Poland in 1939, says that history 'has driven a culture mad.'

REVIEW EXERCISE FOR CHAPTER 34

Use quotation marks correctly.

Correct any errors in the use of quotation marks and related punctuation.

Child psychologist Bruno Bettelheim wrote that fairy tales, with their archetypal evil characters, terrifying situations, and improbable happy endings, could tell children a great deal, "about the inner problems of human beings and of the right solutions to their predicaments in any society". In a newspaper article called Old Theory Could Explain Love of Harry Potter, Richard Bernstein argues that Bettelheim's analysis of fairy tales reveals the reasons for the staggering popularity of J. K. Rowling's books. Although Bernstein sees the book *Harry Potter and the Sorcerer's Stone* as "a fairly conventional supernatural adventure story", he admits that children find the books "as powerful as the witch of "Hansel and Gretel." Bernstein analyzes the narrative and concludes that, "Harry's story, . . . with its early images of alienation, rejection, loneliness and power-lessness leading to its classically fairy tale ending, contains the same basic message that Bettelheim described."

Bernstein is not alone in writing for adults about the Harry Potter "phenomenon." Academic conferences call for papers on Rowling's books; one asked graduate students and professors to ponder the ways that the books "embody, extend, exploit, or enfeeble the fantasy genre". Although children helped the Rowling books to reach "number one" on the bestseller lists, it is clear—in spite of the reservations of adults like Bernstein— that many adults are equally captivated by Harry Potter.

Chapter **35**

Other Punctuation Marks

35a Dashes

Dashes (—) suggest a change of pace. They alert readers to something unexpected or to an interruption. Form a dash by typing two hyphens, putting no extra space before, between, or after them. Most software will transform the two hyphens into one continuous dash.

▶ **Armed with one weapon—his wit—he faced the crowd.**

▶ **The accused gasped, "But I never—" and fainted.**

▶ **In America there are two classes of travel—first class and with children.**
　　　　　　　　　　—Robert Benchley, in Robert E. Drennan, *The Algonquin Wits*

Commas can be used to set off appositive phrases, but dashes are preferable when the phrase itself contains commas.

▶ **The contents of his closet—torn jeans, frayed jackets, and suits shiny on the seat and elbows—made him reassess his priorities.**

35b Parentheses

Use parentheses to mark an aside or provide additional information.

▶ **Chuck Yeager's feat (breaking the sound barrier) led to increased competition in the space industry.**

Also use parentheses to enclose citations in a documented paper and to enclose numbers or letters preceding items in a list.

▶ **(3) A journalist reports that in the course of many interviews, he met very few people who were cynical about the future of the country (Lamb 5).**

Online Study Center　　This icon will direct you to quick reference tools, Web resources, and research guides on the Web site at http://college.hmco.com/keys.html.

35c Brackets

1. Square brackets ([ ])   When you insert words or make changes to words within a quotation, enclose the inserted or changed material in square brackets. Be careful to insert only words that help the quotation fit into your sentence grammatically or that offer necessary explanation. Do not insert words that substantially change the meaning.

> ▶ **Maxine Hong Kingston agrees with reviewer Diane Johnson that the memoir form "can neither [be] dismiss[ed] as fiction nor quarrel[ed] with as fact."**

On occasion, you may need to use brackets to insert the Latin word *sic* (meaning "thus") into a quoted passage in which an error occurs. Using *sic* tells readers that the word or words that it follows were present in the original source and are not your own.

> ▶ **Richard Lederer tells of a man who did "exercises to strengthen his abominable [sic] muscles."**

Square brackets can also be used in MLA style around ellipsis dots that you add to signal an omission from a source that itself contains ellipsis dots.

2. Angle brackets (<>)   Use angle brackets to enclose e-mail addresses and URLs (Web addresses), particularly in an MLA style works-cited list. See 39a and 51d.

35d Slashes

Use slashes (/) to separate two or three lines of poetry quoted within your own text. For quoting more than three lines of poetry, see 49j.

> ▶ **Philip Larkin asks a question that many of us relate to: "Why should I let the toad *work* / Squat on my life?"**

Slashes are also used in expressions such as *and/or* and *he/she* to indicate options. However, be careful not to overuse these expressions.

35e Ellipsis dots

When you omit material from a quotation, indicate the omission—the ellipsis—by using spaced dots (. . .). The following passage by Ruth Sidel, on page 27 of *On Her Own: Growing Up in the Shadow of the American Dream*, is used in the examples that follow.

These women have a commitment to career, to material well-being, to success, and to independence. To many of them, an affluent life-style is central to their dreams; they often describe their goals in terms of cars, homes, travel to Europe. In short, they want their piece of the American Dream.

1. Words omitted from the middle of a quotation   In MLA and APA styles, use three ellipsis dots when you omit material from the middle of a quotation. MLA style also allows for square brackets around the dots so that readers will know that the dots are not part of the original text (50h).

MLA   **Ruth Sidel reports that the women in her interviews "have a commitment to career . . . and to independence" (27). Or [. . .]**

APA   **Ruth Sidel (1990) reports that the women in her interviews "have a commitment to career . . . and to independence" (p. 27).**

2. Words omitted at the end of your sentence   When you omit part of a quotation and the omission occurs at the end of your own sentence, insert ellipsis dots after the sentence period, followed by the closing quotation marks, making four dots in all.

▶ **Ruth Sidel presents interesting findings about jobs and money: "These women have a commitment to career, to material well-being. . . ."**

When a parenthetical reference follows the quoted passage, put the final sentence period after the parenthetical reference:

▶ **Ruth Sidel presents interesting findings about jobs and money: "These women have a commitment to career, to material well-being . . ." (27).**

3. Complete sentence omitted   When you omit a complete sentence or more, insert three ellipsis dots.

▶ **Sidel tells us how "an affluent life-style is central to their dreams; . . . they want their piece of the American dream" (27).**

4. Line of poetry omitted   When you omit one or more lines of poetry from a long, indented quotation, indicate the omission with a line of dots that is approximately as long as a complete line of poetry

in the original. These can be enclosed in square brackets if you are
using MLA style.

▶ **This poem is for the hunger of my mother**
   . . . .
   who read the Blackwell's catalogue
   like a menu of delights
   and when we moved from Puerto Rico to the States
   we packed 100 boxes of books and 40 of everything else.
                        —Aurora Levins Morales, *Class Poem*

5. When not to use ellipsis dots Do not use ellipsis dots when
you quote only a word or a phrase because it will be obvious that
material has been omitted:

▶ **The women Sidel interviewed see an "affluent life-style" in
their future.**

Note: Also use three dots to indicate uncertainty, a pause, or an
interruption.

▶ **After watching the mystery for two hours, I braced myself for
those annoying words "To be continued . . .".**

REVIEW EXERCISE FOR CHAPTER 35
Use other punctuation marks correctly.

Correct any errors in the use of dashes, parentheses, brackets,
slashes, and ellipsis dots. (Citations should conform to MLA style.)

1. George Harrison—the most reclusive member of the Beatles,
   and the one who urged most strongly that the band stop playing
   live shows, died on November 29, 2001.

2. Beatles fans from all over the world mourned the death of the
   second member of the most famous rock band in history [John
   Lennon had been murdered more than twenty years before
   Harrison died of cancer].

3. Harrison (known to fans everywhere simply as "George," whose
   songwriting took a back seat to that of Lennon and McCartney, still
   wrote some of the Beatles' biggest hits, including "Something,"
   "While My Guitar Gently Weeps," and "Here Comes the Sun."

4. Obituaries noted Harrison's interest in Eastern music and religion (at the time of his death, he remained a follower of a form
   of Hinduism he called Krishna Consciousness.

5. In many of the films in which Harrison either had a starring role or made a cameo appearance, *A Hard Day's Night, Help!*, a Beatles parody called *All You Need Is Cash* starring members of Monty Python (and produced by Harrison), *Monty Python's Life of Brian*, his sly sense of humor was apparent.

6. In *The Beatles Anthology*, Harrison noted, "As a band, we were tight . . . We could argue a lot among ourselves, but we were very, very close". . . . [83]

7. For most music lovers, Harrison will be forever associated with a band that broke up in 1970, but his 1987 album, *Cloud Nine*, "[won] over a new generation of fans (. . .) born after the Beatles' demise." (Rees and Crampton 256)

8. Expressing sorrow at Harrison's death, Paul McCartney said, "He (was) really just my baby brother" (Kozinn A1).

Chapter **36**

Italics and Underlining

Use italic type or underlining to highlight a word, phrase, or title in your own writing. In manuscript form, underlining is more distinctive and therefore often preferred, particularly in MLA bibliographical lists and in material to be typeset. Ask your instructor which form to use. For underlining when writing online, see 39b.

▶ **Woolf's novel *Orlando* was written for Vita Sackville-West. OR Woolf's novel <u>Orlando</u> was written for Vita Sackville-West.**

▶ **In <u>The Psychology of Time</u>, we learn about perceptions of filled and empty time. OR In *The Psychology of Time*, we learn about perceptions of filled and empty time.**

36a Italics or underlining for titles of long, whole works

In the body of an essay, italicize or underline the titles of books, magazines, newspapers, plays, films, TV series, long poems, musical compositions, Web sites, online databases, and works of art.

Online Study Center This icon will direct you to quick reference tools, Web resources, and research guides on the Web site at http://college.hmco.com/keys.html.

▶ <u>**The Sun Also Rises**</u>   ▶ *The Daily Show*   ▶ <u>**Newsweek**</u>

▶ *Nickel and Dimed*   ▶ <u>**Mona Lisa**</u>   ▶ *Wikipedia*

For exceptions, see 36f.

EXERCISE 36.1
Use italics correctly for titles of long, whole works.

In each of the following sentences, correct any errors in the itali-cization of titles. Indicate where to add or eliminate italics or underlining as needed. Some sentences may be correct.

EXAMPLE:

                   New Yorker
A notice in the ~~New Yorker~~ attracted some art lovers to the
                   ^
          New York University
symposium at ~~New York University.~~
                   ^

1. In his book Vermeer's Camera, Philip Steadman argues that Vermeer used a mechanical device to project images onto his canvas that he could trace before painting them.

2. The device, a box containing an optical lens, is known as a cam-era obscura, and Steadman and others believe that Vermeer could not have created paintings like "Kitchen Maid" with such photographic precision without mechanical help.

3. In 2001, the painter David Hockney, believing that Caravaggio, Ingres, van Eyck, and other Old Masters used optical devices to enhance the realism of their paintings, assembled a panel of art historians and scientists in New York to debate the issue.

4. In an article called *Paintings Too Perfect? The Great Optics Debate,* the *New York Times* reported on the spirited disagreements that followed.

5. Even panelists discussing van Eyck's Arnolfini Wedding, a painting that depicts an optical device, were unable to agree on whether the artist had used technological assistance to create the painting; still, after the symposium, Hockney reported, "I learned some things."

36b Italics or underlining for main entries in a list of works cited

If you use the MLA style of documentation, underline main entries (for example, title of book or long work; name of journal, newspaper, or magazine; work of art; name of database; or title of Web site) in your list of works cited. In APA and *Chicago* styles, use italics for the main entries. See chapters 51, 52, and 54 for details and examples.

36c Italics or underlining for names of ships, trains, airplanes, and spacecraft

▶ <u>Mayflower</u>   ▶ *Silver Meteor*   ▶ *Mir*

Do not underline or italicize the abbreviations sometimes preceding these names: USS *Constitution*.

36d Italics or underlining for letters, numerals, and words referring to the words themselves, not to what they represent

▶ **The sign had a large <u>P</u> in black marker and a <u>3</u> in red.**

▶ ***Zarf* is a useful word for some board games.**

36e Italics or underlining for words from other languages

Expressions not commonly used in English should be italicized or underlined. However, do not overuse such expressions because they tend to sound pretentious.

▶ **The headmaster frequently talked to baffled parents about his <u>Weltanschauung</u>.**

▶ **The picture shows the model in a state of *deshabille*.**

Do not italicize common expressions such as these: et al., croissant, nom de plume, and film noir.

36f When not to use italics or underlining

Do not italicize or underline the following:

- the names of sacred works such as the Bible, books of the Bible (Genesis, Psalms), and the Koran (Qur'an)
- the titles of documents and laws, such as the Declaration of Independence, the Constitution, and the Americans with Disabilities Act

- the titles of short works, such as poems, short stories, essays, and articles (use quotation marks for these)
- the title of your own essay on your title page (34f)
- statements that you want to emphasize

▶ The climb was ~~so scary.~~ hair-raising.
                    ^

Instead, select a word that conveys the emphasis you want to express.

REVIEW EXERCISE FOR CHAPTER 36

Use italics and underlining correctly.

Underline any words that need italicization or underlining, and remove any unnecessary underlining or quotation marks.

In the nineteenth century, phrenology—the study of bumps on the skull and their relation to the personality—was a popular pseudoscientific practice, and one of the best-known phrenologists was Lorenzo Fowler. Along with his brother Orson, Lorenzo Fowler headed the Phrenological Institute in New York City, where the two trained other phrenologists, and Lorenzo gave readings to celebrities such as Julia Ward Howe, author of The Battle Hymn of the Republic. The Fowler brothers saw themselves as leaders of a progressive movement; they ran the publishing company that put out the first edition of Walt Whitman's "Leaves of Grass." They also published the Phrenological Journal, hoping that phrenological analysis could lead people to correct defects of character that had been revealed by their cranial protrusions.

In 1872, Samuel Clemens, who had written Huckleberry Finn and many other works under the nom de plume Mark Twain, visited Fowler under an assumed name and obtained a reading and a phrenological chart. Clemens, who was an early champion both of scientific innovations like fingerprinting (which is featured in his novel "Pudd'nhead Wilson") and of inventions that proved to be dismal failures, wanted to put phrenology to the test. The results amused him: in "The Autobiography of Mark Twain," Clemens notes that Fowler found a spot on his skull that "represented the total absence of the sense of humor." Months later, Clemens returned for a second reading, identifying himself both as Clemens and as Mark Twain, and was given a reading and a chart that "contained several sharply defined details of my character, but [. . .] bore no recognizable resemblance to the earlier chart."

Clemens remained convinced that phrenology was quackery, and others soon agreed. By 1900, phrenology had fallen out of favor. Even in the twenty-first century, however, the use of terms such as highbrow and lowbrow, which came from phrenology, demonstrates the influence that this idea once had.

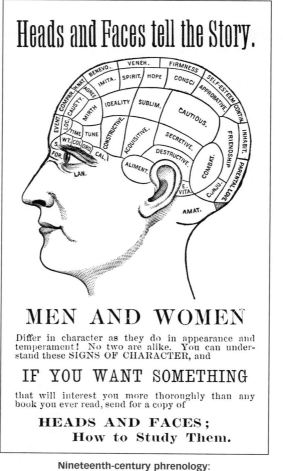

Nineteenth-century phrenology:
A map of the head

Chapter **37**

Capital Letters, Abbreviations, and Numbers

37a Capital letters

Always consult a dictionary if you are not sure whether to capitalize a word. A dictionary will indicate if a noun is a proper noun demanding a capital letter:

▶ **King James Bible**

▶ **King Charles spaniel**

Use the following eight guidelines for capitalization.

1. Always capitalize *I*, even in e-mail communications.

▶ **They announced that I had won the prize.**

2. Capitalize the first word of a sentence, after a period, question mark, or exclamation point.

▶ **Why do the wealthy send their children to residential colleges? They want them to have the benefits of a liberal-arts education.**

3. Capitalize the first word of a sentence quotation—if it is capitalized in the original passage.

▶ **Quindlen says, "This is a story about a name," and thus tells us the topic of her article.**

However, when you quote part of a sentence, do not begin the quotation with a capital letter.

▶ **When Quindlen says that she is writing "a story about a name," she is telling us the topic of her article.**

4. Capitalize proper nouns and proper adjectives. Begin the names of specific people, places, and things with a capital letter.

Online Study Center   This icon will direct you to quick reference tools, Web resources, and research guides on the Web site at http://college.hmco.com/keys.html.

Types of Proper Nouns and Adjectives	Examples
Names of people	Albert Einstein, Bono, T. S. Eliot, Bill Gates
Names of nations, continents, planets, stars, and galaxies	Hungary, Asia, Mercury, the North Star, the Milky Way
Names of mountains, rivers, and oceans	Mount Everest, the Thames, the Pacific Ocean
Names of public places and regions	Golden Gate Park, the Great Plains, the Midwest
Names of streets, buildings, and monuments	Rodeo Drive, the Empire State Building, the Roosevelt Memorial
Names of cities, states, and provinces	Toledo, Kansas, Nova Scotia
Days of the week and months	Wednesday, March
Holidays	Labor Day, the Fourth of July
Organizations and companies	the Red Cross, Microsoft Corporation
Institutions (including colleges, departments, schools, government offices, and courts of law)	University of Texas, Department of English, School of Business, Defense Department, Florida Supreme Court
Historical events, named periods, and documents	the Civil War, the Renaissance, the Roaring Twenties, the Declaration of Independence
Religions, deities, revered persons, and sacred texts	Buddhism, Islam, Muslim, Baptist, Jehovah, Mohammed, the Torah, the Koran (Qur'an)
Races, tribes, nations, nationalities, and languages	the Navajo, Greece, Spain, Farsi
Registered trademarks	Kleenex, Apple, Bic, Nike, Xerox
Names of ships, planes, and spacecraft	the USS *Kearsage*, the *Spirit of St. Louis*, the *Challenger*

Note: Do not capitalize nouns naming general classes or types of people, places, things, or ideas: *government, jury, mall, prairie, utopia, traffic court, the twentieth century, goodness, reason.* For the use of capital letters in online writing, see 39c.

5. **Capitalize a title before a person's name.**

▶ The reporter interviewed Senator Thompson.

▶ The residents cheered Grandma Jones.

However, do not use a capital letter when a title is not attached to a person's name.

▶ Each state elects two senators.

▶ My grandmother is ninety years old.

When a title substitutes for the name of a known person, a capital letter is often used.

▶ Have you spoken with the Senator [senator] yet?

6. **Capitalize major words in a title.** In titles of published books, journals, magazines, essays, articles, films, poems, and songs, use a capital letter at the beginning of all words. However, do not use a capital letter for articles (*the, a, an*), coordinating conjunctions (*and, but, or, nor, so, for, yet*), *to* in an infinitive (*to stay*), and prepositions unless they begin or end a title or subtitle.

▶ "A Matter of Identity"

▶ "Wrestling with the Angel: A Memoir"

▶ *What Lies Beneath*

7. **Capitalize the first word of a subtitle, even if it is an article, a coordinating conjunction, *to*, or a preposition.**

▶ *Reflections from the Keyboard: The World of the Concert Pianist*

8. **Be consistent when using a capital or lowercase letter after a colon.** Usage varies. Usually a capital letter is used if the clause states a rule or principle (32e). Make your usage consistent.

EXERCISE 37.1

Use capital letters correctly.

Capitalize any letters that are incorrectly lowercase, and change any incorrect capital letters to lowercase letters.

EXAMPLE:

           Civil War   *doctor*

During the ~~civil war~~, a ~~Doctor~~ from Kentucky tried to spread

  virus   North

a ~~Virus~~ to cities in the ~~north~~.

1. Biological warfare may strike modern Americans as Barbaric, but during the French and Indian war, smallpox-infected blankets given to Native Americans helped to decimate their numbers.

2. in the 1860s, Dr. Luke blackburn tried the same tactic, giving or selling clothing from patients with Yellow fever to Soldiers in the Union Army.

3. According to some historians, the Doctor hoped to spread Yellow Fever in washington and new York; president Jefferson Davis of the confederate States of America probably knew about and approved of the plan.

4. Fortunately for citizens of the north, yellow fever cannot be passed from one person to another by skin contact. although Dr. Blackburn's plot was discovered on the day of Lincoln's Assassination, he was never prosecuted in a Court of Law.

5. Blackburn eventually became the Governor of Kentucky, where he worked for penal and educational reform. A statue of the good samaritan marks his grave in frankfort cemetery.

37b Abbreviations and acronyms

For abbreviations commonly used in online writing, see 39e. The list below shows you when and how to use abbreviations.

1. Abbreviate titles used with people's names. Use an abbreviation, followed by a period, for titles before or after names. The following abbreviated titles precede names: *Mr., Mrs., Ms., Prof., Dr., Gen.,* and *Sen.* The following abbreviated titles follow names: *Sr., Jr., PhD, MD, BA,* and *DDS.* Do not use a title both before and after a name: *Dr. Benjamin Spock* or *Benjamin Spock, MD.* Do not abbreviate a title if it is not attached to a specific name.

> *doctor*
> ▶ Pat Murphy Sr. went to the ~~dr.~~ twice last week.
>   ^

2. Abbreviate the names of familiar institutions, countries, tests, diplomas, individuals, and objects. Use abbreviations of the names of well-known institutions (*UCLA, YWCA, FBI, IBM*), countries (*USA* or *U.S.A.*), tests and diplomas (*SAT, GED*), individuals (*FDR*), and objects (*DVD*). If you use a specialized abbreviation, first use the term in full followed by the abbreviation in parentheses; then use the abbreviation.

▶ The Graduate Record Examination (GRE) is required by many
graduate schools. GRE preparation is therefore big business.

3. Abbreviate terms used with numbers. Use the abbreviations
such as *BC, AD, a.m., p.m., $, mph, wpm, mg, kg,* and other units of
measure only when they occur with specific numbers.

▶ **35 BC** [meaning "before Christ," now often replaced with
BCE, "before the common era," to avoid reference to one
religion: **35 BCE**]

▶ **AD 1776** [*anno domini,* "in the year of the Lord," now
often replaced with *CE,* "common era," used after the date:
1776 CE]

▶ **2:00 a.m./p.m.** [*ante* or *post meridiem,* Latin for "before" or
"after midday"]

Alternatives are A.M./P.M. or AM/PM. Be consistent. But do not use
these abbreviations and other units of measure when no number is
attached to them.

money
▶ His family gave him a wallet full of $ to spend on vacation.
　　　　　　　　　　　　　　　　　　　　　　　　^

afternoon.
▶ They arrived late in the ~~p.m.~~
　　　　　　　　　　　　　　　　^

4. Abbreviate common Latin terms. In notes, parentheses, and
source citations, use abbreviations for common Latin terms. In the
body of your text, use the English meaning.

Abbreviation	Latin	English meaning
etc.	et cetera	and so on
i.e.	id est	that is
e.g.	exempli gratia	for example
cf.	confer	compare
N.B.	nota bene	note well
et al.	et alii	and others

5. With the plural form of an abbreviation, use *-s* (not *-'s*). Do
not use an apostrophe to make an abbreviation plural (see 33e).

▶ She has more than a thousand CDs.

▶ Both his iPods are broken.

6. Do not abbreviate familiar words to save time and space. In formal writing, write in full expressions such as the following:

&	and
bros.	brothers [Use "Bros." only if it is part of the official name of the business.]
chap.	chapter
Mon.	Monday
nite	night
NJ	New Jersey [Abbreviate the name of the state only in an address, a note, or a reference.]
no.	number [Use the abbreviation only with a specific number: "No. 17 on the list was deleted."]
Oct.	October [Write names of days and months in full, except in some works-cited lists.]
soc.	sociology [Write names of academic subjects in full.]
thru	through
w/	with

EXERCISE 37.2

Use abbreviations and acronyms correctly.

Correct any errors in the use of abbreviations or acronyms.

EXAMPLE:

According to ~~Mister~~ Sid Green, who teaches ~~H.S. hist.~~ in ~~CA,~~ some U.S. colleges and universities no longer require students to take the SAT.
(above "Mister": Mr.; above "hist.": history; above "H.S.": high school; above "CA": California)

1. An early adopter—someone who buys new devices and gadgets as soon as they are available—probably owned CD's when most people still bought records, rented DVD's while others still watched videos on their VCR's, and picked out iPod's as holiday gifts.

2. The acupuncturist's receptionist referred to him as Doctor Loren Selwyn, but I later discovered that he was Loren Selwyn, doctor of philosophy, not Loren Selwyn, medical doctor.

3. Ms Krebs could type so many w.p.m. that the computer printer was spewing out pp. long after she had stopped working for the eve.

4. Sen Hammond helpfully told us that the New Year's Eve party would be held on Dec. 31, but he neglected to say what time we should arrive.

5. Akhenaton, orig. known as Amenhotep, ruled ancient Egypt until his death in about 1358 before the Common Era.

37c Numbers

Conventions for using numerals (actual figures) or words vary across the disciplines.

1. Numbers in the humanities and in business letters

Use words for numbers expressible in one or two words and for fractions (*nineteen, fifty-six, two hundred, one-half*).

Use numerals for longer numbers (*326; 5,625; 7,642,000*).

Use a combination of words and numerals for whole millions, billions, and so on (*45 million, 1 billion*).

2. Numbers in scientific and technical writing

Use numerals for all numbers above nine.

Use numerals for numbers below ten only when they show precise measurement, as when they are grouped and compared with other larger numbers (*5 of the 39 participants*) or when they precede a unit of measurement (*6 cm*), indicate a mathematical function (*8%; 0.4*), or represent a specific time, date, age, score, or number in a series.

Use words for fractions: *two-thirds.*

3. Numbers beginning a sentence
In both the humanities and the sciences, spell out numbers that begin a sentence.

▶ **One hundred twenty-five members voted for the new bylaws.**

▶ **Six thousand fans have already bought tickets.**

ESL NOTE

Singular and Plural Forms of *Hundred, Thousand,* and *Million*

Even after plural numbers, use the singular form of *hundred, thousand,* and *million.* Add -s only when there is no preceding number. *(Continued)*

(Continued)

▶ Five *hundred* books were damaged in the flood.   [not five hundreds]

▶ *Hundreds* of books were damaged in the flood.

4. Special uses of figures (numerals)   In nonscientific writing, use numerals for the following:

Time and dates	6 p.m. on 31 May 2003
Decimals	20.89
Statistics	median score 35
Addresses	16 East 93rd Street
Chapter, page, scene, and line numbers	chapter 5; page 97; scene 2, line 44
Quantities appearing with abbreviations or symbols	6°C (for temperature Celsius), $21, 6'7"
Scores	The Knicks won 89–85.

For percentages and money, numerals and the symbol (*75%, $24.67*) are usually acceptable, or you can spell out the expression if it is fewer than four words (*seventy-five percent, twenty-four dollars*).

5. Plural forms of figures   Be consistent in your usage. MLA style prefers no apostrophe to form the plural of a numeral.

▶ in the 1980s   ▶ They scored in the 700s on the SATs.

Chapter **38**

Spelling and Hyphenation

This chapter provides you with some of the basic hyphenation and spelling rules, which are worth learning, along with some lists of troublesome words for you to refer to, learn, and add to.

Online Study Center   This icon will direct you to quick reference tools, Web resources, and research guides on the Web site at http://college.hmco.com/keys.html.

38a Checking spelling

A spelling checker is of limited use. Even if you check your spelling with computer software, you still need to proofread. A program will not alert you to homonyms (such as *cite* used in place of *sight* or *site*), typographical slips (such as if you write *form* in place of *from),* or variant spellings across dialects of English. So using a spelling checker is only a beginning (6b).

One of the best tools at your disposal is a dictionary, for here you can check spelling, find the various word forms associated with a word (*benefit/benefited*, for example), or discover when a silent *-e* is retained or dropped before a suffix (as in *likable* or *likeness*). See 20b for an example of the amount of information available at your fingertips in a dictionary. If you feel insecure about your spelling, be sure to keep your own list of "My Spelling Words" and add to it whenever you make an error, are surprised by the spelling of a word, or look up a word for confirmation. See 38g and 38h for spelling.

VARIATION   Be aware that differences exist in spelling and meaning among the world's Englishes: British English, American English, African American English, Australian English, Singaporean English, Hong Kong English, Indian English, Caribbean English, and so on. For example, a *cell phone* in the United States is a *mobile phone* in England and a *handphone* in Singapore. The Language and Culture box provides examples of differences in spelling and meaning between British English (the original dialect of one of the authors of this book) and American English.

LANGUAGE AND CULTURE
British and American English

Differences in Spelling

British	American	British	American
colour	color	theatre	theater
humour	humor	centre	center
learnt	learned	criticise	criticize
travelled	traveled	judgement	judgment
cheque	check	defence	defense
neighbour	neighbor	programme	program
towards	toward	jeweller	jeweler

(Continued)

(Continued)

Differences in Meaning Note the potential for confusion.

British	American
bonnet (of car)	hood
windscreen	windshield
boot	trunk
car park	parking lot
dual carriageway	divided highway
roundabout	traffic circle, rotary
lift	elevator
nappy	diaper
dummy	pacifier
pudding	dessert
eiderdown	comforter
braces	suspenders
vest	undershirt
waistcoat	vest
trousers	pants
pants	underwear
chips	french fries
crisps	potato chips
over the road	across the street
mind (verb)	object (I don't mind. Do you mind?)
mind (verb)	watch out for (as in "Mind the gap!")

EXERCISE 38.1

Check the spelling of words.

In the following pairs of words, check (✓) which you think is correctly spelled. If you think both spellings are acceptable in different contexts, check both. Then turn to a dictionary to look up the words. If you make any errors, start your own spelling list with those words.

EXAMPLE:

a. ___✓___ responsible

b. _____ responsable

1. a.	_____ principle	6. a.	_____ truly
b.	_____ principal	b.	_____ truely
2. a.	_____ independance	7. a.	_____ affect
b.	_____ independence	b.	_____ effect
3. a.	_____ address	8. a.	_____ harrass
b.	_____ adress	b.	_____ harass
4. a.	_____ suprise	9. a.	_____ succeed
b.	_____ surprise	b.	_____ suceed
5. a.	_____ Febuary	10. a.	_____ loose
b.	_____ February	b.	_____ lose

38b Plurals of nouns

1. Regular plural forms   The regular plural of nouns is formed by adding -s or -es to the singular word.

essay, essays   match, matches

To form the plural of a compound noun, attach the -s to the main noun in the phrase.

mothers-in-law   passersby

Proofread carefully for plural forms that form the plural with -s but make other changes, too, such as the following:

-f OR *-fe* → *-ves*	
thief, thieves	(*Exceptions:* beliefs, roofs, chiefs)
wife, wives	

-o → *-oes*	*-o* → *-os*
potato, potatoes	hero (sandwich), heros
tomato, tomatoes	photo, photos
hero (man), heroes	piano, pianos

Consonant + *-y* → *-ies*	**Vowel + *-y* → *-ys***
family, families	toy, toys
party, parties	monkey, monkeys

2. Irregular plural forms (no -s ending)

man, men	foot, feet
woman, women	tooth, teeth
child, children	mouse, mice

3. Plural forms borrowed from other languages

Words borrowed from other languages, particularly Greek and Latin words, frequently borrow the plural form from the language, too.

basis, bases	nucleus, nuclei
thesis, theses	vertebra, vertebrae
hypothesis, hypotheses	alumnus (m.), alumni
criterion, criteria	alumna (f.), alumnae

4. Plural forms with no change

Some words have the same form in singular and plural: *moose, deer, sheep, species.*

38c Doubling consonants

Doubled consonants form a link between spelling and pronunciation because the doubling of a consonant signals a short vowel sound.

1. Double the consonant when the verb stem contains one vowel plus one consonant in one syllable.

slip, slipping, slipped   hop, hopping, hopped

The doubled consonant preserves the short vowel sound. Compare the pronunciation of *hop, hopping, hopped* with *hope, hoping, hoped.* Say the words aloud and compare the vowel sounds in *write, writing,* and *written.*

2. Double the consonant when the verb stem contains two or more syllables with one vowel plus one consonant in the final stressed syllable.

refer, referring, referred   control, controlling, controlled

Compare *travel, traveling, traveled* and *cancel, canceling, canceled,* which have the stress on the first syllable. (Note that British English prefers the spellings *travelling, travelled; cancelling, cancelled.*)

3. Double the consonant when the suffix *-er* or *-est* is added to one-syllable adjectives ending in one vowel plus one consonant.

big, bigger, biggest   hot, hotter, hottest

4. Double the *l* when adding *-ly* to an adjective that ends in one *-l*.

careful, carefully   successful, successfully

38d Spelling with *-y* or *-i*

Verb Ends in Consonant + *-y*	*-ies*	*-ying*	*-ied*
cry	cries	crying	cried
study	studies	studying	studied

Verb Ends in Vowel + *-y*	*-ys*	*-ying*	*-yed*
play	plays	playing	played

Exceptions: pay/paid, say/said, lay/laid

Verb Ends in Vowel + *-e*	*-ies*	*-ying*	*-ied*
die	dies	dying	died

Two-Syllable Adjective Ends in *-y*	*-i* with a Suffix	
happy	happier, happily, happiness	

Two-Syllable Adjective Ends in *-ly*	*-lier*	*-liest*
friendly	friendlier	friendliest

38e Internal *ie* or *ei*

This traditional rhyme helps with the decision about whether to use *ie* or *ei*:

I before *e*

Except after *c*

Or when sounded like *ay*

As in *neighbor* and *weigh.*

The following examples illustrate those guidelines:

i Before e	e Before i After c	e Before i When Sounded Like ay
believe	receive	vein
relief	ceiling	reign
niece	deceive	sleigh

But note the exceptions:

i Before e Even After c	e Before i, Not After c	
conscience	height	seize
science	either/neither	foreign
species	leisure	weird

38f Adding a suffix

1. Keep a silent -e before an -ly suffix.

immediate, immediately   sure, surely

Exceptions: true, truly; whole, wholly; due, duly

2. Keep a silent -e before a suffix beginning with a consonant.

state, statement   force, forceful   rude, rudeness

Exceptions: acknowledge, acknowledgment; judge, judgment; argue, argument

3. Drop a silent -e before a suffix beginning with a vowel.

hope, hoping   observe, observant

write, writing   remove, removable

Exceptions: enforce, enforceable; change, changeable. Retaining the -e preserves the soft sound of the preceding consonant.

4. With adjectives ending in -le, drop the -le when adding -ly.

sensible, sensibly

5. With adjectives ending in -ic, add -ally to form the adverb.

basic, basically   characteristic, characteristically

Exception: public, publicly

6. Pay attention to the suffixes *-able, -ible, -ant, -ent, -ify,* and *-efy.*
More words end in *-able* than in *-ible.* Learn the most common *-ible*
words:

eligible	incredible	irresistible	legible
permissible	responsible	terrible	visible

Unfortunately, there are no rules of thumb to help you decide
whether to use the suffix *-ant* or *-ent.* Learn common words with
these suffixes, and have your dictionary handy for others.

-ant	-ent
defiant	confident
observant	convenient
relevant	existent
reluctant	imminent
resistant	independent

The suffix *-ify* is more common than *-efy.* Learn the four *-efy* words:

liquefy	putrefy	rarefy	stupefy

EXERCISE 38.2
Correct misspelled words.

In each of the following sentences, correct any misspelled words.
Some sentences may not contain any errors.

EXAMPLE:

violence
In the wake of high school ~~violance~~, drug use, and other
problems in the last ten years, many schools have adopted a

tolerance
"zero ~~tolerence~~" policy.

1. After school shootings in Jonesboro, Paducah, and elswhere,
   some school administraters decided not to take any chances
   with students carring weapons.

2. A "zero tolerance" policy that called for students to face sus-
   pention if they were caught with guns, knifes, or any potencial
   weapon took effect in many schools.

3. In one school, a seven-year-old boy who had a two-inch-long
   toy gun on his key chain was suspended when the chain fell
   out of his pocket and was noticed by other childs.

4. His mother protestted that suspending students for carrying toies was ridiculous and that schools had an obligation to use common sense.

5. In other areas, many schools have also been declareing "zero tolerance" policys toward posession of drugs and other infractions of the rules.

6. Unbelieveably, a first grader was suspended in Colorado for shareing his candy with freinds because teachers did not recognize the brand (which was sold in the town's major supermarket).

7. A declareation of "zero tolerance" means that schools decide that they will automaticly punish any student who even appears to have broken the rules.

8. The policy allows school personnel no leeway to decide for themselves whether the student's behavior warrants punishment.

9. "Zero tolerance" rules were in place in many school districts even before the horrefying shootings at Columbine High School in Littleton, Colorado, and since then these policys have become even more popular.

10. Although a "zero tolerance" policy probably would have prevented the Littleton killers from showing videoes in class featuring violent attacks, would it realy have alerted anyone in the boys' familys, nieghborhood, or school to the real danger?

38g Multinational characters: accents, umlauts, tildes, and cedillas

Words and names in languages other than English may be spelled with special marks above or under a letter, such as an accent (è or é), an umlaut or dieresis (ö), a tilde (ñ), or a cedilla (ç). Microsoft Word provides ways of producing multinational characters. The basic principle is that you press CTRL and the punctuation key most similar to the mark you need, release the keys, and press the letter. The letter then appears with its mark. Alternatively, you can go to Insert/Symbol, where you have the option to create a "Shortcut Key."

> **TECH NOTE**
>
> **A Useful Web Site for Writing in Other Languages**
>
> *International Accents and Diacriticals: Theory, Charts, and Tips,* prepared by Irene Starr of the Foreign Language Resource Center at the University of Massachusetts, is a useful site. It provides charts of how to use Word, WordPerfect, or a Macintosh computer to produce the multinational characters, instructions on accessing and using the International English keyboard, and links to sites useful for those writing non-Roman alphabets.

38h Hyphens

Use hyphens to divide a word or to form a compound. For the use of hyphens online, see 39d.

1. Hyphens with prefixes   Many words with prefixes are spelled without hyphens: *cooperate, nonrestrictive, unnatural.* Others are hyphenated: *all-inclusive, anti-intellectual.* Always use a hyphen when the main word is a number or a proper noun: *all-American, post-1990.* If you are unsure about whether to insert a hyphen after a prefix, check a dictionary to see if it lists the word as hyphenated.

2. Hyphens in compound nouns and adjectives   Some compound nouns are written as one word (*toothbrush*), others as two words (*coffee shop*), and still others with one or more hyphens (*role-playing, father-in-law*). Always check an up-to-date dictionary.

Hyphenate compound modifiers preceding a noun: *a ten-page essay, a well-organized party, a law-abiding citizen.* When the modifier follows the noun, no hyphen is necessary: *The essay was ten pages long. The party was well organized. Most citizens try to be law abiding.*

Do not insert a hyphen between an *-ly* adverb and an adjective or after an adjective in its comparative (*-er*) or superlative (*-est*) form: *a tightly fitting suit, a sweeter sounding melody.*

3. Hyphens in spelled-out numbers   Use hyphens when spelling out two-word numbers from twenty-one to ninety-nine. (See 37c for more on spelling out numbers.)

▶ **Twenty-two applicants arrived early in the morning.**

Also use a hyphen in spelled-out fractions: *two-thirds of a cup.*

4. End-of-line hyphens Most word processors either automatically hyphenate words or automatically wrap words around to the next line. Choose the latter option to avoid the strange and unacceptable word division that sometimes appears with automatic hyphenation. Do not insert a hyphen into a URL to split it across lines (see 39d).

5. Series of hyphenated prefixes Treat a series of hyphenated prefixes like this:

▶ **Many second- and third-generation Americans celebrate their origins.**

REVIEW EXERCISE FOR CHAPTER 38

Use correct spelling and hyphenation.

Correct any misspellings and hyphenation errors.

Recently, researchers who study chimpanzees have come to the suprising conclusion that groups of chimpanzees have their own traditions that can be past on to new generations of chimps. The chimps do not aquire these traditions by instinct; instead, they learn them from other chimps. When a scientific journal published analysises of chimpanzee behavior, the author revealed that the every day actions of chimpanzees in seperate areas differ in significant ways, even when the groups belong to the same subspecies. For instance, in one West African group, the chimps are often seen puting a nut on a stone and using another peice of stone to crack the nut open, a kind of behavior never observed in other groups of chimpanzees. Sceintists have also observed the chimps teaching there young the nut opening method, and chimps in other places that crack nuts differently teach their young they're own way. Researchers have therefor concluded that chimpanzees have local traditions.

Frans de Waal, who has been studing primates, wrote a book makeing the arguement that these learned behaviors should be considered kinds of culture. The word *culture* has traditionally been used to describe human behavier, but may be, he says, a new definition is needed. Considering this startlingly-new theory of chimpanzee "culture," some researchers think that humans now have an un-deniable obligation to protect the lives of all remaining wild chimpanzees rather than zeroeing in on just a few of the threatenned animals. The lost of a single group of wild chimpanzees would, they say, destroy something irreplacable, a unique culture with its own traditions and way of life.

Chapter **39**

Guidelines for Online Punctuation and Mechanics

39a Punctuation in URLs

Punctuation marks communicate essential information in Web site addresses—Uniform Resource Locators—and in e-mail addresses. Be sure to include all marks when you write an address, and if you need to spread a URL over more than one line, split it after a slash (MLA style) or before a punctuation mark. Do not split the protocol <http://>. Use angle brackets to enclose e-mail and Web addresses. Do not include any additional punctuation within the angle brackets.

▶ **The Modern Language Association, whose Web site is at <http://www.mla.org>, provides examples of documenting Web sources.**

39b Underscoring, underlining, and italics online

In an online source, URLs are hyperlinked and therefore underlined on the screen. When you write for publication on the Web, always use italics to indicate titles and other usually underlined expressions.

39c Captial letters online

Don't let the speed and informal nature of e-mail delude you into thinking that no rules or conventions apply to it. Especially in academic and business settings, e-mail messages written with no capitals for the first word of a sentence, for proper nouns, or for *I* will send readers the somewhat insulting signal that you have not bothered to check what you sent them.

Overdoing capitals is as bad as (maybe worse than) including none at all. Writing an entire message in capital letters can be perceived by readers as "shouting." If you don't want to offend readers

Online Study Center   This icon will direct you to quick reference tools, Web resources, and research guides on the Web site at http://college.hmco.com/keys.html.

in e-mail communications and online discussion groups, avoid the prolonged use of capital letters. See also 12b.

39d Hyphens in online addresses

Some e-mail addresses and URLs include hyphens, so never add a hyphen to indicate that you have split an address between lines. When an online address includes a hyphen, do not break the line at a hyphen: readers will not know whether the hyphen is part of the address. Break the line after @ or after a slash.

Technological vocabulary changes quickly. You will find both *e-mail* and *email*. The MLA prefers the hyphenated spelling, *e-mail*, but the tendency is for common words like this to move toward closing up. Whichever form you use, use it consistently.

39e Abbreviations online

Many abbreviations in the electronics world have become standard usage: *CD-ROM, RAM, HTML, PIN,* and more. In addition, the informal world of online communication leads to informal abbreviations, at least in personal e-mail messages. Abbreviations such as *BTW* ("by the way") and *TTYTT* ("to tell you the truth") are used in informal e-mail but should not appear in more formal written communications.

PART 7

Writing in Standard English: A Guide for Speakers of Other Languages, Other Englishes

ESL

Learning to write well often means learning to write for readers of many different linguistic and cultural backgrounds; it may also mean writing in more than one language and in more than one local version of a language.

Learning to write in college and professional environments can be particularly challenging for those students who did not grow up speaking Standard English. Perhaps you are an international student learning to write in English for audiences and purposes different from those you are accustomed to in your first language. Or maybe you're a recent immigrant learning to discern differences between spoken and written English. Or you may have lived your whole life in the United States but speak a language other than English—or a variety other than Standard English—at home. Even if you move fluently between your home language and Standard English when speaking, you may find that you need to discern language features in your writing that keep readers from understanding what you are trying to communicate. Part 7 is for you.

Chapter **40**

Writing across Cultures: Englishes and Editing

40a English and Englishes

At the same time as we are becoming more aware of diversity and other countries' languages and cultures, we are also experiencing an increase in the use of English. More than 380 million people speak English as their first language, and many more (estimated at more than a billion) use English as a common language spanning local dialects. They use it for special communicative, educational, and business purposes within their own communities. Given those figures, it is no surprise that English is the language most commonly used over the Internet. But it is not the whole story to emphasize the dominance of English in cyberspace. Languages are not fixed and static, and the users of English in their various locations adapt the language for their own needs, as the Circle of World English (1d) shows.

The concept of one English or a "standard" language is thus becoming more fluid, more focused on the situation and the readers than on one set of rules. Consequently, the English regarded as standard in North America is not necessarily standard in Australia, the United Kingdom, Hong Kong, Singapore, Indonesia, India, or Pakistan. Scholars see Englishes—varieties of English—in place of a monolithic English with an immutable set of rules. (See, for example, the Language and Culture box in 38a for examples of words that differ in American English and British English.)

Varieties of English spoken in different geographical locations even have their own names: Spanglish (Spanish English), African American Vernacular, Creole, and Taglish (Tagalog English, spoken in the Philippines) are examples of language varieties that have developed among multiethnic populations. In Singapore, for instance, the official languages of the multiethnic residents are Mandarin Chinese, Malay, Tamil, and English. But the English spoken by many has been adapted and appropriated to what some are now calling *Singlish,* a language meeting local needs.

An example of Singlish on a Singapore wall.

English is thus being reinvented around the world, sometimes to the dismay of academics and government officials, sometimes with the approval of citizens, who see the adaptation as an act of freedom, even rebellion. The Filipino poet Gemino Abad is reported to have claimed, "The English language is now ours. We have colonized it."

While colloquial speech is being adapted and other Englishes, including the English of the Internet, provide colorful global variations, the academic and professional worlds of writing inevitably retain links to the concept of a standard language. To reach the expectations of the largest number of readers, a sense of standard vocabulary, syntax, and grammar still prevails.

40b Difference, not deficit

Students in colleges in North America who grew up speaking another language are often called students of *English as a Second Language* (ESL), and the abbreviation is commonly used in college curricula, professional literature, and the press. However, this term is not really broad enough. Many so-called second-language students speak three or four languages besides English, depending on their lives and educational circumstances and the languages spoken at home. Along with being bilingual or multilingual, such students are frequently multicultural, equipped with all the knowledge and experience that those terms imply.

Whether your first language is a variety of English or a totally different language, it is a good idea to see your knowledge of language and culture as an advantage rather than a problem. Unlike many monolingual writers (individuals who know only one version of one language), you are able to know different cultures in an in-depth way and to switch at will among varied linguistic and rhetorical codes. Rather than having only one language, one culture, and one culturally bound type of writing, you have a broader perspective—more to think about, more to write about, more resources to draw on as you write, and far more comparisons to make among languages, writers, writing, and culture. You bring your culture with you into your writing, and as you do so, you help shape and reshape the culture of North America. Remember, too, that in many situations, the readers you write for will be culturally and linguistically diverse, not all emerging from one educational background. In formal settings, always aim to make your ideas clear to *all* readers by using Standard English, avoiding slang and jargon, and choosing a style appropriate to your subject matter.

TECH NOTE
Web Sites on Language and Writing

Many Web sites provide useful information, exercises, and other resources for multilingual students:

- **Purdue University Online Writing Lab**: ESL resources, handouts, and exercises.

- *Internet TESL Journal:* This site offers crossword puzzles and quizzes, including bilingual quizzes in several languages.

- **Capital Community College Guide to Grammar and Writing**: This site, for students whose native language is not English, provides information and quizzes on words, paragraphs, and essays. In addition, you can send in a question to the site's "Ask Grammar" section, and someone will answer it. The Grammar Logs contain questions and answers and cover interesting points.

Online Study Center **ESL** ESL Center

40c Learning from errors

Even for students who have been learning a new language or the conventions of a standard dialect for a while, errors are inevitable. Welcome and embrace your errors; study them; learn from them. Errors show language learning in progress. If you make no errors while you are learning to speak or write a new language, or the Standard version of English, perhaps you are being too careful and using only what you know to be correct. Be willing to take risks and try new words, new expressions, new combinations. That is the way to expand your repertoire.

Consider keeping a language notebook or setting up your own language blog (3a). Include any new words and unusual structures that you find as you read, write, and converse with others. In addition, use a Sentence Problem Log Sheet (see p. 352) to record errors you make. Consider why you made each error. Was it, for example, transfer from your first language, a guess, a careless mistake, or the employment of a logical but erroneous hypothesis about Standard English (such as "many verbs form the past tense with *-ed;* therefore, the past tense form of *swear* is probably *sweared*")? Analyzing the causes of errors will help you understand how to edit them and avoid them in the future. (The past tense of *swear* is *swore*.)

Readers are most likely to be disturbed by errors when the content and flow of ideas are not clear. A thoughtful, well-written essay that contains a few errors usually is preferable to a sloppy, flimsy piece of work that is grammatically flawless. Errors, however, do distract attentive readers, and you need to learn how to edit for accuracy. Chapters 41–45 address some problems faced by language learners as they grapple with academic English. Consult those chapters as you need to, along with the ESL Notes and Language and Culture boxes appearing throughout this book that address not just Standard English but cultural variations and differences. Chapters 21–29 offer help with common sentence problems faced by many writers, whether they speak one or more than one language.

40d Editing guide to multilingual transfer errors

Errors in writing in a new language can occur when you are grappling with new subject matter and difficult topics. You concentrate on ideas and clarity, but because no writer can do everything at once, you fail to concentrate on editing.

The following language guide identifies several problem areas for multilingual and ESL writers. It shows grammatical features (column 1) of specific languages (column 2) that lead to an error when transferred to English (column 3), and an edited Standard English version (column 4). Of course, the guide covers neither all linguistic problem areas nor all languages. Rather, it lists a selection, with the aim of being useful and practical. Use the guide to raise your awareness about your own and other languages.

If you think of a feature or a language that should be included in the guide, please write to the authors at the publisher's address or send a message to the publisher's Web site at <http://college.hmco .com/keys.html>. This Web site also provides links to sites specifically designed for multilingual students.

Language Guide

Language Features	Languages	Sample Transfer Errors in English	Edited Version
ARTICLES (41c–41f)			
No articles	Chinese, Japanese, Russian, Swahili, Thai, Urdu	*Sun is hot.* *I bought book.* *Computer has changed our lives.*	*The sun is hot.* *I bought a book.* *The computer has changed our lives.*
No indefinite article with profession	Arabic, French, Japanese, Korean, Vietnamese	*He is student.* *She lawyer.*	*He is a student.* *She is a lawyer.*

Language Features	Languages	Sample Transfer Errors in English	Edited Versions
Definite article with days, months, places, idioms	Arabic	*She is in the bed.* *He lives in the Peru.*	*She is in bed.* *He lives in Peru.*
Definite article used for generalization	Farsi, French, German, Greek, Portuguese, Spanish	*The photography is an art.* *The books are more expensive than the disks.*	*Photography is an art.* *Books are more expensive than disks.*
Definite article used with proper noun	French, German, Portuguese, Spanish	*The Professor Brackert teaches in Frankfurt.*	*Professor Brackert teaches in Frankfurt.*
No definite article	Hindi, Turkish	*Store on corner is closed.*	*The store on the corner is closed.*
No indefinite article	Korean (uses *one* for *a*; depends on context)	*He ran into one tree*	*He ran into a tree.*

VERBS AND VERB FORMS (42)

Language Features	Languages	Sample Transfer Errors in English	Edited Versions
Be can be omitted.	Arabic, Chinese, Greek, Russian	*India hotter than Britain.* *She working now.* *He cheerful.*	*India is hotter than Britain.* *She is working now.* *He is cheerful.*
No progressive forms	French, German, Greek, Russian	*They still discuss the problem.* *When I walked in, she slept.*	*They are still discussing the problem.* *When I walked in, she was sleeping.*
No tense inflections	Chinese, Thai, Vietnamese	*He arrive yesterday.* *When I was little, I always walk to school.*	*He arrived yesterday.* *When I was little, I always walked to school.*
No inflection for third person singular	Chinese, Japanese, Korean, Russian, Thai	*The singer have a big band.* *She work hard.*	*The singer has a big band.* *She works hard.*
Past perfect formed with *be*	Arabic	*They were arrived when I called.*	*They had arrived when I called.*
Different tense boundaries from English	Arabic, Chinese, Farsi, French	*I study here for a year.* *He has left yesterday.*	*I have been studying here for a year.* *He left yesterday.*

Language Features	Languages	Sample Transfer Errors in English	Edited Version
Different limits for passive voice	Japanese, Korean, Russian, Thai, Vietnamese	*They were stolen their luggage.*	*Their luggage was stolen.*
		My name base on Chinese characters.	*My name is based on Chinese characters.*
		The mess clean up quick.	*The mess was cleaned up quickly.*
		A miracle was happened.	*A miracle (has) happened.*
No -*ing* (gerund)/ infinitive distinction	Arabic, Chinese, Farsi, French, Greek, Portuguese, Spanish, Vietnamese	*She avoids to go.*	*She avoids going.*
		I enjoy to play tennis.	*I enjoy playing tennis.*
Infinitive not used to express purpose	Korean	*People exercise for losing weight.*	*People exercise to lose weight.*
Overuse of progressive forms	Hindi, Urd	*I am wanting to leave now.*	*I want to leave now.*

WORD ORDER AND SENTENCE STRUCTURE (43)

Verb precedes subject.	Arabic, Hebrew, Russian, Spanish (optional), Tagalog	*Good grades received every student in the class.*	*Every student in the class received good grades.*
Verb-subject order in dependent clause	French	*I knew what would propose the committee.*	*I knew what the committee would propose.*
Verb after subject and object	Bengali, German (in dependent clause), Hindi, Japanese, Korean, Turkish	*. . . (when) the teacher the money collected.*	*. . . (when) the teacher collected the money.*
Coordination favored over subordination	Arabic	Frequent use of *and* and *so*	
Relative clause or restrictive phrase premodifies.	Chinese, Japanese, Korean, Russian	*The enrolled in college student . . .*	*The student (who was) enrolled in college . . .*
		A nine-meter-high impressive monument . . .	*An impressive monument that is nine meters high . . .*
		He gave me a too difficult for me book.	*He gave me a book that was too difficult for me.*

Language Features	Languages	Sample Transfer Errors in English	Edited Version
Adverb can occur between verb and object or before verb.	French, Spanish, Urdu (before verb)	*I like very much clam chowder.* *They efficiently organized the work.*	*I like clam chowder very much.* *They organized the work efficiently.*
That clause rather than an infinitive	Arabic, French, Hindi, Russian, Spanish	*I want that you stay.* *I want that they try harder.*	*I want you to stay.* *I want them to try harder.*
Inversion of subject and verb (rare)	Chinese	*She is leaving, and so I am.*	*She is leaving, and so am I.*
Conjunctions occur in pairs.	Chinese, Farsi, Vietnamese	*Although she is rich, but she wears simple clothes.* *Even if I had money, I would also not buy that car.*	*Although she is rich, she wears simple clothes.* *Even if I had money, I would not buy that car.*
Subject (especially *it* pronoun) can be omitted.	Chinese, Italian, Japanese, Portuguese, Spanish, Thai	*Is raining.*	*It is raining.*
Commas set off a dependent clause.	German, Russian	*He knows, that we are right.*	*He knows that we are right.*
No exact equivalent of *there is/there are*	Japanese, Korean, Portuguese, Russian, Thai (adverb of place and *have*)	*This article says four reasons to eat beans.* *In the garden has many trees.*	*This article says [that] there are four reasons to eat beans.* *There are many trees in the garden.*

NOUNS, PRONOUNS, ADJECTIVES, ADVERBS (41a, 41b, 27, 28)

Personal pronouns restate subject.	Arabic, Gujarati, Spanish (optional)	*My father he lives in California.*	*My father lives in California.*
No human/ nonhuman distinction for relative pronoun (*who/which*)	Arabic, Farsi, French, Russian, Spanish, Thai	*Here is the student which you met her last week.* *The people which arrived . . .*	*Here is the student [whom] you met last week.* *The people who arrived . . .*
Pronoun object included in relative clause	Arabic, Chinese, Farsi, Hebrew	*The house [that] I used to live in it is big.*	*The house that I used to live in is big.*

Language Features	Languages	Sample Transfer Errors in English	Edited Version
No distinction between subject and object forms of some pronouns	Chinese, Gujarati, Korean, Thai	*I gave the forms to she.*	*I gave the forms to* her. Or *I gave* her *the forms.*
Nouns and adjectives have same form.	Chinese, Japanese	*She is beauty woman.* *They felt very safety on the train.*	*She is* a beautiful *woman.* *They felt very* safe *on the train.*
No distinction between *he* and *she, his* and *her*	Bengali, Farsi, Gujarati, Spanish (*his* and *her* only), Thai	*My sister dropped his purse.*	*My sister dropped* her *purse.*
No plural form after a number	Creole, Farsi	*He has two dog.*	*He has two* dogs.
No plural (or optional) forms of nouns	Chinese, Japanese, Korean, Thai	*Several good book . . .*	*Several good* books . . .
No relative pronouns	Korean	*The book is on the table is mine.*	*The book* that is *on the table is mine.*
Different perception of countable/ uncountable	Japanese, Russian, Spanish	*I bought three furnitures.* *He has red hairs.*	*I bought three* pieces of *furniture. Or I bought three* chairs. *He has* red hair.
Adjectives show number.	Russian, Spanish	*I have helpfuls friends.*	*I have* helpful *friends.*
Negative before verb	Spanish	*Jack no like meat.*	*Jack* does not *like meat.*
Double negatives used routinely	Spanish	*They don't know nothing.*	*They don't know* anything. Or *They* know *nothing.*

EXERCISE 40.1

Identify transfer errors.

From samples of your writing marked by instructors, gather samples of transfer errors that you know you need to be aware of. Use a language notebook or blog to keep a list of transfer errors that you make, with an edited version (see p. 579).

40e Editing guide to vernacular Englishes

Many of the varieties of English shown in the Circle of English on page 17 differ from Standard American English in their use of words and grammatical conventions. Speakers of these Englishes have to do a kind of translating, called *code switching*, when they speak or write in Standard English, just as we all switch codes between levels of formality when we interact with different audiences. Consider, for example, situations in which you might say, "'Sup?" ("What's up?") rather than "Good morning." As David Crystal, author of *The Stories of English*, points out, "We need to be very sure of our ground (or very drunk) before we say, 'Yo, Officer.'"

The following table shows some of the common features that confront speakers of African American Vernacular (AAV), Creole, and other varieties of English in North America when they move back and forth between their home culture and the academic world.

Vernaculars and Standard English

Linguistic Feature of Vernacular	Example (Nonstandard)	Edited for Standard English
Omitted form of *be*	Maxine studying.	Maxine *is* studying.
Use of *be* for habitual action	Ray be working at home.	Ray *usually works* at home.
Use of *been* without *have*	I been sleeping all day.	I *have (I've)* been sleeping all day.
Omitted -*ed*	The books arrive this morning.	The books *arrived* this morning.
No -*s* ending for third person singular present tense verb	That model have a big smile.	That model *has a* big smile.
No plural form after a plural number	Jake own two dog.	Jake *owns* two *dogs.*
Verb inversion before indefinite pronoun subject	Can't nobody do that.	*Nobody can* do that.
They instead of possessive *their*	The players grabbed they gear.	The players grabbed *their* gear.
Hisself instead of *himself*	That musician promote hisself too much.	That musician *promotes himself* too much.
Personal pronoun restates subject	His instructor, she strict.	His instructor *is* strict.

Linguistic Feature of Vernacular	Example (Nonstandard)	Edited for Standard English
No apostrophe + -s for possessive	*She my brother wife.*	*She is my brother's wife.*
It used in place of *there*	*It's a gate at the entrance.*	*There is (There's) a gate at the entrance.*
Double negative	*You don't know nothing.*	*You don't know anything./You know nothing.*

Chapter **41**

Nouns and Articles

41a Categories of nouns

Nouns in English fall into various categories.

Proper or common A *proper noun* names a unique person, place, or thing and begins with a capital letter: *Walt Whitman, Lake Superior, Grand Canyon, Vietnam Veterans Memorial, Tuesday*. A *common noun* names a general class of persons, places, or things and begins with a lowercase letter: *bicycle, furniture, plan, daughter, home, happiness*.

Countable or uncountable common nouns A *countable noun* can have a number before it (*one, two,* and so on) and has a plural form. Countable nouns frequently add *-s* to indicate the plural: *picture, pictures; plan, plans*. Use singular countable nouns after *a, an, the, this, that,* and singular quantity words (26i). Use plural countable nouns after *the, these, those,* and plural quantity words (26i).

An *uncountable noun* cannot be directly counted. It has no plural form: *furniture, advice, information*. Use uncountable nouns after *the, this, that,* and certain quantity words (26i and 41b).

Common Nouns

Countable	Uncountable
machine, engine (machines, engines)	machinery
tool, hammer (tools, hammers)	equipment

Online Study Center   This icon will direct you to quick reference tools, Web resources, and research guides on the Web site at http://college.hmco.com/keys.html.

Countable	Uncountable
bicycle, ship (bicycles, ships)	transportation
chair, desk (chairs, desks)	furniture
description, fact (descriptions, facts)	information
necklace, earring (necklaces, earrings)	jewelry
view, scene (views, scenes)	scenery
tip, suggestion (tips, suggestions)	advice
exercise, essay (exercises, essays)	homework

41b Uncountable nouns

Some nouns are usually uncountable and are listed as such in a language learners' dictionary such as *The American Heritage ESL Dictionary*. Learn the most common uncountable nouns and note the ones that end in *-s* but are nevertheless singular:

> *A mass made up of parts:* clothing, equipment, furniture, garbage, homework, information, jewelry, luggage, machinery, money, scenery, traffic, transportation
>
> *Abstract concepts:* advice, courage, education, fun, happiness, health, honesty, information, knowledge, success
>
> *Natural substances:* air, blood, cotton, hair, heat, ice, rice, sunshine, water, wood, wool
>
> *Diseases:* diabetes, influenza, measles
>
> *Games:* chess, checkers, soccer, tennis
>
> *Subjects of study:* biology, economics, history, physics

Follow these guidelines when using an uncountable noun:

1. Do not use a number, a plural word like *these* and *those,* or a plural quantity word (such as *many* or *several*) before an uncountable noun. An uncountable noun has no plural form.

   > ► She gave me ~~several~~ information~~s~~. *(some)*

2. Do not use an uncountable noun with *a* or *an.*

   > ► Puerto Rico has ~~a~~ lovely scenery.

   Exceptions to this rule occur when the phrase *a little* or *a great deal of* is used.

   > ► He has a great deal of antique furniture.

   > ► She has a little modern furniture.

3. Always use a singular verb with an uncountable noun subject.

   ▶ Their advice ~~are~~ useful.

   is

4. Use the following before an uncountable noun:

   ■ no article (called the *zero article*) for a generalization: *Information is free.*

   ■ a singular word such as *this* or *that: This equipment is jammed.*

   ■ a possessive (see 27b): *His advice was useless.*

   ■ a quantity word or phrase for nonspecific reference (see pp. 438–439 in 26i): *They gave us some advice. They gave us a little advice.*

   ■ *the* for specific reference (41d): *The information we found was all wrong.*

5. Give an uncountable noun a countable sense—that is, indicate a quantity of it—by adding a word or phrase that indicates quantity. The noun itself will always remain singular: three pieces of *furniture*, two items of *information*, many pieces of *advice*.

6. Take into account the fact that the concept of countability varies across languages. Japanese, for example, makes no distinction between countable and uncountable nouns. In French, Spanish, and Chinese, the word for *furniture* is a countable noun; in English, it is not. In Russian, the word for *hair* is countable and is used in the plural.

7. Examine the context. Be aware that some nouns can be countable in one context and uncountable in another.

   GENERAL CLASS (UNCOUNTABLE)

   He loves *chocolate*. [All chocolate, in whatever form]

   Time flies.

   We all hang on to *life*.

   He has red *hair*.

   A COUNTABLE ITEM OR ITEMS

   She gave him *a chocolate*. [One piece of candy from a box]

   She then gave him *three chocolates*.

   They are having *a good time*.

   Try it *several times*.

   He is leading *a hedonistic life*.

   A cat is said to have *nine lives*.

   There is *a long gray hair* on her pillow.

SPECIFIC REFERENCE

The chocolate you gave me is delicious. [Specific chocolate]

The time is ripe for action.

The life he is leading is hedonistic.

The hair in his wallet is from his son's first haircut.

KEY POINTS
What to Use before an Uncountable Noun: Summary Chart

YES

Zero article	Furniture is expensive.
This, that	*This* furniture is tacky.
A possessive pronoun: *my, his, their,* and so on	*Their* furniture is modern.
Quantity word: *some, any, much, less, more, most, a little, a great deal (of), all, other* (26j)	She has bought *some* new furniture.

NO

A/an	The room needs ~~a~~ new furniture.
Each, every, another	All furniture ~~Every furniture~~ should be practical.
These, those	That furniture is ~~Those furniture are~~ elegant.
Numerals: *one, two, three,* etc.	two pieces of furniture They bought ~~two furnitures.~~
Plural quantity words: *several, many, a few*	a little furniture She took only ~~a few furniture~~ with her to her new apartment.

EXERCISE 41.1
Use uncountable nouns correctly.

Correct any errors in the use of countable and uncountable nouns. Remember to check for subject-verb agreement when correcting errors.

EXAMPLE:

                paper   *pieces*   *was*
Until about 1810, ~~papers~~ made from ~~piece~~ of cloth ~~were~~ used for
printing books.

1. In most cases, the page of books made before 1840 is still flexible and well preserved.

2. Between 1840 and 1950, however, publishers began to use less expensive paper that was made from wood pulps instead of from cloth.

3. To turn wood into paper, manufacturers added acidic chemicals that could break down and soften the wood. The pages created from these paper still contained some of the acid.

4. The pages of many books printed between 1840 and 1950 are beginning to crumble into dusts because acid is eating away the wood fiber in the pages.

5. The Library of Congress, which owns a huge collection of books, has begun to soak books made with acid paper in chemical bath to remove any remaining acid from the pages; books treated in this way can last for another several hundred years.

41c Basic rules for articles

Articles are *a, an,* and *the.*

1. Use *the* whenever a reference to a common noun is specific and unique for both writer and reader (see 41d).

   ▶ **He loves the museum that Rem Koolhaas designed.** [We know that the museum he loves is the specific one that Koolhaas designed.]

2. Do not use *a* or *an* with a plural countable noun.

   ▶ **They cited ̶a̶ reliable surveys.**

3. Do not use *a* or *an* with an uncountable noun.

   ▶ **He gave ̶a̶ helpful advice.**

4. Use *a* before a consonant sound: *a bird, a house, a blog.* Use *an* before a vowel sound: *an egg, an ostrich, an hour, an ugly vase.* Take special care with the sounds associated with the letters *h* and *u,* which can

have either a consonant or a vowel sound: *a housing project, an honest man, a unicorn, an uprising.*

5. To make a generalization about a countable noun, do one of the following:

- Use the plural form: *Lions are majestic.*
- Use the singular with *a* or *an*: *A lion is a majestic animal.*
- Use the singular with *the* to denote a classification: *The lion is a majestic animal.*

6. A countable singular noun can never stand alone, so make sure that a countable singular noun is preceded by an article or by a demonstrative pronoun (*this, that*), a number, a singular word expressing quantity, or a possessive pronoun.

   A (Every, That, One, Her) nurse
   ▶ ~~Nurse~~ has a difficult job.
          ^

7. In general, though there are many exceptions, use no article with a singular proper noun (*Mount Everest*), and use *the* with a plural proper noun (*the Himalayas*). See 41f for more examples.

41d *The* for a specific reference

When you write a common noun that both you and your readers know refers to one or more specific persons, places, things, or concepts, use the article *the*. You can make a specific reference to something outside the text or inside it.

Specific reference outside the text   References to specific people, places, things, or concepts outside the text point to something unique that both the writer and readers will know. In the following sentences, readers will not wonder which earth, sun, moon, door, or dog the writer means.

- ▶ I study *the* **earth, the sun, and the moon.** [The ones in our solar system]

- ▶ **She closed** *the* **door.** [The door of the room she was in]

- ▶ **Her husband took** *the* **dog out for a walk.** [The dog belonging to the couple, not any other dog]

Specific reference inside the text   A reference to a person, place, thing, or concept can also be made specific by identifying it within the text.

► *The* kitten that her daughter brought home had a distinctive black patch above one eye. [The specific kitten is the one that was brought home.]

► Her daughter found *a* kitten. When they were writing a lost-and-found ad that night, they realized that *the* kitten had a distinctive black patch above one eye. [The second mention is to a specific kitten identified earlier—the one her daughter had found.]

► He bought *the most expensive* bicycle in the store. [A superlative makes a reference to one specific item.]

EXERCISE 41.2

Use articles, including *the*, correctly.

In each of the following sentences, correct any errors in article use.

EXAMPLE:

Many inactive people suffer from ~~the~~ depression.

1. Many scientific studies have proved that exercise helps the people sleep better and lose a weight.
2. A active lifestyle seems to improve not only a person's health but also his or her mood.
3. Endorphins, which are chemicals in human brain that are linked to feelings of well-being, increase when people get the enough exercise.
4. People who do not exercise are twice as likely as active people to suffer a symptoms of depression.
5. However, the scientists are not certain whether people do not exercise because they are depressed or whether they are depressed because they do not exercise.

41e Which article? Four basic questions

Multilingual writers often have difficulty choosing among the articles *a, an,* and *the* and the *zero article* (no article at all). Languages vary greatly in their representation of the concepts conveyed by English articles (see 40d, Editing guide to multilingual transfer errors).

The Key Points box lists four questions to ask about a noun to decide whether to use an article and, if so, which article to use.

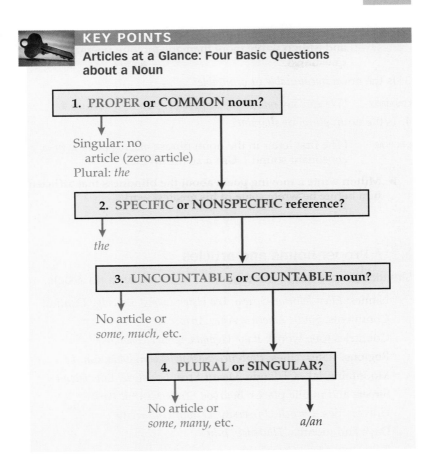

KEY POINTS

Articles at a Glance: Four Basic Questions about a Noun

1. **PROPER or COMMON noun?**

Singular: no
    article (zero article)
Plural: *the*

2. **SPECIFIC or NONSPECIFIC reference?**

the

3. **UNCOUNTABLE or COUNTABLE noun?**

No article or
some, much, etc.

4. **PLURAL or SINGULAR?**

No article or
some, many, etc.   *a/an*

You can use the questions to decide which article, if any, to use with the noun *poem* as you consider the following sentence:

▶ **Milton wrote __?__ moving poem about the blindness that afflicted him before he wrote some of his greatest works.**

1. Is the noun (*poem*) a *proper* noun or a *common* noun?

COMMON   **Go to question 2.**

2. Does the common noun refer to a *specific* person, place, thing, or idea known to both writer and readers as unique, or is the reference *nonspecific*?

NONSPECIFIC [There is more than one "moving poem" in literature, and Milton wrote more than one moving poem.] **Go to question 3.**

3. Is the noun *uncountable* or *countable*?

COUNTABLE [We can say *one poem, two poems*.] **Go to question 4.**

4. Is the noun *plural* or *singular*?

SINGULAR [The first letter in the noun phrase *moving poem* is *m*, a consonant sound.] **Use *a* as the article.**

▶ Milton wrote *a* moving poem about the blindness that afflicted him before he wrote some of his greatest works.

41f Proper nouns and articles

Singular proper nouns: As a general rule, use with no article.

Names: *Ellen Johnson-Sirleaf, Lee Hsien Loong, Edwidge Danticat*
Continents: *South America, Asia, Africa*
Countries (one word): *Italy, Uganda, Greece, Thailand*
Regions, states, cities: *Provence, Saskatchewan, Ohio, Cairo*
Mountains, lakes, islands: *Mount Etna, Lake Erie, Ellis Island*
Streets and public places: *Bourbon Street, Central Park*
Universities: *Cornell University, Oxford University*
Days and months: *Thursday, July*
Religions: *Islam, Catholicism*

There are, however, many exceptions, which you should note in your language notebook or blog (p. 579) as you read.

EXCEPTIONS: SINGULAR PROPER NOUNS WITH *THE*

Proper nouns with a common noun and of as part of the name: *the University of Texas, the Fourth of July, the Museum of Modern Art, the Statue of Liberty*

Highways: *the New Jersey Turnpike, the Santa Monica Freeway*

Buildings: *the Eiffel Tower, the Vertical Campus, the Empire State Building*

Bridges: *the Golden Gate Bridge, the Brooklyn Bridge, the Millan Bridge*

Hotels and museums: *the Hilton Hotel, the Frick Museum, the Louvre*

Countries named with a phrase: *the Dominican Republic, the People's Republic of China*

Parts of the globe and geographical areas: *the North Pole, the West, the Riviera*

Seas, oceans, gulfs, rivers, and deserts: *the Mediterranean Sea, the Atlantic Ocean, the Persian Gulf, the Yangtze River, the Mojave Desert*

Historical periods and events: *the Enlightenment, the October Revolution*

Groups: *the Taliban, the Chicago Seven, the IRA, the Mafia*

Titles: *the President of the United States, the Emperor of Japan*

Plural proper nouns: Use with *the*   Examples are *the United States, the Himalayas, the Philippines, the Chinese* (people), *the Italians.*

REVIEW EXERCISE FOR CHAPTER 41

Use nouns and articles correctly.

In the following passage, correct any errors in article use.

Name of Emmanual "Toto" Constant may not be familiar to everyone in United States, but to Haitian immigrants in this country, he is familiar and controversial figure. Constant, the son of an powerful Haitian military leader, was raised as a aristocrat in the impoverished Caribbean nation. In 1991, he formed political party known as FRAPH. Purpose of FRAPH was to fight against return of exiled president Jean-Bertrande Aristide, whom most poor Haitians supported as a their leader. FRAPH men, armed with the machine guns and machetes, roamed country, terrorizing Aristide supporters with torture, rape, and murder. Constant encouraged Haitians to fear him, claiming that he had the voodoo powers. Observers from United Nations said that FRAPH had been "linked to assassinations and rapes," and a American military official in Haiti warned that FRAPH was turning into "a sort of Mafia."

Even after a American peacekeeping force helped Aristide return to power in the 1994, Toto Constant remained the powerful man in Haiti. He apparently cooperated with an American intelligence officers, revealing details about his group's terrorist activities. Somehow, Toto Constant got out of Haiti and migrated to the New York, where he lived in an Haitian immigrant neighborhood. Many of his neighbors recognized a face of Toto Constant.

In 2000, the most Haitian immigrants in New York wanted Toto Constant deported to Haiti. A trials were being held there to determine if he and other FRAPH members were guilty of the murder and torture. Although Constant did not return to Haiti, the Haitian court convicted him of murder and sentenced him to the life imprisonment. However, Constant remained free, and United States Immigration and Naturalization Service did not deport him. In 2001, after terror attacks on New York City, Haitians in a city demanded that the United States stop sheltering man who had terrorized his own people. Perhaps Constant does have the powerful connections to Central Intelligence Agency, as some Haitian immigrants believe, for United States took no action against him. As 2001 ended, Constant was still the free man.

Chapter **42**

Verbs and Verb Forms

A clause needs a complete verb consisting of one of the five verb forms (25a) and any necessary auxiliaries. Some verb forms cannot serve as the complete verb of a clause; an *-ing* form, an infinitive (*to* + base form), and a past participle (ending in *-ed* for a regular verb) can never function as the complete verb of a clause. Because readers get so much information from verbs, they have a relatively low level of tolerance for error, so make sure you edit with care and use auxiliary verbs whenever necessary.

42a The *be* auxiliary

Inclusion (see also 25d)   The *be* auxiliary must be included in a verb phrase in English, though in languages such as Chinese, Russian, and Arabic it can be omitted.

are
▶ They studying this evening.

been
▶ They have studying since dinner.

Sequence (see also 25d) What comes after a *be* auxiliary? You have two options:

1. The *-ing* form follows a form of *be* in the active voice.

▶ He *is sweeping* the floor.

2. The past participle follows a form of *be* in the passive voice.

▶ The floor *was swept* yesterday.

42b Modal auxiliary verbs: form and meaning

The nine modal auxiliary verbs are *will, would, can, could, shall, should, may, might,* and *must.* Note the following three important points.

1. The modals do not change form.
2. The modals never add an *-s* ending.
3. Modals are always followed by a base form without *to*: *could go, should ask, must arrive, might have* seen, *would be sleeping.*

▶ The committee must ~~to~~ vote tomorrow.

▶ The proposal might improves the city.

▶ The residents could disapproved.

Meanings of Modal Verbs

Meaning	Present and Future	Past
1. Intention	*will, shall*	*would*
	She *will* explain. [*Shall* is used mostly in questions: *Shall I buy that big green ceramic horse?*]	She said that she *would* explain.
2. Ability	*can (am/is/are able to)*	*could (was/were able to)*
	He *can* cook well. [Do not use *can* and *able to* together: *He is able to cook well.*]	He *could* not read until he was eight. [He *was* not *able to* read until he was eight.]

Meanings of Modal Verbs

Meaning	Present and Future	Past
3. Permission	*may, might, can, could*	*might, could*
	May I refer to Auden again? [*Might* or *could* is more tentative.]	Her instructor said she *could* use a dictionary.
4. Polite question	*would, could*	
	Would readers please indulge me for a moment?	
	Could you try not to read ahead?	
5. Speculation	*would, could, might*	*would* or *could* or *might* + *have* + past participle
	If he had more talent, he *could* become a professional pianist. [See also 25f.]	If I had studied, I *might have* passed the test.
6. Advisability	*should*	*should* + *have* + past participle
	You *should* go home and rest.	You *should have* taken your medication. [Implied here is "but you did not."]
7. Necessity (stronger than *should*)	*must* (or *have to*)	*had to* + base form
	Applicants *must* apply for a mortgage.	Theo van Gogh *had to* support his brother.
8. Prohibition	*must* + *not*	
	Participants *must not* leave until all the questions have been answered.	
9. Expectation	*should*	*should* + *have* + past participle
	The author *should* receive a check soon.	You *should have* received your check a week ago.

Meanings of Modal Verbs

Meaning	Present and Future	Past
10. Possibility	*may, might*	*might* + *have* + past participle
	The technician *may* be working on the problem now.	She *might* already *have* revised the ending.
11. Logical assumption	*must*	*must* + *have* + past participle
	She's late; she *must* be stuck in traffic.	She *must have* taken the wrong route.
12. Repeated past action		*would* (or *used to*) + base form
		When I was a child, I *would* spend hours drawing.

EXERCISE 42.1

Use the *be* auxiliary and modal auxiliary verbs correctly.

Correct any errors in the use of the *be* auxiliary and modal auxiliaries.

EXAMPLE:

          are   *should*

Young people who ʌlearning to play an instrument ~~would~~ ʌ practice if they want to improve.

    Most people believe that musicians must to have talent in order to succeed. However, a 1998 study by British psychologist John Sloboda may indicates that the number of hours spent practicing affects musical ability more than inborn talent does. The study included musicians aged ten to sixteen years, from both public and private schools. Sloboda investigated how much each young musician practiced, whether parents and teachers involved in helping each musician improve, and how well each student scored on the British national music examination. Young musicians who had practicing most frequently were most successful on the exam; students whose parents and teachers working closely with them also received high scores. After looking at the exam results, Sloboda cannot help noticing that the students with the highest scores practiced eight hundred times more than the students with the lowest scores. Sloboda believes that individual differences in musical ability would be related to the amount students practice and the amount of support they get from teachers and parents. According to Sloboda's research, even people who do not believe they have musical talent became excellent musicians if they practiced hard enough.

42c Infinitives after verbs and adjectives

Some verbs are followed by an infinitive (*to* + base form or base form alone). Some predicate adjectives also occur with an infinitive. Such combinations are highly idiomatic. You need to learn each one individually as you find it in your reading.

Verb + infinitive

> V   ⌐ inf ⌐
> ▶ His father *wanted to rule* the family.

These verbs are commonly followed by an infinitive (*to* + base form):

agree	choose	fail	offer	refuse
ask	claim	hope	plan	venture
beg	decide	manage	pretend	want
bother	expect	need	promise	wish

Note any differences between English and your native language. For example, the Spanish word for *refuse* is followed by the equivalent of an *-ing* form.

>   *to criticize*
> ▶ He refused ~~criticizing~~ the system.
>   ^

Position of a negative   In a verb + infinitive pattern, the position of the negative affects meaning. Note the difference in meaning that the position of a negative (*not, never*) can create.

> ▶ He did *not* decide to buy a new car. His wife did.

> ▶ He decided *not* to buy a new car. His wife was disappointed.

Verb + noun or pronoun + infinitive   Some verbs are followed by a noun or pronoun and then an infinitive. See also 27a for a pronoun used before an infinitive.

>   V   pron. ⌐ inf ⌐
> ▶ The librarian *advised them to use* a better database.

Verbs that follow this pattern are *advise, allow, ask, cause, command, convince, encourage, expect, force, help, need, order, persuade, remind, require, tell, urge, want, warn.*

Spanish and Russian use a *that* clause after verbs like *want.* In English, however, *want* is followed by an infinitive.

▶ **Rose wanted ~~that~~ her son ~~would~~ become a doctor.**

(inserted above: *to* before become)

Make, let,* and *have   After these verbs, use a noun or pronoun and a base form of the verb (without *to*).

▶ **He *made his son practice* for an hour.**

▶ **They *let us leave* early.**

▶ **She *had her daughter wash* the car.**

But note the past participle form of the verb in the corresponding passive voice structure.

▶ **She usually *has the car washed* once a month.**

Adjective + infinitive   Some predicate adjectives are followed by an infinitive. The filler subject *it* often occurs with this structure.

infinitive

▶ **It is dangerous to hike alone in the woods.**

Adjectives Followed by Infinitive

anxious	(in)advisable	sorry
dangerous	likely	(un)fair
eager	lucky	(un)just
essential	powerless	(un)kind
foolish	proud	(un)necessary
happy	right	wrong
(im)possible	silly	

For the adjectives *easy, difficult,* and *hard,* see 45f.

42d   Verbs followed by an -*ing* verb form used as a noun

▶ I *can't help laughing* at Jon Stewart's *The Daily Show.*

The *-ing* form of a verb used as a noun is known as a *gerund*. The verbs that are systematically followed by an *-ing* form make up a relatively short and learnable list.

admit	discuss	practice
appreciate	dislike	recall
avoid	enjoy	resist
be worth	finish	risk
can't help	imagine	suggest
consider	keep	tolerate
delay	miss	
deny	postpone	

► We considered ~~to invite~~ his parents.
        inviting ^

► Most people dislike ~~to hear~~ cell phones at concerts.
             hearing ^

Note that a negative comes between the verb and the *-ing* form:

► During their vacation, they enjoy *not* getting up early every day.

42e Verbs followed by either an infinitive or an *-ing* verb form

Some verbs can be followed by either an infinitive or an *-ing* verb form (a gerund) with almost no discernible difference in meaning: *begin, continue, hate, like, love, start.*

► She loves *cooking.*   ► She loves *to cook.*

The infinitive and the *-ing* form of a few verbs (*forget, remember, try, stop*), however, signal different meanings:

► He remembered *to mail* the letter. [an intention]

► He remembered *mailing* the letter. [a past act]

42f *-ing* and *-ed* verb forms used as adjectives

Both the present participle (*-ing* verb form) and the past participle (ending in *-ed* in regular verbs) can function as adjectives (see 25a and

25h). Each form has a different meaning: the *-ing* adjective indicates that the word modified produces an effect; the past participle adjective indicates that the word modified has an effect produced on it.

▶ The *boring* **cook served baked beans yet again.** [The cook produces boredom. Everyone is tired of baked beans.]

▶ The *bored* **cook yawned as she scrambled eggs.** [The cook felt the emotion of boredom as she did the cooking, but the eggs could still be appreciated.]

Produces An Effect	Has An Effect Produced On It
amazing	amazed
amusing	amused
annoying	annoyed
boring	bored
confusing	confused
depressing	depressed
disappointing	disappointed
embarrassing	embarrassed
exciting	excited
interesting	interested
satisfying	satisfied
shocking	shocked
surprising	surprised
worrying	worried

Note: Do not drop the *-ed* ending from a past participle. Sometimes in speech it blends with a following *t* or *d* sound, but in writing the *-ed* ending must be included.

▶ I was surprise~d~ **to see her wild outfit.**

▶ The researchers were ~~worry~~ *worried* **that the results were contaminated.**

See also 25h.

REVIEW EXERCISE FOR CHAPTER 42
Use correct verbs and verb forms.

In the following passage, correct any errors in verbs and verb forms.

Can money makes people happy? A well-known proverb says, "Money can't buy happiness," but some people probably would to agree that money is important for a happy life. A survey by Andrew Oswald and Jonathan Gardner of the University of Warwick in England has investigating the connection between money and happiness for eight years. The results are not surprised. If people suddenly get money that they not expecting—from the lottery, for example—they generally feel more satisfying with their lives.

In general, according to the study, receiving about $75,000 must mean the difference between being fairly happy and being very happy. However, people who admitted to be miserable before they had money needed to get $1.5 million before they considered themselves happy. But Oswald and Gardner advise to recognize that the study is not finished. They not admit knowing whether the happiness from receiving unexpected money lasts for a long time.

People who do not expect getting a large amount of money can find other reasons not to despair. The researchers say that money is not the most important factor in whether a person is happy or not. People who married are happier than those who are not: the researchers estimate that a lasting marriage makes the partners as happy as an extra $100,000 a year can. Perhaps look-ing for love is as important as trying to make—or win—a large amount of money.

Chapter **43**

Word Order and Sentence Structure

Languages structure the information in sentences in many ways. For more on sentence structure, see 21c and chapter 24.

43a Inclusion of a subject

In some languages, a subject can be omitted. In English, you must include a subject in every clause, even just a filler subject such as *it*. Sometimes the subject follows the verb, and the clause begins with the adverb *there*.

Online Study Center   This icon will direct you to quick reference tools, Web resources, and research guides on the Web site at http://college.hmco.com/keys.html.

▶ When the director's business partners lost money, ^there^ were immediate effects on the share prices.

▶ He went bankrupt because ^it^ was too easy to borrow money.

Do not use *it* to point to a long subject that follows.

▶ We can say that ~~it~~ (does not matter) the historical period of

the society.

43b Order of sentence elements

Expressions of time and place   Put adverbs and adverb phrases of time and place at the beginning or end of a clause, not between the verb and its direct object.

▶ The quiz show host congratulated |many times| the winner.

Descriptive adjective phrases   Put a descriptive adjective phrase after, not before, the noun it modifies.

▶ I would go to |known only to me| places.

Order of subject, verb, object   Languages differ in the order of appearance of the subject (S), verb (V), and direct object (DO) in a sentence. In English, the most commonly occurring sentence pattern is S + V + DO ("Children like candy"). See also 21c.

▶ ~~Good grades received every~~ ^Every^ student in the class ^received good grades^.

43c Direct and indirect objects

Some verbs—such as *give, send, show, tell, teach, find, sell, ask, offer, pay, pass,* and *hand*—can be followed by both a direct object and an indirect object. The indirect object is the person or thing to whom or to which, or for whom or for which, something is done. It follows the verb and precedes the direct object (21c).

```
       ┌── IO ──┐ ┌── DO ──┐
```
▶ He gave his mother some flowers.

```
      IO  ┌── DO ──┐
      /
```
▶ He gave her some flowers.

An indirect object can be replaced with a prepositional phrase that *follows* the direct object.

```
       ┌── DO ──┐  prepositional phrase
                   ┌──────────────┐
```
▶ He gave some flowers to his mother.

Some verbs—such as e*xplain, describe, say, mention,* and *open*—are never followed by an indirect object. However, they can be followed by a direct object and a prepositional phrase that begins with *to* or *for.*

> to me
▶ She explained ~~me~~ the election process.

> to us
▶ He described ~~us~~ the menu.

Note that *tell,* but not *say,* can take an indirect object.

> told
▶ She ~~said~~ him the secret.

EXERCISE 43.1

Correct errors in inclusion of a subject, order of elements, direct and indirect objects.

Correct any errors in the inclusion of a subject, in the order of elements, and in the use of direct and indirect objects. Some sentences may be correct.

EXAMPLE:

In the United States, more people are having ~~every year~~ plastic
> every year   there
surgery even though are sometimes side effects from the surgery.

1. Cosmetic surgery had in the past a stigma, but now many people consider changing their appearance surgically.

2. In addition, the price of such surgery was once high, but it has declined in recent years.

3. In 2000, 7.4 million people had for one reason or another cosmetic surgery.

4. Were 370,000 African Americans among those 7.4 million patients, and African Americans represent a growing percentage of wanting plastic surgery people.

5. Cosmetic surgery gives to some people an improved self-image.

6. However, can be drawbacks to changing one's appearance.

7. Psychologists are concerned that some African American women reject their African features because they accept the most commonly seen in magazines standards of beauty.

8. Such women might say, for example, that it is a universal standard of beauty a narrow nose.

9. Some middle-class African Americans may also consider plastic surgery when they see that certain African American celebrities have changed their features.

10. Many psychologists say a patient considering cosmetic surgery that beauty comes from inside.

43d Direct and indirect (reported) quotations and questions

In a direct quotation or direct question, the exact words used by the speaker are enclosed in quotation marks. In a reported quotation or indirect question, the writer reports what the speaker said, and quotation marks are not used. Changes also occur in pronouns, time expressions, and verb tenses (25j).

direct quotation
▶ He said, "I have lost my notebook."

indirect quotation
▶ He said that he had lost his notebook.

direct question
▶ He asked, "Have you seen it?"

indirect question
▶ He asked if we had seen it.

Direct and indirect quotations   Usually you must make several changes when you report a direct quotation as an indirect quotation and use an introductory verb in the past tense. You will do this often when you write college papers and report the views of others. Avoid shifts from direct to indirect quotations (24d).

Direct and Indirect Quotations

Change	Direct/ Indirect Quotation	Example	Explanation
Punctuation and tense	Direct	The young couple said, "The price *is* too high."	Exact words within quotation marks
	Indirect	The young couple said that the price *was* too high.	No quotation marks; tense change (21e)
Pronoun and tense	Direct	He insisted, "*I understand* the figures."	First person pronoun and present tense
	Indirect	He insisted that *he understood* the figures.	Change to third person pronoun; tense change
Command to statement	Direct	"Cancel the payment," her husband said.	
	Indirect	Her husband *told* her *to* cancel the payment.	Verb (*tell, instruct*) + *to*
Expressions of time and place and tense	Direct	The bankers said, "*We will* work on *this* deal *tomorrow*."	
	Indirect	The bankers said *they would* work on *that* deal the next day.	Expressions of time and place not related to speaker's perspective; tense change (21e); change to third person pronoun
Colloquial to formal	Direct	The clients said, "Well, no thanks; *we won't* wait."	
	Indirect	The clients thanked the bankers but said *they would not* wait.	Spoken words and phrases omitted or rephrased; also a tense change (21e)

Direct and indirect questions   When a direct question is reported indirectly, it loses the word order of a question (v + s) and the question mark. Sometimes changes in tense are necessary (see also 21e).

DIRECT QUESTION	The buyer asked, "*Are* the goods ready to be shipped?"

INDIRECT QUESTION	The buyer asked if the goods *were* ready to be shipped.

DIRECT QUESTION	The boss asked, "What *are* they doing?"

INDIRECT QUESTION	The boss asked what they *were* doing.

DIRECT QUESTION	"Why *did* they *send* a letter instead of a fax?" her secretary asked.

INDIRECT QUESTION	Her secretary asked why they [*had*] *sent* a letter instead of a fax.

Use only a question word such as *why* or the words *if* or *whether* to introduce an indirect question. Do not use *that* as well.

▶ Her secretary asked ~~that~~ why they sent a letter instead of a fax.

Direct and Indirect Questions

	Introductory Word	Auxiliary Verb	Subject	Auxiliary Verb	Main Verb and Rest of Clause
DIRECT	What	are	they		thinking?
INDIRECT	Nobody knows what	are	they		thinking.
DIRECT	Where	does	he		work?
INDIRECT	I can't remember where		he		works.

Direct and Indirect Questions

	Introductory Word	Auxiliary Verb	Subject	Auxiliary Verb	Main Verb and Rest of Clause
DIRECT	Why	did	she		write that poem?
INDIRECT	The poet does not reveal why		she		wrote that poem.
DIRECT		Have	the diaries	been	published yet?
INDIRECT	The Web site does not say if (whether)		the diaries	have been	published yet.
DIRECT		Did	the space program		succeed?
INDIRECT	It is not clear if		the space program		succeeded.

EXERCISE 43.2
Rewrite direct speech as reported speech.

Rewrite the following sentences as indirect (reported) speech, making any necessary changes. In each case, use the given tag followed by *that, if,* or a question word.

EXAMPLE

"The soup is too spicy." (She complained)

She complained that the soup was too spicy.

1. "I cannot abide such pretentious prose." (The critic announced)
2. "Who is in charge?" (The mayor wanted to know)
3. "What is the square root of 2209?" (The contestant cannot work out)
4. "The economy will rebound." (The broker predicted)
5. "Will I lose all my savings?" (Investors constantly wonder)
6. "I understand the problems." (The candidate assured everyone)

7. "Who knows the answer?" (The game-show host asked)
8. "We will leave early tomorrow." (The guests hinted)
9. "Did my sweater shrink in the wash?" (Her son asked)
10. "We are going to a new French restaurant this evening." (The committee members said)

43e Dependent clauses with *although* and *because*

In some languages, a subordinating conjunction (such as *although* or *because*) can be used along with a coordinating conjunction (*but, so*) or a transitional expression (*however, therefore*) in the same sentence. In English, only one is used.

NO	*Although* he loved his father, *but* he did not have much opportunity to spend time with him.
POSSIBLE REVISIONS	*Although* he loved his father, he did not have much opportunity to spend time with him.
	He loved his father, *but* he did not have much opportunity to spend time with him.

NO	*Because* she had been trained in the church, *therefore* she was sensitive to the idea of audience.
POSSIBLE REVISIONS	*Because* she had been trained in the church, she was sensitive to the idea of audience.
	She had been trained in the church, *so* she was sensitive to the idea of audience.
	She had been trained in the church; *therefore*, she was sensitive to the idea of audience.

See 31e for the punctuation of transitional expressions.

43f Unnecessary pronouns

Do not restate the simple subject of a sentence as a pronoun. See also 24i.

▶ Visitors to the Statue of Liberty ~~they~~ have worn the steps down.

▶ The adviser who told me about dyslexia ~~he~~ is a man I will never forget.

In a relative clause introduced by *whom, which,* or *that*, do not include a pronoun that the relative pronoun has replaced. See also 29f.

▶ The house that I lived in ~~it~~ for ten years has been sold.

REVIEW EXERCISE FOR CHAPTER 43

Use correct word order and sentence structure.

Correct any errors in word order, missing words, or sentence structure in the following passage.

Many people fear in China and Japan the number *four*. Is a good reason for this fear: in Japanese, Mandarin, and Cantonese, the word for *four* and the word for *death* are nearly identical. A study in the *British Medical Journal* suggests that cardiac patients from Chinese and Japanese backgrounds they may literally die of fear of the number four. According to the study, which looked at U.S. mortality statistics over a twenty-five-year period, Chinese and Japanese hospitalized for heart disease patients were more likely to die on the fourth day of the month. Although Chinese and Japanese cardiac patients across the country were all statistically more likely to die on that day, but the effect was strongest among Californian Chinese and Japanese patients. Is not clear why Californians are more at risk. However, one researcher suggested that because California's large Asian population includes many older people, the older generation may therefore teach to younger generations traditional beliefs.

Chinese and Japanese patients with other diseases they were no more likely to die on the fourth of the month than at any other time. White patients, whether they had heart disease or any other illness, they were no more likely to die on the supposedly unlucky thirteenth of the month than on any other day. Psychiatrist Jiang Wei of Duke University Medical School said, "She still didn't know the biological reason for the statistical effect" on Chinese and Japanese cardiac patients. David P. Phillips, the sociologist who conducted the study, said that the only explanation that makes sense is that the number four causes extra stress in Chinese and Japanese heart patients. More research may someday prove whether or not the stress on the fourth of the month it can be enough to kill.

Chapter **44**

Prepositions and Idioms

Prepositions appear in phrases with nouns and pronouns, and they also combine with adjectives and verbs in various ways. Learn the idioms one by one, as you come across them.

44a Idioms with prepositions

Learn the idiomatic uses of prepositions by writing them down in lists when you come across them in your reading. Here is a start:

IN

in July, in 2004, in the morning, in the drawer, in the closet, in Ohio, in Milwaukee, in the cookie jar, in the library stacks, singing in the rain, in the United States, in his pocket, in bed, in school, in class, in Spanish, in time (to participate in an activity), in love, the letter in the envelope

ON

on the menu, on the library shelf, on Saturday, on 9 September 2006, on Union Street, on the weekend, on the roof, a ring on her finger, an article on education, on the moon, on earth, on occasion, on time (punctual), on foot, on the couch, knock on the door, the address on the envelope

AT

at 8 o'clock, at home, at a party, at night, at work

EXERCISE 44.1

Use prepositions in their proper contexts.

In the following passage, fill in each blank space with the appropriate preposition, choosing among *in, on,* and *at.*

EXAMPLE:

People should save for retirement, but many workers resist putting money ___*in*___ the bank for their future.

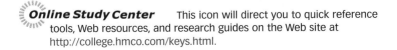

Online Study Center This icon will direct you to quick reference tools, Web resources, and research guides on the Web site at http://college.hmco.com/keys.html.

Everyone hopes to retire _____ some time _____ the future. However, many people fail to invest for retirement, spending most of the money they earn _____ everyday expenses and luxuries. The field of behavioral economics tries to explain why people do not always make rational plans to save for the future.

Behavioral economists also work to find ways to convince people to save money and to get _____ a schedule that will allow them to retire. Although most people are reluctant to decrease the amount of money that is _____ their take-home pay, employers can often persuade workers to promise _____ advance to increase the percentage of the paycheck that they contribute to a retirement account. Many employees get an annual raise _____ work, and the increased contribution can take effect _____ the same time as the raise. In this way, people are likely to feel that they are _____ their way to a comfortable financial future without being forced to make ends meet _____ a smaller paycheck. Some people apparently need to play tricks _____ themselves to make sure that they make wise decisions.

44b Adjective + preposition

When you are writing, use a dictionary to check the specific prepositions used with an adjective.

▶ The botanist is *afraid of* spiders.

▶ E. O. Wilson was *interested in* bees.

Some common idiomatic adjective + preposition combinations are the following. Make your own lists to add to these.

Adjective + Preposition Combinations

Preposition	With Adjectives
about	anxious about, excited about, worried about
in	interested in
to/for	grateful to (someone) for (something), responsible to (someone) for (something)
with	content with, familiar with, patient with, satisfied with
of	afraid of, ashamed of, aware of, capable of, fond of, full of, guilty of, jealous of, proud of, suspicious of, tired of

44c Verb + preposition

Learn the following common idiomatic verb + preposition combinations.

apologize to (someone) for (an offense or error)

arrive in (a country or city); *arrive at* (a building or an event)

blame (someone) *for* (an offense or error)

complain about

concentrate on

congratulate (someone) *on* (success or good fortune)

consist of

depend on

explain (facts) *to* (someone)

insist on

laugh at

rely on

smile at

take care of

thank (someone) *for* (a gift or favor)

throw (an object) *at* (someone not expecting it)

throw (an object) *to* (someone waiting to catch it)

worry about

If you have a language notebook or blog, keep a list of other idiomatic verb and preposition combinations you come across, and learn them.

EXERCISE 44.2

Use adjective + preposition, verb + preposition.

In each of the following sentences, correct any errors in the choice of prepositions.

EXAMPLE:

about
Many Americans have been worried ~~from~~ the possibility ~~of~~
                                      ^   of
biological terrorism, but some doctors are more afraid ~~from~~
the naturally caused influenza than any biological agent.
                                                         ^

1. Although some Americans wanted to take antibiotics as a precaution against anthrax in the fall of 2001, the percentage of people

who asked their doctors of flu shots at that time was no higher than normal.

2. Influenza has been responsible to the deaths of many healthy people in the past century, and doctors do not know when a dangerous strain of flu may appear.

3. Doctors in 1918 were unable to prevent the flu epidemic to killing millions of people around the world; more people died of the flu than as a result of World War I that year.

4. Many people may not be aware to the dangers of influenza.

5. Medical specialists are studying genetic samples from people who died with influenza in 1918 to try to find ways to prevent such a deadly flu from reoccurring.

44d Phrasal verbs

Prepositions and a few adverbs (such as *away* and *forward*) can combine with verbs in such a way that they no longer function as prepositions or ordinary adverbs. They are then known as *particles*. Only a few languages other than English—Dutch, German, and Swedish, for example—have this verb + particle (preposition or adverb) combination, which is called a *phrasal verb*. Examples of English phrasal verbs are *put off* and *put up with*.

The meaning of a phrasal verb is entirely different from the meaning of the verb alone. Note the idiomatic meanings of some common phrasal verbs.

break down [stop functioning]	run across [meet unexpectedly]
get over [recover from]	run out [become used up]
look into [examine]	take after [resemble]

Always check the meanings of such verbs in a specialized dictionary such as *The American Heritage English as a Second Language Dictionary*.

A particle can be followed by a preposition to make a three-word combination:

▶ **She *gets along with* everybody.** [She is friendly toward everybody.]

Other three-word verb combinations are

catch up with [draw level with]   look forward to [anticipate]

| look down on [despise] | put up with [endure] |
| look up to [admire] | stand up for [defend] |

Position of direct objects with two-word phrasal verbs
Some two-word transitive phrasal verbs are separable. The direct object of these verbs can come between the verb and the accompanying particle.

▶ She *put off* her dinner party. [She postponed her dinner party.]

▶ She *put* her dinner party *off*.

When the direct object is a pronoun, however, always place the pronoun between the verb and the particle.

▶ She *put* it *off*.

Some commonly used phrasal verbs that follow that principle are listed here. They can be separated by a noun as a direct object; they must be separated when the direct object is a pronoun.

call off [cancel]	give up [surrender]	make up [invent]
fill out [complete]	leave out [omit]	turn down [reject]
find out [discover]	look up [locate]	turn off [stop]

Most dictionaries list phrasal verbs that are associated with a particular verb, along with their meanings and examples. Develop your own list of such verbs from your reading.

44e Preposition + -*ing* verb form used as a noun

The -*ing* verb form that functions as a noun (the *gerund*) frequently is placed after a preposition as its object.

▶ They congratulated him *on winning* the prize.

▶ Sue expressed interest *in participating* in the fundraiser.

▶ He ran three miles *without stopping*.

▶ The cheese is the right consistency *for spreading*.

Note: Take care not to confuse *to* as a preposition with *to* used in an infinitive. When *to* is a preposition, it is followed by a noun, a pronoun, a noun phrase, or an -*ing* form, not by the base form of a verb.

┌ infinitive ┐
▶ They want *to adopt* a child.

preposition + -*ing* form (gerund)
▶ They are looking forward *to adopting* a child.

Check which to use by testing whether a noun replacement fits the sentence:

▶ They are looking forward to parenthood.

Note also *be devoted to, be/get used to* (see 45i).

REVIEW EXERCISE FOR CHAPTER 44

Use prepositions and idiomatic expressions correctly.

Correct any errors in idiomatic structures with prepositions and adverbs in the following passage.

How important is an American's cultural identity? According to Walter Benn Michaels, the author of *Our America*, people at the United States have been preoccupied of belonging to a particular ethnic or racial group since the 1920s. In that time, some U.S. residents thought that too many immigrants were arriving to the country, and Congress strictly limited immigration in 1924. But other Americans during that decade wanted to find up more about their ancestors' culture and preserve their traditions; they were not happy at the idea that immigrants might change their customs at a new country. Although the Americans who were afraid about immigrants changing the country and the Americans who were interested in preserve different cultures did not agree with the issue of identity, both sides shared an interest on the subject.

More than seventy-five years later, the question on identity still concerns people in the United States, no matter what their political views are. Dr. Michaels argues that an emphasis on culture and diversity ends out putting people on groups according to their ancestry. Either people feel that Americans belong to a group based of their ethnic or racial background, or they feel that Americans all share the country's past and should all take pride of its accomplishments. At his book, Dr. Michaels asks, "Why should any past count as ours?" Dr. Michaels argues that identity should not matter. He believes that Americans should take pride in to have their own accomplishments and stop worrying on the groups to which they belong.

Chapter 45

Frequently Asked ESL Editing Questions

45a When do I use *no* and *not*?

Not is an adverb that negates a verb, an adjective, or another adverb. *No* is an adjective and therefore modifies a noun.

▶ She is *not* wealthy.   ▶ She is *not* really poor.

▶ The author does *not* intend to deceive the reader.

▶ The author has *no* intention of deceiving the reader.

45b What is the difference between *too* and *very*?

Both *too* and *very* intensify an adjective or adverb, but they are not interchangeable. *Too* indicates excess. *Very* indicates degree, meaning "extremely."

▶ It was *very* hot.

▶ It was *too* hot to sit outside. [*Too* occurs frequently in the pattern *too* + adjective or adverb + *to* + base form of verb.]

▶ The Volvo was *very* expensive, but he bought it anyway.

▶ The Volvo was *too* expensive, so he bought a Ford instead.

45c Does *few* mean the same as *a few*?

A few is the equivalent of *some*. *Few* is the equivalent of *hardly any*; it has more negative connotations than *a few*. Both expressions are used with countable plural nouns. Although *a* is not generally used with plural nouns, the expression *a few* is an exception.

Online Study Center   This icon will direct you to quick reference tools, Web resources, and research guides on the Web site at http://college.hmco.com/keys.html.

some

▶ **She feels fortunate because she has *a few* helpful colleagues.**

hardly any

▶ **She feels depressed because she has *few* helpful colleagues.**

You might prefer to use only the more common *a few* and use *hardly any* in sentences in which the context demands *few*. Similar expressions used with uncountable nouns are *little* and *a little*.

⌐some⌐

▶ **She has *a little* time to spend on work-related projects.**

hardly any

▶ **She has *little* time to spend on recreation.**

EXERCISE 45.1

Use *no* and *not*, *too* and *very*, *few* and *a few* correctly.
Correct any errors in the use of *no* and *not*, *too* and *very*, or *few* and *a few*.

EXAMPLE:

not
A wildfire in a wilderness area is ~~no~~ necessarily a disaster.
^

1. Natural disasters such as fires, floods, and storms are usually seen as terrible events, but sometimes they have few positive results.
2. For example, a forest with many tall trees may be very dark for new plant growth, but fires can change the situation to allow sunlight to reach the ground.
3. A river that has no flooded for many years collects silt, which often means that a few fish can spawn.
4. Few human attempts to control disasters have been successful, and trying to ensure that not fire or flood can occur often means that fires and floods are more damaging when they do happen.
5. Although many ecologists have found it too difficult to stop trying to prevent natural disasters, they are now working instead to keep disasters from being too devastating.

45d How do I know when to use *been* or *being*?

In speech, these words often sound similar. In writing, it is absolutely necessary to distinguish them. See also 25d, page 405.

Been *Been* is the past participle of the verb *be.* Use it after auxiliaries *has, have,* and *had.* Follow *been* with an *-ing* form for the active voice and with the past participle form for the passive voice.

▶ It has *been* **snowing.** [active]

▶ They have *been* **indicted.** [passive]

Being *Being* is the present participle *-ing* form of the verb *be.* Use it after a *be* auxiliary: *am, is, are, was, were.* In the active voice, *being* is followed by an adjective or a noun phrase.

▶ He *is being* **pretentious. He is also** *being* **a bore.** [active]

In the passive voice, *being* is followed by a past participle.

▶ They are *being* **watched.** [passive]

45e How do I distinguish *most, most of,* and *the most*?

Most expresses a generalization, meaning "nearly all."

▶ *Most* **Americans like ice cream.**

When a word such as *the, this, these, that,* or *those* or a possessive pronoun (such as *my, their*) precedes the noun to make it specific, *most of* is used. The meaning is "nearly all of."

▶ I did *most of* **this needlework.**

▶ *Most of* **his colleagues work long hours.**

The most is used to compare more than two people or items.

▶ Tarun is *the most* **efficient of all the technicians.**

45f What structures are used with *easy, hard,* and *difficult*?

All of the following patterns are acceptable in English.

▶ It is *easy* **for me to change a fuse.**

▶ It is *easy* **to change a fuse.**

▶ To change a fuse is *easy* **for me.**

▶ To change a fuse is *easy.*

▶ Changing a fuse is *easy* for me.

▶ Changing a fuse is *easy*.

▶ I find it *easy* to change a fuse.

However, a sentence like the following needs to be edited in English into one of the patterns just listed or as shown here:

▶ I ~~am~~ *easy* to change a fuse.

45g How do I use *it* and *there* to begin a sentence?

Use the adverb *there* to indicate that something exists (or existed) or happens (or happened). See also 17b.

There
▶ ~~It~~ was a royal wedding in my country two years ago.

There
▶ ~~It~~ is a tree on the corner of my block.

Use the pronoun *it* for weather, distance, time, and surroundings.

▶ It is a long way to Tipperary.

▶ It is hot.

Use *it* also in expressions such as *it is important, it is necessary,* and *it is obvious*, emphasizing the details that come next. See also 17b.

▶ It is essential for all of you to sign your application forms.

It or *there* cannot be omitted as a filler subject.

it
▶ As you can see, is dark out already.

45h Which possessive pronoun do I use: *his* or *her*?

In some languages, the form of the pronoun used to indicate possession changes according to the gender of the noun that follows it, not according to the pronoun's antecedent. In French, for instance, *son* and *sa* mean, respectively, "his" and "her," the form being determined by the noun the pronoun modifies.

▶ Marie et sa mère [Marie and her mother]

▶ **Pierre et sa mère** [Pierre and his mother]

▶ **Pierre et son père** [Pierre and his father]

In English, however, the gender of a possessive (*his, her,* or *its*) is always determined by the antecedent.

▶ **I met Marie and her mother.**   ▶ **I met Pierre and his mother.**

45i What is the difference between *get used to* and *used to*?

For multilingual writers of English, the distinction between *used to +* base form and *be/get used to + -ing* (gerund) is difficult.

▶ **He *used to work* long hours.** [He did in the past but doesn't anymore. The infinitive form follows *used* in this sense.]

▶ **Air traffic controllers are *used to dealing* with emergencies.** [They are accustomed to it. The *-ing* form follows *be/get used to.*]

EXERCISE 45.2

Use phrasal verbs, preposition + *-ing*, *get used to*, and *used to* correctly.

Correct any errors in the use of phrasal verbs, gerunds after prepositions, and the phrases *get used to* and *used to.*

EXAMPLE:

     used to be
AIDS ~~is used to being~~ a death sentence, but more people now survive for years with the disease.

     Since scientists began to learn about AIDS more than twenty-five years ago, many people have been counting up a cure for the disease. The cure has not yet been found, but today many people with AIDS in this country used to live with the medications and other treatments that allow them to having a reasonably healthy life. In poorer countries, unfortunately, fewer people can look forward on living with AIDS, but AIDS researchers are excited about a recent discovery in the central African country of Rwanda. In Kigali, Rwanda's capital, a study has been following a group of sixteen people who tested positive for HIV at least twelve years ago but have neither taken medicine to treating the illness nor gotten sick. In most AIDS patients, the virus breaks out the immune system; in many patients in the Rwandan study, however, the virus shows an unusual mutation that seems to allow the body to put the virus up with. Researchers do not yet know whether this discovery will assist them in find a cure for the AIDS virus, but every new piece of information in this puzzle may be helpful in fight the disease.

REVIEW EXERCISE FOR CHAPTER 45
Correct errors.

In the following passage, correct any errors.

In the 1970s, market researchers discovered that the most young children were unable to tell the difference between the television shows they watched and advertisements for products. Because of this discovery, it was an attempt in 1978 to put legal restrictions on television advertisements aimed at too young children, but advertisers objected. The industry of marketing to children has being growing steadily since then. Between 1978 and 1998, the amount of money directly spent by children age four to twelve increased from less than three billion dollars a year to almost twenty-five billion dollars, and is not end in sight. Researchers believe that children in that age group also convince their families to spend another two hundred billion dollars a year—such as when a young boy, for example, convinces her mother to purchase a more expensive computer than she might otherwise have bought. Marketers are easy to decide to target this young market—there is their job to aim at consumers who can be convinced and who will spend most money.

However, few other groups have also helped marketers figure out the best way to target a too young audience. Many child psychologists are now been asked to join market-research firms to provide information about how to reach children more effectively. Some members of the American Psychological Association lobbied their organization in 2002 to discipline APA members who have helped advertisers target children, but the APA has no taken action yet. The most psychologists feel that the marketers and their advisers have being allowed very much freedom to appeal to children who cannot make informed decisions about products, but the situation does no seem likely to change.

Research

Finding, Using, and Documenting Sources

PART 8
Writing a Research Paper

PART 9
Documenting Sources: MLA Style

PART 10
Documenting Sources: APA, CSE, and *Chicago* Styles

W hat is research and why do it? You think you might have chronic fatigue syndrome, and you try to find out what are the symptoms and the best way to treat them. That's research. You need to buy a new cell phone, but you are not sure about the features, prices, and plans. You read the ads, talk to sales-people, go to stores, ask friends what they recommend, read con-sumer magazines, and roam the Web. That's research. When you do research, you begin by identifying a need to find information.

When an instructor in one of your courses assigns a research paper, you engage in similar activities, but in a more systematic and formal way. You find out what the issues are, focus on one important issue, formulate a research question about that issue, and then attempt to find an answer or answers to that question, considering the opinions of experts who have studied the question. The answer then becomes the thesis (claim or main idea) of your research paper (see 3g and 46f).

Research—finding information for a purpose—is the at the heart of "information literacy." The Association of College and Research Libraries, at <http://www.ala.org/ala/acrl/acrlstandards/informationliteracycompetency.htm>, describes what that literacy involves:

> Information literacy forms the basis for lifelong learning. It is common to all disciplines, to all learning environments, and to all levels of education. It enables learners to master content and extend their investigations, become more self-directed, and assume greater control over their own learning. An information literate individual is able to
>
> - determine the extent of information needed
> - access the needed information effectively and efficiently
> - evaluate information and its sources critically
> - incorporate selected information into one's knowledge base
> - use information effectively to accomplish a specific purpose
> - understand the economic, legal, and social issues surrounding the use of information, and access and use information ethically and legally

PART 8
Writing a Research Paper

RESEARCH

Online Study Center Research Online exercises

Chapter **46**

Planning

46a The requirements of the research assignment

For a college research assignment, be sure to understand your instructor's expectations for

- length
- due date
- purpose
- audience
- information to be included
- recommended approaches
- number and types of sources
- documentation style
- manuscript format and document design
- presentation: paper versus screen

If you are relatively new to research paper writing, let your instructor know; ask for advice and for sample papers from previous semesters. For advice on writing research papers in the various disciplines, turn to 50e. You can also turn to sample papers and excerpts included throughout this book to see how other students have tackled their assignments:

Papers in English courses (humanities)—MLA style: 7l, 8j, 51g

Papers in sociology and psychology courses (social sciences)— APA style: 9d, 52f

Papers in history, art history, and linguistics (humanities)— *Chicago* style: 9b, 54f

Papers in computer science and biology (sciences)—CSE style: 9d, 53f

46b Organizing your research

Research brings a heavy load, in more than one way. You will collect and carry around books, papers, notes, and drafts. If there is ever a

> ### KEY POINTS
> **Overview of the Research Process**
>
> 1. Start early and plan. Allot time to tasks. Fill out the schedule in 46c, copy it, and put it right next to a copy of the assignment in a place where you can look at it every day.
>
> 2. Don't be afraid to ask questions of your instructor or librarians. No questions are "silly questions" if you need to know the answer to proceed. All instructors and librarians expect students to feel somewhat bewildered by the size and scope of the task. They know how to help and are glad to do so.
>
> 3. Gather the tools that you will need: a flash drive or disks, ink for your printer, a pack of paper, a notebook, index cards, highlighting pens, folders, paperclips, money or a prepaid card for the library photocopier, a stapler, and self-stick notes.
>
> 4. Do the following to get started, though not necessarily in this order (see the sections listed for more details):
>   - Make sure you understand the requirements (46a).
>   - Plan which sources to begin with: primary or secondary (46d).
>   - Select or narrow a topic (3f, 46f).
>   - Compose a purpose statement (46e), a research question, and a tentative working thesis (46f).
>
> 5. Find and evaluate sources (47, 48), make notes (49e), and prepare a working bibliography (49f).
>
> 6. Plan your paper and write an outline (3i) and a draft (50d).
>
> 7. Evaluate the draft and get feedback (4c, 4d).
>
> 8. Revise your draft for ideas and organization—as many times as necessary (50d).
>
> 9. Prepare a list of works cited (51c, 52c, 53c, or 54d).
>
> 10. Edit, proofread, and design the format of your paper (6i, 21–29, 12a).

time in your life when you need to be organized, this is it. If you work mostly on paper, buy several folders of different colors and label them for each part of your research. Keep your research for, say, an English course separate from your notes for a chemistry course.

A research notebook   Keep a research notebook, either a paper version or a handheld computer notebook, so that you can keep track of what you find, where, and when. When an idea occurs to you or you see or hear something relevant to your topic, jot down notes. Make sure that both on paper and in your computer documents you indicate clearly which words and ideas come from what you find in your source materials and which words and ideas are your own. See chapter 49 for more on the importance of avoiding plagiarism.

Computer files   Use your computer not just for writing but also for organizing your work.

TECH NOTE

How to Organize Computer Files

1. In the Save As window, click on Create New Folder, and name it "Research Project."

2. Save in that folder all the files you create pertaining to research: notes on sources, freewriting and brainstorming, ideas for a topic and research question, thesis possibilities, outline, numbered drafts, working bibliography, works-cited list, and so on.

3. If a folder gets unwieldy, move some files into new folders, and rename the first so that you establish a system such as "My Drafts," "Notes from Sources," and "Works Cited."

46c   Making a tentative schedule

Get started as early as you can. As soon as a project is assigned, set a tentative schedule, working backward from the date the paper is due and splitting your time so that you know when you absolutely must move on to the next step. On the next page is a sample time block schedule that you can download, print, or adapt. You will find in reality that several tasks overlap and the divisions are not neat. If you finish a block before the deadline, move on and give yourself more time for the later blocks.

The amount of time suggested in the sample schedule assumes that your instructor gives the assignment five weeks before the paper is due. You will need to recalculate the time allotted to each block of activities if more or less time is available.

Online Study Center   **Research**   Sample research schedule

RESEARCH SCHEDULE

Starting date:
Date final draft is due:

Block 1: Getting started
Understand the requirements.
Select a topic or narrow a given topic.
Determine the preliminary types of sources to use.
Do preliminary research to discover the important issues.
Organize research findings in computer files.
Write a purpose statement.
1 week. Complete by _____

Block 2: Reading, researching, and evaluating sources
Find and copy print and online sources.
Annotate and evaluate the sources.
Write summaries and paraphrases, and make notes.
Set up a working bibliography.
1 week. Complete by _____

Block 3: Planning and drafting
Formulate a working thesis.
Write a purpose statement, a proposal, and/or an outline.
Write a first draft.
1 week. Complete by _____

Block 4: Evaluating the draft and getting feedback
Put the draft away for a day or two—but continue collecting useful sources.
Outline the draft, and evaluate its logic and completeness.
Plan more research as necessary to fill any gaps.
Get feedback from instructor and classmates.
1 week. Complete by _____

Block 5: Revising, preparing list of works cited, editing, presenting
Revise the draft.
Prepare a list of works cited.
Design the format of the paper.
Edit.
Proofread the final draft.
1 week. Complete by _____
(final deadline for handing in)

46d The types of sources: Basic, primary, and secondary

Even at the very beginning of the research process, consider the types of sources you are likely to use as you work on your project. See 47 for more on finding specific print and online sources.

Basic sources to get you started Encyclopedias and general or specialized reference works can help you choose or focus a topic. Because they provide an overview of the issues involved in a complex topic and some may also provide extensive bibliographies of other useful sources, these encyclopedias can also help you develop your research and formulate a research proposal if you are asked to provide one.

Caution: Use encyclopedias as a way to start investigating your subject, but do not rely on them for most of your project.

Below is a list of encyclopedias for initial explorations. Some, such as the first one listed, are available to everyone online. Others may be available free online only though your local library, your college library system, or your Internet service provider. The online *Wikipedia* is also useful, but be aware that it is a work in progress and constantly subject to error and revision.

Encyclopedias to Get You Started

General	*Columbia Encyclopedia* <http://www.bartleby.com> *Encyclopaedia Britannica*
Art	*Encyclopedia of World Art*
Biology	*Encyclopedia of the Biological Sciences*
Business	*International Encyclopedia of Business and Management*
Chemistry	*Encyclopaedia of Chemistry*
Communications	*International Encyclopedia of Communications*
Computer science	*Encyclopedia of Computer Science*
Economics	*Oxford Encyclopedia of Economic History*
Education	*Encyclopedia of Educational Research*
Engineering	*McGraw-Hill Encyclopedia of Engineering*
English literature	*Oxford Companion to English Literature*
Environmental science	*Encyclopedia of the Environment*
Ethnic studies	*Gale Encyclopedia of Multicultural America*
Geography	*Encyclopedia of World Geography*
Geology	*Encyclopedia of Earth System Science*
History	*Dictionary of American History*

Linguistics	*Cambridge Encyclopedia of Language*
Mathematics	*CRC Concise Encyclopedia of Mathematics*
Music	*New Grove Dictionary of Music and Musicians*
Nursing	*Encyclopedia of Nursing Research*
Philosophy	*Encyclopedia of Philosophy*
Physics	*Encyclopedia of Physics*
Political science	*International Handbook of Political Science*
Popular culture	*St. James Encyclopedia of Popular Culture*
Psychology	*Encyclopedia of Psychology*
Religion	*Encyclopedia of Religion*
Sciences	*McGraw-Hill Encyclopedia of Science and Technology*
Sociology	*Encyclopedia of Sociology*
Women's studies	*Routledge International Encyclopedia of Women*

Primary sources   Primary sources are the firsthand, raw, or original materials that researchers study and analyze. You can consult historical documents, visuals, journals and letters, autobiographies, memoirs, government statistics and studies, and speeches. You can examine works of art, literature, and architecture or watch or listen to performances and programs. You can study or initiate case studies or scientific experiments and take extensive field notes. You can also conduct interviews and use data collected from questionnaires. The use of such primary sources can bring an original note to your research and new information to your readers.

INTERVIEWS   Interview people who have expert knowledge of your topic. Plan a set of interview questions, but do not stick so closely to your script that you fail to follow up on good leads in your respondent's replies. Ask permission to tape-record the interview; otherwise, you will have to take quick and accurate notes, particularly if you want to quote. Check the functioning of your tape recorder beforehand. Make note of the date, time, and place of the interview. See 53f for a student's research using paper interviews.

QUESTIONNAIRES   Designing useful questionnaires is tricky because much depends on the number and sample of respondents you use, the types of questions you ask, and the methods you employ to analyze the data. Embark on questionnaire research only if you have been introduced to the necessary techniques in a college course or have consulted experts in this area. You may also need permission to conduct research on human subjects.

SECONDARY SOURCES Secondary sources are analytical works that comment on and interpret other works, such as primary sources. Examples include reviews, discussions, biographies, critical studies, analysis of literary or artistic works or events, commentaries on current and historical events, class lectures, and electronic discussions.

46e Writing a statement of purpose

To focus your ideas and give yourself something to work with, write a simple statement of purpose after you have done some preliminary research (see 2b and 3i). This statement may become more developed or even later change completely, but it will serve to guide your first steps in the process. Here is an example:

> The purpose of this documented paper is to persuade general adult readers that historical films—such as Gladiator—should give precedence to a good story over historical accuracy because readers expect entertainment rather than education when they go to the movies.

As you progress with your research, you can develop your simple statement into a proposal (3i, 46g) and then an outline (3i, 50c).

46f Moving from topic to research question to working thesis

At the planning stage, you may not move far beyond establishing a topic and forming a research question. For this, you will turn to sources (see especially 47b and 47c for sources to use to select and narrow a topic). Move toward a research question and a working thesis as soon as you can so that your search for sources will be guided and productive. The secret is to be flexible. If a topic, a question, or a working thesis appears to be not producing good results, be prepared to find a new topic, question, or working thesis. That is why it is essential to start work early.

Searching for a good topic Try these tools and techniques to help yourself find a good topic—usually a more productive approach than staring at the ceiling hoping for a good idea.

- Look through your college textbooks in various fields for issues worth exploring.
- Consult general and specialized encyclopedias (see 46d for a list). These sources sketch out important issues and provide bibliographies for further reading.

- Browse the Web and subject directories (see the TechNote that follows) by searching for the keywords that interest you. You may find material that illuminates new issues or new sides of an issue.

- Use the *Library of Congress Subject Headings* (LCSH—in the Reference section of your library) to get ideas for topics and the books available on those topics and to learn the terminology used to search catalogs and databases. For instance, in a search for information on "doping in sports," the LCSH would provide the search term "anabolic steroids" and many narrower related terms. See more on LCSH in 47e.

- Talk, listen, and write. Talk to classmates and your instructors about possible topics. Listen to people around you: what topics engage their interest? Above all, carry your research notebook with you, and jot down any good ideas and leads.

TECH NOTE

How to Find Topics on the Web

1. Log on to the *Librarians' Index to the Internet* <http://lii.org> or, for general-interest topics, commercial search directories such as Google or Yahoo! See 47f.

2. Find a subject area that interests you, such as education, literature, health, sports, politics, business, or science. A click on a specific subject area will produce lists of many different topics within that category.

3. Keep clicking on a topic until you narrow the search to one that interests you and is appropriate for your assignment.

Online Study Center Research Search engines

Keep the search for a topic in mind as you go about your daily life. Think to yourself, "What would I like to know more about? What am I curious about?" Reading a magazine, watching TV, and thinking about the things that really matter to you—all these simple everyday activities can generate ideas for research. Carry a notebook and pencil or computer notebook with you so that you can jot down every idea that seems promising.

Selecting a topic Select your own topic with two criteria in mind:

1. Does the topic interest you? Your topic should engage and sustain not only readers' interests but also your own. Readers recognize a bored writer who is simply going through the motions.

2. Is the topic appropriate (for example, in terms of the assignment, length, materials available)? Check with your instructor.

Narrowing a topic You may need to narrow a topic so that it is manageable for the number of pages you intend to write. Narrow by limiting place, time, or issues you will address.

Too Broad	Narrowed
Parkinson's disease	Current treatments for Parkinson's disease
Pollution	Remedies for PCBs in U.S. rivers
Genetic engineering	The hazards of genetically altered foodstuffs
Computers	Health issues of computers
Popular music	The appeal of hip-hop to the young

To find a narrow enough topic, you may have to do background reading to discover the important issues. Even if you begin with what you think is a clear response to your topic, make sure you explore any historical background or complexity that you may have overlooked. Spend time looking at what others have said about the issues before you settle on a direction for your research.

If your instructor assigns a topic, make sure you understand the terms used in the assignment, such as *analyze, interpret,* and *argue* (see 10c for definitions). You may also have to narrow a subject area your instructor assigns to a manageable topic for a short paper.

Moving from topic to question After one student, Claudia Esteban, narrowed her topic to automobile safety, she then needed to decide what aspect of the topic to investigate. Here is her brainstorming list on the topic of automobile safety:

Child seats
Air bags
Seat belts
SUVs
Restrictions on drinking
Punishments for driving while intoxicated
Speeding
Using a cell phone while driving

Esteban then did some preliminary reading and research to find out which areas offered useful material. From the narrowed list of topics she framed two possible research questions and concentrated on discovering what material was available in these two areas:

> What effects would increasing the speed limit on highways to 75 mph have?
> What measures would make SUVs less dangerous on the roads?

Designing a research question   For a research paper, design a research question that gets at the heart of what you want to discover. Your question should contain concrete keywords that you can search (see 47d) rather than general terms or abstractions. The answer you find as you do research is likely to become your thesis. If you find huge amounts of material on your question and realize that you would have to write a book (or two) to cover all the issues, narrow your question.

Questions Needing Narrowing	Revised Questions
How important are families? *Too broad: Important to whom and for what? No useful keywords to search.*	In what ways does a stable family environment contribute to an individual's future success?
What problems does the Internet cause? *Too broad: What types of problems? What aspects of the Internet?*	What types of Internet controls would protect individual privacy?
What are the treatments for cancer? *Too wide-ranging: Volumes could be and have been written on this.*	For which types of cancer are the success rates of radiation therapy the most promising?

A research question will give you a sense of direction. Frequently, as you read and take notes, you will have in mind a tentative response to your question. Sometimes that hypothesis will be confirmed. Sometimes, though, your research will reveal issues you have not previously considered and facts that are new to you, so you will refine, adapt, or even totally change your working thesis (see 3g and 7d for more on a working thesis). If you either cannot find enough material on your topic or discover that all the information is dated, flimsy, or biased, select another topic, narrow it down, and design a new research question. (See chapter 48 on evaluating sources.)

Formulating a working thesis As you do your preliminary work of examining the assignment, planning which types of sources to use, and moving toward a topic, you will probably have in mind the point you want to make in your paper. If your research question is "Should Internet controls be established to protect individual privacy?" you probably favor either a "yes" or "no" answer to your question. At this point, you can formulate a working thesis in the form of a statement of opinion to help drive the organization of your paper.

> Internet controls to protect individual privacy should be established.

> *Or* Internet controls to protect individual privacy should not be established.

KEY POINTS
Writing a Working Thesis

- Make sure the thesis is a statement. A phrase or a question is not a thesis: "Internet controls" is a topic, not a thesis statement. "Are Internet controls needed?" is a question, not a thesis statement.

- Make sure the thesis statement is not merely a statement of fact: "NUA Internet Surveys estimate that 605.6 million people were online as of September 2002" is a statement that cannot be developed and argued. A statement of fact does not let readers feel the need to read on to see what you have to say.

- Make sure the thesis statement does more than announce the topic: "This paper will discuss Internet controls." Instead, your thesis statement should give information about or express an opinion on the topic: "Service providers, online retailers, and parents share the responsibility of establishing Internet controls to protect an individual's privacy."

- Above all, be prepared to change and refine your thesis as you do your research and discover what your topic entails.

When you have a working thesis, your research becomes more focused. You look for material that relates to your thesis. If you find none, you can revise your thesis. If you find huge amounts of material, that is a signal for you to refine your thesis to make it more narrow and more focused on specific issues. Then you are ready to find sources and evaluate their relevance and reliability (chapters 47 and 48). As you read and make notes, you may find that your initial working thesis—"Internet controls should be established to protect individual privacy"—is too broad, and you may decide to narrow it: "Parents need to establish controls to protect their family's privacy on the Internet."

46g Writing a proposal

While you move from topic to research question to working thesis, you may be asked to submit a proposal to ensure that you are on the right track. View it as a mapping-out of the territory you are exploring as well as a plan for where you need to go. While not as precise as an outline (50c), a proposal helps to focus your research project. It can be written as a narrative or a numbered list, whichever fits your topic. For the research paper assignment in her expository writing course, Diana Fatakhova submitted to her instructor a proposal to research the controversial use of antidepressants for youths.

Depression has been an acute psychiatric disorder for decades, and the emergence of antidepressants has given hope to those diagnosed with this illness. Some of these antidepressants, called selective serotonin reuptake inhibitors (SSRIs), include Prozac, Paxil, Effexor, and Zoloft. They have been taken by adults for years and have also been prescribed for children and teenagers at lower doses as well. However, the use of SSRIs for young people has not been endorsed by the FDA, and recent findings have shown that youths who take these medications are at a greater risk of committing suicide because they exhibit an increase in suicidal thoughts and behaviors.

Background information

This subject is controversial since both benefits and dangers go along with youths taking SSRIs. The use of drugs has resulted in a decrease in suicides, but risk factors had not been previously taken into account. Both scientists and parents are now torn between taking a risk and hoping that the child will be able to refrain from committing suicide by staying on the medication. I plan on researching how antidepressants work and what specific effects they have on young people. For a paper directed to my classmates, instructor, and general readers, my research question is this: Do the risks of antidepressants outweigh the benefits, and if so, what alternatives are available?

Purpose

Audience

Research question

Chapter **47**

Finding Sources

47a Using the Web and the library

The Internet provides access to reference works, complete texts, and reliable sources such as databases of scholarly articles. It can be seen as a virtual library, available at the click of a mouse. It also provides a means of access to what were once seen as traditional print sources and to information that exists only online.

Using the Internet as a means to access information can lead you to many sources once viewed as traditional—reference works, books, scholarly articles, newspaper reports, government documents, and other traditional reference works, as well as to many reputable sources available only online, such as scholarly online journals and professional sites. Check at your library reference desk and on your library's Web page to find out which scholarly reference works and databases are available to you online and which Web sites might be particularly pertinent to your topic.

Online Study Center This icon will direct you to quick reference tools, Web resources, and research guides on the Web site at http://college.hmco.com/keys.html.

Not everything you need is going to be available from a computer. Your search may not be comprehensive if you limit yourself to online sources. You may still need to consult reference works, find books in library stacks, check your library's print holdings for articles published more than a few years ago, and use the library catalog to locate the actual articles in bound print journals or on microform.

Get to know your college or community library, its layout, and what its holdings include: What online databases and indexes does it subscribe to? Can you access the online holdings from your home or workplace? Should you print, save, or e-mail sources you find online? The greatest resource of all is the librarians at your library's reference desk. Get to know them and ask for their help.

Consider where you are likely to find the most appropriate sources for your topic. For tracing historical development or looking back to the past, scholarly articles, books, and primary documents such as diaries, memoirs, and speeches are your best bet. For contemporary political or cultural issues, you will probably search newspapers, magazines, Web sites, and online discussion groups. If in doubt about whether time spent in the library or time at your home or work computer will be more productive for your topic, get advice from your instructor or a reference librarian.

Searching for, evaluating, and recording source information are crucial parts of research. Each is discussed here in sequence, but in reality you will be searching, evaluating, and recording all through the process of writing a research paper. In particular, as you search for sources, be sure to keep full records of the sources you find and may use. See 49e on how best to do this.

47b Basic reference works: bibliographies, biographical sources, directories, dictionaries, and others

The reference section of your college or local library is a good place to gather basic information. Reference books cannot be checked out, so they are in the library at all times. Also, as more and more reference works are made available online, the accessibility of material increases. Check Google or your college's online resource page to find out which sources are available online, or ask a librarian.

Reference works provide basic factual information and lead to other sources. However, use the same caution with other reference works as with encyclopedias—use them to get started with basic information, and then quickly move beyond them. (See 47c–47g for details on finding sources other than basic reference works.) Find out if your library subscribes to the huge online database for reference books, *xreferplus*.

Bibliographies (also known as *guides to the literature*)   You can find lists of books and articles on a subject in online bibliographic databases such as the following: *Books in Print, International Medieval Bibliography, MLA International Bibliography of Books and Articles on the Modern Languages and Literature, New Books on Women and Feminism,* and *Political Science Bibliographies.*

Biographies   Read accounts of people's lives in biographical works such as *Who's Who, Dictionary of American Biography, Biography Index: A Cumulative Index to Biographic Material in Books and Magazines, Contemporary Authors, Dictionary of Literary Biography, African American Biographies, Chicano Scholars and Writers, Lives of the Painters,* and *American Men and Women of Science.*

Directories   Directories provide lists of names and addresses of people, companies, and institutions. These are useful for setting up interviews and contacting people when you need information. Examples are *Jane's Space Directory* and *Communication Media in Higher Education: A Directory of Academic Programs and Faculty in Radio-Television-Film and Related Media.*

Dictionaries   For etymologies, definitions, synonyms, and spelling, consult *The American Heritage Dictionary of the English Language,* 4th edition; *Oxford English Dictionary* (multiple volumes—useful for detailed etymologies and usage discussions); *Facts on File* specialized dictionaries; and other specialized dictionaries such as *Dictionary of Literary Terms* and *Dictionary of the Social Sciences.*

Dictionaries of quotations   For a rich source of traditional quotations, go to *Bartlett's Familiar Quotations;* for more contemporary quotations, searchable by topic, go to *The Columbia World of Quotations* (both are available online at <http://www.bartleby.com>). Also, consult specialized dictionaries of quotations, such as volumes devoted to chess, law, religion, fishing, women, and Wall Street.

Collections of articles of topical interest and news summaries   *CQ (Congressional Quarterly)* weekly reports, *Facts on File* publications, and *CQ Almanac* are available in print and online by subscription. *Newsbank* provides periodical articles on microfiche, classified under topics such as "law" and "education," and *SIRS (Social Issues Resources Series)* appears in print and online.

Statistics and government documents   Among many useful online sources are *Statistical Abstract of the United States, Current Index* to Statistics, Handbook of Labor Statistics, Occupational Outlook Handbook, U.S. Census publications, GPO Access, UN Demographic Yearbook, Population Index, and Digest of Education Statistics.

Almanacs, atlases, and gazetteers   For population statistics and boundary changes, see The World Almanac, Countries of the World, or Information Please. For locations, descriptions, pronunciation of place names, climate, demography, languages, natural resources, and industry, consult a gazetteer such as Columbia-Lippincott Gazetteer of the World and the CIA World Factbook series.

General critical works   Read what scholars have to say about works of art and literature in Contemporary Literary Criticism and in Oxford Companion volumes (such as Oxford Companion to Art and Oxford Companion to African American Literature).

Online Study Center   **Research** Online reference works

47c Indexes and databases

Indexes   Indexes of articles appearing in periodicals will start you off in your search for an article on a specific topic. Print indexes, such as Readers' Guide to Periodical Literature, will list works published before 1980. More recent publications are listed in online indexes, such as Applied Science and Technology Index, Engineering Index, and Art Index. An index will provide a complete citation: author, title, periodical, volume, date, and page numbers, often with an abstract. That information will narrow your search. Then you have to locate the periodical in a library or a database and find the actual article.

Online databases   Online databases of journal articles provide sources that have been previously published and referred to by experts.

Online databases and citation indexes owned or leased by a library can be accessed in the library itself. Many libraries also make the databases they subscribe to available on the Internet through their home pages. For example, many libraries provide online access to

- databases of abstracts in specific subject areas, such as ERIC (for education), PAIS (for public affairs), PsycINFO (for psychology), and Sociological Abstracts (for sociology)

- general databases of full articles published in the last twenty or thirty years, such as InfoTrac Expanded Academic ASAP, LexisNexis Academic Universe, and EBSCO Academic Search Premier

- databases of abstracts (with some full texts) of nonspecialized magazine articles, such as the Readers' Guide to Periodical Literature

- databases devoted to quantitative statistics, such as the Millennium Development Goal Indicators Database
- the *JSTOR* database, providing access to less-recent sources
- databases devoted to images such as The J. Paul Getty Trust Web site
- The *InfoTrac Literature Resource Center,* for basic information on authors and literary works
- the database *Ethnic Newswatch,* for ethnic magazines and newspapers

See 47g for a summary of online indexes and databases.

Access to databases in university library Web sites, from both library and home computers, is often limited to enrolled students, who need to verify their status when they log on. Check with your college library to learn which databases it subscribes to. Articles that you find in a database have for the most part been previously published in print, so evaluate them as print sources for currency, objectivity, and reputation (see 48c).

Before you begin a search, read the instructions on the database to learn how to perform a simple search and an advanced search. Knowing what you are doing can save you a great deal of frustration! Generally, begin a search by using keywords or subject terms, if you know them. Use what the database provides to limit a search as to type of source, date, full-text articles or not, and scholarly, peer-reviewed articles, as shown in the following screenshot.

Advanced Search Screen: EBSCO Academic Search Premier Database

47d Keyword searches

Use keywords to search for any material stored electronically. Keyword searching is especially effective for finding material in journal and newspaper articles in databases such as *EBSCO, InfoTrac, LexisNexis,* and specialized subject-area databases because a computer can search not only titles but also abstracts (when available) or full articles. See 47c for more on searching databases.

Keywords are vital for your Web searches, too. Spend time thinking of the keywords that best describe what you are looking for. If a search yields thousands of hits, try requiring or prohibiting terms and making terms into phrases. If a search yields few hits, try different keywords or combinations, or try another search engine or database. In addition, try out variant spellings for names of people and places: *Chaikovsky, Tchaikovsky, Tschaikovsky.* Some search engines, such as Google, automatically suggest alternate spellings.

Use the results to help refine your search. If your search produces only one useful source, look at the terms used in that one source and its subject headings and search again, perhaps using those terms with a different search engine or on a different database. Above all, be flexible. Each database or search engine indexes only a portion of what is available in the published literature or on the Web. Once you find a promising reference to a source that is not available online in full text, check whether your library owns the book or journal. If your search yields a source available only on microfilm or microfiche, you might need a librarian's help to learn how to use the reading machines and how to make copies.

KEY POINTS

Doing a Keyword Search

1. *Know the system used by the database or search engine.* Use the Search Tips or Help link to find out how to conduct a search. Systems vary. Some search for any or all of the words you type in, some require you to indicate whether the words make up a phrase (item 4), and some allow you to exclude words or search for alternatives (items 5, 6, and 8).

2. *Use Advanced Search features in a search engine or database.* Google (<http://www.google.com/help/refinesearch.html>) provides a simple grid to indicate whether you want to find results with all the words, with the exact phrase, with at least one of the words, or without the words, as shown in the

(Continued)

(Continued)

screenshot below. In addition, databases often provide ways to limit results, such as a box you can check to retrieve only full-text or "peer-reviewed" articles (scholarly articles, approved for publication by peer reviewers). See the EBSCO screenshot on page 645.

Google Advanced Search

3. *Use a wildcard character to truncate a term and expand the search.* A wildcard allows you to use at the end of a phrase a character that indicates that more letters can be attached. Common wildcard characters are * for several characters and ? for one character. The truncated search term *addict** will produce references to *addict, addicts, addiction, addictive,* and so on. (Google does not provide this feature.)

4. *Narrow a search by grouping words into phrases.* You can use quotation marks (or in some cases parentheses) to surround search terms to group the words into a phrase, a useful technique for finding titles, names, and quotations. A half-remembered line from a poem by Wordsworth ("the difference to me") entered as a Google search without quotation marks

does not produce a Wordsworth poem on the first page of hits. However, putting quotation marks around this phrase produces a hit to the full text of Wordsworth's Lucy poem right on the first page of results.

5. ***Use Boolean terms to narrow or expand a search.*** Some advanced searches operate on the Boolean principle, which means that you use the "operators" *AND, OR,* and *NOT* in combination with keywords to define what you want the search to include and exclude. Imagine that you want to find out if and how music can affect intelligence. Using only the term *music* would produce vast numbers of hits. Using *AND* narrows the search. The term *music AND intelligence* would find sources in the database that include both the word *music* and the word *intelligence* (the overlap in the circles below).

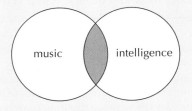

Parentheses can aid in searches, too. The search term *music AND (intelligence OR learning)* would expand the previous search. You would find sources in the database that include both the word *music* and either the word *intelligence* or the word *learning.*

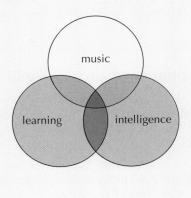

(Continued)

(Continued)

In Boolean searches, *AND* and *NOT* narrow the search: *chicken AND salmonella; tigers NOT Detroit.* The operator *OR* expands the search: *angiogram OR angioplasty.* Not all databases and search engines use this system. Google, for instance, deliberately ignores the words *and* and *not* in a search, so there the search string *tigers NOT Detroit* actually produces sites dealing with the baseball team the Detroit Tigers. Google recommends using the minus sign (always after a space) to exclude a term, as in *tigers −Detroit.* Always check the instructions with each search engine or database.

6. ***Require or prohibit a term to narrow a search.*** Many search engines allow you to use a symbol such as + (plus) before a term that must be included in the document indexed; a − (minus) symbol prohibits a term: + "Civil War"− Gettysburg.

7. ***Take advantage of the "proximity" search feature if available.*** Some search engines and many databases let you indicate when you want your search terms to occur close to each other in the text, a useful feature when you can only remember part of a quotation. Check in the Help or Tips file to determine whether the engine you are using has this feature. Proximity is indicated in various ways in various search engines. *NEAR* or *ADJ* (adjacent) are common: "Virginia Woolf" *NEAR* "Bloomsbury group" would search for the two phrases near each other in the text.

8. ***Be flexible.*** If you don't get good results, try using synonyms—in Google, type a tilde (~) immediately before the search term, as in *~intelligence.* Or try a different search engine or database.

47e Finding print sources: Books and articles

Types of search   When you use library catalogs or periodical databases, decide whether to search by T (title), A (author), S (subject), or K (keyword)(47d). Exact wording and exact spelling are essential for all these searches.

SUBJECT SEARCHES   To find sources focused on one topic, try subject searching. For that, you need to know the specific subject headings the catalogers used to identify and classify material. Consult a reference source such as *Library of Congress Subject Headings,* or ask a librarian for help. For example, you won't find *cultural identity* or *social identity* in *Library of Congress Subject Headings,* but you can look up *culture* and find a list of thirty-two associated headings, such as "language and culture" and "personality and culture."

In addition, these subject headings show related terms, which can suggest ways to narrow or broaden a topic and can help you in other searches, particularly in electronic keyword searches. *Bilingualism,* for example, takes you to topics such as "air traffic control," "code-switching," and "language attrition." An entry in a library catalog will appear with the subject descriptors, so if you find one good source, use its subject classifications to search further. A search in a library online catalog using the keywords *bilingual, education,* and *politics* finds forty-two records. One of these (on page 650) provides some subject terms to help with further searching: *education and state, educational change,* and *educational evaluation.* Similarly, a keyword search of an online database of full-text articles will produce articles with subject descriptors attached, as in the source shot on page 728.

Finding books

ONLINE LIBRARY CATALOGS   The Web gives you access to the online resources of many libraries (actual and virtual), which are good browsing sites. Some useful sites are Library of Congress, LibWeb, New York Public Library, and Smithsonian Institution Libraries.

Online Study Center   **Research**   Online library catalogs

CALL NUMBER   Most college libraries use the Library of Congress classification system, which arranges books according to subject area and often the initial of the author's last name and the date of publication. The call number tells where a book is located in the stacks (the area where books are shelved). Write down this number immediately if a book looks promising, along with the book's title and author(s) and publication information (49e). If a library has open stacks, browse through books on a similar topic on the same shelf or on one nearby. If your college library does not own a book you want, it may be available through an interlibrary loan. Ask a librarian.

INFORMATION IN THE CATALOG   Most screens of electronic catalogs contain the name of the system you are using; the details of your search request and of the search, such as the number of records found; and detailed bibliographical information.

Library Catalog Screen for a Book

CUNY

My Account | Display Options | Folder | End Session | Help
You are searching: CUNY Union Catalog
Search | Results List | Search History | Select all CUNY Libraries | Select Individual CUNY Libraries

Add to Folder Save/Mail

Record Display   Back

Choose format: Full View | Brief View | MARC

Record this information for documentation

Record 1 out of 3   ◀ Previous Record   Next Record ▶

Call number	All Items —— Click here for call number
Author	Hacsi, Timothy A.
Title	Children as pawns : the politics of educational reform / Timothy A. Hacsi.
Publisher	Cambridge, Mass. : Harvard University Press, 2002.
Description	ix, 261 p. ; 25 cm.
Notes	Includes bibliographical references (p. 217-252) and index.
Contents	Introduction -- What difference does Head Start make? -- Is bilingual education a good idea? -- Does class size matter? -- Is social promotion a problem? -- Does more money make schools better? -- Conclusion.
Subjects	Education and state -- United States.
	Educational change -- United States.
	Educational evaluation -- United States.
Call number	Brooklyn ⓘ
Call number	Hunter Main ⓘ

Useful subject search terms

Information about library location and status of book

—Reprinted with permission of The City University of New York Library.

The screen shown here, which extends to links to the call number (LC89.H215202) and the locations of the holdings (locations where the book is housed), provides all the essential information you will need to document the source at the end of your paper: author, title, place of publication, publisher, and date of publication. In addition, it lets you know the number of pages in the book and shows that the book contains a bibliography and an index—useful research tools. The subject search terms shown can help structure further searches.

Once you find a book that seems to be related to your topic, you do not have to read the whole book to use it for your paper. Learn what you can from the catalog entry; then skim the table of contents, chapter headings, and bibliography. Your best time-saver here is the index. Turn to it immediately, and look up some key words for your topic. Read the section of the book in which references to your topic appear; take notes; annotate a photocopy of the relevant pages (49e). A book's bibliography and references are useful, too. The research the author has done can help you in your search. It is a good idea to make a copy of the title page and the page on which the copyright notice appears. If you find nothing remotely connected to your research question, do not cite the book as a resource, even though you looked at it.

***BOOKS IN PRINT* AND ALTERNATIVES**   If you want to find a book or to check on bibliographical details, use *Books in Print* (available in print and online). If your library does not subscribe to the online version, you can use the Amazon.com site at or any other large commercial online bookseller to look up the details of a book—free. Amazon does not, however, list the place of publication, but it may be visible if you "search inside the book."

Finding articles   Find articles in periodicals (works issued periodically, such as scholarly journals, magazines, and newspapers) by using keywords in a periodical database. Use electronic databases for recent works, print indexes for earlier works—especially for works written before 1980. Check which databases your library subscribes to and the dates they cover. Some provide abstracts; some, such as EBSCO, InfoTrac, and LexisNexis Academic Universe, provide the full text of articles. (See also 47c for more on articles in databases.)

Search methods for articles are similar to those used for book searches. If the periodical index does not provide the full text or provide a link to it, you will need to find out first whether your library owns the periodical and then in which form it is available: in bound volumes or in film form, with pages shown in a strip (microfilm) or on a sheet (microfiche), which you will need to read with a special machine. The catalog for your library will tell you on the screen which issues are available in your library and in which format and location. For articles not available in your library, ask about interlibrary loan.

47f Online searches and search engines

URLS   If you already know the Web address (the uniform resource locator or URL) of a useful site, type it exactly, paying attention to spaces (or, more often, lack of spaces), dots, symbols, and capital or lowercase letters. Just one small slip can prevent access. Whenever you can, copy and paste a URL from a Web source so that you do not make mistakes in typing. If you ever get a message saying "site not found," check your use of capitals and lowercase letters (and avoid inserting spaces as you type an address), and try again. You may find that the site is no longer available. Or try adding "l" to an ".htm" suffix, or deleting "l" from ".html."

Search engines and directories   If you do not know the exact Web site you want, you need to use search tools. Some search the whole

Web for you; some search selected sites; some search only the first few pages of a document; still others search only a specific site, such as a university library system or a noncommercial organization; or they search other search engines (these are called *metasearch engines*). Some (Google, Yahoo!) offer subject directories to help you search by topic (see also 3f). Make sure you try all types to find information on your topic. You will miss many useful sources if you do only a Google search.

A note of caution about using search engines: An opinion article by Edward Tenner in the *New York Times* has pointed out that despite their increasing ability to evaluate and "present useful information on the first screen," search engines display "irrelevant or mediocre sites on a par with truly expert ones." Go to 49e to learn how to evaluate sources originating on the Internet and 48d to learn how to develop your "junk antennae."

TECH NOTE

Some useful search engines

- Google (the favorite of many academics) searches more than eight billion Web pages and other search engines. It organizes and ranks results by the number of links to a site. Google also offers a directory of sites grouped by topic and an image search. Google Book Search, a new feature, helps you find books addressing your search terms.

- Google Scholar offers searching limited to scholarly content on the Web, though the site's interpretations of what is scholarly may not always agree with your instructor's interpretation.

- INFOMINE provides scholarly resources in social sciences, humanities, and general reference, selected and annotated.

- Internet Public Library is run by librarians. It includes a guide to subject collections and an "Ask a question" feature, which allows you to e-mail a question about a research project to librarians for evaluation and possible response within three days.

- Metasearch engines extend your search by searching the results of other search engines. Recommended are Dogpile, which searches Google, Yahoo! and others, and jux2, which searches two chosen search engines at one time and presents "best results."

Some useful directories

- WWW Virtual Library is a directory of sources in a large number of academic disciplines.

- Yahoo! is a subject index and directory of the Web. You can keep narrowing down your subjects, or you can use specific keywords. Such a tool is particularly useful when you are trying to find a topic. Yahoo! Picture Gallery finds images.
- University of Michigan's Documents Center Directory supplies statistical, legal, and government documents.
- Librarians' Internet Index is a directory of academic sources.

In addition, consider using subject-specific start pages for more efficient searches than those using general search engines.

47g Finding Web sources

The democratic nature of the Internet means that many Web pages have no editorial control, so although you will probably find a great deal of material, much of it could be mindless and inaccurate (see 48d). As you plan your research, consider which Web resources described in this section might be the most trustworthy and appropriate for your topic. A reference librarian can help you decide.

Online magazines and online scholarly journals   Online magazines and online scholarly journals are proliferating. Some online magazines and journals are available free; some allow you to view only the current issue at no cost. Many, however, require a subscription through your library computer network or a personal subscription. Some scholarly journals have no print versions.

Online Study Center   Research   Online magazines and journals

Online literary texts   Literary texts that are out of copyright and in the public domain are increasingly available online for down-loading. The following are useful sites to consult, although the versions of texts you see may not always be authoritative: *Project Bartleby, Project Gutenberg,* and *University of Virginia's Electronic Text Center.*

eBooks   Many books are becoming available as eBooks, either to be read online at a computer or to be downloaded and read in an eBook reader. If your library subscribes to its database, check its offerings when you are looking for a book.

Online news sites The Web sites of major newspapers, magazines, and television networks provide up-to-date news information; some offer archived information but often only to subscribers. These include *New York Times on the Web* and *CNN Interactive. LexisNexis* also provides access to articles from many newspapers.

Online Study Center **Research and Documentation** Online news sites

Nonprofit research sites Many nonprofit sites offer valuable and objective information. For example, see *Public Agenda Online, American Film Institute,* and *San Francisco Bay Bird Observatory.*

Web pages and hypertext links Many universities and research institutes provide information through their own Web home pages, with hypertext links that take you with one click to many other sources. Individual Web pages can provide useful information, too, but need careful evaluation since anyone can publish anything on the Web (48f).

E-mail discussions With e-mail, you have access to many discussion groups. Messages go out to a list of people interested in specific topics. Without charge, you can join a list devoted to a topic of interest (48e). However, most of the lists are not refereed or monitored, so you have to evaluate carefully any information you find.

For academic research, personal blogs, Usenet newsgroups, and chat rooms provide little that is substantive. Evaluating the reliability of a contributor's comments can be difficult.

Chapter **48**

Evaluating Sources Critically

How can you identify good, relevant sources? Use the following guidelines.

Online Study Center This icon will direct you to quick reference tools, Web resources, and research guides on the Web site at http://college.hmco.com/keys.html.

48a How to read sources critically

Reading what others have written always provides you with ideas, but not just the ideas you absorb from the page or screen. When you read critically, you generate ideas of your own as you read and make your own contributions to the issues under discussion. The principles of critical analysis discussed in 1a can be extended to reading sources critically.

> **KEY POINTS**
> **Reading Sources Critically**

- Ask questions about the credentials and reputation of the author and the place of publication. What do you learn about the writer's purpose and the audience whom the author is addressing? Make sure you subject any material you find on Web pages to especially careful scrutiny (48e).

- Ask questions about the ideas you read. An easy way to do this is to write your annotations in the margin. If you find yourself thinking, "But . . ." as you read, go with that sense of doubt and make a note of what troubles you. Examples of annotated readings are in 1a.

- Be on the lookout for assumptions that may be faulty. If you are reading an article on home-schooling and the writer favors home-schooling because it avoids subjecting students to violence in schools, the unstated assumption is that all schools are violent places. For more on the logic of argument, see 7.

- Make sure the writer's evidence is adequate and accurate. For example, if the writer is making a generalization about all Chinese students based on a study of only three, you have cause to challenge the generalization as resting on inadequate evidence.

- Note how the writer uses language. Which terms does the writer use with positive—or negative—connotations, signaling the values the writer holds? Does the writer denigrate the views of others with phrases such as "a ridiculous notion" or "laughably inept policies"?

- Be alert for sweeping generalizations, bias, and prejudice: "Atheists are evil." "Women want to stay home and have children." "Men love to spend Sundays watching sports."

Do your reading when you can write—not while on the treadmill or watching TV. Note any questions, objections, or challenges on the page (see example in 1a); on self-stick notes; on index cards; in a response file on your computer or in a journal or blog (3a). Your critical responses to your reading will provide you with your own ideas for writing.

48b How to recognize a scholarly article

Learn to distinguish scholarly from nonscholarly articles. A scholarly article is not usually found in a popular magazine. A scholarly journal is peer reviewed—that is, other scholars read all the articles and approve them for publication. Just looking at the cover of the journal, noting the length of the article and the length of each paragraph, and scanning the beginning and end of the article should help make the distinction between a scholarly and a nonscholarly periodical obvious. See pages 656–659 for examples of a scholarly journal.

Cover of a scholarly journal

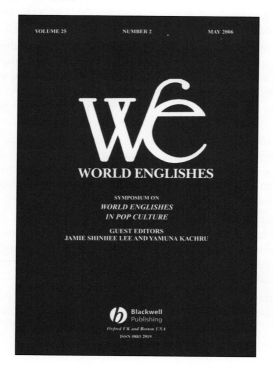

VOLUME 25   NUMBER 2   MAY 2006

we

WORLD ENGLISHES

SYMPOSIUM ON
*WORLD ENGLISHES
IN POP CULTURE*

GUEST EDITORS
JAMIE SHINHEE LEE AND YAMUNA KACHRU

Blackwell
Publishing
Oxford UK and Boston USA
ISSN 0883 2919

KEY POINTS
What a Scholarly Article Does

A scholarly article

- refers to the work of other scholars (look for in-text citations and a bibliographical list of works cited, footnotes, or endnotes)
- names the author and usually describes the author's credentials
- includes notes, references, or a bibliography, and may include an abstract
- deals with a serious issue in depth
- uses academic or technical language for informed readers
- appears in journals that do not include colorful advertisements or eye-catching pictures (a picture of two stunning models is an indication that you are not looking at a scholarly article)

Table of contents of a scholarly journal

Vol. 25, No. 2   **WORLD ENGLISHES**   2006

CONTENTS

SYMPOSIUM ON
WORLD ENGLISHES IN POP CULTURE
Guest editors: Jamie Shinhee Lee and Yamuna Kachru

When you read scholarly articles, look for any section headings, read the abstract and any section headed "Summary" or "Conclusions," and determine the author's main idea to find out whether the article addresses your topic. If you are working on a topic related to current events, you probably will need to consult newspapers, magazines, and online sources as well as or in place of scholarly journals.

Recognizing scholarly articles in general databases

Some databases are specialized and will yield only research articles (or only abstracts) published in scholarly journals. Other databases, such as those hosted by *EBSCO* and *InfoTrac,* are more general, including popular magazines as well as serious and scholarly periodicals. In several databases, you can search for scholarly articles by opting to find "peer-reviewed" articles; these are articles that have been approved by an editorial board. *EBSCO* databases provide this feature.

Article abstract and first page of a scholarly article

World Englishes, Vol. 25, No. 2, pp. 279–297, 2006.   0883–2919

Super-heroes to super languages: American popular culture through South Asian language comics

TEJ K. BHATIA*

ABSTRACT: Although under immense pressure from television, movies, and video games, comics are a very effective and non-intrusive means of introducing American popular culture in South Asia in the age of globalization. The introduction of American comic books in South Asian languages, although a recent phenomenon, has already stimulated the South Asian/Indian appetite for American super-heroes and comics and has added various new cognitive and (psycho) linguistic dimensions to traditional Indian comics. The paper attempts to account for the creative linguistic strategies employed in the representation of super-heroes through super languages (Sanskrit and English) in South Asian language comics and to explain the highly diverse appeal and positive perception of comics in South Asia.

INTRODUCTION[1]

A couple of years ago, while doing field work for my advertising book (Bhatia, 2000) in Dhakar Kheri, a village in the colorful desert state of Rajasthan, bordering with Pakistan, I witnessed a situation which inspired me to undertake a long-range study of American popular culture in South Asian language comics. The situation involved a group of young teenagers sharing an English comic book with elderly gentlemen on a relaxed summer evening; they were translating and paraphrasing the comic book in creative ways, both into Hindi and its rural variety. Even more surprising was that the comic book did not deal either with Indian mythology or Indian super-heroes – it dealt with Superman! This event not only revealed a newfound passion and appetite for American comic books in India, but it also underscored what Bhabha (1996) identifies as the "transcendental" and "translational" capacity of art.

The storytelling session ended with a curious query by one of the village elders: "How come Superman doesn't speak Hindi?" The question was culturally loaded, which cast some doubt about the superpowers of Superman. The driving force behind this question was skepticism that, unlike Lord Buddha, who could communicate not only with humans in different tongues but also with animals, a monolingual, tongue-tied, English-speaking Superman couldn't be a true super-hero if he was limited in his linguistic competence and reach. Fortunately, the situation has changed since then. Superman speaks Indian languages and so do other American super-heroes. Not only this, Superman is the only character who knows how to greet a balloon seller using the Hindi/Sanskrit greeting, *namaste: namaskaar bhaaii, mujhe apne saare gubbaare bec do* 'Hello brother, sell me all of your balloons' (*Superman,* issue 3). Not only does Superman stand out in his ability to use Indian language greetings, but his use of the kinship word *bhaaii* 'brother' further highlights the Indianness of the expression. Other characters do not show such a linguistic talent; they exclusively rely on English greetings.

* 312 HBC, Syracuse University, Syracuse, New York 13224-1160, USA. E-mail: tkbhatia@syr.edu

only abstracts) published in scholarly journals. Other databases, such as those hosted by *EBSCO* and *InfoTrac,* are more general, including popular magazines as well as serious and scholarly periodicals. In several databases, you can search for scholarly articles by opting to find "peer-reviewed" articles; these are articles that have been approved by an editorial board. *EBSCO* databases provide this feature.

TECH NOTE

Databases of Journal Information

- Genamics JournalSeek provides links to the Web sites of journals to help you identify journals as scholarly.

- The Cornell University Web site *Distinguishing Scholarly Journals from Other Periodicals* provides definitions and examples of four categories of periodical literature: scholarly, substantive news and general interest, popular, and sensational.

Article last page and references (APA style)

Super-heroes to super languages   297

of comic books favors English and Sanskrit (as super languages) over Hindi and other South Asian languages and exploits the multilingual context of India effectively.

NOTES

1. This work was funded by the Center for the Study of Popular Television, S. I. Newhouse School of Public Communications, Syracuse University. I am grateful to Professor Robert J. Thompson for his support and comments on the earlier version of this paper. I wish to acknowledge Amar Chitra Kathra for the content in Figure 1 and to acknowledge Sharad Devarajan, President and CEO of South Asian Language Gotham Comics for the content in Figures 2–7.
2. According to the 1991 census, the incidence of bilingualism with English was 8.85 percent and 9.045 percent in the Hindi and Bengali speaking areas, respectively. See Census of India (2004).

REFERENCES

Bhabha, Homi K. (1996) Postmodernism/postcolonialism. In *Critical Terms for Art History.* Edited by Robert S. Nelson and Richard Shiff. Chicago: University of Chicago Press, pp. 307–22.
Bhatia, Tej K. (2000) *Advertising in Rural India: Language, Marketing Communication and Consumerism.* Tokyo Press, Tokyo: Japan (Institute for the Study of Languages and Cultures of Asia and Africa, Tokyo University of Foreign Studies).
Bhatia, Tej K. (2004) Bilingualism in South Asia. In *The Handbook of Bilingualism.* Edited by Tej K. Bhatia and William C. Ritchie. Oxford: Blackwell, pp. 780–807.
Bhatia, Tej K. and Ritchie, William C. (eds.) (2004) *The Handbook of Bilingualism.* Oxford: Blackwell.
Banerjee, Sudeshna (2004) Comics power for serious posers of life. *The Telegraph.* http://www.telegraphindia.com/1041223/asp/calcutta/index.asp.
Canagarajah, Suresh A. (2002) *Geopolitics of Academic Writing.* Philadelphia: University of Pennsylvania Press.
Canagarajah, Suresh A. (2005) *Reclaiming the Local in Language Policy and Practice.* Mahwah, NJ: Lawrence Erlbaum.
Census of India (2004) *Language Atlas of India 1991.* New Delhi: Government of India, S. Narayan and Sons.
CNNFN (2002) Maverick in the morning (transcript). January 10.
Hakuta, Kanji (1985) *Mirror of Language.* New York: Basic Books.
Kachru, Braj B. (1997) Language in Indian society. In *Ananaya: A Portrait of India.* Edited by S. N. Sridhar and N. K. Mattoo. New York: The Association of Indians in America, pp. 555–85.
Kachru, Yamuna (1997) Culture and communication in India. In *Ananaya: A portrait of India.* Edited by S. N. Sridhar and N. K. Mattoo. New York: The Association of Indians in America, pp. 645–63.
Kannan, K. (2004) A renaissance in comics. *The Hindu.* August 30. http://www.thehindu.com/2004/08/30/stories/2004083010590400.htm.
Kuntzman, Gersh (2001) There's more than one way to fight for truth, justice and the American Way. *New York Post.* December 17.
Labov, William (1972) The transformation of experience in narrative syntax. In *Language in the Inner City.* Philadelphia: University of Pennsylvania Press, pp. 354–96.
Lent, John A. (1995) *Asian Popular Culture.* Oxford: Westview Press.
Lent, John A. (ed.) (2001) *Illustrating Asia: Comics, Humor Magazines and Picture Books.* Honolulu: University of Hawaii Press.
Malhotra, Rajiv (2003) RISA Lila-2-Limp scholarship and demonology. http://www.sulekha.com/expressions/column.asp?cid=305890.
McCabe, Allyssa and Peterson, Carole (1991) *Developing Narrative Structures.* Hilldale, NJ: Lawrence Erlbaum.
McCloud, Scott (1994) *Understanding Comics: The Invisible Art.* New York: HarperPerennial.
Pecora, Norma (1992) Superman/Superboys/Supermen: the comic book hero as socializing agent. In *Men, Masculinity and the Media.* Edited by Steve Craig. Newbury Park: Sage, pp. 61–77.
Pratt, Mary Louise (1992) *Imperial Eyes: Travel Writing and Transculturation.* London: Routledge.
Rao, Aruna (2001) From self-knowledge to super heroes: the story of Indian comics. In *Illustrating Asia: Comics, Humor Magazines and Picture Books.* Edited by John A. Lent. Honolulu: University of Hawaii Press, pp. 37–63.
Said, Edward (1978) *Orientalism.* New York: Pantheon Books.
Sardar, Ziauddin (1999) *Orientalism.* Philadelphia, PA: Open University Press.
Spivak, Gayatri Chakravorty (1987) *In Other Worlds: Essays in Cultural Politics.* New York: Methuen.
Walters, Keith and Brody, Michael (2005) Policing usage in comics. In *What's Language Got to Do with It?* Edited by Keith Walters and Michael Brody. New York: W. W. Norton, pp. 109–11.

 *Online Study Center* Research Journal information

48c How to evaluate print sources

Before you make detailed notes on a book or an article that began its life in print, be sure it will provide suitable information to help answer your research question.

Print books Check the date of publication, notes about the author, table of contents, and index. Skim the preface, introduction, chapter headings, and summaries to give yourself an idea of the information contained in the book and of the book's theoretical basis and perspective. Do not waste time making detailed notes on a book that deals only tangentially with your topic or on an out-of-date book (unless your purpose is to discuss and critique its perspective or examine a topic historically). Ask a librarian or your instructor for help in evaluating the appropriateness of sources you discover. If your topic concerns a serious academic issue, readers will expect you to consult books and not limit your references to popular magazines, newspapers, and Internet sources.

Periodical articles in print Take into account the type of periodical, any organization with which it is affiliated, and the intended audience. Differentiate among the following types of articles (listed in descending order of reliability, with the most reliable first):

- scholarly articles (see 48b)
- articles, often long, in periodicals for nonspecialist but serious, well-educated readers, such as the *New York Review of Books, Atlantic Monthly, Economist, Scientific American,* and *Nation*
- shorter articles, with sources not identified, in popular magazines for a general audience, such as *Ebony, Time, Newsweek, Parents, Psychology Today,* and *Vogue,* or in newspapers
- articles with dubious sources, written for sensational tabloid magazines, such as the *National Enquirer, Globe,* and *Star*

Newspaper articles The *New York Times, Washington Post,* and *Chicago Tribune,* for example, provide mostly reliable accounts of current events, daily editorial comments, and reviews of books, films, and art. Be aware that most newspapers have political leanings, so reports of and comments on the same event may differ.

KEY POINTS

Questions to Evaluate a Print Source

1. *What does the work cover?* It should be long enough and detailed enough to provide adequate information.

2. *How objective is the information?* The author and publisher or periodical should not be affiliated with an organization that has an ax to grind—unless, of course, your topic entails examining the ax, reading critically, and making comparisons with other points of view.

3. *How current are the views?* Check the date of publication. The work should be up-to-date if you need a current perspective.

4. *How reputable are the publisher and author?* The work should be published by a reputable publisher in a source that is academically reliable, not one devoted to gossip, advertising, propaganda, or sensationalism. Check *Books in Print, Literary Market Place,* or *ACQWEB's Directory of Publishers and Vendors*

for details on publishers. The author should be an authority on the subject. Find out what else the author has written (in Google, in *Books in Print,* or at Amazon.com) and what his or her qualifications are as an authority.

48d How to evaluate Web sources: Developing junk antennae

What makes the Internet so fascinating is that it is wide open, free, and democratic. Anyone can "publish" anything, and anyone with Internet access can read it. However, when you are looking for information and well-presented, informed opinion, the Internet can pose a challenge.

If you find an article in a subscription database (*InfoTrac* or *LexisNexis,* for example), you will know that the article has been published in print, so you can use the criteria for print works (47e) to evaluate it. If the article has been published in a reputable periodical or in an online journal sponsored by a professional organization or a university, you can assume that it is a valid source for a research paper.

For works devised specifically for the Web, use the strategies in the Key Points box to separate the information from the junk.

KEY POINTS
Developing Your Junk Antennae

1. *Scrutinize the domain name of the URL.* Reliable information can be found on .gov and .edu addresses that are institutionally sponsored (but see item 2). With .com ("dot com") or .org sources, always assess whether the source provides factual information or advocates a specific point of view on an issue.

2. *Assess the originator of an .edu source.* Check that the institution or a branch of it is sponsoring the site. A tilde (~) followed by a name in the URL indicates an individual posting from an academic source. Try to ascertain whether the individual is a faculty member or a student. Increasingly, though, individuals are setting up Web sites under their own domain names.

(Continued)

(Continued)

3. *Check the home page.* Always take the link from a Web site to its "About" page or its home page, if you are not already there. These pages often provide more information about the author, the sponsor, the purpose, and the date of posting.

4. *Determine who is the author, and discover what you can about him or her.* Look for a list of credentials, a home page, a résumé, or Web publications. In Google or Google Scholar, use the author's name as a search term to see what the author has published on the Internet or who has cited the author. If no individual or institutional author is to be found anywhere, check the purpose and the sponsor of the site.

5. *Investigate the purposes of a Web page author or sponsor.* Objectivity and rationality are not necessarily features of all Web pages. The sponsor of a site may want to persuade, convert, or sell. Even if the message is not obviously biased and extreme, be aware that most authors write from some sense of conviction or purpose. (Note, though, that a Web site can be oriented toward a specific view without necessarily being irresponsible.)

6. *Evaluate the quality of the writing.* A Web page filled with spelling and grammatical errors should not inspire confidence. If the language has not been checked, the ideas probably haven't been given much time and thought, either. Don't use such a site as a source. Exceptions are discussion lists and Usenet postings. They are written and posted quickly, so even if they contain errors, they can also contain useful ideas to stimulate thinking on your topic.

7. *Follow the links.* See whether the links in a site take you to authoritative sources. If the links no longer work (you'll get a 404 message: "Site Not Found"), the home page with the links has not been updated in a while—not a good sign.

8. *Check for dates, updates, ways to respond, and ease of navigation.* A recent date of posting or recent updating; information about the author; ways to reach the author by e-mail, regular mail, or phone; a clearly organized site; easy navigation; and up-to-date links to responsible sites are all indications that the site is well managed and current.

9. *Corroborate information.* Try to find the same information on another reliable site. Also look for contradictory information elsewhere.

TECH NOTE

Web Sites on Evaluating Sources

Useful information on evaluating sources is available at a Widener University (Chester, PA) site. An interactive tutorial on evaluating Internet sources is at the Online Study Center.

Online Study Center **Research** Evaluating sources

48e Anatomy of a Web site

Using the flowchart Use the following flowchart to find on a Web site the information that will help you evaluate its reliability. In addition, if you record the information for every accessed site that you might refer to or quote from in your paper, you will then be able to construct your citation without retracing your steps (see 49f). Although different styles of documentation, such as MLA and APA, ask for different chunks of information in different configurations, the five items listed in the chart are common to most of them. As you read the chart, refer to the Web page (below), an annotated screenshot of a site with an explicitly stated agenda "dedicated to restoring democratic authority over corporations, reviving grassroots democracy, and revoking the power of money and corporations to control government and civic society."

Web Page

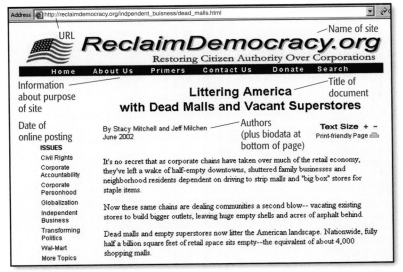

How to Evaluate a Web Site

What to Look For and Record; Where and How to Find It	Additional Things You May Need to Do
1. Name of author →	

1. Name of author

Look at the top or bottom of the page. For Web documents with no author named, look for an organization, government agency, or business that serves as the author.

- Follow any links on the document page to a résumé, publications, purpose statement, or home page. Try to establish the purpose of the site.
- Do a Google search for details about the author, whether an individual, institution, organization, business, or government agency.
- Do not confuse the Web site manager or the person maintaining the site with the author of the information.
- If you cannot find an author, look on the "Home" or "About" page, or go to #2, "Title."

2. Title of document

Find it at the top of the page. Note, though, that some sites will contain documents with titles, and some will not.

- For online sources previously in print form, record any print publication details provided.
- Record page numbers only for PDF documents, in which page numbers appear on the screen.
- Record the name of the document section in which relevant information appears (e.g., Introduction).
- Record paragraph numbers *only* when they are part of the document and appear on the screen.

3. Name of site

If it is not visible at the top or bottom of the page, go to "Home" or "About." Or delete the URL progressively back to each single slash, and click to see which part of the site you access.

Also record what you can of the following, if available:
- name of the organization in charge of the content of the site (owner or sponsor)—usually indicated in the root domain of the URL (before the first single slash)
- for an online journal, the volume and issue numbers
- the date when material was posted online or updated (often not available)

4. Your date of access

Because Web sites come and go and change, always record the exact date on which you access the site.

Save any page that provides you with crucial information or is likely to update or change its content, such as blogs or files ending with *.asp* or *.shtml*.

5. URL

Copy and paste this from your browser into your working bibliography. Copying by hand may introduce errors.

If a page is divided into sections ("frames"), and you want to refer to one frame only, right-click in the frame, and select "Save (or Add) as Favorite"; then retrieve the material in the frame with its own URL.

Recognizing the difficulties Note that on many sites you may have difficulty finding a date of posting, a document title as well as a Web site name, or an exact identification of the author of the material, whether an individual or an organization. Just record whatever you can find on a thorough search of the site, always scrolling down to the bottom of the page. Try using the root domain of the URL—the material just before the dot preceding the first single slash (as in <http://www.library.ucla.edu/>)—to identify the owner, also referred to as the *publisher* or *sponsor*, of the site, who is responsible for its content. If the "Home" and "About" links provide no useful information, consider whether you should use a source if you are unsure about the identity of the author, the author's credentials, or the owner and purpose of the site.

Chapter **49**
Using Sources

Once you have found (47) and evaluated (48) sources for your paper, you then need to know how to document the information and use your sources to support your points. It is especially important to know how to cite any source that you refer to, summarize, paraphrase from, or quote from so that you avoid plagiarizing. First, though, understand what plagiarism is and how careful documentation can steer you clear of it.

49a What is plagiarism? The seven sins— and the consequences

The ease of finding, copying, and downloading information from the screen has its attendant dangers: that researchers lose sight of what is theirs and what isn't, that they forget where they read something, that information seems so prolific that surely it must be there for the taking. Unfortunately, though, that is not the case, especially in the academic world, where presenting somebody else's words or ideas without acknowledging where those words and ideas come from is a punishable offense.

Online Study Center This icon will direct you to quick reference tools, Web resources, and research guides on the Web site at http://college.hmco.com/keys.html.

The word for the offense, *plagiarism,* is derived from a Latin verb meaning "to kidnap," and if you use someone else's words and ideas without acknowledging them, you are in effect kidnapping or stealing those words and ideas.

KEY POINTS
The Seven Sins of Plagiarism

1. *Intentional grand larceny* Presenting as your own work a whole essay bought from paper mills, "borrowed" from a friend, or intentionally copied and pasted from an online source (where such a practice may be compared to ordering "a takeout essay"—see 49i)

2. *Premeditated shoplifting* Using passages from a book, article, or Web site that you intentionally insert in your paper without any attribution (a type of plagiarism differing from point 1 only in that passages, not the whole paper, are copied)

3. *Tinkering with the evidence* Using unattributed source material, making only a few word changes, and trusting that those changes are enough to avoid charges of plagiarism

4. *Idea kidnapping* Using ideas written by others (even if you do use your own words) and neglecting to cite the source of the ideas

5. *Unauthorized borrowing of private property* Using the words or sentence structure of a source and citing the source—but following it too closely and not including actual words from the source within quotation marks

6. *Trespassing over boundaries* Failing to indicate in your paper where ideas from a source end and your ideas take over

7. *Writing under the influence* Being too tired, lazy, or late for an imminent deadline and turning to any of the six previous sins in desperation

---

Consequences Obviously, these "sins" vary in their severity and in the intention to deceive. The types of plagiarism described in items 4 through 6 in the Key Points box sometimes occur unintentionally, but they may be perceived as plagiarism nevertheless. You have to work hard at avoiding them, especially since the consequences of plagiarism can be severe, ranging from an F on a paper or an F in a course to disciplinary measures or expulsion from college. In the world at large, it can lead to lawsuits and ruined careers. Those are reasons enough to work hard at resisting the temptation to plagiarize.

LANGUAGE AND CULTURE
Ownership Rights across Cultures

The Western view takes seriously the ownership of words and text. It respects both the individual as author (and authority) and the originality of the individual's ideas. Copyright laws define and protect the boundaries of intellectual property. However, even the Western world acknowledges that authors imitate and borrow from others' work, as Harold Bloom notes in *The Anxiety of Influence*. In some cultures, memorization and the use of classic texts are common in all walks of life. And worldwide, the ownership of language, texts, music, and videos is continually called into question by the democratic, interactive nature of the Internet. In short, therefore, plagiarism is not something universal and easy to define. In Western academic culture, basic ground rules exist for the "fair use" of another writer's writing without payment, but easy access to music and media sources poses interesting questions about intellectual property and the opportunities to create and remix culture.

TECH NOTE
A Web Site on Plagiarism

For more on the topic of plagiarism, see the Plagiarism Prevention Zone at the Online Study Center for this book. Another resource is the excellent Georgetown University Web site *What Is Plagiarism?*

Online Study Center **Research** More on avoiding plagiarism

49b What is documentation?

When you write, you are expected to provide all the necessary information in an organized system of documentation. The need to acknowledge and document sources is not merely academic pickiness. It is a service to readers. When you document a source, you provide readers with exact details about where to find the reference, the fact, or the quotation. (For a book, for example, you need to supply information about who wrote it, what the title is, the publisher, the place of publication, and the date of publication.) Then it will be quick and easy for interested readers to locate the exact source that you found. Readers may want to find all or some of your sources for any of the following reasons: you have made them curious and they want to read more; they want to explore the topic in greater depth; they find it hard to believe that a source says what you say it says, so they want to read it for themselves.

You do yourself a service, too, every time you cite and document sources. When you acknowledge ideas and words that you have found in the works of reputable authors, you bolster your own case. Readers are far more likely to treat your claim seriously and heed your argument if you show that you can support it with documented evidence, instead of presenting it as something you happened to think of in a random moment or something you heard from a friend. Readers will be impressed by a judicious use of sources, both those that support your claim and those that run counter to it—which you, of course, will refute. Such an approach reveals a thoroughness that readers find impressive and convincing. From the beginning, then, treat source material and the documenting of it as an aid to your argument.

Acknowledging your sources not only gives credit where it is due but also shows how much research you have done. The first step is careful recording of source information and precise note-taking (49e and 49f). The second step is careful acknowledging and citing of sources in your paper and listing of the sources you have used. Chapters 51–54 show you how to use four different styles of citation and documentation: MLA, APA, CSE, and *Chicago*. Once you have recorded the basic information about each source, you will be able to use it in whatever documentation style your instructor or discipline requires.

49c How to avoid plagiarizing

Research and clear documentation open a channel of communication between you and your readers. They learn what your views are and what has influenced those views. They will assume that anything not documented is your original idea and your wording. So if you even accidentally present someone else's actual words or ideas as if they were your own, readers might suspect you of plagiarizing.

To avoid plagiarism, begin with accurate recording and careful management of source material so that you do not end up confused about which parts of your notes contain your ideas and which are derived from the works of others.

KEY POINTS
How to Avoid Plagiarizing

- Start your research early enough to avoid panic mode.
- Make a record of each source so that you have all the information you need for appropriate documentation.
- Set up a working annotated bibliography.
- Take notes from the sources, using a systematic method of indicating quotation, paraphrase, and your own comments. For example, use quotation marks around quoted words, phrases, sentences, and passages; introduce a paraphrase with a tag, such as "Laird makes the point that . . ."; in your notes about a source, write your own comments in a different color. Then, later, you will see immediately which ideas are yours and which come from your source.
- Always acknowledge and document the source of any passage, phrase, or idea that you have used or summarized from someone else's work.
- Never use exactly the same sequence of ideas and organization of argument as your source.
- When you use a single key word from your source or three or more words in sequence from your source, use the appropriate format for quoting and documenting.
- Be aware that substituting synonyms for a few words in the source or moving a few words around is not enough to counter a charge of plagiarism.
- Don't use in your paper passages that have been written or rewritten by a friend or a tutor.
- Never even consider buying, finding, downloading, or "borrowing" a paper or a section of a paper that you turn in as your own work.

49d What to cite and document

When you do refer to a source in your work, carefully cite and document it. Systematically provide information about the author, title, publication data, page numbers, Internet address, dates—whatever is available (see 49g for the information you need to collect). (See chapters 51–54 for guides to specific systems of documentation.) You also document sources so there will be no question about which words and ideas are yours and which belong to other people.

KEY POINTS
What to Cite

1. Cite all facts, statistics, and pieces of information unless they are common knowledge and are accessible in many sources.

2. Cite exact words from your source, enclosed in quotation marks.

3. Cite somebody else's ideas and opinions, even if you restate them in your own words in a summary or paraphrase.

4. Cite each sentence in a long paraphrase (if it is not clear that all the sentences paraphrase the same original source).

Note how James Stalker, in his article "Official English or English Only," does not quote directly but still cites the source of the specialized facts:

> By 1745 there were approximately 45,000 German speakers in the colonies, and by 1790 there were some 200,000, nine per cent of the population (Anderson 80).

Citation is not necessary for facts regarded as common knowledge, such as the dates of the Civil War; facts available in many sources, such as authors' birth and death dates and chronological events; or allusions to folktales that have been handed down through the ages. When you are in doubt about whether a fact is common knowledge, cite your source.

TECH NOTE
The Instability of Internet Information

Information on the Internet is constantly changing. The source material you find today might disappear by tomorrow. The bounty, collaborative nature, and flux of online information mean that you have to be especially careful as you conduct Internet research and record information. When in doubt, even if you are using information from a blog to which you have contributed, always keep a copy of the source on your computer or in print, and cite your source in your essay.

49e Keeping track of sources

The first step toward avoiding plagiarism is keeping track of what your sources are and which ideas come from your sources and which from you. You will find that the most frustrating moments for you as a researcher occur when you find some notes about an interesting point you read but cannot remember where you found the passage, who wrote it, or whether your notes represent an author's exact words. Keep track as you go along. However rushed you feel or however little time you have, save and record your source material. (See 49g for details on exactly what type of information to record about each source.)

Use the Bookmarks or Favorites feature.   Many browsers have a Bookmarks or Favorites feature that allows you to compile and save a list of useful sites you have visited. You can then easily revisit these sites by simply clicking on the bookmark. Bookmarks can be deleted later when you no longer need them. If you work on a networked computer in a lab where you cannot save your work on the hard drive, export your bookmarks to your own computor or use a free online bookmark service.

Online Study Center   **Research** Online bookmark services

Record URL and date of access.   Note that bookmarking will not always last with a long, nonpersistent URL, such as URLs of online subscription services. To be safe, also use the Copy and Paste features to copy the URL on your hard drive, flash drive, or CD, along with the date on which you access the source. As a last resort, copy the URL by hand, but take care to get it exactly right: every letter, symbol, and punctuation mark is important.

Highlight, copy, and paste.   As you read material on the Web, highlight a passage you find, copy it, and then paste it into your own file. Make sure that you indicate clearly in your new document that you have included a direct quotation. Use quotation marks and/or a bigger or colored font along with an author/page citation, as in the following example.

> Novelist John Lanchester has made a telling point about our image of self by having his narrator declare that we **"wouldn't care so much about what people thought of us if we knew how seldom they did"** (62).

Save as much information as you can about the original document in your working bibliography.

Make photocopies of print sources.   Photocopying print articles allows you to devote research time to locating relevant sources and taking notes from reference works and books; you can take the copies of articles with you and use them when you are unable to be in the library. As soon as you have time, though, evaluate the usefulness of your copies by highlighting and commenting on relevant sections or by taking notes.

Make copies of Web sources. When you print a useful Web page, the URL and your date of access will often be excluded. Unlike print sources, the content on many Web sites changes frequently; a download date does not allow for access to a site that has changed. Unless you are absolutely sure that a Web site is stable, save a copy of a source and include it in your paper.

49f Annotating and making notes

Printing and saving from online sources make a source text available for you to annotate. You can interact with the author's ideas, asking questions, writing comments, and jotting down your own ideas. Here is a passage from an article by Ellen Laird on plagiarism (see the bibliographical information on p. 675). As Laird, a college professor, discusses the case of Chip, a student who has plagiarized, she is considering her own role and her student's explanation. The passage shows student Juana Mere's annotations as she gave the article a critical reading.

> *But what if her instructions weren't as clear as she thought?*
> To save face with myself, I must assume that Chip understood that downloading an essay and submitting it as his own was an
> *Look up* egregious act. Why, then, did he do it? *Can she ever really know?*
> *But it's* Chip explained he had been "mentally perturbed" the weekend *Sounds*
> *specula-* before the paper was due and that the essay he had written failed *like a*
> *tion on* to meet his high standards. But I sensed that Chip felt he had made *very*
> *her part* a choice akin to having a pizza delivered. He had procrastinated *general*
> on an assignment due the next day, had no time left in which to *excuse*
> prepare his work from scratch, and had to get on to those pressing
> *Is this* matters that shape the world of an 18-year-old. He dialed his
> *conde-* Internet service provider, ordered takeout, and had it delivered.
> *scending?* *Nice analogy Good quotation*

Annotating is useful for comments, observations, and questions. You also will need to make notes when you do not have a copy that you can write on or when you want to summarize, paraphrase, and make detailed connections to other ideas and other sources. Write notes on the computer, on legal pads, in notebooks, or on index cards—whatever works best for you (see 49i for sample notes). Index cards—each card with a heading and only one note—offer the advantage of flexibility: you can shuffle and reorder them to fit the organization of your paper. In your notes, always include the author's name, a short version of the title of the work, and any relevant page number(s) whenever you summarize, paraphrase, or quote, as shown on page 680. Include full bibliographical information in your working bibliography, as shown on page 675. (See 49g) Then when you start to write your paper, you will have at your fingertips all the information necessary for a citation.

49g Setting up a working bibliography

From the first steps of your research, keep accurate records of each source in a working bibliography. Record enough information so that you will be able to make up a list of references in whichever style of documentation you choose, though not all the points of information you record will be necessary for every style of documentation.

Important: Essential information for an online source is always the URL and the date on which you access the material. Always make a note of that information.

Sort your sources into four categories: print books, print articles, Web sources, and online database sources. The table on page 674 summarizes what you should record. For each category, download or print the templates provided in the Online Study Guide that prompt you to record the information you need to cite your sources.

Online Study Center **Research** Templates for recording sources

---

KEY POINTS
Helpful Hints for Recording Source Information

Print book Photocopy the title page and the copyright page, where much of the information is available.

Print article Photocopy the table of contents of the periodical or anthology.

Web source Save, e-mail yourself a copy, or print out the Web source. Set your computer so that the URL appears on the printout along with the date of access. Use the Copy and Paste functions to copy the URL accurately into your own document.

Online database source Save, e-mail yourself a copy, or print out the online database source.

Source Essentials: What to Record

	Print Book	Print Article	Web Source	Online Database Source
Author(s), editor(s), translator(s) OR Name of company or government agency	✓	✓	✓ (if available on site)	✓
Title and subtitle	✓	✓	✓	✓
Print publication information	✓	✓	✓ (if available on site)	✓
Volume/edition/issue	✓	✓		✓
Call number	✓	✓		
Page numbers of document	✓	✓	✓ Only for PDF documents. Include number of paragraphs only if numbers appear on screen.	✓ Only for PDF documents. Otherwise include start page if given.
Name of Web site			✓	✓ Name of database and service
Other essential information to include	Place: Publisher, date	**Scholarly article:** Include volume number, issue number, date of publication, inclusive page numbers. **Article in a book:** Include title, editor, place, publisher, year of publication, inclusive page numbers of the article.	**Web site:** Include name of sponsor, date of online publication or update, URL, and date of access. **Article in online journal:** Include volume number. Always include URL and your date of access. **E-mail message or discussion list posting:** Include name of sender, subject line, date of posting, name of list, and your date of access to the list.	**Article in a database:** Include volume, issue number, date of print publication, and name and location of library. Also include URL of home page of database or persistent URL of article and your date of access.

Keep your list of sources in a form that you can work with to organize them alphabetically, add and reject sources, and add summaries and notes. Note cards and computer files have the advantage over sheets of paper or a research journal. They don't tie you to page order.

Here is a sample bibliographical record for an article accessed in an online subscription database.

Laird, Ellen. "Internet Plagiarism: We All Pay the Price." Chronicle of Higher Education 13 July 2001: 5. Research Library. ProQuest. New York University Lib. 7 May 2006 <http://proquest.umi.com>.

Annotate the working bibliography If you need to prepare an annotated bibliography, one that summarizes the contents of each source, write a brief summary on the back of the index card or hardcopy template. Or if you are using a computer to record information, keep a separate file for the summaries you will need for an annotated bibliography.

Here are entries from Diana Fatakhova's annotated bibliography, which accompanied her proposal (see 46g). Notice how Fatakhova's annotations not only focus on main points but also include information on how the source will help her paper and what type of source it is. She has even evaluated her sources here.

Cohan, John Alan. "Psychiatric Ethics and Emerging Issues of Pychopharmacology in the Treatment of Depression." Journal of Contemporary Health Law & Policy, Winter 2003: 115–. Academic Universe: Medical Journals. LexisNexis. City U of New York Lib. 31 Oct. 2004 <http://lexisnexis.com>.

This lengthy article covers much ground concerning different tests taken to ascertain the risks of antidepressants. It discusses whether or not antidepressants actually provide the cure they are supposedly meant for or if they merely act as placebos. The author poses the question: is depression due to biology, thus leading to whether it could be cured through drugs? He lists risks associated with these antidepressants, some admitted by drug manufacturers, some by scientific journals, some listed as separate mental syndromes in the DMS-IV, and still others caused by withdrawal. This article will help me identify the risks of taking antidepressants to discover whether or not they are really worth it, and ascertain what other treatments are possible. This is a reliable source that comes from an academic journal and provides its readers with a number of references.

Rivinus, Timothy. "Do The New Antidepressants Cause Youth Suicide?" The Brown University Child and Adolescent Behavior Letter 20 (2004): 8. Academic Search Premier. EBSCO. City U of New York Lib. 28 Oct. 2004 <http://search.epnet.com>.

The author is an advocate for the use of SSRI's and criticizes those who assume that these drugs cause suicidal behavior merely because they are associated with it. He states that creating panic over the use of these drugs may be preventing some youths from getting the treatment they need. He discusses the reasons why people tend to associate antidepressants with suicide and deems them unwarranted. In his opinion, the benefits of SSRI's outweigh the risks. This article will allow me to comment on the opposing view of this issue. It is a reliable source from a credible university journal, written by an MD.

49h Introducing source material

When you provide a summary, paraphrase, or quotation to support one of the points in your paper, set up the context. Don't just drop in the material as if it came from nowhere. Think about how to introduce and integrate the material into the structure of your paper.

NO   **Teachers might feel that Internet plagiarism is just too easy and that students plagiarize too easily by downloading material just like ordering takeout and "having a pizza delivered" (Laird 5).** [If this is your first mention of Laird, readers may wonder who the author is, what the context is, and how the quotation is relevant.]

YES   **Teachers might feel that Internet plagiarism is just too easy and that students plagiarize too easily by downloading material. In fact, college teacher Ellen Laird compares this practice to the ease of ordering takeout and "having a pizza delivered" (5).** [You would cite the original source fully in your works-cited list.]

Introducing source material   If you quote a complete sentence or if you paraphrase or summarize a section of another work, it is advisable to prepare readers for your summary, paraphrase, or quotation by mentioning the author's name in an introductory phrase, rather than just adding a parenthetical citation. In your first reference to the work, give the author's full name. To further orient readers, you can also include a brief statement of the author's expertise or credentials and thesis so that readers understand why this is an important source for you to cite. Here are some useful ways to introduce source material:

X has pointed out that

X, in a seminal article on the topic, has made it clear that

X makes it clear from the evidence she provides that

X uses the evidence to suggest that

According to the expert opinion of X,

In 1999, X, the vice president of the corporation, declared

Varying the introductory verb   The introductory verbs *say* and *write* are clear and direct. For more nuances, though, consider using verbs that offer shades of meaning, such as *acknowledge, agree, argue, ask, assert, believe, claim, comment, contend, declare, deny, emphasize, insist, note, observe, point out, propose, speculate, suggest.*

In the humanities, for instance, many research findings offer interpretation and speculation, so they may be relevant for years, decades, or centuries. Publication dates in the MLA (Modern Language Association) style, therefore, occur only in the works-cited list and do not make an appearance in the in-text citation. Such a practice also serves to minimalize interruptions to the text.

In the sciences and social sciences, however, in APA style, the dates of the works are put at the forefront because timeliness of research is an issue in the fields.

See Parts 9 and 10 for more details on MLA and APA documentation styles.

49i Summarizing and paraphrasing

Summary Summaries are useful for giving readers basic information about the work you are discussing. To summarize a source or a passage in a source, select only the main points as the author presents them, without your own commentary or interpretation. Be brief, and use your own words at all times. To ensure that you use your own words, do not have the original source in front of you as you write. Read, understand, and then put the passage away before writing your summary. If you find that you must include some particularly apt words from the original source, put them in quotation marks.

Use summaries in your research paper to let readers know the gist of the most important sources you find. When you include a summary in a paper, introduce the author or the work to indicate where your summary begins. At the end of the summary, give the page numbers you are summarizing. Do not include page numbers if you are summarizing the complete work or summarizing an online source; instead, indicate where your summary ends and your own ideas return (see 49j). When you write your paper, provide full documentation of the source in your list of works cited at the end.

After reading the article by Laird on plagiarism, Mere decided to write a research paper on Internet plagiarism. She wrote this 65-word summary of an article of 1,635 words in a computer file headed "Laird on college plagiarism." (She could also have used an index card.)

Laird   Summary

"Internet plagiarism"

College professor Ellen Laird explores the possible reasons why a student might have plagiarized a whole essay. She concludes that Chip, otherwise a good student, knew what he was doing, but taking material from the Internet while at home might not have seemed unethical. Laird connects his behavior to our contemporary culture and laments that teaching will have to change to counteract opportunities for plagiarism.

Paraphrase When you need more details than a summary provides, paraphrasing offers a tool. Use paraphrase more often than you use quotation. A paraphrase uses your words and your interpretations of and comments on the ideas you find in your sources. It is commonly accepted that if you cannot paraphrase information, then you probably do not understand it. So paraphrase serves the purpose of showing that you have absorbed your source material.

A paraphrase is similar in length to the original material—maybe somewhat longer. In a paraphrase, present the author's argument and logic, but be very careful not to use the author's exact words or sentence structure.

KEY POINTS
How to Paraphrase

- Keep the source out of sight as you write a paraphrase so that you will not be tempted to copy the sentence patterns or phrases of the original.

- Do not substitute synonyms for some or most of the words in an author's passage.

- Use your own sentence structure as well as your own words. Your writing will still be regarded as plagiarized if it resembles the original in sentence structure as well as in wording.

- Do not comment or interpret: just tell readers the ideas that the author of your source presents.

- Check your text against the original source to avoid inadvertent plagiarism.

- Cite the author (and page number if a print source) as the source of the ideas, introduce and integrate the paraphrase, and provide full documentation. If the source does not name an author, cite the title.

When Mere was making notes for her paper on Internet plagiarism, she decided to paraphrase one of the key paragraphs from Laird's article, one that she had previously annotated (49f, p. 672).

ORIGINAL SOURCE

Chip explained that he had been "mentally perturbed" the weekend before the paper was due and that the essay he had written failed to meet his high standards. But I sensed that Chip felt that he had made a choice akin to having a pizza delivered. He had procrastinated on an assignment due the next day, had no time left in which to prepare his work from scratch, and had to get on to those pressing matters that shape the world of an 18-year-old. He dialed his Internet service provider, ordered takeout, and had it delivered.

—Ellen Laird, "Internet Plagiarism: We All Pay the Price"

You can use common words and expressions such as "made a choice" or "due the next day." But if you use more unusual expressions from the source ("a choice akin to having pizza delivered," "pressing matters," "dialed his Internet service provider"), you need to enclose them in quotation marks. In Mere's first attempt at paraphrase, she does not quote, but her words and structure resemble the original too closely.

PARAPHRASE TOO SIMILAR TO THE ORIGINAL

Laird   Paraphrase, p. 5, ninth paragraph

Laird knew that Chip was mentally perturbed before he wrote

his paper and his high standards prevented him from writing

his own essay. But she felt that what he did was like having a

pizza takeout. He had procrastinated so long that he could not

write an essay from scratch and wanted to enjoy his life. So he

ordered a takeout essay from his ISP (5).

Mere gives the name of the author and the page number of the source material (given in the online version) using the MLA style of documentation. Documentation, however, is not a guarantee against plagiarism. Mere's wording and sentence structure follow the original too closely. When classmates and her instructor pointed this out, she revised the paraphrase by keeping the ideas of the original, using different wording and sentence structure, and quoting what she regarded as a unique phrase.

REVISED PARAPHRASE

Laird   Paraphrase, p. 5, ninth paragraph

Laird's student Chip might have felt psychologically stressed and

that might have affected his attitude to the paper he wrote, forcing

him to reject it as not good enough to hand in for a grade. Laird,

however, sees his transgression not so much as one of high moral

principles as of expediency. He chose the easiest way out. He had

left the assignment until the last minute. He had no time to do the

work. He wanted to go out and have fun. So what did he do? He

went on the Web, found an essay, and "ordered takeout" (5).

49j Quoting

Readers should immediately realize why you are quoting a particular passage and what the quotation contributes to the ideas you want to convey. They should also learn who said the words you are quoting and, if the source is a print source, on which page of the original work the quotation appears. Then they can look up the author's name in the list of works cited at the end of your paper and find out exactly where you found the quotation.

The Modern Language Association (MLA) format for citing a quotation from an article by one author is illustrated in this chapter and in Part 9. See Part 10 for examples of citations of other types of sources in APA, CSE, and *Chicago* styles. For punctuation with quotation marks, see also chapter 34.

Deciding what and when to quote   Quote when you use the words of a well-known authority or when the words are particularly striking. Quote only when the original words express the exact point you want to make and express it succinctly and well. Otherwise, paraphrase. When you consider quoting, ask yourself: Which point of mine does the quotation illustrate? Why am I considering quoting this particular passage? Why should this particular passage be quoted rather than paraphrased? What do I need to tell my readers about the author of the quotation?

Quoting the exact words of the original   To understand how to deal with quotations in your paper, consider the following beginning of a newspaper article that a student used as she was working on a paper on the ethics of marketing to children.

> Think your talkative, trendy, Web-surfing 13-year-old might have a future in sales? She might already be in business. New forms of peer-to-peer, buzz-marketing campaigns—ignited and fanned by firms—are growing fast.
>
> In a practice still widely unregulated, marketers enlist youths they see as having real sway over friends. The goal? Solicit the help of these influential kids in broadening sales in exchange for products and the promise of a role in deciding what the marketplace will offer.
>
> Review a not-yet-released CD, score free concert tickets. Talk up a movie at a party, earn a DVD. The stakes are high: The 12-to-19 set reportedly spends about $170 billion a year.
>
> Marketers insist their efforts are transparent, that kids' reactions are unscripted, and that word of mouth, done right, is inherently authentic.
>
> At its first conference this week, the new Word of Mouth Marketing Association (WOMMA) will invite input on an evolving code of ethics aimed, in part, at protecting children.
>
> But opponents call the industry's youth-targeted component the odious next step in the commercialization of childhood, one that eyes ever-younger age groups, bribing them in a bid to cement brand loyalty and prompting them to wring friends for useful market data.
>
> "Some of the forms that [buzz marketing] takes have to do with recruiting kids to be marketers and encouraging them to keep their identities as marketers secret," says David Walsh, president and founder of the National Institute on Media and the Family (NIMF) in Minneapolis. "So kids end up being junior ad people, and they're encouraged not to share this [even] with their friends."
>
> Teens, he says, also often endanger themselves by sharing too much personal information, opening themselves to different kinds of exploitation. NIMF points out that at one marketer-facilitated online community, kids can create their own Old Spice "Girls of the Red Zone" calendar. And that signing up for membership at Soul-Kool.com, one of a handful of buzz-marketing firms that

double as online communities, requires entering an instant-messenger address.

> —Clayton Collins, "Marketers Tap Chatty Young Teens, and
> Hit a Hot Button," *Christian Science Monitor* 30 March 2005: 11

Any words you use from a source must be included in quotation marks (unless they are long quotations) and quoted exactly as they appear in the original, with the same punctuation marks and capital letters. Do not change pronouns or tenses to fit your own purpose, unless you enclose changes in square brackets (see the examples on pp. 416–417).

NOT EXACT QUOTATION

▶ Collins reports that marketers think "that word of mouth is authentic when it is done correctly."

EXACT QUOTATION, WITHOUT CITATION

▶ "Marketers," Collins reports, think that "word of mouth, done right, is inherently authentic."

EXACT QUOTATION, WITH CITATION

▶ "Marketers," Collins reports, think that "word of mouth, done right, is inherently authentic" (11).

Note that if your quotation includes a question mark or exclamation point, you must include it within the quotation. Your sentence period then comes after your citation.

> Collins asks, "Think your talkative, trendy, Web-surfing 13-year-old might have a future in sales?" (11).

Quoting part of a sentence   You can make sure that quotations make a point and are not just dropped into your paper if you integrate parts of quoted sentences into your own sentences. When it is obvious that parts of the quoted sentence have been omitted, you do not need to use ellipsis dots.

> According to Collins, David Walsh believes that teenagers "endanger themselves by sharing too much personal information, opening themselves to different kinds of exploitation."

Not rigging the evidence   Quoting means quoting an author's ideas without omitting or adding any of your own contextual material to substantially change the author's intent. For example, it would distort the author's views and rig the evidence the wrong way to write this, even though what is quoted is there in the original article:

> Clayton Collins sees "talkative, trendy" teenagers as having a bright "future in sales" (11).

Omitting words in the middle of a quotation If you omit as irrelevant to your purpose any words from the middle of a quotation, signal the omission with an ellipsis mark, three dots separated by spaces. See 35e.

> Collins points out that "signing up for membership at Soul-Kool.com . . . requires entering an instant-messenger address."

In MLA style, if your source passage itself uses ellipses, place the dots within square brackets to indicate that your ellipsis mark is not part of the original text: [. . .].

Omitting words at the beginning of a quotation If you omit as irrelevant to your purpose any words from the beginning of a quotation, *do not* use an ellipsis.

NO **Collins reports that WOMMA's conference ". . . will invite input on an evolving code of ethics aimed, in part, at protecting children."**

YES **Collins reports that WOMMA's conference "will invite input on an evolving code of ethics aimed, in part, at protecting children."**

Omitting words at the end of a quotation If you omit the end of the source's sentence at the end of your own sentence, and your sentence is not followed by a page citation, signal the omission with three ellipsis dots following the sentence period—four dots in all—and then the closing quotation marks.

> Alarmed, Collins establishes the role of youths in "broadening sales. . . ."

When you include a page citation for the print source within your sentence, place it after the ellipsis dots and the closing quotation marks and before the final sentence period.

> Alarmed, Collins establishes the role of youths in "broadening sales . . ." (11).

Also use three dots after the period if you omit a complete sentence (or more). Use a line of dots for an omitted line of poetry (35e).

Adding or changing words If you add any comments or explanations in your own words or if you change a word in the quotation to fit it grammatically into your sentence, enclose the added or changed material in square brackets (35c). Generally, however, it is preferable to rephrase your sentence because bracketed words and phrases make sentences difficult to read.

AWKWARD **Collins reports that the "practice [is] still widely unregulated [in which] marketers enlist youths they see as having real sway over friends."**

REVISED **Collins reports that marketers freely "enlist youths they see as having real sway over friends."**

Quoting longer passages If you quote more than three lines of poetry or four typed lines of prose, do not use quotation marks. Instead, begin the quotation on a new line and indent the quotation one inch or ten spaces from the left margin in MLA style, or indent it five spaces from the left margin if you are using APA or *Chicago* style. Double-space throughout. Do not indent from the right margin. You can establish the context for a long quotation and integrate it effectively into your text if you state the point that you want to make and name the author of the quotation in your introductory statement.

Author mentioned in introductory statement
> Despite his impartial detachment, Collins gives short shrift to marketers and waxes eloquent when introducing the National Institute on Media and the Family (NIMF):

No quotation marks around indented quotation

Quotation indented one inch or 10 spaces (MLA)

> But opponents call the industry's youth-targeted component the odious next step in the commercialization of childhood, one that eyes ever-younger age groups, bribing them in a bid to cement brand loyalty and prompting them to wring friends for useful market data. (11)   Page citation (only for a print source) after period

Note: After a long indented quotation, put the period before the parenthetical citation.

Avoiding a string of quotations Use quotations, especially long ones, sparingly and only when they bolster your argument. Readers do not want to read snippets from the works of other writers. They want your analysis of your sources, and they are interested in the conclusions you draw from your research.

Fitting a quotation into your sentence When you quote, use the exact words of the original, and make sure that those exact words do not disrupt the flow of your sentence and send it in another direction.

A BAD FIT   **It's obvious that Walsh finds the recruiting tactics duplicitous since they "encouraging them to keep their identities as marketers secret."**

A BETTER FIT   **It's obvious that Walsh finds the recruiting tactics toward teenagers duplicitous since they encourage the youngsters "to keep their identities as marketers secret."**

A BAD FIT   **Citing another insidious tactic of buzz-marketers, Collins adds "And that signing up for membership at Soul-Kool.com, one of a handful of buzz-marketing firms that double as online communities, requires entering an instant-messenger address."**

A BETTER FIT   **Citing another insidious tactic of buzz-marketers, Collins adds "that signing up for a membership at Soul-Kool.com, one of a handful of buzz-marketing firms that double as online communities, requires entering an instant-messenger address."**

KEY POINTS

Using Quotations: A Checklist

Examine a draft of your paper, and ask these questions about each quotation you have included.

☐ Why do you want to include this quotation? How does it support a point you have made?

☐ What is particularly remarkable about this quotation? Would a paraphrase be better?

☐ Does what you have enclosed in quotation marks exactly match the words and punctuation of the original?

☐ Have you told your readers the name of the author of the quotation?

☐ Have you included the page number of the quotation from a print source?

☐ How have you integrated the quotation into your own passage? Will readers know whom you are quoting and why?

☐ What verb have you used to introduce the quotation?

☐ Are there any places where you string quotations together, one after another? If so, revise. Look for quotation marks closing and then immediately opening again. Also look for phrases such as "X goes on to say . . ."; "X also says . . ."; "X then says. . . ."

☐ Have you indented quotations longer than four lines of type and omitted quotation marks?

☐ Have you used long quotations sparingly?

49k Indicating the boundaries of a citation

Naming an author or title in your text tells readers that you are citing ideas from a source, and citing a page number at the end of a summary or paraphrase lets them know where your citation ends. However, for one-page print articles and for Internet sources, a page citation is not necessary, so indicating where your comments about a source end is harder to do. You always need to indicate clearly where your summary or paraphrase ends and where your own comments take over. Convey the shift to readers by commenting on the source in a way that clearly announces a statement of your own views. Use expressions such as *it follows that, X's explanation shows that, as a result, evidently, obviously,* or *clearly* to signal the shift.

UNCLEAR CITATION BOUNDARY

According to a Sony Web site, <u>Mozart Makes You Smarter</u>, the company has decided to release a recording on the strength of research indicating that listening to Mozart improves IQ. The products show the ingenuity of commercial enterprise while taking the researchers' conclusions in new directions.

[Does only the first sentence refer to material on the Web page, or do both sentences?]

REVISED CITATION, WITH SOURCE BOUNDARY INDICATED

According to a Sony Web site, <u>Mozart Makes You Smarter</u>, the company has decided to release a recording on the strength of research indicating that listening to Mozart improves IQ. Clearly, Sony's plan demonstrates the ingenuity of commercial enterprise, but it cannot reflect what the researchers intended when they published their conclusions.

Another way to indicate the end of your citation is to include the author's name or authors' names at the end of the citation instead of (or even in addition to) introducing the citation with the name.

UNCLEAR CITATION BOUNDARY

For people who hate shopping, Web shopping may be the perfect solution. Jerome and Taylor's exploration of "holiday hell" reminds us that we get more choice from online vendors than we do when we browse at our local mall because the online sellers, unlike mall owners, do not have to rent space to display their goods. In addition, one can buy almost anything online, from CDs, cell phones, and books to cars and real estate.

REVISED CITATION, WITH SOURCE BOUNDARY INDICATED

For people who hate shopping, Web shopping may be the perfect solution. An article exploring the "holiday hell" of shopping reminds us that we get more choice from online vendors than we do when we browse at our local mall because the online sellers, unlike mall owners, do not have to rent space to display their goods (Jerome and Taylor). In addition, one can buy almost anything online, from CDs, cell phones, and books to cars and real estate.

Chapter **50**

Writing the Research Paper

50a Putting yourself in your paper

You have done hours, days, maybe weeks of research. You have found useful sources. You have a working bibliography and masses of photocopies, printouts, and notes. You have worked hard to analyze and synthesize all your material. You have made a scratch outline. Now comes the time to write your draft.

Get mileage out of your sources. Let readers know about the sources that support your point effectively. Don't mention an author of an influential book or long, important article just once and in parentheses. Let

Online Study Center This icon will direct you to quick reference tools, Web resources, and research guides on the Web site at http://college.hmco.com/keys.html.

readers know why this source adds so much weight to your case. Tell about the expert's credentials, affiliations, and experience. Tell readers what the author does in the work you are citing. A summary of the work along with a paraphrase of important points may also be useful to provide context for the author's remarks and opinions. Show readers that they should be impressed by the expert opinions and facts you present.

Synthesize your sources—don't string them. Large amounts of information are no substitute for a thesis with relevant support. Your paper should *synthesize* your sources, not just string them together, one after the other. When you synthesize, you connect the ideas in individual sources to create a larger picture, to inform yourself about the topic, and to establish your own ideas on the topic. So leave plenty of time to read through your notes, think about what you have read, connect with the material, form responses to it, take into account new ideas and opposing arguments, and find connections among the facts and the ideas your sources offer. Avoid sitting down to write a paper at the last minute, surrounded by library books or stacks of photocopies. In this scenario, you might be tempted to lift material, and you will produce a lifeless paper. Remember that the paper is ultimately *your* work, not a collection of other people's words, and that your identity and opinions as the writer should be evident.

As you gather information and take notes, always remember to relate your notes to your research question and working thesis (46f). All the notes on your source materials (49f) should contribute something to the issue you are researching. As you read and prepare to summarize, to paraphrase (49i), or to record a quotation (49j), ask yourself, "Why am I telling readers this? How does it relate to my topic, my research question, or my thesis?" Those questions should determine the type of notes you take. Then, when you review your notes later, consider what you know about the authors and whether you share their perspectives on the issue and find their evidence convincing. List the ideas and arguments that emerge from your research, and group various authors' contributions according to the points they make.

50b Driving the organization with ideas, not sources

Let your ideas, not your sources, drive your paper. Resist the temptation to organize your paper in the following way:

1. What points Leki makes
2. What points Krashen makes
3. What points Harklan makes

4. What points Smitherman makes

5. What points Horner and Lu make in opposition

6. What I think

That organization is driven by your sources, with the bulk of the paper dealing with the views of Leki, Krashen, and the rest. Instead, let your points of supporting evidence determine the organization:

Thesis

1. First point of support: what evidence I have to support my thesis and what evidence Harklan and Krashen provide

2. Second point of support: what evidence I have to support my thesis and what evidence Leki and Harklan provide

3. Third point of support: what evidence I have to support my thesis and what evidence Smitherman, Leki, and Krashen provide

4. Opposing viewpoints of Horner and Lu

5. Common ground and refutation of those viewpoints

6. Synthesis

 ESL NOTE

Cultural Conventions about Texts

Be aware that the conventions regarding the use of source materials, especially classic texts, differ from culture to culture. When you are writing in English, readers will expect you to propose and explain your ideas and not to rely too heavily on classic well-known texts from thinkers in the field.

To avoid producing an essay that reads like a serial listing of summaries or references ("Leki says this," "Harklan says that," "Harklan also says this"), spend time reviewing your notes and synthesizing what you find into a coherent and convincing statement of what you know and believe. Do the following:

- Make lists of good ideas your sources raise about your topic.

- Look for the connections among those ideas: comparisons and contrasts.

- Find links in content, examples, and statistics.

- Note connections between the information in your sources and what you know from your own experience.

If you do these things, you will take control of your material instead of letting it take control of you.

50c Making use of an outline

Some people—those who find their way into a paper as they write it—like to make a rough scratch outline of the points of the paper before they begin to write; then, once they have a draft on paper, they try to make a detailed sentence outline of what they have written to check the completeness and logic of the draft. Other people like to prepare a detailed outline before they start to write—they have usually done a great deal of research and have planned the paper before they begin to write. Whichever type of researcher you are, try to pause at some point to make an outline, especially if your paper is long and your topic complex. It will help you avoid gaps and repetition and will give you a way to see how well you take readers from one point to the next and how well all your points connect with your thesis. See 3i for examples of a scratch outline and a formal sentence outline. Here is an outline Jared Whittemore made for his research paper on community colleges. He highlighted the key words in his thesis and developed each point in turn in his essay. You can read the fifth draft of his paper in 51g.

Thesis: With their policy of open access, community colleges provide exceptional opportunities especially to students from low-income families, minorities, those with inadequate primary and secondary schooling, and women.

Support I: Historically, community colleges have provided open access.

    A. Statistics in California

    B. Statistics in the U.S.

Support II: Community colleges help low-income students.

    A. Examples of costs

        1. California

        2. Texas

        3. Florida

    B. Cost of community college vs. four-year college

Support III: Minorities especially can benefit from a community
college opportunity.

    A. Statistics for public and private two-year colleges

    B. Statistics for two-year and four-year colleges

    C. Statistics on race nationwide

    D. Statistics on race in California; example of student

Support IV: Community colleges help students with limited
academic skills.

    A. Preparation for a four-year school

    B. Preparation for work

    C. Preparation for older students' lives

Support V: Community colleges provide women with
opportunities.

    A. Increased earning power for women

    B. Lifestyle change for returning women

50d Using visuals

In a research paper, consider where tables and charts could present visual data concisely and clearly. Images may also help you strengthen an argument (see 7b). Use visuals to illustrate and enhance a point or to present information clearly and economically. Do not use visuals merely to fill up space or to look trendy (for more on this see 11c).

    If you look at the sample paper in chapters 51 and 52, you'll see how the visuals used there work well to highlight specific information, to convey quantitative information to number-phobic readers, or to capture the essence of an argument and thus make a point convincingly.

Finding appropriate visuals   Several of the major search engines offer specific image searches, including Google, AltaVista, and Yahoo!. And by using the advance search from there, you are able to narrow your search to certain types of images.

Another useful online source is Flickr, a depository for photos only. It allows people to upload their photos in the database independent of any Web site. This is, therefore, a complementary site providing access to a large volume of amateur photos.

Searching for images can often be difficult and frustrating and many "hits" may not be of interest to you. Image searches use keywords or tags attached to the image, and often they are not accurate or do not describe the image the same way you would describe it. So rather than doing a general image search, it may be more productive to look for images at the Web sites where you find relevant textual information in the first place. Many Web sites, including government sites like the U.S. Bureau of the Census or nonprofit organizations like "Public Agenda," make great efforts to present information on their sites in a visually attractive form. In addition, the National Telecommunications and Information Administration is a good source for tables and charts analyzing Internet use, and the College Board and the UCLA Higher Education Research Institute provide annual studies of first-year students with useful visuals.

If you find an appropriate visual in a book or a journal while you are conducting your research, consider scanning it to use in your research paper. Or ask a librarian if you are able to use a print copy of the journal to create an image in the library. Use of a visual from a journal must conform to copyright laws. However, there often are a number of places in campus libraries where you can create visuals, including a computer center, studio labs, and a reference center.

When you use a visual, "read" it critically and evaluate its appropriateness for your research paper (1b). When you create a visual, ensure that it provides accurate, truthful information (see 11e). Above all, whenever you use a visual, provide the appropriate citation in your paper and documentation in your bibliography (51e, 52d, 53d, 54d).

50e Guidelines for drafting research papers

What not to do

- Do not expect to complete a polished draft at one sitting.
- Do not write the title and the first sentence and then panic because you feel you have nothing left to say.

- Do not constantly imagine your instructor's response to what you write.
- Do not worry about coherence—a draft by nature is something that you work on repeatedly and revise for readers' eyes.
- Do not necessarily begin at the beginning; do not think you must first write a dynamite introduction.

What to do

- Carve out a block of time and begin writing a draft of your paper.
- Turn off your cell phone, log out of your e-mail and IM accounts, close the door, and tell yourself you will not emerge from the room until you have written a good chunk of your draft.
- Promise yourself a reward when you meet your target—a refrigerator break or a trip to the gym, for instance.
- Assemble your copy of the assignment, your thesis statement, all your copies of sources, your research notebook and any other notes, your working bibliography, and your proposal or outline.
- Write the parts you know most about first.
- Write as much as you can as fast as you can. If you only vaguely remember a reference in your sources, just write what you can remember—but keep writing, and don't worry about gaps:

  As so and so (who was it? Jackson?) has observed, malls are taking the place of city centers (check page reference).

- Write the beginning—the introduction—only after you have some ideas on paper that you feel you can introduce.
- Write at least something on each one of the points in your outline. Start off by asking yourself: What do I know about this point, and how does it support my thesis? Write your answer to that in your own words without worrying about who said what in which source. You will check your notes and fill in the gaps later.
- Write until you feel you have put down on the page or screen your main points and you have made reference to most of your source material.

Try not to go back over your draft and start tinkering and changing—at least not yet. Congratulate yourself on having made a start and take a break. Save your draft and do not look at it for a while. In the meantime, you can follow up on research leads, find new sources, discuss your draft with your instructor or with a tutor at your campus writing center, and continue writing ideas in your research notebook.

50f Writing research papers in the disciplines

When you write research papers in different disciplines such as sociology, physics, psychology, art history, and English, you not only use different sources and different systems of documentation; you may also approach the research and the writing in ways that fit the conventions of the discipline. This section outlines approaches to researched writing in the humanities, the natural sciences and mathematics, and the social sciences.

LANGUAGE AND CULTURE
The Cultures of the Academic Disciplines

Each discipline has its own culture and its own expectations of the people who practice in the discipline and write about it. When you take a course in a new discipline, use the following strategies to get acquainted with its ways of thinking and operating.

- Listen carefully to lectures and discussion; note any specialized vocabulary.
- Read the assigned textbook and note the conventions that apply in writing about the field.
- Talk with your instructor about the field, its literature, and readers' expectations.
- When given a writing assignment, ask your instructor for examples of similar types of writing in that discipline.

Before you begin work on a research project, try to find out as much as you can about the following:

- the types of data you should gather: primary or secondary sources? print or Web?
- the standard sources in the field to consult for reliable information
- the design of the paper: headings, title page, visuals
- the documentation style preferred: MLA, APA, CSE, *Chicago*, or other?
- the terminology specific to the field
- the type of language in common use: active or passive voice? first or third person?

See 9a for examples of writing in different disciplines.

Writing research papers in the humanities and arts When you do research in the humanities and the arts, you may be called on to consult both primary and secondary sources. Using secondary sources such as critical works will help you set the art, literature, or issues you discuss in context and will show you the reactions and interpretations of others.

Consider the following when you write research papers in literature, language, philosophy, art, communications, music, or theater. (History, too, is sometimes categorized with the humanities; otherwise, it is placed within the social sciences.)

- Consult primary sources, such as original works of literature, radio and television programs, original documents, and informational Web sites, or attend original performances, such as plays, films, poetry readings, and concerts.

- Form your own interpretations of works. The first person *I* is used in personal and expository writing more than in other disciplines.

- Look for patterns and interpretations supported by evidence, not for one right answer to a problem.

- Use the present tense to refer to what writers have said (*Rushdie points out that . . .*). See 25f.

- Use MLA guidelines (51) or *The Chicago Manual of Style* (54) for documentation style. See 50g for useful resources for research in art, architecture, classics, communications, ethnic studies, history, literature, music, philosophy, religion, and women's studies.

Writing about literature is common in research papers in the humanities. See chapter 8 for more on writing about literature.

Writing research papers in the natural sciences, applied sciences, and mathematics Research in the natural sciences (astronomy, biology, zoology, geography, geology, physics, chemistry), applied sciences (engineering, computer science), and mathematics calls for exact accounts of firsthand experiments and observations. Consider the following when you write a research paper in the natural sciences, applied sciences, or mathematics.

- Focus on empirical data. (See also 9d.)

- Report firsthand original experiments and calculations.

- Be exact, complete, and precise in all descriptions.

- Present a hypothesis.
- Discuss the results in light of procedural problems, previous experiments, and future directions.
- Provide supporting tables, graphs, and charts to illustrate the findings.
- Give background information in the introductory section of your paper, a section sometimes called "Review of the Literature."
- Avoid personal anecdotes.
- Use the present perfect tense to refer to what researchers and writers have reported in published works (*Several studies have established that . . .*).
- Use the past tense for details of specific studies (*Cocchi et al. isolated the protein fraction . . .*).
- Use the passive voice more frequently than in other types of writing (25l) (*the muscle was stimulated . . .*).
- Be prepared to write according to a set format, using sections with headings: Abstract, Review of Literature, Method, Results, Discussion, Conclusion.
- Use APA (52) or CSE (53) documentation style, or follow specific style manuals in scientific areas.

Writing research papers in the social sciences The social sciences (for example, anthropology, business, economics, education, political science, psychology, and sociology) examine the forms and processes that contribute to the construction of society and social institutions. Consider the following when you write a research paper.

- Examine research studies in the field, evaluate their methodology, compare and contrast results with those of other studies, and draw conclusions based on the empirical evidence uncovered.
- Look for accurate, up-to-date information, and evaluate it systematically against stated criteria.
- Use the first person (*I* and *we*) less frequently than you use it in the humanities.
- Use the past tense to refer to what researchers and writers have reported (*Winnicott (1951) showed that . . .*).
- Use the passive voice as appropriate when reporting on scientific and experimental procedures (for example, *The stimulus was repeated* in place of *I repeated the stimulus*).

- Where possible and appropriate, present graphs, charts, and tables to illustrate your data and support your conclusions (see 11c).

- Use APA documentation style (chapter 52) or *Chicago* style (chapter 54), or ask your instructor what is recommended.

50g Research sources in 27 subject areas

Twenty-one college librarians from eighteen colleges in thirteen states helped with the compilation of a list of useful print and online starting points for research across the curriculum in twenty-seven subject areas—from art and architecture to women's studies. That list has recently been updated and revised by Professor Trudi Jacobson, coordinator of User Education Programs at the University Libraries of the University at Albany State University of New York.

Online Study Center **Research** Sources in 27 subject areas

PART 9
Documenting Sources: MLA Style

A full At a Glance Index of examples appears on the pages listed below.

Source shots, illustrating what to cite, appear on pages 718, 724, 728, and 732

You need to document the sources of your information, not only in research papers but also in shorter essays in which you mention only a few books, articles, or other sources to illustrate a point or support your case. Chapter 51 provides information on the style commonly used to document sources in the humanities, the Modern Language Association (MLA) system, as recommended in Joseph Gibaldi, *MLA Handbook for Writers of Research Papers,* 6th ed. (New York: MLA, 2003), and on the MLA Web site at <http://www.mla.org>.

Be accurate and consistent when you follow any documentation style. With the MLA style of citing author and page number, learn the basic principles (51a), and use the detailed examples in 51c and 51d for help with citations and references. Do not try to rely on memory; instead, always look up instructions and follow examples. Your

MLA

college may provide free access to documentation software that helps you compile citations and bibliographies in any documentation style. Ask a librarian if a program such as Endnotes, Refworks, or NoodleBib is available.

Chapter **51**

MLA Style of Documentation

When you refer to, comment on, paraphrase, or quote another author's material, you have to indicate that you have done so by inserting what is called a *citation*. All you need is the name of the author(s) and the page number(s) where you found the material. You can put the author's name in your own text to introduce the material, with the page number in parentheses at the end of the sentence; or, especially for a source you have cited previously, you can put both author and page number in parentheses at the end of the sentence in which you cite the material. Then all more detailed information about your sources goes into a works-cited list at the end of your paper (51d). Sections 51a–51c show you examples and variations on the basic principle of citation—for instance, what to do when no author is named or when you cite an online source that has no page numbers.

51a Two basic features of MLA style

KEY POINTS

Two Basic Features of MLA Style

1. *In your paper,* include an author/page citation for each source: the **last name(s)** of the author (or authors) or title if no author is known and **page number(s)** where the information is located, unless the source is online or only one page long. See 51b for examples.
2. *At the end of your paper,* include a list of all the sources you refer to in the paper, alphabetized by the author's last name or by title if the author is not known. Begin the list on a new page, and title it "Works Cited." See 51e for sample entries.

Online Study Center   This icon will direct you to quick reference tools, Web resources, and research guides on the Web site at http://college.hmco.com/keys.html.

Illustrations of the Basic Features

In-Text Citation	Entry in List of Works Cited

Book:

The renowned scholar of language, David Crystal, has promoted the idea of "dialect democracy" (168).

or

A renowned scholar of language has promoted the idea of "dialect democracy" (Crystal 168).

Crystal, David. The Stories of English. Woodstock: Overlook, 2004.

Print article:

Barry Gewen questions the role of an art critic if "anything goes" in art (29).

or

The role of an art critic is questioned if "anything goes" in art (Gewen 29).

Gewen, Barry. "State of the Art." New York Times Book Review 11 Dec. 2005: 28–32.

Article in online database:

Barry Gewen questions the role of an art critic if "anything goes" in art.

Gewen, Barry. "State of the Art." New York Times Book Review 11 Dec. 2005: 28–. Academic Universe: News. LexisNexis. City U of New York Lib. 14 Dec. 2005 <http://web .lexis-nexis.com>.

A model of non-violent protest against the war is as simple as refusing to attend a White House dinner (Olds).

Olds, Sharon. "No Thanks, Mrs. Bush." Nation 10 Oct. 2005: 5–6. Academic Search Premier. EBSCO. City U of New York Lib. 13 Dec. 2005 <http://search .epnet.com/login.aspx?direct=tr ue&db=aph&an=18335004>.

Web document with no author:

Researchers have explored the link between the social rank of chimpanzees and their mating privileges ("Jane Goodall's").

"Jane Goodall's" Nation. Educational Broadcasting Corporation. 14 Dec. 2005: <http://www.pbs.org/wnet/ nature/goodall/index.html

51b FAQs about MLA in-text citations

Frequently Asked Questions	Short Answer	Examples
What information do I put into the body of my essay?	Give only the name of the author(s) (if available) and the page number (for a print source of more than one page). Include the page numbers in parentheses, never in your own text.	51c
Where do I supply that information?	Usually name the author as you introduce the information, and put the page number(s) in parentheses. Alternatively, put both author and page number in parentheses at the end of the sentence containing the citation.	51b, A, B
How do I refer to an author?	In your text, use both names (and maybe a brief identification of position or credentials) for the first mention. Use only the last name for subsequent references and within parentheses. If you name the author in your text, you will not need parentheses for a work with no page numbers.	51b, A, B
What if no author or editor is named for a source?	Give the title of the work or, in a parenthetical citation, an abbreviation containing the word of the title alphabetized in the works-cited list so that readers can find the source immediately. See 8e on finding the author of an online source.	51b, I, J
How do I give page numbers?	Do not use "p." or "pp." Give inclusive page numbers for information that spans pages: 35–36; 257–58; 305–06; 299–300. (Omit a shared first digit in numbers over 100.)	51b, A–F

Frequently Asked Questions	Short Answer	Examples
Is a page number always necessary?	No. Omit page numbers for a reference to a whole work, to a work only one page long, or to an online or multimedia work with no visible page numbers.	51b, G, H, J, K

See the samples in 51c to answer other questions.

51c MLA author/page citations in text

A. One author, named in your introductory text The first time you mention an author (or authors) whose work you discuss in detail in your text or make several references to, give the full name and, if useful to readers, a brief statement about expertise or credentials. Thereafter, use the author's last name only.

┌─ author ─┐
The sociologist Ruth Sidel's interviews with young women provide
                                      ┌─── quotation ───┐   page number
examples of what Sidel sees as the "impossible dream" (19).──period

When a quotation ends the sentence, as in that example, close the quotation marks before the parentheses, and place the sentence period after the parentheses. (This rule differs from the one for undocumented writing, which calls for a period *before* the closing quotation marks.)

When a quotation includes a question mark or an exclamation point, also include a period after the citation:

>   question mark   period
> Mrs. Bridge wonders, "Is my daughter mine?" (Connell 135).

B. Author not mentioned in your text If you do not mention the author while introducing the reference, include the author's last name in the parentheses before the page number, with no comma between them.

> Many young women, from all races and classes, have taken on the idea of the American Dream, however difficult it might be for them
>   author and page
>   ┌ numbers ┐
> to achieve it (Sidel 19–20).

C. Two or more authors For a work with two or three authors, include all the names, either in your text sentence or in parentheses.

> (Lakoff and Johnson 42)

> (Hare, Moran, and Koepke 226–28)

For a work with four or more authors, use only the first author's name followed by "et al." (*Et alii* means "and others.") See 51e, item 2.

> Some researchers have established a close link between success at work and the pleasure derived from community service (Bellah et al. 196–99).

D. Author with more than one work cited You can include the author and title of the work in your text sentence.

> Alice Walker, in her book <u>In Search of Our Mothers' Gardens</u>, describes revisiting her past to discover more about Flannery O'Connor (43–59).

If you do not mention the author in your text, include in your parenthetical reference the author's last name, followed by a comma, an abbreviated form of the title, and the page number.

> O'Connor's house still stands and is looked after by a caretaker
>   abbreviated title
> comma~ ┌──────┐ /page number
> (Walker, <u>In Search</u> 57).

E. Work in an edited anthology   Cite the author of the included or reprinted work (not the editor of the anthology) and the page number in the anthology. The entry in the works-cited list will include the author, the title of the work, its inclusive page numbers, and full bibliographical details for the anthology: title, editor(s), place of publication, publisher, date. See 51e, items 5 and 6, for examples.

> Des Pres asserts that "heroism is not necessarily a romantic notion" (20).

F. Work quoted in another source   Use "qtd. in" (for "quoted in") in your parenthetical citation, followed by the last name of the author of the source in which you find the reference (the indirect source) and the page number where you find the quotation. List the author of the indirect source you use in your list of works cited. In the following example, the indirect source, Douthat, would be included in the list of works cited, not Mansfield (51e, item 23).

> Harvey Mansfield of Harvard University has attributed grade inflation to "the prevalence in American education of the notion of self-esteem" (qtd. in Douthat 96).

G. Reference to an entire work and not to one specific page   If you are referring not to a quotation or idea on one specific page but rather to an idea that is central to the work as a whole, use the author's name alone. Include the work in your works-cited list.

> We can learn from diaries about people's everyday lives and the worlds they create (Mallon).

H. One-page work   If an article is only one page long, cite the author's name alone; include the page number in your works-cited list (51e, item 23).

I. Author or editor not named   If no author is named for a source, refer to the book (underlined) or article (within quotation marks) by its title. Within a parenthetical citation, shorten the title to the first word alphabetized in the works-cited list (51e, item 8).

> According to The Chicago Manual of Style, writers should always "break or bend" rules when necessary (xiii).

> Writers should always "break or bend" rules when necessary (Chicago xiii).

If you need help in determining the author of an Internet source, see 48d and 48e. For a Web site with no author indicated, use the name of the site.

For an unsigned entry in an encyclopedia or dictionary, give the title of the entry and a page number. Begin the entry in the works-cited list with the title of the alphabetized entry (51e, item 7).

> Drypoint differs from etching in that it does not use acid ("Etching" 312).

J. Electronic and Internet sources Electronic database material and Internet sources, which appear on a screen, have no stable page numbers that apply across systems or when printed, unless they are in PDF files. If your source as it appears on the screen includes no visible text divisions, numbered pages, or numbered paragraphs, provide information about the author in your text rather than in a parenthetical citation. In the first mention, it is common practice to establish the expertise or credentials of authors or the authority of your source.

> In the online journal 21st Century, science writer Stephen Hart describes how researchers Edward Taub and Thomas Ebert conclude that for musicians, practicing "remaps the brain."
>
> No page citation: online source has no numbered pages or paragraphs.

With no page number to indicate the end of a citation, be careful to define where your citation ends and your own commentary takes over. See 50i for more on defining the boundaries of a citation.

To document an online source with no author, give the title of the Web page or the posting, either in full or abbreviated, beginning with the first word you alphabetize. Then begin your works-cited entry with the name of the site (see 51e, item 38).

> A list of frequently asked questions about documentation and up-to-date instructions on how to cite online sources in MLA style can be found on the association's Web site (MLA).

If possible, locate online material by the internal headings of the source (for example, *introduction, chapter, section*). Give paragraph numbers only if they are supplied in the source and you see them on the screen (use the abbreviation "par." or "pars."). If paragraph numbers do appear, include the total number of numbered paragraphs in your works-cited list (see 51e, item 46).

> Hatchuel discusses how film editing "can change points of view and turn objectivity into subjectivity" (par. 6).

Film editing provides us with different perceptions of reality (Hatchuel, par. 6).

K. Multimedia and other nonprint sources

For radio or TV programs, interviews, live performances, films, computer software, recordings, and other nonprint sources, include only the title or author (or, in some cases, the interviewer, interviewee, director, performer, or producer, and so on, corresponding to the first element of the information you provide in the entry in your list of works cited). (See 51e, items 57–60).

> The musical <u>Mirette</u> weaves together music, song, and a warmly inspiring story to make a magical theatrical experience.

> This season, playwright Elizabeth Diggs has given us a delightfully inspiring story of courage on the high wire.

L. Work by a corporation, government agency, or other organization

Give the complete name of the organization in the introductory passage, or give a shortened form in parentheses.

Cite the organization as the author, making sure it corresponds with the alphabetized entry in your works-cited list. Use the complete name in your text or a shortened form in parentheses. The following examples cite a Web site, so page numbers are not included.

> ┌─────── full name ───────┐
> The United States Department of Education has projected an increase in college enrollment of 11% between 2003 and 2013.

> An increase in college enrollment of 11% between 2003 and 2013 has
> ┌ shortened name ┐
> been projected (US Dept. of Educ.).

See 51e, item 9, for an example of a corporation as author in the works-cited list.

If you do not know the name of the author or editor of a report by a government agency, include in your text the name of the agency as you enter it in your works-cited list.

> According to statistics prepared by the United States Department of Education in 2000, students in four-year public colleges paid an average tuition cost of $2617 (346).

See 51e, item 40, for an example of the above in the works-cited list.

M. Two authors with the same last name   Include each author's first initial or the whole first name if the authors' initials are the same.

> A writer can be seen as both "author" and "secretary" and the two roles can be seen as competitive (F. Smith 19).

N. Multivolume work   Indicate the volume number, followed by a colon, a space, and the page number. List the number of volumes in your works-cited list. (See 51e, item 12.)

> Barr and Feigenbaum note that "the concept of translation from one language to another by machine is older than the computer itself" (1: 233).

O. More than one work cited in your sentence   Use a semicolon to separate two or more sources in the same citation. Avoid making a parenthetical citation so long that it disrupts the flow of your text. Consider adding a footnote or an endnote to provide lists of additional source material, as in the second example here.

> The links between a name and ancestry have been noted before (Waters 65; Antin 188).

> Many writers and researchers have discussed the links between a name and ancestry.[1]

If sources refer to different points in your sentence, cite each one after the point it supports. For the use of footnotes and endnotes in MLA documentation, see 51f.

P. Lecture, speech, or personal communication such as a letter, an interview, an e-mail, or a conversation   In your text, give the name of the lecturer or person you communicated with. In your works-cited list, indicate the type of communication after the author or title (see 51e, items 61–66).

> According to Roberta Berstein, professor of art history at the University at Albany, the most challenging thing about contemporary art is understanding that it is meant to be challenging. This may mean that the artist wants to make us uncomfortable with our familiar ideas or present us with reconceived notions of beauty.

Q. Literary works: fiction, poetry, and drama   For well-known works published in several different editions, include information so readers may locate material in whatever edition they are using. In your works-cited list, include the edition you use.

FOR A NOVEL   Give the chapter or section number in addition to the page number in the edition you used: (104; ch. 3).

FOR A POEM   Give line numbers, not page numbers: (lines 62–73). Subsequent line references can omit the word lines. Include up to three lines of poetry sequentially in your text, separated by a slash with a space on each side (/) (see 35d). For four or more lines of poetry, begin on a new line, indent the whole passage one inch from the left, double-space throughout, and omit quotation marks from the beginning and end of the passage (see 49j).

**FOR CLASSIC POEMS, SUCH AS THE *ILIAD*   Give the book or part number, followed by the line numbers, not page numbers: (8.21–25).

FOR A PLAY   For dialogue, set the quotation off from your text, indented one inch with no quotation marks, and write the name of the character speaking in all capital letters, followed by a period. Indent subsequent lines of the same speech another quarter inch (three spaces). For a classic play, one published in several different editions (such as plays by William Shakespeare or Oscar Wilde), omit page numbers and cite in parentheses the act, scene, and line numbers of the quotation, in Arabic numerals. In your works-cited list, provide the bibliographical details of the edition you use.

> Shakespeare's lovers in A Midsummer Night's Dream appeal to contemporary audiences accustomed to the sense of loss in love songs:
>
>> LYSANDER. How now, my love! Why is your cheek so pale?
>>   How chance the roses there do fade so fast?
>> HERMIA. Belike for want of rain, which I could well
>>   Beteem them from the tempest of mine eyes.
>> LYSANDER. Ay me! for aught that ever I could read,
>>   Could ever hear by tale or history,
>>   The course of true love never did run smooth;
>>   (1.1.133-39)

For a modern play available in only one published edition, such as a work by Tony Kushner, cite author and page numbers as you do for other MLA citations.

FOR SHAKESPEARE, CHAUCER, AND OTHER LITERARY WORKS   Abbreviate titles cited in parentheses, such as the following: *Tmp.* for *The Tempest*; *2H4* for *Henry IV, Part 2*; *MND* for *A Midsummer Night's Dream*; *GP* for the *General Prologue*; *PrT* for *The Prioress's Tale*; *Aen.* for *Aeneid*; *Beo.* for *Beowulf*; *Prel.* for Wordsworth's *Prelude*.

R. The Bible and other sacred texts. (Qur'an, Torah, etc.) In a parenthetical citation, give the title of the sacred text (underlined), along with book (abbreviated), chapter, and verse. Note, though, that in a reference to a sacred text that is not directing readers to a specific citation in the list of works cited, the title of the sacred text is not underlined, as in the example that follows (see also 31a and 31f on underlining).

Of the many passages in the Bible that refer to lying, none is more apt today than the one that says that a wicked person "is snared by the

Specific citation underlined

transgression of his lips" (Holy Bible, Prov. 12, 13).

Name of book (Proverbs) abbreviated

See 51e, item 19, for this entry and others in a list of works cited.

S. Two or more sequential references to the same work If you rely on several quotations from the same page within one of your paragraphs, one parenthetical reference after the last quotation is enough, but make sure that no quotations from other works intervene. If you are paraphrasing from and referring to one work several times in a paragraph, mention the author in your introductory phrase; cite the page number at the end of a paraphrase and again if you paraphrase from a different page. Make it clear to readers where a paraphrase ends and your own comments take over (49k).

T. A long quotation Indent by one inch a quotation of four or more lines, without enclosing the quotation in quotation marks. See 49j for an example.

U. A footnote or footnotes To cite a footnote in a work, give the page number followed by "n" or "nn" (as in 65n). For a footnote in an annotated edition of the Bible, give the edition, book, chapter, and verse, followed by "n" or "nn" (New Oxford Annotated Bible, Gen. 35.1-4n). See 51e, item 19, for the entry in a works-cited list.

V. Historical or legal document Cite any article and section number of a familiar historical document, such as the Constitution, in parentheses in your text (US Const., art. 2, sec. 4), with no entry in the works-cited list. Underline the name of a court case (Roe v. Wade), but do not underline laws and acts. List cases and acts in your works-cited list (see 51e, item 67)

51d Guidelines for the MLA works-cited list

The references you make in your text to sources are very brief—usually only the author's last name and a page number—so they allow readers to continue reading without interruption. For complete information about the source, readers can use your brief in-text citation as a guide to the full bibliographical reference in the list of works cited at the end of your paper.

Features of the list   Before you begin to prepare your list, familiarize yourself with the basic features of MLA style. For examples of an MLA works-cited list in students' papers, see 7l, 8j, and 51g.

KEY POINTS

Guidelines for the MLA List of Works Cited

1. *What to list* List only works you actually cited in the text of your paper, not works you read but did not mention, unless your instructor requires you to include all the works you consulted as well as those mentioned in your text.

2. *Format of the list* Begin the list on a new numbered page after the last page of the paper or any endnotes. Center the heading (Works Cited) without quotation marks, underlining, or a period. Double-space throughout the list. Do not add space between entries.

3. *Organization* Do not number the entries. List works alphabetically by author's last name. Begin each entry with the author's name, last name first (or the corporate name or the title of the work if no author is stated). Omit titles ("Dr.") or degrees, but include a suffix like "Jr." or a Roman numeral, as in "Patterson, Peter, III." Use normal order—first name first—for the names of authors after the first name. List works with no named author by the first main word of each entry (51e, item 27).

4. *Indentation* To help readers find an author's name and to clearly differentiate one entry from another, indent all lines

(Continued)

(Continued)

of each entry, except the first one-half inch (or five spaces). A word processor can provide these "hanging indents" (see 11b for how to format hanging indents).

TECH NOTE

Posting Your Paper Online

For an online list of works cited, do not use indentation, which HTML does not support well. Instead, keep all lines flush left and follow each entry with a line space. In addition, use italics in place of underlining for the titles of books or journals because underlining is a signal for a hypertext link.

---

5. *Periods* Separate the main parts of an entry—author, title, publishing information, online information—with a period, followed by one space.

6. *Capitals* Capitalize all words in titles of books and articles except the coordinating conjunctions; the articles, *a, an, the; to* in an infinitive; and prepositions (such as *in, to, for, with, without, against*)—unless they begin or end the title or subtitle.

7. *Underlining or italics* Underline the titles of books and the names of journals and magazines as in the examples in this section. You may use italics instead if your instructor approves and if your printer makes a clear distinction from regular type.

8. *Month* When citing articles in journals, newspapers, and magazines, abbreviate all months except May, June, and July. For the abbreviations to use, see page 714.

9. *Publisher* Use a short form of the name of book publishers (*Random,* not *Random House; Columbia UP,* not *Columbia University Press*). See page 714 for some common abbreviations. For place of publication when more than one office is mentioned, list only the first city mentioned on the title page.

10. *Page numbers* Give inclusive page numbers for articles and sections of books. Do not use "p." ("pp.") or the word *page* (or *pages*) before page numbers in any reference. For page citations over 100 and sharing the same first number, use only the last two digits for the second number (for instance,

683–89, but 798–805). For an unpaginated print work, write "n. pag." Do not include page numbers for online works unless they are PDF documents in which the page numbers appear on the screen. For what to do about page numbers in works in databases, see page 728.

Authors

NAME OF AUTHOR(S) Put the last name first for a single author or the first author: *Fussell, Paul.* For two or more authors, reverse the names of only the first author: *Engleberg, Isa, and Ann Raimes.*

ALPHABETICAL ORDER Alphabetize entries in the list of authors' last names. Note the following:

- Alphabetize by the exact letters in the spelling: *MacKay* precedes *McHam.*
- Let a shorter name precede a longer name beginning with the same letters: *Linden, Ronald* precedes *Lindenmayer, Arnold.*
- With last names using a prefix such as *le, du, di, del,* and *des,* alphabetize by the prefix: *LeBeau, Bryan F.*
- When *de* occurs with French names of one syllable, alphabetize under *d: De Jean, Denise.* Otherwise, alphabetize by last name: *Maupassant, Guy de.*
- Alphabetize by the first element of a hyphenated name: *Sackville-West, Vita.*
- Alphabetize by the last name when the author uses two names without a hyphen: *Thomas, Elizabeth Marshall.*

NO AUTHOR NAMED For a work with no author named, alphabetize by the first word in the title other than *A, An,* or *The* (see 51e, items 8 and 27).

SEVERAL WORKS BY THE SAME AUTHOR(S) For all entries after the first, replace the name(s) of the author(s) with three hyphens followed by a period, and alphabetize according to the first significant word in the title. If an author serves as an editor or translator, put a comma after the three hyphens, followed by the appropriate abbreviation ("ed." or "trans."). If, however, the author has coauthors, repeat all authors' names in full and put the coauthored entry after all the single-name entries for the author.

Goleman, Daniel. <u>Destructive Emotions: A Scientific Dialogue with the Dalai Lama.</u> New York: Bantam-Dell, 2003.

---. <u>Working with Emotional Intelligence</u>. New York: Bantam, 2000.

Goleman, Daniel, Paul Kaufman, and Michael L. Ray. "The Art of Creativity." <u>Psychology Today</u> Mar.–Apr. 1992: 40–47.

AUTHORS WITH THE SAME LAST NAME   Alphabetize by first names: *Smith, Adam*, precedes *Smith, Frank*.

Abbreviations for months   When you give the date of a journal or newspaper article or of an online source, spell out the months May, June, and July in full. Otherwise, use the following abbreviations:

Jan.	Feb.	Mar.	Apr.	Aug.
Sept.	Oct.	Nov.	Dec.	

Abbreviations for names of publishers   Shorten the names of publishers.

- Omit any articles: *A, An, The*.
- Omit abbreviations such as *Co.* and *Inc.*
- Give only first name if name of company consists of several last names: *Little*, not *Little, Brown and Company, Inc.*
- If the publisher's name includes a first and a last name, give only the last name: *Abrams*, not *Harry N. Abrams*.
- Use abbreviations: *Acad.* for *Academy*, *Assn.* for *Association*.
- Use *UP* for *University Press*: *U of Chicago P, Cambridge UP*.
- Use abbreviations that will be familiar to your readers: *MLA, GPO*

Some sample abbreviations:

Basic Books	Basic
Department of Education	Dept. of Educ.
The Feminist Press at the City University of New York	Feminist
Government Printing Office	GPO
Houghton Mifflin Co.	Houghton
National Center for Education Statistics	Natl. Center for Educ. Statistics
Simon and Schuster, Inc.	Simon

51e Examples of entries in MLA list of works cited

WHICH TYPE OF SOURCE?	HOW TO DOCUMENT? GO TO
Print book, part of book, or pamphlet (including government publication)	51e, p. 716, items 1–20
Print article, review, editorial, letter to the editor, or abstract	51e, p. 722, items 21–30
Work found in an online library subscription database (such as *LexisNexis, EBSCO, InfoTrac,* and *PsycINFO*)	51e, p. 726, items 31–36
Web source (such as Web site, government publication, online book, poem, article, online reference work, and e-mail document)	51e, p. 730, items 37–52
Visual, performance, or multimedia source: live, print, or online	51e, p. 736, items 53–60
Miscellaneous source: live, print, or online (including interview, lecture, letter, legal or historical source, and CD-ROM)	51e, p. 739, items 61–68

On the title page of a book and on the copyright page, you will find the information you need for an entry. Use the most recent copyright date. Use a shortened form of the publisher's name; usually one word is sufficient: *Houghton* (not *Houghton Mifflin*); *Basic* (not *Basic Books*). For university presses, use the abbreviations "U" and "P" (no periods).

1. Basic form for a book with one author   See Source Shot 1 on page 718 for an example.

2. Book with two or more authors   Use authors' names in the order in which they appear in the book. Separate the names with commas. Reverse the order of only the first author's name.

Lakoff, George, and Mark Johnson. <u>Metaphors We Live By</u>. Chicago:
    U of Chicago P, 1980.

(annotations above the entry: "comma" pointing to the comma after "George"; "second author's name not reversed" pointing to "Mark Johnson")

For a work with four or more authors, either list all the names or use only the first author's name followed by "et al." (Latin for "and others").

Bellah, Robert N., et al. <u>Habits of the Heart: Individualism and
    Commitment in American Life</u>. Berkeley: U of California P, 1985.

3. Edited book   Use the abbreviation "ed." or "eds.," preceded by a comma, after the name(s) of the editor or editors.

Gates, Henry Louis, Jr., ed. <u>Classic Slave Narratives</u>. New York: NAL, 1987.

For a work with four or more editors, use only the name of the first, followed by a comma and "et al."

4. Author and editor When an editor has prepared an author's work for publication, list the book under the author's name if you cite the author's work. Then, in your listing, include the name(s) of the editor(s) after the title, introduced by "Ed." for one or more editors. "Ed." stands for "edited by" in the following entry.

⌐ author of letters ⌐   name ⌐ of editor ⌐

Bishop, Elizabeth. <u>One Art: Letters</u>. Ed. Robert Giroux. New York: Farrar,

     1994.

If you cite a section written by the editor, such as a chapter introduction or a note, list the source under the name of the editor.

     name   author of letters
⌐ of editor ⌐ editor

Giroux, Robert, ed. <u>One Art: Letters</u>. By Elizabeth Bishop. New York: Farrar,

     1994.

5. One work in an anthology (original or reprinted) For a work included in an anthology, first list the author and title of the included work. Follow this with the title of the anthology, the edition number, the name of the editor(s), publication information (place, publisher, date) for the anthology, and then, after the period, the pages in the anthology covered by the work you refer to.

    author of article   means
⌐ or chapter ⌐   "edited by"

Des Pres, Terrence. "Poetry and Politics." <u>The Writer in Our World</u>. Ed.

      name of editor
     ⌐ of anthology ⌐

     Reginald Gibbons. Boston: Atlantic Monthly, 1986. 17–29.

                    inclusive page numbers of article or chapter

Alvarez, Julia. "Grounds for Fiction." <u>The Riverside Reader</u>. 8th ed.

     Ed. Joseph F. Trimmer and Maxine Hairston. Boston: Houghton,

     2005. 125–39.

If the work in the anthology is a reprint of a previously published scholarly article, supply the complete information for both the original publication and the reprint in the anthology.

Gates, Henry Louis, Jr. "The Fire Last Time." <u>New Republic</u> 1 June 1992:

     37-43. Rpt. in <u>Contemporary Literary Criticism</u>. Ed. Jeffrey W.

     Hunter. Vol. 127. Detroit: Gale, 2000. 113-19.

SOURCE SHOT 1

Listing a Book (MLA)

Find the necessary information for documenting a book on its title page. If the date is not on the title page, look on the copyright page. Include the following:

❶ **Name of author(s)** Last name, first name, followed by a period

❷ **Title of Book: Subtitle** Underlined, with capitals for main words, followed by a period

❸ **Place of publication** The first city mentioned on the title page—not the state, but country or Canadian province if needed—followed by a colon

❹ **Name of publisher** In short form: *Houghton*, not *Houghton Mifflin*; *Basic*, not *Basic Books*; *Abrams*, not *Harry N. Abrams*. Omit abbreviations such as *Co.* and *Inc.*: *Simon*, not *Simon & Schuster, Inc.* For university presses, use the abbreviations "U" and "P" with no periods: *Columbia UP*; *U of Chicago P*, and so on.

❺ **Year of publication** Separated from the publisher's name with a comma; look for ©. Put a period at the end.

Items 1–20 give examples and provide information on variations.

Listing a Book with One Author (MLA)

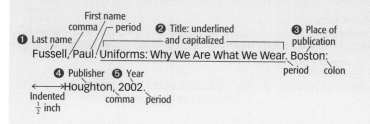

6. More than one work in an anthology, cross-referenced   If you refer to more than one work from the same anthology, list the anthology separately, and also list each essay with a cross-reference to the anthology. Alphabetize in the usual way, as in the following three examples.

```
                            title of article
   ┌─ author of article ─┐   ┌─ in anthology ─┐   editor of anthology
   Des Pres, Terrence. "Poetry and Politics." Gibbons 17–29.
                                                   page numbers of article
```

Title Page

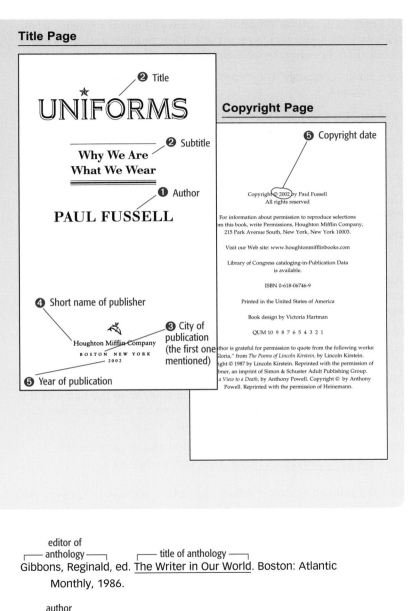

Title Page

★
UNIFORMS ❷ Title

Why We Are
What We Wear ❷ Subtitle

❶ Author

PAUL FUSSELL

❹ Short name of publisher

🪶
Houghton Mifflin Company ❸ City of
BOSTON NEW YORK publication
2002 (the first one
mentioned)
❺ Year of publication

Copyright Page

❺ Copyright date

Copyright © 2002 by Paul Fussell
All rights reserved

For information about permission to reproduce selections
om this book, write Permissions, Houghton Mifflin Company,
215 Park Avenue South, New York, New York 10003.

Visit our Web site: www.houghtonmifflinbooks.com

Library of Congress cataloging-in-Publication Data
is available.

ISBN 0-618-06746-9

Printed in the United States of America

Book design by Victoria Hartman

QUM 10 9 8 7 6 5 4 3 2 1

thor is grateful for permission to quote from the following works:
loria," from *The Poems of Lincoln Kirstein*, by Lincoln Kirstein.
ight © 1987 by Lincoln Kirstein. Reprinted with the permission of
bner, an imprint of Simon & Schuster Adult Publishing Group.
a View to a Death, by Anthony Powell. Copyright © by Anthony
Powell. Reprinted with the permission of Heinemann.

editor of
┌─ anthology ─┐ ┌── title of anthology ──┐
Gibbons, Reginald, ed. The Writer in Our World. Boston: Atlantic
 Monthly, 1986.

author
┌─ of article ─┐ ┌── title of article in anthology ──┐ editor of anthology
Walcott, Derek. "A Colonial's-Eye View of America." Gibbons 73–77.
 page numbers of article

7. Entry in a reference book For a well-known reference book, such as a dictionary, give only the edition number and the year of publication. For encyclopedia entries, also give page numbers.

Kahn, David. "Cryptology." Encyclopedia Americana. Internatl. Ed. 2001.
116–118.

"Etching." The Columbia Encyclopedia. 6th ed. 2000. 312.

For works that are not widely known, also give details of editors, volumes, place of publication, and publisher.

8. Book or pamphlet with no author named Put the title first. Do not consider the words *A, An,* and *The* when alphabetizing the entries. The following entry would be alphabetized under *C.*

The Chicago Manual of Style. 15th ed. Chicago: U of Chicago P, 2003.

9. Book written by a corporation or some other organization Alphabetize by the name of the corporate author or branch of government. If the publisher is the same as the author, include the name again as publisher.

Hoover's Inc. Hoover's Handbook of World Business. Austin: Hoover's,
2005.

10. Government publication If no individual author is named for a government publication, begin the entry with the name of the federal, state, or local government, followed by the agency. See item 40 for an online government publication.

United States. National Commission of Terrorist Attacks upon the U.S.
The 9/11 Commission Report. New York: Norton, 2004.

11. Translated book After the title, include "Trans." for "Translated by" followed by the name of the translator, first name first.

Grass, Günter. Novemberland: Selected Poems, 1956–1993. Trans.
Michael Hamburger. San Diego: Harcourt, 1996.

12. Multivolume work If you refer to more than one volume of a multivolume work, indicate the number of volumes (abbreviated "vols.") after the title.

Barr, Avon, and Edward A. Feigenbaum, eds. The Handbook of Artificial
Intelligence. 4 vols. Reading: Addison, 1981–86.

If you refer to only one volume of a work, limit the information in the entry to that one volume.

Richardson, John. A Life of Picasso. Vol. 2. New York: Random, 1996.

13. Book in a series   Give the name of the series after the book title.

Connor, Ulla. Contrastive Rhetoric: Cross-Cultural Aspects of Second
    Language Writing. Cambridge Applied Linguistics Ser. New York:
    Cambridge UP, 1996.

14. Book published under publisher's imprint   State the names of both the imprint (the publisher within a larger publishing enterprise) and the larger publishing house, separated by a hyphen.

Atwood, Margaret. Negotiations with the Dead: A Writer on Writing.
    New York: Anchor-Doubleday, 2003.

15. Foreword, preface, introduction, or afterword   List the name of the author of the book element cited, followed by the name of the element, with no quotation marks. Give the title of the work; then use "By" to introduce the name of the author of the book (first name first). After the publication information, give inclusive page numbers for the book element cited.

Remnick, David. Introduction. Politics. By Hendrik Hertzberg. New York:
    Penguin, 2004. xvii–xxiv.

16. Republished book   After the title, give the original date of publication. Then cite information about the current publication.

King, Stephen. On Writing. 2000. New York: Pocket, 2002.

17. Edition other than the first   After the title, give the edition number, using the abbreviation "ed."

Raimes, Ann. Keys for Writers. 4th ed. Boston: Houghton, 2005.

18. Book title including a title   Do not underline a book title that is part of the source title. (However, if the title of a short work, such as a poem or short story, is part of the source title, enclose it in quotation marks.)

Hays, Kevin J., ed. The Critical Response to Herman Melville's
    book title not underlined
    Moby Dick. Westport: Greenwood, 1994.

19. The Bible or other sacred text Take the information from the title page and give the usual bibliographical details for a book. Also include the edition and the name of a translator or editor where appropriate.

Enuma Elish. Ed. Leonard W. King. Escondido: Book Tree, 1998.

The Holy Bible. King James Version. Peabody: Hendrickson, 2003.

The Koran. Trans. George Sales. London: Warne, n.d. (n.d. means no
    date given)

The New Oxford Annotated Bible. 3rd ed. Ed. Michael D. Coogan.
    Oxford, Eng.: Oxford UP, 2001.

20. Dissertation For an unpublished dissertation, follow the title (in quotation marks) with "Diss." and the university and date.

Hidalgo, Stephen Paul. "Vietnam War Poetry: A Genre of Witness." Diss.
    U. of Notre Dame, 1995.

Cite a published dissertation as you would a book, with place of publication, publisher, and date, but also include dissertation information after the title (for example, "Diss. U of California, 2006.").

If the dissertation is published by University Microfilms International (UMI), underline the title and include "Ann Arbor: UMI," the date, and the order number at the end of the entry.

Diaz-Greenberg, Rosario. The Emergence of Voice in Latino High School
    Students. Diss. U of San Francisco, 1996. Ann Arbor: UMI, 1996.
    9611612.

If you cite an abstract published in *Dissertation Abstracts International* (*DAI*), give the relevant volume number, date, and page numbers.

Hidalgo, Stephen Paul. "Vietnam War Poetry: A Genre of Witness." Diss.
    U of Notre Dame, 1995. DAI 56 (1995): 0931A.

The conventions for listing print articles (or older articles, preserved on microform) depend on whether the articles appear in newspapers, popular magazines, or scholarly journals. For distinguishing scholarly journals from other periodicals, see 49b. In all cases, omit from your citation any introductory *A, An,* or *The* in the name of a newspaper, magazine, or scholarly journal. For page citations over 100 and sharing the same first number, use only the last two digits for the second number (for instance, 528–39, but 598–605).

21. Article in a scholarly journal: continuously paged by volume
For journals with consecutive pagination through a volume (for example, the first issue of volume 1 ends with page 174, and the second issue of volume 1 begins with page 175), give only the volume number and year. See Source Shot 2 on page 724 for an example.

22. Article in a scholarly journal: paged by issue   For journals in which each issue begins with page 1, include the issue number after the volume number, separated from the volume number by a period, or include the issue number alone if no volume number is given.

Ginat, Rami. "The Soviet Union and the Syrian Ba'th Regime: From Hesitation
to Rapprochement." Middle Eastern Studies 36.2 (2000): 150–71.

volume number   issue number

23. Article in a magazine   Do not include *The* in the name of a magazine: *Atlantic,* not *The Atlantic.* For a magazine published every week or biweekly, give the complete date: date (numeral), month (abbreviated if necessary—see 52d), and year, in that order, with no commas between them. For a monthly or bimonthly magazine, give only the month and year. In either case, do not include volume and issue numbers. If the article is no longer than one page, give that page number. If the article covers two or more consecutive pages, list inclusive page numbers.

Douthat, Ross. "The Truth about Harvard." Atlantic Mar. 2005: 95–99.
Tyrangiel, Josh. "Barrel of Monkeys." Time 20 Feb. 2006: 62.

Article only one page long

24. Article in a newspaper   After the newspaper title (omit the word *The*), give the date, followed by any edition given at the top of the first page (*late ed., natl. ed.*). For a newspaper that uses letters to designate sections, give the letter before the page number: "A23." For a numbered section, write, for example, "sec. 2:23."

Franklin, Deborah. "Vitamin E Fails to Deliver on Early Promise." New
York Times 2 Aug. 2005, late ed.: F5.

SOURCE SHOT 2

Listing a Periodical Article (MLA)

Include the following when listing a periodical article:

❶ **Name of author(s)** Last name, first name, followed by a period

❷ **"Title of Article: Any Subtitle."** In quotation marks

❸ <u>Name of journal or periodical</u> Omitting any *A, An,* or *The,* underlined, with no period following, and including **volume** and **issue** number where necessary (items 21 and 22)

❹ **Date of publication** Whatever is available and necessary for type of periodical (items 21–30), with year in parentheses (items 21 and 22) or day, month, year, in that order, with all months except May, June, and July abbreviated. Follow the date with a colon.

❺ **Page number or range of pages** (such as 24–27; 365–72). End with a period. For newspapers, see items 24 and 25.

See items 21–30 for examples.

---

25. Article that skips pages   When an article does not appear on consecutive pages (the one by Spencer Reiss begins on page 136–141, then skips ten pages and continues on 151–152), give only the first page number followed by a plus sign.

Reiss, Spencer. "The Dotcom King and the Rooftop Solar Revolution."
<u>Wired</u> 20 July 2005: 136+.

26. Review   Begin with the name of the reviewer and the title of the review article, if these are available. After "Rev. of," provide the title and author of the work reviewed, followed by publication information for the review.

Weintraub, Arlene. "Men in White." Rev. of <u>World as Laboratory:
Experiments with Mice, Mazes, and Men</u>, by Rebecca Lemov.
<u>Business Week</u> 5 Dec. 2005: 108–109.

Listing an Article in a Scholarly Journal

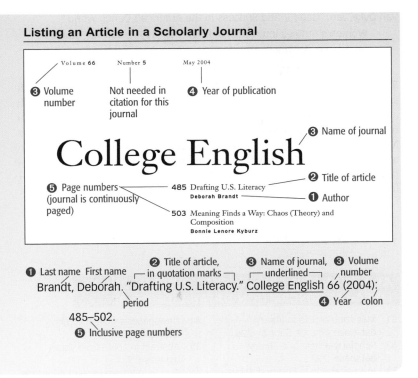

27. **Unsigned editorial or article** Begin with the title. For an editorial, include the label "Editorial" after the title. In alphabetizing, ignore an initial *A, An,* or *The.*

"Resident Evil." New Republic 19 Dec. 2005: 7.
"Spark the Revolution." Editorial. Wall Street Journal 27 Dec. 2005: A20.

28. **Letter to the editor** Write "Letter" or "Reply to letter of . . ." after the name of the author or after the title, if there is one.

Nichol, Christina J. Letter. Harper's Jan. 2006: 6.

29. **Abstract in an abstracts journal** For abstracts of articles, provide exact information for the original work, and add information about your source for the abstract: the title of the abstract journal, volume number, year, and item number or page number. (For dissertation abstracts, see 51e, item 20.)

Van Dyke, Jan. "Gender and Success in the American Dance World."
    Women's Studies International Forum 19 (1996): 535–43. Studies
    on Women Abstracts 15 (1997): item 97W/081.

30. Article on microform (microfilm and microfiche) To cite
sources that are neither in hard copy nor in electronic form, provide
as much print publication information as is available along with the
name of the microfilm or microfiche and any identifying features.
Many newspaper and magazine articles published before 1980 are
available only in microfiche or on microfilm, so you will need to use
this medium for historical research. However, be aware that such collections may be incomplete and difficult to read and duplicate clearly.

"War with Japan." Editorial. New York Times 8 Dec. 1941: 22. UMI
    University Microfilms.

**AT A GLANCE INDEX: WORKS FOUND IN ONLINE
LIBRARY SUBSCRIPTION DATABASES (MLA)**

Libraries subscribe to large information services (such as *InfoTrac,
FirstSearch, EBSCO, SilverPlatter, Dialog, SIRS,* and *LexisNexis*) to
gain access to extensive databases of online articles and to specialized databases (such as *ERIC, Contemporary Literary Criticism,* and
PsycINFO). You can use these databases to locate abstracts and full
texts of thousands of articles.

The URLs used to access databases are useful only to those
accessing them through a subscribing organization such as a college
library or a public library. In addition, database URLs tend not to
remain stable, changing day by day, so providing a URL at the end of
your citation will not be helpful to your readers unless you know it
will be persistent. Cite articles in library databases by providing the
information in Source Shot 3 on page 728.

31. Magazine article in a library database See Source Shot 3 on
page 728 for an example.

32. Scholarly article in a library database

Lowe, Michelle S. "Britain's Regional Shopping Centres: New Urban Forms?"
> volume number for print version of scholarly article
> Urban Studies 37.2 (2000): 261– . MasterFile Premier. EBSCO. Brooklyn
>
> ┌──────── persistent URL ────────┐
> Public Lib., Brooklyn, NY. 20 Feb. 2005 <http://search.epnet.com/
>
> login.aspx?direct=true&db=f5h&an=2832704>.

33. Journal article in a library database

Bailey, Martin. "Van Gogh: The Fakes Debate." Apollo Jan. 2005: 55– .
> Expanded Academic ASAP. Infotrac. University at Albany Lib., Albany,
>
> ┌──── URL of home page ────┐
> NY. 22 Feb. 2005 <http://www.galegroup.com>.

34. Newspaper article in a library database

Weeks, Linton. "History Repeating Itself; Instead of Describing Our Country's
> Past, Two Famous Scholars Find Themselves Examining Their Own."
> Washington Post 24 Mar. 2002: F01– . Academic Universe: News.
>
> URL of home page: no persistent URL available
> LexisNexis. City U of New York Lib. 3 Aug. 2005 <http://
>
> web.lexis-nexis.com>.

35. Abstract in a specialized library database   If the URL is
impossibly long, give the URL of the home page of the subscription
service, with any details of the path followed.

Kofman, Eleonora. "Gendered Global Migrations: Diversity and Stratification."
> Intl. Feminist Jour. of Politics 6 (2004): 643–65. Abstract. Sociological
> Abstracts. CSA Illumina. City U of New York Lib. 28 Feb. 2005
> <http://www.csa.com>. Path: Gender and migration.

36. Article in a database with no visible URLs   If a library or
service provider links directly to a licensed database without dis-
playing the URL of the accessed database, give the name of the database, the name of the service or library, and your date of access.
Specify any path or keywords that you used to access the source.

"Parthenon." The Columbia Encyclopedia. 6th ed. 2000. America Online.
> 12 Apr. 2003. Keywords: Reference; Encyclopedias;
> Encyclopedia.com; Bartleby.com; Columbia Encyclopedia 6th ed.

SOURCE SHOT 3

Listing an Article from a Library Database (MLA)

❶ **Name of author(s)** Last name, first name, followed by a period

❷ **"Title of Article: Any Subtitle."** In quotation marks

❸ **Print information for the article** Name of journal underlined plus **date** of publication plus **page numbers** of the print document if given or shown on the screen or the starting page, followed by a hyphen and a space, for example, 26– . Use page numbers from a printout only if you cite a PDF document.

❹ **Name of the database** Underlined, for example, Academic Search Premier, and followed by a period

❺ **Name of service providing database** For example, *EBSCO, LexisNexis, InfoTrac,* plus a period

❻ **Name of library system** With city and state if necessary, abbreviated to "Lib."

❼ **Your date of access** Day month year, as shown on a printout of the work, with a period at the end

❽ **<URL>** Enclosed in angle brackets, followed by a period, with hyperlinks removed (Tools/AutoCorrect/AutoFormat or Insert/Hyperlink/Remove). Note the specific advice given in the *MLA Handbook for Writers of Research Papers*: "If possible, conclude with the URL of the specific document" (that is, with any persistent URL shown on the screen, provided it is not too long or complicated), but if the database provides no persistent or short URL, give the URL "of the service's home page" (229).

See items 31–36 for examples.

Listing an Article from an EBSCO Database

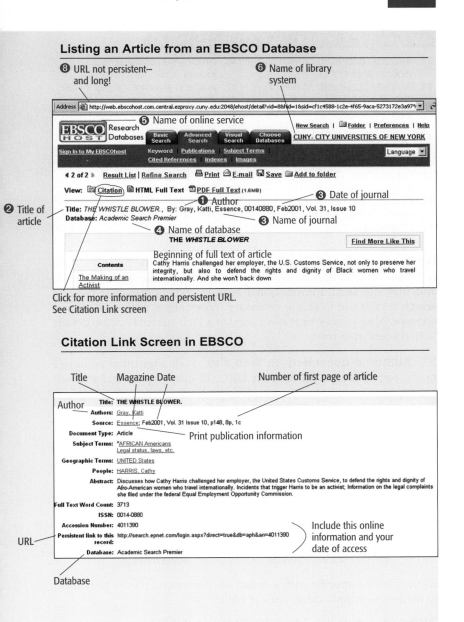

8 URL not persistent— and long!

6 Name of library system

5 Name of online service

2 Title of article

1 Author

3 Date of journal

3 Name of journal

4 Name of database

Beginning of full text of article

Click for more information and persistent URL.
See Citation Link screen

Citation Link Screen in EBSCO

Title

Magazine Date

Number of first page of article

Author

Print publication information

Include this online information and your date of access

URL

Database

With whatever system of documentation you use, the basic question is "What information do readers need to access the same Web site and find the same information I found?" Sometimes you have to search a Web site to locate necessary information, such as date and sponsor. Always save or make a copy of a Web source because details may change over time.

37. Authored document on Web site Web sites often comprise many pages, each with its own URL. To cite a specific document rather than the whole site, provide the URL for the specific page. Source Shot 4 on page 732 shows an example.

38. Web site document, no author For a Web site document for which no author is named, begin with the title. Continue with the details of site, date, sponsor, date of access, and URL.

┌─────── title ───────┐ ┌─────────── site ────────────┐
"Freedom of Information Act." Federal Relations and Information Policy.

       date of   date of
    ┌─ posting ─┐ ┌─────── sponsor ───────┐ ┌─ access ─┐
    1 June 2005. Assn. of Research Libraries. 22 Dec. 2005 <http://

www.arl.org/info/frn/gov/foia/index.html#overview>.

If you follow a specific path to reach the document, it may be helpful to readers to supply details of the path:

"Archeologists Enter King Tut's Tomb: November 26, 1992."
    HistoryChannel.com. 2005. History Channel. 20 Feb. 2005
    <http://www.historychannel.com>. Path: This Day in History;
    November 26.

39. Entire Web site or professional site, no author named

Federal Relations and Information Policy. 6 Dec. 2005. Assn. of Research
Libraries. 21 Dec. 2005 <http://www.arl.org/info/frn/copy/
copytoc.html>.

$$\overbrace{\text{MLA: Modern Language Association}}^{\text{title of site}}. \overbrace{\text{27 Jan. 2006.}}^{\substack{\text{date of}\\ \text{update}}} \overbrace{\text{Mod. Lang. Assn. of Amer.}}^{\text{sponsor}}$$

$$\overbrace{\text{17 Feb. 2006}}^{\substack{\text{date of}\\ \text{access}}} \text{<http://www.mla.org>.}$$

40. Government publication online

Begin with the government and agency and title of the work. Follow this with the date of electronic posting or update, your date of access, and the URL. Government sites often post documents online before publishing them in print form.

United States. Dept. of Educ. Office of Educ. Research and Improvement.
Natl. Center for Educ. Statistics. Digest of Education Statistics, 2003.
30 Dec. 2004. 18 Feb. 2006 <http://nces.ed.gov/programs/digest/d03>.

41. Scholarly project online

$$\overbrace{\text{Perseus Digital Library}}^{\substack{\text{title of scholarly}\\ \text{project}}}. \overbrace{\text{Ed. Gregory Crane.}}^{\text{editor}} \overbrace{\text{Updated daily.}}^{\substack{\text{date of electronic}\\ \text{publication}}} \overbrace{\text{Dept. of Classics,}}^{\text{sponsor}}$$

$$\overbrace{\text{Tufts U.}}\ \overbrace{\text{1 Feb. 2003}}^{\substack{\text{date of}\\ \text{access}}} \text{<http://www.perseus.tufts.edu>.}$$

42. Personal Web site/home page

If a personal Web page has a title, supply it, underlined. Otherwise, use the designation "Home page."

$$\text{Gilpatrick, Eleanor. Home page. } \overbrace{\text{Feb. 2006.}}^{\substack{\text{date of}\\ \text{update}}} \text{ 9 Feb. 2006 <http://}$$
www.gilpatrickart.com>.

43. Course page

For a course home page, give the name of the instructor and the course, the words *Course home page,* the dates of the course, the department and the institution, and then your access date and the URL.

Parry, Katherine. History of the English Language. Course home page.
Feb. 2006. Dept. of English, Hunter Coll. 20 Feb. 2006
<http://bb.hunter.cuny.edu>.

SOURCE SHOT 4

Listing Web Sources (MLA)

Include these five basic items if they are available:

❶ **Name of author(s)** Last name, first, middle initial *or* corporation, institution, or government agency. Begin with the title if you find no author credited on the site. Put a period at the end.

❷ **"Title of Work."** In quotation marks plus any **print publication information**, if available. Give page numbers *only* for print documents in PDF format. Otherwise, give no page numbers.

❸ **Site information** <u>Name of Web Site</u> (underlined) plus **date** of posting or update plus **sponsor** (if available). A Webmaster is not the sponsor of the site.

❹ **Your date of access** Day month (abbrev.) year, with no period after the year. Make a copy of the Web page as soon as you find it; the date will appear on your printout.

❺ **<URL>** Enclosed in angle brackets, followed by a period; hyperlinks removed (Tools/AutoCorrect/AutoFormat). Line split only after a slash. No spaces or hyphens inserted.

See examples in items 37–52.

44. Online book or part of book Give whatever is available of the following: author, title, editor or translator, and any print publication information, as shown in items 1–19. Follow this with the available electronic publication information: title of site or database, date of electronic posting, sponsor, your date of access to the site, and the URL.

Listing an Authored Web Site Document

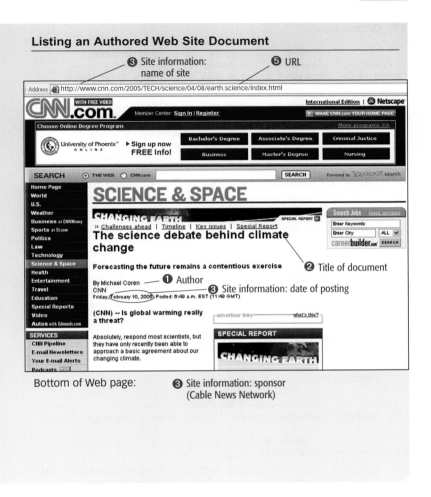

Bottom of Web page: ❸ Site information: sponsor
(Cable News Network)

print publication
author ─── ─── title of work ─── ─── information ───
Darwin, Charles. The Voyage of the Beagle. New York: Collier, 1909.

date of
electronic   name of
─── title of database ─── ┌ publication ┐ ┌─── sponsor of site ───
Oxford Text Archive. 27 Jan. 2005. Arts and Humanities Data

date of   URL enclosed
─── ┌ access ┐   ┌─── in angle brackets ───
Service. 22 Dec. 2005 <http://ota.ahds.ac.uk>.

45. Online poem

title of print print publication
┌─ author ─┐ ┌─ poem ─┐ ┌─ source ─┐ ┌──── information ────┐
Levine, Philip. "What Work Is." What Work Is. New York: Knopf, 1991.

date of electronic sponsor
┌──── title of database ────┐ ┌ updating ┐ ┌──── of site ────┐
Internet Poetry Archive. 4 Apr. 2000. U of North Carolina P.

date of URL enclosed
┌─ access ─┐ ┌──────── in angle brackets ────────┐
19 Dec. 2005 <http://www.ibiblio.org/ipa/levine/work.html>.

46. Article in an online scholarly journal Give the author, title of
article, title of journal, volume and issue numbers, and date of issue.
Include page number or the number of paragraphs only if pages or
paragraphs are numbered in the source, as they are for the first example below. End with date of access and URL.

┌── author ──┐ ┌──────────── title of article ────────────┐
Hatchuel, Sarah. "Leading the Gaze: From Showing to Telling in Kenneth

name of volume and
┌──────────────────────────┐ ┌── online journal ─┐ issue numbers
Branagh's Henry V and Hamlet." Early Modern Literary Studies 6.1

date of online number of paragraphs date of
publication (numbered in the text) access
(2000): 22 pars. 21 Dec. 2005 <http://www.shu.ac.uk/emls/06–1/
hatchbra.htm>.

┌── author ──┐ ┌──────── title of article ────────┐ ┌──
Hart, Stephen. "Overtures to a New Discipline: Neuromusicology." 21st

volume and date of
title of online journal issue numbers access
┌──────────┐ ┌──────┐ ┌── access ──┐
Century 1.4 (July 1996). 22 Dec. 2005 <http://www.columbia.edu/cu/
└ date of ┘ └──── no numbered pages or paragraphs ────┘
electronic publication
21stC/issue-1.4/mbmmusic.html>.

47. Article in an online magazine Two dates can appear one after
the other. The first is the date of posting or update; the second is your
date of access.

Gross, Daniel. "One Word: Logistics." Slate 20 Jan. 2006. 23 Jan. 2006
<http://www.Slate.com/id/2134513/?nav=tap3>.

48. Article in an online newspaper Give the author, title of article, name of newspaper (underlined) and date, name of online site
(underlined), your date of access, and the URL of the article.

Silverstein, Stuart. "More Undergrads Playing Hooky when Class Notes
Go Online." <u>Los Angeles Times</u> 23 Jan. 2006. <u>Chicago Tribune</u>. 25
Jan. 2006 <http://www.chicagotribune.com/news/nationworld/
chi-0601230142jan23,1,6644364.story>.

49. Online review, editorial, letter, or abstract   After the author
and title, identify the type of text: "Letter," "Editorial," "Abstract," or
"Rev. of . . . by . . ." (see 51e, items 25–28). Continue with details of the
electronic source.

Raimes, Ann. Rev. of <u>Dog World: And the Humans Who Live There</u> by
Alfred Gingold. <u>Amazon.com</u>. 18 Feb. 2005. <http://www.amazon.com>.

**50. Entry in an online encyclopedia, dictionary, or other refer-
ence work**   When entries are not individually authored, begin with
the title of the entry. Give the latest date of posting. Provide details of
the sponsor, your date of access, and the URL.

title of article	title of database	date of electronic updating	sponsor	date of access

"Atheism." <u>Wikipedia</u>. 27 Dec. 2005. Wikipedia Foundation. 3 Jan. 2006
<http://en.wikipedia.org/wiki/Atheism>.

"Vicarious." <u>Cambridge Advanced Learner's Dictionary</u>. 2004.
Cambridge UP. 6 Jan. 2006 <http://dictionary.cambridge.org/
define.asp?key=88182&dict=CALD>.

51. Online posting on a discussion list, blog, Usenet, etc.   Give
the author's name, the document title (as written in the subject
line), the label "Online posting," and the date of posting. Follow this
with the name of the forum in the discussion list or of the Web log
(blog), date of access, and URL or address of the list.

Tubbs, Brian. "Washington and Lincoln—Both Great Men." Online posting.

                       ┌── name of forum ──┐
21 Feb. 2005. American Revolution. 21 Feb. 2005 <http://

boards.historychannel.com/forum.jspa?forumID=90>.

Brattina, Tiffany. "The Life of a Salesman." Online posting. 16 Mar. 2004.

       name of
    ┌── blog ──┐
Luna Dreams. 22 Feb. 2005 <http://blogs.setonhill.edu/

TiffanyBrattina/002755.html>.

For a Usenet newsgroup, give the name and address of the group, beginning with the prefix *news*:

Zimmer, Ben. "Eggcorn Database." Online posting. 19 Feb. 2005. 21 Feb.
    2005 <news:alt.usage.english>.

To make it easy for readers to find a posting, refer whenever possible to one stored in Web archives.

Schwalm, David. "Re: Value of an Education." Online posting. 15 Feb. 2005.

      name of
    ┌── archive ──┐
    WPA-L Archives. 21 Feb. 2005. <http://lists.asu.edu/

    archives.wpa-L.html>.

To cite a forwarded document in an online posting, include the author, title, and date, followed by "Fwd. by" and the name of the person forwarding the document. End with "Online posting," the date of the forwarding, the name of the discussion group, date of access, and address of the discussion list.

Gold, Tami. "Update on PSC-CUNY Contract." 16 Feb. 2005. Fwd. by Ken
    Sherrill. Online posting. 17 Feb. 2005. Hunter-L. 20 Feb. 2005
    <http://hunter.listserv.cuny.edu>.

52. Personal e-mail message Provide the subject line heading.

Bernstein, Roberta. "Challenges." E-mail to the author. 12 Feb. 2006.

**AT A GLANCE INDEX: VISUAL, PERFORMANCE, AND
MULTIMEDIA SOURCES (LIVE, PRINT, AND ONLINE) (MLA)**

Identify online visual, performance, and multimedia sources as you would sources that are not online, with the addition of electronic publishing information (site name and date) as well as your date of access and the URL. Items 53, 56, 57, and 58 include citations of online works.

53. Work of art, slide, or photograph List the name of the artist; the title of the work (underlined); the name of the museum, gallery, site, or owner; and the location. You can also include the date the work was created.

Christo. <u>The Gates</u>. Central Park, New York. Feb. 2005.

Duchamp, Marcel. <u>Bicycle Wheel</u>. 1951. Museum of Mod. Art, New York.
     22 Feb. 2005 <http://www.moma.org/collection/depts/paint_sculpt/
     blowups/paint_sculpt_020.html>.

Johns, Jasper. <u>Racing Thoughts</u>. Whitney Museum of Amer. Art, New York.

For a photograph in a book, give complete publication information, including the page number on which the photograph appears.

Johns, Jasper. <u>Racing Thoughts</u>. Whitney Museum of Amer. Art, New
     York. <u>The American Century: Art and Culture 1950–2000</u>. By Lisa
     Phillips. New York: Norton, 1999. 311.

For a slide in a collection, include the slide number (Slide 17).

54. Cartoon   After the cartoonist's name and the title (if any) of the cartoon, add the label "Cartoon." Follow this with the usual information about the source, and give the page number for a print source.

Shanahan, Danny. "The Lawyer Fairy." Cartoon. <u>New Yorker</u> 7 Feb. 2005: 49.

55. Advertisement   For an advertisement, give the name of the product or company, followed by the label "Advertisement" and any publication information. If a page is not numbered, write "n. pag."

Xerox. Advertisement. <u>Fortune</u> 7 Feb. 2005: 1.

For a placards such as a label on a museum wall, provide the label "Placard" after the name of the work. Also give the museum and the dates of the show.

Rauschenberg, Robert. <u>Collection</u>. Placard. New York: Metropolitan
     Museum of Art, 20 Dec. 2005–2 Apr. 2006.

56. Map or chart   Underline the title of the map or chart, and include the designation after the title.

<u>Auvergne/Limousin</u>. Map. Paris: Michelin, 1996.

<u>Pearl Harbor</u>. Multimedia attack map. <u>Nationalgeographic.com</u>. 19 Feb.
     2005. <http://plasma.nationalgeographic.com/pearlharbor>.

57. Film or video List the title, director, performers, and any other pertinent information. End with the name of the distributor and the year of distribution.

<u>Million Dollar Baby</u>. Dir. Clint Eastwood. Perf. Hilary Swank. Warner, 2004.

<u>Office Ninja</u>. Dir. Matthew Johnston. iFilm, 2004. 19 Feb. 2005
    <http://www.ifilm.com/ifilmdetail/2659387>.

When you cite a videocassette or DVD, include pertinent details and the date of the original film, the medium, the name of the distributor of the DVD or cassette, and the year of the new release.

<u>Casablanca</u>. Dir. Michael Curtiz. Perf. Humphrey Bogart and Ingrid
    Bergman. 1943. DVD. MGM, 1998.

58. Television or radio program Give the title of the program episode; the title of the program; any pertinent information about performers, writer, narrator, or director; the network; and the local station and date of broadcast.

"My Big Break." <u>This American Life</u>. Narr. Ira Glass. WBEZ, Chicago. 21
    Jan. 2005. 22 Feb. 2005 <http://www.thislife.org>.

"Seeds of Destruction." <u>Slavery and the Making of America</u>. Narr.
    Morgan Freeman. Thirteen, WNET. WLIW, New York. 22 Feb. 2005.

59. Sound recording List the composer or author, the title of the work, the names of artists, the production company, and the date. If the medium is not a compact disc, indicate the medium, such as "Audiocassette," before the name of the production company.

Turner, Alex, and Arctic Monkeys. <u>Whatever People Say, That's What I'm
    Not</u>. Domino, 2006.

Walker, Alice. Interview with Kay Bonetti. Audiocassette. Columbia:
    American Audio Prose Library, 1981.

60. Live performance Give the title of the play, the author, pertinent information about the director or performers, the theater, the location, and the date of performance. If you are citing an individual's role in the work, begin your citation with the person's name.

Diggs, Elizabeth. <u>Mirette</u>. Dir. Drew Scott Harris. Perf. Robert Cuccioli.
    Saint Peter's Theatre, New York. 17 Dec. 2005.

<u>Mirette</u>. Book by Elizabeth Diggs. Dir. Drew Scott Harris. Perf. Robert
    Cuccioli. Saint Peter's Theatre, New York. 17 Dec. 2005.

61. Personal interview Include the type of interview (telephone, e-mail, personal, etc.).

Gingold, Toby. Telephone interview. 4 Mar. 2006.

62. Published interview Give the name of the person interviewed, followed by the word "Interview" or "Interview with . . .". Include information about the print publication.

Parker, Dorothy. Interview with Marion Capron. Writers at Work: The Paris Review Interviews. London: Secker and Warburg, 1958. 66–75.

63. Broadcast interview Provide information about the broadcast source and the date of the interview.

Gladwell, Malcolm. Interview with Leonard Lopate. The Leonard Lopate Show: Think without Thinking. WNYC, New York. 18 Feb. 2005.

64. Online interview

Gladwell, Malcolm. Interview with Leonard Lopate. The Leonard Lopate Show: Think without Thinking. WNYC, New York. 18 Feb. 2005 <http://www.wnyc.org/shows/lopate/episodes/0218005>.

For a sound recording of an interview, see item 59.

65. Lecture or speech Give the author and title, if known. For a presentation with no title, include a label such as "Lecture" or "Address" after the name of the speaker. Also give the name of any organizing sponsor, the venue, and the date.

Gourevitch, Philip. Lecture. Hunter College, New York. 28 Feb. 2006.

66. Letter or personal communication For a letter that you received, include the phrase "Letter to the author" after the name of the letter writer. Describe the type of any other personal communication ("Telephone call," for example). (See also item 49, for letters published online.)

Rogan, Helen. Letter to the author. 3 Feb. 2006.

Cite a published letter in a collection as you would cite a work in an anthology. After the name of the author, include any title the editor gives the letter and the date. Add the page numbers for the letter at the end of the citation.

Bishop, Elizabeth. "To Robert Lowell." 26 Nov. 1951. One Art: Letters. Ed.
      Robert Giroux. New York: Farrar, 1994. 224–26.

67. Legal or historical source For a legal case, give the name of the case with no underlining or quotation marks, the number of the case, the name of the court deciding the case, and the date of the decision.

Roe v. Wade. No. 70–18. Supreme Ct. of the US. 22 Jan. 1973.

If you mention the case in your text, underline it.

Chief Justice Burger, in Roe v. Wade, noted that . . .

Give the Public Law number of an act, its date, and the cataloging number for its Statutes at Large.

USA Patriot Act. Pub. L. 107–56. 26 Oct. 2001. Stat. 115.272.

Well-known historical documents should not be included in your works-cited list (see 51c, item V).

68. CD-ROM or DVD Cite material from a CD-ROM or DVD in the same way you cite an article in a book, but after the title of the CD or DVD, add the medium of publication and any version or release number.

Flanner, Janet. "Führer, I." New Yorker 29 Feb. 1934: 20–24. The
      Complete New Yorker. DVD-ROM. New York: Random, 2005.
Keats, John. "To Autumn." Columbia Granger's World of Poetry. CD-ROM.
      Rel. 3. New York: Columbia UP, 1999.

51f When to use footnotes and endnotes

With the MLA parenthetical style of documentation, use a footnote (at the bottom of the page) or an endnote (on a separate numbered page at the end of the paper before the works-cited list) only for notes giving supplementary information that clarifies or expands a point you make. You might use a note to refer to several supplementary bibliographical sources or to provide a comment that is interesting but not essential to your argument. Indicate a note with a raised number (superscript) in your text, after the word or sentence your note refers to. Begin the first line of each note one-half inch (or five spaces) from the left margin. Do not indent subsequent lines of the same note. Double-space endnotes. For footnotes, single-space within each footnote, but double-space between notes.

NOTE NUMBER
IN TEXT

Ethics have become an important part of many writing classes.[1]

CONTENT
ENDNOTE

five spaces _____ raised number followed by space
←——→[1] For additional discussion of ethics in the classroom, see Stotsky 799–806; Knoblauch 15–21; Bizzell 663–67; Friend 560–66.

The *MLA Handbook* also describes a system of footnotes or endnotes as an alternative to parenthetical documentation of references.

51g Students' MLA papers

The first paper was written by Jared Whittemore in a required composition course at San Diego City College. Whittemore, the oldest of seven children, grew up in a military family, moving around often. When he graduated from a typical California high school in the San Francisco Bay Area, he knew that he wanted to go to college, but economically it was difficult. However, he had always wanted to be a firefighter, and most of the Fire Technology courses were offered at the  community college level, where tuition was affordable for him. He works as a firefighter with the Federal Fire Department in San Diego. Having attended three community colleges, he remains enthusiastic about their mission.

In his required composition course, Whittemore chose to write his research paper on a topic that was important to him. He wrote a proposal for the paper, prepared an extensive annotated bibliography (see an excerpt from it in 9b, p. 174), drafted an outline (see 50c), and wrote several drafts, refining his thesis and his supporting points as he did so. Here is his fifth draft.

½"

Whittemore 1

1"

Jared A. Whittemore

1"
Professor K. Lim

English 101

14 March 2005

No extra space below title

Community Colleges:

Providers of Opportunity

Title centered not underlined

Community colleges open doors to a better life. Because

of their small size, high level of accessibility, and low tuition

Double-spaced throughout fees, community colleges have been successful in providing

postsecondary education to those who most need it. Four-year

colleges do not provide access to all. Their doors are closed

to students who cannot commit to or afford to pay for a full

four-year education or who do not meet the standards of the

entrance requirements. With their policy of open access,

community colleges have provided exceptional opportunities,

especially to students from low-income families, minorities,   **Thesis statement**

those with inadequate primary and secondary schooling, and

women.

Paragraph indent ½" ⟶ Such access is illustrated by the system of schools that   **Point I: history of open access**

has grown to be the California Community College system,

originally set up to bridge the gap and smooth the transition

between high school and four-year colleges. The schools were

originally known as "junior colleges," offering an education

comparable to thirteenth and fourteenth grades. In their early

stages, the junior colleges were often looked upon as a daring

1"

Whittemore 2

experiment. Then in 1967, when Governor Ronald Reagan authorized the organization of the Board of Governors of the California Community Colleges, they began to be known as community colleges and to gain recognition as institutions of higher education. The original intent was to make the colleges economically and geographically available to all residents of California who were high school graduates and at least eighteen years of age. Thirty-three years later, in 2000, the Chancellor of the California community colleges, Thomas Nussbaum, reports that California has in five years increased the number of students in the state's 108 community colleges by 260,000 students—"approximately twice the entire undergraduate enrollment of the University of California" (2000, 5) with the system serving 1.6 million students (2000, 2) and helping them achieve self-reliance, self-improvement, and increased productivity.

Community colleges provide opportunities for further education not just in California but across the country. The statistics assembled for the annual Digest of Education Statistics, 2000 found that of the total number of 14,549,189 students enrolled in degree-granting institutions in 1998, 5,516,444 (37.9%) of them were enrolled in two-year colleges (United States, Dept. of Educ., table 179). Community colleges are obviously filling a need for many who want to continue their education beyond high school.

Page numbers for a PDF source

Full name for first mention

Exact words quoted

Year for sources with same author and title

Statistics to support point of access

Whittemore 3

While many students aim to improve their status in life by getting vocational training in the community colleges, others will choose a two-year school for purely financial reasons. Particularly benefiting from the community college system are those who come from low-income families. Even with scholarships available, the reality is that a four-year college is geared to full-time students. However, many students cannot afford not to work to make a living while still attending school; they have to find ways to improve their social status, and this is where the community colleges have stepped in. Students perceive the training offered by the colleges as a means of escape from dependency on social welfare programs, so much so that Robert McCabe, Senior Fellow with the League for Innovation in the Community College, claims that "community colleges are the key to avoiding a national crisis by moving underprepared and dependent individuals into productive self-sufficiency" (23).

The state of California again provides striking evidence of this trend. California has the lowest average tuition and fees of all community colleges in the United States. For the 1999–2000 academic year, for example, the national average in-state tuition was $1,136. Students in Texas and Florida paid $895 and $1,330 respectively, while students in California community colleges paid only $317 (United States, Dept. of Educ., table 314). Beginning in the fall of 1999, California students paid just

Transition to Point II: Access for low-income students

Page number for a print source

Statistics to support point: California example

Whittemore 4

$12 per credit unit, far lower than the tuition rates in other states. In addition, students in California enjoyed a 7.7% drop in student fees between the 1997–98 and 1998–99 school year (Higher).

Another overwhelming financial reason for attending a community college is the cost of tuition in comparison to that in public four-year colleges. For a four-year public institution in California, for instance, in 1999–2000, the average cost of tuition alone was $2,617 (United States, Dept. of Educ., table 314). When we compare that to the community college tuition of $317, we see what a cost-effective alternative a community college provides for lower-income students.

Quite possibly the most conspicuous citizens to have enjoyed the benefits of community colleges are minorities. As early as 1973, Sidney Brossman, the first Chancellor of the California Community Colleges, and Myron Roberts, professor of English at Chaffey College, made this claim: "Community colleges have proven uniquely suited to meeting the educational needs of minority-group students in terms both of numbers of such students enrolled and of success achieved in the classroom" (9).

Minorities, a rapidly growing portion of the country's population, are largely turning to the public sector rather than the private for their college education, as the 1997 enrollment statistics in Table 1 show.

First word of article title with no author named

Statistics: costs in two-year and four-year colleges

Point III: access for minorities

Minorities in public colleges

Whittemore 5

Table 1

Minority Enrollment at Degree-Granting Institutions, 1997

	Public		Private	
	Minorities	Total enrolled	Minorities	Total enrolled
2-year	1,675,467	5,360,686	79,328	244,883
4-year	1,365,473	5,835,433	650,942	3,061,332
Total	3,040,940	11,196,119	730,270	3,306,215

Source: United States, Dept. of Educ., Office of Educ. Research and Improvement, Natl. Center for Educ. Statistics, Digest of Education Statistics, 2000 (Washington: GPO, 2001) table 210.

These figures show that nationwide, in 1997, minorities formed 27% of total enrollment in public colleges, with higher figures for community colleges: 31% of total enrollment in two-year schools. In California, statistics tell an encouraging story. The student population in community colleges closely reflects the overall demographics of the state's population. Nussbaum reports on minority enrollment figures:

> As of 1995, the students attending our colleges rather closely mirrored the adult population of the state: Whites—45%, as compared with 55% in the population; African American—8%, as compared with 7% in the population; Hispanics—23%, as compared with 27% in the population; and Asian—13%, as compared with 12% in the population. (1997, 4)

Whittemore 6

Community colleges can, therefore, provide a diverse, multicultural experience to the students enrolled as the numbers of minorities increase. And the numbers are increasing. For example, in the fall of 1999, of the 1.6 million students enrolled in California community colleges, Whites still make up the largest group—41.9%; Hispanics rank second with a percentage of 25% (13.1% of whom are Mexican, Mexican American, Chicano); Asians are the third largest group with a total of 11.8% enrolled (3.7% of Chinese origin); Blacks make up 7.4%; and the last ethnic group with substantial numbers is Filipinos, with 3.2% (CCC Statewide). It is interesting to note that white enrollees decreased by 22.5% between 1990 and 1999, with a dramatic increase in the enrollment of students of minority groups in that same time period. The largest increase has been in the Latino population, with an increase of 65.6%. Two other groups that have shown an increase in numbers are the Asian/Pacific Islanders, with an increase of 44.6%, and Blacks, with an increase of 8.7% (California Postsecondary Education Commission, Sec. 2-10C).

In addition to welcoming low-income students and minorities, community colleges offer significant education opportunities to students whose secondary education has been inadequate or interrupted and who require remedial education. Community colleges serve these students by providing a wide range of classes and programs to establish the basics in

Statistics on race

Article title abbreviated

Transition to Point IV: access for those needing remediation

Whittemore 7

reading, writing, and mathematics. These programs can help ease students into the postsecondary education experience or prepare them for the workforce.

Students who begin higher education with limited academic skills feel unprepared for the education demands of a four-year college and so turn to community colleges:

> Community colleges have been "second chance" institutions, providing courses and services that raise the level of literacy and prepare students for college-level work. The skills include reading, writing, basic math, thinking, and problem solving. (Community College League of California 5)

Preparation for a four-year school

Students who might otherwise become frustrated, struggle, and ultimately fail in a four-year college that offers no programs designed for their specific need have discovered that they can flourish in a community college and then successfully transfer to a four-year school. The remedial courses provide knowledge and skills that secondary education has failed to provide. Community colleges have always had an interest in the successful articulation and transfer of students. Ray Giles, the director of special services at the Community College League of California, points out the recognition of the importance of this mission: "In 1989, remedial education was recognized by the legislature as a function of the community colleges."

No page number for an online source

Whittemore 8

However, some community college students in need of basic preparation courses have no intention of transferring into four-year institutions. Rather, they benefit from the remedial programs that bring them up to speed and allow them to be more competitive as they enter the workforce. Growing numbers of students are already in the workforce, but they attend community colleges seeking advancement in their jobs, new skills, or training to branch out to new careers. For this group of students, community colleges offer a wide range of occupational and technical programs. In our ever-changing hi-tech society, the task of training a technical workforce is one of the community colleges' basic missions. Many of these students already have associate degrees or even bachelor degrees but find it necessary to continue their education to be economically competitive or to seek new job opportunities in other career fields.

The "National Community College Snapshot" prepared by the American Association of Community Colleges shows that the average national age for community college students is approximately 29 years, suggesting an upsurge in students returning to community colleges in pursuit of marketability. Community colleges have made a commitment to continued workforce development, with a wide range of programs and schedules that accommodate students with busy family and work schedules. They offer intensive courses in the evenings

Preparation for career advancement

Whittemore 9

and on weekends, with more and more online courses adding to flexibility in education for students with busy lives. In return, the community and businesses reap the benefits from the large numbers of educated students who are prepared to use their newly acquired education and skills to better themselves and become more productive.

Point V: access for women

One group that has especially responded to the offering of a wide and flexible range of courses and schedules is women. In 1997, women made up 57.6% of the total enrollment in public two-year institutions as opposed to only 40.3% in 1970 (United States, Dept. of Educ., table 179). In California, too, the statistics continue to show a steady increase: in 1990, the total enrollment for women in the fall term was 785,300, and by 1999 the fall term enrollment of women had grown to 799,438 (California Postsecondary Education Commission, Sec. 2-7C).

Many women have returned to college using the community colleges as a portal. In the past, women traditionally held the role of homemaker and were largely responsible for raising children. However, due to changes in economic needs and social attitudes, women see their roles more broadly defined. Women who attend community colleges see a dramatic rise in economic benefit. Ernest Pascarella, a professor at the University of Iowa, cites supporting statistics: "On average, women with associate degrees had about a 26

Whittemore 10

percent advantage over the annual earnings of their

counterparts with a high school degree" (12).

Page
number
in a print
source

Women who enroll in community colleges often do so

after a life-changing event. They return to school after their

children leave home, after divorces, or after being laid off from

jobs. Many are also seeking to learn job skills so they can

contribute to their families' income. For all these reasons,

women are either enrolling for the first time or returning to

college in large numbers. The community colleges with their

wide variety of vocational programs are well suited to help this

large portion of the population in their educational pursuits and

play an integral part in the improvements seen in the status of

women within society, such as higher pay and increased

opportunities for advancement.

Community colleges clearly play a major role in providing

a postsecondary education to wide-ranging groups of

individuals. These schools make higher education available and

accessible to all, making their hopes and dreams reality. These

dreams are embodied by Cynthia Inda, who took remedial

courses at Santa Barbara City College. This is what she says

about her experience:

Without the opportunity to study at my local

community college, I probably wouldn't have gone

to college at all. My high school grades would have

sufficed to get me into a decent university, but I

Long
quotation
indented

Example
reinforces
all the
points
about
access

Whittemore 11

didn't consider myself college material. After all,
none of my six brothers and sisters had attended
college, and most didn't even finish high school.
My parents have the equivalent of a second-grade
education, Mexican immigrants who do not speak
English; my mother worked as a maid and my
father as a dishwasher. But enrolling in a
community college was one of the smartest
decisions I ever made. Despite my slow start, I
learned the skills I needed to move ahead

Passage omitted from original

academically. . . . I also began to explore
educational alternatives. And transferring to a
reputable four-year university became my most
important goal. (qtd. in Nussbaum, 2000, 3)

Passage quoted as indirect source in Nussbaum

Inda thrived in the community college system and went
on to graduate magna cum laude from Harvard University. Can
anyone doubt that community colleges truly provide a gateway
to self-reliance, personal improvement, higher education, and
success?

Whittemore 12

Works Cited

Brossman, Sidney W., and Myron Roberts. <u>The California</u>
⟵⟶ <u>Community Colleges</u>. Palo Alto: Field Educ., 1973.

California Postsecondary Education Commission. <u>Student</u>
<u>Profiles, 2000</u>. Nov. 2000.

<u>CCC Statewide Student Population: Fall 1999 Enrollments</u>. 3
Feb. 2001. California Comm. Colleges. 13 Feb. 2001
<http://misweb.cccco.edu/mis/statlib/stw/studF99.htm>.

Community College League of California. <u>Achieving the</u>
<u>Diversity Commitment: A Policy and Resource Paper of</u>
<u>the California Community College Trustees</u>. Dec. 2000. 2
Mar. 2001 <http://www.ccleague.org/pubs/policy/
diversity.pdf>.

Giles, Ray. "Curriculum Changes Triggered by Changing
Student Needs, Social Trends." <u>The News</u>. Comm.
College League of California. Spring 2000. 3 Mar. 2001
<http://www.ccleague.org/pubs/news00sp.htm>.

<u>Higher Education Update: 1998–99 State Appropriations for</u>
<u>California Postsecondary Education, Update 98-6</u>. Oct.
1998. California Postsecondary Educ. Commission. 3
Mar. 2001 <http://www.cpec.ca.gov/HigherEdUpdates/
Update1998/UP98-6.ASP>.

McCabe, Robert H. "Can Community Colleges Rescue
America?" <u>Community College Journal</u>. Apr./May 1999:
20–23.

Whittemore 13

"National Community College Snapshot." <u>About Community</u>
<u>Colleges</u>. American Assoc. of Comm. Colleges. 11 Feb
1999. 3 Mar. 2001 <http://www.aacc.nche.edu/Content/
ContentGroups/Statistics/
Community_College_Snapshot.htm>.

Nussbaum, Thomas J. "The State of California Community
Colleges Address, 1997." California Comm. College
Chancellor's Office. Sept. 1997. 6 Feb. 2001
<http://www.cccco.edu/executive/chancellor/speeches/
sos0997.pdf>.

---. "The State of California Community Colleges Address,
2000." California Comm. College Chancellor's Office. 28
Sept. 2000. 13 Feb. 2001 <http://www.cccco.edu/
executive/chancellor/speeches/sos0900.pdf>.

Pascarella, Ernest T. "New Studies Track Community College
Effects on Students." <u>Community College Journal</u>
June/July 1999: 8-14.

United States. Dept. of Educ. Office of Educ. Research and
Improvement. Natl. Center for Educ. Statistics. <u>Digest of</u>
<u>Education Statistics, 2000</u>. Washington: GPO, 2001.

Govern-
ment publi-
cation in
print

Here is Lindsay Camp's documented paper written in her required first-year composition course. She developed her argument about the need for both safety and equality because she was planning to become a police officer. If your instructor requires a separate title page, see 12a or ask for guidelines.

Camp 1

Lindsay Camp

Professor Raimes

English 120, section 129

5 December 2003

Safety First: Women and Men in Police and Fire Departments

If any of us were caught in a fire, we would almost

certainly prefer to see a man rather than a woman coming to

carry us down a ladder out of the flames and smoke--though

we would certainty be grateful to either. In an interview, a

firefighter made precisely that point about perceptions of size

and strength (Mignone). However, because society is

increasingly conscious of discrimination based on gender,

police and fire departments have implemented quotas to hire

more women. In many cases, though, in order to meet the

quotas they have used different physical standards for women

and men, so women who want equality have been treated

unequally, men have experienced reverse discrimination, and

public safety has been threatened. To meet standards of both

safety and equality, women and men should pass the same

physical tests.

In order to become police officers, candidates have

to pass a series of exams and evaluations, among them

psychological tests (Wexler) and a physical fitness test, which

"assumes that being physically fit is a good predictor of job

success for fire and police department personnel" (Rafilson,

Camp 2

"Legislative"). In most departments around the country, this test consists of sit-ups, a mile-and-a-half run, bench press repetitions, and a flexibility test (Rafilson, Police Officer 39). Women are encouraged to apply, but in the tests they are judged by lower standards than men.

Table 1 Minimum Fitness Standards for Entry to the Academy

Female Candidates		
Age Group	20–29	30–39
Sit-ups (1 minute)	35	27
Sit & Reach (inches)	20	19
Push-ups	18	14
1.5-Mile Run (minutes)	14:55	15:26
Male Candidates		
Age Group	20–29	30–39
Sit-ups (1 minute)	40	36
Sit & Reach (inches)	17.5	16.5
Push-ups	33	27
1.5-Mile Run (minutes)	12:18	12:51

Source: Rafilson, Police Officer 47.

Table 1 shows that women are given from 2 minutes and 37 seconds to 3 minutes and 15 seconds extra to run a mile-and-a-half. That could mean the difference between catching a suspect and not catching a suspect. Men have to complete 13 to 15 more push-ups than women because women generally do not have the same amount of upper body strength as men.

Author and title for author with more than one work cited

Provides data visually in a table

Comments on table and explains data

Uses data to appeal to logic

Camp 3

But police officers may need to climb fences, lift heavy items, or carry injured people; certainly firefighters may need to carry injured people and heavy hoses.

Recognizing that the physical fitness tests are flawed, police and fire departments have been turning to a different test, called a physical agility exam, in which the candidate must complete an obstacle course. For the New York Police Department's agility exam, candidates are required to wear a 10.5 lb utility belt as they run out of a patrol car, climb a six-foot wall, run up four flights of stairs, drag a 160 lb dummy 30 feet, run back down four flights of stairs, climb a four-foot wall, and run back to the patrol car (Rafilson, Police Officer 40–42). Such tasks are seen as relevant to what a police officer actually encounters while on duty. All candidates must complete every part of the obstacle course in the same amount of time in order to pass the exam, regardless of sex, age, or weight. The obstacles in the course and the time allotted may vary between departments, but there is no partiality given based on ethnicity, gender, or age. Women may need to be provided with preparation and training for the test, as an article in The Police Chief points out (Polisar and Milgram), but they should still be required to take and pass it.

More and more police and fire departments are now using the physical agility test instead of the fitness test. According to Dr. Fred M. Rafilson, the fitness model was

Gives page numbers for print source

Cites online source-- no page number

Gives author's credentials

Camp 4

Fig. 1: From Robie Liscomb, "Preparing Women for Firefighting in B.C."

Uses a visual to strengthen the argument that women can perform heavy physical work

popular because it "allows fire departments to hire more women because passing standards are adjusted based on a person's age, sex, and weight," but, as he says, a "woman can pass a fitness model test for the fire service and still not be able to perform essential job functions that require a great deal of upper body and leg strength" ("Legislative"). Some programs have been established to help prepare women for the new tests. The program at the University of Victoria in British Columbia, Canada, culminates in having women carry "65-pound pumps and heavy fire hoses across the infield of the warm-up track" (Liscomb). Figure 1 shows a participant in action.

Camp 5

Many see upper body strength as crucial. Firefighters are very much like a family, trust each other like brothers, and in a fire emergency may have to make life and death decisions. They need to know that the person next to them can handle all of the duties of the job. Thomas P. Butler, a spokesperson for the Uniformed Firefighters Association, the firefighters' union, points out that "this is a job where one firefighter's life and safety depends on another. It is important that we attract the best and the brightest" (qtd. in Baker). Any person who cannot perform the tasks of a firefighter poses "a direct threat to human life and safety" (Rafilson, "Legislative") and does not belong on the job.

> Cites a one-page work where quotation appears—no page number necessary in citation

> Considers opposing views

Frances Heidensohn's thorough study of women in law enforcement in the U.S.A. and in Britain does, however, point out that many women have "questioned the relevance and purpose of the physical standards as . . . irrelevant to policing" (170). Women in the police force testified that while they had been tested on doing a "body drag," they never had seen it done or had to do this on the job. And, of course, we all can recognize that having different (and lower) standards for women does allow more women to be hired as career officers and helps departments with affirmative action requirements.

> Establishes common ground ("we all")

Those who put themselves on the line on the job, however, still question the wisdom of different testing criteria for men and women. Douglass Mignone, a first lieutenant of

> Refers to introduction and uses evidence from interview to refute the opposing views

Camp 6

the Purchase Fire Department and a New York City Fire

Ethical appeal

Department applicant, for example, makes the case for equal

safety requirements and training:

Indents a long quotation

> If you were in a burning building and had the choice
>
> between my girlfriend Sinead, a five-foot-five, 130 lb
>
> woman, or myself, a six-foot-two, 200 lb man, to get you
>
> out alive, who would you choose? I have no problem with

Emotional appeal

> women being firefighters as long as they meet the same
>
> requirements and undergo the same training as myself.

This view is the consensus among male police officers and

male firefighters, but not that of the general public. The general

idea of safety seems to be slipping past the newspapers and

television. There are no activists standing outside City Hall

crying, "What about our safety?" "Make physical requirements

equal" (Rafilson, "Legislative"). There will be no activists, no

protests, and no media until someone dies or until there is a

tragedy.

Transition from safety to equality

Added to the issue of safety is the issue of equality. In

1964, Congress prohibited discrimination based on race, color,

sex, national origin, or religion under the Civil Rights Act of

1964 (Brooks 26). In 1991, Congress passed the 1991 Civil

Broadens the picture to legislation

Rights Act, which made it "an unlawful employment

practice" to adjust any tests or scores "on the basis of race,

Cites work in which quotation appears

color, religion, sex, or national origin" (qtd. in Rafilson,

"Legislative").

Camp 7

Title VII under this Act claims that the employer accused of "disparate impact" would have to prove business necessity. This has left police and fire departments all over the country confused and asking themselves what to do and whom to hire next. Are police and fire departments going to claim that the physiological differences between men and women make different physical standards a business necessity? According to Special Agent Michael E. Brooks:

> The challenge comes when a male cannot meet the male standard but can meet the female standard. Such an action amounts to express disparate treatment of the male. Disparate treatment, like disparate impact, is only permissible under the business necessity justification. The administrator who uses different physical selection standards for female applicants would, therefore, have to show what business necessity justifies such a practice. (31)

Controversy and confusion abound, and male applicants are filing lawsuits claiming reverse discrimination. The Edmonton Fire Department has a "diversity" policy in which the 12 positions that were available did not go to the top 12 applicants but to women and minorities (Champion). Two groups of rejected applicants filed complaints with the Alberta Human Rights Commission claiming that "the City of Edmonton exercised race and gender bias in denying them employment"

Question draws readers into issue

Provides specific factual details

Camp 8

(Champion). Such practices make it clear that reforms are necessary.

Reminds readers of main point

The process of applying to be hired in a police or fire department must be clear to all and equitable to all. Only those with the highest scores on the written exam should be eligible to take the physical agility test. Then only the candidates who pass the physical should qualify for further testing and employment. Men who fail any of the tests should not be hired--nor should women. If police and fire departments lower standards for anyone, they are putting the general public's safety on the line as well as their fellow officers'. Peter Horne, an assistant professor at Meramec Community College, puts it succinctly: "Females and males should take the same physical agility test. Then it would not matter whether a recruit is 5'8" or 5'4", or a male or female, but only whether he/she possesses the physical capability to do the job" (33–34). The

Ends on a strong note

cost to safety is much too great for women to be held to lower requirements than men.

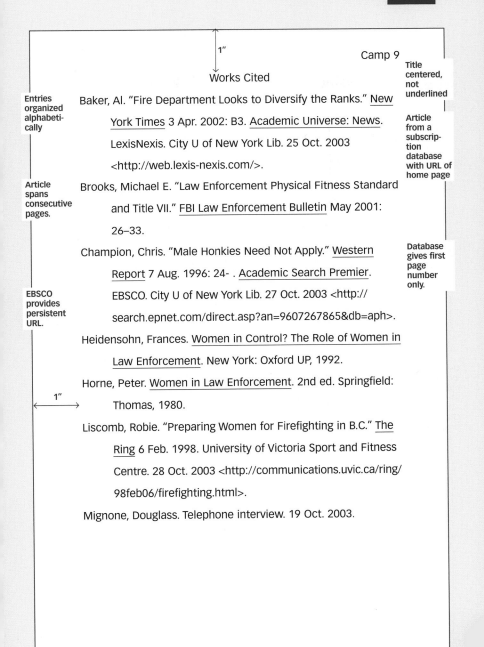

Camp 9

Works Cited

Baker, Al. "Fire Department Looks to Diversify the Ranks." New
York Times 3 Apr. 2002: B3. Academic Universe: News.
LexisNexis. City U of New York Lib. 25 Oct. 2003
<http://web.lexis-nexis.com/>.

Brooks, Michael E. "Law Enforcement Physical Fitness Standard
and Title VII." FBI Law Enforcement Bulletin May 2001:
26–33.

Champion, Chris. "Male Honkies Need Not Apply." Western
Report 7 Aug. 1996: 24- . Academic Search Premier.
EBSCO. City U of New York Lib. 27 Oct. 2003 <http://
search.epnet.com/direct.asp?an=9607267865&db=aph>.

Heidensohn, Frances. Women in Control? The Role of Women in
Law Enforcement. New York: Oxford UP, 1992.

Horne, Peter. Women in Law Enforcement. 2nd ed. Springfield:
Thomas, 1980.

Liscomb, Robie. "Preparing Women for Firefighting in B.C." The
Ring 6 Feb. 1998. University of Victoria Sport and Fitness
Centre. 28 Oct. 2003 <http://communications.uvic.ca/ring/
98feb06/firefighting.html>.

Mignone, Douglass. Telephone interview. 19 Oct. 2003.

Annotations (margin notes):

1"

Title centered, not underlined

Entries organized alphabetically

Article from a subscription database with URL of home page

Article spans consecutive pages.

Database gives first page number only.

EBSCO provides persistent URL.

1"

Camp 10

Polisar, Joseph, and Donna Milgram. "Recruiting, Integrating and

Retaining Women Police Officers: Strategies That Work."

The Police Chief Oct. 1998. IWITTS in the News. Institute

for Women in Trades, Technology, and Science. 27

Oct. 2003 <http://www.iwitts.com/html/

the_police_chief.htm>.

Rafilson, Fred M. "Legislative Impact on Fire Service Physical

Fitness Testing." Fire Engineering Apr. 1995: 83– .

Academic Search Premier. EBSCO. City U of New York

Lib. 23 Oct. 2003 <http://search.epnet.com/

direct.asp?an=9505024136&db=aph>.

---. Police Officer. 15th ed. United States: Arco, 2000.

Wexler, Ann Kathryn. Gender and Ethnicity as Predictors of

Psychological Qualification for Police Officer Candidates.

Diss. California School of Professional Psychology, 1996.

Ann Arbor: UMI, 1996. 9625522.

Published work on Web site

List includes only sources actually cited in the paper.

Second entry for author

PART 10
Documenting Sources: APA, CSE, and *Chicago* Styles

In Part 10, you will find descriptions of documentation systems other than the MLA system. Chapter 52 focuses on the style recommended for the social sciences by the *Publication Manual of the American Psychological Association,* 5th ed. (Washington, DC: Amer. Psychological Assn., 2001), and on the APA Web site. It includes a sample of a student's paper written in APA style. Chapter 53 describes the citation-sequence and the citation-name styles recommended by the Council of Science Editors (CSE). Chapter 54 describes the endnote and footnote styles recommended in *The Chicago Manual of Style,* 15th ed. (Chicago: U of Chicago P, 2003), for writing in the humanities; it is sometimes used as an alternative to MLA style.

Chapter **52**

APA Style of Documentation

A full At a Glance Index of examples appears on the pages listed below.

52a Two basic features of APA style

KEY POINTS

Two Basic Features of APA Style

1. *In the text of your paper,* include these two pieces of information (if they are available) each time you refer to a source:

   - the last name(s) of the author(s)

   - the year of publication

   For quotations, paraphrase, and reference to a specific idea, also include the page number of a print source or any visible paragraph number or section location for an online source.

2. *At the end of your paper,* include on a new numbered page a list entitled "References," double-spaced and arranged alphabetically by authors' last names (or title if no author is named), the date in parentheses, and other bibliographical information. See 52d for examples of what to include in an APA-style reference list.

Online Study Center   This icon will direct you to quick reference tools, Web resources, and research guides on the Web site at http://college.hmco.com/keys.html.

Illustrations of the basic features

In-Text Citation Entry in List of References

Book:

The speed at which we live is seen as cause for concern and derision (Gleick, 1999).

Gleick, J. (1999). *Faster: The acceleration of just about everything.* New York: Pantheon.

The renowned scholar of language, David Crystal, has promoted the idea of "dialect democracy" (2004, p. 168).

Crystal, D. (2004). *The stories of English.* Woodstock, NY: Overlook Press.

[Page number included for quotation]

Print Article:

Ambition is seen as an impulse that "requires an enormous investment of emotional capital" (Kluger, 2005, p. 59).

(Kluger, J. (2005, November 14). Ambition: Why some people are most likely to succeed. *Time, 166,* 48–54, 57, 59.

[Page number included for quotation]

or

Kluger (2005, p. 59) sees ambition as an impulse that "requires an enormous investment of emotional capital."

Article in Online Database:

Research has shown that cross-cultural identification does not begin before eight years of age (Sousa, Neto, & Mullet, 2005).

Sousa, R. M., Neto, F., & Mullet, E. (2005). Can music change ethnic attitudes among children? *Psychology of Music, 33,* 304–316. Retrieved December 15, 2005, from Sage Psychology, CSA database.

Document on Web Site:

Contributing to global warming in the past century is a considerable rise in sea levels (Coren, 2006).

(Coren, M. (2006, February 10). *The science debate behind climate change.* Retrieved April 13, 2006, from http://www.cnn.com/2005/TECH/ science/04/08/earth.science/index.html

52b APA author/year style for in-text citations

AT A GLANCE: INDEX OF APA IN-TEXT CITATIONS

A. One author   If you mention the author's last name in your own sentence, include the year in parentheses directly after the author's name.

> author year
> Wilson (1994) has described in detail his fascination with insects.

(See 52d, item 1, to see how this work appears in a reference list.)

If you do not name the author in your sentence, include both the name and the year, separated by a comma, in parentheses.

> The army retreated from Boston in disarray, making the rebels realize that they had achieved a great victory (McCullough, 2001).
> author comma year

If you use a direct quotation, a paraphrase, or a reference to a specific idea in a work, help readers locate the passage by including in parentheses the abbreviation "p." or "pp." followed by a space and the page number(s). Separate items within parentheses with commas.

> Memories are built "around a small collection of dominating images" (Wilson, 1994, p. 5).
> comma comma page number
> with a quotation

B. More than one author   For a work by two authors, name both in the order in which their names appear on the work. Within parentheses, use an ampersand (&) between the names in place of *and*. Use the word *and* for a reference to the authors made in your text.

> Kanazawa and Still (2000) in their analysis of a large set of data show that the statistical likelihood of being divorced increases if one is male and a secondary school teacher or college professor.

> Analysis of a large set of data shows that the statistical likelihood of being divorced increases if one is male and a secondary school teacher or college professor (Kanazawa & Still, 2000).
> ampersand in parentheses

(See 52d, item 13, to see how this work appears in a reference list.)

For a work with three to five authors or editors, identify all of them the first time you mention the work. In later references, use only the first author's name followed by "et al." (Latin for "and others") in place of the other names.

> Jordan, Kaplan, Miller, Stiver, and Surrey (1991) have examined the idea of *self*.

> Increasingly, the self is viewed as connected to other human beings (Jordan et al., 1991).

(See 52d, item 2, to see how this work appears in a reference list.)

For six or more authors, use the name of the first author followed by "et al." both for the first mention and in a parenthetical citation. However, include the names of the first six authors on your reference list, using "et al." to indicate only authors beyond the first six.

C. Author with more than one work published in one year Identify each work with a lowercase letter after the date: (Zamel, 1997a, 1997b). Separate the dates with a comma. The reference list will contain the corresponding letters after the dates of each work. (See 52c for how to order the entries in the list of references.)

D. Work in an anthology In your text, refer to the author of the work, not to the editor of the anthology. In the reference list, give the author's name, title of the work, and bibliographical details about the anthology, such as the editor, title, publisher, and date (52d, item 4).

> Seegmiller (1993) has provided an incisive analysis of the relationship between pregnancy and culture.

E. Work cited in another source Give the author or title of the work in which you find the reference, preceded by "as cited in" to indicate that you are referring to a citation in that work. List that secondary source in your list of references. In the following example, *Smith* will appear in the list of references with details of the source; *Britton* will not.

> The words we use simply appear, as Britton says, "at the point of utterance" (as cited in Smith, 1982, p. 108).

F. An entire work or an idea in a work Use only an author and a year to refer to a complete work; for a paraphrase or a comment on a specific idea, a page number is not required but is recommended.

G. No author named In your text, use the complete title if it is short (capitalizing major words) or a few words for the title in parentheses, along with the year of publication.

> According to *Weather* (1999), one way to estimate the Fahrenheit temperature is to count the number of times a cricket chirps in 14 seconds and add 40.

> Increasing evidence shows that glucosamine relieves the symptoms of arthritis (*The PDR Family Guide,* 1999).

(See 52d, item 5, to see how the latter work is listed.)

H. Internet or electronic source Give author, if available, or title, followed by the year of electronic publication or of the most recent update. To locate a quotation in a source with no page or paragraph numbers visible on the screen, give the section heading, and indicate the paragraph within the section, such as "Conclusion section, para. 2."

Be wary of citing e-mail messages (personal, bulletin board, discussion list, or Usenet group) as these are not peer reviewed or easily retrievable. If you need to refer to an e-mail message, cite from an archived list whenever possible (see the example in 52d, item 30); otherwise, cite the message in your text as a personal communication (see 52c, item O), but do not include it in your list of references.

I. Entire Web site Give the complete URL in the text of your paper. Do not list the site in your list of references.

> Research on the "Mozart effect" has generated an institute with a Web site providing links to research studies (http://www.mindinst.org).

J. Multimedia or nonprint source For a film, television or radio broadcast, recording, live performance, or other nonprint source, include in your citation the name of the originator or main contributor (such as the writer, interviewer, director, performer, or producer) or an abbreviated title if the originator is not identified, along with the year of production—for example, "(Berman & Pulcini, 2003)." (See 52d, item 34, for how to list this work.)

K. Work by a corporation or government organization In the initial citation, use the organization's full name; in subsequent references, use an abbreviation, if one exists.

first mention: full name

A survey by the College Board (CB, 2005) shows that in 2005–2006, tuition increases slowed at public colleges (CB, 2005).

(52d, item 6, shows how to list this work.)

L. Two authors with the same last name   Include the authors' initials, even if the publication dates of their works differ.

F. Smith (1982) first described a writer as playing the two competitive roles of author and secretary.

(For the order of entries in the list of references, see 52c.)

M. Multivolume work   In your citation, give the publication date of the volume you are citing: (Barr & Feigenbaum, 1982). If you refer to more than one volume, give inclusive dates for all the volumes you cite: (Barr & Feigenbaum, 1981–1986). (See 52d, item 8, for how this work appears in a reference list.)

N. More than one work in a citation   List the sources in alphabetical order, separated by semicolons. List works by the same author chronologically (earliest source first) or by the letters *a, b,* and so on, if the works were published in the same year.

Criticisms of large-scale educational testing abound (Crouse & Trusheim, 1988; Nairn, 1978, 1980; Raimes, 1990a, 1990b; Sacks, 2000).

O. Personal communication, such as a conversation, a letter, an e-mail, or an unarchived electronic discussion group   Mention these only in your paper; do not include them in your list of references. Give the last name and initial(s) of the author of the communication and the exact date of posting.

According to V. Sand, Executive Director of the Atwater Kent Museum of Philadelphia, "Museums are essential to the educational fabric of the United States. They engage our spirit, help us understand the natural world, and frame our identities. They help us see our lives as having value within the continuum of human experience" (personal communication, February 7, 2006).

For archived online postings, see 52d, item 30.

P. A classical or religious work If the date of publication of a classical work is not known, use in your citation "n.d." for "no date." If you use a translation, give the year of the translation, preceded by "trans." You do not need a reference list entry for the Bible or ancient classical works. Just give information about book, chapter, verse, and line numbers in your text, and identify the version you use: Gen. 35: 1–4 (New Oxford).

Q. Long quotation If you quote more than forty words of prose, do not enclose the quotation in quotation marks. Start the quotation on a new line, and indent the whole quotation half an inch or five spaces from the left margin. Double-space the quotation. See page 797 for an example. Any necessary parenthetical citation should come after the final period of the quotation.

52c Guidelines for the APA list of references

How to format the APA list The APA *Publication Manual* and Web site provide guidelines for submitting professional papers for publication, and many instructors ask students to follow those guidelines to prepare them for advanced work. This section follows APA guidelines. Check with your instructor, however, as to specific course requirements for the reference list.

KEY POINTS
Guidelines for the APA List of References

- **What to list** List only the works you cited (quoted, summarized, paraphrased, or commented on) in the text of your paper, not every source you examined.

- **Format** Start the list on a new numbered page after the last page of text or notes. Center the heading "References," without quotation marks, not underlined or italicized, and with no period following it. Double-space throughout the list, with no additional space between entries. Place any tables and charts after the "References" list.

- **Conventions of the list** List the works alphabetically by last names of primary authors. Do not number the entries. Begin each entry with the author's name, last name first, followed by an initial or initials. Give any authors' names after the first in the same inverted form, separated by commas. Use "et al." only to indicate authors beyond the first six. List works with no author by title, alphabetized by the first main word.

- **Date** Put the year in parentheses after the authors' names. For journals, magazines, and newspapers, also include month and day, but do not abbreviate the names of the months.
- **Periods** Use a period and one space to separate the main parts of each entry.
- **Indentation** Use hanging indents. (Begin the first line of each entry at the left margin; indent subsequent lines one-half inch.)
- **Capitals** In titles of books, reports, articles, and Web documents, capitalize only the first word of the title or subtitle and any proper names.
- **Italics** Italicize the titles of books, but do not italicize or use quotation marks around the titles of articles. Italicize the names of newspapers, reports, and Web documents. For magazines and journals, italicize the publication name, the volume number, and the comma.
- **Page numbers** Give inclusive page numbers for print articles, online PDF articles, and sections of books, using complete page spans ("251–259"). Use the abbreviation "p." or "pp." only for newspaper articles and sections of books (such as chapters or anthologized articles). Use document sections in place of page numbers for online HTML articles.
- **Online sources** Include whatever is available of the following: author(s), date of work, title of work, any print publication information, and identification of the type of source in square brackets (for example, "[letter to the editor]"). For an online library subscription service, end with the name of the service and the document number (as in items 21 and 22). For a Web site, always include retrieval information of the date of access and the URL of the actual document, not simply the home page (as in items 23–26). Do *not* underline the URL as a hyperlink unless you are posting the paper online (see 24a) and do *not* put a period after the URL at the end of your entry. Provide page numbers only for documents accessed as PDF files.

Authors

Name of author(s)   Put the last name first, followed by a comma and then the initials.

> Gould, S. J.

Reverse the names of all authors listed, except the editors of an anthology or a reference work (52d, item 4). Use an ampersand (&), not the word *and*, before the author's name.

Alphabetical order   Alphabetize letter by letter. Treat *Mac* and *Mc* literally, by letter.

MacKay, M.	D'Agostino, S.
McCarthy, T.	De Cesare, P.
McKay, K.	DeCurtis, A.

A shorter name precedes a longer name beginning with the same letters, whatever the first initial: *Black, T.* precedes *Blackman, R.*

For a work with no known author, list by the first word in the title other than *A, An,* or *The.*

Alphabetize numerals according to their spelling: 5 ("five") will precede 2 ("two").

Individual author(s) not known   If the author is a group, such as a corporation, agency, or institution, give its name, alphabetized by the first important word (52d, item 6). Use full names, not abbreviations. If no author or group is named, alphabetize by the first main word of the title (52d, item 5).

Several works by the same author   List the author's name in each entry. Arrange entries chronologically from past to present. Entries published in the same year should be arranged alphabetically by title and distinguished with lowercase letters after the date (*a, b,* and so on). Note that entries for one author precede entries by that author but written with coauthors.

Goleman, D. (1996a, July 16). Forget money; nothing can buy happiness, some researchers say. *The New York Times*, p. C1.

Goleman, D. (1996b). *Vital lies, simple truths.* New York: Simon & Schuster.

Goleman, D. (2000). *Working with emotional intelligence.* New York: Bantam.

Goleman, D., Kaufman, P., & Ray, M. L. (1992, March–April). The art of
creativity. *Psychology Today, 25,* 40–47.

Authors with the same last name   List alphabetically by first initial: *Smith, A.* precedes *Smith, F.*

Format and indentation

UNDERLINING OR ITALICS? The fifth edition of the APA *Publication Manual* includes instructions that "take advantage of the nearly universal use of sophisticated word processors." It recommends that authors use italics (not underlining) to represent text that would eventually be converted to italics in print.

HANGING INDENTS IN THE LIST OF REFERENCES   The APA guidelines specify hanging indents for manuscript and final copy. A hanging indent sets the first line of each item in the reference list at the left margin, with subsequent lines of the entry indented five to seven spaces or one-half inch.

Klein, D. F. (1995). Response to Rothman and Michels on placebo-controlled
clinical trials. *Psychiatric Annals, 25,* 401–403.

Rothman, K. F., & Michels, K. D. (1994). The continuing unethical use of
placebo controls. *New England Journal of Medicine, 331,* 394–398.

However, the fifth edition of the *Publication Manual* also notes that if a word processing program makes it difficult to achieve a hanging indent, then a paragraph indent (first line of entry indented five spaces) is acceptable. In either case, the usage should be consistent throughout.

52d Examples of entries in APA list of references

AT A GLANCE: DIRECTORY OF APA SAMPLE ENTRIES

WHICH TYPE OF SOURCE?	HOW TO DOCUMENT? GO TO
Print book, part of book, or pamphlet (including a government publication and technical report)	52d, p. 776, items 1–12

(Continued)

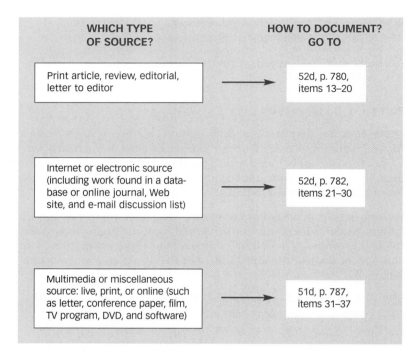

1. Book with one author Give the last name first, followed by the initials. See Source Shot 5 on page 778 for an example.

2. Book with two or more authors List all authors' names in the order in which they appear on the book's title page. Reverse the order of each name: last name first, followed by initials. Do not use "et al." Separate all names with commas, and insert an ampersand (&) before the last name.

all names reversed ————————— ampersand

Jordan, J. V., Kaplan, A. G., Miller, J. B., Stiver, I. P., & Surrey, J. L. (1991).

Women's growth in connection: Writings from the Stone Center.

New York: Guilford Press.
indented
5 spaces

3. Edited book Use "Ed." or "Eds." for one or more editors, in parentheses.

Denmark, F., & Paludi, M. (Eds.). (1993). *Psychology of women: A handbook
of issues and theories*. Westport, CT: Greenwood Press.

4. Work in an edited collection or reference book List the author, date of publication of the edited book, and title of the work. Follow this with "In" and the names of the editors (not inverted), the title of the book, and the page numbers (preceded by "pp.") of the work in parentheses. End with the place of publication and the publisher. If you cite more than one article in an edited work, include full bibliographical details in each entry.

names of editors
not reversed

Seegmiller, B. (1993). Pregnancy. In F. Denmark & M. Paludi (Eds.),
Psychology of women: A handbook of issues and theories
(pp. 437–474). Westport, CT: Greenwood Press.

For a reference book with unsigned entries, begin with the title of the entry and include the page number(s).

Antarctica. (2000). In *The Columbia encyclopedia* (6th ed., pp. 116–118). New
York: Columbia University Press.

For a reference book with an editorial board, list the name of the principal editor.

5. Book or pamphlet with no author identified Put the title first. Ignore *A, An,* and *The* when alphabetizing. Alphabetize the following under *P*.

The PDR family guide to natural medicines and healing therapies. (1999).
New York: Three Rivers-Random House.

6. Book or pamphlet by a corporation or some other organization Give the name of the corporate author first. If the publisher is the same as the author, write "Author" for the name of the publisher.

College Board. (2005). *Trends in college pricing* 2005. New York: Author.

SOURCE SHOT 5

Listing a Book (APA)

On the title page and copyright page of the book, you'll find the information you need for an entry in the list of references.

❶ **Author(s)** Last name, initials (see item 2 for when to use "et al.")

❷ **(Year of publication)** In parentheses; the most recent copyright © date or "n.d." if no date is supplied

❸ *Title of book: Any subtitle* In italics, with capital letters only for the first word of the title and subtitle and proper names

❹ **Place of publication** City and state (abbreviated), but state omitted for a major city, such as New York or San Francisco, or when state is shown in name of publisher, as in "University of Illinois Press"

❺ **Publisher** In a short but intelligible form, including *University* and *Press* but omitting *Co.* and *Inc.*

See items 1–12 for examples.

        initials periods
❶ Last name   / / ❷ Year in parentheses
   /comma / / period ❸ Title italicized
Wilson, E. O. (1994). *Naturalist.* Washington, DC: Island Press.
             ❹ Place of publication colon ❺ Publisher final period

---

If no author is named for a government publication, begin with the name of the federal, state, or local government, followed by the agency.

United States. Department of Homeland Security. (2004). *Preparing for disaster for people with disabilities and other special needs.* Washington, DC: FEMA.

7. Translated book In parentheses after the title of the work, give the initials and last name of the translator, followed by a comma and "Trans."

                        name of translator not reversed
Jung, C. G. (1960). *On the nature of the psyche* (R. F. C. Hull, Trans.). Princeton, NJ: Princeton University Press.

8. Multivolume work When you refer to several volumes in a work of more than one volume, give the number of volumes after the title, in parentheses. The date should indicate the range of years of publication, when appropriate.

Title Page

3 Title

NATURALIST

EDWARD O. WILSON

1 Author

5 Publisher

ISLAND PRESS / Shearwater Books
Washington, D.C. • Covelo, California

4 Place of publication

Copyright Page

A Shearwater Book
published by Island Press

2 Year of publication

Copyright © 1994 by Island Press
Illustrations copyright © 1994 by Laura Simonds Southworth

The excerpt from "Daybreak in Alabama" is from
Selected Poems by Langston Hughes, copyright © 1948
by Alfred A. Knopf Inc., and renewed 1976
by The Executors of the Estate of Langston Hughes.
Reprinted by permission of the publisher.

All rights reserved under International and Pan-American
Copyright Conventions. No part of this book may be
reproduced in any form or by any means without permission
in writing from the publisher: Island Press, 1718 Connecticut
Avenue, N.W., Suite 300, Washington, DC 20009.
SHEARWATER BOOKS is a trademark of
The Center for Resource Economics.

LIBRARY OF CONGRESS
CATALOGING-IN-PUBLICATION DATA
Wilson, Edward Osborne, 1929–
Naturalist / Edward O. Wilson.
p.   cm.
Includes index.
ISBN 1-55963-288-7 (cloth)
1. Wilson, Edward Osborne, 1929–   . 2. Naturalists—
United States—Biography.   I. Title.
QH31.W62A3   1994
508'.092—dc20   94-13111   CIP
[B]

Printed on recycled, acid-free paper
Manufactured in the United States of America

10 9 8 7 6 5 4 3 2 1

Barr, A., & Feigenbaum, E. A. (1981–1986). *The handbook of artificial intelligence* (Vols. 1–4). Reading, MA: Addison-Wesley.

9. Foreword, preface, introduction, or afterword List the name of the author of the book element cited. Follow the date with the name of the element, the title of the book, and, in parentheses, the page numbers on which the element appears.

Weiss, B. (Ed.). (1982). Introduction. *American education and the European immigrant, 1840–1940* (pp. xi–xxviii). Urbana: University of Illinois Press.

10. Revised, republished, or reprinted work For a revised edition of a book, give the edition number after the title in parentheses.

Raimes, A. (2006). *Pocket keys for writers* (2nd ed.). Boston: Houghton Mifflin.

For a republished work, give the most recent date of publication after the author's name, and at the end in parentheses add "Original work published . . ." and the date. In your text citation, give both dates: (Smith 1793/1976).

Smith, A. (1976). *An inquiry into the nature and causes of the wealth of nations.* Chicago: University of Chicago Press. (Original work published 1793)

For a reprint, begin the details in the parentheses with "Reprinted from," followed by the title, author, date, place, and publisher of the original work.

11. Technical report Give the report number ("Rep. No.") after the title.

Morgan, R., & Maneckshana, B. (2000). *AP students in college: An investigation of their course-taking patterns and college majors* (Rep. No. SR–2000–09). Princeton, NJ: Educational Testing Service.

12. Dissertation or abstract For a manuscript source, give the university and year of the dissertation and the volume and page numbers of DAI.

Salzberg, A. (1992). Behavioral phenomena of homeless women in San Diego County (Doctoral dissertation, United States International University, 1992). *Dissertation Abstracts International, 52,* 4482.

For a microfilm source, also include in parentheses at the end of the entry the university microfilm number. For a CD-ROM source, include "CD-ROM" after the title. Then name the electronic source of the information and the DAI number.

For an abstract published in a collection of abstracts, put "[Abstract]" after the title of the work and before the name of the source. For an online abstract, see 52d, item 23.

13. Article in a scholarly journal: pages numbered consecutively through each volume Give only the volume number and year for journals with consecutive pagination through a volume (for example, the first issue of volume 1 ends on page 174, and the second issue of volume 1 begins on page 175). Italicize the volume number and the following comma as well as the title of the journal. See 48b on recognizing a scholarly journal.

no quotation marks around
article title

Kanazawa, S., & Still, M. C. (2000). Teaching may be hazardous to your

journal title, volume number,
and commas italicized

marriage. *Evolution and Human Behavior, 21,* 185–190.

no "p." or "pp." before page numbers

14. Article in a scholarly journal: Each issue paged separately

For journals in which each issue begins with page 1, include the issue number—in parentheses but not in italics—immediately after the volume number.

Ginat, R. (2000). The Soviet Union and the Syrian Baíth regime: From

hesitation to *rapprochement. Middle Eastern Studies, 36*(2), 150–171.

issue number not in italics

15. Article in a magazine
Include the year and month or month and day of publication in parentheses. Italicize the magazine title, the volume number, and the comma that follows; then give the page number or numbers. See Source Shot 6 on page 782 for an example.

16. Article in a newspaper
In parentheses, include the month and day of the newspaper after the year. Give the section letter or number before the page, where applicable. Use "p." and "pp." with page numbers. Do not omit *The* from the title of a newspaper or a magazine. For articles with no author, begin with the title.

Blakeslee, S. (2006, January 10). Cells that read minds. *The New York Times,*

pp. F1, F4.

17. Article that skips pages
When an article appears on discontinuous pages, give all the page numbers, separated by commas, as in item 16.

18. Review
After the title of the review article, add in brackets a description of the work reviewed and identify the medium: book or motion picture, for example.

Madrick, J. (2006, January 12). The way to a fair deal [review of the book *The*

moral consequences of economic growth]. *The New York Review of*

Books, 53, 37–40.

19. Unsigned editorial or article
For a work with no author named, begin the listing with the title; for an editorial, add the label "Editorial" in brackets.

SOURCE SHOT 6

Listing a Periodical Article (APA)

When listing a print periodical article, include the following:

❶ **Author(s)** Last name, initials (see also 52c on how to list authors)

❷ **(Date of publication of article)** In parentheses: year, month (not abbreviated), day, according to type of periodical (items 13–20)

❸ **Title of article: Any subtitle** No quotation marks; capitals only for first word of title, subtitle, and proper names

❹ *Name of journal or magazine, volume number,* or *name of newspaper* All italicized

❺ **Inclusive range of page numbers** All digits included (167–168). Do not use *p.* or *pp.* (except with pages of newspaper articles).

See items 13–20 for examples.

```
                                              ❹ Magazine
     ❶ Author   ❷ Date            ❸ Title       and volume
    ┌──────┐ ┌────────────┐  ┌──────────────────┐ ┌──────────────────┐
    Stix, G. (2006, February). Owning the stuff of life. Scientific American, 294,
          ❺ Page numbers
       ┌──────────┐
       76–83.
```

Spark the revolution [Editorial]. (2005, December 27). *The Wall Street Journal*, p. A20.

20. Letter to the editor Put the label "Letter to the editor" in brackets after the date or the title of the letter, if it has one.

Nichol, C. J. (2006, January). [Letter to the editor]. *Harper's Magazine*, *312*, 6.

AT A GLANCE INDEX: INTERNET AND ELECTRONIC SOURCES (APA)

Table of Contents

Note: The American Psychological Association supplements the fifth edition of its *Publication Manual* with a Web site offering citation examples, periodic updates, and tips.

21. Work in an online database   Many universities, libraries, and organizational Web sites subscribe to large searchable databases, such as *InfoTrac, EBSCO, LexisNexis, OCLC, First Search, PsycINFO,* and *WilsonWeb*. These databases provide access to large numbers of published scholarly abstracts and full-text articles.

See Source Shot 7 on page 784 for an example.

22. Newspaper article retrieved from database or Web site Newspaper articles, as well as journal articles, are often available from several sources, in several databases and in a variety of formats, such as in a university online subscription database. Do not insert a period when the entry ends with a URL.

Eisenberg, A. (2005, February 24). For simpler robots, a step forward. *The New York Times*. Retrieved January 3, 2006, from http://www.nytimes.com

no period at end of URL

SOURCE SHOT 7

Listing a Work in an Online or Electronic Database (APA)

To cite a work in an electronic database, provide as much of the following information as you can find:

❶ **Author(s)** Last name, initials

❷ **(Date of work)** In parentheses, including whatever is necessary (items 13–16) and available of year, month (not abbreviated), day ("n.d." if no date is available)

❸ **Title of work: Any subtitle** No quotation marks; capitals only for first word of title and subtitle and for proper names

❹ **Print publication information** *Name of periodical* (italicized) with *volume number* for journals and magazines (volume number and surrounding commas italicized) and inclusive **page numbers** if given on screen

❺ **Retrieval statement** "Retrieved" followed by your date of access (month, day, year) and comma; "from" followed by name of database and period

See examples and variations in items 21–23.

```
            ┌───── ❶ Authors ─────┐  ┌─ ❷ Date ─┐   ┌────── ❸ Title ──────┐
Goldstein, B. S. C., & Harris, K. C. (2000). Consultant practices in two

            ┌──────────────────────────────────┐  ┌── ❹ Print publication information ──
        heterogeneous Latino schools. The School Psychology Review, 29,
        page numbers
        ┌──────────────────────┐  ┌───────── ❺ Retrieval statement ─────────┐
        368–377. Retrieved January 25, 2006, from WilsonWeb Education
                                                  comma
        ┌──────────────────┐
        Full Text database.
                          └ final period
```

Wade, N. (2000, May 9). Scientists decode Down syndrome chromosome. *The New York Times*, p. F4. Retrieved January 2, 2006, from LexisNexis Academic Universe database.

23. Online abstract For an abstract retrieved from a database or from a Web site, begin the retrieval statement with the words "Abstract retrieved" followed by the date and the name of the database or by the URL of the Web site, with no period at the end.

Online Database

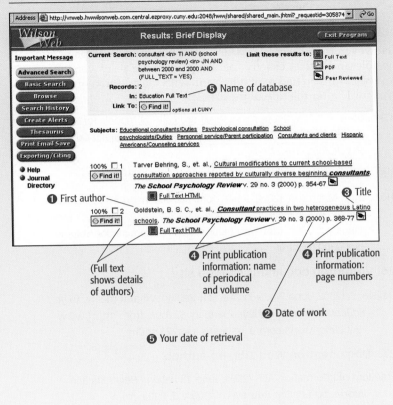

Frith, H., & Gleeson, K. (2004). Clothing and embodiment: Men managing
    body image and appearance. *Psychology of Men & Masculinity, 5,* 40–48.
    Abstract retrieved January 5, 2006, from http://content.apa.org/journals/
    men/5/1/40.html

24. Online article with a print source If information such as
page numbers or figures is missing (as in HTML versions) or if the
document may have additions or alterations, give full retrieval
information.

Jones, C. C., & Meredith, W. (2000, June). Developmental paths of psychological health from early adolescence to later adulthood. *Psychology and Aging, 15,* 351–360. Retrieved January 6, 2006, from http://content.apa.org/journals/pag/15/2/351.html

However, if you access an article in PDF format (with page numbers visible and charts exactly the same as in the print version), cite it exactly as if you had read it in print, with the addition of "[Electronic version]" after the title of the article.

Campos, G. P. (2004, September). What are cultural models for? Child-rearing practices in historical perspective [Electronic version]. *Culture & Psychology, 10,* 279–291.

25. Article in an online journal with no print source

Holtzworth-Munroe, A. (2000, June). Domestic violence: Combining scientific inquiry and advocacy. *Prevention & Treatment, 3,* Article 22. Retrieved January 2, 2006, from http://journals.apa.org/prevention/volume3/pre0030022c.html

26. Authored document on Web site

Delisio, E. (2002, June 24). No Child Left Behind: What it means to you. *Education World.* Retrieved January 5, 2006, from http://www.educationworld.com/a_issues/issues273.shtlm

27. Document on Web site, no author

Freedom of Information Act. (2005, June 1). *Federal Relations and Information Policy.* Retrieved January 3, 2006, from http://www.arl.org/info/frn/gov/foia/index.html#overview

28. Entire Web site, no author   Italicize the title of the Web page. Alphabetize by the first major word of the title.

NPR/Kaiser/Kennedy School Education Survey. (1999). Retrieved January 5, 2006, from http://www.npr.org/programs/specials/poll/education/education.results.html

29. Document on a university or government site   Italicize the title of the document. In the retrieval statement, give the name of the university or government agency (and the department or division if it is named). Follow this with a colon and the URL.

McClintock, R. (2000, September 20). *Cities, youth, and technology: Toward a pedagogy of autonomy.* Retrieved January 1, 2006, from Columbia

University, Institute for Learning Technologies Web site: http://www.ilt
.columbia.edu/publications/cities/cyt.html

30. Blogs and archived discussion lists Make sure that you
include in your list only reliable material posted on archived discussion lists or blogs. If no archives exist, cite the source in your text as
a personal communication (52b, item O).

Gracey, D. (2001, April 6). Monetary systems and a sound economy [Msg 54].
Message posted to http://groups.yahoo.com/group/ermail/message/54

Schwalm, D. (2005, February 15). Re: Value of an education. Message posted
to WPA–L electronic mailing list, archived at http://lists.asu
.eduto WPA–L electronic mailing list, archived at http://lists.asu.edu

Sullivan, A. (2005, November 17). Department of tough issues. In *Daily Dish*
blog. Retrieved February 12, 2006, from http://www.andrewsullivan.com/
index.php?dish_inc=archives/2005_11_13_dish_archive.html

**31. Personal communication (letter, telephone conversation,
interview, personal e-mail)** Cite only in the body of your text as
"personal communication." Do not include these communications in
your list of references (see 52b, item O).

32. Conference paper

Szenher, M. (2005, September). Visual homing with learned goal distance
information. Paper presented at the 3rd International Symposium on
Autonomous Minirobots for Research and Edutainment, Fukui, Japan.

33. Poster session

Szenher, M. (2005, September). Visual homing in natural environments.
Poster session presented at the annual meeting of Towards
Autonomous Robotic Systems, London, UK.

34. Motion picture Identify the medium (motion picture, videocassette, DVD, etc.) in brackets after the title. Give the country where
a motion picture was released, or give the city for other formats. Give
the name of the movie studio.

Berman, S. S. & Pulcini, R. (Directors). (2003). *American Splendo*r [Motion picture]. United States: Fine Line Features.

Jacquet, L. (Director). (2005). *The March of the Penguins* [DVD]. Burbank, CA: Warner Home Video.

35. Television or radio program

Gazit, C. (Writer). (2004). The seeds of destruction [Television series episode]. In D. J. James (Producer) *Slavery and the making of America*. New York: WNET.

36. CD-ROM or DVD   Identify the medium in square brackets after the title.

Jones, M. (2005). *Who is Mike Jones?* [CD-ROM]. Houston, TX: Swishahouse. *World of Warcraft* [CD-ROM] (2004). Irvine, CA: Blizzard Entertainment.

37. Computer software   Do not use italics for the name of the software.

Scilab (Version 3.1.1) [Computer software]. (2005). France: Institut National de Recherche en Informatique et en Automatique. Retrieved from http://www.scilab.org

52e Notes, tables, and figures

Notes   In APA style, you can use content notes to amplify information in your text. Number notes consecutively with superscript numerals. After the list of references, attach a separate page containing your numbered notes and headed "Footnotes." Use notes sparingly; include all important information in your text, not in footnotes.

Tables   Place all tables at the end of your paper, after the references and any notes. Number each table and provide an italicized caption.

Figures   After the references and any notes or tables, provide a separate page listing the figure captions, and place this page before the figures.

52f A student's research paper, APA style

The paper that follows was written by Katelyn Davies when she was a junior at Trinity University, San Antonio, Texas, majoring in Communication. She wrote the paper in June 2005 for Dr. Aaron Delwiche's course "Games for the Web: Ethnography of Massively Multiplayer Games" in the communication department. The assignment was designed to introduce the students to quantitative and qualitative research methods within the limitations of the research setting, as expressed by the instructor.

> Time was too short to pursue in-depth ethnographic research, and sample sizes were too small to extrapolate with confidence to the broader gaming community. For many of the students, it was the first time that they had undertaken a research project of this scope. Nevertheless, this work reflects the efforts of a new generation of scholars grappling with the social significance of this vital medium. (Delwiche: http://www.trinity.edu/adelwich/mmo/students.html)

Davies concentrated on the game *World of Warcraft*, playing it herself to study her own reactions in comparison to what she discovered in her research survey. Her avatar in the game (the physical representation of her character on screen in the game) was Llandellyse, as shown in the attached image. Her paper is excerpted here to highlight formatting and documentation issues. For her complete, interesting, and well-documented study, go to the Online Study Center.

World of Warcraft® provided courtesy of Blizzard Entertainment, Inc.

An online avatar

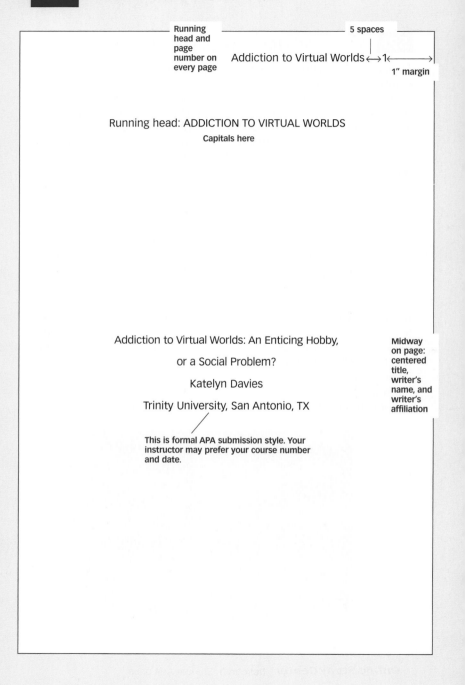

Running head and page number on every page

5 spaces

Addiction to Virtual Worlds ←→ 1 ←——————→

1" margin

Running head: ADDICTION TO VIRTUAL WORLDS

Capitals here

Addiction to Virtual Worlds: An Enticing Hobby,

or a Social Problem?

Katelyn Davies

Trinity University, San Antonio, TX

Midway on page: centered title, writer's name, and writer's affiliation

This is formal APA submission style. Your instructor may prefer your course number and date.

Addiction to Virtual Worlds   2

Abstract

This paper investigates Massively Multi-Player Online Role Playing Games (MMORPGs) in society and the effects they have on players and their real-life responsibilities. While some scholars and media professionals have expressed concern regarding the addictive aspects of these games, players compare their habits and motivations for playing to other hobbies that provide escape and an enjoyable experience. The author conducted in-depth interviews and questionnaires with gamers in order to examine the social, psychological, and emotional needs that players satisfy in virtual worlds, such as *World of Warcraft.* The attractions and motivations that compel gamers to participate in virtual worlds are examined with respect to symptoms and behaviors that illustrate an addiction. A disparity between levels of experience in players and their reactions to addictive aspects of the game suggests a learning curve where more experienced players learn to recognize and disregard those factors in the game that may facilitate "addictive" behaviors.

Heading centered

Length: 151 words (aim for 100–175)

Passive voice common in accounts of research

Summary of results of study

Addiction to Virtual Worlds   3

Addiction to Virtual Worlds: An Enticing Hobby,

or a Social Problem?

MMORPGs such as *World of Warcraft* have instigated
concern in scholars and the press about the usage patterns and
habits of the players. Often, doctors cite extreme cases of neglect
of oneself and others in order to bring attention to this social
phenomenon of popularity and addiction (Orzack, as cited in
Steinkuehler, 2004). Indeed, certain factors and attributes that
can promote or amplify addictive behaviors are present in these
games and are also cited as reasons for playing. The amount
of time players spend in virtual worlds, as well as real life
consequences of playing, are seen by some as indicators of a new
and dangerous addiction. However, players themselves compare
their playing habits to any other hobby or activity that pleases and
excites its user. Where can the line be drawn between addiction
and proclivity? Does the fact that MMORPGs entice people and
keep them playing necessarily mean that these games facilitate
addictive behavior and negligence towards responsibilities?
Doesn't it make a difference that these games often satisfy some
important emotional, social, and psychological needs of players?
We can surmise that MMORPGs provide players with valuable
relationships, interactions, and learning experiences that do not
necessarily detract from the real life counterparts of these
fulfillments. However, why is it that players often choose to satisfy

Margin notes: 1" margin · Title centered, not underlined · Indirect citation (52b, item E) · Research questions · Hypothesis

Addiction to Virtual Worlds   4

these needs or desires in virtual worlds? From data collected in research, game play, and interviews, the answer is that a) they *can,* and b) it's *fun.* As simplified as this answer may seem, the nature of the game and the virtual environment promote (mostly) consistent and enjoyable ways for players to satisfy emotional, social, and psychological needs and desires. An attachment can be formed to friends made, avatars created, or environments explored, but the attachment and enjoyment that results from game play should not warrant the same concern that scholars assert toward gambling and narcotic addiction. True, some players allow their habits to negatively affect their responsibilities and obligations, but these players do not represent the majority. My research indicates that the more experience players have with these environments, the easier it is for them to manage both their virtual and real life responsibilities and recreations.

Literature Review

The Psychology of Addiction

Psychologists have studied certain aspects of psychological makeup that may amplify people's susceptibility toward addiction. Apparently, some of these personal qualities are especially catered to by the Internet and online games. Findings by Gabel et al. (1999) state that novelty seeking, or the need for "new, exciting, challenging, or varied experiences," is highly correlated with the misuse and abuse of substances (p. 103).

Margin annotations:

Indicates results of research and confirmation of hypothesis

Subhead italicized

Begins detailing relevant background material

"et al." for 5 authors (52b, item B)

No extra space around headings

Year in parentheses

Page number for a quotation

Addiction to Virtual Worlds 5

Introduces game that is focus of study

World of Warcraft and other MMORPGs present players with a variety of different quests to fulfill, areas to explore, monsters to kill, and people to meet. Shyness has also been a personality trait associated with Internet addiction. The Internet provides a simplified medium for communication that erects a shield between users, thus allowing people with insecure social skills to interact more comfortably and openly (Chak & Leung, 2004).

Ampersand within parentheses

[The Literature Review continues for about four pages, with the subheads *Attractions and Motivations* (focusing on Yee's research) and *Immersion, Engagement, and Flow* (focusing on McMahan's work).]

Main heading centered

Method

The purpose of this project was to determine the qualities of virtual environments that lead players to form attachments and addictive behaviors. Why are players so eager to satisfy their psychological, social, and emotional needs in virtual worlds? What aspects of MMORPGs encourage addiction in players, and how do players respond to the attachment that can result from extensive game play?

In order to answer these questions, open-ended questionnaires were distributed and in-depth interviews were conducted. The content of both methods was generally similar, although the interview allowed for a more interactive setting where responses could incite reactions and further probing where needed. Questions referred to time invested in

Passive voice for description of method

Addiction to Virtual Worlds   6

gaming; habits of game play such as grouping and reward reinforcement; characteristics of relationships with others; motivations such as shyness and escape; novelty seeking; mastery and control; and indications of flow, immersion, and engagement. The interview questions can be found in the appendix at the end of this paper.

Participants and Procedure   Subhead
                                                           italicized

The questionnaires and in-depth interviews were conducted with college students, game developers, and experienced gamers.   Details of
                                                                     participants
The range of experience in MMORPGs varied from five months to eight years; a few gamers admitted to playing seven days of the week, while most said 3–5 days, depending on other time obligations and workload. The final sample for this study was acquired from college students (5 participants) and gamers on forums online (4 participants). I posted a thread on multiple MMORPG forums, requesting responses from gamers about playing habits and motivations and asking them to state a preference of method—a survey sent through e-mail, or an interview in-game or on AOL Instant Messenger. Most of my responses from students were in interview form through AOL Instant Messenger, whereas forum responses were conducted via open-ended questionnaires sent through e-mail. While I requested subjects on multiple forums, one forum in particular was much more willing to assist in research, and my thread stayed on the

first page for a few days, resulting in replies and private messages of interest and encouragement. One interviewee informed me that older players, with an average age of about 28, mostly visited the forum. Their experience in virtual worlds may have contributed to their willingness to help. In addition to interviews and surveys, weblogs and sites of interest were consulted to obtain insight into more player habits and discussions of MMORPG addiction. After the in-depth interviews and questionnaires were conducted, the responses were coded according to which concept discussed in the literature review the response referred to. Each participant was assigned an arbitrary alias in order to ensure confidentiality; these pseudonyms are referred to in the Results section after quotations (axe, bear, jester, etc.).

Results and Discussion

The results from research indicate a definitive player's perspective on the characteristics of play behavior, habits, and investment. The names of the correspondents were created randomly in order to protect the identities of the project participants. The most common game attraction in responses referred to the network of relationships formed and maintained in the game.

> *My friends are pretty much the reason I keep coming back for more—if it wasn't for them I'd have gotten bored ages ago.*—axe

Provides direct evidence from interview responses

The idea that grouping in MMORPGs is almost necessary once a certain level of difficulty in the game is reached is evident in most players' preference to playing in groups, membership in a guild, or at least some experience in group play. Groups and guilds often establish specific times to hold meetings or complete quests and dungeons, and dedication to a group or guild is an important aspect of membership.

> *When I was in a guild . . . we would have scheduled events that most people were expected to attend. . . . There were consequences for those who missed too many events.* —jester
>
> *I'll start a dungeon, and you won't want to get up in the middle of the dungeon because a) your party will f _ _ _ ing hate you forever if you bail on them in a dungeon, and b) sometimes it takes a lot of effort to get a decent party for a dungeon.* —koala

This obligation to fulfill certain roles in groups, along with simply being present for events, can increase a player's time investment as well as provide him/her with a necessary reason for playing. If social relationships are an important aspect of game play, then fulfilling commitments to online friends is a necessary activity. The difficulty of forming valuable groups with strangers to complete certain quests, dungeons, or instances was expressed by multiple players.

I prefer to stick with my friends in groups—by and large

I don't like to look for pick-up groups. —axe

[I usually group with the] same people. I almost never

group with strangers, as they can be self-centered and

extremely immature as a rule. —bear

[The Results section continues for about five pages as Davies uses quotations from her survey responses to make connections with and comment on the important concepts in the literature review. Davies then analyzes the limitations of her research.]

This research has some limitations. First, the sample involved is extremely small and cannot be representative of the entire gaming community in any way; nine interviews from two main sources cannot be generalized to the 1.5 million subscribers to *World of Warcraft* alone, not to mention the plethora of other MMORPGs available. Similarly, the time allotted to conduct this research was much shorter than the amount of time necessary to receive quantifiable data from a multitude of sources. Another problem lies in the ability of potentially addicted players to accurately recognize and portray their gaming habits and behaviors. Whereas a player may say his/her "hobby" is under control, sources close to the subject may beg to differ. I attempted to tackle this problem in one question of the survey, which asked, "If I asked your roommates if your time responses were accurate, would

Discusses limitations of the study and suggests follow-up

they agree with you?" My responses to this question were overwhelmingly positive, which may suggest a problem, but at the same time, heavy players willingly offered up answers of extensive playing times. If more time could be dedicated, a brief interview with a source close to the respondent could clear up any discrepancies in behaviors reported by players.

Another problem may lie in my lack of attention to the extreme cases often cited by doctors and researchers investigating this topic. These cases of addiction and neglect are not hard to find; in fact, an entire forum exists for loved ones of addicted players and "cured" players who once had a serious addiction. The extremes do exist, and serious problems can result from extensive game play. However, my reasons for not focusing on these data lie in the fact that previous researchers used these extremes to imply a norm, and they assumed that an addiction would necessarily lead to dangerous consequences for players and their loved ones. While reviewing the thoughts of players on this topic, I recognized an obvious frustration with these assumptions and the existence of an in-group vs. out-group perspective. Gamers, especially those who were able to control their playing, were exhausted with and annoyed at doctors and journalists who freely applied such a negative label without much experience in the game and with the gaming community.

[Discussion now takes up the term *addiction*, which Davies deliberately did not use in her research in order to avoid "the bias of a preliminary negative assumption." She then moves to her Conclusion section.]

Conclusion

These multiple factors of addiction and symbols of addictive behavior express the ability of games to entice some players into the virtual worlds and keep them there, always wanting more. However, some players experience a few of these aspects and are aware of the rest, but do not allow them to influence their behaviors or habits of game play. It seems as if the more experienced players have caught on to the addictive aspects of the games and allowed themselves to play without being heavily influenced by these qualities of MMORPGs. Although they may play for extended periods of time (some cited seven days a week), they also claim that their responsibilities and obligations in the real world are not negatively influenced by game play. Specific questions were integrated into the survey that were directly taken from Dr. Greenfield's Virtual Addiction Test (1999). When asked about concerns from friends or family members, most experienced players stated that if, or when, these concerns were stated, they scaled down their playing time appropriately.

Supports hypothesis

Others gauged their amount of time spent playing depending on the amount of work and other real world obligations they had at the time. Most did not lose sleep, were

Addiction to Virtual Worlds   12

not preoccupied with the game when not playing, and explicitly
expressed their priorities of work before play. While many
players, experienced and new alike, expressed playing as a
form of escape, they compared this escape to any activity a
person would take to relieve stress or relax, such as watching
television, going out to a bar, or exercising. Rheingold (1993,
p. 152) cites Pavel Curtis, the creator of LambdaMOO, in his
discussion of the addictive nature of MUDs:

> These are very enticing places for a segment of the
> community. And it's not like the kinds of addictions we've
> dealt with as a society in the past. If they're out of
> control, I think that's a problem. But if someone is
> spending a large portion of their time being social with
> people who live thousands of miles away, you can't say
> they've turned inward. They aren't shunning society.
> They're actively seeking it. They're probably doing it more
> actively than anyone around them. It's a whole new
> ballgame.

This concept of communication and relationship-seeking
activities in players can still be applied today to MMORPGs.

[The Conclusion section continues for a few more pages,
describing the responses of less experienced players and relating the desire for procrastination and escape to the general
frustrations of college life, not necessarily tied to games.
Davies finds in her research "a *desire* to play more than a
need."]

Gives author, date, and page of work in which Curtis quotation was found

Long quotation indented five spaces

Interview Questions

- How long have you been playing MMORPGs?
- On average, how many days of the week do you play MMORPGs/*World of Warcraft*?
- How much time do you usually spend online during each gaming session?
- Do you often find that you intend to play for a certain amount of time, but end up spending considerably more time playing than originally planned?
- If I asked your roommates if your time responses were accurate, would they agree with you?
- How many different characters do you play?
- What are the levels of each of these characters?
- Why do you play?
- Do you find yourself extending your play time after a minor setback or when you're close to completing a quest/leveling up/acquiring a desired item, etc., in order to get that one last thing?

[The list continues for a total of 33 questions.]

Addition to Virtual Worlds   14

References

Adams, E. (July, 2002). *Stop calling games "addictive"!* Retrieved
April 23, 2005, from www.gamasutra.com/features/
20020727/adams_01.htm

Chak, K., & Leung, L. (2004). Shyness and locus of control as
predictors of Internet addiction and Internet use [Electronic
version]. *CyberPsychology & Behavior, 7*(5), 559–570.

Chou, T., & Ting, C. (2003). The role of flow experience in cyber-
game addiction. *CyberPsychology & Behavior, 6*(6), 663–676.

Eysenck, H. J. (1997). Addiction, personality and motivation
[Electronic version]. *Human Psychopharmacology, 12,*
S79–S87.

Gabel, S., Stallings, M., Schmitz, S., Young, S., & Fulker, D. (1999).
Personality dimensions and substance misuse:
Relationships in adolescents, mothers and fathers
[Electronic version]. *The American Journal of Addictions, 8,*
101–113.

Greenfield, D. (1999). *Virtual addiction: Help for netheads,
cyberfreaks and those who love them.* Oakland, CA:
New Harbinger Publications.

McMahan, A. (2003). Immersion, engagement, and presence: A
method for analyzing 3-D video games. In M. Wolf and B.
Perron (Eds.), *The video game theory reader* (pp. 67–86).
Oxford, UK: Routledge.

Annotations (margin notes):

New page for references, double-spaced

Year in parentheses after authors

Hanging indents

Last names first (52c)

Alphabetical organization

URL split after a slash

Italics extend through volume number and commas

Names of editors not reversed

Rheingold, H. (1993). *The virtual community: Homesteading on the electronic frontier.* New York: Harper Perennial.

Steinkuehler, C. (2004). American Psychological Association joins the fray. In *TerraNova.* Retrieved April 23, 2005, from http://terranova.blogs.com/terra_nova/2004/06/onlinevideogame.html

Tobold. (2005, February 25). WoW Journal-Day 15. In *Tobold's MMORPG Blog.* Retrieved May 4, 2005, from http://tobolds.blogspot.com/2005_02_01_tobolds_archive.html

Yee, N. (2002). Ariadne: Understanding MMORPG addiction. Retrieved April 12, 2005, from http://www.nickyee.com/hub/addiction/home.html

No period after URL

Retrieved from a blog (52c, item 30)

Commas after date and year

Chapter **53**

The CSE Style of Documentation in the Sciences

This chapter describes the documentation style recommended for all scientific disciplines by the Council of Science Editors (CSE), previously the Council of Biology Editors, in *Scientific Style and Format: The CSE Manual for Authors, Editors, and Publishers*, 7th ed. (New York: Cambridge University Press, 2006). This new edition describes three systems of documentation for citing the elements necessary to "ensure retrievability of the cited documents" (p. xii). One is a name-year system similar to APA style, in which the in-text citation includes author(s) and year of publication. Another is a citation-sequence system that numbers and lists sources in the order in which they are cited in the paper. The third is a citation-name system that also gives numbers to citations but organizes and numbers the list of references alphabetically by author or title so citation numbers in the text are not sequential.

***Online Study Center**___ This icon will direct you to quick reference tools, Web resources, and research guides on the Web site at http://college.hmco.com/keys.html.

This last option is the one used in The *CSE Manual* itself. Because the name-year system is so similar to APA style and because citations for the citation-sequence and citation-name systems differ only in the numbering, this chapter will concentrate on examples of entries for those last two citation systems.

53a Two basic features of CSE citation styles

Always check with your instructors about documentation style guidelines. Some may not specify one particular style but will ask you to select one and use it consistently.

KEY POINTS

Two Basic Features of CSE Citation-Sequence or Citation-Name Style

1. *In the text of your paper,* number each reference with a superscript number in a smaller size than the type for the text, or place the reference number on the line within parentheses. Place punctuation *after* the superscript number (new to the 7th edition).

2. *At the end of your paper,* list the references by number.

   For the *citation-sequence system:* Arrange and number the references in your list in the order in which you cite them in your paper. The first citation that appears in your paper will be 1, and the first reference in your list (also number 1) will give information about that first citation. Therefore, an author's name beginning with Z could be number 1 and listed first if it is the first source to be cited in your paper.

   For the *citation-name system*: Arrange and number the references in your list alphabetically by author (or title when no author is known). The first citation number in your paper will then match the alphabetical placement. The citation numbered 1 in your text could appear anywhere in your text, but the reference will appear first in your alphabetical list of references, probably among the As or Bs. An author's name beginning with Z is therefore likely to appear near the end of your list and to be numbered accordingly, wherever the citation appears in your paper.

   For either system, begin the list on a new page and title it *References*.

Example of documenting a periodical article

In-text Number Citation	Numbered Entry in List of References
The mutation may prevent degradation of unknown substrates leading to their accumulation in Lewy bodies in neuronal cells[6].	6. De Silva HR, Khan NL, Wood NW. The genetics of Parkinson's disease. Curr Opin Genet Dev. 2000 Jun;10(3):292–298.

53b CSE in-text citations (citation-sequence and citation-name styles)

Use superscript numbers to refer readers to the list of references at the end of your paper.

superscript number
One summary of studies of the life span of the fruit fly[1] has shown . . .

Refer to more than one entry in the reference list as follows:

Two studies of the life span of the fruit fly[1,2] have shown that . . .

Several studies of the life span of the fruit fly[1–4] have shown that . . .

Studies of the fruit fly are plentiful[1–4], but the most revealing is . . .

53c How to list CSE references (citation-sequence and citation-name systems)

KEY POINTS
Setting Up the CSE List of Cited References

1. After the last page of your paper, attach the list of references, headed "References" or "Cited References."

2. Arrange and number the works either consecutively in the order in which you mention them in your paper or alphabetically. Invert all authors' names, and use the initials of first and middle names. Use no punctuation between last names and initials, and leave no space between initials.

(Continued)

(Continued)

3. Begin each entry with the note number followed by a period and a space. Do not indent the first line of each entry; indent subsequent lines to align beneath the first letter on the previous line.

4. Do not underline or use quotation marks for the titles of articles, books, or journals and other periodicals.

5. Capitalize only the first word of a book or article title, and capitalize any proper nouns.

6. Abbreviate titles of journals and organizations.

7. Use a period between major divisions of each entry.

8. Use a semicolon and a space between the name of the publisher (not abbreviated in the new 7th edition) and the publication date of a book. Use a semicolon with no space between the date and the volume number of a journal.

9. For books, you may give the total number of pages, followed by a space and "p." For journal articles, give inclusive page spans, using all the digits: 135–136.

10. For online sources, provide author, title, print publication information, date and place of online publication, your date of access, and the URL.

53d Examples of entries in a CSE citation-sequence or citation-name system

1. Whole book, with one author

title not underlined,

no punctuation ┌─────── only first word capitalized ───────┐

    1. Finch CE. Longevity, senescence and the genome. Chicago:

initials with no periods between

┌───────── publisher ─────────┐ semicolon

The University of Chicago Press; 1990. 922 p.

number of pages in book (optional)

2. Part of a book

Include inclusive page numbers for the excerpt, specific reference, or quotation.

2. Thomas L. The medusa and the snail. New York: Viking Press; 1979. On cloning a human being; p. 51–56.

3. Book with two or more authors

List all the authors.

all authors'
┌── names inverted ──┐
3. Ferrini AF, Ferrini RL. Health in the later years. 2nd ed. Dubuque (IA): Brown & Benchmark; 1993. 470 p.
semicolon after publisher

4. Book with editor(s).

4. Aluja M, Norrbom AL, editors. Fruit flies (tephritidae): Phylogeny and evolution of behavior. Boca Raton (FL): CRC Press; 2000. 984 p.

5. Article in a scholarly journal

no spaces in information about journal
┌
5. Kowald A, Kirkwood TB. Explaining fruit fly longevity. Science 1993;260:
volume number

┌──────────┐
1664–1665.
complete page span

In a journal paginated by issue, include the issue number in parentheses after the volume number.

6. Newspaper or magazine article

Give the full name of the newspaper, the edition, and the first page and column number of the article.

6. Pollack A. Custom-made microbes, at your service. The New York Times (Late Ed.). 2006 Jan 17;Sect F:1 (col. 5).

7. Article with no author identified   Begin with the title of the article.

8. Audiovisual materials   Begin the entry with the title, followed by the medium, such as *CD-ROM* or *DVD,* in brackets. Then include the author (if known), producer, place, publisher, and date. Include a

description, such as number of disks or cassettes, length, color or black and white, and accompanying material. End with a statement of availability, if necessary.

8. AIDS in Africa: living with a time bomb [videocassette]. Princeton (NJ): Films for the Humanities and Sciences; 1991. 33 min, sound, color, 1/2 in.

9. Electronic journal article with a print source   Cite as for a print journal article, and include the type of medium in brackets after the journal title. Include any document number, the accession date "[cited (year, month, date)]," and an availability statement with the URL.

9. Jones CC, Meredith W. Developmental paths of psychological health from early adolescence to later adulthood. Psych Aging [Internet]. 2000 [cited 2006 Jan 18];15(2):351–360. Available from: http://www.psycinfo.com

10. Electronic journal article with no print source   If no print source is available, provide an estimate of the length of the document in pages, paragraphs, or screens. Place the information in square brackets, such as "[about 3 p.]," "[15 paragraphs]," or "[about 6 screens]."

10. Holtzworth-Munroe A. Domestic violence: Combining scientific inquiry and advocacy. Prev Treatment [Internet]. 2000 Jun 2 [cited 2006 Jan 20];3 [about 6 p.]. Available from: http://journals .apa.org/prevention/volume3/pre0030022c.html

11. Article in an electronic database   After author, title, and print publication information, give the name of the database, the designation in square brackets "[database on the Internet]," any date of posting or modification, or the copyright date. Follow this with the date of access, the approximate length of the article, the URL, and any accession number.

11. Mayor S. New treatment improves symptoms of Parkinson's disease. BMJ. 2002; 324(7344):997. In: PubMedCentral [database on the Internet]; c2002 [cited 2006 Jan 19]. [about 1 screen]. Available from: http://www .pubmedcentral.gov/articlerender.figi?tool=pmcentrez&artid=1122999

12. Internet home page   Give author (if available) and title of page followed by "[Internet]." Follow this with any available information about place of home page publication and sponsor, and then include date of publication or copyright date, along with any update. End with your date of citation and the URL.

12. Anemia and iron therapy [Internet]. Hinsdale (IL): Medtext, Inc.; c1995-2006 [cited 2006 Jan 20]. Available from: http://www.hdcn.com/ch/rbc/

13. Posting to a discussion list After the author's name and the subject line of the message, give information about the discussion list, including name of list; place and sponsor, if available; year, date, and time of posting; date of citation; and approximate length of the posting. End with an availability statement of the address of the discussion list or the archive.

13. Bishawi AH. Summary: hemangioendothelioma of the larynx. In: MEDLIB-L [discussion list on the Internet]. [Buffalo (NY): State University of NY]; 2002 May 6, 11:25am [cited 2006 Jan 19]. [about 4 screens]. Available from: MEDLIBL@listserv.acsu.buffalo.edu; item 087177.

53e A student's list of references (CSE)

The following list of references for a paper on "Research Findings and Disputes about Fruit Fly Longevity" shows the CSE citation-sequence numbering system (in which Kowald's article is the first to be cited in the paper). Note the use of abbreviations and punctuation.

Fruit fly longevity 17

Cited References

1. Kowald A, Kirkwood TB. Explaining fruit fly longevity. Science 1993;260:1664–5.

2. Finch CE. Longevity, senescence and the genome. Chicago: The University of Chicago Press; 1990. 922 p.

3. Carey JR, Liedo P, Orozco D, Vaupel JW. Slowing of mortality rates at older ages in large medfly cohorts. Science. 1993;258:457.

4. Skrecky D. Fly longevity database. In Cryonet [discussion list on the Internet]. 1997 June 22. [cited 2006 Feb 21]. [about 12 screens]. Available from: http://www.cryonet.org/cgi-bin/dsp.cgi?msg=8339

For the citation-name system, the references would be ordered alphabetically and numbered (in the text as well as in the list) as follows, with the rest of each list entry remaining the same:

1. Carey
2. Finch
3. Kowald
4. Skrecky

53f Student paper excerpt, CSE style

For a paper in an experimental biology course, with further research funded by the Parkinson's Disease Foundation Fellowship, student Jennifer Martinez investigated experimental studies of Parkinson's disease. She used the CSE citation-name style of documentation and followed APA format guidelines (chapter 52) since the CSE Manual supplies no manuscript instructions. She included a title page, numbered as page 1, with the essay title, running head, her name, name of course and instructor, and date. Here are her abstract, references, first page, and selected references.

Abstract

Running head and page number on every page (Title page is page 1.)

Abstract

In neurological disorders, such as Parkinson's disease (PD), an area of the brain known as the substantia nigra is depleted of neurons that are responsible for controlling muscle movement. A dysfunction of the ubiquitin/proteasome pathway, which removes short-lived and abnormal proteins from the cell, is postulated to be involved with the loss of neuronal cells in PD. The proteins are first tagged with a chain of a small protein called ubiquitin, which is recognized by the proteasome, the machinery that breaks down the proteins into small fragments. Proteins that are not rapidly removed from the cell tend to cluster and are unable to be broken down or degraded. These intracellular aggregates remain in the cell and may contribute to cell death. In PD, these intracellular inclusions, known as Lewy bodies, are found in neurons. This paper reviews the most recent findings on PD with a dysfunction of the ubiquitin/proteasome pathway and on the role played by intracellular proteins such as vimentin, parkin, alpha-synuclein, and cyclooxygenase 2 in formation of PD Lewy bodies. The review showed that the proteins vimentin, parkin, alpha-synuclein, and cyclooxygenase 2 were found to be associated with these inclusions.

Technical language in scientific paper

First page of paper

Ubiquitin/Proteasome Pathway 3

The Role of the Ubiquitin/Proteasome Pathway in
Parkinson's Disease

Proteolysis is the breakdown or degradation of proteins
and is an important cellular event involving tightly regulated
removal of unwanted proteins and retention of those that are
essential. The ubiquitin/proteasome pathway plays an important
role in the intracellular quality control process by degrading
mutated or abnormally folded proteins to prevent their
accumulation as intracellular aggregates. Proteolysis by the
ubiquitin/proteasome pathway involves two major steps:
ubiquitination followed by degradation. A de-ubiquitination step
also plays an important role in this pathway[2].

Ubiquitin (Ub) is a small peptide, consisting of 76 amino
acids and is abundant in all eukaryotic cells[2]. Covalent
attachment of ubiquitin to proteins targets them for degradation.
Once ubiquitinated, proteins do not accumulate in cells since
the Ub/proteasome pathway degrades them. Proteins become
ubiquitinated by a series of four enzymatic reactions: the ATP
dependent activation of ubiquitin by Ub-activating enzymes (E1),
binding of activated ubiquitin to Ub-conjugating enzymes (E2),
the covalent conjugation of ubiquitin to the protein substrate
by Ub-ligases (E3), and the formation of a polyubiquitin chain by
the elongation factor E4. Polyubiquitination acts as a tag for
recognition by the 26S proteasome for protein degradation.

Numbered reference to second source in alphabetical list

Second reference to the same numbered source

Selected references

References on new numbered page

References

Entries aligned alphabetically under first word of entry

1. De Silva HR, Khan NL, Wood NW. The genetics of Parkinson's disease. Curr Opin Genet Dev. 2000;10(3):292–298.

2. Figueiredo-Pereira ME, Rockwell P. The ubiquitin/proteasome pathway in neurological disorders. In: Banik NL, Lajtha A, editors. Role of proteases in the pathophysiology of neurodegenerative diseases. New York: Kluwer/Plenum; 2001. 302p.

3. Imai Y, Soda M, Takahashi R. Parkin suppresses unfolded protein stress-induced cell death through its E3 ubiquitin-protein ligase activity. J Biol Chem. 2000;275(46):35661–35664.

4. Parkinson's disease: hope through research [Internet]. Bethesda (MD): Nat Inst of Neurological Disorders and Stroke; updated 2006 June 27 [cited 2006 Jul 6]; [about 20p.]. Available from: http://www.ninds.nih.gov/disorders/parkinsons_disease/detail_parkinsons_disease.htm

5. Shimura H, Hattori N, Kubo S, Mizuno Y, Asakawa S, Minoshima S, Shimizu N, Iwai K, Chiba T, Tanaka K, Suzuki T. Familial Parkinson disease gene product, parkin, is a ubiquitin-protein ligase. Nat Genet. 2000;25(3):302–305.

6. Wigley WC, Fabunmi RP, Lee MG, Marino CR, Muallem S, Demartino GN, Thomas PJ. Dynamic association of proteasomal machinery with the centrosome. J Cell Biol 1999;145(3):481–490.

No italics or underlining in list

Chapter **54**

Chicago **Style of Documentation**

A full At a Glance Index of types of examples appears on the pages listed below.

As an alternative to an author/year citation style similar to the APA system, *The Chicago Manual of Style,* 15th ed. (Chicago: University of Chicago Press, 2003), describes a system in which sources are documented in footnotes or endnotes. This system is used widely in the humanities, especially in history and art history. Use endnotes, not footnotes, for material you publish online. For a *Chicago*-style paper, include an unnumbered title page, and number the first page of your text as page "2."

54a Two basic features of *Chicago* endnotes and footnotes

KEY POINTS

Two Basic Features of *Chicago* Endnotes and Footnotes

1. Place a superscript numeral at the end of the quotation or the sentence in which you mention source material; place the number after all punctuation marks except a dash.

2. List all endnotes—single-spaced, but double-spaced between notes, unless your instructor prefers double-spaced throughout—on a separate numbered page at the end of the paper, and number the notes sequentially, as they appear in your paper. Your word processing program will automatically place footnotes at the bottom of each page (Insert/Footnote). See 11a.

Example of an endnote or footnote for a book

In-Text Citation with Numeral	Endnote or Footnote
For footnote: Mondrian planned his compositions with colored tape.[3] **For endnote (mentioning source):** According to Arnason and Prather, Mondrian planned his compositions with colored tape.[3]	3. H. Harvard Arnason and Marla F. Prather, *History of Modern Art* (New York: Abrams, 1998), 393.

54b Chicago in-text citations, notes, and bibliography

In-text citation   Use the following format, and number your notes sequentially.

> George Eliot thought that *Eliot* was a "good, mouth-filling, easy to pronounce word."[1]

If you use endnotes and not footnotes, mention the source in your text so that readers do not have to go to the end to find the source. If you include at the end of your paper a bibliography listing all the sources cited in your notes (see 54e), then the note citation can be concise. With no bibliography attached, give full information about a source the first time you include it in your notes.

First note for a source when a full bibliography is included   A bibliography includes full publication details, so in a short note, only the author's last name, a shortened form of the title, and the page number (if a specific reference is made) are necessary. Indent the first line of the note.

author's last name   short title   page number for a specific reference or a quotation
1. Crompton, *George Eliot,* 123.

Entry in bibliography (first line not indented)

Crompton, Margaret. *George Eliot: The Woman.* London: Cox and Wyman, 1960.

Online Study Center   This icon will direct you to quick reference tools, Web resources, and research guides on the Web site at http://college.hmco.com/keys.html.

Full first note for a source when no bibliography is included

author's name   title underlined, all important
┌── in normal order ──┐   ┌─── words capitalized ───┐

1. Margaret Crompton, *George Eliot: The Woman* (London: Cox and

comma   page number

Wyman, 1960), 123.

Note referring to the immediately preceding source   In a reference to the immediately preceding source, you may use "Ibid." (Latin *ibidem,* meaning "in the same place") instead of repeating the author's name and the title of the work. All the details except the page number must be the same as in the previous citation. If the page number is the same too, omit it following "Ibid."

2. Ibid., 127.

However, avoid a series of "ibid." notes. These are likely to irritate your reader. Instead, place page references within your text: "As Crompton points out (127), . . ."

Any subsequent reference to a previously cited source   For a reference to a source cited in a previous note but not in the immediately preceding note, give only the author and page number. However, if you cite more than one work by the same author, include a short title to identify the source.

6. Crompton, 124.

54c Guidelines for *Chicago* endnotes and footnotes

KEY POINTS

Guidelines for Chicago Endnotes and Footnotes

1. In the list of endnotes, place each number on the line (not as a superscript), followed by a period and one space. For footnotes, word processing software will often automatically make the number a superscript number—just be consistent with whatever format you use.

2. Indent the first line of each entry three or five spaces. Single-space within a note and double-space between notes, unless your instructor prefers double-spacing throughout.

3. Use the author's full name, not inverted, followed by a comma and the title of the work. Put quotation marks around article titles, and italicize titles of books and periodicals.

4. Capitalize all words in the titles of books, periodicals, and articles except *a, an, the,* coordinating conjunctions, *to* in an infinitive, and prepositions. Capitalize any word that begins or ends a title or subtitle.

5. Follow a book title with publishing information in parentheses (city—and state if necessary: name of publisher, year) followed by a comma and the page number(s), with no "p." or "pp." Follow an article title with the name of the periodical and pertinent publication information (volume, issue, date, page numbers where appropriate). Do not abbreviate months.

6. Separate major parts of the citation with commas, not periods.

7. For online sources, provide the URL, and for time-sensitive material, end with the date on which you last accessed the source.

54d Examples of entries in *Chicago* notes

AT A GLANCE INDEX: PRINT BOOKS AND PARTS OF BOOKS (*Chicago*)

Note the indented first line, the full name of the author, the commas separating major sections of the note, and the publication details in parentheses (City: Publisher, year of publication). If you quote or refer to a specific page of the source, provide the page number following the publication details and a comma, as in item 1. For a general reference or a reference to the work as a whole, end the note after the closing parenthesis, as in item 2.

1. Book with one author

1. Robert A. Caro, *Master of the Senate: The Years of Lyndon Johnson* (New York: Knopf, 2002), 8.

2. Book with two or three authors

2. George Lakoff and Mark Johnson, *Metaphors We Live By* (Chicago: University of Chicago Press, 1980).

3. Book with four to ten authors

For a book with multiple authors, use the name of only the first author followed by "and others" in a note; in a bibliography, include the first six names and use "et al." for the rest.

3. Randolph Quirk and others, *A Comprehensive Grammar of the English Language* (London: Longman, 1985).

4. Book with no author identified

4. *Chicago Manual of Style,* 15th ed. (Chicago: University of Chicago Press, 2003).

5. Book with editor or translator

5. John Updike, ed., *The Best American Short Stories of the Century* (Boston: Houghton Mifflin, 1999).

For a translated work, give the author, title, and then the name of the translator after "trans."

6. Author's work quoted in another work

6. E. M. Forster, *Two Cheers for Democracy* (New York: Harcourt, Brace and World, 1942), 242, quoted in Phyllis Rose, *Woman of Letters, A Life of Virginia Woolf* (New York: Oxford University Press, 1978), 219.

Note, however, that *The Chicago Manual of Style* recommends that a reference be found in and cited from the original work.

7. Government document

7. U.S. Department of Education, National Center for Education Statistics, *The Condition of Education,* 2005 (Washington, DC: GPO, 2005).

8. Scriptures, Greek and Latin works, classic works of literature

Provide the reference in the text or in a note. For the Bible, include the book (in abbreviated form, chapter, and verse, not a page number), and the version used (not italicized).

8. 1 Cor. 7:1–5. (New Revised Standard Version).

You do not need to include the Bible in your bibliography.

For Greek and Roman works and for classic plays in English, locate by the number of the book, section, and line or by act, scene, and line. Cite a classic poem by book, canto, stanza, and line, whichever is appropriate. Specify the edition used only in the first reference in a note.

9. Part of an edited volume or anthology (essay or chapter)

9. Terrence Des Pres, "Poetry and Politics," in *The Writer in Our World*, ed. Reginald Gibbons (Boston: Atlantic Monthly Press, 1986), 17-29.

AT A GLANCE INDEX: PRINT ARTICLES IN PERIODICALS (*Chicago*)

---

10. Article in a scholarly journal, continuously paged through issues of a volume

If journal volumes are paged continuously through issues (for example, if issue 1 ends on page 188 and issue 2 of the same volume begins with page 189) give only the volume number and year, not the issue number. If you refer to a specific page, put a colon after the year in parentheses and then add the page number or numbers. To cite an abstract, include the word *abstract* before the name of the journal. For more on scholarly journals, see 486.

10. Hesse, Douglas, "The Place of Creative Nonfiction," *College English* 65 (2003): 238.

11. Article in a scholarly journal, each issue paged separately

When each issue of a journal is paged separately, with each issue beginning on page 1, include "no." for number after the volume number, and follow it with the issue number.

11. Rami Ginat, "The Soviet Union and the Syrian Ba'th Regime: From Hesitation to *Rapprochement*," *Middle Eastern Studies* 36, no. 2 (2000): 160.

12. Article in a magazine

Include the month for monthly magazines and the complete date for weekly magazines (month, day, year). Cite only a specific page number in a note (after a comma), not the range of pages. Provide the range of pages of the whole article in any bibliographical citation.

12. Andrew Sullivan, "We Don't Need a New King George," *Time,* January 23, 2006, 74.

13. Article in a newspaper Include the complete date, the edition, if relevant, and the section number. Do not include an initial *The* in the name of a newspaper. A page number is not necessary as a newspaper may appear in several editions. You may, however, give the edition and any section number.

13. Michiko Kakutani, "Bending the Truth in a Million Little Ways," *New York Times,* late edition, sec. E, January 17, 2006.

If the city is not part of the newspaper title, include it in parentheses: *Times* (London).

14. Editorial, no author identified When no author is identified, begin the note with the title of the article.

14. "Spark the Revolution," *Wall Street Journal,* December 27, 2005, sec. A.

15. Letter to the editor

15. Christina J. Nichol, letter to the editor, *Harper's,* January 2006, 6.

16. Review of book, play, or movie

16. Anne Hollander, "Men in Tights," review of *Why We Are What We Wear,* by Paul Fussell, *New Republic*, February 10, 2003, 34.

AT A GLANCE INDEX: ONLINE AND MEDIA SOURCES

17. Online reference work Cite an online dictionary or an encyclopedia in a note, but do not include it in a bibliography. Because reference works are frequently updated, you need to give the date on which you accessed the material. Precede the title of the article with the initials *s.v.* (Latin for *sub verbo*—"under the word").

> 17. *Columbia Encyclopedia,* 6th ed., s.v. "Bloomsbury group," http://www.bartleby.com/65/bl/Bloomsbury.html (accessed January 5, 2006).

18. Online book   Include your date of access only for time-sensitive material or material that may be revised for different editions.

> 18. Mary Wollstonecraft Shelley, *Frankenstein, or, The Modern Prometheus* (London: Dent, 1912), http://ota.ahds.ac.uk.

19. Article obtained through an online database   After any available print information, give the URL of the entry page of the service and other retrieval information, and (only if the material is time-sensitive or may exist in varying editions) the date you accessed the material. Give a page number only if it is indicated on the screen.

> 19. Geoffrey Bent, "Vermeer's Hapless Peer," *North American Review* 282 (1997), http://www.infotrac.galegroup.com.

20. Article in an online journal

> 20. Sarah Hatchuel, "Leading the Gaze: From Showing to Telling in Kenneth Branagh's *Henry V* and *Hamlet,*" *Early Modern Literary Studies* 6 no. 1 (2000), http://www.shu.ac.uk.emls/06-1/hatchba.htm.

21. Article in an online magazine   Cite as for a print publication, but add the URL.

> 21. Daniel Gross, "One Word: Logistics," *Slate,* January 20, 2006, http://www.Slate.com/id/2134513/?nav=tap3.

22. Article in an online newspaper   Cite as for a print publication, but add the URL. See item 13 above.

> 22. John Johnson Jr., "Shining a Light on the Dark Planet," *Latimes.com,* January 15, 2006, http://www.latimes.com/news/printedition/asection/la-sci-pluto15jan15,1,3860080.story?ctrack=1&cset=true.

23. Government publication online

> 23. U.S. Department of Education, National Center for Education Statistics, *Digest of Education Statistics, 2004,* October 12, 2005, http://nces.ed.gov/pubsearch/pubsinfo.asp?pubid=2006005.

24. Web page or document from a Web site   Give the author of the content, if known, the title of the document, the owner or sponsor of the site, the URL, and your date of access if the material is frequently updated.

> 24. "MLA Style," Modern Language Association, http://www.mla.org (accessed January 20, 2006).

25. Personal home page   If a page does not have a title, use a descriptive phrase such as "home page."

> 25. Eleanor Gilpatrick, home page, http://www.gilpatrickart.com.

26. E-mail communication

> 26. George Kane, e-mail message to the author, January 7, 2006.

27. Posting on an electronic discussion list or blog   Whenever possible, cite a URL for archived material. Otherwise, end the note after the date.

> 27. David Schwalm, e-mail to WPA-L mailing list, February 15, 2005, http://lists.asu.edu/archives.wpa-l.html.

28. CD-ROM, DVD, e-book   Indicate the medium.

> 28. Ann Raimes, *Digital Keys* 4.0 (Boston: Houghton Mifflin, 2005), CD-ROM.

29. Interview   Treat a published interview like an article or a book chapter, including the phrase "interview with." For unpublished interviews, include the type of interview and the date.

> 29. Douglass Mignone, telephone interview with the author, October 19, 2003.

30. Lecture or speech   Give location and date.

> 30. Peter Kwong, "Chinese America: The Untold Story of America's Oldest New Community" (lecture, Asian Research Institute, New York, February 10, 2006).

31. Film, slide, videocassette, audiocassette, or DVD End the note with an indication of the type of medium, such as *film, slide, videocassette,* or *DVD.* For online multimedia, include the type of medium, such as *MP3 audio file.*

31. *Citizen Kane,* produced, written, and directed by Orson Welles, 119 min., RKO, 1941, film.

54e *Chicago* **bibliography guidelines and sample**

Check whether your instructor wants you to include a bibliography of works cited (or a bibliography of works consulted) in addition to notes. The bibliography form differs from the note form in several ways:

NOTE FORM

Note number indented   Publication details in parentheses

7. Peter C. Sutton, *Pieter de Hooch, 1629–1684* (New Haven, CT: Yale University Press, 1988), 57.

page number of exact citation

Note that commas are used to separate the major parts of the note.

BIBLIOGRAPHY FORM

No number, no indent in first line

Sutton, Peter C. *Pieter de Hooch, 1629–1684.* New Haven, CT: Yale University Press, 1988.

Indented after first line

Note that periods separate the major parts of the entry.

Bibliography Guidelines

- Begin a bibliography on a new, numbered page after the endnotes.
- List entries alphabetically, by authors' last names.
- Include authors' full names, with the first author's inverted.
- Indent all lines three or five spaces except the first line of each entry.
- Single-space entries and double-space between entries, or double-space the whole list.
- Separate the major parts of each entry with a period and one space.
- If you include a bibliography, you can use the short form for notes (54b).

Here is the bibliography from a student's paper on the seventeenth-century Dutch painter Pieter de Hooch.

Quinones 16

Bibliography

Bent, Geoffrey. "Vermeer's Hapless Peer." *North American Review* 282 (1997). http://www.infotrac.galegroup.com/.

Bruce, Donald. "Vermeer and de Hooch at the National Gallery." *Contemporary Review,* August 2001. http://search.epnet.com.

Franits, Wayne E. "The Depiction of Servants in Some Paintings by Pieter de Hooch." *Zeitschrift für Kunstgeschichte* 52 (1989): 559–66.

Sutton, Peter C. *Pieter de Hooch,1629–1684.* New Haven: Yale University Press, 1988.

54f A student's research paper, *Chicago* style

Eva Hardcastle wrote the following research paper for a writing course with a focus on language use. The class had been discussing slang and Standard English, and she chose to expand the discussion by doing research on slang dictionaries. She was instructed not to include a bibliography, so her endnotes include the full citation for each source. She single-spaced her notes, with a double space between notes, as her instructor required. Some instructors may prefer double-spacing throughout.

SLANG DICTIONARIES:

MIRRORING OUR FLEXIBLE USE OF LANGUAGE

EVA HARDCASTLE

ENGLISH 218

Professor Marino

APRIL 22, 2006

1

Page numbering begins after title page

More information in note

The reference section of every library contains one or more slang dictionaries.[1] At first it is puzzling to consider why there are slang dictionaries and how they are used. People who use slang do not get it out of a slang dictionary, do not check the spelling of slang, and do not look up the meaning of an unfamiliar slang expression they may hear used by a friend or coworker. Close examination of slang dictionaries, however, suggests that these works reflect the flexible ways people shift back and forth between informal and formal speech. On one hand, we often communicate in a standardized way so we can be clearly understood and can successfully fit into the larger society. On the other hand, we often talk in many diverse and free-style ways so we can express our individuality and belong to various subgroups within society. Slang dictionaries convey the message that both types of speech have validity and historical interest.

States thesis

Slang exists largely in relation to what it is not—it is not Standard English. James Stalker makes this point as he summarizes colleagues' attempts to date the beginning of slang:

> Lighter (1994) maintains that we cannot really label words as being slang before c. 1660, the Restoration period, because "standard" English did not exist before that time, hence the concept of slang could not exist before that time, although cant, criminal jargon, could. Partridge (1954) seems to agree. Slang arose as a response to Standard.[2]

Quotation indented at left

Quotation cited in a note

3

In-group slang is informal, irreverent, and edgy, while Standard English is formal, respectful, and mainstream. Slang dictionaries make these distinctions clear, neatly translating slang into Standard English and highlighting the difference between the two in a nonjudgmental way.

These dictionaries let a reader know, for instance, that in Australia *narky* means "upset," that in the Royal Air Force *pukka gen* means "trustworthy information," or that in England in 1811 *Pompkin* meant "A man or woman of Boston in America; from the number of pumpkins raised and eaten by the people of that country."[3] With slang words and their definitions each presented in this straightforward, neutral manner, it is easy to see both as valid ways of expressing oneself. Which you use depends on your choices, aims, priorities, audience, time period, and context.[4]

Interestingly, many people have always felt strongly that Standard English needs to be championed as the only way to communicate. Other people have always felt equally strongly that English must be appreciated and preserved in all its natural exuberance and variety. Tom McArthur, a scholar of global English, writes, for instance, about early "dialectologists," who "pursued their cataloging and commentary under the vast shadow of standardization . . . and so worked with a sense of urgency."[5] Clearly slang dictionary writers are more aligned with this second group, valuing slang's idiosyncrasies. But slang dictionary writers also approve highly of Standard English, as

Specific examples to illustrate a point

Opposing views

Words omitted from a quotation

4

found in their prefaces and definitions. Both slang and Standard English have their place, slang dictionaries seem to say, and are worthy of attention and preservation.[6]

In *Democratic Eloquence,* Kenneth Cmiel considers how nineteenth-century citizens of America wrestled with slang, "the riff-raff of language."[7] Americans were famous for being able to use language in colorful, casual ways, but they actively questioned the role of slang in a democracy. They wondered whether slang was a good thing, embodying friendliness, independence, self-confidence, and a demographic disregard for class distinctions, or a bad thing, indicating boorishness, low sensibility, incivility, poor education, and an embarrassing lack of culture and refinement. Or both? People were ambivalent, in other words. Cmiel writes:

> Americans were pulled in contradictory directions. The new expressive decorum encouraged informal speech, and slang, dialect, and familiarity all contributed to moments of egalitarianism. Popular education, however, encouraged refined and elegant prose.[8]

Cmiel follows the debate in newspapers, grammar guides, speeches, and dictionaries of the day. In the mid-nineteenth century, regular dictionaries condemned slang as vulgar and low, leaving most of it entirely out. By the 1880s and into the twenty-first century, not only do more slang dictionaries appear, but the next generation of general dictionaries includes more slang words. As the editors of *Funk & Wagnalls Standard* (1890) put it in their

Two sides of argument

5

preface to their new edition: "The question that should control the lexicographer is not, should the word be in the English language? But is it?"[9] Expressing this nonjudgmental philosophy, long, new, academic-style slang dictionaries appear. They document in great detail that people in all walks of life and occupations use slang sometimes and that a person sometimes talks freely or rudely, sometimes more delicately. For example, in one slang dictionary is the slang expression—"Blue o'clock in the morning," followed by the definition—"Pre-dawn, when black sky gives way to purple. Suggestive of rollicking late hours."[10] Both parts of this entry seem like fine uses of language, and the mind goes happily back and forth between them. That back-and-forth mirrors how we vary our mode of communication according to mood, audience, and situation.

Provision of interesting example

So, finally, what is the purpose of slang dictionaries? Some slang dictionary prefaces say that their purpose is to preserve a national language and national pride.[11] Some say their purpose is to "help ESL students learn informal English as it is spoken or heard on TV."[12] Some dictionaries of technical terms such as computer slang can have a practical, job-training aspect.[13] But mostly slang dictionaries seem to celebrate the quirkiness of slang. They present old slang, such as *frisk* for search or *racket* for noise (both from c. 1780), and newer slang, such as *24/7* for constantly (from c. 2000), and in the process make clear that people move easily back and forth between the slang and Standard English, usually without any dictionary at all.

Summary of what slang dictionaries do

Positive note at end

First line
of each
note
indented

Complete
biblio-
graphical
informa-
tion
contained
in notes:
no
separate
bibliog-
raphy
needed

NOTES

1. Examples include Eric Partridge, *A Dictionary of Slang and Unconventional English,* 7th ed., ed. Paul Beale (London: Routledge and Kegan Paul, 1984); Harold Wentworth and Stewart Berg Flexner, *Dictionary of American Slang* (New York: Crowell, 1975); Jonathan Lighter, *Random House Historical Dictionary of American Slang,* 2 vols. (New York: Random House, 1994–97).

2. James C. Stalker, "Slang Is Not Novel," paper presented at a meeting of the American Association for Applied Linguistics, Long Beach, California, 1995, 8, ERIC, ED 392 251.

3. Pete Alfano, "Australian for Olympics," *Fort Worth Star Telegram,* 10 September 2000, Sports, p. 13; Eric Partridge, *Dictionary of Slang and Unconventional English,* 5th ed. (New York: Macmillan, 1961), 1103; Francis Grose, *Lexicon Balatronicum: A Dictionary of the Vulgar Tongue: A Dictionary of Buckish Slang, University Wit, and Pickpocket Eloquence* (London: Jones, 1811; reprint, Chicago: Follett, 1971).

4. This concept is discussed in Harvey Daniels, *Famous Last Words: The American Language Crisis Reconsidered* (Carbondale: Southern Illinois University Press, 1983), 68. In his chapter "Nine Ideas about Language," Idea 5 is "Speakers of all languages employ a range of styles and a set of subdialects or jargons."

Note
extended
to provide
additional
informa-
tion

5. Tom McArthur, *The English Languages* (Cambridge, UK: Cambridge University Press, 1998), xiv. See also Tom McArthur, *Living Words: Language, Lexicography, and the Knowledge Revolution* (Exeter: University of Exeter Press, 1998), 37. Here McArthur calls the pro-diversity group "permissivists."

Page
numbers
at bottom
of page
when
page has
a heading

6. In an interview (Janny Scott, "That All-American Dictionary Adds an All-American Coach," *New York Times,* 19 August 2000, sec. A, p. 1), dictionary editor Jesse Sheidlower

7

echoes this point: "You can be interested in slang or dialect or things that people call ungrammatical, but still think that there is a formal way of speech. . . . Our entire conversation has been conducted in a relatively formal standard English despite the fact that I know a lot of words that will make people's hair crawl."

7. Kenneth Cmiel, *Democratic Eloquence: The Fight over Popular Speech in Nineteenth-Century America* (New York: William Morrow, 1990), 127–8.

8. Ibid., 90.

9. Quoted in Cmiel, 224.

10. J. Redding Ware, *Passing English of the Victorian Era: A Dictionary of Heterodox English, Slang, and Phrase* (London: Routledge, 1909), 38.

11. S. B. Flexner, introduction to Wentworth and Flexner, *DAS,* viii.

12. David Burke, *Street Talk: Slang Used in Popular American Television Shows* (Berkeley: Optima, 1992), viii.

13. See, for examples, Constance Hale, ed. *Wired Style: Principles of English Usage in the Digital Age.* San Francisco: Hard Wired Books, 1996, 35–58; and University of Wisconsin–Platteville, "Computer Slang Glossary" http://www.uwplatt.edu/~disted/general/glossary.htm (accessed February 20, 2006).

Same source as in note 7

Citation of online source

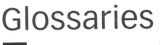

Glossaries

55 Glossary of Usage   **56** Glossary of Grammatical Terms

55

Glossary of Usage

Listed in this glossary are words that are often confused (*affect/effect, elicit/illicit*) or misspelled (*it's/its*). Also listed are nonstandard words (*irregardless, theirself*) and colloquial expressions (*OK*) that should be avoided in formal writing.

a, an   Use *an* before words that begin with a vowel sound (the vowels are *a, e, i, o,* and *u*): *an apple, an hour* (silent *h*). Use *a* before words that begin with a consonant sound: *a planet, a yam, a ukelele, a house* (pronounced *h*).

accept, except, expect   *Accept* is a verb: *She accepted the salary offer. Except* is usually a preposition: *Everyone has gone home except my boss. Expect* is a verb: *They expect to visit New Mexico on vacation.*

adapt, adopt   *Adapt* means "to adjust" and is used with the preposition *to: It takes people some time to adapt to the work routine after college. Adopt* means "to take into a family" or "to take up and follow": *The couple adopted a three-year-old child. The company adopted a more aggressive policy.*

adverse, averse   *Adverse* is an adjective describing something as hostile, unfavorable, or difficult. *Averse* indicates opposition to something and usually takes the preposition *to. The bus driver was averse to driving in the adverse driving conditions.*

advice, advise   *Advice* is a noun: *Take my advice and don't start smoking. Advise* is a verb: *He advised his brother to stop smoking.*

affect, effect   In their most common uses, *affect* is a verb, and *effect* is a noun. To *affect* is to have an *effect* on something: *Pesticides can affect health. Pesticides have a bad effect on health. Effect,* however, can be used as a verb meaning "to bring about": *The administration hopes to effect new health care legislation. Affect* can also be used as a noun in psychology, meaning "a feeling or emotion."

aisle, isle   You'll find an *aisle* in a supermarket or a church. An *isle* is an island.

all ready, already *All ready* means "totally prepared": *The students were all ready for their final examination. Already* is an adverb meaning "by this time": *He has already written the report.*

all right, alright *All right* (meaning "satisfactory") is standard. *Alright* is nonstandard. However, *alright* is used in popular culture to mean "wonderful."

all together, altogether *All together* is used to describe acting simultaneously: *As soon as the boss had presented the plan, the managers spoke up all together. Altogether* is an adverb meaning "totally," often used before an adjective: *His presentation was altogether impressive.*

allude, elude *Allude* means "to refer to": *She alluded to his height. Elude* means "to avoid": *He eluded her criticism by leaving the room.*

allusion, illusion The noun *allusion* means "reference to": *Her allusion to his height made him uncomfortable.* The noun *illusion* means "false idea": *He had no illusions about being Mr. Universe.*

almost, most Do not use *most* to mean a*lmost: Almost* [not *Most*] *all my friends are computer literate.*

alot, a lot of, lots of *Alot* is nonstandard. *A lot of* and *lots of* are regarded by some as informal for *many* or *a great deal of: They have performed many research studies.*

aloud, allowed *Aloud* is an adverb meaning "out loud": *She read her critique aloud. Allowed* is a form of the verb *allow: Employees are not allowed to participate in the competition.*

ambiguous, ambivalent *Ambiguous* is used to describe a phrase or act with more than one meaning: *The ending of the movie is ambiguous; we don't know if the butler really committed the murder. Ambivalent* describes uncertainty and the coexistence of opposing attitudes and feelings: *The committee is ambivalent about the proposal for restructuring the company.*

among, between Use *between* for two items, *among* for three or more: *I couldn't decide between red or blue. I couldn't decide among red, blue, or green.*

amoral, immoral *Amoral* can mean "neither moral nor immoral" or "not caring about right or wrong," whereas *immoral* means "morally wrong": *Some consider vegetarianism an amoral issue, but others believe eating meat is immoral.*

amount, number *Amount* is used with uncountable expressions: *a large amount of money, work, or effort. Number* is used with countable plural expressions: *a large number of people, a number of attempts.* See 41b.

an See *a*.

ante-, anti- *Ante-* is a prefix meaning "before," as in *anteroom. Anti-* means "against" or "opposite," as in *antiseptic* or *antifreeze.*

anyone, any one *Anyone* is a singular indefinite pronoun meaning "anybody": *Can anyone help me? Any one* refers to one from a group and is usually followed by *of* + plural noun: *Any one* [as opposed to any two] *of the suggestions will be considered acceptable.*

anyplace The standard *anywhere* is preferable.

anyway, anywhere, nowhere; anyways, anywheres, nowheres *Anyway, anywhere,* and *nowhere* are standard forms. The others, ending in *-s,* are not.

apart, a part *Apart* is an adverb: *The old book fell apart. A part* is a noun phrase: *I'd like to be a part of that project.*

as, as if, like See *like.*

as regards See *in regard to.*

assure, ensure, insure All three words mean "to make secure or certain," but only *assure* is used in the sense of making a promise: *He assured us everything would be fine. Ensure* and *insure* are interchangeable, but only *insure* is commonly used in the commercial or financial sense: *We wanted to ensure that the rate we paid to insure our car against theft would not change.*

awful Avoid using *awful* to mean "bad" or "extremely": <u>not</u> *He's awful late* <u>but</u> *He's extremely late.*

a while, awhile *A while* is a noun phrase: *a while ago; for a while. Awhile* is an adverb meaning "for some time": *They lived awhile in the wilderness.*

bad, badly *Bad* is an adjective, *badly* an adverb. Use *bad* after linking verbs (such as *am, is, become, seem*): *They felt bad after losing the match.* Use *badly* to modify a verb: *They played badly.*

bare, bear *Bare* is an adjective meaning "naked": the *bare* facts, a *bare*-faced lie. *Bear* is a noun (the animal) or a verb meaning "to carry" or "to endure": *He could not bear the pressure of losing.*

barely Avoid creating a double negative (such as *can't barely type*). *Barely* should always take a positive verb: *She can barely type. They could barely keep their eyes open.* See *hardly.*

because, because of *Because* is a subordinating conjunction used to introduce a dependent clause: *Because it was raining, we left early. Because of* is a two-word preposition: *We left early because of the rain.*

being as, being that Avoid. Use *because* instead: *Because* [not *Being as*] *I was tired, I didn't go to class.*

belief, believe *Belief* is a noun: *She has radical beliefs. Believe* is a verb: *He believes in an afterlife.*

beside, besides *Beside* is a preposition meaning "next to": *Sit beside me. Besides* is a preposition meaning "except for": *He has no assistants besides us.*

Besides is also an adverb meaning "in addition": *I hate horror movies. Besides, there's a long line.*

better See *had better.*

between See *among.*

brake, break When we apply the *brake* in a car, we can *break* a window or even get a bad *break.*

breath, breathe The first word is a noun, the second a verb: *Take three deep breaths. Breathe in deeply.*

bring, take Use *bring* to suggest carrying something from a farther place to a nearer one, and *take* for any other transportation: *First bring me a cake from the store, and then we can take it to the party.*

can't hardly This expression is nonstandard. See *hardly.*

censor, censure The verb *censor* refers to editing or removing from public view. *Censure* means to criticize harshly. *The new film was censored for graphic content, and the director was censured by critics for his irresponsibility.*

cite, site, sight *Cite* means "to quote or mention"; *site* is a noun meaning "location"; *sight* is a noun meaning "view": *She cited the page number in her paper. They visited the original site of the abbey. The sight of the skyline from the plane produced applause from the passengers.*

compare to, compare with Use *compare to* when implying similarity: *They compared the director to Alfred Hitchcock.* Use *compare with* when examining similarities or differences: *She wrote an essay comparing Hitchcock with Orson Welles.*

complement, compliment As verbs, *complement* means "to complete or add to something," and *compliment* means "to make a flattering comment about someone or something": *The wine complemented the meal. The guests complimented the hostess on the fine dinner.* As nouns, the words have meanings associated with the verbs: *The wine was a fine complement to the meal. The guests paid the hostess a compliment.*

compose, comprise *Compose* means "to make up"; *comprise* means "to include." *The conference center is composed of twenty-five rooms. The conference center comprises twenty-five rooms.*

conscience, conscious *Conscience* is a noun meaning "awareness of right and wrong." *Conscious* is an adjective meaning "awake" or "aware." *Her conscience troubled her after the accident. The victim was still not conscious.*

continual, continuous *Continual* implies repetition; *continuous* implies lack of a pause. *The continual interruptions made the lecturer angry. Continuous rain for two hours stopped play.*

could care less This expression is often used but is regarded by some as nonstandard. In formal English, use it only with a negative: *They could not care less about their work.*

council, counsel A *council* is a group formed to consult, deliberate, or make decisions. *Counsel* is advice or guidance. *The council was called together to help give counsel to the people. Counsel* can also be a verb: *We counseled the students to withdraw from the course.*

credible, creditable, credulous *Credible* means "believable": *The jury found the accused's alibi to be credible and so acquitted her. Creditable* means "deserving of credit": *A B+ grade attests to a creditable performance. Credulous* means "easily taken in or deceived": *Only a child would be so credulous as to believe that the streets are paved with gold.* See also *incredible, incredulous.*

criteria, criterion *Criteria* is the plural form of the singular noun *criterion*: *There are many criteria for a successful essay. One criterion is sentence clarity.*

curricula, curriculum *Curricula* is the plural form of *curriculum. All the departments have well-thought-out curricula, but the English Department has the best curriculum.*

custom, customs, costume All three words are nouns. *Custom* means "habitual practice or tradition": *a family custom. Customs* refers to taxes on imports or to the procedures for inspecting items entering a country: *go through customs at the airport.* A *costume* is "a style of dress": *a Halloween costume.*

dairy, diary The first word is associated with cows and milk, the second with daily journal writing.

decease, disease *Decease* is a verb or noun meaning "die" or "death." *Disease* is an illness: *The disease caused an early decease.*

decent, descent, dissent *Decent* is an adjective meaning "good" or "respectable": *decent clothes, a decent salary. Descent* is a noun meaning "way down" or "lineage": *She is of Scottish descent. Dissent,* used both as a noun and a verb, refers to disagreement: *The dissent about freedom led to civil war.*

desert, dessert *Desert* can be pronounced two ways and can be a noun with the stress on the first syllable (*the Mojave Desert*) or a verb with the stress on the second syllable: *When did he desert his family?* The noun *desert* means "a dry, often sandy, environment." The verb *desert* means "to abandon." *Dessert* (with stress on the second syllable) is the sweet course at the end of a meal.

device, devise *Device* is a noun: *He said they needed a device that could lift a car. Devise* is a verb: *She began to devise a solution to the problem.*

different from, different than   Standard usage is *different from*: *She looks different from her sister.* However, *different than* appears frequently in speech and informal writing, particularly when *different from* would require more words: *My writing is different than* [in place of *different from what*] *it was last semester.*

differ from, differ with   To *differ from* means "to be unlike": *Lions differ from tigers in several ways, despite being closely related.* To *differ with* means to "disagree with": *They differ with each other on many topics but are still good friends.*

discreet, discrete   *Discreet* means "tactful": *Be discreet when you talk about your boss. Discrete* means "separate": *He writes on five discrete topics.*

disease   See *decease.*

disinterested, uninterested   *Disinterested* means "impartial or unbiased": *The mediator was hired to make a disinterested settlement. Uninterested* means "lacking in interest": *He seemed uninterested in his job.*

dissent   See *decent.*

do, due   *Do* is a verb. Do not write "*Do* to his absences, he lost his job"; instead use the two-word preposition *due to* or *because of.*

drag, dragged   Use *dragged* for the past tense of the verb *drag. Drug* is nonstandard.

drown, drowned   The past tense of the verb *drown* is *drowned; drownded* is not a word: *He almost drowned yesterday.*

due to the fact that, owing to the fact that   Wordy. Use *because* instead: *They stopped the game because* [not *due to the fact that*] *it was raining.*

each, every   These are singular pronouns; use them with a singular verb. See also 26i and 27d.

each other, one another   Use *each other* with two; use *one another* with more than two: *The twins love each other. The triplets all love one another.*

effect   See *affect.*

e.g.   Use *for example* or *for instance* in place of this Latin abbreviation.

elicit, illicit   *Elicit* means "to get or draw out": *The police tried in vain to elicit information from the suspect's accomplice. Illicit* is an adjective meaning "illegal": *Their illicit deals landed them in prison.*

elude   See *allude.*

emigrate, immigrate   *Emigrate from* means "to leave a country"; *immigrate to* means "to move to another country": *They emigrated from Ukraine and immigrated to the United States.* The noun forms *emigrant* and *immigrant* are derived from the verbs.

eminent, imminent *Eminent* means "well known and noteworthy": *an eminent lawyer. Imminent* means "about to happen": *an imminent disaster.*

ensure See *assure.*

etc. This abbreviation for the Latin *et cetera* means "and so on." Do not let a list trail off with *etc.* Rather than *They took a tent, a sleeping bag, etc.,* write *They took a tent, a sleeping bag, cooking utensils, and a stove.*

every, each See *each.*

everyday, every day *Everyday* (one word) is an adjective meaning "usual": *Their everyday routine is to break for lunch at 12:30. Every day* (two words) is an adverbial expression of frequency: *I get up early every day.*

except, expect See *accept.*

explicit, implicit *Explicit* means "direct": *She gave explicit instructions. Implicit* means "implied": *A tax increase is implicit in the proposal.*

farther, further Both words can refer to distance: *She lives farther (further) from the campus than I do. Further* also means "additional" or "additionally": *The management offered further incentives. Further, the union proposed new work rules.*

female, male Use these words as adjectives, not as nouns in place of *man* and *woman: There are only three women* [not *females*] *in my class. We are discussing female conversational traits.*

few, a few *Few* means "hardly any": *She feels depressed because she has few helpful colleagues. A few* means "some"; it has more positive connotations than *few: She feels fortunate because she has a few helpful colleagues* (45c).

fewer, less Formal usage demands *fewer* with plural countable nouns (*fewer holidays*), *less* with uncountable nouns (*less sunshine*). However, in informal usage, *less* with plural nouns commonly occurs, especially with *than: less than six items, less than ten miles, fifty words or less.* In formal usage, *fewer* is preferred.

first, firstly Avoid *firstly, secondly,* and so on, when listing reasons or examples. Instead, use *first, second.*

flammable, inflammable, nonflammable Both *flammable* and *inflammable* mean the same thing: able to be ignited easily. *Nonflammable* means "unable to be ignited easily." *Dry wood is flammable* or *Dry wood is inflammable. Asbestos is nonflammable.*

flaunt, flout *Flaunt* means "to show [something] off," or "to display in a proud or boastful manner." *Flout* means "to defy or to show scorn for." *When she flaunted her jewels, she flouted good taste.*

former, latter These terms should be used only in reference to a list of two people or things: *We bought lasagna and rhubarb, the former for dinner* *and the latter for dessert.* For more than two items, use *first* and *last: I had some pasta, a salad, and rhubarb; though the first was very filling, I still had room for the last.*

get married to, marry   These expressions can be used interchangeably: *He will get married to his fiancée next week. She will marry her childhood friend next month.* The noun form is *marriage: Their marriage has lasted thirty years.*

go, say   Avoid replacing the verb *say* with *go,* as this is nonstandard usage: *Jane says* [not *goes*], "*I'm tired of this game.*"

good, well   *Good* is an adjective; *well* is an adverb: *If you want to write well, you must use good grammar.* See 28a.

had better   Include *had* in Standard English, although it is often omitted in advertising and in speech: *You had better* [not *You better*] *try harder.*

hardly   This is a negative word. Do not use it with another negative: not *He couldn't hardly walk* but *He could hardly walk.*

have, of   Use *have,* not *of,* after *should, could, might,* and *must: They should have* [not *should of*] *appealed.*

height   Note the spelling and pronunciation: not *heighth.*

heroin, heroine   Do not confuse these words. *Heroin* is a drug; *heroine* is a brave woman. *Hero* may be used for an admirable person of either sex.

hisself   Nonstandard; instead, use *himself.*

hopefully   This word is an adverb meaning "in a hopeful manner" or "with a hopeful attitude": *Hopefully, she e-mailed her résumé.* Avoid using *hopefully* in place of *I hope that:* not *Hopefully, she will get the job* but *I hope that she will get the job.* The former usage is, however, quite common.

I, me   Do not confuse *I* and *me.* Use *I* only in the subject position, and use *me* only in the object position. To check subjects and objects using *and,* simply drop any additional subject or object so that only the pronoun remains: not *The CFO and me were sent to the conference* but *The CFO and I were sent* (I was sent); not *Please send copies to my secretary and I* but *Please send copies to my secretary and me* (send copies to me). See 27a.

illicit   See *elicit.*

illusion   See *allusion.*

immigrate   See *emigrate.*

imminent   See *eminent.*

implicit   See *explicit.*

imply, infer   *Imply* means "to suggest in an indirect way": *He implied that further layoffs were unlikely. Infer* means "to guess" or "to draw a conclusion": *I inferred that the company was doing well.*

incredible, incredulous *Incredible* means "difficult to believe": *The violence of the storm was incredible. Incredulous* means "skeptical, unable to believe": *They were incredulous when he told them about his daring exploits in the whitewater rapids.*

infamous *Infamous* is an adjective meaning "notorious": *Blackbeard's many exploits as a pirate made him infamous along the American coast.* Avoid using it as a synonym for "not famous."

inflammable See *flammable.*

in regard to, as regards Use one or the other. Do not use the nonstandard *in regards to.*

insure See *assure.*

irregardless Nonstandard; instead use *regardless: He selected a major regardless of the preparation it would give him for a career.*

it's, its The apostrophe in *it's* signals not a possessive but a contraction of *it is* or *it has. Its* is the possessive form of the pronoun *it: The city government agency has produced its final report. It's available upon request.* See also 33f.

kind, sort, type In the singular, use each of these nouns with *this* and a singular noun: *this type of book.* Use in the plural with *these* and a plural noun: *these kinds of books.*

kind of, sort of Do not use these to mean "somewhat" or "a little." *The pace of the baseball game was somewhat* [not *kind of*] *slow.*

knew, new *Knew* is the past tense of the verb *know. New* is an adjective meaning "not old."

lend, loan *Lend* is a verb, and *loan* is ordinarily used as a noun: *Our cousins offered to lend us some money, but we refused the loan.*

less See *fewer.*

lie, lay Be sure not to confuse these verbs. *Lie* does not take a direct object; *lay* does. See 25e.

like, as, as if In formal usage, *as* and *as if* are subordinating conjunctions and introduce dependent clauses: *She walks as her father does. She looks as if she could eat a big meal. Like* is a preposition and is followed by a noun or pronoun, not by a clause: *She looks like her father.* In speech, however, and increasingly in writing, *like* is often used where formal usage dictates *as* or *as if: She walks like her father does. He looks like he needs a new suit.* Know your audience's expectations.

likely, liable *Likely* means "probably going to," while *liable* means "at risk of" and is generally used to describe something negative: *Eddie plays the guitar so well he's likely to start a band. If he keeps playing that way, he's liable to break a string. Liable* also means "responsible": *The guitar manufacturer cannot be held liable.*

literally   Avoid overuse: *literally* is an adverb meaning "actually" or "word for word" and should not be used in conjunction with figurative expressions such as *my jaw literally hit the floor* or *he was literally bouncing off the walls. Literally* should be used only when the words describe exactly what is happening: *He was so scared his face literally went white.*

loan   See *lend.*

loose, lose   *Loose* is an adjective meaning "not tight": *This jacket is comfortable because it is so loose. Lose* is a verb (the past tense form and past participle are *lost*): *Many people lose their jobs in a recession.*

lots of   See *alot.*

man, mankind   Avoid using these terms, as they are gender-specific. Instead, use *people, human beings, humankind, humanity,* or *men and women.*

marital, martial   *Marital* is associated with marriage, *martial* with war.

may be, maybe   *May be* consists of a modal verb followed by the base form of the verb *be; maybe* is an adverb meaning "perhaps." If you can replace the expression with *perhaps,* make it one word: *They may be there already, or maybe they got caught in traffic.*

me, I   See *I.*

media, medium   *Media* is the plural form of *medium: Television and radio are both useful communication media, but his favorite medium is the written word.*

most   See *almost.*

myself   Use only as a reflexive pronoun (*I told them myself*) or as an intensive pronoun (*I myself told them*). Do not use *myself* as a subject pronoun: not *My sister and myself won* but *My sister and I won.*

no, not   *No* modifies a noun: *The author has no intention of deceiving the reader. Not* modifies a verb, adjective, or adverb: *She is not wealthy. He does not intend to deceive.*

nonflammable   See *flammable.*

nowadays   All one word. Be sure to include the final *-s.*

nowhere, nowheres   See *anyway.*

number   See *amount.*

off, off of   Use only *off,* not *off of: She drove the car off* [not *off of*] *the road.*

oftentimes   Do not use. Prefer *often.*

OK, O.K., okay   Reserve these forms for informal speech and writing. Choose another word in a formal context: not *Her performance was OK* but *Her performance was satisfactory.*

one another   See *each other.*

owing to the fact that   See *due to the fact that.*

passed, past   *Passed* is a past tense verb form: *They passed the deli on the way to work. He passed his exam. Past* can be a noun (*in the past*), an adjective (*in past times*), or a preposition (*She walked past the bakery*).

peak, peek, pique   *Peak* is the top of a summit: *She has reached the peak of her performance. Peek* (noun or verb) means "glance": *A peek through the window is enough. Pique* (also a noun or a verb) has to do with feeling indignation: *Feeling insulted, he stormed out in a fit of pique.*

personal, personnel   *Personal* is an adjective meaning "individual," while *personnel* is a noun referring to employees or staff: *It is my personal belief that a company's personnel should be treated like family.*

phenomena, phenomenon   *Phenomena* is the plural form of the noun *phenomenon: Outer space is full of celestial phenomena, one spectacular phenomenon being the Milky Way.*

plus   Do not use *plus* as a coordinating conjunction or a transitional expression. Use *and* or *moreover* instead: *He was promoted, and* [not *plus*] *he received a bonus.* Use *plus* as a preposition meaning "in addition to": *His salary plus his dividends placed him in a high tax bracket.*

pore, pour   To *pore* is to read carefully or to ponder: *I saw him poring over the want ads before he poured himself a drink.*

precede, proceed   *Precede* means "to go or occur before": *The Roaring Twenties preceded the Great Depression. Proceed* means "to go ahead": *After you pay the fee, proceed to the examination room.*

prejudice, prejudiced   *Prejudice* is a noun. *Prejudice is harmful to society. Prejudiced* is a past participle verb form: *He is prejudiced against ethnic minorities.*

pretty   Avoid using *pretty* as an intensifying adverb. Use *really, very, rather,* or *quite: The stew tastes very* [not *pretty*] *good.* Often, however, the best solution is to avoid using any adverb: *The stew tastes good.*

principal, principle   *Principal* is a noun (*the principal of a school*) or an adjective meaning "main" or "most important": *His principal motive was monetary gain. Principle* is a noun meaning "standard or rule": *He always acts on his principles.*

quite, quiet   Do not confuse the adverb *quite,* meaning "very," with the adjective *quiet* ("still" or "silent"): *We were all quite relieved when the audience became quiet.*

quote, quotation   *Quote* is a verb. Do not use it as a noun; use *quotation: The quotation* [not *quote*] *from Walker tells the reader a great deal.*

real, really   *Real* is an adjective; *really* is an adverb. Do not use *real* as an intensifying adverb: *She acted really* [not *real*] *well.*

reason is because   Avoid *the reason is because.* Instead, use *the reason is that* or rewrite the sentence. See 24f.

regardless   See *irregardless.*

respectable, respectful, respective   *Respectable* means "presentable, worthy of respect": *Wear some respectable shoes to your interview. Respectful* means "polite or deferential": *Parents want their children to be respectful to adults. Respective* means "particular" or "individual": *The friends of the bride and the groom sat in their respective seats in the church.*

respectfully, respectively   *Respectfully* means "showing respect": *He bowed respectfully when the queen entered. Respectively* refers to items in a list and means "in the order mentioned": *Horses and birds gallop and fly, respectively.*

rise, raise   *Rise* is an intransitive verb: *She rises early every day. Raise* is a transitive verb: *We raised alfalfa last summer.* See 25c.

sale, sell   *Sale* is a noun: *The sale of the house has been postponed. Sell* is a verb: *They are still trying to sell their house.*

should (could, might) of   Nonstandard; instead use *should have: You should have paid.* See 25k, pages 418–19.

since   Use this subordinating conjunction only when time or reason is clear: *Since you insist on helping, I'll let you paint this bookcase.* Unclear: *Since he got a new job, he has been happy.*

site, sight   See *cite.*

sometimes, sometime, some time   The adverb *sometimes* means "occasionally": *He sometimes prefers to eat lunch at his desk.* The adverb *sometime* means "at an indefinite time": *I read that book sometime last year.* The noun phrase *some time* consists of the noun *time* modified by the quantity word *some: After working for Honda, I spent some time in Brazil.*

sort, type   See *kind.*

sort of   See *kind of.*

stationary, stationery   *Stationary* is an adjective meaning "not moving" (*a stationary vehicle*); *stationery* is a noun referring to writing paper.

supposedly   Use this, not *supposably: She is supposedly a great athlete.*

taught, thought   Do not confuse these verb forms. *Taught* is the past tense and past participle form of *teach; thought* is the past tense and past participle form of *think: The students thought that their professor had not taught essay organization.*

than, then   *Then* is a time word; *than* must be preceded by a comparative form: *bigger than, more interesting than.*

their, there, they're   *Their* is a pronoun indicating possession; *there* indicates place or is used as a filler in the subject position in a sentence; *they're* is the contracted form of *they are*: *They're over there, guarding their luggage.*

theirself, theirselves, themself   Nonstandard; instead, use *themselves.*

threat, treat   These words have different meanings: *She gave the children some cookies as a treat. The threat of an earthquake was alarming.*

thusly   Incorrect form of *thus.*

to, too, two   Do not confuse these words. *To* is a sign of the infinitive and a common preposition; *too* is an adverb meaning *also*; *two* is the number: *She is too smart to agree to report to two bosses.*

undoubtedly   This is the correct word, not *undoubtably.*

uninterested   See *disinterested.*

unique   The adjective *unique* means "the only one of its kind" and therefore should not be used with qualifying adjectives like *very* or *most*: *His recipe for chowder is unique* [not *most unique* or *quite unique*]. See 28h, "Absolute adjectives."

used to, get (become) used to   These expressions share the common form *used to*. But the first, expressing a past habit that no longer exists, is followed by the base form of a verb: *He used to wear his hair long.* (Note that after *not*, the form is *use to*: *He did not use to have a beard.*) In the expression *get (become) used to, used to* means "accustomed to" and is followed by a noun or an *-ing* verb form: *She couldn't get used to driving on the left when she was in England.* See also 45i.

way, ways   Use *way* to mean "distance": *He has a way to go. Ways* in this context is nonstandard.

wear, were, we're   *Wear* is a verb meaning "to have on as covering adornment or protection" (*wearing a helmet*); *were* is a past tense form of *be*; *we're* is a contraction for *we are.*

weather, whether   *Weather* is a noun; *whether* is a conjunction: *The weather will determine whether we go on the picnic.*

whose, who's   *Whose* is a possessive pronoun: *Whose goal was that? Who's* is a contraction of *who is* or *who has*: *Who's the player whose pass was caught? Who's got the ball?*

your, you're   *Your* is a pronoun used to show possession. *You're* is a contraction for *you are*: *You're wearing your new shoes today, aren't you?*

56

Glossary of Grammatical Terms

absolute phrase   A phrase consisting of a noun phrase followed by a verbal or a prepositional phrase and modifying an entire sentence: *Flags flapping in the wind,* the stadium looked bleak.

acronym   A pronounceable word formed from the initials of an abbreviation: *NATO, MADD, NOW.* 37b.

active voice   Attribute of a verb when its grammatical subject performs the action: The dog *ate* the cake. 25l, 17c.

adjective   The part of speech that modifies a noun or pronoun: She wears *flamboyant* clothes. His cap is *orange.* 21a, 28. See also *comparative; coordinate adjective; cumulative adjective; superlative; parts of speech.*

adjective clause   A dependent clause beginning with a relative pronoun (*who, whom, whose, which,* or *that*) and modifying a noun or pronoun: The writer *who won the prize* was elated. Also called a *relative clause.* 21e, 29.

adverb   The part of speech that modifies a verb, an adjective, another adverb, or a clause: She ran *quickly.* He is *really* successful. The children were *well* liked. Many adverbs end in *-ly.* 21a, 28. See also *comparative; conjunctive adverb; frequency adverb; parts of speech; superlative.*

adverb clause   A dependent clause that modifies a verb, an adjective, or an adverb and begins with a subordinating conjunction: He left early *because he was tired.* 21e.

agent   The person or thing doing the action described by a verb: *His sister* won the marathon. The marathon was won by *his sister.* 25l.

agreement   The grammatical match in person, number, and gender between a verb and its subject or between a pronoun and its antecedent (the word the pronoun refers to): The *benefits continue; they are* pleasing. The *benefit continues; it is* pleasing. 26, 27d.

antecedent   The noun that a pronoun refers to: My son who lives nearby found a *kitten. It* was black and white. 27c, 27d, 29a.

appositive phrase   A phrase occurring next to a noun and used to describe it: His father, *a factory worker,* is running for office. 21d, 27a, 31d.

article   *A, an* (indefinite articles), or *the* (definite article). Also called a *determiner.* 41c, 41d, 41e.

auxiliary verb   A verb that joins with another verb to form a complete verb. Auxiliary verbs are forms of *do, be,* and *have,* as well as the modal auxiliary verbs. 25d, 42a. See also *modal auxiliary verb.*

base form　The dictionary form of a verb, used in an infinitive after *to: see, eat, go, be.* 25a.

clause　A group of words that includes a subject and a verb. 21e. See also *dependent clause; independent clause.*

cliché　An overused, predictable expression: *as cool as a cucumber.* 20g.

collective noun　A noun naming a collection of people or things that are regarded as a unit: *team, jury, family.* For agreement with collective nouns, see 26g, 27d.

comma splice　The error that results when two independent clauses are incorrectly joined with only a comma. Chapter 23g.

common noun　A noun that does not name a unique person, place, or thing. Chapter 21a, 41a. See also *proper noun.*

comparative　The form of an adjective or adverb used to compare two people or things: *bigger, more interesting.* 28h. See also *superlative.*

complement　A *subject complement* is a word or group of words used after a linking verb to refer to and describe the subject: Harry looks *happy.* An *object complement* is a word or group of words used after a direct object to complete its meaning: They call him a *liar.* 21c, 26d.

complete verb　A verb that shows tense. Some verb forms, such as *-ing* (present) participles and past participles, require auxiliary verbs to make them complete verbs. *Going* and *seen* are not complete verbs; *are going* and *has been seen* are complete. 23d, 25a.

complex sentence　A sentence that has one independent clause and one or more dependent clauses: *He wept when he won the marathon.* 21f.

compound adjective　An adjective formed of two or more words often connected with hyphens: a *well-constructed* house. 28d, 38h.

compound-complex sentence　A sentence that has at least two independent clauses and one or more dependent clauses: *She works in Los Angeles, but her husband works in San Diego, where they both live.* 21f.

compound noun　A noun formed of two or more words: *toothbrush, merry-go-round.* 21a, 38h.

compound predicate　A predicate consisting of two or more verbs and their objects, complements, and modifiers: He *whistles and sings in the morning.* 21c, 23e.

compound sentence　A sentence that has two or more independent clauses: *She works in Los Angeles, but her husband works in San Diego.* 21f.

compound subject　A subject consisting of two or more nouns or pronouns and their modifiers: *My uncle and my aunt* are leaving soon. 21c, 26h, 27a.

conditional clause   A clause introduced by *if* or *unless,* expressing conditions of fact, prediction, or speculation: *If we earned more,* we would spend more. 25k.

conjunction   The part of speech used to link words, phrases, or clauses. 21a, 21e, 26h, 31b. See also *coordinating conjunction; correlative conjunctions; parts of speech; subordinating conjunction.*

conjunctive adverb   A transitional expression used to link two independent clauses. Some common conjunctive adverbs are *moreover, however,* and *furthermore.* 18c, 21e, 31e.

connotation   The meanings and associations suggested by a word, as distinct from the word's denotation, or dictionary meaning. 20c.

contraction   The shortened form that results when an apostrophe replaces one or more letters: *can't* (for *cannot*), *he's* (for *he is* or *he has*), *they're* (for *they are*). 33d.

coordinate adjective   Evaluative adjective modifying a noun. When coordinate adjectives appear in a series, their order can be reversed, and they can be separated by *and.* Commas are used between coordinate adjectives: the *comfortable, expensive car.* 28f, 31g.

coordinating conjunction   The seven coordinating conjunctions are *and, but, or, nor, so, for,* and *yet.* They connect sentence elements that are parallel in structure: He couldn't call, *but* he wrote a letter. 18c, 21e, 31b.

coordination   The connection of two or more ideas to give each one equal emphasis: *Sue worked after school, so she didn't have time to jog.* 18c.

correlative conjunctions   A pair of conjunctions joining equivalent elements. The most common correlative conjunctions are *either . . . or, neither . . . nor, both . . . and,* and *not only . . . but also: Neither* my sister *nor* I could find the concert hall. 24j.

countable noun   A common noun that has a plural form and can be used after a plural quantity word (such as *many* or *three*): one *book,* three *stores,* many *children.* 41a, 41e.

cumulative adjective   An adjective that modifies a noun and occurs in a conventional order with no comma between adjectives: a *new red plastic* bench.

cumulative sentence   A sentence that adds elements after the independent clause. 18b.

dangling modifier   A modifier that fails to modify the noun or pronoun it is intended to modify: <u>not</u> *Turning the corner,* the lights went out. <u>but</u> *Turning the corner, we* saw the lights go out. 24c.

demonstrative pronoun   The four demonstrative pronouns are *this, that, these,* and *those: That* is my glass. 26j.

denotation   A word's dictionary meaning. See also *connotation.* 20b, 20c.

dependent clause   A clause that cannot stand alone as a complete sentence and needs to be attached to an independent clause. A dependent clause begins with a subordinating word such as *because, if, when, although, who, which,* or *that: When it rains,* we can't take the children outside. 21e, 23c.

diction   Choice of appropriate words and tone. Chapter 20.

direct object   The person or thing that receives the action of a verb: They ate *cake* and *ice cream.* 21c, 43c.

direct quotation   A person's words reproduced exactly and placed in quotation marks: *"I won't be home until noon,"* she said. 34b, 43d, 49j.

double negative   The use of two negative words in the same sentence: He does *not* know *nothing.* This usage is nonstandard and needs to be avoided: *He does not know anything. He knows nothing.* 28g.

ellipsis   Omission of words from a quotation, indicated by three dots: "I pledge allegiance to the flag . . . and to the republic for which it stands . . ." 35e, 49j.

etymology   The origin of a word. 20b.

euphemism   A word or phrase used to disguise literal meaning: She *is in the family way* [meaning "pregnant"]. 20g.

faulty predication   The error that results when subject and verb do not match logically: not The *decrease* in stolen cars *has diminished* in the past year. but The *number* of stolen cars *has decreased* in the past year. 24e.

figurative language   The use of unusual comparisons or other devices to draw attention to a specific meaning. See *metaphor; simile.* 8f, 20e.

filler subject   *It* or *there* used in the subject position of a clause, followed by a form of *be: There are* two elm trees on the corner. 17b, 26e, 46g.

first person   The person speaking or writing: *I* or *we.* 27a.

fragment   A group of words that is punctuated as if it were a sentence but is grammatically incomplete because it lacks a subject or a predicate or begins with a subordinating word: *Because it was a sunny day.* Chapter 23.

frequency adverb   An adverb that expresses time (such as *often, always,* or *sometimes*). It can be the first word in a sentence or be used between the subject and the main verb, after an auxiliary verb, or as the last word in a sentence. 28e.

fused sentence   See *run-on sentence.*

gender   Classification of a noun or pronoun as masculine (*Uncle John, he*), feminine (*Ms. Torez, she*), or neuter (*book, it*). 27a, 46h.

generic noun   A noun referring to a general class or type of person or object: A *student* has to write many papers. 27d.

gerund The *-ing* verb form used as a noun: *Walking* is good for your health. 21d, 26f, 42d, 42e. See also *verbal*.

helping verb See *auxiliary verb*.

imperative mood Verb mood used to give a command: *Follow* me. 21b.

indefinite pronoun A pronoun that refers to a nonspecific person or thing: *anybody, something*. 26i, 27d.

independent clause A clause that has a subject and predicate and is not introduced by a subordinating word. An independent clause can function as a complete sentence. *Birds sing. The old man was singing a song.* Hailing a cab, *the woman used a silver whistle.* 21e, 32b.

indicative mood Verb mood used to ask questions or make statements. It is the most common mood. 21b.

indirect object The person or thing to whom or to which, or for whom or for which, an action is performed. It comes between the verb and the direct object: He gave his *sister* some flowers. 21c, 43c.

indirect question A question reported by a speaker or writer, not enclosed in quotation marks: They asked *if we would help them.* 24d, 43d.

indirect quotation A description or paraphrase of the words of another speaker or writer, integrated into a writer's own sentence and not enclosed in quotation marks: He said *that they were making money.* 24d, 43d, 49j.

infinitive The base form, or dictionary form, of a verb, preceded by *to: to see, to smile.* 21d, 42c, 42e.

infinitive phrase An infinitive with its objects, complements, or modifiers: *To wait for hours* is unpleasant. He tries hard *to be punctual.* 21d.

intensive pronoun A pronoun ending in *-self* or *-selves* and used to emphasize its antecedent: They *themselves* will not attend. 27h.

interjection The part of speech that expresses emotion and is able to stand alone: *Aha! Wow!* Interjections are seldom appropriate in academic writing. 21a.

interrogative pronoun A pronoun that introduces a direct or indirect question: *Who* is that? I don't know *what* you want. 26l, 27i.

intransitive verb A verb that does not take a direct object: Exciting events *have occurred.* He *fell.* 21c, 25a. See also *transitive verb*.

inverted word order The presence of the verb before the subject in a sentence; used in questions or for emphasis: *Do you expect* an award? Not only *does she do* gymnastics, she also wins awards. 21c, 26e.

irregular verb A verb that does not form its past tense and past participle with *-ed: sing, sang, sung; grow, grew, grown.* 25b.

linking verb   A verb connecting a subject to its complement. Typical linking verbs are *be, become, seem,* and *appear: He seems* angry. A linking verb is intransitive; it does not take a direct object. 21c, 27a, 28c.

mental activity verb   A verb not used in a tense showing progressive aspect: *prefer, want, understand: not* He *is wanting to leave.* <u>but</u> He *wants* to leave. 25e.

metaphor   A figure of speech implying a comparison but not stating it directly: a *gale* of laughter. 8f, 20e.

misplaced modifier   An adverb (particularly *only* and *even*) or a descriptive phrase or clause positioned in such a way that it modifies the wrong word or words: She showed the ring to her sister *that her aunt gave her.* 24b.

mixed structure   A sentence with two or more types of structures that clash grammatically: *By doing* her homework at the last minute *caused* Meg to make many mistakes. 24a, 24f.

modal auxiliary verb   The nine modal auxiliaries are *will, would, can, could, shall, should, may, might,* and *must.* They are followed by the base form of a verb: *will go, would believe.* Modal auxiliaries do not change form. 25d, 42b.

modifier   A word or words that describe another noun, adverb, verb, phrase, or clause: He is a *happy* man. He is smiling *happily.* Chapter 28.

mood   The mood of a verb tells whether the verb states a fact (*indicative:* She *goes* to school); gives a command (*imperative: Come* back soon); or expresses a condition, wish, or request (*subjunctive:* I wish you *were* not leaving). 21a, 25a, 25h. See also *imperative mood; indicative mood; subjunctive mood.*

nonrestrictive phrase or clause   A phrase or clause that adds extra or nonessential information to a sentence and is set off with commas: His report, *which he gave to his boss yesterday,* received enthusiastic praise. 29b, 31d.

noun   The part of speech that names a person, place, thing, or idea. Nouns are proper or common and, if common, countable or uncountable. 21a, chapter 41. See also *collective noun; common noun; compound noun; countable noun; generic noun; noun clause; parts of speech; proper noun; uncountable noun.*

noun clause   A dependent clause that functions as a noun: I like *what you do. Whoever scores a goal* will be a hero. 21e.

noun phrase   A noun with its accompanying modifiers and articles: *a brilliant, hard-working student.* 21a.

number   The indication of a noun or pronoun as singular (one person, place, thing, or idea) or plural (more than one). 26a, 27d.

object of preposition The noun or pronoun (along with its modifiers) that follows a preposition: on *the beach.* 21d, 44e.

paragraph A group of sentences set off in a text, usually on one topic. 5a.

parallelism The use of coordinate structures that have the same grammatical form: She likes *swimming* and *playing* tennis. 5e, 24j.

participle phrase A phrase beginning with an -*ing* verb form or a past participle: The woman *wearing a green skirt* is my sister. *Baffled by the puzzle,* he gave up. 21d. See also *verbal.*

particle A word (frequently a preposition or adverb) that combines with a verb to form a phrasal verb, a verb with an idiomatic meaning: get *over,* take *after.* 44d.

parts of speech Eight traditional categories of words used to form sentences: noun, pronoun, verb, adjective, adverb, conjunction, preposition, and interjection. See 21a and the listing for each in this glossary.

passive voice Attribute of a verb when its grammatical subject is the receiver of the action that the verb describes: The book *was written* by my professor. 17c, 25l. See also *active voice.*

past participle A verb form that in regular verbs ends with -*ed.* The past participle needs an auxiliary verb to function as the complete verb of a clause: *has chosen, was cleaned, might have been told.* The past participle can function alone as an adjective. 25a, 25b, 25d, 25h, 42f.

perfect progressive tense forms Verb tenses that show actions in progress up to a specific point in present, past, or future time. For active voice verbs, use forms of the auxiliary *have been* followed by the -*ing* form of the verb: *has/have been living, had been living, will have been living.* 25e.

perfect tense forms Verb tenses that show actions completed by present, past, or future time. For active voice verbs, use forms of the auxiliary *have* followed by the past participle of the verb: *has/have arrived, had arrived, will have arrived.* 25e.

periodic sentence A sentence that uses words and phrases to build up to the independent clause. 18b.

person The form of a pronoun or verb that indicates whether the subject is doing the speaking (first person, *I* or *we*), is spoken to (second person, *you*), or is spoken about (third person, *he, she, it,* or *they*). 26a, 27a.

phrasal verb An idiomatic verb phrase consisting of a verb and a preposition or adverb called a *particle: put off, put on.* 44d.

phrase A group of words that lacks a subject or predicate and functions as a noun, verb, adjective, or adverb: *under the tree, has been singing, amazingly simple.* 21d. See also *absolute phrase; appositive phrase; infinitive phrase; participle phrase; prepositional phrase.*

possessive The form of a noun or pronoun that indicates ownership. Possessive pronouns include *my, his, her, their, theirs,* and *whose: my* boat, *your* socks. The possessive form of a noun is indicated by an apostrophe or an apostrophe and *-s: Mario's* car, the *children's* nanny, the *birds'* nests. 26h, 27b, 33a, 33b.

predicate The part of a sentence that contains the verb and its modifiers and that comments on or makes an assertion about the subject. To be complete, a sentence needs a subject and a predicate. 21c.

prefix Letters attached to the beginning of a word that change the word's meaning: *un*necessary, *re*organize, *non*stop. 38a.

preposition The part of speech used with a noun or pronoun in a phrase to indicate time, space, or some other relationship. 21a, 29d, chapter 44. The noun or pronoun is the object of the preposition: *on the table, after dinner, to her.*

prepositional phrase A phrase beginning with a preposition and including the object of the preposition and its modifiers: The head *of the electronics company* was waiting *for an hour.* 21d, 23b, 44b.

present participle The *-ing* form of a verb, showing an action as being in progress or continuous: They are *sleeping.* Without an auxiliary, the *-ing* form cannot function as a complete verb but can be used as an adjective: *searing* heat. When the *-ing* form is used as a noun, it is called a gerund: *Skiing* can be dangerous. 25a, 25f, 42d, 42f. See also *verbal.*

progressive tense forms Verb tenses that show actions in progress at a point or over a period of time in past, present, or future time. They use a form of *be* + the *-ing* form of the verb: They *are working;* he *will be writing.* 25e, 25f, 25g.

pronoun The part of speech that takes the place of a noun, a noun phrase, or another pronoun. 21a, 26h, chapter 27. See *parts of speech.*

pronoun reference The connection between a pronoun and its antecedent. Reference should be clear and unambiguous: Mr. Estern picked up *his* hat and left. 27c.

proper noun The capitalized name of a specific person, place, or thing: *Golden Gate Park, University of Kansas.* 21c, 37a, 41f. See also *common noun.*

quantity word A word expressing the idea of quantity, such as *each, every, several, many,* and *much.* Subject-verb agreement is tricky with quantity words: *Each* of the students *has* a different assignment. 26i. See also *agreement.*

reflexive pronoun A pronoun ending in *-self* or *-selves* and referring to the subject of a clause: They incriminated *themselves.* 27h.

regular verb Verb that ends with *-ed* in its past tense and past participle forms. 25a.

relative clause　See *adjective clause.*

relative pronoun　Pronoun that introduces a relative clause: *who, whom, whose, which, that.* 29a.

restrictive phrase or clause　A phrase or clause that provides information essential for identifying the word or phrase it modifies. A restrictive phrase or clause is not set off with commas: The book *that is first on the bestseller list* is a memoir. 29b, 31j.

run-on sentence　The error that results when two independent clauses are not separated by a conjunction or by any punctuation: <u>not</u> *The dog ate the meat the cat ate the fish.* <u>but</u> *The dog ate the meat; the cat ate the fish.* Also called a *fused sentence.* 23g, 23h.

second person　The person addressed: *you.* 27a, 27g.

shifts　Inappropriate switches in grammatical structure, such as from one tense to another or from statement to command or from indirect to direct quotation: <u>not</u> Joan asked *whether I was warm enough* and *did I sleep well* <u>but</u> *Joan asked whether I was warm enough and had slept well.* 24d, 25i.

simile　A figure of speech that makes a direct comparison: She has a laugh *like a fire siren.* 8f, 20e.

simple tense forms　Verb tenses that show present, past, or future time with no perfect or progressive aspects: they *work,* we *worked,* she *will work.* 25e, 25f, 25g.

split infinitive　An infinitive with a word or words separating *to* from the base verb form: *to successfully complete.* This structure has become acceptable. 24b.

Standard English　"The variety of English that is generally acknowledged as the model for the speech and writing of educated speakers." This *American Heritage Dictionary,* 4th edition, definition warns that the use of the term is "highly elastic and variable" and confers no "absolute positive evaluation." 1b, 40a.

subject　The noun or pronoun that performs the action of the verb in an active voice sentence or receives the action of the verb in a passive voice sentence. To be complete, a sentence needs a subject and a verb. 21a, 23d, 24i, 43a.

subjunctive mood　Verb mood used in conditions and in wishes, requests, and demands: I wish he *were* here. She demanded that he *be* present. 25h.

subordinate clause　See *dependent clause.*

subordinating conjunction　A conjunction used to introduce a dependent adverb clause: *because, if, when, although, since, while.* 18c, 21e, 23c.

suffix   Letters attached to the end of a word that change the word's function or meaning: gentle*ness*, humor*ist*, slow*er*, sing*ing*. 38a.

superlative   The form of an adjective or adverb used to compare three or more people or things: *biggest; most unusual; least effectively.* 28h, 41d. See also *comparative*.

synonym   A word that has the same or nearly the same meaning as another word.

tense   The form of a verb that indicates time. Verbs change form to distinguish present and past time: he *goes*; he *went.* Various structures are used to express future time, mainly *will* + the base form, or *going to* + the base form. 25e. See also *perfect progressive tense forms; perfect tense forms; progressive tense forms; simple tense forms.*

third person   The person or thing spoken about: *he, she, it, they,* or nouns. 26a, 27a.

topic chain   Repetition of key words or related words throughout a passage to aid cohesion. 18a, 25l.

transitional expression   A word or phrase used to connect two independent clauses, such as *for example, however,* and *similarly.* 5e, 31e, 32b.

transitive verb   A verb that takes an object—the person or thing that receives the action (in the active voice): Dogs *chase* cats. When transitive verbs are used in the passive voice, the subject receives the action of the verb: Cats *are chased* by dogs. 21c, 25c, 25l. See also *intransitive verb.*

uncountable noun   A common noun that cannot follow a plural quantity word (such as *several* or *many*) is never used with *a* or *an,* is used with a singular third person verb, and has no plural form: *furniture, happiness, information.* 21a, 26f, 41b.

verb   The part of speech that expresses action or being and tells (in the active voice) what the subject of the clause is or does. The complete verb in a clause might require auxiliary or modal auxiliary verbs to complete its meaning. 21a, chapter 25, chapter 42.

verbal   A form, derived from a verb, that cannot function as the main verb of a clause. The three types of verbals are the infinitive, the *-ing* participle, and the past participle (for example, *to try, singing, stolen*). A verbal can function in a phrase as a noun, adjective, or adverb. Chapter 42, 45e.

verb chain   Combination of an auxiliary verb, a main verb, and verbals: She *might have promised to leave*; they *should deny having helped* him. Chapter 42.

verb phrase   A complete verb formed by auxiliaries and the main verb: *should have waited.* 25a.

voice Transitive verbs (verbs that take an object) can be used in the active voice (*He is painting the door*) or the passive voice (*The door is being painted*). 17c, 25l.

zero article The lack of an article (*a, an,* or *the*) before a noun. Uncountable nouns are used with the zero article when they make no specific reference. 41b, 41c, 41e.

TEXT CREDITS

Part 1: Page 9, from "The Economics of Fair Play" by Karl Sigmund, Ernst Fehr, and Martin A. Nowak. Copyright © 2002 by Scientific American. All rights reserved; pages 11–12, excerpt from Gloria Anzaldua, "How to Tame a Wild Tongue," from *Borderlands/La Frontera*, The New Mestiza. Copyright © 1987, 1999 by Gloria Anzaldua. Reprinted by permission of Aunt Lute Books; page 16, Hetty Hughes, Untitled poem on text messaging from Guardian Newspaper Competition, England. Reprinted by permission of the author; page 17, Tom McArthur's Circle of World English, from "The English Languages?," *English Today* 11 (July 1987), p. 11, Cambridge University Press. Reprinted with the permission of Cambridge University Press; page 59, screen capture reprinted by permission from Microsoft; page 75, from Malcolm Gladwell, "The Social Life of Paper," *New Yorker*, March 25, 2002, p. 93. Reprinted with permission from The New Yorker Magazine; page 81, definition of "life" is from *The Columbia Encyclopedia Online*. Copyright © Columbia University Press. Reprinted with the permission of the publisher; page 82, Matthew Gilbert, "All Talk, All the Time," *Boston Globe Magazine*, June 4, 2000, p. 9. Copyright 2000 by Globe Newspaper Company, Massachusetts. Reproduced with permission of Globe Newspaper Company, Massachusetts in the format Textbook via Copyright Clearance Center; page 93, Malcolm Gladwell, "The Moral-Hazard Myth," *New Yorker*, August 29, 2005, p. 49. Reprinted by permission of the author; page 99, screen captures reprinted by permission from Microsoft.

Part 2: Page 140, Gerald Moore, "Letter to the Editor," *The Independent*, Tuesday, July 3, 2001, p. 13. Reprinted by permission of the author; page 144, from Rita Dove, "Rosa," *On the Bus with Rosa Parks*. Copyright © 1999 by Rita Dove. Used by permission of W. W. Norton & Company, Inc.; page 145, Gwendolyn Brooks, "We Real Cool," *Blacks*. Reprinted by consent of Brooks Permissions; page 161, Emily Dickinson, "There's a Certain Slant of Light." Reprinted by permission of the publishers and the Trustees of Amherst College from *The Poems of Emily Dickinson*, Thomas H. Johnson, ed., Cambridge, Mass.: The Belknap Press of Harvard University Press, copyright © 1951, 1955, 1979, 1983 by the President and Fellows of Harvard College; pages 165–166, Jenny Hung, "Surviving a Year of Sleepless Nights," *Newsweek*, September 20, 2000. All rights reserved. Reprinted by permission; pages 190–191, permission to reprint granted by Charles Mak and the LaGuardia Center for Teaching and Learning, coordinators of the e-portfolio initiative at LaGuardia Community College, CUNY, available at <http://www.lagcc.cuny.edu/ctl>.

Part 3: Pages 203–205, screen captures reprinted by permission from Microsoft; page 239 top and bottom, screens reproduced courtesy of the InterReligious Council of Central New York and Daniel Suave; pages 246–258, sample documents in 14b–15 are adapted from Scot Ober's *Contemporary Business Communication*, sixth edition (Houghton Mifflin Company, 2006). Used with permission; page 258, letter adapted from Scot Ober, *Business Communication*, Fifth Edition (Houghton Mifflin Company, 2003); page 259, Scot Ober, condensed version of Chapter 15, Employment Communication, *Contemporary Business Communication*, Sixth Edition (Houghton Mifflin Company, 2006). Copyright © 2006 by Houghton Mifflin

Company. Reprinted with permission; page 260, line graph from Al Gore, *An Inconvenient Truth: The Planetary Emergency of Global Warming and What We Can Do about It*, 2006, 66–67. By arrangement with Rodale, Inc.

Part 5: Pages 495–496, adapted from Randy Cassingham, *The Dvorak Keyboard* (1986), www.Dvorak-keyboard.com. Used with permission of the author.

Part 6: Page 547, the quotation from "Toads" by Philip Larkin is reprinted from *The Less Deceived* by permission of The Marvell Press, England and Australia; page 549, "Class Poem" by Aurora Levins Morales from *Getting Home Alive*, Aurora Levins Morales and Rosario Morales, eds. Copyright © 1986 by Aurora Levins Morales and Rosario Morales. Used with permission from Firebrand Books, Ann Arbor, Michigan.

Part 8: Page 645, screen capture of Advanced Search for EBSCO Academic Search Premier Database (search for Global Warming Glaciers). Image reproduced with permission of EBSCO Publishing; page 646, screen capture reprinted courtesy of Google; Page 650, screen capture courtesy The City University of New York; page 663, screen capture courtesy of Reclaim Democracy.org; pages 678–681, Ellen Laird, "Internet Plagiarism: We All Pay the Price," *Chronicle of Higher Education*, July 13, 2001, p. 5. Reprinted by permission of the author. Ellen Laird teaches in the English Department at Hudson Valley Community College; pages 682–683, by Clayton Collins. Excerpted with permission from the March 30, 2005 issue of *The Christian Science Monitor* (www.csmonitor.com). © 2005 The Christian Science Monitor. All rights reserved.

Part 9: Page 729, EBSCO citation link screen (listing an article and citation link screen) entry for Gray, Katti, *The Whistle Blower*. Image reproduced with permission of EBSCO Publishing; page 733, reprinted by permission of CNN ImageSource.

Part 10: Page 785, reprinted by permission of the H. W. Wilson Company. Copyright © 2006. Material reproduced with permission of the publisher; page 789, screen from Katelyn Davies.

PHOTO CREDITS

Part 1: Page 14, Chris Anderson; page 15, Courtesy American Indian College Fund; page 79, Corbis; page 80, The Library of the London School of Economics and Politics.

Part 2: Page 112, Courtesy www.Adbusters.org; page 113 left and right, Susanne Wustmann; page 119, Courtesy of Scenic Hudson Inc.; page 120, Courtesy Friends of the Hudson; page 135, screen from Vegsource.com at <http://vegan.uchicago.edu/nutrition/01.html>; page 145 left, Tim Wright/Corbis; page 145 right, Bettmann/Corbis; page 161, Hulton/Archive/Getty Images; page 171, *Trafalgar Square*, 1939–43, by Piet Mondrian (1872–1944). Oil on Canvas, 57¼" x 47¾", gift of Mr. and Mrs. William A. M. Burden (510.1964). © 2002 Mondrian/ Holtzman Trust, c/o Beeldrecht/ Artists Rights Society, NY. Digital image © The Museum of Modern Art. Licensed by SCALA/Art Resource, NY; pages 190–191, Charles Mak, LaGuardia Community College, City University of New York.

Index

Note: An asterisk (*) refers to a Glossary entry.

LIST OF BOXES AND NOTES

 **Key Points Boxes**

Language and Culture Boxes

Tech Notes

ESL Notes

Source Shots

CORRECTION GUIDE

Note: Numbers refer to sections in the book.

Abbreviation	Meaning/Error
ab or abbr	abbreviation, **37b, 39e**
adj	adjective, **21a, 28**
adv	adverb, **21a, 28**
agr	agreement, **26, 27d**
art	articles, **41**
awk	awkward, **17, 18, 24**
bias	biased or sexist language, **20f, 27e**
ca or case	case, **27a**
cap (t̲om)	use capital letter, **37a, 39c**
coh	coherence, **5e**
comp	comparative, **28h, 28i**
coord	coordination, **21e, 31b, 18c**
cs	comma splice, **23**
d	diction, **20**
db neg	double negative, **28g**
dev	development, **5d**
dm	dangling modifier, **24c**
doc	documentation, **49, 51–54**
-ed	error with -*ed* ending, **25h**
exact	exactness, **20c**
frag	sentence fragment, **23**
fs	fused sentence, **23g, 23h**
hyph	hyphenation, **38h, 39d**
id	idiom, **44**
inc	incomplete sentence or construction, **24h, 43a**
ind quot	indirect quotation, **24d, 25j, 43d**
-ing	error with -*ing* ending, **42**
ital	italics/underlining, **36, 39b, 51d, 52c, 53c, 54e**
jar	jargon, **20d**
lc (M̶e)	use a lowercase letter, **37a**
log	logic, **7d, 7j**
mix or mixed	mixed construction, **24a**

Abbreviation	Meaning/Error
mm	misplaced modifier, **24b**
ms	manuscript form, **12, 14, 15**
nonst	nonstandard usage, **1d, 21, 40a**
num	faulty use of numbers, **37c**
//	parallelism, **24j**
p	punctuation, **30–35, 39a**
pass	passive voice, **17c, 25l**
prep	preposition, **21a, 44**
pron	pronoun, **27**
quot	quotation, **30, 49j**
ref	pronoun reference, **27c**
rel cl	relative clause, **29, 31d**
rep or red	repetitive or redundant, **16a, 16d**
-s	error with -*s* ending, **26b**
shift	needless shift, **24d, 25i**
sp	spelling, **38**
s/pl	singular/plural, **26a, 38b**
sub	subordination, **21e, 31b, 18c, 43e**
sup	superlative, **28h**
s-v agr	subject-verb agreement, **26**
t	verb tense, **25e–25j**
trans	transition, **31e**
und	underlining/italics, **36, 39b, 51d, 52c, 53c, 54e**
us	usage, **55**
v or vb	error with verb, **25**
var	[sentence] variety, **21f, 21g**
w	wordy, **16**
wc	word choice, **20**
wo	word order, **43**
ww	wrong word, **20**